Re<sup></sup>

KU-208-809

# Multilingual Matters

Afrikaner Dissidents
    JOHA LOUW-POTGIETER
Aspects of Bilingualism in Wales
    COLIN BAKER
Bicultural and Trilingual Education
    MICHAEL BYRAM and JOHAN LEHMAN (eds)
Bilingualism or Not: The Education of Minorities
    TOVE SKUTNABB-KANGAS
Citizens of This Country: The Asian British
    MARY STOPES-ROE and RAYMOND COCHRANE
Fourth International Conference on Minority Languages
    D. GORTER, J.F. HOEKSTRA, L.G. JANSMA and J. YTSMA
Key Issues in Bilingualism and Bilingual Education
    COLIN BAKER
Language, Culture and Cognition
    LILLIAM MALAVÉ and GEORGES DUQUETTE (eds)
Language Distribution Issues in Bilingual Schooling
    R. JACOBSON and C. FALTIS (eds)
Language in Education in Africa
    CASMIR M. RUBAGUMYA (ed.)
Language and Ethnic Identity
    WILLIAM GUDYKUNST (ed.)
Language and Ethnicity in Minority Sociolinguistic Perspective
    JOSHUA FISHMAN
Language Planning and Education in Australasia and the South Pacific
    R. B. BALDAUF and A. LUKE (eds)
Minority Education: From Shame to Struggle
    T. SKUTNABB-KANGAS and J. CUMMINS (eds)
Minority Education and Ethnic Survival
    MICHAEL BYRAM
Multilingualism in India
    D. P. PATTANAYAK (ed.)
The Use of Welsh: A Contribution to Sociolinguistics
    MARTIN J. BALL (ed.)

**Please contact us for the latest book information:**
**Multilingual Matters Ltd,**
**Bank House, 8a Hill Road**
**Clevedon, Avon BS21 7HH**
**England**

16-95

**MULTILINGUAL MATTERS 76**
Series Editor: Derrick Sharp

# Reversing Language Shift

Theoretical and Empirical Foundations of Assistance to Threatened Languages

## Joshua A. Fishman

**MULTILINGUAL MATTERS LTD**
Clevedon • Philadelphia • Adelaide

**Library of Congress Cataloging in Publication Data**

Fishman, Joshua A.
Reversing Language Shift: Theoretical and Empirical Foundations of Assistance to
Threatened Languages/Joshua A. Fishman.
p. cm. (Multilingual Matters: 76)
Includes bibliographical references and index.
1. Code switching (linguistics). 2. Linguistic minorities. 3. Language planning. I. Title.
II. Series: Multilingual Matters (Series): 76.
P115.3.F5    1991
306.4'49    dc20

**British Library Cataloguing in Publication Data**

A CIP catalogue record for this book is available from the British Library.

ISBN 1-85359-122-X
ISBN 1-85359-121-1 pbk

**Multilingual Matters Ltd**

*UK:* Bank House, 8a Hill Road, Clevedon, Avon BS21 7HH, England.
*USA:* 1900 Frost Road, Suite 101, Bristol, PA 19007, USA.
*Australia:* PO Box 6025, 83 Gilles Street, Adelaide, SA 5000, Australia.

Index compiled by Meg Davis (Society of Indexers).
Typeset by Editorial Enterprises, Torquay.
Printed and bound in Great Britain by the Longdunn Press Ltd.

נעלען,
אַ דאַנק װעמען
כ׳האָב אַזוי פֿיל פֿרײד
אין לעבן געפֿונען, באַטש
אַ נאַנץ לעבן זובן מיר
צוזאַמען די אומה
ולשון װאָס אונדזער
דור האָט פֿאַרלוירן,
אי דאָ, אי דאַרטן.

... to every province according to the writing thereof, and to every people after their language, that every man should bear rule in his own house, and speak according to the language of his people.

Book of Esther 1: 22

Many distinguished linguists seem to me excessively cautious about publishing a scientific conclusion before it can be finally established. I think that such a procedure unnecessarily delays the progress of science. The one requirement is that before a conclusion is proposed, its author must think it through and make it harmonize with the available evidence. No scientific conclusion is final; every one of them should be held subject to immediate revision in the light of new evidence.

Sturtevant and Hahn, 1951,
*A Comparative Grammar of the Hittite Language*, v.1 (revised).
New Haven: Yale University Press, p. 16.

When one significant section of the community burns with the sense of injustice, the rest of the community cannot safely pretend that there is no reason for their discontent.

*Waitangi Tribunal* (New Zealand) 1986, p. 46.

... men build their cultures by huddling together, nervously loquacious, at the edge of an abyss.

Kenneth Burke, 1954,
*Permanence and Change* (rev. edn).
Hermes, p. 136.

# Contents

# Author's Preface

My first sociolinguistic monograph was *Yiddish in America* (1965); my first sociolinguistic book: *Language Loyalty in the United States* (1966). It is clear to me now, that I was writing the present book even then.

Although I have struggled to approach language maintenance and language shift as fields of dispassionate scientific inquiry, I have never tried to hide (neither from myself nor from the careful reader) the value positions in support of cultural pluralism and cultural self-determination to which I personally subscribe. Indeed, my work of the 60s began as a quest for any possibly overlooked successes, amidst all of the clearly obvious failures, in the efforts to secure minority language maintenance in the United States. The intellectualization of this quest has led me to a constant review of the circumstances of modern life, even under democratic and multicultural auspices, which lead overwhelmingly in the direction of language shift. That intellectualization has helped me realize that every failed societal effort on behalf of greater ethnolinguistic self-regulation nevertheless hides, within itself, many minor successes (first and foremost, the community-fostering experience of a common struggle on behalf of a shared verity) and some memorable 'near misses' that reveal the direction in which 'success' might lie.

I deeply regret that I did not react to those realizations more quickly. Perhaps as a result of the initial language shift momentum that I provided for this field of study, and my negligence with respect to offering more focused insight into the few cases of actual language maintenance success and near-success that I had come across, the entire positive side of the ledger is far less represented in the intellectual economy of the macro-sociolinguistic enterprise than it could and should be. In a sense, therefore, this book not only represents the continuation of a long felt interest, but, also, the payment (or, at least, the partial payment) of a long regretted debt.

In 1963–64, when Einar Haugen and I were both at the Center for Advanced Study in the Behavioral Sciences, that great sociolinguist, some 20 years my senior, inquired whether I did not find my work to be full of sadness, dealing as it did with a topic as sad as language shift. I replied that doctors always realize that all of their patients will ultimately die and that they are powerless to do anything to counteract that unhappy fact. On the other hand, they can still derive considerable satisfaction from understanding the causes of various illnesses and, accordingly, attempting to avoid or overcome those causes and, thereby, to delay the inevitable as long as possible.

In 1980 I began to teach a graduate course in medical anthropology at Yeshiva University's Ferkauf Graduate School of Psychology (Albert Einstein College of Medicine Campus), for students majoring in health psychology and clinical psychology. As a result of a decade of involvement in that connection, I became increasingly aware that my reply to Haugen had been inadequate. The practice and the sciences of modern medicine attempt not only to combat illness, but to cultivate 'wellness' and, in doing so, they have come to recognize that health care which does not correspond to the patient's culture and that does not prescribe accordingly is both less just and less effective than optimal health care requires. The same is true in the sociology of language. It too must arrive at understandings and develop practices which address themselves explicitly to 'wellness' and which recognize that ethnolinguistic 'wellness' is unattainable without theoretical knowledge and applied efforts that correspond to the ethnolinguistic and ethnocultural preferences and commitments of specific speech networks and speech communities.

The problems of maintenance are particularly severe for speech communities which are undergoing language shift that is already so advanced that they cannot even control informal intergenerational usage within the confines of the home, family, neighborhood and face-to-face community. This certainly becomes the initial desideratum of language maintenance, although it does not free the speech community from a constant barrage of outside ethnolinguistic influences. Once the former goal (immediate protection of the intimate intergenerational language transmission context) is attended to, the latter too can be successively attempted. However, both of these goals are exceptionally difficult ones to realize, particularly in modern interactive society. Therefore, to attempt the latter, via stylish efforts to control the language of education, the workplace, the mass media and governmental services, without having sufficiently safeguarded the former, is equivalent to constantly blowing air into a tire that still has a puncture. It is very difficult to achieve a steady state merely based upon the incoming air, because of losses due to the unmended puncture. I have attempted to explicate this truism both by addressing it theoretically as well as by returning to it via twelve case studies derived from both the Old World and the New.

Although my cases are drawn primarily from speech communities that I have visited many times in the course of more than a quarter century, and that I have continued to read about as exhaustively as is humanly possible throughout this same period of time, nevertheless, I could never have reached the necessary degree of detailed and integrated understanding with respect to most of them without the substantial assistance of local specialists, many of them scholars of great renown. I have thanked them in person, I have thanked them in the notes to the particular chapters in which their individual aid and guidance was most vital, and I now thank them again as a definable cluster of truly devoted friends and colleagues. Our collective dedication to the welfare of the world's threatened languages, in general (as well as our more intimate concern for a certain one or another 'most favorite threatened [or recently threatened] language', in particular), have made this volume possible. They must be held blameless, however, with respect to the interpretations that I have made of the data they provided or helped me obtain.

If one of the benefits of being a sociolinguist in a psychology department on a medical campus is the necessary development of broader, less traditional theoretical and methodological interests than is common when one works primarily within a more usual mono-disciplinary context, one of the prices that one pays for that benefit is the absence of real library depth in areas outside of psychology and medicine. Four individuals have made it possible for me to have long-term access to just that depth at the Stanford University and University of California (Berkeley) graduate libraries well before, during and after the time that this book was being conceptualized, written and rewritten. It is, therefore, both my pleasure and my duty to acknowledge the silent but major contributions of Charles A. Ferguson, Shirley B. Heath, Sonia Moss, Michelle Murray, Gina Wien and John Rawlings, all of Stanford University, to this volume. But for them, the endless quiet and the equally endless bibliographic depth that such a book requires could never have been even approximated and I would like my gratitude to them to be a matter of public record. As always, however, my greatest thanks go to Gella, to whom this book is dedicated.

# 1   What This Book is About and Why It is Needed

At one level this book is about exactly what its title implies: the theory and practice of assistance to speech communities whose native languages are threatened because their intergenerational continuity is proceeding negatively, with fewer and fewer users (speakers, readers, writers and even understanders) or uses every generation. The world is full of languages like this. Many are demographically rather small, with only a few hundred thousand (and, frequently, far, far fewer) users, whereas some are still demographically quite sizeable, with a million or more users, but the process of outflow exceeding inflow for three generations or more has applied to them as well. In most cases, these languages have a small band of conscientious (and often contentious) advocates, and, not infrequently, even some token governmental support. Nevertheless, the efforts expended on behalf of these languages often usually produce few, if any, positive intergenerational results, the tides that they are battling are not reversed, and their situations proceed from bad to worse.

In the main, this book is about why most efforts to reverse language shift are only indifferently successful, at best, and outright failures or even contra-indicated and harmful undertakings, at worst. It attempts to diagnose such difficulties and to prescribe ameliorative and restorative efforts in a sociolinguistically informed way, i.e. in a way that combines more narrowly ethnolinguistic with more broadly sociocultural and econotechnical considerations. It draws upon the experience of past and current practitioners of language restoration, it reviews pertinent sociolinguistic research and theory, it examines a fairly large number of cases of attempted reversals of language shift on several continents, and it seeks to suggest a more rational, systematic approach to what has often hitherto been a primarily emotion-laden, 'let's try everything we possibly can and perhaps something will work', type of dedication.

## Are Reversing Language Shift Efforts Outmoded, Provincial or Trivial 'in the Larger Scheme of Things'?

One of the first problems tackled is the problem of whether reversing language shift (hereafter: RLS) efforts *should* be undertaken at all. Such efforts are often denigrated as 'revealing romantic fixations with the early to mid-nineteenth century', at a time when the problems of the late twentieth century are already out of hand and the coming problems of the twenty-first century promise to be even more intractable. Is this the time to worry about 'sickly languages', of whatever size? When some nations are still at each others' throats while others are belatedly preoccupied with the major headaches of working out their own approaches to pluralism in government and in production, when cities the world over are crumbling due to crime and industrial pollution, when drugs are decimating the young, when poverty and incurable illnesses are ravaging hundreds of millions throughout the world, when natural resources are being destroyed or depleted at an awesome rate, when serious climatic disturbances due to environmental abuse are foreseeable but, nevertheless, probably unavoidable, when totalitarianism, of the left and of the right, both secular and religious, still dominates such sizeable proportions of mankind, when basic moral values and the very institution of the family are under siege, when new mass media of communication and new means of mass production and international trade arrangements can finally foster one 'global village' out of the endless variety of estranged and cantankerous peoples in the world ... is this the time to worry about, much less try to do anything on behalf of, threatened languages (mostly, small threatened languages to boot) whom history and the majority of their own former speakers 'have [apparently] consigned to the dustbin'?

What can one say in response to the above litany of 'more serious illnesses' and 'more encompassing concerns and possibilities'? Perhaps only that different peoples ache in different places and at different times. The fact that we need to concentrate more resources on the war against cancer and AIDS does not make either patients or doctors unconcerned about a huge variety of other, still recalcitrantly extant physical and mental disorders. On the one hand, even earaches, sore throats, toothaches or warts can be greatly disconcerting and disabling to those who suffer from them and, on the other hand, one must be particularly careful about classifying as 'merely minor or imaginary' the problems that are of concern to others. Moreover, speech communities that realize that they are in danger of dying are certainly not complaining about a 'mere' toothache, but, rather, about a very painful and dangerous disorder within their sociocultural realm. Thus, this book does not advocate overlooking or down-playing other, perhaps equally or even more serious societal aches and pains. Rather, it addresses itself to a societal issue which is often overlooked and which deserves attention, if only because it represents a hurt that more people feel than is commonly recognized, and because this hurt (and the lack of recognition for it) is indicative not only of social disorganization but of social injustice as well, the latter being a malady which must not be sloughed off as merely being of interest to the provincial or the antiquarian.

## Will the 'Global Village' Render RLS Unnecessary?

Yes, Western European integration is advancing on several fronts ('1992' is drawing nigh and the new problems that it will generate while solving old ones will be with us for a long time) and, yes, as these words are being written, there is considerable hope and concern for the success of industrial and political democratization and pluralization in Eastern Europe. Nevertheless, the European Community itself has called several times for increased use of, respect for and assistance to the non-state minority languages of that continent,[1] out of a deep recognition that a united Europe does not mean a centrally organized, regulated or uniformized Europe. A significantly more unified, integrated Europe (a goal which will not be reached tomorrow, by the way) is not necessarily in contradiction to the local identities, loyalties and behaviors that predate and undergird the pan-European counterparts (but not substitutes) that may now be arising as supplementary to them.

Although the age of the 'global village' may have arrived in some very few parts of the globe, even there people will continue to live their daily lives, to raise their children and to transmit their linguistic and non-linguistic heritages largely in terms of more particularistic, co-existing villages. Furthermore, the apparent victory of the pluralistic political model and of the competitive economic model throughout much of Europe does not mean that cultural pluralism *within the nation states* of that part (and of other parts) of the world is either assured or self-evident.

Unfortunately, democratic regimes can be just as blind to cultural pluralism and to the needs of minorities for cultural recognition and support, as are autocratic regimes. Unfortunately, too, most of the world remains unsafe for and generally unsympathetic to or unaware of the need for pluralistic cultural democracy. It is quite obvious, therefore, that there will long be a need for reversing language shift efforts to continue to be carried on, and that, as heretofore, they will need to be carried on primarily by the minorities themselves, rather than by any of the 'big brothers' or international integrative frameworks that exist today or are likely to come into existence in the foreseeable future. These efforts are easily overlooked by those whose gaze is directed elsewhere.

They do not usually get headline treatment, but that does not make their quiet, often desperate struggles any less justified or any less related to the basic human dignity of those involved in them.

## The Destruction of a Language is the Destruction of a Rooted Identity

Which brings us to what this book is about at a second or deeper level. The destruction of languages is an abstraction which is concretely mirrored in the concomitant destruction of intimacy, family and community, via national and international involvements and intrusions, the destruction of local life by mass-market hype and fad, of the weak by the strong, of the unique and traditional by the uniformizing, purportedly 'stylish' and purposely ephemeral. Once more, this book is not a denial of the legitimacy of the national and international spheres of responsibility, involvement and concern, nor does it constitute an attack upon modern life and its technological and intellectual advances and advantages. However, this book does claim that the foregoing do not constitute the sum total or the essence of social life and of language transmission, and that societally based RLS cannot be accomplished at all if it is not accomplished at the intimate family and local community levels.

Indeed, for RLS to 'take hold' these 'lower levels' constituting face-to-face, small-scale social life must be pursued in their own right and focused upon directly, rather than merely being thought of as obvious and inevitable by-products of 'higher level' (more complex, more encompassing, more power-related) processes and institutions. Which is not to say that no such by-product effect occurs at all, but, rather, that initial focusing on RLS-efforts *per se* is crucial, particularly on such efforts as can be engaged in by local communities and by their constituent families by means of their own efforts, resources and dedication. It counsels greater sociocultural self-sufficiency, self-help, self-regulation and initiative at the 'lower level', so to speak, before seriously pursuing such 'higher level' arenas, almost always conducted in a contextually stronger, established rival language, as secondary or even more advanced education, the extra-communal work sphere, the national mass media and other governmentally controlled services and operations.

This book does not question the importance of the latter arenas, particularly their importance *vis-à-vis* access to power in modern, urban life, but it does question the need or the ability of all languages to function in these particular spheres, as well as the advisability of *such* goals when the more foundational spheres — more foundational insofar as intergenerational mother tongue transmission is concerned — of family and community have not yet been safeguarded. Particularly, it rejects the view that intimate 'language-in-culture' concerns are 'merely folkloric romanticism' in comparison to purportedly worthier interests of power and conflict. There cannot be any secure RLS without both the one and the other, and the issue that must preoccupy us is *when to pursue which* and the true nature of the relationships between them both and intergenerational mother tongue transmission.

What hope or purpose is there for a community's sociocultural, econotechnical and political self-regulation if the upper societal spheres are dominated by another language? Well, there is still the opportunity to function in these latter spheres via societal bilingualism, i.e. via the co-mastery of the generally employed language of those spheres, by means of exposure to institutions of education and work and to other life experiences that go beyond intimacy, family and local community. Would not such exposure then proceed once more to undermine the language of intimacy, family and community? Not necessarily; not if the latter are protected by hallowed and conscious sociocultural boundaries: values, rituals, traditions, belief-systems and a unifying and encompassing vision of 'being an Xman-via-Xish', i.e. of using the traditional own-ethnicity-associated language for purposes of ethnic self-definition and association. Indeed, intimacy, family, community, identity and affiliation are the essences of ethnocultural creativity and continuity and by *initially* disengaging them from the confrontation with the pursuit of power (at least until such time as there is a sufficiently firm primary base from which this pursuit can take its point of departure) they are rendered *more*, rather than *less*, viable and are ever more strongly related to some of the very processes and pursuits that humans value most. Is this mere romanticism? Can the weak have no other alternatives than the hobson's choice of either 'dreaming the impossible dream' and perishing culturally due to inaction, on the one hand, or engaging in a totally hopeless struggle, and perishing culturally due to erroneous actions, on the other hand?

This book counsels a third alternative, namely, *initial* conflict avoidance (but not, by any means, the avoidance of the voluntary struggle for ethnolinguistic existence), emphasizing the advocacy of cultural democracy and the attainment of diglossic bilingualism, demographic concentration, and the studied strengthening of ethnocultural boundaries in connection with friendship, family and community, rather than premature and risky functional confrontations with the powers that be. It does not counsel the postponement of overt promotion of RLS, but in that connection it advises patient and diligent concentration on the 'home front', before serious attention and scarce resources are devoted to the higher order spheres. Those spheres extend significantly beyond the minority community, and the attainment of basic control over them, and successes in connection with them, is much more problematic and must depend on basic changes in the demographic, juridical and, therefore, political realities surrounding RLS-efforts, if they are to be attained in a lasting fashion.

By attending to the emphases, phases and rationales suggested here, it is hoped that RLS will be more successfully attained and, at the same time, that the very ethnocultural purposes for which RLS is desired will be fostered rather than lost in the process of ever expanding and prematurely competitive aspirations for political power and economic success. It is not enough, it will be argued, to 'be like everyone else, but in Xish', for if that were enough then Xish really would be no more than a culturally redundant and cliquishly self-serving flourish. It is identity, rather than power, and *Gemeinschaft* (intimate community), rather than *Gesellschaft* (impersonal society), that Xish must fundamentally and studiously pursue at the outset, since power spheres are always embedded in and manipulated by even greater power spheres, whereas cultural spheres can be both ethnoculturally self-protective and econotechnically syncretistic at the same time. More than anything else, pro-RLS-efforts must take pains not to confuse and compromise their goals via the means that they pursue, in order to better attain and preserve these goals. The priorities at various points in the RLS struggle must vary but they must, nevertheless, derive from a single, integrated theory of language-in-society processes that places intergenerational mother tongue transmission at the very center and that makes sure to defend that center before setting out to conquer societal processes that are more distant, dubious and tenuous *vis-à-vis* such transmission.

## Fostering 'Small-Scale Community Life' is Difficult but Crucial for RLS, particularly in the More Weakened Cases

Thus, it is the twentieth and the twenty-first century that this book is about: about efforts to make the post-modern present and the future more meaningful and more comforting for ordinary folk, more creative and humanistically nurturing for all, rather than merely about giving late-comers and losers a leg up in the ongoing race toward new records in popular consumerism, cultural pap and governmental pomp. 'Good problems' may be defined as problems whose solutions contribute to the solutions of related problems rather than to their exacerbation. Language shift is a by-product of unequal rates of social change and of growth in econotechnical power and, therefore, of self-regulation, i.e. the very same processes that also contribute to the widespread anomie and alienation that typify so much of modern life among the culturally dominant and the culturally recessive alike. Reversing language shift deals with a 'good problem' because it is itself a potential contribution to overcoming some of the endemic sociocultural dislocation of modernity. In this sense, then, RLS is potentially a contribution to the solution of problems that are greater than the one that is first on its own agenda. Indeed, RLS is a contribution to many of the central problems that eat away at modern life, at modern man and at modern society. As such, it deserves the serious attention and the heartfelt cooperation of one and all, regardless of whether our own favorite language is involved or implicated in the efforts that it requires. It is not a problem restricted to the provincial, peripheral boondocks, but, rather, a problem that relates to the very heartland and the cutting edge of worldwide modernity in all of its assets and in all of its debits. It is a problem whose solution deserves our collective understanding and involvement.

The study and practice of RLS proceeds from the theoretically informed study of cases[2] to the fostering of intergenerational mother tongue transmission viewed as a cultural right and a societal resource. The cases that we will examine are either fundamentally Western or, at the very least, substantially impacted by longer exposure to Western-derived values, processes and dislocations. This is necessarily so because it is precisely in such Western or Western-impacted contexts that RLS is both most necessary practically and best justified and most fully precedented philosophically. The even larger number of RLS problems now brewing in localities that have only more recently been seriously impacted by the West (in the past 25–50 years) will require separate and additional treatment in the future.

## Language as a Resource that Can Be Augmented, Developed and Modified

The fundamental point of departure for RLS-efforts is the view that language is a resource at the level of societal integration and social identification. This point of departure does not imply the reification of ethnocultural identity nor the assumption that such identity can ever be 'preserved' in some pure and unaltered state. It does assume that every human aggregate defines its history and works toward a desired model of its future in accord with that definition. Majorities do so as well as minorities and it is no more reprehensible for the latter to engage in such a quest than it is for the former. A preferred, historically associated mother tongue has a role in this process of individual and aggregative self-definition and self-realization, not merely as a myth (i.e. as a verity whose objective truth is less important than its subjective truth) but also as a genuine identificational and motivational desideratum in the ethnocultural realm. While it is true that culture is a construct rather than a 'thing' to be molded, fashioned, changed or pointed in a particular direction, the same is also true of other targets of organized societal efforts, e.g. education, mass communications, public health, justice and their various related societal institutions and goals. Thus, it is by no means inherently ludicrous, wicked or stupid to plan or seek to influence or to modify the ongoing interaction between language and culture, even though one must grant that such planning and modification, like all social planning and modification, is sometimes done ludicrously, wickedly and stupidly[3].

Nor is it at all necessary to be a primordialist oneself in order to recognize the emotional strength of the common linkage of language with formative ties to family, community and history. The fact that these ties can come asunder does not negate the right of those who are so inclined to combat the sundering of the very ties that mean so very much to them. However, and this is more to the point, the fact that these ties are often so strongly and directly experienced does not mean that those who seek to foster them can successfully do so in a spontaneous and untutored way. Indeed, weakened and endangered languages pertain to cultures that no longer significantly regulate the daily lives of their members. That is also why RLS is so difficult to attain.

RLS requires reversing the tenor, the focus, the qualitative emphases of daily informal life — always the most difficult arenas in which to intervene. Indeed, RLS resists being programmed or planned, not only because its would-be planners and programmers are frequently poor in resources and weak in numbers, but because it is initially necessary for the weak in numbers and poor in resources to tackle some of the most elusive behaviors and interactions of social and communal life. Nevertheless, it is my hope and conviction that a sense of priorities can be conveyed in this connection, a sense that is derived from a theory of intergenerational mother tongue transmission and the particular circumstances in which a particular threatened speech community finds itself. That too, then, is what this book is about and why it is needed.

## Notes

1. For analyses of the pro-minority-language concerns and pronouncements of the European Community Parliament and the implications of '1992' for these languages, as well as for the state languages that are not considered official for EC purposes, see Coulmas, 1989. A briefer treatment is provided by O'Riagáin, 1989.
2. The most immediate predecessor of the current volume is Ellis and mac a' Ghobhainn, 1971. It too attempts to derive its conclusions and recommendations from a detailed examination of cases. All in all it examines 20 cases (17 European and three Asian), the majority of which are by now so well established that some may find it difficult to imagine that they were 'threatened' at some point in the past. There is only one case in common between that book and this one (Hebrew) and the

theoretical emphases of the two volumes are quite different. The former book stresses the 'will to survive' while this one stresses a theory that incorporates ideology (motivating and activating belief) and concrete applications of the right step at the right time. (I am greatly indebted to Nancy Dorian for calling this out-of-print book to my attention and for making a copy of it for me. It is a book which not only deserves to be better known but to be reprinted as well.)

3. For a recent exposé of many of the conceptual errors involved in treating constructs such as culture and language as if they were tangible physical entities that can be fixed, molded or manipulated at will, see Handler, 1988. Although his treatment is quite telling, it, nevertheless, somehow overlooks a very important fact, namely, that different languages do, after all, relate to different cultural identities and that these identities serve to orient and to mobilize human aggregates. One does not have to be a 'believer' to be able to appreciate the similar role of religion; one should not have to be a language nationalist in order to appreciate the crucial role of specific languages and of preferences for a specific language in the fashioning of both political and ethnocultural agendas.

# References

COULMAS, Florian 1989, European integration and the idea of the national language: Ideological roots and economic consequences. In his (ed.), *Wanted: A Language Policy for the European Community*

ELLIS, Peter Berresford and MAC A'GHOBHAINN, Seumas 1971, *The Problem of Language Revival: Examples of Language Survival*. Inverness: Club Leabhar.

HANDLER, Richard 1988, *Nationalism and the Politics of Culture*. Madison: University of Wisconsin Press.

O'RIAGAIN, Donall 1989, Nations and states: Some reflections on Europe after 1992. *Contact Bulletin* 6, 2, 1–2.

# 2 Why Try to Reverse Language Shift and Is It Really Possible to Do So?

Before a task can be undertaken, it is desirable that those involved in the undertaking be maximally clear in their minds and united in their hearts as to why that task *should* be undertaken. This is particularly true with respect to a collective task undertaken by those purporting to labor not only on behalf of themselves, but on behalf of an ethnocultural entity. Individuals can sometimes afford to be less than fully conscious and less than maximally unconflicted about their individual actions, i.e. to hope to attain consciousness and inner unconflictedness as they go along. Even so, a lack of clarity *vis-à-vis* goals and means at the individual level often exacts a price in that many things that are done subsequently need to be undone, repaired, discarded or redone. 'That's life', we say, shaking our heads sadly; 'Live and learn!' Collective undertakings, however, just cannot afford to proceed in this fashion, both because their goals are typically more complex to begin with than are the goals of individuals, and because collective action inevitably elicits a degree of collective counter-action as well. Therefore, the success of collective action is limited, at best, by the extent to which at least the individuals whom such action attracts are able to work in concert rather than at cross-purposes.

Of course, there is no sure way to predict the future and all our collective efforts are constantly exposed to unanticipated side-effects and to co-occurrences beyond our control. In addition, there are *always* more things that it would be good to know *before* one undertakes a collective task, but we are always limited in time, talent and wherewithal, and most tasks must, inevitably and unfortunately, be undertaken under less than fully optimal circumstances, if they are to be undertaken at all.

True though all these observations may be, their truth only makes it particularly and all the more desirable for collective tasks, tasks involving many people on behalf of an ethnocultural goal such as 'reversing language shift' (RLS), to be undertaken only after careful consideration of the goals, prospects and circumstances of the prospective undertaking. Language issues in society are usually fraught with emotions, values, ideals and loyalties and, as with most 'matters of the heart', they seem so compelling that to pause for clarification may seem, to many who favor reversing language shift (pro-RLSers we will call them from now on), to be not only unnecessary but unfeeling, uncaring and rigid. However, without such prior clarification and deliberation, there is a very substantial risk that a disparity of goals and a diversity of levels of commitment will remain hidden, only to erupt later in the form of schisms, defections, animosities and other disturbances that will do far greater damage to 'the language cause' than could have been brought about by a modicum of delay for clarification and possible unification originally (McPherson, 1973). Some such disruptive problems are likely to arise anyway, because collective action is always exposed to an irreducible minimum of rivalry for leadership and difference of opinion, interpretation and prioritization. However, without prior, honest clarification of both goals and doubts, circumstances and possibilities, the likelihood of future ruptures and difficulties is literally built-in into societal reform efforts (and attempts to reverse language shift must be understood to constitute just such an effort) from their very outset. While it is irksome it is nevertheless inescapable: the established sociocultural order often requires no reason, no conscious rationale or justification, while its reversal or modification is usually beset with just such requirements.

## Why Bother?

Obviously, not all members of any endangered ethnocultural entity can be united *vis-à-vis* the desirability of reversing language shift, i.e. not all of them will favor more frequent and more functionally diversified use of Xish [pro-nounced: Ex-ish] (Xish will stand for the name of any language, since so many language names in English are formed on this model, e.g. Swedish, Spanish, Danish, Polish, Yiddish, etc.) by the members of the community (let us call them Xmen [pronounced: Ex-men], on the model of Englishmen, Frenchmen, Irishmen, etc.) with which that language has been historically associated. Were that not the case, then the problem itself, language shift away from Xish and the resulting need to consider how to reverse this process (whether in general or in specific pursuits), probably would not exist. Indeed, not only do many Xmen seem oblivious to the need for reversing language shift, but some may actually deny the need for pro-RSL efforts and oppose efforts along those lines. What are the rationales and what are the motives of anti-RLSers [are-el-esers]? These rationales and motivations must be well known and understood by the advocates of reversing language shift, not only because without such familiarity it will be more difficult to cope with the arguments of those who deny the desirability of reversing language shift, but because some of these arguments may also be sub-consciously accepted, at least in part, by some pro-RLSers too.

## 'It Is Too Late; Nothing Can Be Done About It Anymore!'

The most defeatist claim by anti-RLSers is that RLS cannot succeed because it is 'too late', i.e. because the speakers and supporters of Xish are already too few in number and/or too weak in social influence or power for their efforts to be crowned with success. This charge must be carefully considered. It is true, unfortunately, that some irremediable language shift situations may exist insofar as certain RLS goals are concerned and that some languages and their associated cultures have already been so eroded that they can no longer be returned to their former statuses, let alone promoted beyond those statuses. However, even for them something can be done. Therefore, the question of success must not be approached in absolute terms (achieving full success vs. doing nothing at all) but, rather, in functional, contextual or situational terms as well as in terms of Time 1 vs. Time 2 vs. Time 3, i.e. in terms of immediate vs. longer-range goals. *There is no language for which nothing at all can be done*, and, therefore, the crux of any RLS solution is to decide what is the best that can be done for Xish in a particular context and in a given time-frame, and then to go on from there. Just as a physician faced by a patient with many different complications must decide which ailments to leave for later (if they are to be tackled at all) and which to tackle first (since not all ailments are similarly critical) and with which cures (since some cures of ailment A may engender 'complications' with respect to ailment B), so RLS advocates must decide which *functions* (i.e. which ethnolinguistic contexts) to tackle first, because they are the most critical, and which specific steps to take in order to (re)gain those functions *among specific target populations*. Over and over again pro-RLSers must remind themselves that it is intergenerational mother tongue transmission that they are after, rather than merely 'good things (or impressive symbolic splashes) for Xish'.

Much language policy is discussed in terms of the nationwide level only; however, that is not the only or even necessarily the optimal level for RLS and for language status planning more generally. Indeed, the more disadvantaged a particular language is the less productive (and the less feasible) macro-level (nationwide, regionwide) policies may actually be. Under such circumstances, more pinpointed goals must be focused upon first, goals that are oriented toward much smaller societal units such as families, clubs or neighborhoods, or to speaking (rather than writing), or to schools (rather than businesses), or to kindergartens (rather than high schools), etc.

## Example 1: Differentiating Between Functional Alternatives in RLS-Efforts

In the late nineteenth/early twentieth century 'revival' (actually, revernacularization) of Hebrew, priority was given to speaking the language over writing it. In addition, in preparing new terminologies so that speakers could cope with the exigencies of modern daily life, the Hebrew Language Academy started with carpentry and 'kitchenry' (artifacts and activities of the modern kitchen), rather than with terminologies for the natural sciences.

RLS-efforts recently undertaken on behalf of Maori have concentrated on childcare/nursery schools more than on other societal institutions, such as mass media or government. This is a frequent decision of RLS movements, because early childhood schools afford an organized and long-term opportunity to reach and influence the young. An RLS movement on behalf of a language spoken primarily by individuals already past school-age might best start elsewhere.

Some Amerindian languages are already in such disarray, and have been neglected for such a length of time, that it is necessary to piece their grammars and vocabularies together first, from various oral and written sources, before any efforts on behalf of active spoken use, by either adults or children, can be undertaken.

Thus, the general conclusion that 'nothing can be done about it anymore' is likely to be correct only if totally inappropriate goals are being entertained. The strongest adherents of inappropriate goals are likely to be some of the pro-RLSers themselves. It may be hard for true and complete believers to settle for less than the full demographic and functional pie. But this is as defeatist a position as is the taunt of anti-RLSers that anything less than full and exclusive dominion is unworthy and demeaning, and, therefore, nothing at all can or should be done for the language. A more realistic counsel is to realize that 'a bird in the hand is worth two in the bush'. A few well-chosen smaller victories earlier on will do much more for the eventual larger-scale and longer-term success of pro-RLS efforts than will lack of success *vis-à-vis* more grandiose but impossible goals.

The argument between those who want everything for Xish (and, presumably, right away too) and those who say that *that* is impossible to attain and, therefore, nothing at all should be tried, is ultimately easier for judicious RLSers to resolve than is the argument between those who advocate *certain* immediate measures and those who advocate others. Both of these latter folks are in the pro-RLS camp and yet they may disagree profoundly; so profoundly, indeed, that some of the purportedly pro-RLS steps advocated by those in one sub-camp will strike those in another as being useless or even contraindicated, i.e. damaging *vis-à-vis* the RLS goal. Obviously, it is almost as bad to settle for less when more could be gained, than to aspire to more than can be gained and, therefore, by over-reaching, to suffer further reverses, such as loss of motivation, time, funds and supporters. This then, rather than the argument with anti-RLSers who believe in the 'nothing can be done about it anyway' position, is the area on which pro-RLS forces should concentrate their analytic, persuasive and ameliorative talents. Those who claim that 'nothing can be done about it' because it is already too late, because even to try to do anything is a public admission of and an intensification of the terrible straits in which Xish finds itself, should be answered that the problem is not *'whether to do anything?'* but *'what* to do?; *when* to do it?; *where* to do it?; and *how* to do it?' That is a good problem* (actually, a problem-series), one that deserves an answer and one that requires much study. We will return to *this* problem (it is a 'good problem') in Chapter 4 (and in several subsequent chapters), below.

## Mothing Should be Done about It Because RLS Is Unnecessary or even Undesirable

Defeatism is still fundamentally an empirical position. It implies agreement with respect to the desirability of the RLS goal in principle, but pessimism, often very profound pessimism, with respect to the attainability of one or another type of RLS goal or practice. As we have already pointed out, differences between optimists and pessimists may be difficult to resolve, but not nearly as difficult as it is to resolve differences pertaining to the desirability of RLS *per se*. The latter differences are differences *vis-à-vis ends*. They are profoundly philosophical/ideological/value-related and are generally not as bridgeable via empirical analysis and rational discussion as are differences with respect to *means*.

The first thing to realize, in connection with differences with respect to whether RLS is or is not even 'theoretically' desirable, is that *any* answer to this question is based on philosophical premises. This is important to recognize, because, frequently, one side will view itself as 'entirely realistic' while viewing the other side as 'hopelessly ideological'. The maintenance and advancement of disadvantaged languages, these being the ultimate goals of RLS, do not need to be justified *any more* than does the position that such languages deserve no special attention and that they should be permitted to sink into oblivion if they cannot make it on their own. Of course, the maintenance and advancement of disadvantaged languages requires *no less* justification than does its opposite. Furthermore, since the adherents of RLS are likely to be fewer in number and with less access to the media, the schools, the church, the government and the various other opinion-forming institutions of society, their views are *less* likely to be known to others at the same time as they themselves are more likely to be exposed to the views of their opponents. Accordingly, it is of special importance that the pro-RLS views be well and unembarrassedly put, not only so that others may be influenced by them (after all, there are usually many folks who are neither decidedly pro- nor anti-, and some of these can still be influenced in the pro-direction), but so that pro-RLSers themselves can be reassured that their minority position is well taken.

Views about the desirability of RLS are, in essence, views as to the relationship between language and culture. It is very hard to tell the truth about the relationship between language and culture; it is even harder to tell the whole truth and nothing but the truth in this connection. It is hard to tell the truth about language and culture because anything that one says about the relationship between them is likely to be perspectival, that is, it is likely to be strongly influenced by the 'teller's' involvement in the very relationship that he or she is discussing. Most cultures, and minority or threatened cultures in particular, have very definite views of the relationship between languages and cultures in general and, most specifically, about the relationship between their own language and their own culture. To some extent, scientific methods of experimental design and of cross-cultural comparison help safeguard against such sources of bias, but it is impossible to escape from them entirely, precisely because they are both unconscious and pervasive.

In addition, 'the whole truth' about the relationship between language and culture may be too complex and too subtle, as well as too subjective and self-fulfilling to be fully told. In all realms of cultural behavior, those factors that are believed to be true have very definite consequences, whether or not they were initially or demonstrably true above and beyond the beliefs about them. Thus, beliefs about the relationship between language and culture are part of any culture itself and they are culturally transmitted from one generation to the next. Such beliefs have definite consequences for child socialization and education, for second language learning and intergroup relations, for cultural borrowing and culture planning. The consequences of the beliefs, therefore, need to be examined in any consideration of the 'whole truth' about the relationship between language and culture. Cultures are feedback systems and they tend to produce those very results which they take to be inevitable, regardless of whether or not they are truly inevitable.

As a result of all of the foregoing, no claim can be made to tell 'the truth, the whole truth and nothing but the truth' about the desirability or advisability of RLS. What follows is inevitably and admittedly a perspectival effort in that direction. Clearly, however, contrary views would be equally perspectival.

## We Can Be Xmen without Xish (i.e. We Can Be Xmen via Yish [Y-ish] or via Zish [Z-ish])

The longer the process of language shift away from Xish has gone on, the longer the phenomenon of Xmen who do not speak or even understand Xish has existed. Jews who do not speak Hebrew have existed for millennia, Irishmen who do not speak Irish have existed for centuries, and Puerto Ricans who do not speak Spanish (usually these are third generation, American mainland-born individuals of 'insular' Puerto Rican 'grandparentage') have existed for only about a quarter century at most. In all cases, however, they have become powerful examples of the detachability of a traditionally and historically associated language with respect to the continuity of individual and collective ethnocultural identity. If Yish is a language of greater power and opportunity than is Xish, and if Yish speakers of Xish parentage or ancestry continue to believe that they can still be Xmen (or Xmen in addition too, i.e. they believe that they can be Xmen and Ymen simultaneously and entirely in Yish), then the need for Xish for the purposes of Xishness (Swedishness, Danishness, Spanishness) will seem to many to be greatly decreased, if not eclipsed entirely.[1]

While it is important to grant the reality of the phenomenon 'Xmen who know no, or hardly any, Xish', it is even more important to examine this reality. The traditionally associated language of any ethnocultural collectivity is associated with the total ethnocultural pattern of that collectivity at a particular time and place. Jews who have lost their familiarity with Hebrew have lived a different daily life-pattern (a different Jewishness) than have Jews who did not, regardless of whether both groups continued to call themselves Jews and to be so called by others. The discontinuance of Hebrew in daily life was often lamented by rabbis and other Jewish community leaders (rabbis are not merely religious spokesmen; they are often community leaders in all other respects as well), because this discontinuance was associated with other profound changes as well: with a greater incidence of leaving the historic homeland, with a greater incidence of non-observance of then-current traditions, with a greater incidence of intermarriage, with a greater incidence of new customs (not hallowed as were the original ones), with a greater incidence of mispronunciation of hallowed ritual texts — all in all, therefore, with a greater incidence of culture change.

An examination of the Irish and the Puerto Rican cases (and countless others, yet to be discussed) will reveal counterparts to the Jewish case among them as well. Language shift generally and basically involves culture change as well indeed, initially, quite devastating and profound culture change, all the more so in cases where the ethnocultural collectivity does not also represent a distinctive religious tradition dissimilar from and discontinuous with those religious traditions surrounding it and where the vernacular traditionally and historically associated with this tradition is, therefore, not also sanctified.

Thus, while ethnocultural label-maintenance and self-concept-maintenance may long outlast language-maintenance, the detailed pattern of culture, and any community's ability to maximize self-regulation of culture change and the regulation of culture contact, is invariably different when the historically associated language is present than when it is absent. Of course, the language alone will not be either the sole and sufficient cause or the guarantor of all the cultural patterns associated with it. Anthropologists are quite capable of finding small peoples who retained their 'identity' because they retained their traditional agricultural system, or their traditional kinship system, even though they lost their languages. However, given the ambiguity of 'identity' under such circumstances, it is necessary to add that most cultures reveal the 'domino principle' in operation and when any of their main props, such as language, are lost, most other props are seriously weakened and are far more likely to be altered and lost as well. Ultimately, therefore, RLS and language maintenance are not about language *per se*; they are about language-in-culture. RLS is an attempt to foster, to fashion, to attain and to assist a particular language-in-culture content and pattern.

A call for RLS must, therefore, also be seen and explained as a call for cultural reconstruction and for greater cultural-self-regulation. If this is not understood then RLS-efforts must, inevitably, fail, as all ethnocultural planning that lacks a central and crucial integrative component must fail. RLS is an indication of dissatisfaction with ethnocultural (and, often, also with ethnopolitical and ethno-economic) life as it currently is, and of a resolve to undertake planned ethnocultural reconstruction. This change does not need to be backward-looking in its thrust, regardless of the historical metaphors that it may utilize (because of their recognized symbolic and emotional significance). Indeed, most RLS-efforts are actually syncretistic and modernistic with respect to their cultural implications and goals. If that is the case, then what is the exact difference between their ethnocultural goals and the goals pursued by those who maintain that 'one can be a good Xman without knowing Xish'? Normally, it is a difference in precise self-definitions, in the minutiae of cultural implementations and in self-regulatory preferences and capacity *vis-à-vis* outside influences. These differences are felt to be representative of a different ethnocultural pattern, symbol-system and value-system, but it is exactly these differences that must be explained and detailed in order to convey 'the RLS idea'.

## Example 2: Successful RLS is Invariably Part of a Larger Ethnocultural Goal

Since the restoration of post-Franco democracy in Spain, RLS-efforts on behalf of Basque have been an aspect of a broader movement seeking greater cultural autonomy for 'the Basque community'. Thus far, Spain has granted 'the Basque community' only a modicum of self-regulatory authority, exercised by a 'Basque Government', particularly in matters of local cultural concern. The exact limits of this authority continue to be jointly explored and is ofconcern to more than RLSers, since many non-Basques and non-Basquephone Basques now live in the Basque provinces.

The movement on behalf of French in Quebec has been part and parcel of a movement to become 'masters in our own house'. Although the pursuit of independence from Canada has (thus far) been rejected by the Quebecois electorate, the furtherance of French has gone hand in hand with the Francization of industrial, commercial and provincial- governmental operations.

The recovery and reintroduction of Amerindian languages on many Indian reservations has been accompanied by the recovery and reintroduction of traditional dances, songs, handicrafts and a strengthening of traditional worship and curative rituals.

Sore Shenirer's movement of Orthodox Day Schools for Jewish girls in interwar Poland argued that genuine Orthodoxy in daily practices and values was not possible without the use of Yiddish, 'the language of traditional Orthodoxy', just as Yiddish without Orthodoxy was decried as a senseless parroting of Gentile secular nationalisms. Laborite and left-wing secular nationalists also fostered Yiddish (as 'a' or even 'the' Jewish national tongue), but did so as part of a platform that viewed Jews as a modern, secular nationality, with its own schools (in Yiddish), its own theaters (in Yiddish), its own books, journals and publishing houses (in Yiddish), and with its own governmentally recognized local courts (in Yiddish).

RLS is rarely, if ever, pursued 'for its own sake'. Only linguists, translators, some language teachers and a few other clearly atypical individuals are interested in languages 'for their own sake'. However, pro-RLS partisans often make the impression that this *is* so, i.e. that language *is* their exclusive concern. As a frequently embattled and sometimes besieged minority, they often become so accustomed to speaking only to each other that they forget how to speak effectively to others. What they no longer need to explain to each other they often no longer know how to explain to others. They often need to remind themselves and to make themselves more conscious of their own RLS 'basic principles', so that they can then make others more conscious of these principles as well. RLSers should not be embarrassed about the fact that theirs is *basically a value position* (a position relative to the ethnocultural saliency, content and regulation of their lives), because the position of their opponents is also no more than a value position. On the other hand, they must become more adept at explaining what this position is, because in doing so they will be able to better design the steps that are needed in order to implement it, whether at the macro-level or at the micro-level. They must realize that RLS is, essentially, a societal reform-effort that involves both the *abandonment* of widely accepted (but ideologically contra-indicated) cultural patterns and the attainment of their stipulated replacements. To realize this is to realize why RLS is so difficult to attain; not to realize it is to forgo the slim chances that exist for the success of RLS-efforts.

RLS essentially entails a critique of Xish society (and probably also of Yish society) as it is and, therefore, a resolve to pursue specific revisions in ethnocultural content, process and self-regulation. Sometimes this involves political and economic revisions as well, but the latter need not imply power aspirations of a seditious, separatist or social strife nature. All sociocultural efforts (including all anti-RLS-efforts as well) involve leadership (and, therefore, political and power aspirations at the organizational level) and wherewithal (and, therefore, economic concerns at the organizational level, as well as individuals whose own economic success will be bolstered by 'the cause'). The levels of political and economic preoccupation, and the existence of leadership with self-focused goals in addition to the collectively shared ones, these do not define the differences between pro- or anti-RLS-programs and philosophies. Such preoccupations, when they obtain, are not necessarily evil and exploitative when found among pro-RLSers and innocuous, benign or salutary when encountered among anti-RLSers[2].

The entire intellectually fashionable attempt to reduce all ethnocultural movements to problems of 'who attains power' and 'who gets money' is exactly that: reductionistic. It reduces human values, emotions, loyalties and philosophies to little more than hard cash and brute force. These misguided attempts, regardless of the great names associated with them and the pseudo-intellectual fashionableness that they occasionally enjoy because of their purported 'realism', inevitably impoverish rather than enrich our understanding of the complexity of human nature and of sociocultural reality. They cannot help us grasp the intensity of ideals and idealism, of commitments and altruism, that are at the very heart of much social behavior in general and of RLS behavior in particular.

And it is not the flea but the elephant that is being overlooked by such reductionist schools of thought. Human beings individually and collectively, when functioning in groups and in historically defined collectivities, often champion causes that are unpopular and that cannot be calculated to bring them nearly as much gain nor as much power as would any of various concurrently 'more likely to succeed' causes, movements or undertakings. Irrational? Perhaps, but cultures, unlike computers, are fundamentally irrational. Their function is to be integratively 'different' ('authentic', 'unique', 'themselves'), both in values or *Weltanschauungen* and in their prescriptions for daily life, rather than to be efficient — a task that can be left to cost, time and motion specialists and to other well paid representatives of efficiency and rationality 'for their own sake'. Cultures and cultural differences are inherently irrational, but it is this same irrationality (or is it super-rationality?) that is at the heart of religion, love, emotion, altruism, creativity, art, music and individuality, rather than only being at the heart of conflict, competition and various forms of self-aggrandizement (as anti-RLSers sometimes charge, conveniently overlooking thereby both the irrationality and the conflict that accompany their own views). Just as it is not the power and self-interest focus of RLS-efforts that differentiate them from any and all other social efforts (including anti-RLS-efforts which necessarily have their own carefully hidden power and self-interest agendas), so it is not the basic irrationality of RLS-efforts that differentiates them from other sociocultural efforts (definitely including anti-RLS-efforts). Rather, it is the particular content and direction of RLS — its focus on a particular language-and-ethnoculture link expressed via a particular cultural content, cultural process and cultural self-regulatory pursuit — that is differentiating, and it is this content, process and direction that RLSers must have firmly and unembarrassedly in mind. RLSers are implicitly saying: 'We want a different kind of Xman from that which is currently ascendant and from that which is predictable without the particular language-in-culture linkage we espouse'. It is this 'different kind' and that kind's *link to Xish* that must be spelled out if those who are not yet convinced are to become persuaded to mend their ways.

## A language is indexically related to its culture

Languages are linked to particular ethnocultures in three major ways: indexically, symbolically and in a part/whole fashion. That language which has traditionally been linked with a given ethnoculture is, at any time during which that linkage is still intact, best able to name the artifacts and to formulate or express the interests, values and world-views of that culture. Since the two, the language and the ethnoculture (if we may permit ourselves to separate them for a moment), have 'grown up together' over an extensive period of time, they are better attuned to each other, at any time when the linkage between them is generally intact, than is any other language to that culture at that time. That is not to say that the traditionally associated language is a perfect or isomorphic road-map to its traditionally related culture. The two, language and culture, change at related but not at identical rates. For a while, languages may preserve terms and expressions appropriate to cultural artifacts and reflecting cultural interests that are no longer available or implemented. Nevertheless, they do not long lack for consensual terms for those that are currently available and implemented. This is usually well known to all RLS advocates and they will boast to each other (or to any opponents who will listen) that there is no way of saying *x* in Yish whereas 'in Xish it is so easy, so natural and so lovely to say ...'. What pro-RLSers are less likely to admit, or even to realize, is that Yish or Zish could, in time, come to achieve comparable felicity of expression were they to remain associated with the culture that has *x*'s or is concerned with them. The 'necessary but lacking' word could be borrowed directly from Xish, or a translation-loan (a Yish word translated from Xish) or a neologism (a newly created Yish word) could be created to cope with the hitherto 'missing' word or concept. After all, in the long run, all languages are equally capable of expressing any and all sociocultural realities. However, no one lives in the long run; we all live in the short run, in the here and now, and in the short run the pro-RLSers are right: in the short run (which is to say, at any particular point in time) no language but the one that has been most historically and intimately associated with a given culture is as well able to express the artifacts and the concerns of that culture.[3]

## Example 3: Languages are Lexically 'Most Appropriate' for their Traditionally Associated Cultures

Eskimo has several words for various different types of snow (wet and dry, thick and thin) and Beduin Arabic, for different types of horses and camels, precisely because their associated cultures are crucially concerned with the distinctions between these types. Other cultures, in which snow, horses or camels play little if any important role, can get by with only one or two words subsuming all of them.

Kinship terminologies pertain to culture-specific kinship systems. Yiddish has a word for the relationship between the parents of the bride and the parents of the groom: this relationship is called *mekheto'nemshaft*. The two fathers address each other as *mekhu'tn* and the two mothers, as *mekhetey'neste*. Both sets of parents have rights and obligations toward the young couple (e.g. arranging and paying for the wedding) and toward each other (e.g. sharing the latter expense in ways that they agree upon).

Japanese and Indonesian/Malaysian have had (and to a more minor degree still have) a variety of pronouns that relate to the status differences that are recognized (or politely implied) to exist between interlocutors. When post-World War II Indonesian required a second person pronoun that would not have such status implications, it went outside of its traditional system to borrow such a term ($U$, from Dutch).

American English has sports terminology unknown to British English, and vice versa. Australian English has terms for animal life that have no counterparts in either American or British English. The same is true for typically regional foods, articles of apparel and aspects of material culture within each of these three English varieties. Increased contact between speakers of various varieties of English has erased many of these differences, but others remain and new differences are constantly being generated between them.

However, true though the lexical link between language and culture may be, it is both an ephemeral and a peripheral truth. It is ephemeral because ethnocultures are changing all of the time and receding languages may actually come to be *less* attuned to many of the most recent changes that have occurred than are their competitors. (As we will discuss at length in Chapter 11, below, if this anomaly is to be avoided it is crucial that a modicum of corpus planning — the authoritative creation of new terms, at least for the purposes of daily life, including daily technology, as RLSers actually live it and advocate that it be lived — be conducted throughout the course of RLS-efforts, regardless of how well RLSers believe they already know the language). It is peripheral because felicity of expression is not, in and of itself, either the central goal of RLS or an important ideal for most ordinary members of an ethnoculture (although humanities professors and literary folk are apt to forget that). The indexical superiority of Xish, if any, must pertain to the particular brand and content of Xish culture (Xishness) that RLSers advocate and, accordingly, it is the cultural advocacy that is crucial, rather than the lexical/semantic felicity *per se*.

## A language is symbolically linked to its culture

A more germane argument on behalf of the traditionally associated language championed by RLS-efforts is that language and culture are linked symbolically. By dint of long-term association, the two are not only well attuned to each other, but they stand for each other in the minds of insiders and of outsiders too. During World Wars I and II, German-Americans (and even Swiss-German-Americans) were careful not to speak German in public in the USA. This was not because America was at war with the German language, but because the German language 'stood for' (i.e. it had become symbolic of) the German nation and America was at war with the latter. When RLSers tell us that the language is a major (even, in their eyes, 'the' major) component of their (ethnocultural) identity, what they mean, feel and believe (and what they would like others to mean, feel and believe) is that the language stands for being an Xman, 'a true Xman', one who lives, breathes and implements a particular Xish-enriched-Xishness with his/her whole being. The language, for RLSers, stands for their ideal Xishness and their ideal Xman. This ethnoculturally symbolic role of language is not a strange phenomenon. After all, language is the major symbol-system of our species. The word 'table' is not a table itself, as General Semanticists never tire of telling us, but it consensually 'stands for' a table, so that all who understand the word know what to buy, set, fix, move, fold or paint when the word is heard or read. Little wonder then, that almost all of the languages of the world have also come to stand for the particular ethnic collectivities that speak them, for the ethnocultures that traditionally utilize them and, where we are dealing with official languages of nations or regions, for the polities that implement them. Speakers of English (and other languages used across national boundaries) sometimes tend to forget this. English is so omnipresent in the world (at least, in the world of native English speakers) that it is easy to begin to think that it is simply neutral and natural everywhere. Speakers of languages that are regionally competitive with or conflicted with English have an understandably different view. They know that English is symbolic of Anglo-American might, money and life-styles, not all of which may be congenial to their own interests, views and goals.[4]

Unfortunately, the symbolic link between a language and its traditionally associated ethnoculture is a sword that cuts both ways. For receding languages, the language also is symbolic of the process of receding, of the disadvantages popularly ascribed to a receding language, of the atypicality of the life-style of those who hang on to a receding language after most others have shifted to a language of greater currency and, therefore, also to a language of seemingly greater advantage in status, income, social acceptance and social participation. RLSers are often loath to admit that their dearly beloved language could be symbolic of anything else than what *they* feel it to be symbolic of and what *they* want it to be symbolic of. However, where a mass re-ethnization process has gone on for a long time, that is, where Xmen in droves have come to be primarily (or solely) speakers of Yish instead, Yish may also stand for (may also be symbolic of, at least in their own eyes) remaining an Xman-of-a-certain-kind,-saliency-and-intensity, while, at the same time, benefiting from many typically Yish/Yishness advantages as well. 'But what are all of these other payoffs worth in comparison with being fully and truly Xmen by speaking Xish?', the RLSers may ask. Perhaps they are right, but this ('fully and truly') is an appeal, ultimately, to more than symbolism alone. It is an appeal to the implementation of a certain kind (a certain content) of Xishness, a certain priority for that content

and a certain degree of commitment to it even when its material rewards may
not be in accord with its 'real [moral, spiritual, ethical and, therefore, core-cul-
tural] worth'. Once again, therefore, we conclude that it is cultural content and
outlook, the cultural style or way of life, the *raison d'être*, rather than language
alone, that differentiates pro-, non- and anti-RLSers and it is this content and
outlook that RLSers need to spell out and exemplify in order that others may be
attracted to it.

## A language is linked to its culture in part–whole fashion

The above two discussions of how language is linked to culture bring us to
the realization that there must be yet another link between an ethnoculture and
its traditionally associated language: the link that is due to the fact that there is
a partial identity between the two, i.e. that parts of every culture are expressed,
implemented and realized via the language with which that culture has been
most intimately associated. So much of any culture is primarily verbally constituted: its songs and its prayers, its laws and its proverbs, its tales and its greetings, its curses and its blessings, its philosophy, its history and its teachings, and
on and on, encompassing almost all of non-material culture. All of the foregoing
are conventionally and consensually expressed via the culture's traditionally
associated language, to such a degree that, at least for those who learned them in
the original language, they do not have the same 'flavor', the same 'charm', the
same 'magic', not to mention the same 'associations and memories', when translated into any other language. It is in this fashion, via the part–whole relationship (that is, via the partial identity and extensive interdependence) that exists
between an ethnolanguage and its traditionally associated ethnoculture, that
child socialization patterns come to be associated with a particular language, that
cultural styles of interpersonal relations come to be associated with a particular
language, that the ethical principles that undergird everyday life come to be
associated with a particular language and that even material culture and aesthetic
sensibilities come to be conventionally discussed and evaluated via figures of
speech that are merely culturally (i.e. locally) rather than universally applicable.

## Example 4: Every Language Utilizes Figures of Speech that are Specific to the Specific Content of its Associated Culture

Because of its fascination with baseball, American English uses the expression 'to take a seventh inning stretch' to indicate a pause for relaxation,
somewhere past the midpoint of any undertaking. Whether individually or

in groups, a seventh inning stretch may be taken, requested or offered ('Coffee time, folks! Let's take our seventh inning stretch now!') in the midst of non-urgent pursuits that have nothing at all to do with baseball. Perhaps the habit of such a 'break', rather than merely the expression referring to it, was also borrowed from baseball.

Spanish speakers both in the USA and in Spain itself (and perhaps those in Latin America as well), refer to speaking Spanish as *'hablar cristiano'* (speaking Christian). This goes back to the historic period, more than half a millennium ago, when Spain was partially controlled by the Arabic-speaking Moors and also had a substantial Hebrew-praying and Judezmo- (Judeo-Spanish) speaking Jewish population (both in the Christian and in the Islamic parts of the Peninsula). Since Spanish was the unifying language of Christians (Basque, Catalan and other regional languages were also spoken, of course), to speak Spanish was to speak as a Christian.

Things that are done often are referred to in Yiddish as being done 'every Monday and Thursday', regardless of whether they are done on these particular days or not. Mondays and Thursdays are the weekdays on which the Torah is taken out and part of the weekly lection is read (in Orthodox synagogues). Because of the week in, week out and year in, year out nature of this practice, it came to be acceptably applied to (i.e. to be the cultural figure of speech for designating) any frequently and regularly occurring event.

The part–whole relationship between traditionally associated languages and cultures is also a two-way relationship, of course. Not only are most cultural acts and events linguistically encoded and linguistically suffused, but the languages themselves become replete with figures of speech that are by-products of frequent hearings, sayings, recitations and (in literate cultures) readings. Untranslatable figures of speech are often of this nature. It is not so much that they are completely untranslatable as that any translation requires a host of explanatory phrases (footnotes, so to speak). In order to render such sayings intelligible and to convey their vivid cultural appropriateness, explanations and footnotes must, at least initially, be resorted to. These rob the translations of spontaneous impact and are totally unnecessary for native members of the language's traditionally associated culture. Ethnosemantics and ethnotypologies constitute fields of academic inquiry that have attempted to analyze the cultural specificity of any language, but these fields have only begun to scratch the surface of the complete cultural specificity that is part and parcel of each and every natural language. They are interested primarily in tight-knit systems (such as the traditional kinship terminology, the traditional body-parts terminology or the traditional pronoun system). Such systems are often quite strikingly and literally unavoidably culture-specific. However, they do not begin to exhaust all that which is culture-specific in any language. To really know any language well, one must know its associated culture (indeed, even the history of that culture), every bit as much as it is necessary to know the associated language if one wants to know a culture well. This truism brings us back to RLS and culture and to the general cultural outlook, as well as to the cultural specifics and behavioral goals that RLSers favor.

## RLS and Its Preferred Model of Xish Culture

Many ethnic identities have managed to survive wholesale language shifts in connection with their historically associated languages. The Irish, the Jews, the Afro-Americans and many Amerindian peoples have been pointed to again and again as evidence that ethnic identity can survive language shift, although many of the conclusions along such lines may well overlook the differential contributions of internal pull and external push factors in arriving at this purported continuity of identity.

The critics of Xmen-via-Yish claims, however, are also quick to point out that identity continuity and ethnocultural continuity proper are often two quite different phenomena, with the latter being greater than and encompassing of the former. If it is ethnocultural continuity proper that is the desideratum, then linguistic discontinuity must be recognized as always (and at least initially) accompanied by and resulting in great cultural disruption and dislocation. While it is true that the substantial relinguification of a culture is theoretically possible (and that it has, indeed, occurred in some few cases), it is also true, however, that such relinguification-plus-continuity exacts a very substantial cost in time, effort and attrition before fully adequate new lexical associations, fully adequate new verbal-cultural replacements or substitutions, and fully adequate ethnolinguistic symbolic structures and identities are fashioned. In the end, the new ethnocultural system may be experienced by some as fully adequate but it is not really isomorphically the same as the old one that it replaced.

Thus, the champions of the Xmen-via-Xish point of view quite rightly point out, if ethnic identity *is* retained, notwithstanding all of the dislocation and disruption that an ethnic group undergoing relinguification must experience, that identity does not really pertain to the same culture that was initially associated with that identity. The ritualized High Culture may make the transition from Language₁ to Language₂, and so may snatches of the Low Culture, but the ethnoculture as a whole, the very texture of daily life and its daily rounds, responsibilities and relationships between traditional roles, places and topics, is no longer the same when Yish replaces Xish.

While it must be granted that the content of any ethnoculture will inevitably change over time, even without wholesale disruption and language shift, such change is also likely to be more internally regulated, screened and evaluated, resulting in more continuity (or, at least, the sense of continuity) than discontinuity in the finely patterned and intermeshed outlooks, goals, behaviors and relationships that constitute any culture. Furthermore, the Xmen-via-Xish goal has a particular version of Xishness in mind and it cannot, therefore, lightly accept the view that this particular version (including Xish as its vehicle and symbol) is just as easily attained via Yish, because that is not, indeed, the case at some level of the total *Gestalt* or 'feel' of what Xishness and Xish culture 'really are' or 'really should be'. Ultimately, the advocates of Xish and of Yish have different definitions of Xishness in mind, particularly at the transitional stage when some Xmen are shifting from Xish to Yish, and although these differences may ultimately come to be regarded as minimal, they are very likely to be regarded as much more than merely minimal during some fairly extensive period of dislocation. Some differences in the two brands of Xishness are likely to remain on a long-term basis, if only due to the fact that the two expressions of Xishness will be subject to different degrees and types of change, as well as to different degrees and types of fidelity to earlier stages in the development of Xishness.

Therefore, to answer the oft-encountered taunt that 'I can be just as good an Xman without understanding and speaking Xish', RLSers need to clarify the cultural life-style and ethnocultural ideal that they stand for. Is it only 'to be modern, like all the others, but in our own language'? This was the slogan of many nineteenth century nationalist movements (and, indeed, of many twentieth century ones as well), but most RLS-efforts arise at a much more enfeebled stage of ethnocultural coherence and solidarity than do nationalist movements. Of course, some nationalist movements involve RLS-efforts too, but the overlap between the two is not nearly as great nor as important as the differences between them. Most RLS movements, particularly those that have been most active since World War II, are not as basically motivated by political aspirations such as political separatism or even political autonomy. They generally seek not so much an impact on the general body politic, as, rather, a focus on 'those of their own kind' and on their internal cultural order. Indeed, an RLS movement that has a surrounding nationalist movement to fall back upon already has an advanced organizational and ideological thrust, a clientele and a definition of its desired future. However, even such movements often find that independence is not enough to guarantee ethnocultural and ethnolinguistic distinctiveness and find it necessary, therefore, to institute 'cultural policies' and 'language policies' (viz. policies on behalf of French in Quebec, Flemish in Belgium, Irish in Ireland, even after the attainment of cultural autonomy or even political independence) calculated to provide the ethnolinguistic breathing space that small cultures always require for their co-existence in a world dominated by ethnolinguistic behemoths. Those RLS movements that cannot and do not aspire to political separatism, that cannot and do not place their hopes in political boundaries as their ultimate safeguards against foreign ethnolinguistic domination, who envision a future that will permanently leave them relatively exposed to a more powerful culturally different environment, such movements are, therefore, all the more in need of a definition of their cultural norms, practices and goals with respect to the content and saliency of their own ethnocultural distinctiveness.

Such definitions are not easy to come by (and once attained, they must be re-examined and revised periodically), but they are essential. The usual RLS claim is that Xish is needed in order 'to be a better, a more authentic, a more loyal, a more committed, Xman'. However, such superlatives do not constitute a programmatic definition, as is clear from the usual response by non-RLSers: 'Nowadays, I can be all that in Yish and without any (or without much) Xish at all'. The two most common ingredients of programmatic definitions of the cultural goals of RLS movements are (i) mining the past for inspiration to meet the challenges of the future and (ii) strengthening cultural boundaries so as to foster greater intergenerational cultural continuity. The ethnocultural past (more precisely, an interpretation of the ethnocultural past) is of major importance to RLS movements, because ethnocultural values, ethnocultural differences and the ethnolanguage itself are all derived from and linked with the past. Some RLS movements may actually be associated with 'return to the past', 'nativization' or 'revitalization' philosophies, but this is very unusual. The past is generally merely a treasure-trove to be utilized in the solution of problems of today and tomorrow. It is a *useful* past that RLS movements define, in order to extract from it implications for current practices, current beliefs, current challenges, current attitudes and current commitments defining their image of the real, authentic, proud and responsible Xman.

RLS movements and efforts necessarily imply a dissatisfaction with things as they are now, just as they imply a quest for solutions with respect to a better future. This better future necessarily includes greater ethnocultural (and, of course, ethnolinguistic) continuity, distinctiveness and creativity. All of this, in turn, implies our point (ii) above, namely, the desirability of maintaining cultural boundaries. In our modern, interactive and interdependent world, where re-ethnization into obviously more powerful, purportedly more rewarding and more encompassing ethnocultural and ethnolinguistic categories is a prevalent, worldwide phenomenon, the very desirability of minority (and particularly of weakened minority) ethnocultural continuity must be defended. Many modern intellectuals (including the popular Solomonic wisdom of the *New York Times*) are basically integrationists or assimilationists insofar as minority cultures are concerned, many of them still throwing off the imaginary 'shackles' of their own minority ethnicity, believing firmly that larger, wealthier cultures are obviously better (more forward-looking, more progressive, more in tune with the times, indeed, the wave of the future) and that it is sheer folly (and the result of being brainwashed by a self-serving ethnic leadership) to remain aloof from them, particularly when they hold out explicit or implicit 'welcome' signs to one and all. In response, it is not enough for RLSers to point to the cultural invidiousness and unacknowledged ethnocentrism of such 'enlightened' and 'liberated' anti-RLS views ('racist', many members of the modern younger generation would properly call them). It is not enough to point to the fact that anti-RLSers and assimilationists also have *their* leaders who benefit directly from the success of their own movements. Rather, it is necessary to delineate the specific tune of the 'different drummer' that pro-RLSers wish to march to, in the hope that they can thereby more nearly approximate the concept of cultural fidelity that motivates them.

## Why Should I Be so Concerned about Being or Remaining an Xman?

Our argument began with whether RLS is possible. Once an opponent of RLS grants that some degree of reversal is always possible, he or she may then shift to the topic of whether it is really necessary to know Xish in order to be a good Xman. If, thanks to the success of an RLS movement's educational efforts, any hitherto anti-RLSers become unable to deny this claim (or to do so as adamantly as was previously the case), then they may still withdraw to the inevitable fall-back position which claims that it is not really all that necessary or desirable to be an Xman or 'just an Xman'. Re-ethnization in the direction of greater rewards has gone on throughout history, so why not now? In addition, isn't there something wrong about the insistent preservation of a smaller identity when a larger one is in the offing? Finally, wouldn't the whole world be better off if there were just one universal culture and one universal language, and we were all simply 'citizens of the world', rather than members of mutually exclusive and necessarily parochial and mutually non-comprehensible local cultures? Clearly, these are serious questions involving fundamental philosophical and value-laden considerations and RLS movements need to have serious and well thought-out answers to them.

## Is the maintenance of ethnocultural and ethnolinguistic differences a 'parochial' and harmful pursuit?

A preference for one's own ethnolinguistic group has been called ethnocentric and even racist. Perhaps it is best to admit that this may, at times, be so, but then an avoidance of one's own original ethnolinguistic group has been referred to as self-hatred and identity-insecurity. Clearly, none of the above designations *need* be true and whether or not they are true in any particular case must be determined, rather than assumed in advance.

Almost all animal species naturally live primarily among their own. Among humans, this is appreciably a by-product of socialization and enculturation, that is, of being raised in a particular society and culture and taught to behave in accord with its norms (which includes: to 'value' and to 'believe' along culturally rewarded lines). It is only natural, therefore, to come to prefer one's kith and kin, to feel more comfortable in their company, to appeal to them for help and to help them, in turn, when they are in need, to be concerned for their welfare and for the continuity of the practices and values that are shared with them. Members of any reasonably functional culture value it (consciously or not, consciousness of one's cultural values being a stage that is crucial for and heightened by collective organization on behalf of that culture and its values), for it is their guide to life, and when it is threatened they tend to come to its defence or assistance. Culture becomes hallowed, not only because religion is a part of culture but because cultural norms and expectations have about them the aura of right and wrong, of morality, decency and propriety. These beliefs, convictions and attitudes may vary somewhat from person to person and from period to period, within a culture, but without their consistency and coherence the culture itself can have no intergenerational continuity.

Whether ethnocultural concerns and preferences are ethnocentric or racist depends on what their concurrent views and behaviors toward outsiders are. If outsiders are looked down upon as biologically inferior, then racism is involved. If outsiders are not respected and valued in their own right, not presumed to have their own legitimate ways and customs, if the rhyme and reason for the whole world is attributed only and completely to one's own ethnocultural group, then ethnocentrism is clearly involved. Note, however, that strong and dominant cultures are at least as likely to hold such views as small and threatened ones. Those who throw stones at RLSers often live in glass houses (indeed, in gilded ghettos) themselves, ghettos of such power that their parochiality is conveniently ignored. Indeed, the negation of RLS 'in principle' is part of the majority establishment's 'rhetoric of futility' which begins by actively undercutting the minority's survival chances and then follows up this injury with the additional insult of projecting its own biases upon minority efforts on behalf of cultural survival.

Without a doubt, RLSers may become ethnocentric, but so may non-RLSers. Those who transethnify into broader group memberships may be just as ethnocentric (or even more so) relative to their new ('broader') membership as RLSers may be to their traditional (and 'narrower') ones. Either group may adopt exclusionary practices and may be prejudiced against 'others' and 'outsiders'. It is not unheard of for majorities to be unfair, nor for world-cultures to be self-seeking, defamatory and altogether too taken with their own concerns, their own needs and their own gratifications. Essentially, then, RLS has nothing particularly to do with either racism or ethnocentrism and may well be accompanied by the view that although all peoples are created equal and deserve to live in happiness, charity begins at home. Indeed, an accepting and unconflicted view of one's own culture may be a building block of and a pre-condition for accepting unconflicted views of other cultures. Security begets security.

### Wouldn't it be better if we could all be Ymen, or, better yet, Citizens of the World?

It may be possible for 'broader' (supra-local) and 'narrower' (primarily local) self-definitions to co-occur. Such possibilities depend on intercultural views and definitions that can be collectively arrived at only after years of mutually positive experience. Being French does not need to keep one from being European too, and being a Pennsylvanian does not need to keep one from being American, or Jewish, or Republican at the same time. However, just one and the same broader loyalty and identity for everyone is not really possible and may not even be desirable. Local identities stem from the preponderance of local experiences throughout our most formative years and the continued comfort of such experiences even after maturity. These identities and experiences add color and diversity to the human landscape, which would otherwise be merely irrelevant and unrelated to local conditions, local institutions and local opportunities. Uniformation is never an optimal *human* solution. It necessarily involves subjugation of the weak by the strong, of the few by the many: in short, the law of the jungle. It represents an impatience with the most human qualities and the imposition of a 'mass market' or 'efficiency' model in intergroup and interpersonal relations. Thus, while it is true that the world is slowly also tending toward higher order identities, the lower order ones (the family, the friendship network, the ethnic bond) still have many functions to fulfill and many satisfactions to provide.[5] The triumph of science has not killed off religion and the triumph of internationalism will not kill off local identities nor local socialization goals. The modern and the traditional coexist, each fulfilling different needs in society and in personality.

When intergroup relations are not negatively charged, many multiple memberships are viewed as commensurable, particularly if they are viewed as pertaining to different dimensions or levels of identity. Thus, while one cannot normally be both a Baptist and a Catholic simultaneously, there is usually no reason why one cannot be both a daughter and a Republican. Similarly, both broader and narrower ethnicities are sometimes simultaneously possible (e.g. Flemish and Belgian), where the one is not viewed as invalidating the other, but, rather, as complementing it. The availability of such complementary definitions depends on the local acceptance of culturally-based theories of ethnicity that are compatible with complementary definitions, on historical experiences of positive intergroup cooperation and interdependence, and on the long-term interaction of the one (the culturally based theories of ethnicity) with the other (the historical experiences of positive intergroup relations). If it is recognized by Western academics that it may be difficult to teach college freshmen Western and Non-Western Civilization in a single, integrated course and to do so in a mutually accepting and appreciating fashion (see *New York Times*, January 19, 1988, p. A12), then it should not be too difficult for these same academics and assorted man-in-the-street intellectuals to realize that the working out of simultaneous and non-conflictual ethnolinguistic identities may be no easy matter to arrive at and that such syncretism is definitely not helped along by a triumphalist, Western intellectual stance claiming cognitive and moral superiority. It may not be easy to attain this goal of reciprocally accepted multiple ethnocultural identities but it is a goal that is possible of attainment.

However, to 'trade in' narrower memberships, merely because broader ones have also become available, may be exploitative, self-seeking, opportunistic as well as self-impoverishing. To abandon one's own because they are few or weak, and to do so in their time of need, is hardly considered the height either of responsibility or of humanity. There is no reason why one cannot be both Basque and human too, both Basque and European too, both an advocate of RLS (on behalf of Basque) and an advocate of UNESCO too. Indeed, it is the European Community, looking forward to 1992, that has recently paid most attention to assisting and defending the continued and increased use of its 'lesser used' languages (Coulmas, in press). Whether one can be both Basque and Spanish too, however, is a question of sensitivities of time and place. If the two are not considered to be displacive, antagonistic or competitive then they are more likely to be viewed as possible co-occurrences rather than as incommensurables. Even as commensurables they require cultural consensus as to 'which comes first', i.e. which is more fundamental in socialization and intergenerational identity. Is one a Finno-Swede or a Swedo-Finn? They are not the same thing. One part of the identity is adjectival, implying 'added color'; the other part is substantive, implying origins. Finally, 'commensurists' too can fully support RLS, if they take both parts of their identity seriously. Even those who prefer to transethnify must grant that those who do not are neither necessarily narrow-minded nor provincial. Many of them are simply more capable of preserving old loyalties and combining them with new ones than are the majority of those who have opted out of their original identities entirely. At any rate, the 'why bother' knee-jerk response to RLS-efforts is hardly a completely rational one. It is replete with biases of its own and, ultimately, implies a competitive world-view in which human intelligence and loyalty are not to be 'wasted' on smaller or struggling ethnocultural entities.

## Is RLS Desirable? A Value Issue

The desirability of RLS is a value issue of great complexity and many ramifications. It involves a view of humanity and of the legitimacy and necessity of humanity's manifold cultural constituents. RLSers should view local cultures (all local cultures, not only their own) as things of beauty, as encapsulations of human values which deserve to be fostered and assisted (not merely 'preserved' in a mummifying sense). They should view such planned assistance to language-in-culture as being no more reprehensible than is agricultural planning (rather than just letting things grow 'naturally', as they would without organized planning and human intervention), or than are educational planning, economic planning or family planning as expressions of social policy. Indeed, RLS-efforts are a type of language status planning, an involvement in language-in-culture that is no way unprecedented (much less 'necessarily contraindicated, reprehensible or undesirable') and RLSers need not feel embarrassed, defensive or unsure of themselves for engaging in or advocating such efforts. They should, however, fully realize the complexity, the subtlety and, therefore, the potential for mismanagement of such efforts due to ignorance and arrogance. Such efforts involve philosophical commitments that are just as defensible as those of anti-RLSers and that are just as commensurable with progress, humanity and greater mutual acceptance between peoples. But RLS is hard to achieve, because it entails an effort of the weak to rebuild and defend their cultures at the very times that these cultures are under the domination or influence of stronger outside forces. Accordingly, RLS-efforts must at least be admired for their temerity and devotion, rather than merely dismissed out of hand or caricatured for either practical or philosophical reasons.

## General Conclusions

Cultural continuity and cultural change are always and inevitably intertwined with each other.[6] Indeed, by their co-presence they define each other, as do the half empty and the half full glass of water. Those who cling to Xish and who accept the challenge of overcoming all difficulties (the empty half of the glass of water) in order to foster the Xmen-via-Xish model, are bound by the same relationships between language and culture as are those who pursue the new Xmen-via-Yish goal and who, like Whorf's Hopi informants, do not see that part of the glass that has no water as 'empty' at all, but, rather, as full of a different and quite useful content. The indexical relationship between language X and Xish culture can be undone and a new relationship can be established between language Y and some version of Xish culture. The fact that this can be done, given sufficient time and effort, does not mean that it should be undertaken or that 'Xish culture' will be identical at all under the two sets of linguistic circumstances. The traditional implementation of Xish culture via Xish acts, events and texts can be undone and new or translated replacements can be implemented via Yish. The fact that this can ultimately be done does not mean that it should be done or that the cultural significance of these acts, events or texts will be identical under both sets of linguistic circumstances. The fact that the traditional symbolic relationship between Xish and Xishness can ultimately be replaced by a new symbolic relationship between Yish and Xishness merely indicates that in the fullness of time such transformations are possible and they have, indeed, occurred throughout human history. This does not mean that such symbolic redefinitions and self-redefinitions are either desirable or easily attained, or that Xishness is the same under both sets of linguistic circumstances. Only linguistic determinism claims that the above dissociations and recompositions of Xishness without Xish are theoretically impossible *ab initio*, and it has not been able to support the heavy burden of proof that its own convictions require.

The differences between Xishness (or Xish culture) under traditional circumstances of association with Xish and under revised circumstances of association with Yish may be great or small, depending on the rapidity and extent of ongoing social change and social dislocation that occurs *pari passu* to the replacement of Xish by Yish. Any detailed ethnographic analysis will reveal, however, that there is inevitably some difference in Xishness (i.e. in Xish culture) under these two sets of circumstances, but the question still remains as to whether the degree of difference that obtains also 'makes any difference' phenomenologically, i.e. in terms of intracultural interpretation. Small differences, objectively noted by disinterested parties, can be magnified and become *causes célèbres* phenomenologically, just as large differences, objectively noted, can come to be intraculturally disregarded and made light of. The role of vested elites and of rebellious counter-elites in the interpretation of such differences is a crucial one and the role of self-interest is as appreciable in this connection as it is in all other social behavior, and on both sides of the fence rather than on one side of it only. The one thing that is certain is that both RLS-efforts and anti-RLS-efforts are essentially value-based. They are philosophically and ideologically determined and are neither confirmable nor disconfirmable on a purely objective basis alone.

RLS appeals to many because it is part of the process of re-establishing local options, local control, local hope and local meaning to life. It basically reveals a humanistic and positive outlook *vis-à-vis* intragroup life, rather than a mechanistic and fatalistic one. It espouses the right and the ability of small cultures to live and to inform life for their own members as well as to contribute thereby to the enrichment of humankind as a whole.

## Notes

1.  I originally documented the detachability of languages from their traditional language-in-ethnoculture contexts in my *Language Loyalty in the United States* (1966), which is also replete with examples of the extent to which the continuity of ethnic labels may survive after the language-in-ethnoculture link has come undone. Such survival of ethnic labels should not be confused, however, with the implementational continuity of ethnocultures. The 'after' stage (after substantial language shift has occurred) is only nominally (denominally) continuous with the 'before' stage. This is so, first of all, because the 'before' identity too was necessarily in a state of ongoing change before the linkage to its customarily associated language began to come undone, and, second, because the 'after' identity (without the traditional language linkage) was necessarily exposed to different influences, both conceptually and implementationally, than was the identity of those who retained the linkage. These considerations are discussed at length in my *Rise and Fall of the Ethnic Revival* (1985). Three different identity phenomena are involved (and it is, unfortunately, both common and easy to gloss over the differences between them due to the fact that they are each referred to by the single term, 'identity'): continuity of label, continuity of self-concept and continuity of cultural implementation (overt observances and the acceptance and implementation of cultural values and attitudes). Generally speaking, the last (continuity of cultural implementation) changes more quickly than either of the others when the original language-in-ethnoculture linkage is substantially weakened as culture change occurs. In the long run, the loss of the linkage sometimes leads to re-ethnization into another contextually co-existing primordial (deeply historical and essentially already formed) ethnicity, sometimes to ethnogenesis or to the (co-)formation of a new and still relatively open-ended ethnicity (sometimes a 'broader' one: 'American', 'Amerindian', 'Soviet', 'Yugoslav', 'Black' [in South Africa], and sometimes a 'narrower' one: 'Anglo-Chinese', 'Dutch-Indonesian', 'Franco-Algerian'), and sometimes to the continuation of the 'same' identity on a vastly altered implementational basis (Jewish, Irish, Scots, Breton). Which of these

three courses will obtain in any particular case is largely governed by contextually available cultural definitions, intergroup experiences and material opportunities. In each instance, however, the loss of the linkage results in a profound disturbance of the original language-in-culture model among those populations undergoing relinguification (and, on occasion, also among the remaining and numerically fewer 'true believers'). Therefore, to conclude that their 'identity' has remained the same even though their culture and language-in-culture has undergone profound changes is to confuse continuity of label with continuity of the phenomenon to which the label originally applied (see Sookdeo, 1987; Roosens, 1989).

2. I initially pointed to the differences that may exist between the leaders of ethnocultural reconstitutive movements and their rank-and-files in my *Language and Nationalism* (1972). Such differences, e.g. in mastery of the traditionally associated language and in personal knowledge of and implementation of ethnocultural observances, have sometimes been seized upon by anti-RLSers, charging that the RLS leadership is (i) self-seeking (which means, not really committed to the language-in-ethnoculture 'cause', but, rather, exploiting it for its [the leadership's] own material and power goals) and (ii) non-representative of those whom they seek to mobilize and on behalf of whom they speak (which also translates into a charge of lack of commitment or dishonesty). Those who make such blanket charges overlook several pertinent facts: (1) leaders must be different from their rank-and-file, by definition, or they would lack the drive, the personality and the vision to lead; and (2) the more recent personal 'return' to the language-in-ethnoculture link, which characterizes some RLS leaders who had previously lost or abandoned this link (not all RLS leaders in any case), is a type of conversion experience that often results in a more altruistic and less self-interested leadership than is otherwise and more generally the case. All in all, the charge that the RLS leadership (and ethnic leadership more generally) is corrupt, and that it leads its followers astray out of self-interest, can just as justifiably be turned against the anti-RLS leadership (or against any leadership whatsoever, for that matter). This charge is basically unfair. It places the rank-and-file membership in a two-way bind. If the leadership is supported, this confirms the charge of 'brainwashing by a self-interest-governed leadership', and if the leadership is abandoned, this weakens and potentially defeats the movement. Such hypotheses tend to obfuscate rather than clarify the basic differences in goals, values and opinions that should be under discussion by introducing a separate variable (nature of the leadership) which could be studied comparatively in both pro-RLS and anti-RLS contexts but which is rarely really studied in either.

3. The indexical appropriateness of any language to its traditionally associated culture has contributed to, but is distinct from, another facet of the Whorfian hypothesis, a facet which I have called $W_2$, which claims that languages are *causal or determining* (hence: linguistic determinism) *vis-à-vis* the culturally specific behaviors and worldviews of their speakers (see Culjak, 1968 for evidence of the Euroasian antiquity of this view; and also Fishman, 1960, 1980, 1982). What I have described here, in connection with the indexical relationship between a language and its traditionally associated culture, is a much weaker relationship, one which I have called $W_1$. This view maintains that the traditionally associated language reflects or conveys its culture and, moreover, does so more felicitously and succinctly than do other languages, for as long as the language-in-culture linkage remains generally intact. Most RLS-efforts are $W_1$ related and $W_2$ views are quite rare in literature intended for educated readers. It should be mentioned that $W_2$-type views can also be found in the linguistically secure mainstream, rather than in RLS circles alone.

4. For evidence of much-belated academic recognition of the non-neutral and highly partisan and symbolic status of English, see Fishman, 1987; Skutnabb-Kangas and Phillipson, 1986; Phillipson and Skutnabb-Kangas, 1986; and, particularly, Flaitz, 1988.
5. For recent samples of the commonly available Marxist, capitalist and 'progressivist' defenses of larger ethnocultural identities and their principled rejections of smaller ones, particularly if the latter are in need of special collective efforts for reconstituting and reasserting their weakened intergroup boundaries, see Patterson, 1977; van den Berghe, 1981; and Edwards, 1985. For examples of the literature on ethnogenesis, i.e. the formation of new ethnicities and, therefore, the re-'designation' of previously differently- identifying and identified populations, see Lamy, 1979; Magosci, 1978; Roosens, 1989; and the bulk of the papers (particularly those by Keyes and by Abner Cohen) in Keyes, 1981. For a superabundance of the racism that can (but that need not) accompany language-in-culture emphases, see Mosse, 1966 and Römer, 1985. For the democratic potential in language-in-culture efforts see Fishman, 1978; Royce, 1982; and Fishman, 1981, all of which are based upon the earlier writings by Barth (1969) and on the now classic contributions of Herder, Kallen and Whorf. The latter's advocacy of a linguistically pluralistic world that would be safe for and sympathetic toward small languages has been referred to as $W_3$ (Fishman, 1983).
6. The interpretation of change and continuity, and the necessity of accurately estimating the one in order to estimate the other, is mentioned several times in the work of Spicer (see, e.g. his 1980) and is specifically focused upon by J. R. Moore (1981) in a volume in honor of Spicer.

## References

BARTH, Fredrik 1969, *Ethnic Groups and Boundaries*. Boston: Little-Brown.
COULMAS, Florian in press, European integration and the idea of the national language: Ideological roots and economic consequences. In his (ed.) *Wanted: A Language Policy for the European Community*.
CULJAK, M. 1968, The Theory of Linguistic Weltanschauung and B. L. Whorf's Hypothesis: Historical Sources and Critical Assessment. Ph.D. Dissertation, University of Delhi.
EDWARDS, John R. 1985, *Language, Society and Identity*. Oxford: Blackwell.
FISHMAN, Joshua A. 1960, A systematization of the Whorfian hypothesis. *Behavioral Science* 8, 323–39.
— 1972, *Language and Nationalism*. Rowley, MA: Newbury House. Completely reprinted in his *Language and Ethnicity* (1989). Clevedon: Multilingual Matters, 105–75 and 269–367.
— 1978, Positive bilingualism; some overlooked rationales and forefathers. *Georgetown University Round Table on Languages and Linguistics*. Washington, D.C.: Georgetown University Press, 42–52.
— 1980, The Whorfian hypothesis: varieties of valuation, confirmation and disconfirmation. *International Journal of the Sociology of Language* 26, 25–40.
— 1981, Cultural pluralism and the American school. *Plural Societies* 12, 5–12.
— 1982, Whorfianism of the third kind: ethnolinguistic diversity as a worldwide societal asset (The Whorfian hypothesis: varieties of valuation, confirmation and disconfirmation II). *Language in Society* 11, 1–14.

—    1987, English: neutral tool or ideological protagonist? A 19th century East-Central European intellectual views English from afar. *English World Wide* 8, 1–10.

FISHMAN, Joshua A. *et al.* 1966, *Language Loyalty in the United States.* The Hague: Mouton.

—    1985, *The Rise and Fall of the Ethnic Revival.* Berlin: Mouton.

FLAITZ, Jeffra 1988, *The Ideology of English; French Perceptions of English as a World Language.* Berlin: Mouton.

KEYES, Charles F. (ed.) 1981, *Ethnic Change.* Seattle: University of Washington Press.

LAMY, Paul (ed.) 1979, Language planning and identity planning. *International Journal of the Sociology of Language* 20 (entire issue).

MCPHERSON, William (ed.) 1973, *Ideology and Change.* Palo Alto, CA: National Press Books.

MAGOCSI, Paul Robert 1978, *The Shaping of a National Identity.* Cambridge: Harvard University Press.

MOORE, Janet R. 1981, Persistence with change: a property of sociocultural dynamics. In G. P. CASTILE and G. KUSHNER (eds.) *Persistent Peoples: Cultural Enclaves in Perspective.* Tucson: University of Arizona Press, 228–42.

MOSSE, George L. 1966, *Nazi Culture: Intellectual, Cultural and Social Life in the Third Reich.* New York: Grosset and Dunlap.

PATTERSON, Horace Orlando 1977, *Ethnic Chauvinism: The Reactionary Impulse.* New York: Stein and Day.

PHILLIPSON, Robert and SKUTNABB-KANGAS, Tove 1986, English: the language of wider colonialisation. In: R. PHILLIPSON and T. SKUTNABB-KANGAS, *Linguicism Rules in Education.* Roskilde: Roskilde University Centre, Institute VI, 344–77.

RÖMER, Ruth 1985, *Sprachwissenschaft und Rassenideologie in Deutschland.* Munich: Wilhelm Fink.

ROOSENS, Eugene E. 1989, *Creating Ethnicity: The Process of Ethnogenesis.* Newbury Park: Sage.

ROYCE, Aya Peterson 1982, *Ethnic Identity: Strategies of Diversity.* Bloomington: Indiana University Press.

SKUTNABB-KANGAS, Tove and PHILLIPSON, Robert 1986, The legitimacy of the arguments for the spread of English. In: R. PHILLIPSON and T. SKUTNABB-KANGAS, *Linguicism Rules in Education.* Roskilde: Roskilde University Centre, Institute VI, 378–415.

SOOKDEO, Anil 1987, The transformation of ethnic identities: the case of the 'coloured' and Indian Africans. *Journal of Ethnic Studies* 15 (4), 69–83.

SPICER, Edward H. 1980, *The Yaquis: A Cultural History.* Tucson: Arizona University Press.

VAN DEN BERGHE, Pierre L. 1981, *The Ethnic Phenomenon.* New York: Elsevier.

WHORF, Benjamin L. 1956 *Language, Thought and Reality.* New York: Wiley.

# 3 'Where' and 'Why' Does Language Shift Occur and How Can It Be Reversed?

## Locating Language Shift in Social Space and in Societal Dynamics

When a patient is sick, there are several crucial preliminaries before a successful cure can be undertaken. First of all, it is necessary for those who would be curers to *believe that finding a cure is worthwhile*. This is a profoundly subjective and culturally embedded decision, as medical anthropology has thoroughly demonstrated. Not all cultures, nor all individuals within the same culture, will necessarily agree that a given patient, particularly if he or she be very old and ill, without funds, family or other advantageous material and psychological support systems and without any particularly meritorious accomplishments in life, is 'worth' the attention and the costs in time, effort and funds that the available cures entail. When the patient is someone we love and respect, however, we become extremely annoyed at 'nit-picking' and 'heartless' questions about the advisability of attempting all possible cures while the patient's life hangs in the balance. On the other hand, doctors become similarly annoyed and 'burned out' when they spend year after year saving the lives of individuals who are then returned to the same hapless and hopeless social neglect that occasioned or contributed to the original life-threatening conditions that doctors were called in to reverse. For a cure to 'take', there needs to be, at the very least, a resolve that 'yes', it is 'worth' trying to cure the patient and, therefore, 'yes' it is worth trying to find out what his/her illness is due to, so that its cure can be attempted and *so that the patient's life circumstances afterwards can be altered* in order that a relapse need not be a foregone conclusion.

After considering Chapter 2, we have presumably passed beyond at least the first point in the above metaphor in connection with assisting threatened languages to reverse the language shift that engulfs them. Of course, there are many differences between an individual patient and a language-in-culture nexus (one major difference being that cultures have no 'natural life-span', as do human beings,[1] and, therefore, the very notion of 'it's too late to do anything about the illness' is a much more dubious and subjective one in connection with cultures), but the above metaphor, if we do not over-extend it, may be a useful one nevertheless. We have already discussed, in Chapter 2, whether 'our patient' is 'worth saving'. We have already seen that this is basically a subjective, value-laden decision, rather than a strictly factual or obvious one. Its answer implies the kind of intergroup life and the kind of intercultural world we want to have and build, insofar as ethnic diversity, cultural democracy and the equal moral worth and legitimacy of small cultures (alongside the large ones) are concerned. We have tried to utilize constructive arguments, rather than potentially embarrassing moral posturing, in order to persuade others to accept our view, and this approach is recommended to all others who are engaged in pro-RLS efforts *vis-à-vis* those who differ with them. It is the only way to 'win friends and influence (reasonable) people', although extreme opponents are probably 'unreachable' by any means.

If we have reached a reasonably satisfyingly positive answer to the question 'should RLS (= finding a cure for the disease, LS) be attempted?', then we must go on in this chapter to seek greater familiarity with the nature and causes of the disease, so that a more *generally* suitable (as well as a more *individually* suitable) cure can be prescribed in subsequent chapters for various cases of the disease. This chapter, then, will be more diagnostic whereas subsequent chapters will attempt to be more remedial.

## Has LS Really Occurred and, If So, Where?

Our first task is to confirm that LS has indeed occurred. Equally trained and qualified observers will sometimes differ in making that diagnosis because a language-in-culture nexus is far more difficult to diagnose than any individual patient (and even in connection with patients, diagnostic disagreements are far from being unknown). Language shift is often a slow and cumulative process, thereby making 'before vs. after' data hard to come by. Rarely have competent and reasonably impartial observers been collecting the necessary diagnostic data over several years so that a detailed analysis can be made when and as needed. Even where language census reports are available spanning several decades, they more often than not present problems of their own, such as asking too few language-focused questions, changes over time in how the language questions asked have been worded, and changes in the surrounding social/cultural/political contexts such that respondents may have been led to overclaim Xish on some occasions and to underclaim it on others. The most important thing to remember is that censuses, admirable research tools though they may sometimes be,[2] are, after all, the tools of a given sociocultural and ethnolinguistic establishment and are instituted to serve their masters' purposes, not only with respect to *what* is asked, but with respect to *when* and *how*, as well as with respect to *what particular analyses are undertaken, how they are performed* and *what findings are reported* with respect to the data on hand. For all these reasons, Yish establishment census data with respect to Xish language shift is often suspect, to say the least. In that case, alternatives are needed. What alternatives exist?

Due to the time-interval requirement for the most convincing study of language shift, so that the incidence of language use in Time A can be compared, for an equivalent sample of Xmen, with the incidence of corresponding use in Time B, the major tactical problem for the study of LS is often that of finding an earlier study that can serve as a benchmark for a currently contemplated comparative study. Sometimes pro-RLSers are fortunate and they discover that someone (someone whose objectivity and credentials are relatively acceptable to them) completed a suitable benchmark study at some point in the past (in Time A), so that they merely need to replicate it now (in Time B). With the growth and spread of sociolinguistics/sociology of language during the past quarter century (and, in some very few parts of the world, going back even half a century or more[3]) it is becoming increasingly possible to find a previous governmental or non-governmental study of Xish language use that can serve as a benchmark relative to a current study. However, the number of minority languages that can expect to be this fortunate is still relatively small, and our current critical standards *vis-à-vis* earlier studies are now so advanced that the most that can normally be expected is that earlier studies, where available, will be 'taken into account', because rarely will they be found to be fully adequate for current comparative purposes.

This being the usual case, there is often no alternative but to conduct a single 'cross-sectional' study *now*, and to build into it those intergenerational comparisons that will enable us to draw inferences, imperfect though they may be, as to Time A ('then') vs. Time B ('now') differences. In some such studies, the 'then' data is sometimes based on recollections, i.e. on the memory of current respondents with respect to Xish language use at one or more points in the past. Such recollections are colored, as are all self-report studies, by the attitudes and opinions of the respondents, by their varying needs to make favorable impressions ('social desirability' impressions) on those who are questioning them, and by the various social, cultural and political pressures that typify the time when any particular study is being carried out. If the 'now' data is also of the self-report type, then it too will be marked by all of the above problems and the differences noted between recollected self-report on Time A and current self-report on Time B will be far less valid than one would optimally hope for. However, cross-sections of memory constitute only one of two major types of cross-sectional studies; the other type makes use of cross-sectional comparisons based upon current ('now') reports on sub-populations that differ in age (and possibly in other characteristics as well).

Age cross-sectional studies avoid the issue of selective memory for times gone by through sampling a variety of ages 'now', in Time B, and then performing an age-related analysis based on this one probe. If there is an age-gradient with respect to use-claiming, that is, if subjects between 20 and 29 years of age, for example, claim to use Xish less than do subjects between 30 and 39, whereas subjects between 30 and 39 claim to use it less than do those between 40 and 49, who, in turn, claim to use the language less than do subjects between 50 and 59, etc., etc., then this gradient is taken to be the reflection of use-changes that have taken place over time. Although this assumption may be quite correct, it may also be less than completely valid. We are dealing with *different subjects at each age*, rather than with *the same subjects at different ages*, and there is no way of being completely sure that the former (the different subjects at each age) are really comparable in all relevant language-related respects. It is possible that they might be different in their degrees of language use — *even if they were all of the same age, i.e. even if they all grew up at the same time* — due to factors on which they have not been or cannot be equated (e.g. the different youth (or other sub-) cultures to which they were exposed when growing up, differences in number of years of formal education, differences in amount of exposure to foreigners, etc.), and these factors could be responsible for the differences between the age groups with respect to language-use claiming, rather than the passage of time per se. Such other possible factors must be built into the survey design itself, via appropriate questions and stratified sampling methods, so that the implications of age cross-sectional studies can be taken seriously. Ultimately not age per se (neither ossification of the bones nor even just the passing of time) interests us but, rather, age-related *cultural experiences*, i.e. things that increasingly or decreasingly happened to Xish-speaking Xmen as time passed. Note, however, that the language use data that we have been discussing in this second type of cross-sectional study is still of the self-report variety.

Of course, the 'now' data need not be (or need not be entirely) of the self-report type. It may, instead or in part, rely on the notations of trained observers, sometimes even on the observations of several such at the same time, so that individual researcher errors in observation and record-keeping can later be found and corrected. Although such ethnographic or participant observation studies may be optimal in terms of data validity (fidelity) and reliability (dependability), they are, nevertheless, so costly in time, staffing and funding that they are usually simply out of the question on any large sample basis for pro-RLS purposes, given all of the resource pressures under which these purposes are usually pursued. The sense of lack of time is often particularly oppressive for pro-RLS advocates. They frequently feel, and very rightly so, that the clock is ticking away and that every day is witness to a further erosion of the 'health' of their language. Not only is this often so, but, to make a bad case worse, the establishment authorities often utilize 'studies' and 'research' precisely for the purpose of delay. Weak languages have literally been studied to the point of exhaustion, if not extinction, in recent years and many pro-RLSers have come to suspect the worst, accordingly, of any study, particularly if it is not under their own control insofar as staff, schedule and focus are concerned. Where a study is felt to be both desirable and possible, some combination of a large-scale (and, therefore, less intensive) self-report study (usually called a survey) and one or more small-scale (and, therefore, more intensive or detailed) observational studies is probably optimal, with the latter coming after the former and following them up so as to elicit further detailed information relative to particularly crucial or striking large-scale findings.[4]

However, pro-RLSers rarely can afford the optimal and usually have to settle for the minimal, however unsatisfactory that may be. Minimally, what can be hoped for is an opportunity for trusted informants, drawn from various social and geographic segments of the speech community, to get together in order to compare their judicious impressions. For these impressions to be commensurable (i.e. for them to be expressed in the same terms or units so that impressions can be compared, combined, or partitioned), a jointly accepted outline may be helpful by detailing in advance the areas of language-life that each informant should think about and report upon, relative to any particular population with which he or she is expertly familiar.

## The dimensionality of LS

### 1. Media of possible LS

The first differentiation that needs to be made, in order to arrive at a consensus as to whether LS has occurred and, if so, *where* in the entire language-use arena it has occurred, is the differentiation between speaking, reading and writing. This distinction is obviously of great importance *vis-à-vis* any remedial steps that may be suggested subsequently. If fewer people now have any understanding of the language at all, then this is commonly regarded as a limiting factor with respect to the number that can speak it, and if fewer are speaking the language at all, then this is commonly regarded (except in the case of religious classical tongues) as a limiting factor with respect to its use in reading and writing. Similarly, writing itself almost always presupposes reading. Thus, in modern society, these four 'media', understanding, speaking, reading and writing, constitute an 'implicational scale', such that those whose highest attainments come later in the list can be assumed to be in control of the earlier attainments as well. No similar implicationality is usually found between those skills coming earlier in the list and those skills coming later. The existence of speakers does not imply readers and the existence of readers does not imply writers. Observers should, therefore, be encouraged to report separately the command of skills *vis-à-vis* each medium and their reports should be checked for monotonic decline, i.e. for a decrease in magnitude in accord with their expected implicational order, since this provides a minor check on informant accuracy (or 'data validity').

## 2. Overtness: attitude/volition, competence and performance

Within several media the differences between attitude/volition, competence and performance are rather crucial ones and truly expert observers can be trained to report upon them as well. It makes an important difference, with regard to which future RLS steps are to be advocated, whether the number of speakers of Xish has dropped because the number who *can* speak has decreased or because the number who *want to* (dare to?) speak has decreased. The same distinction between *wanting to (attitude/volition), being able to (competence)* and *actually doing so (performance)* also obtains for reading and writing, and probably for understanding as well. Some people may not want to let on that they understand Xish even though they do. All in all, however, the implicationality of overtness levels should not always be taken for granted and needs to be confirmed. Some people may be able to speak without wanting to and, even more pathetically, in some LS settings, some individuals may actually speak a few words or phrases without understanding what they are saying. The major point being made here, therefore, is that medium and overtness inevitably interact and, therefore, should be reported interactively rather than in isolation from each other. However, since the judgments involved here are rather subtle and intricate, it may often not be possible to take the time and to find the wherewithal to train observers to make them reliably or validly.

## 3. Domains and role relations

Another major dimension that characterizes LS is the sociocultural context in which Xish is being realized or implemented. Such contexts can be conceptualized on a broader or on a narrower basis. Broadly speaking, they are conceptualized as all of the interactions that are rather unambiguously related (topically and situationally) to one or another of the major institutions of society: e.g. the family, the work sphere, education, religion, entertainment and the mass media, the political party, the government, etc. These are referred to as 'domains'.[5] More narrowly viewed, the contexts of language use are conceptualized as the role relations that are most congruent with particular domains. In the family domains there are such obvious role relations as husband–wife, parent–child, sibling–sibling, grandparent–grandchild, etc., etc. In the work sphere the most common role relations are employer–employee, supervisor–lower employee, employee–employee (where both are on the same level of the status hierarchy), etc. There are LS settings where it is common to speak (or read or write) Xish to one's parents and grandparents but not to one's children or younger siblings. In the work sphere, co-workers often speak Xish to each other, but not employers to employees or vice versa. Individuals may be simultaneously parents at home, employees in the work sphere, congregants in a house of worship, students in an educational program, members of a political party, reservists in the armed forces and voters or otherwise active citizens *vis-à-vis* the government. Across these various domains, and even in their several different role relations within the same domain, their incidence of use of Xish may vary considerably. It is exactly such variation, both from person to person and from situation to situation for the same person, that must ultimately be sketched out, across a large and representative sample of persons and, optimally, for two periods in time (but minimally for one), if the LS picture for Xish is to be clarified.

## What to Count in an Informed Evaluation of LS?

Thus far we have merely been presenting the framework of an informed evaluation of LS. This framework is needed in order to more accurately detect uneven shift, i.e. shift that is not 'across the board', but, rather, as is more usually the case, differential, being more rapid and fargoing in some connections and in some sub-populations than in others. However, a *framework* for specifying the social location of LS should not be confused with either the LS *data* to which this framework will be applied, nor to the *causes* of LS which produce or bring about the findings obtained. It is precisely because these three (framework, LS data, LS causes) are often confused that this chapter devotes separate attention to each of them.

### Counting Individuals

Most usually, individuals are the unit of enumeration in LS studies. Sometimes this is directly so, as when we count the population of certain districts (e.g. districts historically known for their greater language maintenance), the membership of certain organizations (e.g. those dedicated to language maintenance), the circulation of certain periodicals (e.g. those committed to RLS), or the attendance at certain schools (e.g. those traditionally successful in imparting good Xish language skills and pro-Xish attitudes and behaviors). Individuals are the safest thing to count and demographic statistics is a very sophisticated science that has been developed over many centuries in order to do so with increasing accuracy.[6] However, even the counting of individuals is not free of complications, and some prior definitions are required in order to count them in such a fashion as to facilitate comparability across time, across districts and, above all, across enumerators. If population size is being counted then the definition of a 'resident' must be kept constant. Are seasonal workers to be counted? Refugees destined to be resettled elsewhere? Prison inmates and hospital patients? Armed forces personnel temporarily absent from (or present in) the district? Tourists and vacationers? Similar definitional problems are related to the designations 'member', 'subscriber', 'enrollee', etc. All of these definitional issues must be straightened out before enumerations are undertaken, so that the data obtained can have maximal validity and, therefore, maximal value.

The same definitional clarity is also required *vis-à-vis* the social *descriptors* that are commonly associated with counts of individuals: age (to determine if residents, members, or readers are older or younger in one district than in another or than they used to be at some previous point in time) should be determined in a uniform way (e.g. exact age, nearest birthday, last birthday, next birthday), as should occupation/social class, amount of education and various other descriptors. Many of these are really continuous variables and they can be sliced in different ways, all of them ultimately somewhat arbitrary. What is important, therefore, first of all, is to pick a uniform set of definitions (because social class and all other descriptors can be defined in different ways) and a uniform set of 'slices' for the descriptors selected and, secondly, to try to stick with these definitions and slices over time, otherwise longitudinal data will become non-comparable over time. Although an LS evaluation may start out as a one-time cross-sectional enterprise, it is good to keep in mind that another such evaluation may be required or desired a decade later and that hastily arrived at descriptor definitions and descriptor 'slices' *now* will pose mighty problems and 'revisionist temptations' *later*. Obviously, 'narrow slices' can be combined subsequently into broader ones, whereas overly 'broad slices' cannot as easily be broken up into narrower ones (data reprocessing being required for that purpose).

## Counting Xish attitude, competence and performance

If there are technical, definitional difficulties just in connection with counting people, then it should come as no surprise that it is much more difficult to *count people in accord with certain of their language-use characteristics*. In

EXAMPLE 1 (Counting individuals): Mother-tongue claiming of the native of native parentage in the USA, 1940-1970, for 25 languages, with percent increase (decrease) 1940-1970 and 1960-1970

| Mother Tongue | 1940 | (Estim) 1960 | 1970 | Change 1940-1970 | 1949-1970 % Increase (Decrease) | Change 1960-1970 | 1960-1970 % Increase (Decrease) |
|---|---|---|---|---|---|---|---|
| Total | 84,124,840 | 145,275,265 | 169,634,926 | 85,510,086 | 101.65 | 24,359,661 | 16.77 |
| English | 78,352,180 | — | 149,312,435 | 70,960,255 | 90.57 | — | — |
| Norwegian | 81,160 | 40,000 | 204,822 | 123,662 | 152.37 | 164,822 | 412.06 |
| Swedish | 33,660 | 17,000 | 113,119 | 79,459 | 236.06 | 96,119 | 565.41 |
| Danish | 9,100 | 6,000 | 29,089 | 19,989 | 219.66 | 23,089 | 384.82 |
| Dutch | 65,800 | 74,000 | 102,777 | 36,977 | 56.20 | 28,777 | 38.89 |
| French | 518,780 | 383,000 | 1,460,130 | 941,350 | 181.45 | 1,077,130 | 281.23 |
| German | 925,040 | 588,000 | 2,488,394 | 1,563,354 | 169.00 | 1,900,394 | 323.70 |
| Polish | 185,820 | 87,00 | 670,335 | 484,515 | 260.74 | 583,335 | 670.50 |
| Czech | 81,760 | 34,000 | 148,944 | 67,184 | 82.18 | 114,944 | 338.07 |
| Slovak | 29,260 | 10,000 | 86,950 | 57,690 | 197.16 | 76,950 | 769.50 |
| Magyar (Hungarian) | 13,180 | 16,000 | 52,156 | 38,976 | 295.72 3 | 6,156 | 225.98 |
| Serbo-Croatian | 5,200 | 7,000 | 24,095 | 18,895 | 363.37 | 17,095 | 244.21 |
| Slovenian | 5,780 | 3,000 | 9,040 | 3,260 | 56.40 | 6,040 | 201.33 |
| Russian | 13,980 | 18,000 | 30,665 | 16,685 | 119.35 | 12,665 | 70.36 |
| Ukrainian | 2,780 | 10,000 | 22,662 | 19,882 | 715.18 | 12,662 | 126.62 |
| Armenian | 1,880 | — | 13,785 | 11,905 | 633.24 | — | — |
| Lithuanian | 9,400 | 8,000 | 34,744 | 25,344 | 269.62 | 26,744 | 334.30 |
| Finnish | 14,880 | 4,000 | 58,124 | 43,244 | 290.62 | 54,124 | 1353.10 |
| Rumanian | 2,060 | 2,000 | 5,166 | 3,106 | 150.78 | 3,166 | 158.30 |
| Yiddish | 52,980 | 39,000 | 170,174 | 117,194 | 221.20 | 131,174 | 336.34 |
| Greek | 6,160 | 12,000 | 56,839 | 50,679 | 822.71 | 44,839 | 373.66 |
| Italian | 125,040 | 147,000 | 605,626 | 480,585 | 384.35 | 458,625 | 311.99 |
| Spanish | 718,980 | 1,291,000 | 4,171,050 | 3,452,070 | 480.13 | 2,880,050 | 233.09 |
| Portuguese | 11,380 | 7,000 | 62,252 | 50,872 | 447.03 | 55,252 | 789.31 |
| Arabic | 3,720 | 4,000 | 25,765 | 22,045 | 592.61 | 21,765 | 544.13 |
| Total Non-English | 2,917,780 | 2,807,000 | 10,646,701 | 7,728,922 2 | 64.89 | 7,826,017 | 278.80 |
| Total Non-English minus Spanish | 2,198,800 | 1,516,000 | 6,475,652 | 4,276,852 | 194.51 | 4,945,867 | 328.41 |

Source: Fishman et al. (1985) pp. 139-40

EXAMPLE 2A (Counting radio and TV stations): USA radio and television stations, 1960 and 1981-82, nationwide and non-English using

| | 1960 | | | | 1980/1982 | | | | %Change 1960-1981/1982 | |
| | USA as a Whole | | Non-English Using | | USA as a Whole 1981 | | Non-English Using 1982 | | USA | Non-English Using |
| | n | % | n | % | n | % | n | % | | |
|---|---|---|---|---|---|---|---|---|---|---|
| Radio | 3,688 | 87.43 | 1,622 | 100.00 | 7,847 | 91.26 | 2,333 | 90.08 | 112.77 | 43.84 |
| TV | 530 | 12.57 | — | — | 752 | 8.74 | 257 | 9.92 | 41.89 | — |
| Total | 4,218 | 100.00 | 1,622 | 100.00 | 8,599 | 100.00 | 2,590 | 100.00 | 103.86 | 59.68 |

Source: Fishman et al. (1985), p. 225

EXAMPLE 2b (Counting the circulation of specific periodicals): Circulation trends in five foreign language dailies published in New York City, 1925-1956

| Newspaper | Date founded | Circulation (Daily) | | | | | | Sunday 1956 |
| | | 1925 | 1935 | 1945 | 1950 | 1954 | 1956 | |
|---|---|---|---|---|---|---|---|---|
| Staat/Zeitung*a | 1834 | 56336 | 54006 | 26586 | 25840 | 22814 | 21049 | 38937 |
| Forverts | 1897 | 143716 | 136082 | 98969 | 79719 | 74451 | 7621 | 79949 |
| Tog^b | 1914 | 78901 | 82332 | 48843 | 51929 | 66446 | 59179 | 57765 |
| Prensa | 1913 | 10800 | 15628 | 14614 | 11439 | 16882 | 17787 | 13765 |
| Diario | 1948 | — | — | — | 12803 | 25195 | 33286 | 30390 |

aCombined with Herold in 1936    bCombined with Morgn-Zhurnal in 1953    Source: Fishman et al. (1968), p. 230

addition to definitional issues alone (what is a language attitude?; how does it differ from a belief? from an opinion? from a sentiment?), there is also the problem of the inherent covertness of much of the attitudinal and competence data that may be of crucial interest to an LS study. In small-scale and in long-term studies, skilled and specially trained observers can infer and estimate such covert variables for a limited population (with whom they have been in protracted face-to-face interaction) from various indirect bits and pieces of overt behavior. Attitudes are inferred or inferrable from things occasionally said and done (as well as from things never said or done, even though one is in an environment in which it is common to do or say such things). Competence is often inferred or inferrable from observed listening-to-Xish behavior, e.g. observed laughing or smiling at the right time when in earshot of Xish humor, observed correct following of oral or written instructions conveyed in Xish, etc. However, all of these approaches are time-consuming, expensive and, because of their covert 'criteria' (i.e. that which would prove the correctness of the inferences), of uncertain or unprovable validity. As a result, it is not really conceivable that RLS advocates will often be able to engage in the luxury of studying them. If attitudes and competencies *do* become of overriding interest or importance, there is usually no practical alternative to either collecting self-report data about them via 'scales' or 'questionnaires',[7] on the one hand, or, on the other hand, to letting trustworthy and informed observers[8] report their impressions as well and as uniformly as they can.

## Language use

Language use is somewhat easier to evaluate than language attitude and language competence; after all, much of it is overt and available for others to see and hear. However, its accurate depiction is beset by various difficulties, not unlike those we have already mentioned above. The greatest of these difficulties is finding the proper unit of performance that is to be counted. In connection with speaking, should it be the number of utterances that are judged (or self-reported) to be predominantly in Xish, this number then being convertible to a 'proportion of Xish utterances to all utterances'? For this to be a feasible goal (for self-reports or for observer notation) in terms of time, manpower and funds, it requires a prior uniform definition both of 'utterance' and of 'predominantly', a requirement that not only presupposes advanced linguistic and sociolinguistic training, but one that is not completely attainable today even by those with such training.

The usual escape hatch in the rating of observable behaviors, particularly for large-scale studies (country-wide, region-wide, and even city-wide), is not

EXAMPLE 3 (*Counting attitudes and opinions*): *Positive replies to attitude and opinion questions by native-born (NB) and foreign-born (FB) community activists in three different ethnic groups*
*Note*: Fr 1 = Franco-Americans in Louisiana; Fr 2 = Franco-Americans in New England; Sp 1 = Chicanos in California; Sp 2 = Cubans in Florida; Sp 3 = Puerto Ricans in New York.

| Question | | French | | | Spanish | | | | Yiddish | Grand |
|---|---|---|---|---|---|---|---|---|---|---|
| | | Fr1 | Fr2 | Fr tot | Sp1 | Sp2 | Sp3 | Sp tot | Y tot | total |
| 1. Was there an ethnic boom revival | NB | 63.6 | 73.7 | 68.3 | 92.9 | 100.0 | 77.8 | 88.0 | 87.5 | 78.0 |
| | FB | 100.0 | 50.0 | 66.7 | 100.0 | 95.0 | 93.9 | 95.4 | 78.6 | 90.0 |
| | T | 65.2 | 71.4 | 68.2 | 95.4 | 95.4 | 87.5 | 92.6 | 83.3 | 83.1 |
| 2. Did it increase respondent's EMT use? | NB | 31.8 | 42.1 | 36.6 | 78.6 | 50.0 | 55.6 | 68.0 | 43.8 | 47.6 |
| | FB | 00.0 | 00.0 | 00.0 | 37.5 | 45.0 | 53.3 | 46.5 | 00.0 | 33.3 |
| | T | 30.4 | 38.1 | 34.1 | 63.6 | 45.4 | 54.2 | 54.4 | 23.3 | 41.6 |
| 3. Did it improve respondent's attitudes toward EMT? | NB | 45.4 | 47.4 | 46.3 | 85.7 | 100.0 | 88.9 | 88.0 | 50.0 | 59.8 |
| | FB | 00.0 | 00.0 | 00.0 | 50.0 | 60.0 | 80.0 | 65.1 | 7.1 | 65.0 |
| | T | 43.5 | 42.9 | 43.2 | 72.7 | 63.6 | 83.3 | 73.5 | 30.0 | 62.0 |
| 4. Did it renew respondent's customs of culture? | NB | 4.6 | 36.8 | 19.5 | 92.9 | 50.0 | 44.4 | 72.0 | 18.8 | 35.4 |
| | FB | 00.0 | 00.0 | 00.0 | 75.0 | 75.0 | 40.0 | 62.8 | 7.1 | 46.7 |
| | T | 4.4 | 33.3 | 18.2 | 86.4 | 72.7 | 41.7 | 66.2 | 13.3 | 40.1 |
| 5. Did it increase EMT use (community)? | NB | 13.6 | 42.1 | 26.8 | 85.7 | 100.0 | 66.7 | 80.0 | 62.5 | 50.0 |
| | FB | 00.0 | 00.0 | 00.0 | 75.0 | 95.0 | 66.7 | 81.4 | 57.1 | 71.7 |
| | T | 13.0 | 28.1 | 25.0 | 81.8 | 95.4 | 66.7 | 80.9 | 60.0 | 59.2 |
| 6. Did it improve attitudes toward EMT (community)? | NB | 27.3 | 42.1 | 34.2 | 92.9 | 100.0 | 100.0 | 96.0 | 87.5 | 63.4 |
| | FB | 00.0 | 00.0 | 00.0 | 87.5 | 80.0 | 86.7 | 83.7 | 71.4 | 76.7 |
| | T | 26.1 | 38.1 | 31.4 | 90.9 | 81.8 | 91.7 | 88.2 | 80.0 | 69.0 |
| 7. Did it renew customs of culture (community)? | NB | 4.6 | 31.6 | 17.1 | 85.7 | 100.0 | 66.7 | 80.0 | 56.2 | 43.9 |
| | FB | 00.0 | 00.0 | 00.0 | 100.0 | 95.0 | 60.0 | 83.7 | 50.0 | 71.7 |
| | T | 4.4 | 28.6 | 15.9 | 95.4 | 95.4 | 62.5 | 82.8 | 53.3 | 55.6 |

| | | (1) | (2) | (3) | (4) | (5) | (6) | (7) | (8) | (9) |
|---|---|---|---|---|---|---|---|---|---|---|
| 8. What caused revival? INTERNAL FORCES? | NB | 72.7 | 52.6 | 63.4 | 78.6 | 100.0 | 77.8 | 80.0 | 87.5 | 73.2 |
| | FB | 100.0 | 00.0 | 33.3 | 75.0 | 75.0 | 80.0 | 76.7 | 57.1 | 70.0 |
| | T | 73.9 | 47.6 | 61.4 | 77.2 | 77.3 | 79.2 | 77.9 | 73.3 | 71.8 |
| 9. local group? | NB | 68.2 | 31.6 | 51.2 | 78.6 | 00.0 | 11.1 | 48.0 | 6.2 | 41.5 |
| | FB | 00.0 | 50.0 | 33.3 | 75.0 | 40.0 | 13.3 | 37.2 | 7.1 | 30.0 |
| | T | 65.2 | 33.3 | 50.0 | 77.3 | 36.4 | 12.5 | 41.2 | 6.7 | 36.6 |
| 10. local person? | NB | 40.9 | 00.0 | 22.0 | 14.3 | 00.0 | 11.1 | 12.0 | 18.8 | 18.3 |
| | FB | 00.0 | 00.0 | 00.0 | 25.0 | 10.0 | 6.7 | 11.6 | 00.0 | 8.3 |
| | T | 39.1 | 00.0 | 20.4 | 18.2 | 9.1 | 8.3 | 11.8 | 10.0 | 14.1 |
| 11. national group? | NB | 00.0 | 00.0 | 00.0 | 14.3 | 00.0 | 11.1 | 12.0 | 6.2 | 4.9 |
| | FB | 00.0 | 00.0 | 00.0 | 50.0 | 15.0 | 33.3 | 27.9 | 14.3 | 21.7 |
| | T | 00.0 | 00.0 | 00.0 | 27.3 | 9.1 | 25.0 | 20.6 | 10.0 | 12.0 |
| 12. national figure? | NB | 4.6 | 00.0 | 2.4 | 42.9 | 00.0 | 00.0 | 24.0 | 00.0 | 8.5 |
| | FB | 00.0 | 00.0 | 00.0 | 50.0 | 10.0 | 6.7 | 16.3 | 7.1 | 13.3 |
| | T | 4.4 | 00.0 | 2.3 | 45.4 | 9.1 | 4.2 | 19.1 | 3.3 | 10.6 |
| 13. What caused revival? EXTERNAL FORCES? | NB | 00.0 | 21.0 | 9.8 | 00.0 | 00.0 | 44.4 | 16.0 | 31.2 | 15.8 |
| | FB | 00.0 | 00.0 | 00.0 | 12.5 | 30.0 | 53.3 | 34.9 | 28.6 | 31.7 |
| | T | 00.0 | 19.0 | 2.3 | 4.6 | 27.3 | 50.0 | 27.9 | 30.0 | 22.5 |
| 14. government program? | NB | 9.1 | 5.3 | 7.3 | 7.1 | 00.0 | 11.1 | 8.0 | 00.0 | 6.1 |
| | FB | 00.0 | 00.0 | 00.0 | 12.5 | 15.0 | 6.7 | 11.6 | 00.0 | 8.3 |
| | T | 8.7 | 4.8 | 6.8 | 9.1 | 13.6 | 8.3 | 10.3 | 00.0 | 7.0 |
| 15. other ethnic movement? | NB | 9.1 | 31.6 | 19.5 | 92.9 | 100.0 | 55.6 | 80.0 | 25.0 | 39.0 |
| | FB | 00.0 | 00.0 | 00.0 | 87.5 | 70.0 | 73.3 | 74.4 | 14.3 | 56.7 |
| | T | 8.7 | 28.6 | 18.2 | 90.9 | 72.7 | 70.8 | 76.5 | 20.0 | 46.5 |
| 16. legislation? | NB | 45.4 | 10.5 | 29.3 | 64.3 | 50.0 | 88.9 | 72.0 | 00.0 | 36.6 |
| | FB | 00.0 | 00.0 | 00.0 | 12.5 | 90.0 | 60.0 | 65.1 | 00.0 | 46.7 |
| | T | 43.5 | 9.5 | 27.3 | 45.4 | 86.4 | 70.8 | 67.6 | 00.0 | 40.8 |

Source: Fishman et al. (1986), pp. 288-9

only utilized at the level of self-report. It is undertaken in terms of ratings of 'relative frequency clusters'. Such ratings are technically known as 'Likert-type' ratings[9] and utilize such designations as 'always', 'frequently', 'sometimes', 'rarely' and 'never'. Ratings such as these normally do not tell us how often 'frequently' is, nor do they tell us exactly what 'frequently' means to the respondents (or whether it means the same thing to all respondents). These difficulties or indeterminacies are *not* overcome by changing the relative designations to absolute ones such as 'more than 20 times a day', 'between 15 and 20 times a day', 'between 10 and 15 times a day', 'between five and 10 times a day' and 'fewer than five times a day', because the notion of 'times' is dubious and variable from respondent to respondent. Is a 'time' an Xish interjection ('Hello!') in an otherwise non-Xish conversation? Is it a phrase? a sentence? a single turn-to-talk (of whatever length) in a dyadic conversation? 'Times' *can* be defined, of course, but the more precise the definition of 'times' (or of other frequency cluster boundaries) the more unmanageable become the questions about them insofar as most 'ordinary respondents' are concerned.

As a result of quandaries such as the above, where greater rating or self-rating accuracy is either unattainable or attainable only at prohibitive costs (including diminution of the scale on which information will be available), the response categories used in language surveys are most commonly left undefined, i.e. they are presented as intuitively understandable and interpretable 'relative frequency clusters'. Fortunately, our dependence on such categories is not entirely an article of faith. It has been demonstrated many times, and even in connection with sociolinguistic data on LS concerns, that where there is no overpowering reason for dissimulation (e.g. giving spurious anti-Xish social desirability responses under circumstances where respondents can be identified and 'punished' for pro-Xish self-reports) the responses on self-report Likert-type instruments are significantly related to independently obtained daily behavioral records of a more precise type[10]. Thus, the saving grace of response categories is two-fold: that they can be reasonably valid and reliable and that the 'next best thing' (detailed observation) would provide information on a far smaller sample of the target population and would do so at a far greater price in time, funds and manpower, without materially overcoming most of the major methodological difficulties that normally beset social science research.

### An even more minimal solution to the problem of estimation

Minimalism is *not* a greatly desirable state of affairs when it comes to estimating the degree and nature of erosion with respect to Xish. The more accurately the erosion of the language can be estimated, and the more fully

EXAMPLE 4 (*Using relative frequency response categories*): *Relative frequency replies to language census questions*

| Item | Yes | Little | No | NP | $r_{12}{}^a$ |
|---|---|---|---|---|---|
| 1. Can Understand Spanish conversation? | 779 | 135 | 019 | 067 | 80 |
| 2. Can Speak Spanish (conversation)? | 833 | 077 | 016 | 074 | 83 |
| 3. Can Read newspapers/books in Spanish? | 397 | 049 | 318 | 237 | 84 |
| 4. Can Write letters in Spanish? | 390 | 030 | 339 | 241 | 86 |
| 5. Can Understand English conversation? | 571 | 176 | 183 | 070 | 83 |
| 6. Can Speak English (conversation) | 536 | 181 | 216 | 067 | 83 |
| 7. Can Read newspapers/books in English? | 455 | 130 | 206 | 209 | 83 |
| 8. Can Write letters in English? | 387 | 063 | 327 | 223 | 81 |

| | Span | Eng | Both | NP | |
|---|---|---|---|---|---|
| 9. First language understood (conversation)? | 886 | 002 | 039 | 072 | 50 |
| 10. First language spoken (conversation)? | 884 | — | 023 | 093 | 50 |
| 11. First language read (newspapers/books)? | 401 | — | 297 | 302 | 92 |
| 12. First language written (letters)? | 383 | 002 | 276 | 339 | 90 |
| 13. Most frequently spoken at home? | 657 | 088 | 183 | 072 | 57 |
| 14. Most frequently read at home? | 267 | 051 | 357 | 325 | 85 |
| 15. Most frequently written at home? | 339 | 014 | 255 | 392 | 93 |
| 16. Most frequently spoken with fellow workers? | 137 | 049 | 137 | 677 | 84 |
| 17. Most frequently spoken with supervisor? | 046 | 009 | 264 | 680 | 57 |
| 18. Most frequently spoken with clients/customers? | 032 | 014 | 035 | 919 | 79 |
| 19. Language of instruction in school? | 339 | 237 | 167 | 257 | 79 |
| 20. Language liked most (conversation)? | 362 | 285 | 286 | 267 | 61 |
| 21. Language of priest's/minister's sermon? | 452 | 137 | 193 | 206 | 46 |
| 22. Language of silent prayer? | 469 | 123 | 151 | 257 | 75 |
| 23. Language of church service? | 427 | 160 | 293 | 220 | 48 |

*Note*: Percentages carried to three places (decimals omitted) based upon $n = 431$

[a]Reliability of response after one week (census–recensus)

*Source*: Fishman *et al.* (1971), p. 161

the true state of affairs confronting pro-RLSers is known to them, the more refined and well chosen can be the ameliorative steps and the more revealing the follow-up evaluations *vis-à-vis* the success of steps already underway. However, sometimes there is simply no alternative to minimalism on the evaluation front. Then it may be necessary to utilize methods even rougher than any of those sketched above, namely: the use of a panel of individuals, each individual optimally familiar with a different population segment (region, social class, ethnic group, etc.) and each individual rating that segment, in accord with a uniform and maximally cross-classified rating form but with respect to only a few simplified and global questions. Given the manifold possible interactions between various media, overtness levels, domains and role relationships discussed earlier, a panel can be asked to rate whether Xish or Yish 'is the most frequently used language' or whether Xish is 'used as frequently (or by the same proportion of people [or of teenagers]) today as was the case in Time $A_1$ or in Time $A_2$ years ago'. This approach yields no more than informed opinion, but it may have to suffice until better research can be planned. Even informed opinion can be useful, particularly for internal purposes, and the use of a grid such as that shown in Example 5 provides a structured and uniform approach for collecting such opinion from various specialists and for comparing such opinion from one specialist to the other and from one time to the next.

What Example 5 reveals is a structured sociolinguistic approach to the changes from 1957 to 1987 that an informed observer has noted. They generally boil down to impressions that there has been a decrease in Basque use at home and in private, intimacy-related (family/friendship) interactions, but a slight increase in Basque use in public and in formal domains and role relations. This is a summary portrait, of course, drawn out of experience with all the speech networks and individuals that the informant has been familiar with during more than a quarter century. In a later chapter, we will discuss what the particular pattern of impressions revealed by this particular informant summary implies. At this point we merely introduce it as an example of what a brief, informed, impressionistic summary looks like. Were it less impressionistic there would be empirical entries in its various cells, such as numbers of Basque speakers or frequencies of Basque use (or even — most difficult of all to obtain and far beyond the level of our presentation in this volume — frequencies of Basque usages of various lexical and syntactic kinds). The information that Example 5 yields is far less than what we would optimally like to have. However, until more optimal data is at hand, it provides a basis for discussion and planning among pro-RLSers. The first such discussion that is needed deals with the issue of how the depicted state of affairs came about. That is the topic to which we will now turn.

EXAMPLE 5: *A minimal evaluation of 'predominant patterns re speaking Basque in urban Gipuzcoa, 1957 and 1987*
(B = Basque; S = Spanish)

| Media | Overtness | Domain | Role relations | 1957 | 1987 |
|---|---|---|---|---|---|
| Speaking | Production | Family | Husband–wife | B | B/S |
| | | | Parent–child | B/S | S |
| | | | Grandparent–grandchild | B | B/S |
| | | | Siblings (at home) | S/B | S |
| | | | Others (parent's generation) | B | B/S |
| | | | Others (children's generation) | S/B | S |
| | | Neighborhood | Friends | B/S | S |
| | | | Acquaintances | S/B | S |
| | | Sports/ Entertainment | Others in attendance | S | S/B |
| | | Education | Pupil–teacher | S | S/B |
| | | | Pupil–pupil | S | S/B |
| | | Work | Employer/Employee | S | S/B |
| | | Government | Officer (Civil Servant)/citizen | S | S/B |

*Source*: A Basque activist attending the Second Basque World Congress, San Sebastian, September 1987.

# Why Does Language Shift Occur?

The *where* and *why* of language shift are necessarily intimately related, particularly so at earlier stages of the shift process. The location of shift in the total 'sociocultural space' of a speech community is an indication of just where the stresses and strains of cross-cultural contact have eroded the ability of the smaller and weaker to withstand the stronger and larger. However, social processes transpire along a time continuum, and both historical time and current time must be of concern to those who wish to fully understand language shift in order to counteract it. Immediate sore-points must be treated immediately, of course, but unless their relationship to more ultimate causes is understood, the immediate treatments may be no more than patchworks and palliatives, rather than ameliorative steps of any lasting value.

We will set aside from our consideration of *why* LS occurs such factors as obvious prohibitions of minority language use and advocacy. Such prohibitions must be removed and their negative implications for justice and democracy more generally, i.e. their demoralizing and corroding effects on the moral and ethical sensibilities of the majority, must be pointed out.[11] Minorities have no other means at their disposal, in this connection, than moral suasion, on the one hand, and the building of coalitions with other unfairly disadvantaged groups, on the other. Majorities that are deaf to their own injustice in the sphere of cultural democracy are usually equally deaf to other injustices of the system they control, whether racial, economic, religious and/or sexual, so that ethnolinguistic minorities rarely need to bear the load of opposition entirely by themselves. The court of world opinion can also be appealed to and many professional societies exist that can help spread far and wide a familiarity with the grievances of ethnolinguistic minorities, thereby enlisting understanding, sympathy, material support and moral pressure for their very elementary human dreams (dreams that majorities take for granted), namely dreams of enabling one's own children to live according to one's own cultural norms, values and preferences[12]. This is a difficult struggle, but the long-term trend has proven it to be a rewarding one, since out-and-out prohibitions of minority ethnolinguistic efforts are increasingly rare and restricted to obviously unreconstructed and morally offensive totalitarian regimes.

More generally, the legal problems faced by minority ethnolinguistic groups are less obviously adversary and more in the nature of customary disinterest, footdragging and unresponsiveness to grievances pertaining to rights that are clearly a matter of record and provided for in law. Such approaches to the curtailment of minority ethnolinguistic rights are not limited to obviously antidemocratic regimes and may be encountered almost anywhere in the world. They are probably inevitable, to some degree, and constitute the most common means utilized, both consciously and unconsciously, by establishments seeking to preserve their perquisites and their power. Here, however, the field is even more open for minority sponsored protests, lawsuits and coalition building, in order that rights may be more fully respected, laws more completely and quickly implemented, and bureaucratic roadblocks more expeditiously removed. Most frequently, RLS-efforts begin with the voluntary, self-supported efforts of minorities, even in the face of majority disinterest and partial intragroup apathy. All in all, therefore, subtle opposition and studied disregard by majorities and an ongoing political and public relations effort to overcome or counteract such opposition and disregard on the part of minorities (both *vis-à-vis* majorities and *vis-à-vis* many if not most networks within the minorities themselves) must be viewed as constantly ongoing accompaniments of RLS-efforts, including all of the efforts focused upon the LS factors per se, to which we now turn.

## Physical and demographic dislocation

There is obviously a physical basis to all of life, whether individual, social or cultural. When this physical basis is dislocated, the continuity of life itself becomes threatened. At the ethnocultural level one of the major physical threats to intergenerational language-in-culture continuity is population transfer and voluntary or involuntary out-migration. Any ongoing process of demographic diminution, particularly if it becomes a historical constant such that successive generations come to take it for granted and come to prepare for their own role in its further continuation (see the Irish, Basque, Catalan and Frisian cases in subsequent chapters), cannot be anything other than dislocative of the language-in-culture pattern (and of the language-in-society and language-in-economy patterns as well), even of those who stay behind. Physical dislocation may be brought about by severe and recurring famines (note the history of a thousand years of famines in Ireland[13]), by natural catastrophes such as floods, earthquakes, major temperature changes, droughts and pestilences of man, beasts or crops, etc. But human intervention may also be involved in the physical dislocation of populations, as in the case of warfare, genocide, scorched earth policies of invasion or resistance to invasion, slave-hunting expeditions, population expulsion policies (often euphemistically referred to as 'resettlement', 'transfer' or 'exchange'), soil exhaustion and mineral or forest depletion, and, most recently, toxic poisoning of air, water, soil, plants, animals or humans. LS in various parts of the USA, USSR, Brazil, Australia and New Guinea, for example, has clearly transpired as a result of environmental changes brought about by the industrialization of agriculture, forestry, animal husbandry and mineral exploitation, in addition to and in conjunction with the industrialization of production and the intrusion and 'relocation' of populations.

All of the above circumstances, some of them recurring and stretching over longer periods of time and some of them abruptly cataclysmic, leave the remaining populations demographically, socially and culturally weakened via the direct impact on intergenerational mother tongue transmission within the family and neighborhood occasioned by foreign occupants, 'protectors', settlers, immigrants and visitors, on the one hand, or *vis-à-vis* intergroup cultural influences and contacts (via trade, mass media and even aid efforts), on the other hand. Furthermore, those who leave, or are driven or carried off, are usually even in worse straits, insofar as intergenerational ethnolinguistic continuity is concerned. As voluntary or involuntary migrants to places of relocation they are exposed to an overwhelming array of unfamiliar and power-imbalanced circumstances which make language-in-culture maintenance 'problematic', to say the least. Cultures are dependent on familiar and traditional places and products, as much as they are on familiar coparticipants and on an established consensus among them as to cultural values, norms and processes. Demographic dislocation may undermine the latter (culturally familiar interlocutors) every bit as much as it does the former (culturally familiar contexts), the two, the demographic and the cultural, being intimately linked to each other.

Even such a widespread and seemingly innocuous demographic process as the urbanization of a hitherto rural or non-sedentary population usually has drastically negative physical and therefore, ultimately, negative sociocultural dislocative consequences. Urbanization of hitherto rural newcomers involves interacting with strangers at almost every step: in the neighborhood, at work, at school, in shopping, in transportation, in entertainment and at civic functions, on the one hand; and a greatly increased density of communication, on the other hand. The result of this co-occurrence is an endless deluge of ethnolinguistic messages in the lingua franca which any urban environment either develops or adopts, a language which is different from that of most Xish homes and families and which easily comes to rival and displace the language of dislocated home and family, particularly for the young. Urbanization neatly exemplifies the basic point that we are trying to make here. There are few, if any, culturally innocent physical and demographic arrangements, just as there are few, if any, physically and demographically unencumbered cultural ones. Physical and demographic arrangements have cultural (and, therefore, language-in-culture) consequences. Physical and demographic dislocation is immediately translatable into cultural (and, therefore, into language-in-culture) dislocation. Pro-RLS efforts, on their part, must also have a physical and demographic counterpart, rather than merely an ethnocultural aspect. Pro-RLS activists must be concerned with *where* Xish speakers live, *how closely* they live to each other, how preponderant they are in the districts in which they reside, how easily available basically Xish neighborhood institutions (nurseries, schools, houses of worship, clubhouses, athletic centers, meeting houses, libraries, theaters, etc.) are to Xish speakers of various ages. As we will see later on, the disadvantages of physical dispersion can be somewhat compensated for by modern technology, but, when it comes to intergenerational mother tongue transmission and maintenance, there is nothing like not having such disadvantages to compensate for to begin with. Every pro-RLS movement must strive to provide physical breathing-space for its constituency, demographically concentrated space where Xish can be on its own turf, predominant and unharassed. Such spaces may appear abnormal or atypical *vis-à-vis* the outside, non-Xish surrounding reality; but *vis-à-vis* internal Xish reality, such spaces become potential oases of authenticity and centers of increased cultural self-regulation that seek to counteract the physical dislocation that minority life is so commonly afflicted with.

Will such efforts at physical 'normalization' lead to self-ghettoization? Unlikely. The bulk of minority life is still exposed to and dependent upon interactions with others and with other-dominated societies, economies, cultures and governments. Physical 'normalization' merely represents an effort at minimal balance, at boundary maintenance and demographic preponderance in at least a few areas of basic, normal daily interaction, so that Xish can have some space to call its own, some space in which it is the normal and self-evident channel, expression and accompaniment of at least some crucial cultural transmission and maintenance processes. We will attend at greater length to possible 'solutions' to dispersion later; at this point, we are merely trying to point out a problem area that is so self-evident that, like the air we breathe, it has often been overlooked: LS occurs because interacting languages-in-cultures are of unequal power and, therefore, the weaker ones become physically and demographically dislocated.

**Social dislocation**

'Of unequal power' also means that members of minority ethnolinguistic groups are frequently (but not inevitably) socially disadvantaged, i.e. less educationally and economically fortunate than the average of the population surrounding them. This disadvantage is a by-product of their frequent relative powerlessness numerically, politically and in terms of resource control of almost every kind. This is quite obviously so in terms of unselected immigrants to a more advantaged host-context, particularly in the early years after their arrival. However, it is also true of minoritized indigenous populations who have been peripheralized (some would say 'colonized') even while remaining in some of their traditional areas of residence. They too are commonly characterized by briefer school attendance and by lower income, by lower literacy in any language and by poverty, by lack of social graces as defined by the majority population and by lack of the conveniences of everyday life that are so common among the majority population. If such is the picture of the bulk of the remaining speakers of Xish, then it becomes part of what Xish stands for or symbolizes, both in the eyes of most Ymen and in the eyes of many Xmen too. This is a problem for pro-RLSers, because many — including many who consider themselves Xmen — will oppose RLS on the grounds that such efforts will lead to prolonging disadvantage, rather than to counteracting it.

The obvious solutions to ignorance, coarseness and poverty consist of providing opportunities for education, refinement and better jobs, but since all or most of the latter are controlled or under the auspices of Ymen and Yish society, they obviously require mastery of Yish. Willy-nilly, Xmen who seek social mobility become dependent on Yish society and are not only coopted into that society, but try to make sure that their own children gain entry into it at as early an age as possible. Dependency interaction between Xmen and Ymen, a process in which those Xmen who are most like Ymen are the ones most rewarded by the power structure of Yish, continually erodes Xish: its demography, its society and its culture. Given the continuance of the original power and resource differentials between Xish and Yish, and given the continuance of the incorporative capacity as well as the incorporative ideology of many modern Yish societies and cultures, the transethnification and translinguification of former Xmen inexorably continues as well.[14] Xmen are seemingly faced by a cruel dilemma: either to remain loyal to their traditions and to remain socially disadvantaged (consigning their own children to such disadvantage as well), on the one hand; or, on the other hand, to abandon their distinctive practices and traditions, at least in large part, and, thereby, to improve their own and their children's lots in life via cultural suicide. Furthermore, Ymen who favor and support the ethnic and linguistic 'mainstreaming' of Xmen, pose as (and consider themselves to be) both humanitarians and realists, with nothing but their less fortunate neighbors' best interests in mind. The counterpart of the foregoing is the unenviable position of pro-RLSers, who may come to be accused of being the enemies of their own people, however unconsciously and unmeaningly, foolishly prolonging their needless ignorance, boorishness and poverty. The stance of accusing those who are victims of discrimination of bringing about their own misfortune (rather than recognizing the mainstream's culpability in that regard) is a common one for anti-RLSers and among spokesmen of fortunate establishments more generally. Actually, this stance is merely an accompaniment to the parallel stance that Xish is not being persecuted or denied its place in the sun at all, but, rather, that those who are abandoning it are doing so voluntarily. Whether made in the USSR or in the USA, neither charge is true.

Although the dilemma posed by dependency interaction is certainly a real and a cruel one, it is neither as inescapable nor as easily remediable as simplistic 'either–or' thinking would have it. The promise of social mobility via Yish is far from universally realized and the need to leave Xish behind in order to pursue that promise is far from entirely justified. Transethnification and translinguification bring with them their own problems and exact their own steep prices, medically (as revealed by elevated and aggravated illness patterns among dislocated assimilating populations), psychologically (as revealed by mental stress patterns among dislocated assimilating populations) and socioculturally (as revealed by crime and violence patterns among dislocated assimilating populations).[15] Accordingly, pro-RLSers must become adept at combinatorial rather than at mutually exclusive solutions. They must pursue stable bilingualism, at least among Xmen, if not among the generality of the population at large, and cultural pluralism, at least as an intra-Xish platform, if not as a national policy. In either case, it is the dilemma per se that needs to be combated. Good education should not necessarily be only in Yish and only under Yish auspices. Boorishness and Xishness need not be synonymous at all, since Xish too can develop (or recover) its own high culture, with intellectuals and a 'polite society' as part of its social structure. Economic mobility requiring Yish can and should be available to those Xmen who wish to 'acquire Yish but retain Xish and Xish culture as well'. An economic base under Xish control need not be entirely out of the question, thereby providing employment and mobility to Xish speakers who remain in a cultural environment and in a physical space more nearly their own. The creation of an economic base often requires the assistance and cooperation of a prior economic base (the Yish economic base), but if the much touted Yish 'good will' is really there, and, more importantly yet, if the potential for 'profits in the Xish sector' is really there, such cooperation too should be forthcoming. At any rate, the reduction of the entire problem of Xish language maintenance to that of economic advantage pure and simple, is overly simplistic and reductionistic. It is akin to other brands of reductionism (e.g. that 'only schools in Xish will save us', 'only mass media in Xish will save us', 'only full fledged cultural autonomy will save us') in that it offers a mechanistic and pre-packaged solution that is automatically applied to every RLS case, even before its particular problems are fully examined or well understood. Since the economy associated with Xish will always be smaller that that associated with Yish, pro-RLSers must focus their gaze on other avenues of solution than those which are basically no more than the 'counsel of futility'.

Social dislocation, the syphoning off of the talented, the enterprising, the adventurous, the imaginative and the creative, is a serious problem for the future of any ethnocultural community. Mighty nations take steps to curb and to avoid a braindrain and Yish society would do so too, if that were its problem. If Xish society cannot take unilateral steps along these lines, it can at least engage in internal clarification efforts, oriented toward Xmen, that 'the best of all possible worlds' is an ethnolinguistically syncretistic one, one that involves Xish and Yish in stable co-existence among Xmen, rather than either Xish or Yish alone[16] in two totally distinct and antagonistic populations. Languages and cultures need not be mutually exclusive or replacive zero-sum-games, any more than do the various multiple memberships which Ymen currently entertain and even take for granted at the individual level. The utilization of Yish by Xmen in given, delimited intergroup domains need not ultimately imperil Xish intragroup identity, nor ultimately alter the core of Xish intragroup culture. However, for such utilization to be non-dislocative of Xish, it ultimately requires the formation of a new type of Xman, an Xish leader and intellectual who may be more capable of engaging in RLS than was previously the case (rather than merely a type more eager to transethnify), a type whose greater ability along these positive lines may be directly attributed to his or her greater ability to meet and interact with Ymen in Yish in certain pursuits *and to do without them completely in others*, on the one hand, while cultivating Xishness in certain areas at a higher intellectual and more creative cultural level than was the case before, on the other hand. Obviously, the solution to social dislocation requires newer responses than those that have existed before to the problems of intergroup dependency relationships, responses that locate advantages for Xish rather than merely catalog its disadvantages. We plan to return to this topic again and in greater detail in the immediately following chapters as well as in others that come subsequent to it.

**Cultural dislocation**

As with physical and social dislocation, so also the overall impact of cultural dislocation and the possibility of its reversal depends greatly on its surrounding overall context. Brutally repressive regimes consciously engage in the 'blackest' and most reprehensible cultural dislocation of ethnolinguistic minorities and the efforts of such regimes along such lines (via massive arrests and executions of cultural leaders, wholesale deportations and genocide, blanket prohibition of languages and other ethnocultural features in public life and even their control in private life via a network of informers, etc.) must constantly be exposed to the light of public criticism and to the pressure of internal reform by external and sympathetic humanitarian forces. It is because this is so obvious that we do not belabor that point here, but rather, turn our attention directly to the avowedly 'democratic' contexts in which 'white' genocide is practiced, more slowly, more discreetly, more or less gently, but, nevertheless, continually and cumulatively. Even in democratic settings indigenous populations are enticed and rerouted from their customary areas and distributed in small numbers to a variety of new and less advantageous areas in which their traditional cultural pursuits cannot be successfully reestablished. Even in such settings indigenous populations are robbed of control of the natural resources that could constitute the economic bases of a more self-regulatory collective life and, therefore, robbed also of a possible avenue of cultural viability as well. And, above all and most commonly, even in such settings 'dependency interaction' is foisted upon indigenous populations in such fashion as to erode their psychological and their cultural independence.[17]

Indeed, it is precisely because most modern democracies engage in conscious or unconscious cultural genocide, and precisely because they do so via many of their most central and most prized and admired social, economic

WHERE AND WHY DOES LANGUAGE SHIFT OCCUR?                    63

and political processes, that LS is so common and that RLS is so difficult to attain and so heartbreaking to pursue. This is particularly so, because all that is highly desirable, in the general interest and 'sauce for the (majority) goose', frequently turns out to be dislocative for the (disadvantaged minority) gander, unless special self-regulatory safeguards and precautions are available and implemented.

At a superficial level of analysis, modernization and democratization themselves constitute cultural dislocation risks as far as RLS is concerned. Modernization and democratization lead to increased interaction between individuals from different cultures (in the neighborhood, in the playground, in education, at work, in worship, in governmental service, etc.) and, therefore, to increased impact of the strong on the weak. Modernization and democratization erode 'parochial' cultural differences, even religious differences, and lead to universal dependence on the same media, political parties, educational institutions and programs, and economic endeavors, which, although they may be ideologically fractionated, are, nevertheless, not segmented along ethnocultural lines but along highly generalized socioeconomic and sociopolitical lines, such that substantial proportions of Xmen and Ymen are on both sides of every issue.

The result of such nominally 'free access of everyone to everything and everywhere' is that the majority culture, Yish culture, is endemic and omnipresent; and minority cultures, having very little, if any, public legitimization and private space, thereby constantly decline in survival potential, the more their members participate in 'the greater general good'. For ethnocultural minorities, the predictable outcome of such untrammeled participation in 'the greater general good' is dependency interaction, intermarriage, de-ethnification and re-ethnification. On the basis of a scenario such as the above, it is easy to argue that modernization and democratization themselves are the enemies of RLS because *they undercut the very cultural and identity distinctions on which minority language maintenance must be based*. However, such a conclusion is misguided. It is based on the half-truths that inevitably derive from either–or thinking, since underlying such a mis-analysis is a Hobson's choice. This is the choice of 'either' parochial language-in-culture maintenance and withdrawal from benefiting in 'the greater general good' and the latter's maximization of the intellectual and material promise of modernization and democratization, on the one hand, 'or' abandoning purportedly primordial and primeval sentiments and wholeheartedly joining the forward march of humanity 'under the leadership of the united Yish front' locally and, who knows, perhaps even regionally and internationally as well, on the other hand.

However, the choices need not be so unbalanced and the blessings of democratization and modernization need only be seasoned or leavened by a concern for 'cultural democracy' in order for the implied incommensurability between RLS and 'the greater general good' to evaporate into thin air. Pro-RLSers need not become opponents of democracy in order to advocate and foster RLS. They need merely champion the logical and ethical continuation and culmination of democracy by extending it to the cultural realm as well, that is, to the protection and cultivation of the cultural (and, therefore, of the language-in-culture) rights of minorities that seek such protection and cultivation. Not all Xmen will seek such protection for the cultivation of Xish language-in-culture and they should certainly be free to join the Yish mainstream entirely, or to consciously or unconsciously develop a 'Yish-speaking Xish culture', as they prefer. In either of these latter instances, the material advantages associated with Yish culture will certainly be available to them, to help build the kinds of life and the kinds of neighborhoods that they prefer for themselves and their children, if only because their Yishness will be viewed as in the national interest and as contributory to 'the greater general good'.

But those Xmen who prefer to remain identified with the 'Xmen-via-Xish' ideal should also be seen as contributing to the national interest and the greater general good. Many of them, often most of them, will opt for a stable 'Xish in certain contexts plus Yish in other contexts' bilingual and bicultural solution to the problem of RLS and Xish language maintenance. As such, they will be involved in the general economy and in the general political process and will be concerned that Yish be effectively taught to their children in the (bilingual) schools that will be established by and for them. They will not be cut off, isolated or ghettoized from the general good, from general problems or from general responsibilities, but they will assiduously maintain a treasured Xish corner of their lives and will aspire to be happier, more productive and more contributory citizens as a result. Indeed, their ethnocultural and language maintenance problems will be far from solved. They will still be surrounded by the dominant culture, by its media, its higher education, its more rewarding positions in the economy and in government. They may pay a certain price for their choice, but it will be a price they have chosen to pay, a price they can opt out of whenever they come to consider it too steep, and it will be a price not unlike that of religious minorities (Quakers) or occupational minorities (small farmers), who are generally valued and even assisted to overcome discrimination (and sometimes even compensated for their extra burdens) as part and parcel of the democratic ethos.

Our major stress here has been that democracy and modernization engender problems for RLS and for minority language-in-culture maintenance which can be coped with and ameliorated by means of *recognizing cultural democracy as a component and as a responsibility of the general democratic promise*. Spokesmen and apologists for the Yish mainstream often do not recognize any such responsibility. Instead, they often advocate its diametric opposite: the cultural homogenization of the population via a common language and a common education, regardless of the implicit anti-democratic nature of such homogenization, attacking minority aspirations as contraindicated for 'the greater general good' and as self-punitive for the minorities themselves. Even more often, however, the mainstream establishment is simply unaware of minority ethnocultural and ethnolinguistic aspirations. It is in the very nature of mainstream life to be unknowingly provincial and self-centered (while ascribing such traits only to others, who are outside the mainstream), and, therefore, to interact primarily with its own members, or with former Xmen who have opted to become Ymen (or, at best, with self-styled Xmen-via-Yish) and, therefore, to be unfamiliar with or even totally ignorant of the Xmen-via-Xish pro-RLS views and aspirations. The first step along the long road to changing the views of Ymen (and of many, many Xmen too) is, therefore, an essentially permanent public information and education campaign, and an accompanying legal campaign aimed at obtaining favorable court decisions, that will seek to bring overlooked and unheard of views out into the open, to bring these views to the courts, to the media, to a larger general public and into greater general awareness, to foster greater sensitivity to the call for cultural democracy and to foster more widespread opposition to the needless and harmful attrition of ethnolinguistic resources within modern and democratic contexts.

However, until much needed long-range general political reforms can be instituted,[18] innumerable short-range and local concrete steps on behalf of RLS are possible and indispensable. These are the kinds of steps that we will focus upon in most of our subsequent chapters. Language maintenance has often been discussed as if it were a global, 'total language' task. Our goal here will be to demonstrate that it is a functionally specific process which must be tackled on well chosen, functionally specific grounds. Its success is highly dependent on convictions that are basically philosophical rather than materialistic. Its difficulties are reversible, precisely because RLS basically depends on processes that are just as mundane and normal as are those pertaining to language convergence, language attrition and language death. The fact that all of the latter have already been closely studied by sociolinguists while RLS has languished in neglect is merely an indication that the modern, liberal, rational mind is generally biased in incorporative directions that it itself rarely recognizes. This volume represents an effort to redirect attention in an hitherto overlooked direction.

## A General Perspective on RLS: Boundary Maintenance

Is it inevitable that the stronger will destroy the weaker, either by quickly dispatching him, by wearing him down slowly or by so disorienting or deracinating him that he commits suicide? There are certainly many examples of such 'law of the jungle' relationships between coterritorial or adjoining languages-in-cultures. However, if culture groups do not want *such* primitive law to regulate their interactions, they can seek other and better arrangements between themselves. Other types of wars that were once far more common have been widely recognized in more recent times as unnecessary and undesirable: for example, religious wars, social class wars and economic wars, some of these being wars between nations and some of them wars within nations. Thus, it is not completely visionary to strive for arrangements that will make intercultural warfare and attrition (for that is what the ongoing language shift amounts to, even if quietly and democratically conducted) less common than they are today. Humankind is capable of the additional necessary level of appreciation of and sensitivity for the self-defined identity and beauty of others, so that cultural warfare too will fall out of favor and come to be viewed as an unnecessary and undesirable waste of human lives, talents and resources. When such a blissful state of values and affairs is finally arrived at it will be recognized as requiring less and offering more than is generally dreamed of today.

All that is basically required, to begin with, is greater local self-management of cultural processes and institutions, to the effect that families, neighborhoods, schools, libraries, theaters, entertainment groups, youth groups (hobby groups, skill groups) and even lower-level work-sites and media units can function in the languages preferred by a sufficiently large and dedicated clientele. Of course, such self-management is easier sought than attained. Until the RLS-efforts of units such as the above can benefit from public support, particularly given that they are 'merely' specific counterparts of more general units already receiving such support in most parts of the world, *they will usually have to struggle for their existence by operating on a self-supporting basis*. In either case, they are all instances of boundary maintenance devices, systems and processes. The basic desiderata of language-in-culture maintenance are cultural boundaries within which Xish is consensually accepted and relatively protected for certain pursuits. These boundaries need not be, should not be, and in modern life they really cannot be fully isolating. Cultural boundaries need not co-occur with simultaneous geographic, political, economic or social boundaries. They *do* involve a concentrated demographic base, however, the exact size and concentration requirements of which may be modified downward in the light of modern communication capabilities. Within this base, RLS measures can have widespread popular legitimacy, being connected, as such measures inevitably are, with cultural ideals, with cultural values and with cultural identities, all of which are at a sufficiently high level of consciousness and of focused technical capability to locally compensate for and be in a state of balance with the stronger forces of the larger, surrounding society by which they had previously been outflanked. The initial, basic problem of RLS boils down to attaining a greater demographic concentration of the faithful, on the one hand, and judicious decisions as to which intercommunal boundary maintaining or reviving institutions to give priority to, on the other hand.

Judicious decisions as to *what* to do and *when* are at the very heart of successful RLS-efforts. Unsuccessful efforts are often characterized by undertaking less, but even more often by undertaking more, than can be effectively sustained. But why is it, one may ask, that language shift often comes about without sustained planning, whereas RLS requires so much thought, effort and conviction? Perhaps it is because the very heart of mother tongue transmission (the usual but not the inescapable goal of RLS) involves precisely those natural collective processes (home, family, neighborhood) which are not easily accessible to or influenced by social planning. As a result of the relative inaccessibility of the very core processes on which intergenerational mother tongue transmission depends, RLS-efforts are often lured or goaded into concentrating their resources on measures that are more easily plannable and manipulable (like schools or mass media). The latter, however, operate at too great a distance from the nexus of intergenerational mother tongue transmission and, therefore, instead of contributing parsimoniously (directly and quickly) to such transmission they contribute largely to 'atmosphere building' which is further away from the heart of the matter. Planning effective RLS is difficult, therefore, because, as we will soon see in case after case, RLS (particularly for the most weakened cases) requires a constant process of goal approximation, of inching in closer and closer to hard-to-reach natural social processes, in order to get them going again in a self-priming fashion, rather than focusing on more easily influenced aspects of language-in-society that are simultaneously more distant from the intergenerational nexus of mother tongue transmission.

## Notes

1. The 'life' and 'death' metaphor with respect to cultural phenomena is difficult to avoid entirely, and is obviously and intuitively instructive up to a point, but it is good to remember that it is, after all, no more than a metaphor, a figure of speech based upon certain superficial similarities. In addition to the absence of a natural life-span for cultural phenomena, as mentioned above, it is also necessary to recognize the 'gray area' with respect to the boundary between 'life' and 'death' even in connection with individual phenomena, a 'gray area' which modern medical ethics and religious

thought have been forced to deal with due to the vast changes in recent medical technology. Finally, however, the constant ability of cultures to change, to combine continuity with change, to interpenetrate one another, to fuse, to develop in unexpected and
unforeseeable directions, all reveal capacities and characteristics which have no
strong counterparts at the level of individual life phenomena. The boundedness of
individuals is such that it is relatively simple to tell when a given individual is or is
not present; the changing boundaries of cultures and the changing content and patterns of cultures are such that it is much more difficult, perhaps even impossible, to
determine whether a culture 'is the same culture' that it was previously, whether it is
entirely absent or completely present on a subsequent occasion (historical period),
etc. The same is also the case for languages. Nevertheless, important though these
boundary problems may be for philosophical or abstract theoretical discussion, social
movements such as pro- or anti-RLS efforts, being cultural phenomena themselves,
consensually define these boundaries much more pragmatically, in terms of perceived
consequences for major value positions and for their primary symbolic markers, and
undertake concerted social action accordingly. Without such 'simplification for the
purposes of clarity' neither RLS nor any other (and even opposite) social action
would be possible.

2.  The assets and debits of sociolinguistic censuses and surveys have been discussed at
    length and at various times in the sociolinguistic literature. Among the more exhaus-
    tive references in this connection are Ohannessian, Ferguson and Polome, 1975;
    Lieberson, 1981 (see particularly pp. 281–303) and Mehrotra, 1985. Although cen-
    suses (and the language surveys with which they are so closely aligned methodolog-
    ically) should not and cannot be the be-all and end-all of RLS research, they do have
    one asset that other, more detailed methods lack, namely, they provide an estimate of
    their own degree of unreliability and, therefore, an estimate of their maximal validity
    via their computed 'standard errors' of estimation. This self-correcting feature in
    censuses humbles the researcher and keeps him or her from unjustifiably inflated
    views of the degree of perfection achieved, even more so than does the criticism of
    anti-census researchers who nevertheless remain ignorant of the degree of error that
    continues to be unrecognized within their own favorite alternative methods.

3.  Among the oldest traditions of language censuses, going back to the earliest years of
    this century or even before, are those of the Irish language censuses, the Czarist and
    Austro-Hungarian language censuses, the Indian language censuses, the American
    language censuses, and the language census work that was part of the German
    Auslandsdeutsche Volksforschung school (see Fishman *et al.*, 1966, Appendix B)
    and which came through most professionally (and prior to that school's contamina-
    tion by Nazi views) in the early work of Heinz Kloss (1929).

4.  My *Bilingualism in the Barrio* (Fishman *et al.*,1971) is still the prime example of
    consciously interdisciplinary and cross-methodological research on a single speech
    community, so that broad focus and narrow focus data on the same individuals can
    be compared, combined and used to arrive at a fuller understanding both of the com-
    munity and of the assets and limitations of the various methods used to study it.

5.  The 'domain' concept was first successfully introduced, tested and confirmed in
    my *Bilingualism in the Barrio (op. cit.)*. It has subsequently gained rather
    widespread acceptance as a macro-level locator of LS *in a manner corresponding
    to the major social institutions of a particular culture*. Obviously, it is not intended
    to be an explanatory notion along dynamic (i.e. causal) lines, but, rather, a locator
    of LS in sociocultural space, thereby enabling a researcher to address a variety of
    hypothesized dynamic processes with respect to a variety of possible loci of LS.

As a locator, however, domain analysis also enables researchers to determine whether LS is (still) ongoing and, if so, precisely where (i.e. in what types of social interactions) its documented impact can be noted. The empirical validation of 'domains' implies that ordinary members of speech communities not only can but do conceptualize their own and their interlocutors' language use in somewhat global, macro-stuctural terms, rather than only in terms of specific micro-structural interactions, i.e. that they recognize the distinction between domain and situation, even though the former is constituted out on institutionally related aggregates of the latter.

6. Counting individuals is both the oldest and the most advanced branch of social measurement. See Duncan (1984) for the view that counting individuals is still the safest and the most perfected (and, therefore, the preferred) type of measurement available to the social sciences. See Fishman *et al.*, 1968 and 1985 for numerous examples of counting publications, schools, radio and TV stations and local religious institutions relevant to language maintenance and language shift.

7. The construction of attitude scales and other self-report instruments is an area of longstanding and sophisticated psychometric expertise in which few sociolinguists have acquired adequate training. Preliminary familiarity with this area can be obtained from texts such as Allen and Yen (1979), Anastasi (1988), Brown (1983), Ghiselli, Campbell and Zedeck (1981), Nunnally (1959) or Thorndike and Hagen (1977). The problems of adapting instruments for culturally 'different' (i.e. non-mainstream) subjects are well discussed in Deutsch *et al.* (1964), Samuda (1975), Samuda and Wolfgang (1985), and Schwarz and Krug (1972). This literature should be carefully reviewed before constructing instruments that are to be administered alike to Xish-dominant Xmen, to Yish-dominant Xmen, and to individuals of various degrees of bilingualism and biculturism in between. For problems of measurement bias (and therefore, lowered validity of findings) in this connection see Jensen, 1980; Feuerstein, 1980; and Novick and Ellis, 1977.

8. The literature on ethnographic observation and description is huge and is almost completely discontinuous with that on the construction of formal measures which differentiate maximally and conscientiously between the measure and the measurer (see note 7, above). Useful introductions to this literature are provided by Bogdan and Taylor (1975), Ellen (1984), Fetterman (1984), Goetz and LeCompte (1984), Johnson (1975), Leiter (1980), Lincoln and Guba (1985), Lofland (1976), Lonner and Berry (1986; note the very relevant essay by Berry, Trimble and Olmedo on the assessment of acculturation, pp. 291–324), Mehan and Wood (1975), Schwartz and Jacobs (1979), Spradley (1979), Spradley and McCurdy (1972), Stocking (1983), Wepner (1977), Werner and Schoepfle (1987, two vols) and Whyte (1984), most of which also refer to the sociolinguistically relevant ethnographic and ethnomethodological work of Hymes, Garfinkle, Gumperz, Sacks, Schegloff and others. To my knowledge, the only effort to link the psychometric and the ethnographic traditions within sociolinguistics is the study by Hoffman and Fishman (1971). The general issue of combining and comparing quantitative and qualitative research is analyzed in Merton, Coleman and Rossi (1979).

9. The construction of Likert-type measures was first detailed in Likert, 1932 and can now be reviewed in most introductory measurement texts. For introductions to research findings and research methods in the area of attitude change see Campbell, 1963; Cohen, 1964; and Sherif *et al.*, 1965. For examples of the many attitudinal measures that have proved valuable in social-psychological research see Robinson and Shaver, 1973. For discussions of language attitude research specifically, see

Agheyisi and Fishman, 1970; Shuy and Fasold, 1973; Cooper, 1974 and 1975; Cooper and Fishman, 1977; and Ryan and Giles, 1982.

10. See Fishman and Terry (1969). The issue of determining validity is a major preoccupation of social measurement. The assessment of validity requires that an independently measurable criterion be located so that the relationship between the proposed measure and this criterion can be determined. Given that measures of language shift are themselves exceedingly hard to come by, it should come as no surprise that the validity of the LS measures that have been constructed to date remains generally undemonstrated and undocumented. LS research, and sociolinguistic research more generally, is, therefore, hugely dependent on methodological research in the social sciences more generally in order to support its claims to validity. The Fishman and Terry study referred to above presents a type of criterion validity and, together with the large variety of other measures referred to in it and throughout Fishman *et al* (1971), constitutes an attempt to demonstrate construct validity as well insofar as sociolinguistic census study is concerned.

11. The denial of cultural rights to minorities is as disruptive of the moral fabric of mainstream society as is the denial of civil rights. Civil rights, however, are focused on the individual, while cultural rights must focus on ethnocultural groups. Such groups have no recognized legal standing in many Western democracies where both establishment capitalist thought and anti-establishment Marxist thought prophesies the eclipse of culturally distinct formations and the arrival of a uniformized, all-inclusive 'modern proletarian' culture. The more recent recognition of collective cultural rights and the resulting efforts to add such rights to the usual post-American Revolution list of individual civil rights, and to do so entirely outside of the framework of grievances of one or another minority nationalist 'liberation movement', is a by-product of social-democratic thinking of the latter part of the nineteenth and the earlier part of the twentieth centuries, both in Central Europe (e.g. Birnbaum, 1906; Kahn, 1950; Rocker, 1978) and in the USA (e.g. Horace Kallen, 1915, 1924, 1956, 1971; also see Konvitz, 1987). The deeper historical roots of Western appreciation for cultural diversity and, therefore, for the need for cultural rights, trace back to Herder and the latter part of the eighteenth century. See Fishman, 1978, 1980 and 1982 for a discussion of Herder and Whorf, the latter's restatement of the benefits of ethnolinguistic pluralism having had the greatest impact on anthropology and, ultimately, on sociolinguistics itself.

12. Ethnolinguistic supression of indigenous, non-Westernized populations everywhere is highlighted in *Survival International News* (also available in Spanish), *Survival International Review* and *Urgent Action Bulletin*, all publications of Survival International, an organization with branches in France, Spain and the USA and with an International Secretariat at 310 Edgware Road, London W21 1DY, England. Recent issues of *SI* publications have dealt with governmental expropriation of tribal lands and the removal of tribal peoples, in favor of private logging, mining, prospecting and other commercial interests, often to the personal benefit of the governmental authorities approving these actions, in Sarawak, the Philippines, Colombia, Ecuador, Argentina, Malaysia, French Guyana, Canada, the USA, and Australia. A very similar American-based publication is the *Cultural Survival Quarterly* of Cultural Survival, 11 Divinity Avenue, Cambridge, MA 02138, USA. Both organizations have tended to overlook cultural genocide in the USSR and in the former Communist bloc more generally, due primarily to their preoccupation with the Third World. Far less guilty of such blindspots is *Europa Ethnica*, a quarterly, published (primarily in German) by Wilhelm Braumuller Publishers, Servitengasse 5, A-1092, Vienna,

Austria, that, nevertheless, focuses entirely on the problems of ethnolinguistic minorities in Europe. This journal publishes official notices of the Föderalistischen Union Europäischer Volksgruppen (FUEV) and of the Internationalen Instituts fur Nationalitatenrecht und Regionalismus (INTEREG). More specifically Western European in focus is The European Bureau for Lesser Used Languages which 'seeks to preserve and promote the lesser used autochthonous languages [of Western Europe] ... together with their associated cultures'. The Bureau is an independent body that works in close cooperation with the Commission of the European Communities and the European Parliament, its member state institutions, the Council of Europe and other bodies. It publishes a quarterly, *Contact Bulletin*, and maintains its Secretariat at 7 Cearnog Mhuirfean, Baile Atha Cliath [= Dublin] 2, Ireland. The Bureau's primary emphases are devoted to (a) providing consultation to language movements as to how to attain their local and immediate goals and (b) fostering positive resolutions and supportive actions *vis-à-vis* the lesser used European languages on the part of the various intergovernmental groups with which it is in ongoing contact. Although the Bureau and its periodical publication do protest the LS efforts and processes underway in Western Europe, both are more oriented toward long-term education and persuasion within democratic contexts, rather than toward the rapid redress of grievances or priority assistance in the face of rapid deterioration.

Most of the above-mentioned publications bring extensive reviews of books, journals and films dealing with efforts for and against language-in-culture maintenance, but, unfortunately, they all reach a rather small, previously sympathetic and primarily academic, lay intellectual and international civil service audience, thereby still leaving the RLS cause without media that are suitable for and capable of reaching the more ordinary reading public and local decision makers everywhere. As a result, RLS advocates certainly cannot rely substantially on outside media and must engage all the more in both local and broader informational, educational and, where possible, court-centered efforts of their own or in coalition with other aggrieved parties. The organization that comes closest to reaching the general media, including educational units and authorities, on a worldwide basis, is the Minority Rights Group, 29 Craven Street, London WC2N 5NT, England (with branches in Argentina, Australia, Austria, Belgium, Canada, France, West Germany, India, Italy, Japan, Netherlands, Norway, Sweden and Switzerland), which publishes and distributes to the world press five *MRG Reports* a year and continually revises and updates its earlier issues. To date, some 80 such reports have been published and further investigations are financed from the sales of these reports. Note, however, that MRG is concerned with all types of oppressed minorities, e.g. women and children, migrant workers, religious groups, the mentally ill, etc., rather than with disadvantaged ethnolinguistic groups alone.

Regrettably inaccessible to the English-encapsulated world are the publications and conferences of the Gesellschaft für bedrohte Völker, with offices in West Germany, Switzerland, Luxembourg and France. Its journal, *progrom!* (sic) has featured abrogations of ethnolinguistic rights in all parts of the world and is both well-informed and written in a non-technical fashion that is easily understandable by laymen. The Gesellschaft also publishes brochures, organizes demonstrations and letter-writing campaigns, issues press releases and raises and contributes funds on behalf of populations suffering from persecution and discrimination. Its headquarters are currently at Postfach 2024, 3400 Gottingen, West Germany.

Aiming even more directly at RLS is the Association Internationale pour Defense des Langues et Cultures Menacées. Founded in 1964 by 50 Scandinavian

72 REVERSING LANGUAGE SHIFT

professors, this organization has convened academics every other year to hear reports of efforts on behalf of various threatened languages (primarily those of Western Europe) and to issue reports and resolutions directed at UNESCO and individual governments. Its current headquarters are at 9, rue du Beau-Mur, B-4030 Liege, Belgium.

The above-mentioned organizations and periodicals are but a fraction of the complete list of those concerned in some way with RLS and is not meant to be taken as exhaustive. Additional references are to be in Alfredsson, 1989, and in Skutnabb-Kangas and Phillipson, 1989. The former cites a UN declaration on behalf of the rights of indigenous peoples in which language is mentioned but the right to engage in RLS, much less to receive assistance from one's government for RLS, is totally overlooked.

Finally, it should be pointed out that several of the above-mentioned groups also attempt to contact the United Nations and/or UNESCO. Unfortunately, ethnolinguistic rights to organize for language maintenance and to obtain support for anti-language shift efforts are not clearly included within the UN's purview or in its widely publicized Universal Declaration of Human Rights. Although the latter does specify the right to a nationality (and even the right to change one's nationality), the right of parents to choose the kind of education that shall be given to their children and the right to participate in the cultural life of the community, it is oriented toward individual rather than toward group or community protection in ethnolinguistic matters and, therefore, is essentially inoperative, whether by design or by oversight, insofar as organized and publicly recognized RLS is concerned. For a sampling of texts and analyses of various international declarations in the human rights area see Brownlie, 1981; Capotorti, 1979; Council of Europe, 1985; Hannum, 1984; Humphrey, 1976; Levin, 1982; United Nations, 1983a,1983b; U.S. House Committee on Foreign Affairs, 1983; Vasak and Alston, 1982; and Westerveen, 1986. Skutnabb-Kangas and Phillipson, 1989 and Tabory, 1980 are among the very few to discuss collective (rather than merely individual) language rights as basic human rights.

The relatively recent Universal Declaration of Linguistic Rights (see Appendix to this chapter) may be viewed as a preliminary attempt to support RLS and to reject anti-LS efforts, but, thus far, it has only been adopted by a small number of academic bodies dealing directly or indirectly with ethnolinguistic topics. Unlike 'human rights', which strike Western and Westernized intellectuals as fostering wider participation in general societal benefits and interactions, 'language rights' still are widely interpreted as 'regressive' since they would, most probably, prolong the existence of ethnolinguistic differences. The value of such differences and the right to value such differences have not yet generally been recognized by the modern, Western sense of justice, thereby constituting one of the major philosophical problems for RLS efforts everywhere. Modern Western democratic values are ethnolinguistically disruptive for small languages-in-cultures because they will only recognize the individual's rights to speak, think, write or pray as he or she will, rather than any right to maintain (and to seek public support for the maintenance of) a culture that will enable interested individuals to do these things on a societal and intergenerationally continuous basis.

13. Crawford (1988) brings together a collection of specially written papers that review the Irish experience with famines from 900 to 1900, thereby enabling us to see the Great Famine of 1845–1849 as a cataclysmic event striking more than a third of the population and followed by a profound restructuring of the economy and culture of Irish society. De Freine (1967) reviews much of the same data, but with a very powerful focus on the language-in-culture consequences of the economic events that transpired.

14. Dependency interaction is also, of course, a social class phenomenon, above and beyond any involvement of minority ethnolinguistic aggregates. The most striking recent transferral of this general notion to the ethnocultural realm is that by Hechter (1975) and the many other sociologists and political scientists influenced by his concepts and theories, some of which he himself subsequently revised or withdrew (see, e.g. Hechter *et al.*, 1982), even more so than by his excessively rhetorical vocabulary (e.g. 'internal colonialism').

15. The deleterious impact of cultural dislocation on physical and mental health is a mainstay and *raison d'être* of journals such as *Culture, Medicine and Psychiatry, Medical Anthropology Quarterly* and *Social Science and Medicine*. Several integrative reviews of this topic have appeared and can be sampled in Appell, 1986; Back, 1980; Dasen *et al.*, 1988 (particularly note Chapter 9, by Berry and Kim on 'Acculturation and mental health'), Devereux, 1980; Dressler, 1982; Harwood, 1981 (see particularly the chapter on 'Guidelines for Culturally Appropriate Health Care', pp. 482–507); Kleinman, 1988; Landy, 1977; Romanucci-Ross *et al.*, 1983; Spector, 1979; and Tseng and McDermott, 1981, or in volumes dealing separately with various Hispanic groups, various Oriental groups, various African and Afroamerican groups, various Amerindian groups, etc. Work in this area and in medical anthropology (as well as in ethnopsychiatry) more generally is regularly reviewed in the Annual Review of Anthropology as well as in the Annual Review of Sociology.

16. Widespread and stable (and, therefore, traditional) intragroup bilingualism is known as 'diglossia' in the sociolinguistic literature. A substantial literature has developed on this topic in the brief period since Ferguson suggested the term (1959), much of which (through 1983) is reviewed in Fishman (1984). The fruitfulness of this concept is evidenced by more recent and endlessly ongoing work on it, e.g. Britto, 1986; Chantefort, 1970; De Silva, 1976; Giacomelli, 1983; Krishnamurti *et al.*, 1986; Suleiman, 1986; Talmoudi, 1984; and Tollefson, 1978. The initial establishment of diglossia, as a language maintenance tactic, is, nevertheless, a cultural innovation and, therefore, a departure from prior cultural norms. It is, however, a withdrawal to a position of relative strength, focusing on certain domains (usually: intimacy and/or tradition-religion), in connection with which cultural boundaries favoring Xish can be successfully maintained, even though Yish continues to be normatively utilized by Xmen in pursuits related to other domains.

17. The culturally dislocative influences of democracies upon the cultural minorities within their borders are particularly great because of the 'open society' self-images that democracies hold dear. The voluntarism of assimilation is widely assumed, primarily because there are no laws requiring it and because, in a free country, all are presumably free to do as they like in matters ethnocultural as in all others, to such a degree that minorities themselves become oblivious of the degree to which their slow-but-sure re-ethnization is a by-product of established social, cultural and economic practices and arrangements. Even flagrant exceptions to the usual democratic 'hands off' posture *vis-à-vis* minority ethnocultural continuity, such as the currently ongoing 'English Only' campaign in the USA (Fishman, 1988), are legitimized as efforts to facilitate more widespread minority access to the full measure of material rewards of living in 'the great society'. In the absence of values and expectations *vis-à-vis* cultural-democracy obligations of the majority toward minorities, a useful metaphor may be found in the anti-monopoly and anti-restraint-of-trade legislation that exists in the economic realm within democratic capitalism. Just as it is considered 'unfair' for large firms to drive small firms out of business, and thereby to control entire fields of economic endeavor for their own direct benefit, so it is eminently

unfair for large cultures to do so to small cultures, particularly when the latter still reveal aggregates that are actively pursuing aspirations of cultural continuity for themselves and for their children. The sanctity of the struggling 'small family business', which is so easily grasped and defended by champions of the free marketplace, needs to be transferred to the struggling small culture as well.

18. Genuine reforms favoring minority language maintenance and even providing it with a modicum of general fiscal support are not unknown under democratic-capitalist and democratic-socialist auspices. For cases other than those reviewed in the various chapters of this volume see: re Switzerland, Billigmeier (1979); re Italy, Sonino (1989); re Canada (re French in Anglo-Canada as well as the so-called Heritage languages [= immigrant languages] there) see Cummins (1986), Cartwright (1985) and Arnopolous (1982); in India, Khubchandani (1983), etc. The gains made under pre-*glasnost* communist auspices are also not to be overlooked (although, in several instances, particularly in the USSR, these were no more than temporary and exploitative accommodations which the establishment literature there masks by providing blind apologetics rather than factual functional analyses): see Allsworth (1973), Bromley (1988), Desheriev (1978), Isayev (1977), Kreindler (1982, 1985), Niedzielski (1979), Rockett (1981), Schmalstieg and Magner (1978), Sugar (1980), Tollefson (1978); but they can obviously (and have obviously) just as easily be(en) centrally removed as they have been centrally granted. The real test of the newly trumpeted democratization of Eastern Europe will be whether RLS fares any better there than it did under Soviet and communist domination.

# References

AGHEYISI, Rebecca and FISHMAN, Joshua A. 1970, Language attitude studies. *Anthropological Linguistics* 11, 137–57.

ALFREDSSON, Gudmundur 1989, International discussion of the concerns of indigenous peoples. *Current Anthropology* 30, 255–64.

ALLEN, Mar J. and YEN, Wendy M. 1979, *Introduction to Measurement Theory.* Monterey: Brooks/Cole.

ALLSWORTH, Edward (ed.) 1973, *The Nationality Question in Soviet Central Asia.* New York: Praeger.

ANASTASI, Anne 1988, *Psychological Testing* (6th edn). New York: Macmillan.

APPELL, George N. 1986, The health consequences of development. *Sarawak Museum Journal* 36, 57 (New Series), 43–74.

ARNOPOLOUS, S. McLeod 1982, The spirit of Regulation 17. In his *Voices from French Ontario.* Kingston and Montreal: McGill University Press and Queens University Press, 53–91.

BACK, Kurt W. 1980, Uprooting and self-image: catastrophe and continuity. In George V. COELHO and P. I. AHMED (eds.) *Uprooting and Development: Dilemmas of Coping with Modernization.* New York: Plenum, 177–230.

BILLIGMEIER, Robert H. 1979, *A Crisis in Swiss Pluralism; The Romansh and Their Relations with the German- and Italian-Swiss in the Perspective of a Millennium.* The Hague: Mouton.

BIRNBAUM, Nathan 1906, Judische Autonomie. *Ost und West* 6, no. 1, January. Translated into English in Joshua A. FISHMAN 1977, *Ideology, Society and Language.* Ann Arbor: Karoma, 185–9.

BIRNBAUM, Nathan 1906, Judische Autonomie. *Ost und West* 6, no. 1, January. Translated into English in Joshua A. FISHMAN 1977, *Ideology, Society and Language.* Ann Arbor: Karoma, 185–9.

BOGDAN, Robert and TAYLOR, Steven J. 1975, *Introduction to Qualitative Research Methods: A Phenomenological Approach to the Social Sciences.* New York: Wiley.

BRITTO, Francis 1986, *Diglossia.* Washington, D. C.: Georgetown University Press.

BROMLEY, Yulian 1988, *Major Ethnosocial Trends in the USSR.* Moscow: Progress.

BROWN, Frederick G. 1983, *Principles of Educational and Psychological Testing.* New York: Holt, Rinehart & Winston.

BROWNLIE, I. (ed.) 1981, *Basic Documents on Human Rights.* (2nd edn). Oxford: Clarendon.

CAMPBELL, Donald T. 1963, Social attitudes and other acquired behavioral dispositions. In Sigmund KOCH (ed.) *Psychology: A Study of a Science*, vol. VI. New York: McGraw-Hill, 94–172.

CAPOTORTI, Francesco 1979, *Study of the Rights of Persons Belonging to Ethnic, Religious and Linguistic Minorities.* New York: United Nations.

CARTWRIGHT, Don 1985, An official language policy for Ontario. *Canadian Public Policy* 11, 561–77.

CHANTEFORT, Pierre 1970, *Diglossie au Québec.* Quebec City: International Research Center on Bilingualism.

COHEN, Arthur R. 1964, *Attitude Change and Social Influence.* New York: Basic Books.

COOPER, Robert L. 1974, Language Attitudes I. *International Journal of the Sociology of Language* no. 3 (entire issue).

— 1975, Language Attitudes II. *International Journal of the Sociology of Language* no. 6 (entire issue).

COOPER, Robert L. and FISHMAN, Joshua A. 1977, A study of language attitudes. *Bilingual Review* 4, 7–34.

COUNCIL OF EUROPE, DIRECTORATE OF HUMAN RIGHTS 1985, *Human Rights in International Law: Basic Texts.* Strasbourg: Council of Europe.

CRAWFORD, E. Margaret 1988, *Famine: The Irish Experience, 900–1900.* Edinburgh: John Donald.

CUMMINS, Jim (ed.) 1986, *Heritage Languages in Canada: Research Perspectives.* Toronto: Ontario Institute for Studies in Education.

DASEN, P. R., BERRY J. W. and SARTORIUS N. (eds) 1988, *Health and Cross-Cultural Psychology: Toward Applications.* Newbury Park: Sage.

DE FREINE, Sean 1978 [1967], *The Great Silence; The Study of a Relationship between Language and Nationality* (2nd edn). Dublin: Mercier.

DESHERIEV, Junus D. 1978, *Natsionalni yazik i natsionalnaya kultura.* Moscow: Nauk.

DE SILVA, M. W. S. 1976, *Diglossia and Literacy.* Mysore: Central Institute of Indian Languages.

DEUTSCH, Martin, FISHMAN, Joshua A., NORTH, Lawrence and WHITEMAN, Martin 1964, Guidelines for testing minority group children. *Journal of Social Issues.* 20, 127–45.

DEVEREUX, George 1980, *Basic Problems of Ethnopsychiatry.* Chicago: University of Chicago Press.

DRESSLER, William W. 1982, *Hypertension and Culture Change.* South Salem: Redgrave.

DUNCAN, Otis 1984, *Notes on Social Measurement: Historical and Critical.* New York: Russel Sage.

ELLEN, R. F. 1984, *Ethnographic Research: A Guide to General Conduct.* London: Academic Press.

FETTERMAN, David M. (ed.) 1984, *Ethnography in Educational Evaluation*. Beverley Hills: Sage.

FEUERSTEIN, Reuven 1980, *Instrumental Enrichment: An Intervention Program for Cognitive Modifiability*. Baltimore: University Park.

FERGUSON, Charles A. 1959, Diglossia. *Word*. 15, 325–40.

FISHMAN, Joshua A. 1978, Positive bilingualism: some overlooked rationales and forefathers. *Georgetown University Round Table on Languages and Linguistics, 1978*. Washington, D.C.: Georgetown University Press, 42–52.

—    1980, The Whorfian hypothesis; varieties of valuation, confirmation and disconfirmation I. *International Journal of the Sociology of Language* 26, 25–40.

—    1982, Whorfianism of the third kind: ethnolinguistic diversity as a worldwide societal asset. (The Whorfian hypothesis: varieties of validation, confirmation and disconfirmation II). *Language in Society* 11, 1–14.

—    1984, Epistemology, methodology and ideology in the sociolinguistic enterprise. In: A. Z. GUIORA (ed.) *An Epistemology for the Language Sciences*. Detroit: Wayne University Press, 33–47.

—    1988, English only: its ghosts, myths and dangers. *International Journal of the Sociology of Language* 74, 125–40.

FISHMAN, Joshua A. and TERRY, Charles 1969, The validity of census data on bilingualism in a Puerto Rican neighborhood. *American Sociological Review* 34, 636–50. Reprinted, 1971, in J. A. FISHMAN *et al.*, *Bilingualism in the Barrio*. Bloomington: Indiana University Publications, 177–97.

FISHMAN, Joshua A. *et al.* 1966, *Language Loyalty in the United States*. The Hague: Mouton.

—    1971, *Bilingualism in the Barrio*. Bloomington: Indiana University.

—    1985, *The Rise and Fall of the Ethnic Revival*. Berlin: Mouton de Gruyter.

GHISELLI, Edwin E., CAMPBELL, John P. and ZEDECK, Sheldon 1981, *Measurement Theory in the Behavioral Sciences*. San Francisco: Freeman.

GIACOMELLI, Roberto 1983, *Graeca Italica; studi sul bilinguismo-diglossia nell' Italia antica*. Brescia: Paideia.

GOETZ, Judith P. and LeCOMPTE, Margaret D. 1984, *Ethnography and Qualitative Design in Educational Research*. Orlando: Academic Press.

HANNUM, H. (ed.) 1984, *Guide to International Human Rights Practice*. Philadelphia: University of Pennsylvania Press.

HARWOOD, Alan (ed.) 1981, *Ethnicity and Medical Care*. Cambridge: Harvard University Press.

HECHTER, Michael 1975, *Internal Colonialism; The Celtic Fringe in British National Development*. Berkeley: University of California Press.

HECHTER, Michael, FRIEDMAN, Debra and APPELBAUM, Malka 1982, A theory of ethnic collective action. *International Migration Review* 16, 412–34.

HOFFMAN, Gerard and FISHMAN, Joshua A. 1971, Life in the neighborhood. *International Journal of Comparative Sociology* 12, 85–100.

HUMPHREY, J. 1976, The International Bill of Rights: scope and implementation. *William and Mary Law Review* 17, 527–41.

ISAYEV, M. I. 1977, *National Languages in the USSR: Problems and Solutions*. Moscow: Progress.

JENSEN, Arthur R. 1980, *Bias in Mental Testing*. New York: Free Press.

JOHNSON, John M. 1975, *Doing Field Research*. New York: Free Press.

KAHN, Robert A. 1950, *The Multinational Empire; Nationalism and National Reform in the Habsburg Monarchy, 1848–1918*. 2 vols. New York: Columbia University Press.

KALLEN, Horace M. 1915, Democracy versus the melting pot. *Nation*. February 18, 190–4 and February 25, 217–20.
— 1924, *Culture and Democracy in the United States*. New York: Boni and Liverright.
— 1956, *Cultural Pluralism and the American Idea: An Essay in Social Philosophy*. Philadelphia: University of Pennsylvania Press.
— 1971, *What I Believe and Why-Maybe*. New York: Horizon.
KHUBCHANDANI, Lachman M. 1983, *Plural Languages, Plural Cultures; Communication, Identity and Sociopolitical Change in Contemporary India*. Honolulu: University of Hawaii Press.
KLEINMAN, Arthur 1988, *Rethinking Psychiatry: From Cultural Category to Personal Experience*. New York: Free Press.
KLOSS, Heinz 1929, Sprachtabellen als Grundlage für Sprachstatistic, Sprachenkarten un für eine allgemeine Sociologie der Sprachgemeinschaften. *Vierteljahrschrift für Politik und Geschichte* 1, 7, 103–17.
KONVITZ, Milton R. (ed.) 1987, *The Legacy of Horace M. Kallen*. Rutherford and Cranbury: Fairleigh Dickensin Press and Associated University Presses.
KREINDLER, Isabelle (ed.) 1982, The Changing Status of Russian in the Soviet Union. *International Journal of the Sociology of Language* no. 33 (entire issue).
— 1985, *Sociolinguistic Perspective on Soviet National Languages*. Berlin: Mouton.
KRISHNAMURTI, Bh., MASICA, Colin P. and SINHA, Anjani K. 1986, *South Asian Languages: Structure, Convergence and Diglossia*. Delhi: Motilal Barnardidase.
LANDY, David (ed.) 1977, *Culture, Disease and Healing*. New York: Macmillan.
LEITER, Kenneth 1980, *A Primer on Ethnomethodology*. New York: Oxford University Press.
LEVIN, L. 1982, *Human Rights: Questions and Answers* (2nd edn). Paris: UNESCO.
LIEBERSON, Stanley 1981, *Language Diversity and Language Contact*. Stanford: Stanford University Press.
LIKERT, Rensis A. 1932, A technique for the measurement of attitudes. *Archives of Pyschology* no. 140.
LINCOLN, Yvonna S. and GUBA, Egon G. 1985, *Naturalistic Inquiry*. Beverley Hills: Sage.
LOFLAND, John 1976, *Doing Social Life; The Qualitative Study of Human Interactions in Natural Settings*. New York: Wiley.
LONNER, Walter J. and BERRY, John W. (eds) 1986, *Field Methods in Cross-Cultural Research*. Beverley Hills: Sage.
MEHAN, Hugh and WOOD, Houston 1975, T*he Reality of Ethnomethodology*. New York: Wiley.
MEHROTRA, Raja Ram (ed.) 1985, Sociolinguistic Surveys in South, East and Southeast Asia. *International Journal of the Sociology of Language* no. 55 (entire issue).
MERTON, Robert K., COLEMAN, James S. and ROSSI, Peter H. (eds) 1979, *Qualitative and Quantitative Social Research; Papers in Honor of Paul F. Lazarsfeld*. New York: Free Press.
NIEDZIELSKI, Henry 1979, Language consciousness and language policy in Poland. *Word* 30, 134–59.
NOVICK, M. R. and ELLIS, D. D. 1977, Equal opportunity in educational and employment selection. *American Psychologist* 32, 306–20.
NUNNALLY, Jum C. Jr 1959, *Tests and Measurements: Assessment and Prediction*. New York: McGraw-Hill.
OHANNESSIAN, Sirarpi, FERGUSON, Charles A. and POLOME, Edgar C. (eds) 1975, *Language Surveys in Developing Nations; Papers and Reports on Sociolinguistic Surveys*. Arlington: Center for Applied Linguistics.

PHILLIPSON, Robert and SKUTNABB-KANGAS, Tove 1986, English: the language of wider colonisation. In: Robert PHILLIPSON and Tove SKUTNABB-KANGAS, *Linguicism Rules in Education*, 3 vols. Roskilde: Roskilde University Centre Institute VI, 344–77.

ROBINSON, John P. and SHAVER, Phillip R. 1973, *Measures of Social Psychological Attitudes*. Ann Arbor: Survey Research Center.

ROCKER, Rudolf 1978, *Nationalism and Culture*. St Paul: Coughlin.

ROCKETT, Rocky L. 1981, *Ethnic Nationalities in the Soviet Union*. New York: Praeger.

ROMANUCCI-ROSS, Lola, MOERMAN, Daniel E. and TANCRED, Laurence R. (eds) 1983, *The Anthropology of Medicine: From Culture to Method*. South Hadley: Bergin.

RYAN, Ellen B. and GIKES, Howard (eds) 1982, *Attitudes Toward Language Variation*. London: E. Arnold.

SAMUDA, Ronald J. 1975, *Psychological Testing of American Minorities: Issues and Consequences*. New York: Dodd Mead.

SAMUDA, Ronald J. and WOLFGANG, Aaron 1985, *Intercultural Counselling and Assessment: Global Perspectives*. Livingstone: Hogrefe.

SCHMALSTEIG, William R. and MAGNER, Thomas F. (eds) 1978, *Sociolinguistic Problems in Czechoslovakia, Hungary, Romania and Yugoslavia*. Columbus: Slavica.

SCHWARTZ, Howard and JACOBS, Jerry 1979, *Qualitative Sociology. A Method to the Madness*. New York: Free Press.

SCHWARTZ, P. A. and KRUG, R. E. 1972, *Ability Testing in Developing Countries: A Handbook of Principles and Techniques*. New York: Praeger.

SHERIF, Carolyn W., SHERIF, Muzafer and NEBERGALL, Roger E. 1965, *Attitudes and Attitude Change: The Social Judgment-Involvement Approach*. London: Rube.

SHUY, Roger and FASOLD, Ralph W. (eds) 1973, *Language Attitudes: Current Trends and Prospects*. Washington, D.C.: Georgetown University Press.

SKUTNABB-KANGAS, Tove and PHILLIPSON, Robert 1989, Wanted! Linguistic human rights. *Rolig papir* no. 44 (entire issue).

SONINO, Elisabetta Zuanelli (ed.) 1989, Italian sociolinguistics: Trends and issues. *International Journal of the Sociology of Language* no.76 (entire issue).

SPECTOR, Rachel E. 1979, *Cultural Diversity in Health and Illness*. New York: Appleton-Century-Crofts.

SPRADLEY, James P. 1979, *The Ethnographic Interview*. New York: Holt, Rinehart and Winston.

SPRADLEY, James P. and MCCURDY, David W. 1972, *The Cultural Experience; Ethnography in Complex Society*. Chicago: Science Research Associates.

STOCKING, George W. Jr 1983, *Observers Observed; Essays on Ethnographic Fieldwork*. Madison: University of Wisconsin Press.

SUGAR, Peter (ed.) 1980, *Ethnic Diversity and Conflict in Eastern Europe*. Santa Barbara: ABC-Clio.

SULEIMAN, Saleh M. Kh. 1986, *Jordanian Arabic between Diglossia and Bilingualism*. Amsterdam: John Benjamins.

TABORY, Mala 1980, *Language Rights as Human Rights. Israel Yearbook on Human Rights* 10, 167–223.

TALMOUDI, Fathi 1984, *The Diglossic Situation in North Africa*. Gotheborg: Acta Universitatis Gothoburgensis.

THORNDIKE, Robert L. and HAGEN, Elizabeth L. 1977, *Measurement and Evaluation in Psychology and Education*. New York: Wiley.

TOLLEFSON, James William 1978, Diglossia and language policy with special reference to Slovenia. PhD Thesis, Stanford University. (Published, 1980, as *The Language Situation and Language Policy in Slovenia*. Lanham: University Press of America.)

TSENG, Wen-Shing and MCDERMOTT, John F. 1981, *Culture, Mind and Therapy*. New York: Brunner/Mazel.
UNITED NATIONS 1983a, *Human Rights: A Compilation of International Instruments*. Mew York: United Nations.
— 1983b, *United Nations Actions in the Field of Human Rights*. New York: United Nations.
UNITED STATES HOUSE COMMITTEE ON FOREIGN AFFAIRS 1983, *Human Rights Documents: Compilation of Documents Pertaining to Human Rights*. Washington, D.C.: US Government Printing Office.
VASAK, K. and ALSTON, P. (eds) 1982, *The International Dimension of Human Rights*. 2 vols. Westport and Paris: Greenwood and UNESCO.
WERNER, Oswald and SCHOEPFLE, G. Mark 1987, *Systematic Fieldwork*. Newbury Park: Sage.
WERNER, Robert S. (ed.) 1977, *Street Ethnography*. Beverley Hills: Sage.
WESTERVEEN, G. 1986, *The International Bill of Human Rights: Normative and Institutional Developments, 1948–1985*. Utrecht: Netherlands Institute of Human Rights.
WHYTE, William F. 1984, *Learning from the Field: A Guide from Experience*. Beverly Hills: Sage.

# Appendix 1: Universal Declaration of Linguistic Rights

At its 22nd seminar on Human Rights and Cultural Rights (7–9 October 1987; Recife, Brazil; Franciso Gomes de Matos, Chair), the International Association for the Development of Cross-Cultural Communication issued the following:

## The Recife Declaration

*Considering* that the ideals and principles of equality, solidarity, freedom, justice, peace and understanding, which have inspired national and international legislation an dinstruments on human rights, share a crucial linguistic dimension.

*Recognizing* that the learning and use, maintenance and promotion of languages contribute significantly to the intellectual, educational, sociocultural, economic and political development of individuals, groups, and states.

*Noting* that the Universal Declaration of Human Rights, the International Covenants related to human rights and other international universal instruments make provision for cultural rights.

*Mindful* of the need to arouse and foster awareness, within and across cultures, of the recognition and promotion of the linguistic rights of individuals and groups.

*Asserting* that linguistic rights should be acknowledged, promoted, and observed, nationally, regionally and internationally, so as to promote and assure the dignity and equity of all languages.

*Aware* of the need for legislation to eliminate linguistic prejudice and discrimination and all forms of linguistic domination, injustice and oppression, in such contexts as services to the public, the place of work, the educational system, the courtroom, and the mass media.

*Stressing* the need to sensitize individuals, groups, and states to linguistic rights, to promote positive societal attitudes toward plurilingualism and to change societal structures toward equality between users of different languages and varieties of languages.

*Hence, cognizant* of the need to provide explicit legal guarantees for linguistic rights to individuals and groups by the appropriate bodies of the member states of the United Nations.

The XXII Seminar of the International Association for the Development of Cross Cultural Communication recommends that steps be taken by the United Nations to adopt and implement a Universal Declaration of Linguistic Rights, which would require a reformulation of national, regional, and international language policies.

# 4 How Theatened is 'Threatened'?

## (A typology of disadvantaged languages and ameliorative priorities)

Much to the chagrin of some linguists, people have increasingly organized themselves to 'do something' about their own (or somebody else's) language.[1] Some of these efforts are technically referred to as 'language planning' in the sociolinguistic literature. When people organize to do something about the societal functions or reputation of a particular language, that is referred to as 'status planning'. When they organize themselves to do something about the vocabulary, spelling or any other aspect of the language *per se*, that is called 'corpus planning'. We will be concerned with the role of each in RLS, but with status planning first and foremost. (For a discussion of corpus planning, see Chapter 11, below.)

RLS status planning involves the authoritative allocation of scarce resources, such as intelligence, funds, time, effort and implementational power, to the solution of language status problems, i.e. to problems that are due to the shrinking number of *users* that a language has or to the meager importance of the *uses* with which it is commonly associated in its speech and/or writing community. Threatened languages, for which RLS-efforts are required in order to save them from erosion and ultimate extinction, are languages that are not replacing themselves demographically, i.e. they have fewer and fewer users generation after generation and the uses to which these languages are commonly put are not only few, but, additionally, they are typically unrelated to higher social status (prestige, power) even within their own ethnocultural community, this being a reflection of the relative powerlessness of the bulk of their users. RLS is an attempt on the part of authorities that are recognized by the users and supporters of threatened languages, to adopt policies and to engage in efforts calculated to reverse the cumulative processes of attrition that would otherwise lead to their contextually weak language-in-culture becoming even weaker, while its competitor, a strong language-in-culture, becomes even stronger. RLS implies a social policy (either by the weak alone, on their own behalf, or, more rarely, by the weak and the strong together), to interfere with and to disconfirm the 'predictable course of events', because that course would result in consequences that are consensually viewed as undesirable. Like all social policy, whether undertaken to cure the ill before it is too late, or to feed the starving, or to bring literacy to the illiterate, or to preserve natural resources from being plundered or contaminated, RLS involves a prior value consensus among those who advocate, formulate, implement and evaluate it. Without such prior consensus, RLS policy itself may become a bone of contention even among its own advocates. In the hope of avoiding or at least *anticipating* such contention, we will review a number of value positions before proceeding further.

1. *Much RLS can be implemented without compulsion.* There is an aspect of compulsion to any governmental activity, even to such innocuous services as the postal service or the sanitation department's service, and, accordingly, if RLS becomes governmental policy it too will inevitably have an aspect of compulsion about it, if only because tax levies will be expended on its behalf and some taxpayers may object to their taxes being put to any such purposes. However, we must not jump to the conclusion that RLS is inevitably and necessarily a governmental policy at all. Many RLS-efforts can be undertaken on a small and voluntary scale by organized individuals who are wholeheartedly in agreement with specific RLS goals and willing to devote their means to them. Indeed, it is highly preferable for RLS advocates to initially seek out those things that they themselves, as an organized and legitimate constituency, can do for the strengthening of their own language-in-culture, even without governmental or broader societal assistance, just as it is preferable for governmental funding, when and if it becomes available, to be facilitatory and enabling rather than compulsory and punitive. Certainly, the earliest stages of RLS-efforts usually require the generous and voluntary devotion of committed individuals, organized into voluntary associations which no one but such individuals themselves support and accept as authoritative.

   This initial level of RLS activity may be insufficient to fully reverse the dangers faced by threatened languages and it may also be insufficiently satisfying for those who have more advanced goals in mind requiring governmental action and material support. However, more advanced goals and governmental action are frequently ineffective, precisely because there is no grassroots community and neighborhood initiative, involvement, commitment and follow-through. A voluntary rank and file effort is at least a beginning. It may be possible and desirable to go further, thereafter, but without that early level of strong intra-Xish support, nothing done subsequently will be enduring and governmental efforts may either be purely pro-forma or even calculated to 'turn off' more people than they 'turn on', as pro-Irish advocates learned to their sorrow in the late 60s and early 70s. Pro-Frisian efforts, on the other hand, seem to have successfully avoided the danger of compulsion thus far, perhaps because of recent and more general Netherlandish experience with providing support for a large variety of voluntary, community-based efforts. At any rate, the lower level of initial RLS activity is 'lower' only because it is foundational; it need not be less intensive or less crucial by any means. Its goal is to achieve signs of RLS momentum, without compulsion, as indications of popular sentiment and support, much before politicization becomes apparent.

2. *'Minority rights' need not interfere wih 'majority rights'*. Threatened languages are frequently surrounded not so much by hostile outsiders (Ymen, we have called them before) as by unsympathetic insiders (Xmen-without-Xish or Xmen-via-Yish). Because the latter have already begun to fashion a new identity, based, in part, on their greater and seemingly more rewarding association with Yish and with Ymen, RLS-efforts on behalf of Xish make them doubly uncomfortable. On the one hand, such efforts call into question their status as Xmen among Xmen-via-Xish, and, on the other hand, expose them to criticism from anti-RLS Ymen. Caught in the middle betwen pro-RLS-Xmen, on the one hand, and anti-RLS- (or even just potentially anti-RLS) Ymen, on the other hand, the Xmen-via-Yish often bend over backwards to identify with the frustrations, doubts, suspicions, guilt feelings and insecurities of Ymen more generally. This reaction may be a mixture of identification with the aggressor and identity uncertainty/self-hatred, but, whatever its psychological dynamics, it frequently leads to a public apologetic posture which paints pro-RLSers as attempting to curtail the rights of the majority to use Yish and Yish alone or to prohibit the body-politic as a whole from continuing to operate via that language. These are distorted reactions that can be countered only by pointing to the genuinely intra-Xmen goals that pro-RLS efforts pursue.

Ymen themselves, of course, may also become alarmed (often via contagion from Xmen-via-Yish), about the purported insults that pro-RLS efforts, even if voluntary but certainly if governmentally espoused, would perpetrate on the realm, on public order, on national unity, on clear thinking, on morality, on economic productivity, on cultural literacy, on Yish history and tradition and on all Ymen everywhere. RLS advocates can and should stress, therefore, that no infringement of anyone's rights and no rejection of anyone's dignity or legitimacy is part or parcel of their program or goal. This should not be merely a public relations position but, hopefully, a deeply felt conviction. Having suffered themselves from an imbalance of power between Xish and Yish, pro-RLSers must seek a social order in which no new suffering is caused because of any local reversal of the previous imbalance. Cultural democracy *is* possible and its pursuit must be an honest and deep commitment, rather than merely a temporary strategy and a disarming tactic of the pro-RLS forces. Slaves who become cruel masters themselves do great damage to the cause of abolition; previously disadvantaged RLSers who become cultural imperialists themselves, within their newly dominated networks, do great damage to the RLS cause, not only locally or regionally but internationally as well. Francophone Quebec's restriction of the public use of English on store and street signs, now that French has unmistakenly come to the fore there, has harmed the moral and political position of francophone minorities outside of Quebec[2] as well as the position of a variety of RLS-efforts far outside the borders of Canada. Somewhat similar events have occurred in Israel (re Hebrew vs. Yiddish) and, to a far lesser degree, in Catalonia (re Catalan vs. Spanish). It is a problem that must not be overlooked by pro-RLSers if they are to satisfactorily answer the accusation that they merely represent the window-dressing for a *sub rosa* power play.

3. *Bilingualism is a benefit for all, for Xmen and for Ymen alike.* Many people are afraid of bilingualism. Some pro-RLSers accept it as a temporary strategy, secretly longing for a completely monolingual Xish society at the end of the rainbow, a society in which the disruptive and destructive influences and blandishments of Yish will be politically beyond the pale. Many Xmen-via-Yish oppose bilingualism because it always reminds them that they too could have retained Xish or could even now regain Xish rather than opt for Yish alone. Some Ymen oppose bilingualism because it implies questions about their undisputed 'mastery in their own home', and because they have been wrongly taught to associate it with disadvantaged status socially and culturally, with civil strife politically and with lower productivity economically. However, bilingualism should be neither a temporary strategy nor an implicit threat, but rather an enriching concomitant to the multicultural reality of the modern world. Bilingualism represents the potentiality for a mutually advantageous bridge between co-polity neighbors as well as between cross-polity neighbors. Good things as well as bad things can cross that bridge and it is the potential for good (economically, culturally and diplomatically) that makes bilingualism such a worthwhile investment.

Populations experiencing language shift have no alternative, by and large, but to be bilingual. They need not bemoan this price of their weaker status, for it is a price that at least has the potential of adding perspective, opportunity, variety and nuancing to their lives. Some say that 'something is lost' when there is no completely monolingual Xish society anywhere, and, of course that is true in the trite sense that the eclipse of any cultural pattern (even a monolingual one) is a loss. However, a return to Xish monolingualism may be neither practically possible nor philosophically desirable. RLS-efforts along such lines will quickly exhaust the political, economic, physical and emotional resources available to Xmen and will elicit the early opposition of anti-RLSers among Xmen and Ymen alike. Bilingualism, indeed, is the only route via which RLS can proceed before it takes hold, and it is both a good faith indicator to one and all as well as a moral challenge *vis-à-vis* relations with Ymen and with Xmen-via-Xish. Accordingly, rather than bemoan the loss of Xish monolingualism, RSLers must stress the genuinely creative, innovative and enriching gain of bilingualism, a bilingualism that is both protective of a particular definition of Xishness as well as interactive with Yishness.

Modern life makes it impossible for any culture to be entirely independent from its surroundings or from influences coming from afar. That being the case, all one can or should hope for is as much cross-cultural understanding as possible, as accurate cross-cultural communication as possible, and as much development of cultural individuality as modern reality permits, i.e. an individuality which consists of each culture's own, maximally self-regulating fusion of influences from a variety of sources. It is this *self-regulated fusion* that is or becomes authentic and unique and it is this fusion that RLS should genuinely aspire to and that bilingualism serves. Self-regulated bilingualism is not tantamount to cultural suicide but, rather, to self-regulated cultural growth. This is true for Xmen and for Ymen alike, even though they will undeniably differ in the constituents, in the degree of balance and in the fluency that their respective bilingualisms typically achieve.

Bilingualism is neither 'an added burden for the poor' nor 'a luxury of the rich'. Bilingualism is a bridge, as mentioned earlier, with great positive utility for both Xmen and Ymen. Like all bridges, however, it has to be watched and repaired. The early stages of RLS are impossible without this bridge and the later stages are rendered more humane, more sensitive, more creative with it than without it[3]. Finally, it should be stressed that it is a particular societal arrangement with respect to bilingualism that RLS requires, namely, that arrangement we have referred to before as involving 'diglossia'. When intragroup bilingualism among Xish-speaking Xmen is stabilized so that Xish has *its* functions and Yish has *its* functions and these two sets of functions overlap minimally, then Xish will have its 'own space', i.e. functions in which it and it alone is normatively expected, and Yish will no longer be a major danger to it in those functions. Diglossia not only constitutes additive bilingualism (rather than subtractive or replacive bilingualism in which one language pushes the other out of use) but stabilized bilingualism that recognizes the need for internal boundaries as much as (or even more than) external ones (see Strassoldo, 1982). As such, it involves a willingness of RLSers to admit Yish as *an integral part of their lives* — although a far different part, as we will see, at later stages of RLS than at earlier ones — for the foreseeable future and to do so without regrets or recriminations. This does not mean a soft or cringing attitude toward Yish; indeed, it means a very hard and inflexible approach in which Yish is as clearly denied the functions of Xish among pro-RLS Xmen, just as Xish is denied all of the functions of Yish (particularly the intergroup functions) by society at large.

4. *RLS-efforts must vary according to problems faced and opportunities encountered.* The typical RLS scenario presents the problem of too much that needs to be done urgently and too few resources with which to do it all. As a result, the early and felicitous setting of priorities is of exceptional importance, precisely because time is short (language erosion is going on all of the time) and defeats or failures are not only demoralizing for the few who are committed to RLS but they are seized upon and played up by the many who are the active or passive opponents of RLS. A disequilibrium between languages is normal and perhaps even inevitable whenever two languages are used by the same population or in the same polity. RLS implies not the establishment of *equilibrium per se*, certainly not initially, but, rather, the establishment of *stability* between the weaker (Xish) and the stronger (Yish), such that Xish becomes at least intergenerationally transmissible in as many culturally crucial functions as there is a reasonable chance can be attained, given the resources available at any point in time. Accordingly, the setting of priorities requires a sophisticated judgment as to (a) which functions are culturally crucial to intergenerational language use continuity and (b) and in which functions there is a reasonable chance of RLS success. When these two desiderata do not coincide then the optimal compromise between them must be sought, because success in intergenerationally unimportant functions is merely camouflaged failure, and failure with respect to intergenerationally crucial functions necessarily quickly becomes disheartening and irremediably immobilizing. Thus, a sensitive diagnosis of the areas of greatest Xish strength (relative to Yish) is called for, as is a thorough understanding of which sociocultural functions are really fundamental or primary *vis à vis* intergenerational continuity and which are secondary or peripheral in that connection.

Just as not everything that needs to be accomplished in order for RLS to come about can be accomplished simultaneously, because pro-RLS forces are too weak for such grandiosity and, therefore, they need to focus their precious but limited resources on a well chosen, smaller, 'urgent but do-able' agenda, so that which is most 'urgent but do-able' may well vary from community to community. A threatened language is not necessarily similarly or equally threatened in every community or in every social network in which it is still employed. Accordingly, 'tailor-made' efforts are preferable to 'across the board' efforts in which the same goals are pursued (or prescribed) everywhere. Tailor-made efforts also permit more local input, elicit more local commitment and make better use of diverse local talent. Finally, a diversified approach, such that two, three or more different goals are pursued in five, ten or fifteen different places, permits a better evaluation as to what is generalizable in the results that are attained and what is so specific (specific to particular co-occurrences of particular activists and other quite particular local circumstances) that no generalizable lesson can be derived (or derived as yet) from the results attained.

RLS obviously involves all three levels of social planning: *strategy* (i.e. expert diagnosis as to the most crucial intergenerationally continuous functions that can be tackled given the available resources), *tactics* (the organization and administration of specific projects in specific places with respect to those functions) and *operations* (the ongoing monitoring of results relative to resources). This complex of interrelated considerations can best be grasped and appreciated in conjunction with a graded typologyy of sociolinguistic disadvantage. If we more fully realize that not every threatened language community or language network is equally or similarly threatened, nor equally and similarly capable of response to threat, then we can more easily agree that not every RLS-effort must proceed to do the same things in the same way. There are no panaceas in socio-cultural affairs. The 'cure' or 'solution' must 'fit the illness' or 'problem' as precisely as possible, thus making a typology of illnesses (i.e. of types and degrees of threatened statuses within language communities and networks) an extremely important precondition for any systematic approach to RLS strategy.


## A Graded Typology of Threatened Statuses

The well known 'Richter Scale' measures intensity of earthquakes. High numbers are indicative of stronger tremors, i.e of greater disruption of the established, normal geological strata and, accordingly, of greater threat to those living in the vicinity of the quake. What follows here is a similarly graded sociolinguistic disruption scale with respect to language communities or networks and, here too, higher numbers will imply greater disruption and, therefore, more severe or fundamental threat to the prospects for the language to be handed on intergenerationally. In some respects, the GIDS (Graded Intergenerational Disruption Scale) may be thought of as a sociocultural reverse analog to the sociopsychological language vitality measures that several investigators have recently proposed[4]; the higher the GIDS rating the lower the intergenerational continuity and maintenance prospects of a language network or community. The major difference between the two, in addition to their different substantive foci, is that the GIDS is at least a quasi-implicational scale, i.e. higher (more disrupted) scores imply all or nearly all of the lesser degrees of disruption as well.[5]

**Stage 8 on the GIDS (Graded Intergenerational Disruption Scale): most vestigial users of Xish are socially isolated old folks and Xish needs to be re-assembled from their mouths and memories and taught to demographically unconcentrated adults**

The degree of attrition in some language communities and networks is so advanced that the few remaining users (normally speakers but sometimes reciters or 'blessers', 'cursers', 'prayers' or even just 'understanders') of Xish are themselves scattered and, often, also very deficient in proficiency for the ordinary purposes of everyday discourse. They have no one to use Xish with conversationally and, therefore, they often use those words or expressions that they still command with household animals or even with inanimate objects such as family photos and personal mementos. Often such individuals, the last survivors of a formerly vibrant language-in-culture community, live in relatively isolated, rural and inaccessible locations, or, alternatively, in old-age-homes in more urbanized locations.

Stage 8 contexts yield individuals who are well recognized as informants by folklorists and by linguists who are concerned with saving even the last few remnants of language-in-culture already in the most advanced stages of attrition. Such preservative efforts are certainly extremely worthwhile because they help both professional and amateur 'collectors' to piece together and restore folksongs, proverbs and folktales, formulaic expressions (greetings, apologies, benedictions, maledictions, etc.) and, from the foregoing, subsequently, to assemble partial phonologies, grammars and lexicons, piece by piece until a reasonable whole is once more at hand; at first, just on cassette and on paper, and, later, hopefully, once again in the hearts, minds and mouths of somewhat younger users. RLS advocates can help in these tasks too, keeping in mind, however, that not only are these, themselves, the bare rudiments of RLS, but that (given a proper sequencing of efforts) it may be possible to build from this stage toward progressively less disrupted stages.

Pro-RLS advocates working with stage 8 'informants' should be aware that such individuals often remember more Xish than they themselves realize. As fluency in a particular language is lost, it becomes progressively harder to trigger memory for that language. Sometimes a few emotional (humorous or affect-arousing) expressions can help to jog the memory. Sometimes pictures of family members, or of favorite persons, places and things, or of childhood-related activities can serve as memory-joggers, just as they do when utilized by therapists working with the neurologically impaired and even the comatose. After the first isolated informant has produced as much as he (or, more likely, she) can at a particular juncture, the recordings of what has been collected thus far can then be used with subsequent informants, in order to check on their reliability and in order to try to add to them (thereby extending the collected language corpus). This type of work is often discouraging (if not downright depressing) to the RLS worker, because it makes crystal clear the vastness of the erosion that has occurred and the distance that must still be traveled before restoration of the corpus of Xish is relatively complete. However, with sufficient training and perseverance it is often possible to accomplish surprisingly much. The records of many Amerindian and Australian Aboriginal languages and those pertaining to various immigrant varieties have been substantially restored after beginning from this sad starting point. Such restoration is the necessary precursor for working toward RLS at less disrupted stages of languages than stage 8, but even if no less disruptive stages are attainable, because of psychological, societal or material barriers, a record of a language is itself a living testimony to it and should be acknowledged as an accomplishment wherever even that lowly stage of vitality has not hitherto been attained.

A natural consequence of reconstruction (and an effort that can often begin even before reconstruction becomes necessary, i.e. when elderly and demographically sparse and disconnected speakers can still be located) is instruction. Many threatened languages take advantage of such circumstances today, as reflected by the proliferation of 'ethnic community courses' for adults. Although these adults may have strong Xmen community roots themselves, the Xish which they acquire via such courses no longer has, for the learners, any such functional contextualization. The adult learners acquire an emotionally gratifying but functionally meager command of the language, this meager functionality being a reflection of the societal dislocation of Xish from the culture of the adult Xmen who are engaged in efforts to reacquire Xish. Stage 8 demonstrates something that language teachers and language learners are often unaware of, namely, that language learning and the intergenerational language-in-culture use that RLS requires can be two quite separate and unconnectable things.

## Stage 7 on the GIDS: most users of Xish are a socially integrated and ethnolinguistically active population but they are beyond child-bearing age

Sometimes it is not possible to overcome the dislocations of stage 8 on the GIDS, although even at that level it may be possible to engage in a good deal more identity reconstruction than language reconstruction/adult instruction alone. The oral culture that is salvageable at stage 8 is also translatable and can provide a younger generation (one that is going through the various transformations of being Xmen-via-Yish) with a toehold on the 'old culture' and a link with it from which to cultivate either that very point of departure or, alternatively, bolster their attempts at a modified return to being Xmen-via-Xish. Folk cultures are not either vibrant or moribund; nor are they either clearly authentic or artificial and false. All of the foregoing are designations that can easily come from outside of the community of members. Inside the community of members, folk cultures are whatever they are, whatever they are experienced as being, and one of their possibilities is that of being 'emergent', i.e. of reappearing, of undergoing apparent revitalization and development after a period of attenuation.[6] Sometimes this happens, as with some Australian Aboriginal and Amerindian (and even some post-immigration) cultures without attaining RLS; however, *that* is the topic of another inquiry (a fascinating inquiry, to be sure). For our purposes, it is enough to indicate at this point that efforts to cope as best one can with RLS at stage 8 on the GIDS can contribute handsomely along lines that are often initially not imagined, not even by RLS advocates dedicated to a vision of 'being Xmen *with* (and, partially, *due* to or *because* of) Xish' and to a variety of Xishness which strikes them as being obviously more authentic, precisely because of its constant association with a linguistically Xish medium and other Xish symbols.

The major difference between stage 7 and stage 8 RLS remediation-efforts is provided by the fact that the elderly Xish speakers are still societally integrated, living in homes, neighborhoods and communities among their own Yish-speaking children, grandchildren and neighbors. Being beyond child-bearing age, however, they can no longer contribute to the number of Xish users demographically, although they can still contribute to the number of such speakers sociologically, i.e. by dint of social example and by means of social action. This is still so even when older Xish speakers are increasingly located in old-age homes, provided these homes contain several Xish speakers and when the links between their residents and the surrounding community of children, grandchildren and great-grandchildren are still quantitatively and qualitatively vibrant. Unlike stage 8 we are not yet dealing, at stage 7, with the very last Mohicans, but, rather, with a generational phenomenon such that the generation of native users of Xish, though elderly, is still appreciably present, on the one hand, and is still largely societally integrated, on the other hand. Under such circumstances (and they are quite common, within both immigrant-derived and indigenous communities) it is important to realize that 'old folks are a resource'. Indeed, at the outset of RLS-efforts, they are often the major linguistically functional resource available to language activists.

Just as the major goal at stage 8 is to reassemble the language itself and to build up a core of those who have at least some knowledge of it, so that it can, subsequently, once more be mastered for sociofunctional (rather than purely idiosyncratic) purposes, so the major goal at stage 7 is to gain a younger cohort of Xish-as-a-second-language users (or younger 'non-native Xish speakers', as they are referred to by certain RLS movements), a cohort still sufficiently young to have children of its own and to implement Xish as the language (or co-language) of normal socialization for the functions that pro-RLSers stress as part and parcel of their preferred image of Xmen-via-Xish[7] It is vitally important that pro-RLSers keep their eyes on the ball in this connection and not allow themselves to be sidetracked or hoodwinked by the possibly widespread entertainment and education' uses of Xish among some demographically concentrated older generation groups. Just as no amount of 'positive attitudes toward Xish' at stage 8 can substitute for reassembling the language and its verbal culture (the road to societal language death is paved with the good intentions called 'positive attitudes'), so no amount of lectures in Xish, theater performances in Xish, Xish song recitals, books or journals in Xish, prizes and award ceremonies for Xish authors, all of the foregoing generally being arranged for audiences that are advanced in years, nor even endless rounds of 'intergenerational visiting' at stage 7, can substitute for the re-establishment of young families of child-bearing age in which Xish is the normal medium or co-medium of communication and/or of other culturally appropriate home, family, neighborhood and community intergenerational vernacular activity.

*The goal at this stage (as at every stage) must be to transcend itself*, i.e. to attain that which is most crucially lacking so that RLS can be achieved and maintained: a variety of youth groups, young people's associations, young parent groups and, finally, residential communities or neighborhoods, all of which utilize (or lead to the utilization of) Xish. These may be conducted, organized, supported, financed, and ideologically encouraged and reinforced by 'old folks' but it is not the 'old folks' whose pleasure and facility in Xish is the real goal at this stage but, rather, *their activization on behalf of changing the overt behavioral patterns of the young*. The road to societal death is paved by language activity that is not focused on intergenerational continuity, i.e. that is diverted into efforts that do not involve and influence the socialization behaviors of families of child-bearing age.

Of course 'the old folks' must be kept happy, busy and committed too. They must be kept talking Xish, supporting it emotionally and financially and via overt voluntary efforts of various organizational and public relations kinds. Their efforts lend an invaluable public visibility to Xish and this, in turn, has a vital feedback influence on the 'community of interest and commitment'. However, what is often overlooked, at this stage, is the difference between means and ends. Song concerts, theatrical performances, poetry readings, lectures, publications and prizes are RLS-means, not RLS-ends in themselves. As RLS-means they are not intergenerationally continuous. Families are not formed, the daily and intergenerational societal channels of Xish communication are not re-established and the oralcy or literacy of the young are not substantially fashioned by such activities or by the institutions that maintain and conduct them.

However, if the informal interaction between the elderly, the social gatherings, concerts, lectures, prizes, performances, periodic publications and manifold other activist efforts that are the hallmark of stage 7 *are so focused as to bring about and foster intergenerational continuity* then, and only then, have they re-established a link, the missing link, to the future, to the world of young folks, rather than merely being what they otherwise are, no more than *means of social interaction and social expression for the gratification of 'old folks' per se*. If no such further contribution is envisaged or directly confirmable, then the fading generation of Xish speakers is merely engaging in self-gratification rather than in RLS-efforts. Instead of progressing from step 7 to step 6 on the GIDS the next stage will inevitably be a regression to the documentation/reconstruction and dispersed (a-societal) learning phenomena which stage 8 represents.

**Stage 6 on the GIDS: the attainment of intergenerational informal oralcy and its demographic concentration and institutional reinforcement**

Stage 6 is concerned with the reappearance of the intergenerational family. It is an extremely crucial stage for Xish because *the lion's share of the world's intergenerationally continuous languages are at this very stage and they continue to survive and, in most cases, even to thrive, without going on to subsequent ('higher') stages*. At this stage, Xish is the normal language of informal, spoken interaction between and within all three generations of the family, with Yish being reserved for matters of greater formality and technicality than those that are the common fare of daily family life. The major problems with respect to achieving stage 6, given that stage 7 has been achieved, are that the younger generation that has been targeted in stage 7 must somehow (a) leave behind an already ongoing sociolinguistic *modus vivendi* and (b) create another that is demographically concentrated and intergenerationally continuous. These goals need not be attained via the extreme form of esoteric experimental communities established for RLS purposes, although in such specially established communities even a relatively tiny population can most easily attain the new critical mass that metamorphoses them from a minuscule minority into a local majority (note the discussion of pioneering Jewish settlements in late nineteenth and early twentieth century Palestine, Chapter 10, below). Other, more common forms of demographic concentration can more easily be attained and can serve roughly the same purposes, e.g. planned concentration in particular neighborhoods where stage 7 institutions are located or locatable, or, at least, frequently scheduled, and cognitively/emotionally gripping, briefer concentrations for outings and vacations. All of these approaches provide Xish-speaking young folks with additional vital opportunities for the formation of new 'families of procreation' and for informal interaction outside of the confines of their 'families of orientation'. Instead of being the language of linguistically isolated families (however numerous and large these may come to be), Xish must also become the language of interfamily interaction, of interaction with playmates, neighbors, friends and acquaintances. Via demographic concentration, those who initially constitute generationally diverse speakers that are organized only on an individual family basis strive to attain an even higher form of social organization: beginning with family they attain community. Most languages of the world are rather limited, both numerically and sociofunctionally, but are self-perpetuating on this very basis and it is truly foundational if further, higher order RLS-efforts are to be successfully pursued.

Note that this stage also subsumes such neighborhood institutions as local economic, religious, cultural and recreational units as rub shoulders with the daily neighborhood life of ordinary folk. If we do not particularly discuss neighborhood work and religious institutions here, it is only because the former is becoming rarer as urban economies modernize and the latter are not always Xish mother-tonge focused due to their association with one or another classical language (see chapter 12, below, on RLS-efforts on behalf of second or third languages).

Just as stage 8 represents a language-in-culture waiting to be painstakingly reassembled and relearned, and just as stage 7 represents a language-in-culture waiting for its 'old timers' to reconnect with younger generations, so stage 6 represents a language-in-culture waiting for young people to create their own families and for intergenerationally diverse families to achieve the demographic concentration of communities.

Stage 6 is a difficult stage. Some of the families that it contains may not be entirely constituted of Xish speakers or of Xishly fluent speakers. However, the more the Xish speakers are concentrated and the more they reinforce each other, the more they create the social norms and interactive situations that facilitate the acquisition of Xish-as-a-second-language for those who have not hitherto done so, and the more they contribute to the fluency of those who are somewhat less fluent than others. Stage 6 involves the informal daily life of a speech community. As such, it is difficult to plan (planned informality is a contradiction of sorts). It can be facilitated, however; it can be fostered and encouraged. If its fundamental desirability is recognized, then all other RLS-efforts can be evaluated in terms of their feedback or by-product contribution to this stage.

Various additional strategies and tactics may also be called for while demographic concentration is either not yet possible or, at least, not possible for all those whose informal family functioning is already primarily in Xish. The regular use of telephone conference calls, of amateur or local radio, of closed circuit television, of scheduled exchanges of visits, of frequent exchange of taped letters, of taped stories, songs and games for children, the formation of parents' associations (and, if appropriate, separate sessions for mothers/fathers, grandparents) etc., etc., all function to link Xish-speaking families with each other and to establish and reinforce a sense of community even when these families do not have the benefit of the residential propinquity upon which community generally depends. The scattered Friulian language activists in Italy have used some of these methods to great advantage and, at this stage, as in stage 7, it is almost as worthwhile for pro-RLS youngsters to be in touch with each other *across* regional lines as within them. Shared experience, in connection with successes and failures at stage 6, is a great conserver and facilitator of energy and resources and an international clearing house for this purpose is greatly needed.[8] Equally difficult to come by (and even more important) are intrafamilial tactics and strategies for maintaining the interest and dedication and for augmenting the facility and versatility of children or of other family members who are either below par or who are eager for further growth. An 'RLS Family Service' is much needed in this connection,[9] for it is at this stage that the vision of being Xmen-via-Xish becomes an overt, total behavioral, ethnocultural reality rather than being merely a narrowly sociolinguistic one.

It is precisely because stage 6 is such a crucial stage, the stage of daily, intergenerational, informal oral interaction, that it requires full appreciation and extra-careful attention. The core of this stage is the family (although, given demographic concentration, a community of families can be envisaged). The family is an unexpendable bulwark of RLS. The family has a natural boundary that serves as a bulwark against outside pressures, customs and influences. Its association with intimacy and privacy gives it both a psychological and a socio-logical strength that makes it peculiarly resistant to outside competition and sub-stitution. Although it is true that in modern, urban environments the family has lost much of the socialization power that it once had and much of its ability to close itself off from noxious influences, it is, nevertheless, the most common and inescapable basis of mother tongue transmission, bonding, use and stabiliza-tion. The family (and even the immediate community) *may not be enough for RLS to be attained*, particularly where outside pressures are both great and hos-tile (see Kasarda, 1978; White, 1987; Horwitt, 1989), but without this stage safe-ly under Xish control the more advanced stages have nothing firm to build upon. While it is true, of course, that neighborhood change occurs, bringing with it the characteristic anomie of urban life and the estrangement of neighbors from each other, it must be a prime goal of RLS movements not only to challenge and to overcome such processes but, furthermore, to instill the stimulation and purpose-fulness of conscious Xishness into 'their' neighborhoods, because, after all is said and done, that is still the locus within which intergenerational mother tongue transmission occurs.

The clustering of families into communities provides welcome additional defense and facilitative further scope for the family as the core of RLS. This is said not to downgrade the contributions and refinements associated with the further steps in the RLS process, nor to deny that the further steps mentioned below provide valuable feedback and reinforcement for the home-family-neighborhood-community roots of RLS, but merely to make it crystal clear that the centrality of this constellation must be recognized, pondered, and contributed to via RLS social policy as a whole, rather than being undercut or upstaged by the more dramatic and modern arenas and media of sociocultural life. The latter can undoubtedly contribute to, but they cannot substitute for, home-family-neighborhood-community processes, just as inflating a flat tire cannot substitute for making sure that the tire has no leaks from which the air will then escape. The home-family-neighborhood-community complex is the normal 'whole' of childhood life and of intergenerational mother tongue transmission. Accordingly, it must remain at the center of RLS-efforts, no matter what are the stages that necessarily come thereafter.

This presents two major types of dilemmas to RLS-efforts. First of all, families are not captive audiences, as pupils are in school, as workers are in the workplace, or as soldiers are in the armed forces. There is no particular, parsimonious point of assembly where one goes to find families. Secondly, the major societal influences stemming from outside macro-forces must not be permitted to overcome and vitiate the combined efforts of the stage 6 institutions. All of that simply means, however, that one must take special pains to facilitate the formation and concentration of the home-family-neighborhood-community institutions and processes that constitute the heart and soul of stage 6. *One cannot jump across or dispense with stage 6.* That has been tried several times and, uniformly, it has resulted in less success and more wasted resources than RLS can afford. Without an intimate and sheltered harbor at stage 6 an RLS movement tends toward peripheralization from personal and emotional bonds and faces the danger of prematurely tilting at dragons (the schools, the media, the economy) rather than squarely addressing the immediate locus of the intergenerational transmission of Xish.

## Stage 5 on the GIDS: Xish literacy in home, school and community, but without taking on extra-communal reinforcement of such literacy

In stage 6 we have assumed that oralcy is the basic medium of the basic intergenerational continuity of language in the vast majority of language communities and networks. (For the continuity of languages to be utilized in literacy functions alone, see Chapter 12.) Stage 5 is preoccupied with the protection of the oral realization of Xish by providing it with at least a somewhat broadened functional periphery and, furthermore, by doing so in such a way as to still depend overwhelmingly on intragroup resources and processes, i.e. by focusing on Xish literacy primarily under intragroup sponsorship, with respect to both its acquisition, its content and its control.

There are various reasons for advocating a modicum of literacy ('guided literacy' some might call it) for languages that basically function in their spoken form. The most vital of these, insofar as RLS is concerned, is that literacy facilitates interindividual, internetwork and intercommunal communication and goal attainment and, therefore, also the attainment of RLS goals, particularly so when Xish-speaking families are not overwhelmingly clustered into communities. Xish literacy provides entry to ties that themselves become the sinews of community. A farflung community of interest, made up of relatively isolated families and 'settlements' (neighborhoods, quarters, etc.), can be tied together psychologically and integrated culturally via RLS-related correspondence, newsletters, magazines, brochures and books.

The written and printed Xish word, and the RLS message brought in via print and writing, become welcome guests, frequent messengers and reminders, as well as visible symbols of the RLS goal and of the entire image of Xishness that the fostering and promoting of Xish represents. Since, in modern contexts, Yish literacy is almost assuredly present and active (given the centrally instituted requirements of compulsory schooling with which Yish is associated), Xish literacy frees pro-RLSers from complete dependence on Yish print media insofar as informational, attitudinal, ideological/philosophical and recreational communications are concerned. This is an important 'liberation', since without it pro-RLSers are likely to become convinced that there is no way in which *their* views can receive the widespread, informed and elegantly impassioned expression that is needed for Xish to compete with and counteract the pro-Yish views with which even pro-RLSers themselves are so frequently bombarded.

Many sociolinguists and all professional educationists are greatly enamoured of literacy as a key to social mobility and to competitiveness in the modern work sphere. Benefits such as these are not to be sneezed at, but, at this stage, they are not yet directly RLS-related. Indeed, since the lion's share of social mobility and work sphere competitiveness may well require Yish literacy and since such literacy may well undercut RLS-efforts, these particular arguments are problematic when it is RLS that is our primary goal. It is also not particularly convincing to claim, as some do, that without a literacy option at all the 'prestige' of Xish will never measure up to the 'prestige' of Yish, since this is an overly global way of sizing up the relative power potential of the two.

I remember very vividly asking for the daily Rusin newspaper at a hotel in Novi Sad (Yugoslavia) in 1980. The kiosk attendant unhesitatingly told me that Rusin publications could not be obtained at the hotel kiosk because 'People who read Rusin don't stay at hotels'. On an overall 'prestige' rating the fact that Rusin literacy was possible did not begin to equalize the prestige of Rusin with that of its local competitors: Serbocroatian, Hungarian, German, Italian, etc. Furthermore, it might be assumed, as far as nationwide or worldwide news was concerned, that Rusin readers could follow such news (and probably even do so more fully) in newspapers in one or another language of greater 'prestige'. However, insofar as the treatment of Rusin, Rusinness and the attainment of Rusin ethnocultural goals, and, therefore, *insofar as Rusin language advocates and adherents were concerned*, publications in (and, therefore, literacy in) Rusin had greater 'prestige' and had attributed to them infinitely greater importance and urgency than any publications in 'languages of wider communication' could ever attain. They felt infinitely better off with such literacy than they would have felt without it.

How is such 'guided literacy' to be attained, particularly if it is highly pre-dictable that those attaining literacy in Xish will inevitably already be (or will soon become) literate in Yish as well? Often this can be done at home, or in the home of a pedagogically gifted neighbor, or in the quarters of the local religious unit, or in a local (i.e. neighborhood) *Xish literacy center for children and/or adults*, along the lines of the Basque *ikastolas* (see Chapter 6, below) during some of the years of the Franco regime. What all of the above agencies of liter-acy acquisition have in common is that (a) they are under maximal Xish com-munity input and control, (b) they can set their own policies with respect to personnel, methods and content and (c) they also foster Xish socialization among children, young folks and adults when they wear their 'other hat', namely that of cultural and recreational centers. None of them usually require any (or any substantial) governmental (i.e. Yish) approval, supervision or regulation, given the ordinary democratic or quasi-democratic conventions and circum-stances that we have assumed throughout the bulk of our discussion.

On the other hand, the lack of Yish control usually means that such agencies of RLS-oriented literacy acquisition will receive little or no governmental funding, on the one hand, and will not satisfy compulsory education requirements, on the other hand. The direct consequence of the former intra-communal characteristic is that the disadvantaged (pro-RLSers) have yet another burden to bear; the direct consequence of the latter characteristic is that the Xish literacy agency does not become an unwilling or unwitting captive of unwelcome Yish views and processes. This is not to be taken as implying a blanket isolation from Yish views, values, interactions, rewards, opinions and preferences, but, merely, that *there must be some fully Xish agencies where Yish and Yishness are minimized*, if any balance at all is to be maintained between the weak and the strong and if Xish is to have any formal functions entirely unto itself, outside of the strictly oral domains that we have reviewed earlier.

We are carefully distinguishing the acquisition of literacy from education more broadly and more generally. The latter is yet to come, at the next stage (stage 4), and presents its own opportunities and dangers for RLS. Stage 5 deals with only part of the total education domain, a part that is entirely Xish, primarily literacy-focused, socialization-related and entirely under intra-communal control. These features are not accidental. They must be monitored in order to make sure that they are not lost in overly eager haste to build the RLS roof before its foundations have been erected and assured. Stage 5 is itself the roof, if you like, to the first and most difficult phase of RLS, the phase in which the basic existence of Xish and of an Xish-speaking community requires urgent and careful attention. It is as unwise (indeed, even more unwise) to move ahead to more advanced concerns when the more elementary ones have not been answered, as it is to remain at an overly elementary level when more advanced opportunities can be taken advantage of. Furthermore, although it is true that all the stages that we have discussed thus far represent a drain on the resources of those with the fewest resources to spare, it is also true that nothing that we have discussed so far requires really substantial material resources and that what is required of pro-RLSers initially is primarily plentiful initiative, intelligence, dedication, organizational ability and hard work.

It may seem unfair that the poor should have to tax themselves for their own betterment, but that is the way of the world and if Xmen do not labor on behalf of Xish before the world as a whole is changed, no one will do it (or pay someone else to do it) for them, or even believe that Xmen themselves really believe that it is worth doing. The road to RLS is a long and difficult one and most of this road must be paved with self-sacrifice. There is no other way, really, for no language-in-culture can endure if it is dependent on another for the minimal essentials of its intergenerational continuity. Obviously, not all RLS-efforts get this far; those that cannot manage to do so, try to stabilize at the family level and, failing that, slip back to the non-transmissible (and, therefore, empty) pageantry of stage 7 and, ultimately, to the struggle against sociocultural detachment and dismemberment so characteristic of stage 8.

## Stage 4 on the GIDS: Xish in lower education (types a and b) that meets the requirements of compulsory education laws

Thus far, we have dealt with stages of sociolinguistic disarray that are substantially remediable by the self-propelled efforts of pro-RLSers. Such efforts on the part of the socioculturally (and often economically) disadvantaged are obviously burdensome to them, but the price that they exact is also energizing, motivating, commitment fostering and community fostering. The very process of struggling for an Xish-speaking community helps foster just such a community. By paying the price of the early and most crucial stages of RLS themselves, pro-RLSers are saying to themselves and to others that Xish, and the goal of implementing a particular vision of Xmen-via-Xish, commands the basic loyalty and dedication needed to secure its continuity, even if on a numerically small and functionally limited scale. Stage 5 is at almost the outer perimeter of expansion that still leaves all basic intergenerational sociolinguistic needs and processes substantially within the power of Xmen to plan, control and defend. If more advanced stages fail, this (stage 5 and its prerequisite, stage 6) is the perimeter to which 'withdrawal according to plan' can safely regroup, in the hope that future occasions may present themselves for greater success along more ambitious and, therefore, less totally independent and self-sustaining lines.

The first efforts to cross over to 'the other side of the continental divide' is likely to be the effort to gain co-control of the lower (i.e. local and less specialized) educational and lower work domains. We will consider them one step at a time, starting with education, i.e. with the one that impacts earlier and is also more formative *vis-à-vis* skills and attitudes requisite for later stages in life. Subsequently we will turn to the lower work sphere and to even later stages as well.

Modern education is a prerogative of the polity, i.e. of the political arm of society. Compulsory education rests upon the power of the Yish political arm to compel one and all to educate their children in accord with programs that the polity has certified as minimally adequate and desirable from the point of view of its Yish definition of 'the general interest'. Accordingly, public education involves an implicit social compact, just as does government itself. In return for accepting the polity's definition of what is educationally minimally adequate, desirable and in the 'general interest', parents are relieved of (most) direct tuition expenses and these expenses are paid from the general tax coffers: yet another sign that a widely acceptable social consensus is implied. Both the political power underlying the compulsory nature of modern education and the wide societal consensus underlying the use of general tax funds for this purpose point to the use of Yish rather than Xish as the normal medium of compulsory education. However, the use of Xish as a co-medium, in those schools attended only (or primarily) by Xish children and founded and self-supported only (or very largely) by Xish community funds, is, nevertheless, a possible compromise on the part of the polity insofar as the general social consensus is concerned with respect to what is minimally adequate and desirable in education. However, it is also a compromise for the staunch supporters of Xish and for all those who pursue the vision of a particular type of Xmen-via-Xish, for they must accept major Yish authority and input in the ultimate decision as to what is minimally adequate and desirable for Xish children. The polity's permission to conduct part of the education of Xish children in Xish is revokable and is dependent, at any rate, on the Xish community's willingness to pay most of the costs of such education itself. Thus, the risks for Xmen are twofold: the permission of the Yish authorities may be revoked, on the one hand, an inescapable risk precisely because the legitimization of 'majority rule' is employed; and, on the other hand, there is the risk of having to raise substantial amounts of money so that appreciably Yish views of what is a minimally adequate and desirable education can be implemented. These views may, indeed, conflict with Xish philosophy/ideology and manifest needs in conjunction with such matters. We will refer to such schools, that meet compulsory education requirements but that are largely maintained by the Xish community itself (out of recognition of the truth that schools represent Xish 'cultural space' per se, rather than merely agencies for the transmission of neutral knowledge, skills and attitudes), as 'schools of type 4a'.

An even more fundamental compromise on the part of the Yish polity and its educational authorities is involved in an agreement for schools teaching partially in Xish, and utilizing a partially Xish definition of what is adequate and desirable in education, to be conducted and paid for out of general tax funds. Such self-limiting compromises, in which the strong have limited their own power to force the weak to follow the educational pattern so substantially dictated and controlled by the strong, have been made in the name of cultural democracy on several occasions and in various polities, but they require the same twofold compromise on the part of RLSers, even though the latter have obviously been strong enough to elicit a self-limiting compromise on the part of the Yish authorities. Yish authorities must give (and periodically renew or confirm) permission for such education and must agree to (and approve) Xish preferences in connection with at least part of the definition of what is minimally adequate and desirable in publicly funded education. We will call such schools, that provide an Xish component in the definition of minimally adequate and desirable education, but that are entirely funded from general tax funds, 'schools of type 4b'.

Clearly, the major factor in the effectiveness of the types of schooling that also seek to attain the goal of Xmen-via-Xish, above and beyond the more general educational goals of optimal cognitive, social and emotional development, is the effectiveness of the curriculum, of the pedagogic materials and of the teachers, and, in the final analysis, on the dedication of the latter and their ability to effect a mutual compact with the parents whose children they teach. Clearly, there can be effective schools of type 4a and ineffective schools of type 4b, and vice versa, and there is no a priori reason why pro-RLSers should necessarily prefer one to the other on purely pedagogic grounds alone. However, from the point of view of maintaining the social boundaries that undergird minority language-in-culture, the two types of schools may well differ substantially. Schools of type 4a are more completely under Xish control and may better reflect the subtleties of Xish society and culture (e.g. in the school decorations that are employed, in the tunes that come over the public address system, in the sense of 'at homeness' of parents and grandparents who visit, in the very school calendar itself and in innumerable formal and informal ways that are not part of the designated curriculum but that 'build an environment' nevertheless) far better and more fully than can schools of type 4b. Schools of type 4a may be at greater liberty to have a longer school day or a longer school year, in order to provide more time for Xish subjects. They may be more closely linked with other Xish community institutions that also foster the Xmen-via-Xish vision (such as local religious units, Xish youth clubs, Xish sports teams, Xish summer camps, etc., etc.). Schools of type 4a may be able to channel interaction with Yish youngsters and with Yish society and culture as a whole in a far more egalitarian and controllable way. Above all else, schools of type 4a (even more so than the schools of type 5) call upon parental support, involvement and commitment, thereby creating and strengthening that most elusive and vital of all RLS assets: community.

Schooling in lieu of compulsory education is the first RLS step that involves regular contact and cooperation with the world outside of Xish society. In a very crucial sense, formal education implies the exposure of Xish children to Yish influences. That is why such education is not merely an opportunity for Xish but also, in an even larger sense, a risk. It is quite understandable for pro-RLSers to aspire that the education of those of their children who are pursuing the vision of Xmen-via-Xish be paid for out of general tax funds, just as is the education of children who follow the vision of Ymen-via-Yish. However, even if this aspiration is tactically successful, its risks must be carefully evaluated and it may well be undesirable to insist on such type 4b schools prematurely, before it is reasonably certain that the Xish social and cultural boundary can actually be maintained under such circumstances and that the schools themselves can truly function with sufficient Xish co-input and co-control to be institutions on behalf of the vision that they seek to serve. If such certainty requires more Xish demographic and political concentration than is available at any particular time or place, then it may be better to be safe, with at least a *few* schools of type 4a, than to be sorry with *many* schools of type 4b.

Obviously, the first step 'on the other side of the continental divide' must be taken carefully, in full cognizance of the difficulties and dangers inherent in it, rather than precipitously, on the mistaken assumption that it is a universally recognized and obvious goal for Xish to be utilized as a medium of instruction in schools that are maintained from general tax funds. Actually, it is far from being the latter and, indeed, such schools may elicit more public animosity and opposition than they are worth in terms of what they contribute to RLS. If this step is to be taken at all, it is best to be clear about the amount of risk that it entails and the amount of demographic-economic-political power that it requires in order to be successfully implemented. Even if implemented, 4b schools must be 'indigenized' in *fact* (i.e. in their operations: in personnel, in program definition, revision and control, and in budgetary design and approval), as, for example, in some of the schools for Navajos (see Chapter 7, below), rather than merely in principle or in law.

There is no separate and special GIDS step pertaining to 'political party, pressure or power' because political organization (organization to influence the allocation of scarce resources) on behalf of RLS is needed throughout all RLS-efforts where interaction with Ymen is required, and increasingly so (as well as increasingly focused on influencing Ymen and the resources that they control) as the 'continental divide' is crossed.

Of course, there is the matter of expense again, but the maintenance of schools is not merely a matter of finances. Type 4a schools frequently also provide indirect RLS benefits, as centers of adult employment, voluntary adult involvement and activization, adult education, and intergenerational interaction. Similarly, type 4b schools can also provide indirect RLS benefits along many of the above lines, with their possible financial benefits to the Xish community being potentially even more substantial, due to their potentially more ample budgets for salaries for teachers, teacher aids, custodians and buildings and grounds staff, curricular-, materials- and program-specialists and consultants (much used in Wales and in Friesland), kitchen and lunchroom staff, etc., etc. All of the latter benefits, however, also make a larger Xish adult population dependent on Yish-controlled funds for their livelihoods and, more generally, *orient them toward financial success via interaction with Ymen* more than with Xmen, and, most probably, also toward interaction even with Xmen, at least in that context, via Yish. Thus type 4b schools may be the beginning of the interactional dependency route, a route that generally leads away from RLS rather than toward it.

The major point to remember with respect to education and RLS is that education links those who receive it to the reward system controlled by those who provide it. *That is its function and that is what motivates its success.* RLS activists must make sure that the education of Xish children links them as early as possible and as closely as possible to the maximal possible Xish cultural reward system. Any other kind of education inevitably undercuts RLS rather than contributes to it. Yish reward systems that are apparently democratically managed (i.e. democratically managed insofar as Yish interests are concerned) can, nevertheless, be very potent and undemocratic means of relinguifying and re-ethnifying ethnocultural minorities by coopting them and their children into the greater Yish reward system. This need not be an evil, sly or even consciously conducted process; however, it is a process that inevitably destroys the vision of Xmen-via-Xish, even the vision of 'Xmen with Xish who also know Yish and participate in Yish economic and political life'. Therefore, it behoves pro-RLSers to foster greater consciousness of both the gains and the risks of the state-required, formal educational process as far as RLS is concerned. A 4b school may be Xish only in a very pro-forma fashion. Its existence, its staff and its constituency may constantly tremble at the whim of ethnopolitically motivated Yish administrative obstructionism and pettiness (see the discussion of bilingual education for Hispanics in the USA, in Chapter 7, below). It may actually be more trouble for RLS than it is worth, particularly if its community roots are minimized and attenuated by a Yish administrative superstructure. Let us remember that schooling comes after (not before) mother tongue transmission has already transpired. Its role in RLS is dependent on its ability to connect back with and reinforce the Xish family-home-neighborhood-community nexus in a supportive fashion, while children are still impressionable. The question remains whether 4b schools will actually do so, rather than merely remove a financial burden from the shoulders of the RLS leadership.

**Stage 3 on the GIDS: use of Xish in the lower work sphere (outside of the Xish neighborhood/community) involving interaction between Xmen and Ymen.**

The last few lines, above, also bring us to the issue of the lower work sphere. Even at stages 6, 5 and 4 the lower work sphere is also germane, but there it functions safely within the Xish neighborhood. Even in this more sheltered connection, some minorities come to control certain industries, products or areas of specialization and, as such, to provide for themselves the economic foundations of the type of dual or multiple symbiotic societies that have been noted in the Caribbean and in other parts of the developing world and that correspond to economically more fortunate, demographically concentrated minorities more generally,[10] namely the opportunity to meet the Yish market on its own terms. Clearly, there is and must be an economic basis to Xish life and to the advancement of RLS. Although this need not be overestimated as to its importance, it must also not be underestimated. Accordingly, its coordination and development from the point of view of strengthening Xish demographic and political power is an important desideratum at all steps. In stage 3, however, this already important lower work sphere is attended to additionally along two different lines (corresponding to types a and b, above, with respect to education). On the one hand, Xish-controlled and staffed enterprises and services seek to meet the needs of the Yish market; on the other hand, Yish-controlled enterprises and services seek to meet the needs of the Xish market. In each case, we are still restricting ourselves to the lower work sphere outside of the Xish neighborhood and to enterprises of a relatively small scale. Nevertheless, the RLS challenge is quite different in each of these two contexts.

Where Xmen are serving Ymen from the point of departure of an Xish enterprise the RLS emphasis must be on differentiating inter-Xmen interaction from Xmen–Ymen interaction. In an Xish-controlled enterprise that serves Ymen it is still possible for Xmen to interact with each other in Xish, to keep their business records (where permitted by law) in Xish and, more generally, to make the work sphere as Xish as possible in numerous little ways (such as remaining closed on Xish ethnocultural holidays, providing Xish background music, providing on-the-job time for Xish entertainment, discussion, listening to tapes, etc.). The goal of this effort is Xish ethnolinguistic boundary maintenance. Going to work outside of the Xish neighborhood does not necessarily have to mean changing entirely to Yish at work, not even when one's work entails serving the Yish market, and particularly not when the business/workplace itself is in Xish hands (see the discussion of Hasidic efforts at stage 3, in Chapter 7, below). On the other hand, when Yish businessmen are serving the local Xish public, RLS efforts must be oriented to requesting that this service be in Xish. 'Service should be in the language preferred by those served', is a general RLS principle at this stage (akin to the American slogan that 'the customer is always right'), and, accordingly, not only local Yish businesses serving Xish communities but even local governmental or quasi-governmental offices (banks, post offices, registry offices, small claims courts, neighborhood health clinics, etc.) can sometimes be influenced to move in this direction. Pressure on local governmental units is outside the limits of stage 3 and we will turn to it in conjunction with stage 2. The importance of lower work sphere RLS-efforts, however, cannot be doubted, not even in the absence of stage 2 successes.

As in the case of schooling, RLS successes in the realm of work represent the efforts to carry RLS outside of the immediate Xish community itself and into those more general, Yish-controlled, pursuits that nevertheless impinge quite unavoidably upon the daily well-being of the Xish family and neighborhood. If no success is experienced here then stages 5 and below always undergo stress and will always be exposed to unavoidable and uncontrollable influences that tend to counteract their own vision of Xmen-via-Xish. If stages 4 and 3 too can be reached, then a first and second layer of outer defense have been established for the inner defenses (stages 8–5) that are the *sine qua non* of RLS.

Once we are past stage 5 then every further upward step along the way carries its own dangers with it, along with its own opportunities, and there are no longer any 'all win situations'. The greater the industrial success of a minority ethnocultural region ('minority' *vis à vis* the polity as a whole), the more that region must be linked to the polity's reward system and even to the international market-place in connection with obtaining customers, funds, workers and the most advanced equipment and expertise. Catalonia has learned this lesson, partially to its own regret: success in the national and international work sphere generates its own dangers and problems in such areas as the appearance of an immigrant, non-Catalan speaking workforce, federal regulation, dependency on non-local funding, greater exposure to non-local media, etc. Nevertheless, the work sphere must be tackled by successful RLS-efforts, because its alternative, to be overwhelmingly economically dependent upon Ymen and Yish-controlled rewards, is even more troublesome and dislocative.

The effort to 'make Xish safe at work' begins in the lower work sphere. Once stage 5 is relatively assured, then stage 3, like stage 4b, is a risk that cannot long be postponed without thereby also generating serious problems. Finally, having said this, it must also be stressed that stage 3, particularly when prematurely aimed at, is far from being a magical 'open sesame' for RLS. It is neither a necessary stage (see the discussion of Hebrew, Chapter 10, below) nor a sufficient stage (see the discussion of Catalan in that same chapter), economic determinists among pro-RLSers and among sociolinguists notwithstanding. It is merely a highly desirable contributory stage, one that is usually at a considerable distance from the nexus of intergenerational mother tongue transmission and that is even indirectly tied back to that nexus only with considerable forethought and ingenuity. At any rate, it is a stage that is frequently out of reach for RLS movements and they must learn to function without it, as best they can, by stressing stages 6–4 all the more.

**Stage 2 on the GIDS: Xish in lower governmental services and mass media but not in the higher spheres of either**

The final two steps on the GIDS are reached by relatively few RLS movements, although those that do, happen to be the movements that 'hit the headlines' most frequently and, perhaps therefore, the ones that also get the lion's share of attention even among sociolinguists. Those RLS movements that safely secure stage 5 and below can remain intergenerationally secure, provided they can maintain sufficient ethnocultural separation from Yish encroachment on their own family-home-neighborhood-community intragroup institutional bases. Those movements that successfully cope with the dangers of stages 4 and 3 have assured themselves some breathing-space even in connection with lower level (which means: 'local, community based, influenced and influencing') processes. Those movements that enter into stages 2 and 1 are moving into the 'Big Leagues'. Attempting to influence these two stages means taking on the most powerful and the most central institutions and processes of the polity as a whole and, therefore, also the ones most firmly and exclusively under Yish control. This is so precisely because stages 2 and 1 represent the government itself or are most closely governmentally regulated because of their importance in the formation and preservation of integrative attitudes, opinions, identities and the topmost skills and statuses.

As at the other stages that we have reviewed, above, it is best to seek Xish recognition first in connection with those governmentally encumbered processes that have the greatest potential for Xish grass-roots involvement. The larger the pro-RLS contingent, the more concentrated it is demographically, and the more involved it has already become in the educational, economic and political processes at the grass-roots level, the more claim it also has on lower level governmental services and mass media in its language. These services and media are intended to reach everyone and to foster the greatest good for the greatest number. Accordingly, those whose vision of 'the greatest good' includes the vision of being Xmen-via-Xish can claim to be recognized as a bona fide constituency for services in that language which is of supreme importance for them (even if they are proficient in Yish too) and for this recognition to be a matter of regional policy rather than merely a matter of individual accommodation or of once-in-a-while appreciation. Local governmental agencies and services in Xish neighborhoods should be urged to operate bilingually, in Yish and in Xish, using whichever language is preferred by the citizens whom they are serving. Bilingual forms should be requested at their offices. National radio and television too should be asked to provide a certain number of hours of Xish programming (or of Xish-dubbed programming), to supplement the often more readily available (but also less frequently listened to or watched) 'local diet' of Xish programming. In addition to the recognition of Xish that derives from services that are provided in accord with this principle of 'service to the citizen in his or her preferred language', the provision of such services in Xish is also inevitably related to the hiring of more Xish speakers and, therefore, to the greater economic viability of the vision of being 'Xmen with Xish'.

As with the prior steps 'on this (Yishly powerful) side of stage 5', it is also necessary to keep in mind the risks that derive from stage 2, rather than merely focusing upon its benefits. Stage 2 further integrates Xish and Xmen into polity-wide reward systems. This is a stage at which brain-drain possibilities become particularly worrisome, although such possibilities become part of the risk picture even in stages 4 and 3. Yish rewards for excellence are always likely to be greater than Xish rewards and the professionalization of quasi-governmental, civil service and media specialization leads inexorably toward Yish, Yishness and Ymen. It is hard to overcome the pull of the higher salaries and ranks that are to be obtained in the national capital or in major population centers outside of the Xish region. Even those functionaries and specialists who remain physically within the Xish region are likely to be substantially oriented toward colleagues, superiors and constituencies whose roots and loyalties are elsewhere. This danger needs to be acknowledged and guarded against by suitable ideological heightening and organized (and organizational) countersteps. Where bilingualism can be monetarily recognized for the additional capacity that it represents this may prove helpful in slowing down the brain-drain flow. Being and fostering Xmen-via-Xish is basically a philosophical/ideological position and, as such, it requires constant philosophical/ideological restatement and updating if it is to remain effective. In the last analysis, pro-RLSers may have to settle for a certain outflow at the upper reaches of society in order to maintain the essential solidarity and even inflow at the more intermediate segments of Xish society. Finally, the real contribution of stage 2 to intergenerational mother tongue transmission must constantly be monitored empirically. It is often assumed to be greater than it is, on the basis of its contribution to a variety of recreational preferences and adult concerns. Since there will always be more (and probably better) Yish than Xish media, the Xish media are really a weak reed (and a post-mother tongue transmission reed as well) for RLS to lean upon substantially.

## Stage 1 on the GIDS: some use of Xish in higher level educational, occupational, governmental and media efforts (but without the additional safety provided by political independence)

Arrival at stage 1 represents the end of a long and difficult haul, but, most certainly, it does not represent the end of RLS problems and concerns. Indeed, the problems at this stage of the GIDS are often particularly aggravated and politicized ones, but there are definite advantages to being at this stage as well. Stage 1 essentially represents the arrival of the pursuit of cultural autonomy for those who have pursued the vision of Xmen-via-Xish. As the recognized co-language of its region,[11] Xish would not only become co-associated with the highest educational, occupational, governmental and media activities there, but its spokesmen and representatives would become responsible for planning, conducting and evaluating such activities and, therefore, for keeping a very watchful eye on the use of Xish (and on the implementation of Xishness) in conjunction with them. Even if this stage is attained, there will inevitably be some pro-RLSers who are still dissatisfied, perhaps because Xish is not the sole official and ethno-national language of the region, perhaps because there are still many Xmen living outside of the region whose acquisition and maintenance of Xish is still far from certain (and may actually deteriorate there, as more and more Xish-speaking Xmen from peripheral regions move to the Xish regional center in order to enjoy 'daily living among one's own and in one's own language and culture'), or perhaps because even in the 'heartland' and even with cultural autonomy the pressures from Yish may still be omnipresent.

It is unwise to disregard the pessimism of the pessimists, the alarms of those who constantly 'view with alarm' the state of health of Xish language-in-culture. Yish, the constant competitor, is always part of the local 'heartland' scene too, not to mention that its undisputed domination in all other parts of the polity and its role as lingua franca between the regions and the national center usually also remains inviolate. There are also dangers from international languages, English often being first and foremost among them, whose pressure upon higher education, industry and technology and the media is felt even by Yish and, therefore, all the more by Xish. Thus, there is no justification in deriding or dismissing the dire prophecies of the pessimists. 'Eternal watchfulness is the price of RLS' and that price must be paid at stage 1 too. Indeed, some such price must even be paid by the supporters of the languages of smaller, politically independent units;[12] and even larger polities throughout the world, for example France itself, often feel the need of engaging in defensive RLS actions on behalf of their own national languages in order to dispel the spectre of English. The more the speakers of Xish and other smaller languages are drawn into the international orbit the more difficult it becomes for them to completely be 'the masters of their own homes' and the more painful to them is their realization of their relative smallness and unimportance in the overall, international econotechnical and political scheme of things, with or without independence. The proof of the pudding is the immediacy of feedback between stage 1 and stage 6, i.e. the nexus of daily life in general and intergenerational mother tongue transmission in particular. If this feedback is sluggish or questionable in demonstrable empirical terms, then stage 1 is a luxury rather than a necessity insofar as the attainment of RLS goals are concerned. It is a goal that can be tackled later rather than sooner.

Indeed, at the very stage at which cultural autonomy is finally attained, after a struggle that has often taken generations, it is not unusual for the 'victory' to feel unexpectedly hollow, insignificant and useless. 'What is the sense of it all', some may ask, 'if we are now merely moderns, like all other moderns, but in Xish?' This is an existential question of course, i.e. a question of deeply philosophical dimensions, and its answers inevitably reflect more basic answers as to the meaning of life in general and to the meaning or nature of Xishness in particular. There will certainly be those who will reply, as did many of the leaders of late nineteenth- and early twentieth-century nationalist movements, that 'to be modern Xmen but in Xish' is all that they ever had in mind. But there will be others for whom *that* answer and *that* realization at stage 1 will be insufficient. Their vision of 'Xmen with Xish' stressed certain historical commitments to values and behaviors and beliefs that they consider uniquely, traditionally and necessarily Xish, in short: the maximal implementation of the full Xish patrimony or heritage.

Pro-RSLers of the latter kind will certainly remain dissatisfied in stage 1 and will constantly advocate their more authenticity-stressing vision of Xmen-via-Xish. For others, at earlier stages, that vision may have been merely a means to an end, but for them, for the 'true believers', for the traditionalists, the vision was not only the end, the goal, the purpose of their involvement in pro-RLS activities, but it was (like democracy and all of ethics) an unreachable, unattainable 'holy grail', always somewhat out of reach and always justifying redoubled efforts to improve and intensify the Xish component of Xish society and culture. The struggle between the modernists and the traditionalists (and various interstitial compromise positions between these two extremes) can be a healthy one for the future of Xish. As long as neither side wins decisively the benefits that each recognize are available to those who seek them, the penalties that they each fear are held at bay, and no coercive capacity is granted to either of them. In this connection too 'eternal vigilance' is necessary, since cultural democracy is as much a precious verity for intra-Xish life as it is (or was at earlier GIDS stages) for interaction between Xmen and Ymen.

## *Gehobenes primitivgut, gesunkenes kulturgut* and the possibility of feedback

Throughout our presentation we have stressed a 'first things first' approach. This does not mean that each pro-RLS movement must start at stage 8 and laboriously pass through every intervening step until it gets as far as it can go at any particular juncture. Quite the contrary; it means that pro-RLS efforts should carefully gauge what stage they are at (in a particular location or neighborhood) and to undertake to repair lower, foundational stages before moving ahead to more advanced ones. Such a tactic does not entirely deny the possibility of feedback down the line, from more advanced stages to more foundational ones, just as it does not entirely deny the possibility of momentum from the conquest of lower, more fundamental stages to higher, more advanced ones. Indeed, both momentum and feedback exist as societal realities, but a cautious approach requires the recognition of the possibility that both will make relatively minor contributions to intergenerational mother tongue transmission in comparison with the dynamics of stage 6 (or stages 6–4a).

'Castles in the sky' are alluring but they do not make for safe living-quarters. It is definitely more exciting and more newsworthy to work on the more modern and 'flashy' side of the 'continental divide', on the side that deals primarily with the written, formal language and with interactions that are status stressing and/or oriented toward large constituencies. However, it is doubly difficult to dominate the latter steps, not only because it is at these very steps that Yish opposition is most fully and easily crystallized (including the opposition of Xmen-via-Yish) but because these steps are hollow victories and must ultimately crumble unless they rest upon the strong base of the informal, intimate spoken language in daily family, neighborly and community interaction. It is never crystal clear whether it is better to dig in at a lower, more foundational level or move ahead to higher risks and more advanced attainments. Even the most judicious may differ with respect to their judgment in this crucial connection. What is needed is that both views be carefully attended to and that a certain amount of hedging be engaged in, no matter which decision is taken.

The GIDS pinpoints three potentially dangerous decision stages. Stage 7 presents the danger of self-satisfaction with adult 'cultural programs' and 'positive attitudes', paying too little attention to the fact that these are not intergenerationally transmissible and must come to a predictably negative denouement no matter how much or how often the older generation enjoys them. Stage 5 presents the risk of timidity *vis-à-vis* the outside, Yish world of affairs and, therefore, a tendency to remain within the safe and comfortable world 'inside Xishness', thereby resigning Xish and Xishness to a parochialism that cannot satisfy more than a small number of self-isolates. This stage questions the wisdom of crossing the 'continental divide' because after such a crossing the prior *intragroup diglossia* among Xmen-via-Xish must become increasingly complicated by a burgeoning *intragroup diglossia* such that Yish is used only with Ymen while Xish is increasingly reserved for Xmen and preferred by them from Xmen as well. Stage 2 presents the danger of forgetting the 'golden rule': without sociocultural separation, without the most stubborn maintenance of voluntary boundaries between Xmen and Ymen and between Xishness and Yishness the future of Xish is problematic. Indeed, philosophically/ideologically reinforced sociocultural boundaries become more rather than less important the further one is from the 'continental divide' (the crossing over from stage 5 to stage 4) because one is then dealing with increasing Yish influences, invested power and politicized consciousness. When in doubt, it may be best to remember the adage: 'a bird in the hand is worth two in the bush'. As always, there is also the counter-adage: 'nothing ventured, nothing gained'. Nevertheless, in the practical world of resources it is worth stressing that Yish can afford more losses than can Xish and pro-RLSers will be well advised to act accordingly. The case studies to which we will soon turn should serve to exemplify the steps and the cautions expressed above and throughout this chapter.

## Concluding Observation

This chapter focuses on three principal notions:

1. *RLS-efforts must initially be primarily based on the self-reliance of pro-RLSers and on the community of Xish users and advocates whom pro-RLSers seek to mobilize and to activate.* The most crucial ameliorative steps that are undertaken are and must be those that the pro-RLS 'forces' can reasonably support and attempt by dint of their own time, funds and devotion. The time may come when the general, Yish-dominated voluntary magnanimity and tax-coffers will also support some particular RLS-effort or another on behalf of Xish, but Xish cannot afford to wait until that time may (or may not) come. Only a vibrant, self-reliant Xish community can hasten the coming of that time (if it ever comes) and, therefore, if no such community exists, then building it must be the first priority: doubly so, for only such a community, made up of demographically concentrated Xish-using families and neighborhoods, can provide the basic mechanisms that safeguard the processes of intergenerational mother tongue transmission.

RLS involves planned social and cultural change and those who are in control of the current sociocultural order can hardly be expected to be in the forefront of such change or among its early supporters or facilitators. Accordingly, those who seek to foster the changes in low culture (and, later, in high culture too, if possible) that RLS requires, can count only upon themselves, particularly at the earliest and weakest stages of the total effort. Fortunately, there are many things that can be undertaken on that basis and among them are the *sine qua nons* of all RLS stages, stages 8–6 (or, maximally, stages 8–5). These stages are labor-intensive rather than cost-intensive, and, as such, they depend squarely on the dedication, ability and simple sweat and tears that can be mobilized by and on behalf of the vision of being Xmen-via-Xish.

2. *In addition to initial self-reliance, another basic prerequisite for RLS-success is that of the proper sequencing of efforts.* There are instances of

fortunate RLS movements that have come into being while Xish society was still relatively intact and in control of its basic intergenerational mother tongue transmission processes (see Chapter 10 re the cases of francophone Quebec, on the one hand, and Catalonia, on the other hand). But the majority of RLS movements have come into being at far more advanced stages of sociocultural dislocation and, therefore, the remedial efforts that they needed to focus upon were far different from those that were rightfully available to the more fortunate cases. Reluctance to recognize this state of affairs and its necessary consequences underlies the common lack of success of most RLS movements. The premature rush of many such movements to stress goals at stages 4–1 (or even 3–1) has proven to be debilitating to them both emotionally and materially, even more so than would have been the fate of the 'success cases' had they remained fixated at stages 8–5.

For those RLS-efforts that correspond to seriously dislocated language-in-culture realities (earmarked above all by the demographic scattering or thinning out — rather than merely the numerical diminution — of the remaining Xish speakers), nothing can substitute for the rebuilding of society at the level of pockets of basic, everyday, informal life. This is among the hardest language planning goals to accomplish, and for several reasons. First of all, it requires the detachment or withdrawal of pro-RLSers from the ongoing social life dominated by Yish and, in its stead, the establishment of emotionally, attitudinally, ideologically and overtly independent counterpart networks operating via Xish. Secondly, the informality and spontaneity of everyday life does not lend itself to excessive planning, and efforts to impose such planning upon it easily divest it of the bonds of emotionality and intimacy that are the very essence of its being and of mother tongue bonding in particular. It remains to be seen whether the greater awareness of the centrality of stage 6 which this chapter has stressed (and which this volume will stress again and again in the chapters to come) will really help RLS movements approach their tasks with the sense of priorities as well as the gingerliness that stage 6 requires. It is not unlike the weaving of a new gossamer web out of an old one, while the old one is constantly being buffeted by the relentless tides and torrents of social change.

It is much easier, of course, to concentrate on the upper stages (4 or 3–1) immediately and rather exclusively. However, these stages are characterized by two overriding minuses insofar as RLS-efforts on behalf of seriously dislocated language-in-culture constellations are concerned: (a) they do not lead directly to intergenerational mother tongue transmission, being removed, as they are, from the actual nexus of such transmission, and (b) they do lead directly to increased dependence upon, confrontation with or rivalry with the dominant language-in-culture, Yish, at a time when Xish is ill-prepared to cope with such burdens. Stressing the wrong priorities is a very costly example of lacking a proper social theory or model of what RLS entails. Such an error engenders its own dynamics and, therefore, in order to escape from these dynamics, a double detachment or extrication becomes necessary (once, from Yish domination of all daily social processes and, then again, from the 'tradition' of erroneous RLS responses to that domination). Such double detachment is tantamount to a two-front struggle at a time when RLS barely has strength for the more limited appropriate one-front effort.

The sociolinguistic landscape is littered with the relatively lifeless remains of societally marginalized and exhausted RLS movements that have engaged in struggles on the wrong front (or on all eight fronts simultaneously), without real awareness of what they were doing or of the problems that faced them. Societal detachment and societal marginalization and exhaustion are not one and the same, by any means. The former characterizes the effort to establish one's own center of cultural gravity with respect to remedial stages 6–5 and possibly 4a as well. The latter characterize the results of prolonged efforts focused in intergenerationally non-transmissible (or minimally transmissible) directions. The later designations apply to RLS movements that have become little more than the hobbies of eccentric healers who are unaware of the true nature of the disease that they are pretending to cure.

3. *Finally, this chapter implies the need to ponder the interstage connections in RLS-efforts, particularly the feedback between the stages above 4b and those below it.* Another way to raise this point is to ask: '*What* exactly does each stage beyond 4a contribute to intergenerational mother tongue transmission *per se*, *when* (i.e. after how much delay) is that contribution made and *how* can its contribution be empirically traced or confirmed?'

Intergenerational mother tongue transmission and language maintenance are not one and the same, related though they are in the total RLS enterprise. Without intergenerational mother tongue transmission (or the transmission of a written or spoken second language, if that should be the societal goal) no language maintenance is possible. That which is not transmitted cannot be maintained. On the other hand, without language maintenance (which is a post-transmission process) the pool from which successive intergenerational transmission efforts can draw must become continually smaller. If fewer and fewer will maintain Xish, fewer and fewer will be available to transmit it to *their* offspring. Thus, both processes are necessary for successful RLS and neither one alone is sufficient for that purpose. Stage 6 (or, by extension, 6 through 4a) represents the focus on transmission *per se*, whereas stages 4b–1 represent the focus on language maintenance too, i.e. on the creation of the broader societal environment (going beyond childhood and adolescence to adulthood) in which the transmitted language can prosper and move toward a growing pool of speakers for subsequent intergenerational transmission.

Viewed from this perspective it becomes clear why severely dislocated language-in-culture constellations must stress the foundational stages (6–4a) first and then go on to protect and enhance them (stages 4b–1) thereafter. It should also become clear why lack of influence with respect to stages 4b–1 can expose an already dislocated language-in-culture unit to further debilitating dislocation, particularly if it is fully 'engaged' in the world of interactive modernity, while the mere presence (usually it is no more than a symbolic presence at that) of Xish in stages 4b–1 cannot really begin to rebuild the dislocated community or overcome its dislocations. Minoritized language-in-culture constellations can never look forward to as full a sway at stages 4b–1 as that exercised by those constellations dominating them (see Chapter 13 re the widespread but mistaken notion that schools alone or some representation in the media or in the economy are all that RLS requires). This is a true dilemma. Minoritized language-and-culture constellations cannot hope to quickly compete successfully, in connection with stages 4b–1, with those that dominate them. It is only at stages 4a and below that they can hope to build a world (initially a mini-world) of intimacy that is substantially their own and that is intergenerationally transmissible, given sufficiently effective group boundary consciousness, beliefs and practices that foster family-home-neighborhood-community islands of detachment from the larger Yish world of modernity (at least until that larger world can be somewhat regulated and tamed).

All of which brings us back full circle to the ideological realm. RLS is almost always part and parcel of a greater ideological program. Successful intergenerational mother tongue transmission may require priorities and sequential emphases which are at odds with the greater belief and value system of which RLS is but a part. The one may require a prolonged period of regrouping and of partial insulation from the cutting edges of modernity; the other may require a proud and embracing conquest of the very forefront of modernity under proud Xish auspices. Thus, ultimately, part of the heartache of RLS is that it often has an internal conflict or ambivalence to face up to, within the very circle of the true believers themselves, as well as an opposition from the external world of Ymen, Yish (including Xmen-via-Yish) and Yishness. It is this latter double burden that leads to uncrossable barriers for RLS movements, even for those who recognize that there is as much danger in not crossing the 'continental divide' to the degree commensurate with one's strength, as there is in crossing it prematurely, while still in a condition of internal and external weakness.

## Notes

1. At the risk of some minor redundancy with a later chapter (Chapter 11, below), it should be pointed out here that there is not only a very substantial literature on language planning but several professional journals that are devoted to it. Perhaps the best international compendium of recent work in this entire area is that by Fodor and Hagege (4 vols, 1983–89; one additional volume is currently in press), organized on a language by language basis but, unfortunately, still without a topical index that might help the reader trace any particular topic across all volumes. Also useful is Cobarrubias and Fishman (1983), organized topically with particular attention to the distinction between, as well as the relationship between, status planning and corpus planning, but also without a topical index. Cooper (1989) is the best and most recent introductory textbook in this area. See Woolard (1985) for the still all-too-rare stress on individual daily behavior as the acid test of the success of language policy (status planning), an approach which this chapter will seek to follow at various stages and in various domains of language use.

   The major journals for initial orientation in connection with language status planning are *Language Problems and Language Planning and Language Planning Newsletter*. Given that language planning has been studied and implemented by far more linguists and linguistically trained specialists than by social scientists or social science trained specialists, it comes as no surprise that the status planning aspects of language planning have received far less attention than have their corpus planning counterparts. However, even were the same amount of systematic attention to be devoted to them both, there is still good reason to expect status planning to be the more intractable of the two, both intellectually and practically, given the greater complexity of social-cultural-economic-political-demographic reality than of linguistic reality alone. Various RLS movements also publish journals that are of some general interest and value (see, e.g., *Noves SL*, published in Barcelona, and *Afn Shvel*, published in New York), even though their focus is quite specifically on one language alone.

2. It would be incorrect to conclude that all, or even most, anglophone reactions to the rise of French since the mid-60s have been negative. Even Freed and Kalina's (1983) *Anglo Guide to Survival in Quebec* has more humorous and accommodational tones than polemic or critical ones. For other signs of anglo accommodation to 'the French fact and deed', both within and outside of Quebec, see, e.g., Cartwright (1987), the large literature on French immersion education and a fairly limitless number of articles and news items in *Language and Society/Langue et Société*, the journal of the Commissioner of Official Languages (Ottawa). Nevertheless, journalistic and other less scholarly anglo views reveal a high degree and intensity of rejection of 'excessive francization' within Montreal and of uncompromising francophone goals outside of Quebec, particularly so in the western provinces, with the latter (opposition to French west of Quebec) generally being 'justified' as a response to the former (excessive and even insulting francization within Montreal).

   The growing monolingualization of Canadian demography, with displaced francophone minorities moving to Quebec and displaced anglophone minorities moving to Toronto (Ontario) or to even more westerly provinces, is itself an indication of the more general lack of satisfactory provisions for minority language needs in Canada, even in connection with the two founding ('official') languages. Concomitantly with the foregoing, French advocates have increasingly abandoned their former bilingualism quest *vis-à-vis* Canada as a whole in favor of an insistence on public French

monolingualism for Quebec, thereby increasingly abandoning francophones outside
of Quebec or any strong claim upon a nationwide policy that might be of assistance
to them. Obviously, bilingualism within Quebec is viewed by its authorities as a
greater danger to the 'heartland' than the loss of French outside of Quebec. The
future may hopefully see a reversal of this confrontational approach to one that is
more mutually accommodating. For a more extensive discussion of the success of
pro-French efforts and events in Quebec, see Chapter 10, below.

3.  Haugen (1987) provides a fine restatement of the 'Blessings of Babel'. Other serious
    work in this vein, and useful bibliography for its further elucidation, can be found in
    my papers on Whorf, Herder and Kallen (Fishman, 1978, 1982) and in the very size-
    able recent literature on enrichment bilingual education, i.e., the type of bilingual
    education that removes it from its minority mainstreaming vs. minority maintenance
    polemics. Siguan and Mackey's monograph (1987) in UNESCO's (International
    Bureau of Education) 'Educational Sciences' series is a useful introduction to this
    entire area and also provides a preliminary international directory of centers for the
    study and promotion of bilingualism and bilingual education.

4.  'Linguistic vitality' is the crux of much recent work by researchers such as
    Bourhis, Giles and Rosenthal (1981), Johnson, Giles and Bourhis (1983), Labrie
    (1984), Landry and Allard (1984), Allard and Landry (1986), Cartwright (1987),
    Young et al. (1988) and others. An entire issue of the International Journal of the
    Sociology of Language is scheduled to appear on this topic in 1992. Most of this
    admirable work focuses on language attitudes and their relationship to other
    attitudes, values and commitments. There is much in this work that is of value to
    RLS-efforts, notwithstanding the fact that it is more social psychological than
    sociological, more oriented toward measuring and describing individual behavior
    than toward measuring, describing and activating societal processes on behalf of
    RLS. The most noteworthy exception to the foregoing trend is McConnell (1988),
    whose work is macrodimensional and range-of-functions oriented to such an extent
    that a safe and secure oral community would appear to have far less vitality than
    would a community undergoing considerable duress and disarray across a wide
    array of functions.

5.  'Implicationality' is a concept borrowed from social and psychological measurement.
    It connotes a series such that all later occurrences in the series imply or subsume all
    those that have occurred earlier in the series. This notion was initially advanced by
    Louis Guttman (1944, 1947a, 1947b) in conjunction with attitude measurement, but
    it has earlier and ongoing counterparts in object assembly tasks that are ordered by
    complexity and in criterion-referenced testing in which the criteria have an underly-
    ing rationale such that more advanced criteria build upon (depend upon) mastery of
    less advanced criteria. In Guttman attitude scaling items are selected so as to maxi-
    mize their overall implicationality (sometimes also referred to as 'scaleability'),
    those items that do not scale (do not stand in an implicational relationship with each
    other) being omitted at the item-analysis stage of scale construction. To the extent
    that the maximalization of implicationality leads to a subset of all possible items that
    is either (a) atypical of the entire attitudinal domain, (b) too short to be reliable, or
    (c) insufficiently predictive of the phenomena ('criteria') that we want these items to
    predict or explain, there is not much to be gained by its pursuit.

    Many linguistic considerations are genuinely implicational, e.g., those that
    depend on phonological space or on order of acquisition (Rickford, 1987 and in
    press). Thus, among native speakers, formal phonological and morphosyntactic real-
    izations imply the prior acquisition of their informal counterparts whereas among

second language learners this does not obtain, and the opposite may actually be true in the case of school-based second language learning.

Implicationality may be either synchronic, diachronic or both. The GIDS, discussed below, is proposed as a diachronic quasi-implicational scale vis à vis criteria of stability and magnitude of RLS. The GIDS implies that it is generally better (more constructive, more productive) for RLS sub-goals to be pursued and attained in a certain order. It is implicational in 'a first things first' sense, in the sense that arithmetic must come before algebra; foundations must be put down before the walls are erected, and walls must be erected before the roof is put up. This is not to say that a roof is less important than the walls or the walls less important than the foundation, even though it is obviously necessary, since they each presuppose and gain in functionality from what has come before them, for them to be assembled in a given order. Since there appear to be few societal ventures that are implicational in this sense, it is our hope that RLS-efforts will gain in clarity and in attainability when the requirements of implicationality are imposed upon them.

6.  The notion of 'emergent', as utilized here, is parallel to its use by Landy (1974) in his discussion of traditional folk medicine when it is brought face to face with modern Western medicine. Under such circumstances, Landy tells us, traditional folk medicine either is *adaptive*, becoming influenced by (and, in more minor ways, also influencing) the much stronger and more pervasive practices of modern Western medicine, or it becomes *attenuated*, shrinking, crumbling and even disappearing entirely before the onslaught of modern Western medicine, or it demonstrates an *emergent* quality, that is a capacity to spring back and to regain the confidence and trust of many who had either discarded it previously or who knew about it only by word of mouth, based upon the memory of parents and grandparents. Landy implies, and we here explicitly suggest, that there is much in modern Western life that contributes to the dissatisfaction with it and that underlies the re-emergence of smaller scale, simpler, more intimate and more trusting social relationships and processes, the processes of *Gemeinschaft* and Little Culture as contrasted with those of *Gesellschaft* and Great Traditions.

However, the reality of emergent folk medicine, and emergent minority ethnolinguistic phenomena, does not imply the complete displacement of modern medicine, on the one hand, nor of mainstream part-identities, on the other hand. The emergent quality of minority ethnolinguistic reality, dealt with at length in my (1985) *Rise and Fall of the Ethnic Revival*, implies a hierarchy of resort, that is a situational implementation of a more (rather than of a less) complex total repertoire of behaviors (and of linguistic alternatives) than was available before syncretism and emergence came about. There may be a certain irony about the pursuit of simplicity succeeding only via the attainment of greater overall complexity, but, irony aside, the end result is a certain psychological and ethnocultural 'stretching' or growth and the realization that both simplicity/authenticity and complexity/syncretism have their assets and that the combination of their assets seems to outweigh the combination of their debits (which are, at any rate, unavoidable).

7.  I have employed the more neutral '[Xish] users' up to this point, because of my sensitivity to the fact that some RLS movements are on behalf of languages of reading alone, or of reading/writing, or even just of praying/singing, rather than necessarily on behalf of languages of spoken daily interaction, as would be implied by my constant use of 'speakers' rather than 'users'. However, on the whole, RLS movements are overwhelmingly concerned with and based upon the primary spoken use of the languages on whose behalf they labor, reading and writing being implicational of

their prior spoken acquisition and mastery. That being the case, and the point having
been made here that speaking need not be a goal of each and every RLS movement,
I will from here on utilize 'speaking' as the most typical example of early and foundational RLS-efforts.

8.  I have called for research and information 'clearing houses' before in connection
    with RLS-related efforts, with little success (see, e.g., Chapter 14 of my 1966 [1977]
    *Language Loyalty in the United States*), and I do so again here, because there are
    now, finally, at least two potential RLS-relevant 'clearing houses' in this area and
    more may yet come into being. The two that I am aware of are (a) International
    Research Center on Bilingualism (IRCB), Laval University, Cité Universitaire,
    Quebec, Canada, and (b) European Bureau for Lesser Used Languages (EBLUL), 7
    Cearnog Mhuirfean, Baile Atha Cliath (Dublin) 2, Ireland. Both of these may be of
    some help, at least in the 'misery loves company' sense, but neither of them comes
    close enough to the model of the Human Relations Area Files at Yale University
    which permit the retrieval of cases from throughout the world on the basis of data
    that has been pre-coded with respect to a large number of RLS-related descriptive
    and analytic dimensions. In addition, however, RLS requires a clearing house that
    can also provide cost (or, better yet, cost and effectiveness) estimates that can be
    used as rough guides by those considering a variety of alternative steps and solutions
    to their problems. I cannot imagine that budgeting and staffing such a center would
    pose a problem for UNESCO, for example, and must conclude that its absence is a
    sign that the 'natural sponsoring agencies' are governed by priorities dictated by
    great-power interests rather than by small-scale (intra-polity) concerns. That being
    the case, it might be more realistic for EBLUL or IRCB to expand their holdings and
    services, rather than to hope that other bodies will undertake RLS-focused services
    *de novo*.

9.  Currently, the nearest thing to an RLS School and Family Service is the *Bilingual
    Family Newsletter* (Multilingual Matters Ltd, Bank House, 8a Hill Road, Clevedon,
    Avon, England, BS21 7HH). Unfortunately, although it is now (1990) already in the
    seventh year of its existence, it is still forced to devote the lion's share of its attention
    to allaying the doubts, problems, fears and suspicions of its subscribers with respect
    to bilingualism, rather than becoming the forum for successful strategies, tactics,
    materials and programs that would be optimally useful. At any rate, the *BFN* seems
    to primarily serve an 'ethnically mixed family' clientele, where a different language
    is spoken by each parent (or where the child is bilingual but at least one parent is
    monolingual rather than bilingual), and, therefore, it is hardly focused on the type of
    family constellation and societal model that is likely to result in RLS. Since *BFN*'s
    constituency deserves attention too, it would probably be best to hope for a separate
    service and newsletter for RLS-oriented families and schools and, once again, it
    would seem to me that the type of center discussed above (see note 8) would also
    constitute the natural auspices in this connection.

10. Outside of some of the notions developed by Smith (1965), Depres (1975), Madu
    (1978) and Lijphart (1977), all of whom deal primarily with Third World and pre-
    industrialized cases, and a very few others, little concerted social science attention
    has been given to RLS implications of basically modernized, politically integrated
    and culturally differentiated but economically interdependent modern ethnolinguistic
    groups. When attention is finally directed to such arrangements the latter have gen-
    erally already progressed (or is it deteriorated?) to the stage of political separatism
    (see, e.g., the various esssays brought together in Williams, 1982). McRae's work
    (1983, on Switzerland; 1986, on Belgium, and two others yet to come, on Finland

and Canada) is an exception in this connection, but even here we are dealing only with the stage of high consciousness of politically defined intra-polity boundaries and with several systems that are already under significant strain. What is more generally missing is attention to less politicized, community-level institutional (family, neighborhood, club, church, school, workplace) functioning of a situational type and at an intermediate level of abstraction which permits both some process analysis and some quantification of rates and outcomes. Le Page and Tabouret-Keller (1985) is very provocative but is too close to the microscopic and 'stream of consciousness' analytic extreme to permit a clear picture to emerge.

11. Stage 1 will be discussed only from the point of view of the 'territorial principle', since the 'personality principle' (which is not as obviously based upon local demographic preponderance or concentration) seems to be decreasingly available in most modern RLS settings. It is obviously a more difficult and probably a less stable modern arrangement due to the increased intensity of cross-ethnic interaction.

12. The fact that smaller national languages have troubles, both from below and from above, and, in a sense, are in a more unenviable position than 'unrecognized' minority languages, is adumbrated in my 'The peculiar problems of smaller national languages' (1984).

# References

ALLARD, Réal and LANDRY, Rodrigue 1986, Subjective ethnolinguistic vitality viewed as a belief system. *Journal of Multilingual and Multicultural Development* 7, 1–12.

BARTH, Frederik (ed.) 1969, *Ethnic Groups and Boundaries*. Boston: Little-Brown.

BOURHIS, Richard Y., GILES, Howard and ROSENTHAL, D. 1981, Notes on the construction of a subjective vitality questionnaire for ethnolinguistic groups. *Journal of Multilingual and Multicultural Development* 2, 145–55.

BOURHIS, Richard Y. and SACHDEV, Itesh 1984, Vitality perceptions and language attitudes: some Canadian data. *Journal of Language and Social Psychology* 3, 97–127.

CARTWRIGHT, D. 1987, Accommodation among the anglophone minority in Quebec to official language policy: a shift in traditional patterns of language contact. *Journal of Multilingual and Multicultural Development* 8, 187–212.

COBARRUBIAS, Juan and FISHMAN, Joshua A. (eds) 1983, *Progress in Language Planning*. Berlin: Mouton.

COOPER, Robert L. 1989, *Language Planning and Social Change*. Cambridge: Cambridge University Press.

DEPRES, Leo (ed.) 1975, *Ethnicity and Resource Competition in Plural Societies*. The Hague: Mouton, and Chicago: Aldine.

FISHMAN, Joshua A. 1978, Positive bilingualism: some overlooked rationales and forefathers. *Georgetown University Round Table on Language and Linguistics*. Washington: Georgetown University Press, 42–52.

— 1982, Whorfianism of the third kind; ethnolinguistic diversity as a worldwide societal asset. (The Whorfian hypothesis: varieties of validation, confirmation, and disconfirmation 2). *Language in Society* 11, 1–14.

— 1984, On the peculiar problems of smaller national languages. In Andrew GONZALEZ (ed.) *Panagini; Essays in Honor of Bonifacio P. Sibayan on his 67th Birthday*. Manila: Linguistic Society of the Philippines, 24–39.

FISHMAN, Joshua A. *et al.* 1966 [1977], *Language Loyalty in the United States.* The Hague: Mouton [Reprinted, New York: Arno Press].
— 1985, *The Rise and Fall of the Ethnic Revival; Perspectives on Language and Ethnicity.* Berlin: Mouton de Gruyter.
FODOR, Istvan and HAGEGE, Claude (eds) 1983–89, *Language Reform/La réforme des langues/Sprach reform,* vols 1–4. Hamburg: Helmut Buske.
FREED, Josh and KALINA, Jon (eds) 1983, *The Anglo Guide to Survival in Quebec.* Montrel: Eden Press.
GILES, Howard, BOURHIS, Richard Y. and TAYLOR, D. M. 1977, Towards a theory of language in ethnic group relations. In Howard GILES (ed.) *Language, Ethnicity and Intergroup Relations.* London: Academic Press, 307–48.
GUTTMAN, Louis 1944, A basis for scaling qualitative data. *American Sociological Review* 9, 139–150.
— 1947a, Scale and intensity analysis for attitude, opinion and achievement. In G. A. KELLY (ed.) *New Methods in Applied Psychology.* College Park: University of Maryland Press, 173–80.
— 1947b, The Cornell technique for scale and intensity analysis. *Educational and Psychological Measurement* 4, 179–90.
HAUGEN, Einar 1987, *Blessings of Babel; Bilingualism and Language Planning: Problems and Pleasures.* Berlin: Mouton.
HORWITT, Sanford D. 1989, *Let Them Call Me Rebel; Saul Alinsky: His Life and Legacy.* New York: Knopf.
JOHNSON, Pat, GILES, Howard and BOURHIS, Richard Y. 1983, The viability of ethnolinguistic vitality; a reply. *Journal of Multilingual and Multicultural Development* 4, 255–69.
KASARDA, John D. 1978, Urbanization, community and the metropolitan problem. In David STREET *et al. Handbook of Contemporary Urban Life.* San Francisco: Jossey-Bass, 27–57.
LABRIE, N. 1984, *La vitalité ethnolinguistique et les caractéristiques socio-psychologique de l'individu vivant en milieu bilingue.* Quebec: International Research Center on Bilingualism.
LANDRY, Rodrigue and ALLARD, Réal 1984, Bilinguisme additif, bilinguisme soustractif et vitalité ethnolinguistique. *Recherches sociologiques* 15, 337–58.
LANDY, David 1974, Role adaptation: Traditional curers under the impact of western medicine. *American Ethnologist* 1, 103–27
LEPAGE, Robert B. and TABOURET-KELLER, Andree 1985, *Acts of Identity.* Cambridge: Cambridge University Press.
LIJPHART, Arend 1977, *Democracy in Plural Societies.* New Haven: Yale University Press.
MCCONNELL, Grant D. 1988, A model of language development and vitality. Unpublished paper presented at the International Conference on Language and National Development: The Case of India. Osmania University, January 4–8, 1988.
MCRAE, Kenneth D. 1983, *Conflict and Compromise in Multilingual Societies: Switzerland.* Waterloo: Wilfred Laurier University Press.
— 1986, *Conflict and Compromise in Multilingual Societies: Belgium.* Waterloo: Wilfred Laurier University Press.
MADU, Oliver V. 1978, *Models of Class Domination in Plural Societies of Central America.* Washington: University Press of America,
RICKFORD, John R. 1987, The haves and have nots: sociolinguistic surveys and the assessment of speaker competence. *Language in Society* 16, 149–78.

—  in press, Implicational scaling and critical age limits in models of linguistic varia-
tion, acquisition and change. In Charles A. FERGUSON and Thom HUEBNER (eds)
*Second Language Acquisition and Linguistic Theory.* Amsterdam: John Benjamins.
SIGUAN, Miquel and MACKEY, William F. 1987, *Education and Bilingualism.* London:
Kogan-Page in association with UNESCO.
SMITH, M. G. 1965, *The Plural Society in the West Indies.* Berkeley: University of
California Press.
STRASSOLDO, R. 1982, Boundaries in sociological theory: a reassessment. In R.
STRASSOLDO and G. DELLI ZOTTI (eds) *Cooperation and Conflict in Border Areas.*
Milan: Franco Angeli, 245–71.
WHITE, Michael J. 1987, *American Neighborhoods and Residential Differentiation.* New
York: Russell Sage.
YOUNG, Louis, BELL, Nancy and GILES, Howard 1988, Perceived vitality and context: a
national majority in a minority setting. *Journal of Multilingual and Multicultural
Development* 9, 285–9.
WILLIAMS, Colin H. (ed.) 1982, *National Separatism.* Vancouver: University of British
Columbia Press.
WOOLARD, Kathryn 1985, Language variation and cultural hegemony: toward an integra-
tion of sociolinguistics and social theory. *American Ethnologist* 40, 738–48.

# 5 Irish: What More Can Be Done?

## Historical Background

The Irish RLS effort has been different from any other that we will review in this volume because Irish alone, of all the endangered languages within our purview (and, perhaps, one of very few in the world at large) is a language with a state ostensibly dedicated to its protection, a state in which it is declared to be 'the national language' and 'the first official language'. Can this really be so? Can there be a threatened language with a state of its own? Apparently so, anomalous as that appears to be. Indeed, since the rise of modern Irish nationalism, roughly a century ago, the 'revival' or 'restoration' of Irish (so that it would become, at the very least, along with English, one of the 'languages of general communication' of the country), has been a constant verity of almost all of Irish public and organized political expression. Nevertheless, centuries earlier, long before the re-establishment of an independent Ireland during and immediately after World War I, English had already begun to effectively displace Irish as the vernacular of the island's propertied rural and urban population. And, as we will soon see, below, the forces propelling English in Ireland were much more than mere proximity to an aggressive world power utilizing what has become, in this century, the world's major language of wider communication (Luxembourg's vernacular, Letzebuergesch, has retained its vitality despite similar proximity *vis-à-vis* such worldwide languages as French on the one side and German on the other).

An unparalleled combination of culturally, economically, politically and demographically dislocating factors (occupation, warfare, transfer of populations, the establishment of a dominant English-speaking class in towns and urban areas which later developed into all-English cities [and into the country's only centers of commerce, industry, wealth and political power], repeated famines that destroyed indigenous and authentic rural life and its traditions, legal prohibitions against Irish, significant periods of *de facto* abandonment by most major Church authorities, the rise of an Anglo-Irish culture that is not only locally noteworthy but which has solid claims to worldwide attention, and, finally, the constant and still ongoing emigration to English-dominant countries both near and far), these have all contributed to the early, continual and still ongoing erosion of Irish in spite of the very substantial efforts and repeated ingenuity on behalf of RLS for some 100 years (the first 30 under voluntary auspices and the last 70 under combined voluntary and state auspices).

However, even after centuries of erosion and even after three generations of basically disappointing state-directed or -supported RLS-efforts, the visionary goal of the restoration of spoken Irish remains a goal that commands the apparent allegiance of almost the entire spectrum of organized Irish life in the 26 southern counties that constitute the Republic of Ireland. Indeed, except for the past opposition of the British and Irish Communist Party and a brief 'Language Freedom Movement' that successfully opposed the purported 'excesses' of 'compulsory Irish' as a medium of instruction in the nation's schools during the mid- and late 60s, the image of Irish has generally remained a distinctly positive one and one that is widely associated with the exhilarating purposefulness and the affirmation of ethnocultural authenticity and creativity that were the hallmarks of the end of the nineteenth and the beginning of the twentieth centuries in Irish intellectual, political and social life.[1]

## Global Parameters of Irish Language Attitude and Use Today

What does Ireland have to show for some 70 years of post-independence RLS-efforts? In answering this question it is necessary to distinguish, as do the Irish themselves, between two different Irish language realities: that of Western Ireland, known as the Gaeltacht, facing toward the Atlantic and most distant from England and from Dublin, and that of the rest of the country, east of the Gaeltacht. The latter, over 90% of the country both geographically, demographically and economically, began to anglify earliest. Its anglification proceeded to the point that it ultimately not only lost its own native Irish speakers, but that it then contributed mightily to the anglification of those Gaeltacht migrants who resettled there. Those who subsequently undertook to learn and to speak Irish anew ('revivalists'), as a result of RLS-efforts, whether under governmental or voluntary auspices in various parts of the country, learned it as a second language. In the Gaeltacht, however, poor, rural and relatively isolated as it was and often still is, there long remained (and in some cases there still remain) proportionately many native-speaking individuals, families, networks and communities. As a result, RLS policy there has aimed at maintaining (helping, supporting) the native speakers who live there, hopefully adding to their intergenerational numbers via a variety of social and economic policies, and utilizing the Gaeltacht to help with the 'restoration' elsewhere and to serve as an example of Irish as a living and lively language of daily life.

The one thing that the populations in the Gaeltacht and in the East had in common was a huge preponderance of positive attitudes toward Irish. Large majorities of both populations have reported themselves as having positive attitudes toward the language itself as a symbol of Irish independence and authenticity, as supporting government policies on behalf of the language, as vastly favoring the continuation (at least the elective continuation) of Irish in the schools and in other major social institutions of Irish life. However, as soon as we leave the attitudinal sphere and turn to actual language use and to RSL policies on its behalf, the differences between the Gaeltacht and the rest of Ireland become manifold.

## (a) The Gaeltacht

Although the Gaeltacht now constitutes only 2.3% of Ireland's population it still accounts for 7.4% of all Irish speakers and 45% of all Irish-speaking families. Further evidence of the continued disproportionate importance of the Gaeltacht for the vitality of Irish is the fact that its 58,026 Irish speakers over three years of age (in 1981, as recorded in the Census of that year) constitute 77.4% of the total population of that age living in the Gaeltacht, whereas in the country as a whole only 31.6% of the population over three claims to be Irish-speaking. Unfortunately, however, the ability of the Gaeltacht to materially influence the fortunes of Irish are seriously weakened by the fact that it is now a discontinuous or fragmented region whose inhabitants are substantially isolated from each other and cannot, therefore, easily pool their efforts to realize the full potential of their numbers (see map). Furthermore, the ongoing modernization, urbanization and industrialization of the Gaeltacht, intended to improve the lives of its inhabitants and to keep them from moving to the predominantly English East, has often also dramatically resulted in the accelerated anglification of its native population and in a growing influx of English speakers from outside the region. As a result, the proportion of Irish speakers in the Gaeltacht has been continuously and precipitously falling during the past quarter century (86.5% in 1961, 82.9% in 1971 and, as mentioned before, 77.4% in 1981).

Even more ominous, from the point of view of RLS, is the fact that the number of Gaeltacht residents actually using Irish as their habitual language of *daily* life (as distinct from rarer use) has been estimated as being only 29,000, i.e. only about half of those claiming ability to speak it and the majority of Irish-speaking parents there have lately begun to rear their newly born children in English ('so they can be like all other Irish children'), doing so to such an extent that a family still rearing its children in Irish is now often an object of comment and curiosity in many Gaeltacht areas. Some qualified observers now estimate

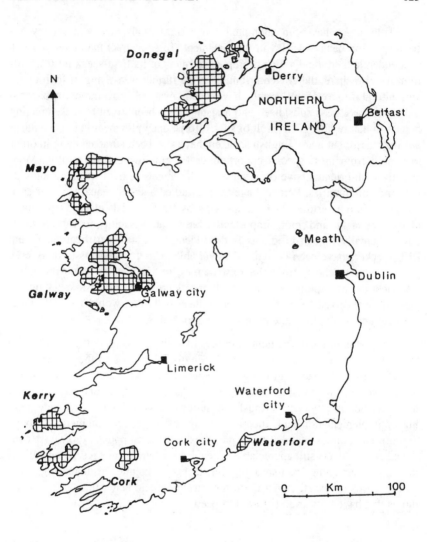

FIGURE 5.1 *Ireland and its Gaeltacht* (*Source*: P. Commins, 1988)

that only about a third of the Gaeltacht communities still can be characterized as consisting primarily of networks of competent and predominant users of Irish, and, to make a bad case even worse, some see various state policies and agencies themselves as seriously implicated in the dislocation of traditional Irish community life and in the consolidation of English in the public domain and in status roles there.[2]

True, much has been attempted and a substantial amount of money has been spent on behalf of RLS in the Gaeltacht. To counteract the poverty which was endemic there (and which prompted so many of its Irish-speaking residents to move elsewhere, thereby contributing to the further weakening of Irish there) agricultural improvement grants have been awarded, government-sponsored industries have been subsidized and assistance has been given to those erecting houses in that region. As a result of such efforts, unemployment in the Gaeltacht *has* decreased, but many English speakers have also been attracted there in order to benefit from these special opportunities for employment and profits. More directly Irish-oriented have been various inducements to Irish-speaking individuals and communities. Parents have been awarded a small annual sum for each of their children certified as Irish-speaking by field officials of the Department of the Gaeltacht, and, more importantly, family admissability to various other governmentally funded programs is dependent upon such certification. Fluent Irish speakers have been designated as suitable hosts for students (largely civil servants and teachers) from the East coming to spend their summers in the Gaeltacht in order to improve their Irish or to learn it *in situ*. Irish-speaking villages have received funds to construct village halls that would facilitate more frequent and more enjoyable programs and meetings.

On the other hand, the large numbers of visitors and tourists now attracted to the Gaeltacht (and the predominantly English signs posted there in order to guide them) have had anglifying consequences by and large. All in all, the indigenous Gaeltacht residents have had things done to them and for them, but they have not usually been seriously consulted or involved *vis-à-vis* policy making or implementation and, therefore, many of the efforts enumerated above seem foreign, imposed and at cross-purposes to the local population, whose continued emigration is still appreciable. The need for 'emergency rescue operations in the still remaining Irish-speaking Gaeltachts' is mentioned increasingly, but no consensus on exactly *what* to do now, different and better than all the many things that have been tried before, has been arrived at.

## (b) The East

If there is a widespread sense of disappointment with respect to what has been accomplished in the Gaeltacht, then there is *some* room for satisfaction with what has been accomplished in the rest of the country. Some of the leading nationalist spokesmen of the mid-nineteenth century (e.g. Thomas Davis [1814–1845]) never imagined that the East could actually attain more than 'that the Irish language should be cherished, taught and esteemed' so that it could be 'preserved and gradually extended", with 'gradually' being defined as encompassing a hundred years or more after the establishment of an independent Ireland. However, others aspired to much, much more and, it now appears, may have overestimated the impact of eventual independent statehood on the total process of language revival in the East.

In the early 1920s, when the State was established, there were approximately a quarter million speakers of Irish and most of these were native speakers. More than 50 years later (in 1975), there were some 220,000 self-styled speakers of Irish, either native speakers (largely in the Gaeltacht) or fairly fluent non-native speakers (largely in the East). Such matters are always difficult to estimate, particularly when self-estimates are involved, and, therefore, it should come as no surprise that soon after the above figures were made available another estimate, based on a different data set (1981), arrived at a total of 1,018,413 self-styled speakers (some 31.6% of the total population) of all levels of fluency. Finally, a third and even more recent data set (1983) estimated 13% of the total population to be fluent or native speakers of Irish, a proportion that would translate into approximately 260,000 individuals.[3]

TABLE 5.1 *Percentage of Self-Claimed 'Irish Speakers', Nationwide, by Age group and Year*

| Year/Age | 3–4 yrs % | 15–19 yrs % | 35–44 yrs % | Total Pop.(3+) % |
|---|---|---|---|---|
| 1926 | 4.6 | 27.6 | 11.9 | 18.3 |
| 1936 | 5.5 | 45.3 | 12.3 | 23.7 |
| 1946 | 4.1 | 43.4 | 11.2 | 21.2 |
| 1961 | 5.9 | 50.5 | 26.2 | 27.2 |
| 1971 | 5.5 | 51.5 | 27.2 | 28.3 |
| 1981 | 4.9 | 51.0 | 30.0 | 31.6 |

*Source:* O'Riagáin (1988), from Census of Population, 1981.

The Census of 1981, which we previously cited as indicating that the proportion of Irish speakers in the Gaeltacht was falling, can also be cited to indicate that the proportion of speakers in the country *as a whole* is rising and, if this be so, such growth must be attributed to the increase in non-native speakers there. As Table 5.1 shows, only 4.9% of three- to four-year-olds in the country are claimed to be Irish speakers (a decline from a high of 5.9% in 1961). However, better results are found among adolescents and young adults: 51% of

15- to 19-year-olds claim to be Irish speakers (practically the same as in 1961) and 30% of 35- to 44-year-olds claim to be Irish speakers (up from 26.2% in 1961). Clearly, it is the high-school years in which Irish speaking is most claimed, and the freer access to secondary education since the 60s has certainly contributed to this. Equally clear is the attrition thereafter. Those who were 15-19-year-old in 1961 are a significant sub-group within the cohort of the 35- to 44-year-olds in 1981. The attrition between these two reference points is roughly 20%. But the decline does not stop at that point. The non-transmissibility of the acquired language is so great, particularly in the East, that only a very tiny proportion of the minority that learns to speak the language in high school then hands it on, a decade later, to its own children.

Two glaring faults appear from further analyses of the adolescent-adult-infant data reported above, namely, the general failure, in the past, to teach Irish to working-class youths who do not attend the good academic high schools in which Irish is most frequently and best taught, on the one hand; and, above all, the failure to follow up the well-educated middle-class youths who have mastered Irish during their high school attendance, on the other hand, so that they could more easily form Irish-speaking (or, at least, bilingual) *speech communities* in their post-school years and, thereby, transmit the Irish which they have acquired to a successive generation.

Obviously, a quarter million or so fluent speakers of Irish, in a time of already growing Europeanization of outlook, of industry and of economic prospects as a whole, cannot be considered a total failure by any means. However, neither Bord na Gaeilge, the government's coordinating body for its vast variety of language efforts (spanning education, the Gaeltacht, communications and public service), nor Comhdháil Náisiúnta na Gaeilge, the coordinating body for voluntary language organizations, appear to be pleased at all with what has been accomplished to date. The appreciable sums expended during the past half century (a relatively small proportion of the total governmental budget every year, but an apparently enormous total sum when tallied across all of these years, although even this total comes to well under 10% of all governmental expenditures during this same period) make the results appear meager indeed, and the glowing rhetoric of many language nationalists of an earlier time, when new sacrifices had to be called for and when the long awaited independent State was finally born amid much travail, make today's reality seem paltry indeed. Other endangered languages might be satisfied with a quarter million fluent speakers, three-quarters of a million semi-speakers, and well over a million more language supporters and well-wishers, but the Irish, living in their own country and apparently the masters of their own fates, expected more from themselves. Two questions often arise: (a) what went wrong? and (b) is the effort and expense of RLS worth it, relative to the more painless approach of pursuing

Irishness via English alone? The option of 'Xmen [and Xness] via Yish' that we have frequently discussed in earlier chapters is a very real option indeed in Ireland, and the revival must cope with the awareness that the entire world admires Yeats, Joyce, Wilde and Shaw as 'Irishmen via English".

## A Stage by Stage Attempt to Analyze the Current State of RLS on Behalf of Irish and its Prospects for the Future

*Stages 8 and 7: Reassembling the language and bringing it to adults, some of whom once learned it and still remember it marginally and others of whom never acquired it before*

Because the Gaeltacht had kept the language alive as a language of everyday life, nothing like a reassembly of a vestigial or nearly completely forgotten tongue was necessary in the case of Irish. However, the Gaeltacht was largely a rustic society and most of the literary treasures of the classic Irish past were generally as little known to its inhabitants and as inaccessible to them as they were to their thoroughly anglified brethren in the East. During the last century, however, a huge amount of scholarship, much of it operating under nationalist influence, has rescued, edited, published in modern Irish and often translated into English this entire body of literature, a literature that stands proudly beside the other classical literatures of the Western world and compares favorably with them. More directly related to RLS, however, has been the huge number of Irish courses made available, either at no cost or at purely nominal cost, to adults throughout the land. In the Gaeltacht, Udaras na Gaeltachta, Roinn na Gaeltachta and the Department of Education provide such courses for newcomers, as well as others, subsidize the boarding of teachers and civil servants interested either in acquiring or in improving their Irish, and also support summer and other special courses for secondary school students and for teacher trainees. Indeed such subsidies have been characterized as 'a sort of cottage industry in the Gaeltacht' because of their economic importance to the local population, above and beyond any language learning importance that they may have for outsiders.

Through the Department of the Gaeltacht (Roinn na Gaeltachta) assistance is also provided to voluntary Irish language organizations (many of whom run their own courses), as well as to Irish-language drama, song recitals and musical performances throughout the entire country. All in all, based upon public and private efforts, a very considerable number of Irish books, magazines, newspapers, films, tapes and records (particularly for children and, therefore, also pertinent to stage 6, below) have been produced and made available inexpensively to all those who might be interested in them. There is no doubt that individuals at all levels of education and sophistication can now live a full, varied and stimulating cultural life via Irish as long as they have the necessary opportunities to (re)learn it and are willing to do so. This claim could not have been made half a century ago and is a distinct accomplishment of the total language restoration and revival movement[4]. Having said this, it should also be said that these efforts do not often lead to a real mastery of the language, let alone to its spoken use in daily life or its intergenerational mother tongue transmission.

*Stage 6: Establishing the vital linkage with youth, family, neighborhood and community*

Clearly, no matter how important they may be, courses, concerts and reading or listening matter — whether for the old or for the young — do not themselves create a speech community. Neither goodwill nor competence nor even leisure-time language use translates automatically into the basic building-blocks of home-family-neighborhood-community life that alone can lead to inter- generational language transmission. For such transmission to occur, RLS-efforts must be specifically oriented toward the level of stage 6 and even that may not do the trick without considerable persistence and ingenuity. Both government and voluntary organizations have made some limited attempts to do so, but, as we will see, unfortunately, not with any great success.

## Éigse-Carlow

Éigse-Carlow is an example of various community-based efforts at promoting the Irish language in a 'festival fun' atmosphere in the town of Carlow. It was begun in 1979, as an antidote to the 'school drudgery' image that Irish often conjured up in the public mind and as a weekend event involving traditional music and entertainment, sports events, drama, poetry contests, quiz shows, slide and film presentations, talent contests, open-school visits to all-Irish elementary schools, etc., etc., all being conducted in Irish at various levels of difficulty. As a result of its success, Éigse-Carlow has expanded from a weekend into a two-week affair which is not only a popular and fashionable part of community life in Carlow but which attracts visitors from afar and has come to serve as a model for other towns. What is particularly noteworthy about Carlow is that its energies have not dissipated with success. Many of the town's shops, restaurants and business establishments not only support Éigse, thereby indicating that the festival has become a matter of widely shared civic pride, but they also participate in it themselves, conducting their operations in Irish for the period of the festival. Carlow also owes its voluntary all-Irish primary school (see stage 4a, below) to the enthusiasm engendered by Éigse. Founded in 1982 with 20 students and one teacher, the school now has 215 students and eight teachers and its entering classes are completely 'booked' for years in advance! This is a good example of how RLS activity at the foundational level of stage 6 can foster the social dynamics to support further activity thereafter, even if the efficacy of the reverse sequence is much more questionable, unless carefully directed to feedback to stage 6. The school meets five days a week for 40 weeks in the year, but yet the community (including most of the pupils who attend the school) speaks Irish only two weeks out of the year.[5]

## Glór na nGael

Éigse-Carlow is a specific example of a more general stage 6 RLS-effort known as Glor na nGael (= 'the voice of the Irish"). The latter is an annual competition, established in 1962, for the residential locality that has done the most in the previous 12-month period to increase community use of Irish. In 1982 Carlow was the winner of this competition for the year. Competing localities need to set up a committee that broadly reflects the various institutions, organizations and enterprises of the immediate area, formulate and implement a plan of action, and stand ready to be evaluated on the extent to which they have achieved their target. The annual competition is given nationwide publicity and the President of the Republic always makes the presentation to the winning town.

What the Glór competitions attempt to measure is the progress made via the plans laid and carried out. The actual standard attained or the amount of Irish spoken is not what is at issue in their evaluation, and Gaeltacht communities that are already Irish-speaking are in a class apart and are judged more demandingly. The Glór headquarters (in Dublin) consider it vital that the whole community be aware of what is being planned and that it be harmoniously involved in the planning and implementation efforts, since what is being aimed at, ultimately, is the fostering of community via the language and of the language via community. The community projects undertaken may cover any and all aspects of daily life: public and social affairs, media, commercial life, religious and other church affairs, sports and pastimes, cultural events and festivals and the use of Irish at home and on the streets.

Awards are given in six different categories (Gaeltacht communities, suburbs and cities, localities with under 1,000 inhabitants, localities with between 1,000 and 5,000 inhabitants, localities with between 5,000 and 10,000 inhabitants and localities with between 10,000 and 25,000 inhabitants), with three annual awards in each category and a number of special awards (e.g. use of Irish in youth activities, public service, the media, etc.) as well. The highest rated overall winner also receives the Glór na nGael Trophy (designed by a well-known artist, with the living language symbolized by chirping birds) and a cash award. Prize-giving is normally on the third Sunday of May and is hosted by the national winner. The assistance offered by Glór headquarters includes professional advice pertaining to publicity, implementation, and so on. Glór is obviously a great help in keeping the struggle for Irish before the public and in converting that struggle into something in which the public itself is directly and actively involved, rather than having the language generally remain the passive beneficiary of the efforts of governmental agencies or of the atypical citizens who are members of voluntary organizations[6].

## A variety of other small-scale community efforts

A common characteristic of the Glór projects, as of the Éigse project discussed before, is that their carry-over to and their influence upon the totality of normal, everyday 'post-event' community life is uncertain at best. They are projects of a more partial nature, of a more circumscribed duration and of a more institutionalized sponsorship than normal life typically is for the average speech network of any 'real life' speech community. Various other community-based attempts on behalf of Irish also suffer from most of these same limitations, but make a contribution, however small and non-cumulative, to the Irish-language side-stream of mainstream (English-language) daily life in Ireland. Some churches (both in the Gaeltacht and in Eastern cities) have sensitively introduced a regular service in Irish and these give the language a function and a sponsorship formerly generally unavailable to it. The Feachtas youth clubs, choral groups and the annual festival for youth that has spread from the Gaeltacht throughout the country, all have their limited beneficial effects. The Gaeltacht seminars on the use and development of local natural resources also include attention to language and culture as among the resources to be attended to and cultivated. (A small negative example, in this connection, is the decision of the national authorities not to post highway signs completely in Irish only unless the Irish and English names of localities are sufficiently similar as to be easily recognizable by monolingual anglophones). All in all, these are efforts that constitute motivational and ideological straws in the wind, rather than major determinants of the informal home, family, neighborhood and community life upon which the intergenerational transmissability of a language rests.

Two additional projects of the stage 6 type are somewhat more ambitious and original and deserve to be discussed separately and at somewhat greater length. In County Tipperary, North Riding (a non-Gaeltacht district), eight vocational secondary schools, four church-conducted secondary schools, and onr comprehensive school, together with a number of elementary schools, have joined together to promote Irish outside of the Irish classrooms to which it is normally relegated. The committees that have been formed to plan and oversee this project are highly representative of the community, including representation from educational administrators and teachers (not only teachers of Irish), parents, pupils and various community interests such as elected officials, the churches, the editor of the local newspaper, the county librarian, local banks and businesses, language agencies (both governmental and voluntary) and the local economic development corporation. The major thrust of the project is to encourage and assist members of the community either to use whatever Irish they have (and to do so without embarrassment as to its fluency or error-freeness) or to learn Irish (or more Irish). In addition to relying on a professional publicity campaign, courses (including Irish for Special Purposes for specific service groups), and family vacations in the Gaeltacht, this project also boasts a directory of individuals and businesses willing to use Irish and plans to institute continuous selective monitoring by the Linguistic Institute of Ireland to determine which of its efforts is working (or not working) and with whom. Obviously, it is hoped that what has been begun as a special project of the Glór na nGael type can gain sufficient momentum to develop into a new, self-sustaining sociolinguistic reality, i.e. the launching of Irish-speaking communities in an area where there were previously only 'Irish-liking' and 'Irish-knowing' communities. It remains to be seen, however, whether the definition of community employed in this connection is sufficiently dynamic and intimate home-family process oriented to foster intergenerational mother tongue transmission.

A more centrally focused and integrated, but also more restricted effort is that of Fundúireacht Chlann Lir. The originator of this project is Domhnall O'Lúbhlaí, a language activist who was actually born in New York, christened in the Church of St Francis, in the Bronx, and then brought back to Ireland as a child. A creative and productive originator of projects on behalf of Irish language, culture and general economic development (the latter, focused on the Gaeltacht), O'Lúbhlaí's Chlann Lir is inspired by the conviction that language is basically a societal activity and, therefore, for Irish to be learned and used in real-life communicative fashion, a special mini-societal context must be created for such learning and use. This mini-society will consist of a school, a chapel, student residences, a leisure center (offering Irish entertainment and opportunity to engage in Irish arts and crafts), a museum, staff quarters and, ultimately, even an industrial base. Irish courses will be provided at all levels, with special courses for foreigners, businessmen and workers, including intensive weekend and summer courses. Courses will also be provided in Irish art, music, singing, dance and drama. The entire community will operate under the guidance of 'animateurs' whose goal will be to foster communication via Irish so as to 'make the present the logical continuation of the past' and to maximize involvement and development on the part of its members. Basically, therefore, what O'Lúbhlaí seeks to create is not so much a real community as a stage which approximates such a community, a stage that 'animateurs' can manipulate in order to take language learning and use out of the classroom and into a semblance of daily life enhanced by beauty and dedication[7]. This project is not yet operational but its conceptualization is of an advanced and even of an inspiring sort. Nevertheless, its artificiality is still apparent and its impact upon or carry-over to post-project 'real, informal, intergenerational life' is basically quite questionable.

What is remarkable about the last two undertakings that we have discussed is that they build Irish-speaking quasi- communities, whether on a permanent or on a short-term (language learning) basis. Our presentation of these efforts attempts to reveal how much ingenuity, coordination and effort, not to mention expense and consensus, is still needed in order to concentrate dispersed Irish speakers into normal (rather than 'event-related") speech communities, i.e. into contexts out of which intergenerational language transmissibility can really be nurtured and realistically hoped for. Only such contexts will enable Generation 2 to *build upon* and, therefore, surpass Generation 1, rather than, as has by and large been the case so far, merely to struggle to *catch up with it*.

This, precisely, had been the goal of 'Scéimeanna Pobail' (= Community Projects), a series of planned efforts of Bord na Gaeilge during the early and mid-80s. What was envisaged was a number of newly planned communities where fluent speakers of Irish could concentrate, a planned expansion of the prior tendency for urban 'revivalist' Irish speakers to cluster residentially roughly in the vicinity of an all-Irish school. In these planned ('basic') communities Irish would be the normal means of communication from the very outset, and their hinterland, with which they would necessarily be in constant touch, would be the 'supportive community', consisting of the vast majority of Irishmen whose main language is still English even though almost all of them are fond of Irish, many of them understand quite a bit of Irish and some have a modicum of conversational capacity in the language. These 'basic' communities were thought of as Eastern, urban counterparts to Gaeltacht communities and although initially six such were discussed, more serious consideration was given to an initial two in the Dublin area. Unfortunately, these plans have most recently been abandoned entirely, partially because of inexperience on Bord na Gaeilge's part insofar as field, interventionist and local efforts are concerned (given the prior administrative/bureaucratic, promotional and national focus of the Bord) and partly because such efforts, even were they to be successful, seemed to compete with the local efforts of voluntary agencies who simply could not fathom and strenuously objected to the necessarily sustained community planning approach (rather than the 'special events' approach) that the projected 'basic communities' focus required. As a result of this combination of difficulties, Bord na Gaeilge has returned to coordinating and facilitating 'choice of Irish' in the media, education and all government-related (and dependent) services rather than pursuing the new departure of building genuine all-Irish local communities whose pay-off could be intergenerational transmissibility.[8]

This failure is not merely a failure for Bord na Gaeilge; the voluntary agencies themselves are implicated, as is public opinion as a whole. In returning to the status quo ante, the prior vicious circle has been returned to, the circle that requires language activists of all kinds to run harder and harder in order, at best, to stay in the same place year after year.

*Stage 5: The attainment of literacy, independent of the public education system*

The situation of Irish is different from that of the other endangered languages that we will be examining in detail in this volume and, indeed, different from that of almost all endangered languages throughout the world. In most cases, endangered languages are the receding languages of minority ethnic groups, i.e. languages of ethnocultural groups that are of a different ethnodemographic origin than is the mainstream of the country in which they reside. Since this is not the case in Ireland, the usual distinction between literacy acquisition under Xish auspices and literacy acquisition under Yish auspices no longer obtains and, as we will see below, the usual distinction between type 4a schools and type 4b schools also requires modification. Ymen (Englishmen, Frenchmen, etc.) are not the immediate problem of Irish. The immediate problem is that which we have designated as 'Xmen-via-Yish' and their long-established and secure mainstream claim to being legitimate Irishmen. In a sense, this is an easier problem than the problem of being opposed by hostile or guilt-laden Ymen, but it is also, in another sense, a more difficult problem, because it is the problem of 'we have met the enemy and they are us', i.e. almost everyone in Ireland is partially an 'Xman-via-Yish' too, no matter how devoted he or she may be to the ideal of 'Xmen-via-Xish'. Be this as it may, we will remain with our usual stagewise model, in order to facilitate subsequent systematic comparisons with other endangered languages wherever possible.

Outside of the regular public school system and somewhat related to literacy-readiness are the Naíonraí pre-schools, whose origins (inspired by the Welsh pre-school movement) date back to the late 60s and whose blossoming has occurred during the past ten years. The Naíonraí, mainly play-groups for three- to four-year-year olds, function entirely in Irish and have increased in number from one in 1968 to 185 in 1988, with only about a quarter of this total number being in the Gaeltacht. These pre-school play-groups do not involve direct teaching. They were initially begun on a voluntary basis by interested parents, concerned with the early introduction of their children to Irish or with the amelioration of their too early immersion in English. There were enough of these groups in 1974 that a voluntary coordinating committee for them was set up (Na Naíonraí Gaelacha) and by 1978 a state-funded coordinating committee (An Comhchoiste Réamhscolaíochta) was established to provide training for the group-leaders and various types of back-up assistance for the supervisors of these groups.

The approach of the group-leaders aims at providing a rich language acquisition environment, largely through informal (but carefully sequenced) play and natural communicative situations, utilizing several ancillary teaching aids (cassettes, videos) that have been specifically developed for this purpose. This approach obviously demands a high level of linguistic competence from the group-leaders, about 40% of whom (in 1986) were native speakers, and 10% 'highly competent' non-native speakers, the rest being rated as of 'good competence'. Since so many prior promising efforts pertaining to the revival of Irish have petered out after a number of years, after routinization sets in and the initial glow of innovative efforts has passed, some of the supporters of the Naíonraí are hesitant about over-claiming in connection with the impact of these play-groups. It is true that their 'graduates' acquire proficiency in both comprehension and expression, often go on to (and therefore foster the growth of) all-Irish primary schools, acquire strongly positive attitudes toward the language and reinforce or gratify such attitudes in their parents as well. The play-groups certainly provide clear evidence of great dedication and concern for the future of the Irish language in an active and resourceful segment of the adult community. Unfortunately, however, the Naíonraí are not, in themselves, a solution to the problem of cumulative transmissibility because a fateful score of years pass between the time of 'graduation' from the Naíonraí and the time when the children of these 'graduates' begin to be born. During that score of years the manifold influences of 'Irishness through English' (and of de-ethnization) are generally much stronger than are the influences that foster transmissibility, even though many Naíonraí-attendees do influence current home use of Irish both during and after their attendance. Finally, of course, the Naíonraí are not in themselves meant to be a solution to the problem of literacy acquisition and, accordingly, other agencies must activate the reading-readiness that the play-groups impart to those that attend them (and, of course, to their parents as well).[9]

Somewhat closer to the goal of literacy acquisition that is independent of the public school system are the all-Irish summer language courses *for* young people, and conducted *by* young people, known as Coláiste na bhFiann. The founder of these particular courses was, once again, Domhnall O'Lúbhlaí, to whom we were introduced at stage 6, above. Today, after many years of effort, Coláiste na bhFiann caters to some 2,000 young people at eight different centers around Ireland. Roughly 200 young leaders are involved and some 50 teachers, all of whom by now have themselves come up through the system. In a sense, therefore, Coláiste na bhFiann is not only teaching Irish to youngsters who do not know it and reinforcing Irish in youngsters who already know some, but it is also training a cadre of young people who will be willing and able to be the leaders of the language revival in the future (and of whom some are already functioning as such).

Early on in its history those in charge of Coláiste na bhFiann realized that the summer courses could not, by themselves, maintain from one summer to the next the competence that they had engendered. Most youngsters returning to their homes after their summer's experience at the Coláiste centers quickly lost most of the language skill and the leadership skills that they had acquired there. It was in order to offset this trend that Cumann na bhFiann was founded. Initially, it restricted itself to providing all-Irish youth clubs from September to April, thereby enabling young people both to reinforce what they had learned during the summer and to use the language in an out-of-school setting. Today, Cumann na bhFiann activities are held on a weekly basis with some 1,200 youngsters attending. In more recent years, it has also opened its activities to all college students in Ireland and, indeed, to all young people interested in the language. By now, there is a small but growing stream consisting of past pupils of the summer and school-year youth programs who have married with one another and are rearing their own children through Irish. This, indeed, is the very cumulative intergenerational transmissibility that we have mentioned so often, but its dimensions are still minute and its geographic concentration (so that real 'community' in the *Gemeinschaft* sense can be fostered among its members) is still unattended to.

The Coláiste na bhFiann idea has had two additional fruitful outcroppings. The first of these is Dúshlán (= challenge). It prepares and involves some of those who have attended Colaiste na bhFiann to function as teachers of Irish to anglophone parents whose children are attending all-Irish schools. By learning Irish, these parents are enabled to continue and reinforce the work of these schools via the home-and-family life of the pupils. By utilizing 'believers' rather than paid teachers, the full impact of commitment is added to the teaching–learning process in which Dúshlán members participate. Finally, there is Clann na bhFiann, the parent section of Coláiste na bhFiann, which sponsors a host of social activities and also, and most important for our discussion here, language classes which involve both listening/speaking but also reading/writing. Soon the Clann's members may increasingly consist of individuals who have themselves gone through the entire Coláiste experience, thereby potentially representing another small gain for transmissibility.[10]

*Stage 4: Education in Irish and learning Irish at school*

As mentioned before, the general contrast between type 4a and type 4b schools does not really apply to Ireland, particularly with the state's eagerness to subsidize and coordinate successful ventures that initially develop in the often more imaginative and innovative voluntary sector. Nevertheless, at various times in recent Irish history, there have been strictly voluntary schools attended in lieu of compulsory education and many of the all-Irish elementary schools functioning today were initiated in that fashion, even though they are today part of the network of governmentally provided education. One of the causes leading to such schools was the complaint of pro-Irish parents concerning the low proficiency of most non-native teachers of Irish and their non-use of Irish outside of class. Another obvious cause has been the increasing number of 'graduates' of the Naíonraí pre-school groups. Their hard-won Irish competence would have been completely lost had they attended the generally available public schools, in 94% of which Irish is taught only as a second language and in which precious little proficiency is generally attained. As a result of both of the above factors, community initiative (rather than governmental policy) has led to a revived interest in all-Irish elementary schools (after the government abandoned its previous 'compulsory Irish' approach) and the overall decline in the *number* of such schools since 1960-61 may ultimately be reversed, now that the decline in

TABLE 5.2 *Types of Elementary Schools in Ireland*

| School Year | Entirely Irish Medium | Partially Irish Medium | Irish as a Second Lang. | Total No. of Schools |
|---|---|---|---|---|
| 1930/31 | 228 = 4% | — | 5,150 = 96% | 5,378 |
| 1940/41 | 623 = 12% | 2,193 = 43% | 2,261 = 45% | 5,077 |
| 1950/51 | 523 = 11% | 1,955 = 40% | 2,509 = 49% | 4,987 |
| 1960/61 | 420 = 9% | 2,055 = 42% | 2,405 = 49% | 4,880 |
| 1970/71* | 194 = 5% | 49 = 1% | 3,874 = 94% | 4,117 |
| 1980/81 | 161 = 5% | 21 = 1% | 3,112 = 94% | 3,294 |

*New assessment criteria introduced
*Source:* Department of Education, Annual Statistical Reports. (Adapted from O'Riagáin, 1988)

the *proportion* of such schools finally ended in 1980/81 (see Table 5.2). Fifty of these schools are now in English-speaking areas and it is there that the bulk of

their more immediate future growth is expected. Unlike the early twentieth century version of this type of program, these latter-day all-Irish schools are genuinely of grass-roots origin, not merely being established by local parental
support, but becoming foci for the establishment of demographically concentrated Irish-speaking networks in their vicinities. The huge majority of the pupils in
these schools meet the high levels of Irish proficiency that are expected of them
and, in addition, their overall academic achievement is on a par with or exceeds
that of children attending those schools in which a negligible dose of Irish as a
Second Language is offered. These all-Irish schools are now governmentally
supported and it remains to be seen whether any real growth in their numbers, in
their proportion of all schools and in their excellence can be maintained and
augmented. At the moment they are a small and still fragile phenomenon, one
that is very promising but also one that reaches only a very limited proportion of
all of Ireland's children, almost all of them being *de facto* restricted to middle-
class clienteles.[11]

As for type 4b schools, there is not much that needs to be said about them.
Those who are highly committed to the maintenance and fostering of Irish have
no confidence at all in the schools that teach Irish as a second language and that
do not use Irish as their medium of instruction. Thus, even in their own country,
i.e. in a country where no ethnic distinction separates pro-RLSers from the
majority or mainstream of society, a distinction is needed between type 4a and
type 4b schools. This distinction is based on the voluntary or self-selected preference of pro-RLSers for type 4a schools. A by-product of this self-selection is
the accentuation of the class bias in the RLS effort, with all-Irish schools being
primarily for middle-class children and most working-class children attending
the ordinary schools and learning very little Irish in the process.

*Stage 3: Irish in the worksphere*

Irish has found a place for itself in the non-governmental work sphere only
in very minor ways outside of the Irish-speaking Gaeltacht. Despite the
economic recession and cutbacks that have typified the 80s, employment has
remained relatively stable in Gaeltacht industries due to the special
governmental concern that the exodus from those areas be kept as small as
possible. In this connection, some essentially non-governmental enterprises have
been established with an express policy of using Irish, e.g. certain cooperatives
and various special projects, some of which have also benefited from short-term
outside support. Nevertheless, emergency measures have recently been
increasingly called for if the economic and social condition of the Gaeltacht,
including its linguistic situation, is to be salvaged. Greater involvement of the
local population in improved planning, and greater self-help programs in
conjunction with such planning, in order to counteract the image of the

Gaeltacht and its inhabitants (and their language) as hopeless and endless 'charity cases", have also frequently been mentioned. On the other hand, no serious plans for Irish in the work sphere, whether with Irish speakers working among other Irish speakers or among English speakers, are currently underway outside of the Gaeltacht. Perhaps this is only to be expected, given the greater consolidation and development that are still urgently needed in connection with stages 6, 5 and 4a, above.[12]

### Stage 2: Local governmental services and media

A few of the Gaeltacht areas operate administratively entirely in Irish (e.g. all of the committees and institutions of the Parish of Cnoc in Cois Fharraige) but this is not generally the case, neither there nor in the Eastern counties. Elsewhere, the Civil Service has units that voluntarily operate in Irish (i.e. in Irish also) and Irish competence exams have long been given to Civil Service employees with promotions and raises as rewards to those scoring well on them. A special agency, Gaeleagras, was founded in 1971, in the Department of Finance, to promote Irish in the Civil Service. Gaeleagras offers day and evening Irish courses, conducted in Irish, throughout the year, and also organizes social and cultural events that are conducted in Irish, in order to create an environment in which Irish is spoken naturally among civil servants. However, the distinction might well be made between civil servants learning Irish for their own personal use and appreciation, and civil servants learning Irish in order to serve the public in Irish. There may well be more of the former than of the latter and, at the same time, there are inevitably some pro-RLSers who want to be served in Irish at their local governmental offices but who cannot be accommodated in that connection because the local civil servants do not always happen to include any Irish speakers in their ranks.

Radio na Gaeltachta, which began regular broadcasts in 1972, provides programs in Irish for the country as a whole and for the Gaeltacht in particular. It has been able to 'introduce' the scattered Gaeltachts to each other, on the one hand, and to enable various accomplished speakers of Irish, from wherever they may hail and wherever they may live, to be recognized far and wide for their 'rare skill". The Irish radio programs are also a resource for language learners, although their efficacy in this connection really remains to be demonstrated. All in all, it is quite possible that more Irish speakers are anglified via the ocean of English radio than English speakers are strengthened in their Irish via the single existing channel of Irish radio. This suspicion is multiplied in connection with television. Quite recently, an all-Irish television station has been announced (initially serving the Gaeltacht) and it is current policy to expand Irish language programs and to transmit them within a designated time band so that those who want them will be less likely to miss them. There is also a new effort to translate children's television programs into Irish. However, none of these efforts are likely to compete with either the amount or the diversity of constantly available English television, and the advisability of concentration on such competition, rather than on more urgent and more intergenerationally transmissible stage 6, 5 and 4b enterprises, is questionable indeed.[13]

### Stage 1: Irish in the higher spheres of work, education and government

Irish at work, Irish in governmental services and Irish in the mass media are all efforts replete with tokenism (as is, basically, Irish in type 4b education). Perhaps that is inevitable in a society in which Xish has been displaced and replaced to such an extent and in which the model of being 'Xmen in Yish' is so well established, in time, in status and in numbers. That being the case, it can come as no surprise that stage 1 as well is so largely an exercise in tokenism, even where Irish is still (decreasingly) required for admission to university study or to government employment. In Parliament, formal motions are usually in Irish and all statutes are published completely in bilingual versions, even though debates are almost entirely in English. The metal coin of the realm is entirely in Irish, while paper money and postage stamps are bilingual, as are the letterheads of government agencies (with the Irish always coming first and in larger typeface). Outside of courses pertaining to specialization in the Irish language itself there is a mere scintilla of Irish medium courses in higher education, and Irish medium tertiary level courses of a non-academic kind are similarly rare and rather humdrum when they do exist. This tokenism is regrettable and regretted by many staunch pro-RLSers, but the latter generally reverse any cause and effect linkage that may exist between such tokenism and the state of Irish today. Today, it may not really be profitable to devote major energies to reversing this tokenism, which does, after all, keep the image of Irish before the public, an image that pro-RLSers must then cultivate and intensify. Major RLS-efforts and energies might be much more crucially and transmissibly applied at stages 6, 5 and 4a, because it is at those stages that the true battle for the future of Irish (i.e. for its steadily increased cumulative transmissibility) is being waged and where additional significant victories must be won, and won relatively quickly, i.e. before the Irish become weary of the lack of success in their pursuit of Irish as a 'generally spoken language' and settle, once and for all (as have most of those in their government), for tokenism alone. The penchant of the politicians for tokenism is truly amazing. At the earliest stage of RLS it was attracted to tokenism in the Gaeltacht. When that failed, it was attracted to tokenism in the schools. When that too failed, it was finally attracted toward tokenism in governmental legal and administrative forms and outer symbols, the ultimate retreat into meaninglessness *vis-á-vis* the daily life of ordinary human beings.

## Concluding Remarks

We have devoted considerable space to Irish RLS-efforts because Irish is a good example of a very difficult (perhaps the most difficult) situation which has been worked at without major success for many years and, nevertheless, one that has produced more good ideas and gratifying accomplishments in recent years than it is generally given credit for. There has been disillusionment, but it has not overcome the RLSers. There has been a surfeit of governmental bureaucracy and monopolization of support or control, but local voluntary initiatives still continue unabated and have, in recent years, begun once again to stress truly basic issues and stages and to recognize that local voluntary efforts are often in a better position to achieve breakthroughs than are ponderous, costly, centrally controlled, nationwide efforts.

Emigration and economic reverses continue to sap the strength of Irish in the Gaeltacht and in the East, but there is also growth in the East and an adamant (and very Irish) RLS stance in the very face of defeat. The amount of governmental financial support for Irish has always been *relatively* small (it is difficult to pinpoint the exact amount, but the total may have been no more than 4 million pounds in 1985 and even somewhat less in 1986; as these lines are being written the Bord na Gaeilge budget and the membership of the Bord itself for 1989–90 have still not been set or approved) but there has been a growing recognition that many crucial things can be done and noteworthy results attained even without funds or with very meager funds. There are still too many attempts to merely translate the Anglo-Irish life style into Irish, but there is a growing realization that the model of being 'Xmen via Xish' yields and requires an authentic legitimacy of its own and must not merely be a translation of the modernity that will always be more plentifully and effectively available in English than in Irish.

It is hard to continue the RLS struggle for so many years without energies being dissipated and without the over- institutionalization or routinization of RLS thinking and acting. Nevertheless, new ideas have appeared and at the most crucial stages at that. Even the European Economic Community has been enlisted so that pro-RLSers can be in a stronger position to bring pressure on their state and on their society to do as much for Irish as some other European governments are doing and preparing to do for their local, indigenous but ethnically side-stream languages (e.g. Catalan and Basque), while at the same time even less fortunate 'lesser used languages' in Europe (e.g. Frisian) are pointing to Irish, in order to obtain more government attention than has been their lot.

Without focusing squarely on the home-family-neighborhood- community concentration of Irish speakers, particularly in the East, it may be unrealistic to pursue the old goal of ultimately making Irish a general language of communication throughout Ireland, but is not unrealistic to seek to socialize an ever larger proportion of the population into more fluent bilingualism and to permanently keep them so as spokesmen and as advocates of one valid model of modern Irish life. RLSers in Ireland give the lie to the claim that Ireland never seriously considered making the Irish language its everyday vehicle of communication[15]. There has been a lot of governmental tokenism, of course, but there has been a lot of RLS dedication, a lot of ingenuity, a lot of hard work and, in recent years, a new recognition of where the brunt of future effort should be placed. Ireland is a test case that all RLSers everywhere must ponder carefully, so that the can benefit from its lessons, including the lesson of how to avoid 'Irelandization', i.e. the peripheralization of Xish in Xland.[16]

Without a century of RLS-efforts, Irish would certainly be in far worse straights than it is today. (Compare Irish with the current state of Scottish Gaelic, for which serious, organized efforts have only recently begun, with only some 80,000 scattered speakers.) Nevertheless, the full potential of the Irish situation never seems to have been tapped, as can be seen from the fact that even today fully two thirds of the population agrees that Irish is crucial for maintaining Irish identity but half of those who agree with this view have no speaking ability with respect to Irish themselves. Obviously there is an opportunity here that is not being addressed. Even today, the Irish government has not interceded to make its 'first official language' a co-official language of the European Community, as many other governments associated with indigenous 'lesser used languages' have done (even when those are not their 'first official languages'). Little wonder then that Irishmen vacationing in Europe often speak Irish to each other when within earshot of locals, so as not to be mistaken for Englishmen, but when they return to Ireland and are no longer in need of a contrastive identity, they wonder whether the 'useless time' spent studying Irish at school shouldn't be 'put to better time studying German' or some other language of importance in the European Community.

Nearly three quarters of a century of combined voluntary and governmental failure to make Irish a 'generally spoken language of Ireland' is a terrible burden for RLS to carry today. It raises the question, particularly after the abandonment of the 'community projects' approach in the late 80s, as to whether that is really a feasible goal anymore, or whether the intergenerational transmission of school-Irish as a second (or third) language isn't all that should be generally aimed at. That too would be a noteworthy accomplishment and one which is even now not too far from realistic attainment. The burden of well-established and world-renowned Irishness-via-English, taken together with the additional burden of 'living down' its own failures to tackle the right tasks at the right time and in the right way during the past three or four generations, may fully justify and even require the honest setting of new and more realistic RLS goals in Ireland in the near future. Having made the 'voluntary' RLS organizations fully dependent on governmental financing, on the one hand, and having become more and more withdrawn from any genuine concern for furthering spoken Irish on a country-wide basis, on the other hand, there may be much to be said for publicly admitting that all that one can hope for in the foreseeable future is focused on stages 7 and 4. Indeed, such an admission would not change very much in practice.

By focusing most of its attention on stages 4a and above, and by limiting its efforts on behalf of stage 6 to episodic experiences, Ireland has achieved most of what schools can be expected to achieve—an intergenerationally transmitted second language primarily associated with late adolescence — and that achievement seems to have been fairly successfully stabilized. That in itself is no mean achievement — indeed, it is an unrecognized (even if non-maximalist) RLS success story. Perhaps the gaze of RLSers should be directed to it more acceptingly (it too would not have been attained without their major input), rather than at the empty half of the glass which cannot be filled by efforts that are so removed from the real nexus of intergenerational mother tongue transmission. Perhaps the RLS tradition of not addressing the real problem is now too well-established to be overcome on any large-scale basis in Ireland. The time for thanking God for minor blessings (or, in more secular terms, to 'either fish or cut bait') may be at hand. This is an issue that now genuinely belongs on the RLS agenda, both tactically and ideologically.

What the revivalists have accomplished against great odds, and their current levels of devotion, achievement and involvement, all border on the miraculous; but the time may have come to realize that these attainments and characteristics cannot set the norm for Ireland as a whole and that future RLS policy may require separate approaches and standards of evaluation for different segments of Irish society. RLSers might do well to realize that not having swept the field or completely reversed the tide is not a sign of defeat but, rather, a level of accomplishment that must be evaluated against what would most probably have obtained had they not entered the fray at all; in the Irish case, this is not only very considerable but enough to safeguard the continuation of Xmen-via-Xish for the foreseeable future. The lack of attainment at the level of mother-tongue acquisition and transmission, particularly when measured at the nationwide level, does not mean that other types of transmission are similarly unlikely (see Chapter 12, below) nor that some reasonable and judicious growth in intergenerational mother tongue transmission *per se* is out of the question. Indeed, many threatened languages in Europe and elsewhere would consider themselves fortunate to achieve during the coming century the level of RLS that Irish has achieved during the past century.[17]

## Notes

1. For a review of the profound sociocultural dislocations that contributed to the original endangerment of Irish, see de Freine, 1965. The rebirth of Irish interest in this topic, one so long overlooked (and, therefore, de Freine's work is entitled 'The Great Silence"), can be gauged from Edward's extensive (but still incomplete) bibliography (1983). For the earlier Communist opposition to the Irish revival see British and Irish Communist Party, 1972. (The current Communist Party of Ireland has adopted a favorable position toward Irish and has appointed Irish speakers to several key positions.) Brief sociolinguistic reviews of the pre-State and early State efforts on behalf of Irish may be found in Dorian (1988), Macnamara (1971), O'Ciosáin (in press) and O'Tuama (1970). For a discussion of the more general long-term decline of Celtic languages see Durkacz (1983). For some indications of the infinitely worse situation of Scottish Gaelic, in contrast to Irish (Irish Gaelic), see Withers (1984).
2. Census figures and other estimates of Irish speakers in the Gaeltacht and elsewhere are reported by Dorian (1988), O'Ciosáin (in press), Fennell (1981), O'Riagáin (1988), and O'Riagáin and O'Gliasáin (1984). The main sources of attitudinal data are Committee on Irish Language Attitudes (1975) and Market Survey Report (1977).
3. The Census estimate for 1975 is reported in Greene (1981); for 1981 and 1983 in O'Riagáin (1988).
4. Stage 7 programs for adults are reviewed in O'Ciosáin (in press).
5. My information on Éigse-Carlow is from an Éigse-Carlow brochure (1988) and from a personal communication from Bride de Roiste (1988).
6. My information concerning Glór na nGael is from a brochure by Nora Welby (1978), the secretary of Glor na nGael.
7. My information on the County Tipperary and the Chlann Lir projects is from a memorandum by Helen O'Murchú (1988a).
8. The 'basic community' project of Bord na Gaeilge is discussed in the Bord's publications dated 1981, 1983 and 1985 as well as in the thoughtful analysis of the Bord's work by Hilary Tovey (1988). That there is still some interest in establishing housing projects in which Irish speakers can concentrate and be close to other RLS institutions is evidenced by the July 1988 'development proposal' *Bath Place Blackrock*, 'a proposed bilingual [housing] complex' in Dublin, aiming at 'a genuinely bilingual ethos' under private auspices but with the 'active encouragement of Bord na Gaeilge and other relevant agencies'.
9. My information concerning the Naíonraí play-groups is derived from Helen O'Murchú (1987) and from Máirtín O'Murchú (memorandum, 1988).
10. My information on Coláiste na bhFiann, Dúshlán, Clann na bhFiann and Chlann Lir is from a memorandum by Helen O'Murchú (1988b). Several of these initially voluntary efforts now receive state support and Irish literacy is a component (although not the major goal) of each of these efforts.
11. Information on type 4a schools is provided by Harris (1988), O'Riagáin (1988) and by O'Riagáin and O'Gliasáin (1984). See O'hAolain (1989) for the lament that as of December 1988 there was no educational software for Irish in primary schools. Although efforts are underway to remedy this situation 'there is a danger that we could end up with the ultimate Orwellian horror of videos and computers speaking Irish Gaelic with adults and children listening uncomprehendingly to the language of their ancestors'.

12. My information on Irish in the work sphere is from a personal communication from O'Baoill (1988) and from O'Ciosáin (in press).
13. The following have contributed to my information regarding Irish on radio and television: O'Baoill, personal communication, O'Ciosáin (in press), O'Fiannachta, personal communication and O'Riagáin, personal communication. As to the linguistic standardization and corpus planning needs of the non-print media (not to mention those of the schools and their primarily print media), see Chapter 11, below.
14. My information on Irish in central government and higher education is derived from O'Baoill, personal communication, O'Ciosáin (in press), Dorian (1988), and O'Fiannachta, personal communication.
15. The view that language revival (in the sense of intergenerational mother tongue transmission) was never a serious goal of the Irish independence movement is expressed by Joan Rubin (1983) in her 'Evaluation of status planning: What has the past decade accomplished?'. I believe that Rubin mistakenly takes routinized governmental actions as adequate definers of the RLS-movement's goals rather than as compromises — often unnecessary and unthinking compromises — with those goals.
16. Additional useful references, beyond those already cited, are Advisory Planning Committee (1986, 1989), Doyle and Rosenstock (1980), Hanly (1931), Irish Marketing Surveys (1988), Little et al. (1986), O'Ciosáin (1983, 1988), O'Murchú and O'Murchú (1988), O'Murchú (1986a, 1986b), O' Riagáin (1986), Verdoodt (1989) and Williams (1988).
17. Helen and Máirtín O'Murchú have commented on an earlier draft of this chapter and I am greatly indebted to them for their assistance, not only throughout this chapter but throughout my many visits to Ireland and many years of 'Irish watching' from afar. Needless to say, however, neither they nor any of the others whom I have named above are in any way responsible for (nor, generally, either aware of or necessarily in agreement with) the interpretations and gratuitous advice contained in this chapter. This chapter reflects the readings, views and circumstances known to me as of mid-1989. Advisory Planning Committee (1989) appeared at that very time, too late for more than a mere mention in these pages. I was subsequently invited by Bord na Gaeilge to comment on this report in detail and was delighted to note extensive areas of agreement between my views and those of the APC as well as, of course, some inevitable areas of disagreement (particularly in connection with the Committee's assumption that informal social life is entirely outside of the grasp of language planning efforts). The report is extremely well done and should be considered required reading by all RLSers everywhere.

# References

ADVISORY PLANNING COMMITTEE 1986, *Irish and the Education System: An Analysis of Examination Results*. Dublin, Bord na Gaeilge.
— 1989, *The Irish Language in a Changing Society; Shaping the Future*. Dublin: Bord na Gaeilge.
BORD NA GAEILGE 1981, Sceimeanna Pobail: Final Report of Coiste Comhairleach to Bord na Gaeilge. Dublin: Bord na Gaeilge (unpublished).
— 1983, *Action Plan for Irish 1983–1986*. Dublin: Bord na Gaeilge.
— 1985, *Tuarascail Bhliantuil/Annual Report*. Dublin: Bord na Gaelige.

BRITISH AND IRISH COMMUNIST ORGANIZATION 1972, *The Irish Language: Revivalism and the Gaeltacht*. Policy Statement No. 5, May. Belfast: British and Irish Communist Party.

COMMINS, Patrick 1988, Socioeconomic development and language maintenance in the Gaeltacht. *International Journal of the Sociology of Language* 70, 11–28.

COMMITTEE ON IRISH LANGUAGE ATTITUDE RESEARCH 1975, *Report; As Submitted to the Minister for the Gaeltacht, October 1975*. Dublin: The Stationery Office.

DAVIS, Thomas [1845] 1945, *Essays and Poems with a Centenary Memoir*. Dublin: Gill.

DE FREINE, Sean 1965, *The Great Silence*. Dublin: Foilseachain Naisiunta Teoranta.

DORIAN, Nancy C. 1988, The Celtic languages in the British Isles In Christina B. PAULSTON (ed.) *International Handbook of Bilingualism and Bilingual Education*. New York: Greenwood, 109– 139.

DOYLE, Bill and Gabriel ROSENSTOCK 1980, *Slógadh*. Dublin: Rialtas na hEireann.

DURKACZ, V. E. 1983, *The Decline of the Celtic Languages*. Edinburgh: John Donald.

EDWARDS, John 1983, *The Irish Language; An Annotated Bibliography of Sociolinguistic Publications 1772–1982*. New York: Garland.

FENNELL, D. 1981, Can a shrinking linguistic minority be saved? In E. HAUGEN *et al.* (eds) *Minority Languages Today*. Edinburgh: Edinburgh University Press, 32–9.

GREENE, David 1981, The Atlantic group: Neo-Celtic and Faroese. In E. HAUGEN *et al.* (eds) *Minority Languages Today*. Edinburgh: Edinburgh University Press, 1–9.

HANLEY, Joseph 1931, *The National Ideal: A Practical Exposition of True Nationality Appertaining to Ireland*. Dublin: Dollard.

HARRIS, John 1988, Spoken Irish in the primary school system. *International Journal of the Sociology of Language* 70, 69–87.

IRISH MARKETING SURVEYS 1988, *Public Attitudes to Irish in Schools; Presentation of National Survey Findings, October 1988*. Dublin: Bord na Gaeilge.

LITTLE, David, Helen O'MURCHU and David SINGLETON 1986, *Towards a Communicative Curriculum for Irish*. Dublin: Center for Language and Communication Studies, Trinity College.

MACNAMARA, John 1971, Successes and failures in the movement for the restoration of Irish. In Joan RUBIN and Bjorn JERNUDD (eds) *Can Language be Planned?* Honolulu: The University Press of Hawaii, 65–94.

MARKET SURVEY REPORT 1979, *Research Report on Attitudes to a Publicity Campaign for the Irish Language*. Dublin: Market Attitude Studies Ltd.

O'BAOILL, Brian 1988, Personal communication.

O'CIOSAIN, Seamus 1983, Bilingualism in public administration: The case of Ireland. *Revista de Llengua i Dret* 1, 11–19.

— 1988, Language planning and Irish: 1965–74. *Language Culture and Curriculum*.

— 1990, *Language Planning: The Case of Ireland (1922–1975)*. In press.

O'HAOLAIN, Pádraig 1989, Information technology and the language. International Conference on Provision for Minority Languages, Stornoway (Isle of Lewis), October 4–6, 1989. Mimeographed, pp. 14–16.

O'MURCHU, Helen 1987, *Pre-Primary Education in Some European Lesser Used Languages*. Dublin: European Bureau for Lesser Used Languages.

— 1988a, Local collaboration towards incremental language use. Personal Memorandum.

— 1988b, A logical progression or necessity is the mother of invention. Personal Memorandum.

O'MURCHU, Máirtín 1986a, The retreat from Irish: the statistical analysis and other aspects. In J. DOOGE (ed.) *Ireland in the Contemporary World; Essays in Honor of*

*Garret Fitzgerald*. Dublin: Gill and Macmillan, 112–21.

— 1986b, Irish and English now. *pogrom* No. 121, 24–5.

— 1988, Pre-schooling in Irish: a success story. Personal Memorandum.

O'MURCHU, Michael W. and Helen O'MURCHU (eds) 1988, *Aspects of Bilingual Education: The Italian and the Irish Experience* . Dublin: Bord na Gaeilge.

O'RIAGÁIN, Padraig 1986, The demise of the Irish language. *pogrom*. No. 121, 20–4.

— 1988, Bilingualism in Ireland, 1973–1983: an overview of national sociolinguistic surveys. *International Journal of the Sociology of Language* 70, 29–51.

O'RIAGÁIN, P. and O'GLIASAIN, M. 1979, *All-Irish Primary Schools in the Dublin Area: A Sociological and Spatial Study of the Impact of All-Irish Schools on Home and Social Use of Irish*` Dublin: Institiuid Teangeolaiochta Eireann.

— 1984, *The Irish Language in the Republic of Ireland, 1983: Preliminary Report of a National Survey*. Dublin: Institiuid Teangeolaiochta Eireann.

O'TUAMA, Sean (ed.) 1970, *The Gaelic League Idea*. Cork and Dublin: Mercier Press.

RUBIN, Joan 1983, Evaluation of status planning: what has the past decade accomplished? In J. COBARRUBIAS and J. A. FISHMAN (eds) *Progress in Language Planning* Berlin: Mouton, 329–44.

TOVEY, Hilary 1988, The state and the Irish language: the role of Bord na Gaeilge. *International Journal of the Sociology of Language* 70, 53–68.

VERDOODT, Albert 1989, *Western Europe* (vol. 3 of H. KLOSS and G. D. MCCONNELL (eds) *The Written Languages of the World: A Survey of the Degree and Modes of Use*). Quebec: Laval University Press, HH3–50. (For Basque and Frisian, see pp. 249–60 and 583–9.)

WELBY, Nora 1987, *Glor na nGael Competition: Irish, the Bond of the Community*. Dublin: Glor na nGael.

WILLIAMS, Colin H. 1988, Language planning and regional development: lessons from the Irish Gaeltacht. In his (ed.) *Language in Geographic Context*. Clevedon: Multilingual Matters, 267–301.

WITHERS, Charles W. J. 1984, *Gaelic in Scotland, 1698–1981: The Geographic History of a Language*. Edinburgh: John Donald.

# 6   The Cases of Basque and Frisian

The RLS status of Basque and Frisian may be instructively compared to that of Irish. The rosy possibilities that glimmer today for Basque are not unlike those that were still envisioned three and four generations ago for Irish, when RLS-efforts in Ireland were still fresh and promising. There is in the Autonomous Basque Community (to be defined below), as there was once in the newly established independent part of Ireland, a sense of practically unlimited opportunities for the language. At last the abused and neglected language seems/seemed to have found a champion who would do battle for it and carry the day against the traditional rival who had, over centuries, syphoned off so many of its best sons and daughters as well as its most crucial and power-and-modernity related functions. Frisian, on the other hand, may represent what is yet in the offing for Irish, if the state and the bulk of society successfully disengage from its cultivation even more than is the case today. Political and cultural establishments tend to withdraw from or seek to find alternatives to seemingly unending and hopeless struggles. In the RLS arena, prolonged and consistent failure to secure intergenerational mother tongue transmission tends to degenerate into mere intergenerational 'heritage language admiration' and the part-time cultivation thereof at the level of a favorite hobby.

It is still too early to tell whether Basque will re-establish the solid links with the home family-neighborhood-community life nexus of intergenerational mother tongue transmission, links that Irish failed to make during the springtime of its own RLS-efforts. The next generation will tell the story *vis-á-vis* Basque, and at the same time it will become clear whether Irish RLS-efforts will slip into the quiet and querulous hush that increasingly surrounds Frisian RLS-efforts today.

The two languages (and language communities) to which we turn our attention in this section are comparable in some important respects. Both the Basques and the Frisians are indigenous minorities within democratic, modern Western European states. Both inhabit moderately prosperous regions and, as a result (and very much unlike Ireland) they have experienced relatively more in-migration than out-migration for many years. The major sociolinguistic consequence of these processes is that both Basques and Frisians are now ethnoculturally threatened within their own regions, the threat being a two-pronged one: from 'co-ethnics' (Xmen) who have relinguified, on the one hand, and from 'other-ethnics' (Ymen) who have imported and imposed the integrative languages of their respective states, Spanish and Dutch respectively, into the very midst of local ('regional") life and culture. The resulting erosion of Basque and Frisian has been massive, to the extent that in both cases use of the indigenous languages has become rather atypical for many Xmen on most occasions. Accordingly larger-scale, more coordinated RLS-efforts on behalf of both languages, going substantially beyond those initiated even as far back as two or more centuries ago, began to be implemented during the past two decades.

## Background to Basque RLS-Efforts

Basque speakers constitute roughly a quarter of the population of the Basque Autonomous Community (hereafter: BAC), an entity consisting of the northern Spanish provinces of Gipuzkoa, Bizkaia and Araba. We will deal here only with Basque in the BAC context, excluding from our consideration both the Basque area in France and the Province of Navarre; see Figures 6.1 and 6.2.) After the death of the Fascist dictator, Francisco Franco (1892–1975), whose relationship with the Basques had consistently been a particularly punitive one in view of their totally uncompromising and unexpectedly prolonged resistance to his ultimately successful insurgency against the Spanish Republic (1936–1939) a Statute of Autonomy was quickly approved (in 1978 by the central [Spanish] government, as part of the new Spanish Constitution, and in 1979, by referendum on the part of the population of the Basque region itself[1]) and a Basque Government was established.

In 1979 the central government acquiesced to pressures emanating primarily from Basques and Catalans alike and also issued a 'Decree on Bilingualism' which, while declaring Spanish to be the nationwide official language and guaranteeing the rights of Spanish speakers everywhere to use their language in all public and institutional functions, provided that all public school pupils in regions with indigenous languages must receive *at least* three to five hours of instruction per week in those languages, during both their elementary and secondary education, and that a modicum of central funding would also be made available for any school giving even greater curricular prominence to its respective regional language. Thus, at long last, there began a new and hopefully happier chapter in Basque cultural history, but this new beginning came at a time when Basque had already suffered centuries of neglect and even persecution and, as a result, was in a seriously weakened position both functionally and attitudinally.

1  SPAIN
2  FRANCE
3  BASQUE  COUNTRY
4  GALICIA
5  CATALONIA

FIGURE 6.1 *'The Basque Country' (including the 'Basque Autonomous Community') and the major other minority language areas of Spain and South-Western France*
(*Source:* Cobarrubias and Lasa, 1987)

Throughout the centuries of Basque history prior to 1979 the Basque language had rarely been effectively nurtured at a dependably continuous societal level, whether for governmental, literary or scholarly purposes. Instead, for centuries, many of the Basques who learned Spanish gave up Basque (with the notable exception of certain Church jurisdictions) and even joined the ranks of those who heaped abuse upon it, as if it were a comical (at best) and barbaric (at worst) monstrosity. Most of those who retained their command of Basque, with the exception of regrettably few churchmen, other intellectuals and outspoken nationalists over a span of centuries, largely lived in isolated rural, agricultural and pastoral districts and learned little or no Spanish. When commercial and industrial centers began to develop in the Basque region, Basque society and culture generally acquired and retained only a relatively small Basque-speaking urban middle class. Finally, as a result of all of the above processes, the Spanish-speaking newcomers to the Basque region — particularly those coming to its more urban areas — typically found it neither possible, desirable nor even imaginable that they learn Basque. This is the heritage that the Basque government must overcome — as evidenced today by the fact that probably only about a quarter (or even less) of the roughly 3 million inhabitants of the BAC can speak Basque reasonably well and only 21% of 15- to 17-year-olds in the region believe that it is even necessary to speak Basque in order to be Basque. There is some small consolation in the fact that the latter percentage is even as high as it is. It falls to only 15% among 25- to 27-year-olds, that is, among young people who were already almost out of school when the new Basquization efforts got underway[2] and, therefore, there is good reason to claim that RLS matters have improved somewhat in quite recent years and that they have done so precisely in the age group most likely soon to begin families of their own.

The efforts of the Basque government on behalf of Basque are guided by the 'Basic Law on the Standardization of the Basque Language (Euskara)' adopted in 1982. Indeed, this law entrusts to the public authorities not only the strengthening of the use of Basque and the standardization of its written form but also its 'normalization', given that it is not only 'part of the cultural heritage of the Basque people' and 'the most viable and objective sign of our Community', but, also, 'together with Spanish, an *official language within the Autonomous Community*'. 'Normalization' may not be an entirely appropriate word for what the Basque government has undertaken in this connection, since what is involved is not really the intra-language task of returning to all the usual ('normal') H-functions (high culture and power functions) which it once discharged. As we have noted above, Basque rarely discharged any such functions in the past. Rather, the task of 'normalization' in the Basque context pertains to acquiring new functions, hitherto ('normally') discharged by Spanish, at the very same time that Spanish remains co-official and very often even dominant in

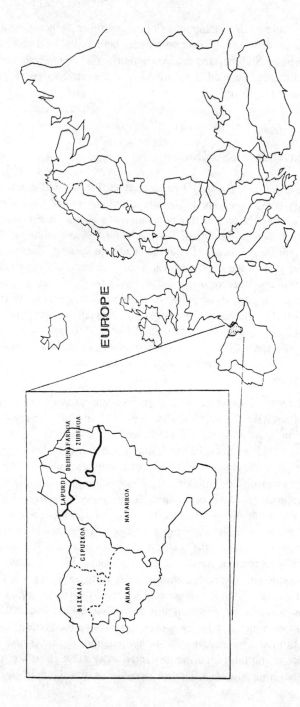

FIGURE 6.2 'The Basque Country' and the part thereof which constitutes the 'Basque Autonomous Community'.
Note: Bizkaia (Viscaya), Gipuzkoa and Araba (Alava) constitute the Basque Autonomous Community. The heavy line denotes the Spanish–French border.

the BAC itself[3]. The Secretariat of Language Policy and other agencies established by the Basque government in order to pursue these goals is, therefore,
charged with more than RLS alone; and the question arises whether these various goals can be productively pursued simultaneously and, even if so, what priorities should be allocated to them.[4]


## Background to Frisian RLS-Efforts

The Province of Friesland, the only Frisian context that we will examine
here, is a northeasterly province of The Netherlands, and has a total population
of some 600,000. Slightly over half of this population (54%) claims Frisian as
its mother tongue, about double the rate of Basque mother tongue encountered
in the Basque Community, and some 73% claim to be able to speak it. These two
percentages imply that 19% of the population for whom Frisian is not the mother tongue have, nevertheless, learned to speak it and even more, of course, have
learned to understand it. In part, these gains or 'surpluses' may be due to the
basic similarity between Frisian and the languages and dialects that surround it:
Dutch, Stellingwerfsk, Stedsfrysk (City Frisian), Biltsk, and a variety of discrepant, smaller Frisian dialects.[5] If so, this too differentiates between the Frisian
and the Basque RLS-efforts, since the linguistic distance between Basque and
Spanish is great indeed.

Although Friesland has its own provincial government, as does the BAC,
that government does not have the autonomy in cultural affairs, nor the consensual statutory definition of its powers *vis-á-vis* the central government, that the
Basque government has enjoyed since 1979. Similarly, it does not have an agency of government similar to the Basque Secretariat of Language Policy, with recognized and funded responsibility for initiating, coordinating, evaluating and
revising language policy on behalf of Frisian. Accordingly, whatever RLS-
efforts transpire are the result of undertakings by a mix of voluntary agencies,
quasi-official bodies and the often unwilling or reluctant acquiescence of provincial or central official bodies. Often the undisguised opposition and foot-dragging of the central government needs to be overcome for even minor
RLS-efforts to be approved. Accustomed as we are to considering The
Netherlands as a democratically governed country, we must realize that majority
rule and majority power can be serious stumbling blocks and even barricades for
RLS-efforts on behalf of minority languages even in democracies.[6] Indeed, just
as Basquization authorities might wish that their region shared some of
Friesland's demographic and interlinguistic characteristics (although as we will
see in a moment, the complete sociolinguistic profile of Friesland is by no

FIGURE 6.3 *Friesland, among the Provinces of The Netherlands*
(*Source:* K. Zondag, 1982)

means entirely a positive one), so would Frisian RLSers wish they had an
autonomous government of their own, at least in the cultural sphere, that was not
dependent on central governmental approval and funds before crucial steps on
behalf of RLS could be undertaken.

From the early 1970s onward sizeable numbers of non-Frisians have moved into Friesland, most of them coming from other parts of The Netherlands, while, on the other hand, many Frisians have moved out of Friesland. It is estimated that only one out of ten young Frisians who leave for university study in other parts of the Netherlands (there are no universities in Friesland itself, as we will see later on) ever returns, and former Frisians who return to the 'homeland' upon retirement are usually thoroughly Dutchified by then. Every one of the above types of migration involves a loss for Frisian and, all in all, about a quarter of the current population of Friesland was born outside of the Province. This figure corresponds exactly to the proportion of people considering themselves 'entirely Dutch' insofar as ethnic identity is concerned, with an additional 36% considering themselves 'primarily Dutch'. Thus, although three quarters of the population of Friesland claims that it can speak Frisian, a much higher percentage than pertains to Basque in the BAC, the proportion who consider themselves to be 'primarily Frisian' is approximately the same as the proportion in the BAC considering itself to be 'primarily Basque'. Indeed, the situation is even somewhat more precarious for Frisian since there are no longer any societally organized monolingual speakers of Frisian whereas there are still some elderly Basque monolinguals living in their ancestral homes and villages.

The extensive erosion that characterizes Frisian as a mother tongue and primary language today is due to a small number of interrelated reasons. First of all, the prevalence of mixed marriages between Frisian and Dutch (or other non-Frisian) speakers has increased greatly in the past century, from 37% in 1850–79 to 59% since 1940. The proportion of young adults who continue speaking (or who acquire) Frisian is very low in such marriages and lower yet among their children, particularly if the mother is Dutch, even in comparison with other young adults among whom the proportion of shifters to Dutch is also generally high. The shift to Dutch is also a concomitant of the movement of young people from rural, predominantly Frisian-speaking environments to predominantly Dutch-speaking urban environments. Whereas in former years urban environments were able to maintain a stable diglossic pattern, this pattern has substantially crumbled in recent years, leaving all of informal life exposed to Dutchification and leaving Frisian with no safe redoubt of it own. This youth-related phenomenon is well exemplified in a small municipality such as It Hearrenfean (Dutch: Heerenveen). In the countryside around the town, where over 95% of the population was Frisian-speaking in the 1950s, 71% of the population is now Frisian-speaking. In the older parts of town that were settled generations ago, 53% are Frisian-speaking. In the newer parts of town into which young adults (including many in-migrants from elsewhere in The Netherlands) have moved, only 42% are Frisian-speaking and only

FIGURE 6.4 *The municipalities and towns of Friesland.*
(*Source:* K. Zondag, 1982)

25% of the offspring of the mixed marriages there learn any Frisian at all at home.

Nevertheless, after all is said and done, much of the original association between Frisian and Frisianness or Frisian identity remains intact. Although only 39% of the total population claims 'primarily Frisian' identity, this identity is claimed by 57% of Frisian speakers, only 5% of whom claim 'entirely Dutch' identity. Beginning in the late 60s a stronger and better coordinated popular

movement to reverse language shift and to foster Frisian in every possible way
came into being, a movement whose earliest origins can be traced back to the
early nineteenth century. A large number of grievances against the ever-present
and overly-meddling central authorities and against the growing presence of
'foreigners' on the Frisian scene, the cultural accommodations made elsewhere
in The Netherlands for 'guest workers' from Southern Europe, and, finally, the
relatively good economic circumstances that provided additional funds for
somewhat unprecedented purposes — all of these circumstances have enabled
the hitherto relatively small coterie of Frisian activists to obtain more of a
following and of a hearing than had previously been the case. Efforts on behalf
of the Frisian language played (and continue to play) a prominent role in their
program.[7]

> *Stages 8 and 7: Reassembling Xish, learning it as a second language dur-*
> *ing adulthood and enriching the ethnocultural and ethnolinguistic experi-*
> *ences of those who are already Xish-speaking.*

While the need to teach Basque to ethnically Basque adults who never
acquired this language during their childhood (not to mention the need to teach
Basque to the many more adults who are not ethnically Basque and who [or
whose forbears] relocated in the Basque region) is clearly a paramount concern,
requiring substantial attention throughout the BAC, there is, of course, still a
core of Basque mother-tongue adults who know the language natively and who
either use it and/or need to be encouraged and assisted to use it at least in some
parts of their normal daily lives. The authentic, pre-modern Basque cultural tradition is one that places a high priority on verbal versatility, but almost entirely
at the level of oral language use. The age-old tradition of extemporaneous oral
poetry ('bertsolaritza'), all improvised in accord with demanding traditional patterns, is still alive and well in some rural settings and even in some urban environments too (particularly in Gipuzkoa). This tradition, in its original format of
improvised poetry for endless hours, has been reinforced and extended in two
respects. Annual local and regional *bertsolaritza* contests that take place in fashionable theaters, cinemas and jai-alai stadiums now bring together contestants
and audiences from near and far. In addition, musical renditions of initially spoken verses, presented in greatly shortened format, have become popular songs
that schools and mass media have spread to thousands who would otherwise
never have engaged in Basque singing.

Other oral traditions are also still creatively functional, but of more
limited participatory potential. Traditional theater ('*pastorales*'), with its
carefully preserved and scrupulously unaltered texts and tales of individual
fortunes and misfortunes, is also still to be encountered, primarily but not
exclusively in rural areas, and the links between it and other Basque theatrical

THE CASES OF BASQUE AND FRISIAN

traditions and to the modern, urban Basque stage are not hard to find. There is a similar link (and a similar tendency for modernization and divergence) between the traditional world of Basque rural sports and contests of physical endurance and the current tendency both to preserve some of the foregoing (particularly for special occasions) on the one hand, and, on the other hand, to modify and relate them (even to export them, as in the case of jai-alai) to the world of modern 'international' sports.

All of the foregoing adult cultural activities are similar in one respect: they involve oralcy far more than literacy. Although there is a continuous Basque literary tradition from the sixteenth century onward, it enjoyed a very limited popular following even among the educated, who generally preferred either Latin (initially) or Spanish (subsequently) for whatever textual functions for which they had any use or interest. The relative neglect of Basque literacy (relative to Spanish literacy) for nearly 500 years exposes Basque RLS-efforts to two hurdles to this very day, even though some 600 'thin market' books are now produced annually thanks to BAC subsidies. On the one hand, the language still lacks a fully accepted, non-controversial literary standard. Even though about 80% of the annual book-production is by now in the Batua (Gipuzkoa-related) standard variety, this is not the preferred variety of 80% of the readers or potential readers of Basque books. On the other hand, many of its best known and most beloved verbal art forms were (and are) so totally dialectal in nature. In addition, to some extent the language still lacks and to an even larger extent it still has the 'image' of lacking much of the up-to-date terminology related to all branches and manifestations of modern secular life. The latter lack is easier to rectify than the former ones. Corpus planning agencies, both governmental and non-governmental, have succeeded in producing huge numbers of new terminologies in various fields of endeavor, popular, professional and scientific. However, these generally still have very little currency, as might be expected, and, taken together, they have not yet overcome the popular expectation that Basque will not have 'a handy, simple word of its own' even for all of the popular items of mass consumption, entertainment and diversion that typify so much of modern life. Often this is a mistaken view, but it is one that has not been easily rectified precisely because the road to modernity ultimately leads not to full reliance upon Basque but, actually, away from such a reliance; i.e. at best, to an uneasy partnership with Spanish.[8]

The Frisian counterpart to the above-mentioned Basque efforts are similarly focused on stage 7 rather than on stage 8. Indeed, this is even more so in the Frisian case, where the genetic similarity between Frisian and Dutch is heavily relied upon (perhaps excessively so) in order to provide adults with an entry into Frisian as a second language, without the necessary intervention of formal courses which are so obviously required in the Basque/Spanish context. In the Frisian case, as in the Basque, the language is also certainly still well and naturally spoken by many rural and by some urban speech networks and both of these engage in a large number and variety of adult speech activities. At the oral level there is Frisian theater (e.g. *Tryater*, a professional group that regularly attracts large audiences) and the popular Frisian Festival of the Fryske Kultuerried (Frisian Culture Council) which is held roughly every five years. It was at the 1985 Festival at which the only full length Frisian feature film to date, *De Dream*, was first screened and viewed by some 150,000 viewers (35,000 within the borders of Friesland and 115,000 in other provinces of The Netherlands). It was subsequently shown on a nationwide TV channel and attracted an estimated two and a half million viewers. There are 'evenings' at which beginning authors read from their still unpublished works. There are musical evenings, evenings of folksongs and folksinging, and literary evenings. There is even something as modern as '*Operaasje Fers*' ('Operation Verse' or, more colloquially, 'Dial-a-Poem'), a telephone number that one can call at any hour in order to listen to a different Frisian poem every week.

There is also quite a literary scene in Frisian, and one that reaches somewhat beyond the most dedicated and conscious or conscientious RLSers alone. Frisian literature reaches beyond the small circle of adults who have received any formal education in Frisian, the latter experience representing, in the main, a rather recent RLS-related accomplishment and, therefore, one that has primarily influenced only young people. Because of the basic similarity between Frisian and Dutch, many adults have little difficulty reading Frisian, based on their Dutch education, provided their attitudes toward Frisian are sufficiently positive, a situation that has no counterpart at all in the Basque country. As a result, Frisian literary production is quite varied, particularly in connection with a plethora of small-circulation journals. Books, which inescapably cost more than journals, are helped to find readers and purchasers by the annual '*De Sutelaksje*'. This is an effort conducted by volunteers who undertake to bring literally wheelbarrows full of Frisian books, door-to-door, to about a hundred different Frisian villages and neighborhoods. This type of activity has not, by any means, overcome the usual dissociation between Frisian and modern literacy, but it has been able to put to good use some of the local goodwill that exists for Frisian, goodwill that is actually easier to activate in connection with the written word (that can be patiently perused) than it can in connection with the spoken word that is not only more fleeting but that often appears to be more dialectally distant than its written counterpart.

Unfortunately, however, when all is said and done, most of the stage 7 activity on behalf of Frisian reaches only those who are already committed to Frisian. This may not be true of one particular effort or another which may succeed in breaking out, momentarily, of the usually narrow bounds of the previously converted and committed Frisianists. Indeed, this is even more so in the case of Frisian than in the case of Basque, regardless of the former's manifold linguistic similarities to Dutch, primarily because Frisian lacks the thrust of a governmental agency like the (Basque) Secretariat for Language Policy that can afford to constantly undertake new initiatives for bringing Frisian to the public both in popularly attractive and in official/quasi-official connections. Indeed, in recent years, there has been a palpable realization that stage 7 activity in Frisian has become more difficult to undertake and its pulse somewhat more lethargic than before. The 'true believers' are becoming older and more tired, even if their convictions have not changed.[9]

*Stage 6: The intergenerational, demographically concentrated family-home-neighborhood-community sphere: the basis of transmission*

Whatever it is that other stages may and can accomplish insofar as RLS is concerned, they are merely 'buying time' in the short run until a sound basis for long run intergenerational transmission can be established. Once stage 6 is established, the subsequent stages add vigor, color and breadth to language life, but they cannot in themselves either counteract or compensate for basic weaknesses at this stage. Both Basque and Frisian are still threatened, notwithstanding all that has been done and is still being done on their behalf, precisely because stage 6 is difficult to manipulate and, therefore, tends to be either overlooked or given a lower priority than it deserves, while other more eye-catching but ephemeral efforts receive the lion's share of attention.

Part of the problem, for example, in connection with Basque, is that stage 6 is still associated with rural and small-town life. Villages and towns of less than 2,000 inhabitants or of between 2,000 and 10,000 inhabitants are still the most heavily Basque-speaking in the BAC. Of course, their Basqueness has more to do with the continuity of rural tradition (bolstered by the pro-Basque efforts of some — not all — of the rural Roman Catholic clergy) than with any impact of the official Basquization efforts, particularly since those efforts have necessarily focused primarily on largetown, city and provincial capital life, that is: on places with more than 10,000 and even more than 50,000 inhabitants, where modernity has replaced much of tradition and where home-family-neighborhood life is much harder either to maintain or to influence. Nevertheless, the recent RLS-efforts have not failed entirely in these respects, as is evidenced by indications that both the capital cities and other larger points of population concentration are beginning to attract sizeable contingents of RLSers and of those dependent on governmentally conducted Basque-language activities. It is also evidenced by the fact that among young folks (14- to 18-year-olds) who know at least some Basque the context in which their Basque is most commonly activated is that of interaction with siblings. Nevertheless, there is still a very long, long way to go to overcome the reverses that still plague RLS-efforts at this stage. Differences between parental and child Basque language use are accelerating because proportionally more young folks are leaving primarily-Basque life behind than are being attracted to it by Basquization efforts. Among parents with a good command of Basque, about 8% of their children now know little if any Basque, whereas among parents with little or no command of Basque at all, only 3% of the children have acquired a good command of Basque. Although the sheer numbers of the latter are greater than those of the former, the former represented an opportunity for intergenerational transmission within a complete home-family-neighborhood context and the latter represent merely a school-acquired competence that may never reach the still far-off juncture of intergenerational language transmission.

As one would expect on theoretical grounds, the mother's role in intergenerational transmission of Basque is far more determining than the father's, even when the mother's command of spoken Basque is merely moderate. As a rule, mothers can compensate for fathers' inability or lesser ability with respect to spoken Basque, but fathers cannot similarly compensate for mothers' inability in that connection, the differences in child acquisition of good Basque being as great as 15% in favor of the mothers, when the Basque mastery of parents is unequal and the mother knows more Basque than the father. Furthermore, in addition to the linguistic composition of the parental household, the family transmission of Basque depends primarily on the linguistic composition of the neighborhood or town in which the family lives. Finally, the language consciousness of the parents is decisive in this process, and it is only here, in third place, that characteristics of subsequent stages come into effect. Without proper parental and neighborhood/town sociolinguistic characteristics the subsequent characteristics of consciousness-building schools, media and official agencies have no way of taking hold and contributing to the foundation of future *intergenerational* transmission (rather than merely to age-specific activities).

In the absence of major RLS focus on stage 6 efforts a number of minor efforts in this area receive undue attention. New road signs are all bilingual, with Basque first and in bolder type, and increasing attention is being given to the Basquization of other features of the 'general environment', such as street and building signs, public advertising, legends on monuments and other points of interest, etc. While it is true that all of these make a contribution to the construction of a more Basquish environment, and are both advocated and opposed on that basis, they do not come to grips with the heart of the intergenerational transmission mechanism: the normal, daily, repetitive and intensively socializing and identity-forming functioning of home, family and neighborhood. If this stage is not Basquized, then the next generation of RLSers will have to reconquer that which its predecessors achieved by dint of much exertion and sacrifice. The BAC will be Ireland all over again.[10]

The stage 6 picture in Friesland is generally quite similar to that which we have just reviewed in connection with the Basque Autonomous Community. Frisian is still the home language of 75% of the inhabitants of the traditionally Frisian rural areas, where it was the home language of 94% of the inhabitants in 1955. On the other hand, this loss has hardly been compensated for by the fact that 38% of the inhabitants of *urban* areas have Frisian as their home language, whereas it was the home language of only 32% there in 1955. Whatever numerical increase there may have been between these two periods, due to the fact that the urban population is constantly being augmented by migration from rural and small town areas, is more than vitiated by the slow but continual disappearance of authentically and fully Frisian primary environments. Indeed, so Dutchified has everyday life become almost everywhere that even RLSers are inclined to believe that Frisian and Dutch culture represent a 'monoculture' rather than two basically different cultures whose inevitable similarities are due to their physical proximity to each other and to their shared modernization experiences.

Other than via Frisian *per se*, the ethnocultural manifestations of Frisianness are few and far between: primarily some foods and drinks (e.g. *beerenburg*, a potent popular alcoholic beverage) and a variety of sports (*fierljeppen* [pole-vaulting over canals], *keatsen* [a variety of outdoor handball], *skutsjesile* [an intervillage sailing competition], *ringriden* [a traditional surrey-race with the goal of putting a ring on the finger of a far-off, outstretched wooden hand]). The growing immigration of Dutch speakers involved in industrial and large-scale agricultural pursuits, and the increasing economic and cultural marginalization of the countryside and its language (to such an extent that new urbanites coming from the countryside quickly shift to Dutch so as not to reveal their rural origins), bring in their wake cultural forms and identities which the Frisian-speaking urban intelligentsia is hard put to counteract or even to fully withstand within its own ranks. If, indeed, a 'monoculture' has come to pass uniting Frisians and Dutchmen, then the case for Frisian is a very difficult one and the stance of being 'Xmen via Yish' is already quite a maximalistic position since it is obviously more demanding than the alternative of being Ymen (or regionally different Ymen) *per se*.

In the face of massive and long-lasting processes such as the above-mentioned, the counteracting Frisian RLS-efforts at the level of stage 6 seem puny indeed. Such undertakings as special theater, musical and song performances and concerts for children and young folks (as were organized in 1987, in commemoration of the 50th anniversary of the permission granted by the central authorities to include Frisian in public education) cannot begin to repair the linguistic damage to the very foundations of the transmission of Frisian engendered by widespread mixed marriages and heterogeneous neighborhoods. Even the more noteworthy recent developments in connection with Frisian in the religious domain are probably not sufficiently intensive, interesting though they undeniably are, to stem the gathering tide.

Since the late 70s, an ecumenical (Protestant and Catholic) revised Frisian translation of the Bible has appeared as well as a revised hymnal, initially intended for Protestant churches but also used by Roman Catholic churches in their occasional Frisian services. Whereas generally only about 20 churches in Friesland will offer Frisian services on any particular Sunday, on the special 'Frisian Sunday' set aside once a year for this very purpose some 50, 60 or even more may do so. By now 6% of Frisian churchgoers (who comprise some 60% of the population of Friesland) attend Frisian church services regularly and a whopping 57% do so occasionally. Indeed, until recently many Frisians doubted that so many clergymen really could give sermons in Frisian as are now evidently doing so without much difficulty. '*Lieteboekdagen*' ('Days of the Hymnal'), organized in 1985 and 1987, attracted so many hundreds of people to the collective singing of Frisian songs that the annual number of such programs was increased from two to five in 1988. All in all, the generations-old (even centuries-old) resistance against Frisian in religion has crumbled and young people, particularly urban young people, are quite accepting of prayers in Frisian. The question still remains, however, whether this represents anything more than a 'liturgicalization' of Frisian, something much different from its vernacularization. Although church and religion more generally can be powerful home and neighborhood forces (perhaps less so in modern Christianity than in more easterly religions, but powerful nevertheless) it still remains true that in modern urban life the church as an institution is usually too marginal to guarantee intergenerational continuity (even the continuity of religious practices *per se*) and shares and reflects the weakness of the family institution, rather than being able to repair that weakness. Since the transmission of Frisian apparently cannot be guaranteed within the family, and since neither Basque nor Frisian (especially not Frisian) have been able to follow the most recent Irish example of directly focusing on neighborhood and family building for RLS purposes, it is no wonder, then, that the next most intensive institution in the lives of children, the school, has come to be depended upon in that connection to an inordinate degree. We turn now, therefore, to a consideration of its contributions to RLS.[11]

*Stage 5: Schools for children (that do not meet the requirements of compulsory education) and courses in language and literacy acquisition for adults*

There was a time in the Basque Country, not too many years ago, when Basque was forbidden and when children could be taught this language only clandestinely, in 'underground' schools that were hidden from the authorities. These schools, known as *ikastolas* (the correct Basque plural is *ikastolak*, but we giving the word an English (or Spanish) plural form), were recognized toward the end of the Franco regime, when the widespread anticipation of the dictator's approaching and inevitable death led to a slow mellowing of the regime's originally repressive nature. Under the Statute of Autonomy the *ikastolas* became fully legitimate private schools with a continued emphasis on Basque immersion and, like all private schools, heavily subsidized. More recently, yet a third incarnation began for the *ikastolas*. They have become totally public institutions, paid for by public funds, and with separate full immersion and partial immersion tracks. The only remaining noteworthy reminder of their former self-supporting stage is the annual *kilometroak*, a five-mile march (in Gipuzkoa) engaged in by Basques from all over the BAC (and even from further afield), over 100,000 marching together, the proceeds of which are still primarily earmarked for the needs of the *ikastolas*. The last such march raised more than a quarter million dollars, a not inconsiderable sum in any budget and a far from negligible expression of solidarity in any RLS movement.

A related mass expression of support pertains to Basquization efforts at the adult level. The annual, regionally sponsored 'walk', mentioned above, as well as one ten-day 'run' on a 2,800 km course, also raise funds for AEK, the major non-governmental organization which teaches Basque and literacy in Basque to adults in nearly 250 centers throughout the BAC. In addition to these, there are, of course, also publicly supported courses for adults, which the government maintains in accord with its statutory obligations to promote the Basque language. The governmental organization for this purpose (HABE) also provides some support to AEK and to practically all non-governmental adult language-teaching organizations. In the latter connection, there are hundreds of very popular (even if usually less effective, more expensive but more conveniently scheduled) private schools and courses for these same purposes (see the discussion of *Euskaltegis* at Stage 4a, below). All in all, this is quite an accomplishment, particularly in the literacy area and especially for a language which has never had a strong literacy tradition and whose standardization still remains somewhat conflicted. The overall utilitarian importance and the functional success of these efforts is attested to by the examinations which follow upon the completion of coursework (see the discussion of EGA examinations at Stage 4a, below). Successful performance on these examinations yields certificates that are useful for obtaining positions and promotions where mastery of Basque has become part of the job description. Nevertheless, notwithstanding the above-mentioned efforts and the good standard which many of the government-sponsored courses have attained and maintained, the number and proportion of adults who have not yet been reached are truly staggering. Even were the number of

the unreached to become substantially smaller, the feedback of these RLS-efforts
to the home-family-neighborhood-community nexus of intergenerational mother
tongue transmission is far from certain, particularly given their occupational orientation and general lack of internal motivation among the adult learners to
whom they were directed.

Nothing corresponding to the huge and multifaceted Basque adult language
teaching effort exists in the Frisian area. There is, of course, the AFUK institute
which provides adult courses in Frisian, both for native Frisians and for newcomers to Friesland. However, its normal operational mode may be described as
'somewhat old-fashioned', making little if any use of the newest approaches to
language teaching and language learning that characterize a substantial segment
of the Basque scene in this connection. On the other hand, AFUK's 1988 brief
and intensive course for civil servants was quite successful and may augur new
and improved efforts in the future. Also worthy of mention is the recent availability (since 1983/84) of improved Frisian/Dutch and Dutch/Frisian desk dictionaries, the first of which appeared in the 1950s. Of lesser significance to all but
academics and the most educated Frisian RLSers are the first five volumes (by
1988) of the planned 18-volume *Larger Dictionary of the Frisian Language*.
Considerable proportions of the total staff and funds of the Frisian Academy are
devoted to this effort and to the related Language Data Bank for Frisian to which
it has contributed. Although this is a matter of considerable prestige it is simply
not the kind of tool that can or will have much direct impact on RLS, particularly insofar as the acquisition of fluency in spoken or written Frisian is concerned
on the part of those who have, thus far, never learned it or who gave it up after
acquiring it early in life.[12] The same observation also applies to the various
Basque dictionary projects currently underway. The most important among the
latter is the historical dictionary (of which one volume has already been published and eight or nine more are at various stages of completion or planning),
known as the *Dictionary of Authorities*, being worked on by the Royal Academy
of the Basque Language and benefiting both from regional BAC and individual
provincial support. This dictionary, based upon sources from the eleventh to the
twentieth century, will 'ultimately' be the basis of shorter dictionaries for everyday use.

It is only to be expected that every RLS movement will have its 'great dictionary' project (linguists are, after all, at or near the very center of most RLS
and language-nationalism movements); what is more surprising, however, is the
largely unrealistic nature of the 'practical consequences for RLS' so often associated with such projects and the large sums of money and the sizeable manpower resources that are, therefore, allocated to them, usually with insufficient
justification or validation. Indeed, the investment is so great that, once several
volumes have been completed, 'great dictionary' projects tend to become sacred

causes in their own right, 'monuments' or icons to their languages rather than stimulants leading to improved intergenerational mother tongue transmission.

*Stage 4a: Schools in lieu of compulsory education and fully under RLS control*

Perhaps the major problem initially faced by the educational authorities and the Secretariat of Language Policy, in conjunction with the government's Basquization goals and responsibilities, was the fact that there were so pitifully few Basque-speaking and Basque-literate teachers for a task of the magnitude and urgency of the Basquization of the BAC's schools. Unlike the case of Frisian, where the language of prior literacy (Dutch) is of considerable help (even given the many contrastive errors to which it must also lead) in the acquisition of the minority language, prior literacy and even sophistication in Spanish is of no value whatsoever in the adult mastery of Basque, the two languages being totally dissimilar. Nevertheless, a far-flung effort aiming at literacy training and Basquization of the teaching staff (known by its initials IRALE) was set up, soon after the Franco regime's collapse, to cope with the 95% of all public school teachers who knew no Basque at all as well as virtually all of the remaining 5% who knew how to speak it but not its still uncertain written conventions. These goals pursued for over a decade via two separate methods: (a) subsidized courses given during after-work hours and summer vacations and (b) for those who had already reached an intermediate level of competence, leaves of absence for up to a year and a half in order to pursue the study of more advanced Basque on a full time basis. In 1985–86 some 5,000 teachers were enrolled in either after-work or summer courses and 500 (the maximum that can currently be accommodated) in the full-time programs.

The special schools to teach Basque to teachers are called *Euskaltegis* (= Basque Language Schools; the final 's' is the English plural) and similar schools for other types of professionals in urgent need of Basque are maintained by a variety of town and village governments, cooperatives, cultural associations, large business enterprises, and so on. Those who complete these courses are then required to take nationwide examinations (known as EGA examinations) in order to certify that they have attained a 'sufficiently professional level of competence' in written and spoken Basque. It is obviously extremely desirable that certified teachers maintain their competence, although no system of periodic re-examinations has thus far been instituted. This would seem to be highly advisable, given the completely Spanish environments in which many if not most of the teachers live out of school. Since the EGA level is a well regarded and demanding one (between 1982 and 1988 slightly more than 19,000 certificates were awarded to more than 59,000 candidates for certification) it has also come to be the standard required by other governmental and private employers with respect to positions with Basque prerequisites. However, after all is said and done, the task remains a herculean one and to this very day there are many teachers, particularly among those in the older generation, who are not really fully competent or comfortable in Basque. Some of the latter individuals are invariably required to teach Basque at a level beyond their current capacity (even though all Basque medium and Basque subject teachers are required to have attained the EGA level. This is particularly so since more and more schools are constantly required that teach more Basque (or in Basque) than has been the case heretofore.

Turning now to the teaching of Basque to children in the BAC, our stage 4a corresponds most clearly to the *ikastolas*, on the one hand, and to other public and private schools also following models D and B, on the other hand. All of these types of schools and models pertain to both elementary and secondary education. In the type D schools, Basque is the virtually exclusive medium of instruction, Spanish being used only to teach Spanish as a subject. In type B schools there is greater parity between Basque and Spanish, each language being used as a medium for half of the schoolday. The attainment of competence in Basque and its use as the medium or co-medium of education has absorbed the lion's share of the government's human and financial resources *vis-á-vis* language since 1978. Indeed, it is clear that other aspects of language policy may have been neglected, relatively speaking, in order to make sure that type B and D schools might have every possible chance of succeeding at the widest possible revernacularization of Basque among the younger generation. It has been a slow uphill battle against substantial odds. Among those who were 25–29 years old in 1986 only 1% had studied in type B or D schools. This proportion was already 14% among those who were then 15–17 years old. Of all those still attending public schools in that year the corresponding proportion was 24% and among kindergarten pupils alone it was already 54%. None of these figures include the *ikastola* pupils who constituted another 66,000 (or 20% of the total school enrollment) in 1986.

It is clear that the proportion of all students who learn Basque to EGA level continues to climb, and may well pass the 50% point quite soon and will continue to climb upward thereafter (with corresponding decreases in the less maximalistic school types, yet to be discussed, below). It is also clear that the level of Spanish mastery of students in schools of the B, D and *ikastola* types has in no way suffered, primarily because Spanish is the mother tongue of most students and the dominant language in their home and neighborhood environments. The question that remains is whether the Basque competence that the schools of these types achieve can subsequently be maintained in out-of-school and in after-school life, to the point that the general environment too can ultimately be Basquized thereby and this Basquization intergenerationally transmitted rather than artificially engendered from without. Failing that, the Spanishness of the out-of-school and after-school and adult worlds will remain dominant and force educators to engage in 'Operation Catch-up' generation after generation. It is clear that Basque educators are aware of the problem that the insufficient Basquization of everyday life poses for the intergenerational transmission of the considerable Basque language competencies that children in type B schools acquire. The after-school Basque clubs available for such children, almost all of whom come from Spanish-speaking homes, are simply insufficiently intensive and 'real life"-like to make Basque into a less artificial vehicle of communication for them. There are also completely Basque-speaking youth clubs for naturally Basque-speaking youngsters but these are generally in the rural areas and would be unsuitable for type B pupils at any rate because neither their Basque nor their urban interests are suitable for membership in such clubs. Accordingly, three 'Basque Atmosphere Short-Stay Boarding Schools' have been established where 8-, 9- and 10-year-old pupils (drawn mostly from type B schools but some also coming from type A) spend two weeks during the school year in the Basque rural areas, both as a self-contained tourism and play group as well as in the company of Basque mother tongue children of those areas. Currently fewer than 2,000 pupils per year can be accommodated in these special schools. While it is hoped to open more schools of this kind in the years ahead even the most generous increase imaginable will still reach only a small proportion of the age-group and will do so for any given group of children only for two weeks at a time out of the year, and probably only once in their lives. Clearly, the time has come to attend more, and more directly, to the intergenerational transmission stage, stage 6, so that the accomplishments of stage 4a will be better able to take hold, rather than be dissipated, generation after generation.[13]

On the Frisian front too some stage 4a progress has been made, although clearly not as much as in the BAC. The first voice on behalf of harnessing the public schools to the task of halting the de-Frisianization of the Frisians was raised as far back as 1897, by S. Bartstra, a Minister who protested against the complete absence of Frisian history in the schools of the province. The first language-related step was taken a decade later, when the Provincial government allocated a subsidy to support voluntary Frisian lessons after regular school hours. The first timid step by the central government (the authority that totally controls educational legislation and funding in The Netherlands), along the thorny path of re-Frisianization came fully 40 years after Bartstra's protest (in 1937), when the upper house of the National Parliament amended the Education Act to *permit* (!) some instruction in Frisian 'where it is in active use'. Nearly 40 more years were destined to pass until the Education Act was again modified (1974), this time to *require* the teaching of Frisian as an elementary school *subject* by no later than 1980. The six years of lead time were to intended to be used for curriculum preparation and teacher training. At the same time, permission was also granted to use Frisian as a *medium* of instruction in elementary education where that was locally desired. By the time these new revisions were adopted, 30% of all elementary schools in Friesland were already teaching Frisian as a subject in one grade or another and another 14% were using it as a medium in the first two or three grades, in accord with a 1955 emendation of the Education Act.

As was the case in the BAC, the first step under the amended Education Act of 1974 was to make sure that elementary school teachers themselves knew Frisian. This goal was more or less achieved by 1981, when 86% of all elementary school teachers in Friesland were reported to be able to read Frisian, 81% to speak it and 64% to write it. Within one year of implementing the newly amended Education law (i.e. in 1981) 78% of all schools were teaching Frisian (note: *not* teaching *via* Frisian but merely teaching Frisian as a subject) in all elementary grades and 14% more were teaching it only in the earliest grades. The remaining 8% of all elementary schools (primarily in Stellingwerven, It Bilt and other non-Frisian areas) were effectively resisting the law. Public opinion was also quite in harmony with the amended education law, since 61% of the population of the province approved of the new requirement and 24% more approved conditionally, either type of approval being related most strongly to the Frisian language fluency of the respondents.

From the very outset of the implementation of the amendment making Frisian at least a mandatory *subject*, nearly every Frisian municipality began giving their schools an additional sum per pupil per year in support of any additional costs engendered by Frisian instruction, plus a one-time payment per pupil for the purchase of teaching materials (books, slides, etc.) pertaining to Friesland or Frisian. At present, the additional costs attributed to Frisian instruction have been made an integral part of the total education budget and each school must then decide what amount of its funds to actually spend for this particular purpose. The total sums allocated for Frisian do not begin to approximate their Basque counterpart, not even on a per capita basis.

It is interesting to note that by 1982 there was already a large minority (44%) in favor of 'spending more time on Frisian in the elementary schools', with 34% more favoring such additional time conditionally. However, very few schools, some 10% in all and almost all of these in the rural areas and, therefore, primarily smaller schools, made Frisian either the primary medium of instruction or even just a substantial co-medium of instruction; and even those few who did so, did so mostly in the kindergarten and first two grades. After all is said and done, Frisian is generally taught no more than an hour per week in most elementary grades, this minimalism being particularly true of the urban schools. This being the case, type 4a schools are in a very distinct minority in Friesland and are limited to rural schools, and even to only one kind of rural school at that. The most Frisian-emphasizing pattern devotes 95% of total school time to Frisian in kindergarten and in the first year and then thereafter, in grades 2 to 6, devotes only 30% of total school time (about one and a half hours per day) to Frisian. Perhaps no more than 5% of all elementary school children attend the (rural) schools of this type.

In 1985, when financial exigencies had already begun to dominate the Dutch educational scene, budgetary school reforms (presumably undertaken primarily for 'pedagogic reasons') provided that nursery schools and elementary schools should be combined into single units and that all schools could opt to teach Frisian only in some grades and not in others, in accord with their own preferences. Both of these developments tended to further decrease the proportion of type 4a schools, or of schools reasonably approximating type 4a schools in the public sector. Unfortunately, this is practically the only sector in Frisian education since RLSers there have never dared assume the burden assumed in the Basque Country (extending beyond what later became the BAC) by the initial *ikastola* founders, namely the burden of supporting private schools of their own in which they would have far greater freedom to give as much emphasis to Frisian as might be required for adequate to higher-cultural mastery of the language and its intergenerational transmission by regional children who may or may not have had it as a mother tongue.

*Type 4b schools: the object of RLS affection as a distinctly part-time 'guest' in the public school arena*

Preliminary evaluations have clearly revealed that pupils of type A schools in the BAC, receiving less than an hour per schoolday of instruction in Basque as a subject, make little if any cumulative progress toward learning Basque from one year to the next. Basque is simply too different and too little present in their total life space for their meager exposure to it (3–5 hours per week!) to produce any functional level of mastery. There may be some consolation in the fact that these schools are slowly attracting ever-smaller proportions of all school-age children, but it is hard to imagine that their proportion will drop below one third in the foreseeable future, and this will leave a huge and relatively permanent reservoir of minimally Basquized individuals in the BAC. The Spanish Constitution explicitly guarantees their right to select Spanish as the major vehicle of their education and of their entire public and private life. Educators and policy makers merely hope that the attitudes of most essentially monolingual Spanish speakers toward the Basque language and toward Basque-speaking society will be positive, rather than negative, and that more and more children from such backgrounds who do not go to type B schools will be able to maintain a smattering of type A school-derived 'emergency Basque' throughout their adult lives, primarily on the basis of their inevitable exposure to the growing Basquization of public life more generally.

Meanwhile, type A schools are subject to a few conventions of the educational system which do tend to bring a little more Basque into their daily functioning. As in all schools in the BAC, new bilingual signs are being put up with the Basque version coming on top and in somewhat bigger and bolder lettering. This has already been done in slightly more than half of all schools and the remaining ones (mostly secondary schools) should all be reached by this policy within a few years. Similarly, type A schools are included in the Department of Education's policy to send general communications (i.e. communications being sent to 10 or more schools) bilingually. Only type D schools receive all such communications in Basque. Nevertheless, the overwhelming majority of all Department of Education communications with schools (indeed, 94% of all communications) are *not* 'general communications' and, therefore, these are still more frequently being sent in Spanish because of the lack of sufficient numbers of Basque-literate personnel in the Department itself to be able to send all communications bilingually.

The very situation which is considered the undesirable *exception* in the Basque country namely: type 4b schooling in which the weakened regional language is given so little attention that it is not really possible to learn it, has become the undesirable *rule* in Friesland. Only in nursery schools/kindergartens in rural areas, where most of the children are still Frisian-speaking and where most of the teachers have Frisian as their mother tongue, is Frisian the normal, daily language of instruction and communication. At the other extreme is a rather sizeable number of elementary schools in which Frisian is taught for the usual 30–45 minutes per week but where the writing of Frisian is not taught at all and, furthermore, where there are some grades in which no Frisian at all is taught. At the secondary school level, no legal obligation to teach Frisian was ever instituted. At that level it is possible, therefore, to offer Frisian as a subject only if at least 20 students request it. As a result, only some 5% of secondary school students in Friesland are studying Frisian at any particular time. Even in the teacher training 'Normal Schools' the time devoted to Frisian is extremely minimal and the availability of the subject may soon be discontinued entirely, or virtually so, as financial cutbacks continue to dominate the entire Dutch educational scene.

Clearly, the efforts to provide 'a little bit of Frisian' have not succeeded in reversing the attrition of the language nor even in becoming 'self-perpetuating minor appendages' to the total public educational processes. On the other hand,

RLS advocates in Friesland have organized virtually no alternative schools of their own of whatever type. The many weaknesses of Frisian that we have encountered at levels 6, 5 and 4 constitute a very serious handicap future possibilities in the RLS arena, particularly insofar as the improvement of the intergenerational transmissibility of the language is concerned.[14]

*Stage 3: The world of work, both within the ethnolinguistic community (among other Xmen),as well as outside it (among Ymen.)*

The constitutional provisions protecting Spanish have, thus far, been interpreted as not permitting the BAC authorities to institute extensive (let alone omnipresent) Basque-on-the-job requirements similar to those on behalf of French in Quebec (see Chapter 10, below). Nevertheless, new civil service positions and vacancies are interpreted as requiring bilingual incumbents and the announcements of the availability of such positions are occasionally published only in Basque. Large employers are encouraged and assisted to Basquize their operations, at least to the point of enabling Basque speakers to carry out their functions in Basque and to serve the public in Basque wherever and whenever there is an opportunity to do so. Many firms and agencies have instituted Basque courses for their employees (including younger executive officers) and have made the EGA certificate of Basque competence a prerequisite for promotion and tenure. Although the work sector is still primarily conducted in Spanish, and perhaps will remain so for the foreseeable future, there is already a widespread and growing view that a fair command of Basque is a very worthwhile employability investment.

A 1986 study reports that 48% of the population is of the opinion that Basque is very useful in finding work; 66% is of the opinion that those who know Basque have better jobs than those who do not. Thus, while publicity campaigns promoting the use of Basque in public cannot be said to have produced any tangible result at the oral level, it does seem that the total emphasis on Basquization has spilled over, at least attitudinally, into the work sphere. Unfortunately, there is very little prospect of the intergenerational transmissibility of 'attitudinal Basquization' if it remains pegged at this level *per se*.

The Frisian picture in this connection is less clear cut. While Frisian plays practically no role at all in trade and industry — probably a lesser role than it plays in the BAC — it is quite normal for Frisian-speaking clients and customers of service-oriented businesses and of local government bureaux to be understood if and when they speak Frisian and even, at times, to be replied to in that language as well. This can happen *vis-á-vis* Basque in urban centers in the BAC too, but its incidence there is so low that even Basque activists rarely act on the common Frisian activist assumption that an unknown interlocutor will understand enough Xish to permit communication to be successfully entered into. This by-product of the greater similarity between Frisian and Dutch (a similarity, by the way, which also simplifies the ongoing 'untutored' lexical Dutchification of Frisian, at the same time that Frisian grammar too is evolving at a deeper level in a direction more similar to Dutch) is also an indicator of the general absence of hostility toward Frisian, since communicability is also in large part an attitudinal variable, rather than merely a reflection of linguistic similarity. RLS benefits from such positive attitudes of Yish speakers toward Xish, but such attitudes are not sufficient to yield Xish intergenerational mother tongue transmissibility.[15]

*Stage 2: Xish in regional mass media and governmental services*

As might be expected, there is considerable official interest in and support for Basque at this level. About 80 towns and villages issue Basque-language newsletters announcing local events and ordinances. Since these are generally very small, rural municipalities, these newsletters are estimated as having a combined circulation of only 32,000. This is no minor matter, however, since, as we have remarked several times before, the tradition of mass literacy in Basque is a rather new one at any rate. There is also a well established weekly, *Argia*, which has a region-wide circulation of roughly 10,000. Additionally, the government is planning to establish a daily in Basque in the near future and is currently sponsoring two experimental weeklies with a combined circulation of about 10,000. Furthermore, each of the four Spanish dailies of the region (*El Correo, El Diario Vasco, Egin* and *Deia*) devotes several pages a week to items in Basque, most of them setting aside about half a page per day for this purpose. Two of them, *El Correo* and *El Diario Vasco*, also devote several pages to Basque on a given day of the week. Finally, there are a fairly large number of small and intellectually or professionally specialized (and subsidized) monthlies and quarterlies of a rather good quality. All in all, there is not yet much of a region-wide all-Basque periodical press in the BAC, perhaps some 20 supra-local periodicals in all (dealing with political, child-oriented, popular science, religious and other topics), but some major growth can be expected in the years immediately ahead. The number of bilingual publications is even larger. Growth in the prevalence of Basque literacy may be occurring slowly, but it is crystal clear that it is occurring.

There is also increasingly more Basque on the radio, there being some Basque not only on the governmentally operated stations but some half dozen or more privately operated all-Basque stations as well. But the true media success is in connection with Basque television. In the latter case, proportionally more people have claimed to understand Basque programs well ('always or usually': 50%) than have claimed to know Basque well in any other functional context whatsoever. An additional 14% claim to watch Basque TV even though they only understand Basque 'poorly'. The BAC authorities have had far less success in connection with influencing the central (state) controlled media to broadcast in Basque, although Article 20 of the Spanish Constitution guarantees access to the state media for the different languages of Spain.

Generally speaking, the expectations aroused by the strengthened role of Basque in the regional non-print media are largely unwarranted. There is no evidence whatsoever that the mass media can overcome or compensate for basic weaknesses in stage 6, and a dozen years of experience with TV in Welsh fully corroborates the view that the time that is bought with TV is expensively bought indeed, given that it has no intergenerational transmission payoff thereafter. A child-oriented TV program now and then is no match for the Spanish competition with respect to such programs and, even were the Basque ones to be technically superior, they cannot act *in loco parenti* nor substitute for the lifetime of daily activities that must transpire before intergenerational mother tongue transmission can take place.

Governmental services, signs and forms are, of course, plentifully available in Basque, both in principle and in practice, and the progressive Basquization of the public administration is clearly foreseen as is the official Basquization of all place names in the BAC. There are also plans underway to send out government notices to each citizen only in one language, namely in the language of each citizen's first choice, on the assumption that more citizens will choose Basque and struggle to read Basque that way, than would be the case with bilingual notices in which their eyes immediately gravitate to the more 'comfortable' Spanish text.

In all of the above respects Basque has succeeded within less than a decade to a far greater extent than Frisian has within a much longer span of years. In the realm of Frisian print media there is only a waning weekly to report and ever so slightly more than a page per week (plus a few ads throughout the year on very special occasions) in each of the local dailies, *Friesch Dagblad* and *Leeuwarder Courant*. There are also a few agricultural journals and a few journals for different factions within intellectual and nationalist circles. All in all, there is not much to show for Frisian in print, particularly since there has been almost no literary renewal via young talent during the past dozen years or more.

Radio Fryslan (since 1988: Omrop Fryslan) broadcasts for about 20 hours per week, generally but not exclusively in Frisian, and enjoys a good but not a growing listenership. There is almost no Frisian TV (30 hours *per year*, if educational TV, for school use, is counted too). The national television channel very rarely broadcasts anything at all in Frisian, even counting news items involving verbatim comments by Frisian speakers. There was something known as 'teleboard' up to 1984, an inexpensive method of transmitting somewhat fuzzy images via radio waves, that was used for teaching Frisian to children at school but that was obviously also watched at home by a number of adults. In 1984 it was replaced by the educational TV programs mentioned above. The prospects for additional Frisian programs on radio are quite meager. As far as TV is concerned, there is a clear prospect of 22 hours more *per year*, as of 1989. At that time there will be a new 'grand total', of 52 hours per year of Frisian TV, the equivalent of one hour per week, half of it during the school day and half during 'prime time' for adult programming.

The official (rather than merely the voluntary and 'off the record') use of Frisian in municipal government and administrative affairs is a matter of considerable current interest to Frisian language activists. It is also an area of longstanding contention. As far back as 1951 it was the basis of '*Kneppelfreed*' (= Cudgel Friday), a street riot in Ljouwert (Leeuwarden) protesting against the inadmissibility of Frisian before the courts. A compromise reached in 1956 permitted oral Frisian (the oath, testimony) in the courts but no written use of Frisian. Written documents were later ruled to be admissible, but only as accompaniments to or translations of the official and obligatory Dutch records and documents. Strictly speaking, a similar situation currently pertains to the records of municipalities and other administrative offices. Operationally, however, as long as Dutch speakers (regardless of the length of time that they have lived in Friesland) can obtain free translations of documents written in Frisian, the validity of Frisian documents is generally not challenged (even though from time to time one challenge or another will escalate to the stage of media notoriety). In this makeshift fashion, without any formal legal recognition of Frisian by the central authorities, municipalities flexibly opt for alternating Dutch or Frisian operations, as topic and target group dictate, and provide translations only on request. This is referred to as the principle of 'equal validity and equal right' and its biggest limitation, aside from the fact that it merely represents a *modus vivendi* rather than any official acceptance of Frisian, is the fact that only a minority of officials are sufficiently comfortable with written Frisian to employ it very frequently or freely.

In the Provincial Assembly, members make their presentations either in Frisian or in Dutch, without translation. Most members regularly utilize Frisian. The provincial government has also begun to announce all of its job vacancies in Frisian, this notwithstanding the fact that only 17% of those whose mother tongue is Frisian (and almost none of those whose second language is Frisian) ever use Frisian in any governmental or administrative context. In some ways this entire area of RLS-effort is very similar to that of

Frisian in education. A great deal of attention has been given to the legalistic niceties of language legislation and policy statements, and the overcoming of Dutch resistance in these areas is greatly stressed as a matter of principle. However, once proper legal provisions are in place in the few areas in which Dutch resistance has finally been worn down, the implementation of new opportunities via RLS funding and concrete institutional procedures leaves much to be desired.

Thus far there has been considerable animosity against Frisian in administration only in conjunction with the imposition of monolingual Frisian placenames in some municipalities. Animosity is far from common, however, and the provincial government has appointed a Language Promoter to assist the four municipalities (out of the 31 in all of Friesland) that have adopted the 'one language at a time' approach in their administrative work. Eleven of the 31 municipalities have adopted local policies fostering the use of Frisian in municipal administration. Two have decided to declare their Frisian names to be official. These are all meaningful symbolic actions, to be sure, but it remains highly questionable whether they will contribute in any way to halting the intergenerational drift away from Frisian. For that purpose they are simply too far removed from the everyday life of the heartland of the intergenerational mother tongue process.[16]

*Stage 1: Government, employment and education at the highest levels*

Government is very strongly represented in the Basquization effort as well as in the very process of self-Basquization (i.e. Basquization of the government itself). Higher education has been less impacted thus far, although some notable advances have been made. Even the spheres of upper management, finance, industry and commerce have been breached, although least has been accomplished here relative to the first-mentioned spheres.

The total RLS-effort is vigorously directed by the Secretariat of Language Policy, an agency which is entrusted with coordinating the language-related work of all governmental departments as well as with overall planning, providing authoritative information, evaluation and research in this regard. The Secretariat's overall priorities are proposed by the 'Advisory Board on the Basque Language', the supreme consultative body for planning and coordinating all government activities regarding Basque. The 'Advisory Board's Plenary' is presided over by the President of the BAC himself and has on it representatives from the Ministry of Education, the Royal Academy of the Basque Language, the University of the Basque Country, the University of Deustu, the Secretariat of Language Policy and a dozen well-known Basque experts. The 'Board' has various standing committees that receive and analyze the respective 'Plans of Action' of various governmental departments, as well as their annual progress reports pertaining thereto. On the bases of these several individual plans the 'Plenary' then proposes to the government the 'General Plan of Action' with respect to Basque and any changes that should be made in the plans previously adopted. Although some of the above bureaucratic superstructure may be excessive, it does accurately convey the deep and abiding BAC governmental dedication to improving the fortunes of the Basque language and to doing so just as quickly and as fully as possible.

The university scene with respect to Basque is less impressive at present. The oldest institution, the University of Deustu, established only a century ago (1887), is not substantially Basque. The relatively new institutions that exist in Bilbao, San Sebastian and Vitoria-Gasteiz (all of them being branches of the University of BAC) are still partially incomplete and generally too young to be taken seriously by the academic world, in comparison to their older and more eminent counterparts elsewhere in Spain and abroad. On the other hand, their Basquization goals are serious and onerous ones: to enable all university disciplines to be taught in both Spanish and Basque. Although this goal is still a long way from being attained (perhaps a third of all UBAC courses are now also being taught entirely or predominantly in Basque to a small but slowly growing cadre of interested students; indeed, there is currently more student demand for such courses than there is Basque-competent faculty capable of gratifying this demand), none the less hundreds of specialized textbooks and academic nomenclatures have been prepared in Basque by cadres of subsidized and volunteer specialists and, for the first time in Basque history, there are young Basque intellectuals who are embarking on academic careers in Basque rather than only in Spanish or French. Unfortunately, even under the best circumstances, universities require many generations in order to develop to levels of real intellectual excellence and it is not clear whether such development is really in store for the fledgling institutions of the BAC. However, that these institutions will contribute to the further modernization of Basque and to the intensification of intellectual life in that language is quite clear. For the moment, that may be their major claim to fame.

The uppermost reaches of corporate enterprise, tied in as they are to national and to international concerns and directed as they usually are by individuals of middle age and beyond, most of them coming for 'tours of duty' from outside the BAC, are undoubtedly among the least Basquized aspects of life in the BAC. Perhaps all that can be expected of them, in most cases, is that they do not appear to be obstructing the Basquization effort but, rather, to be cooperating with it, at least passively.

The Frisian scene at the very highest levels is far less promising and, above all, far less coordinated and vigorous than its Basque counterpart. While it is true that there is some centralized planning with respect to language policy, both at the province-wide and at the municipal levels, these developments are so recent that it is not possible to judge yet whether they really involve more than public posturing and the adoption of well-meaning and good-sounding resolutions that have neither the necessary enthusiasm, funding nor implementation to back them up. The Frisians often succeed in scolding and berating the central authorities for the lack of central (i.e. Hague-funded or approved) support for the Frisianization of Friesland, more than they succeed in consensually adopting and then vigorously following through on anything like a well-considered set of urgent priorities to be accomplished by their own wherewithal and efforts. The Frisian activists are right, of course; they do deserve the central recognition and support that they seek. But the secret of RLS is not merely to be right but, first and foremost, to be effective.

Before Dutch Higher Education began to be cut back in the early and mid-80s, and in some cases it was cut back not only to the bone but into the bone itself, there had been fond plans for the establishment of a university in Friesland (in Ljouwert [Leeuwarden]), in initial affiliation with the nearby distinguished University of Groningen. Such a university, it was hoped, could be a center not only for Frisian studies but for studies of minority language and culture issues, including the various expressions of individual and societal bilingualism, more generally. These plans have now been scrapped, at least for the foreseeable future, and the only functioning Frisian institutions of intellectual prominence are the non-degree granting Frisian Academy, the Provincial Educational Council and the Frisian Center for Bilingual Schooling. The Academy's work has long received international recognition for its solid research and publications contributions to a variety of humanistic disciplines, but neither it nor the educational agencies mentioned above can substitute for the breadth and depth of intellectual leadership that a university can provide. This is particularly true in The Netherlands where Frisian students studying at the various distinguished universities in other parts of the country are 'naturally' perceived as Netherlanders, rather than as Frisians, and where the tendency to adopt this self-view by the Frisians themselves is quite irresistable, regardless of what their self-image may have been in Friesland proper. Universities are far from sufficient for guaranteeing the success of RLS-efforts, but their absence 'at home' and their plentiful presence among Ymen provide a commonly used exit-door from Xish and Xishness, for Frisian youngsters and for other Xmen the world over,[17] even though it must be mentioned that there are chairs in Frisian linguistics at the universities in Groningen, Amsterdam (with chairs at two different universities), Leiden and Utrecht, none of these being in Friesland *per se*.

## Concluding Remarks

All the major drawbacks to Basque RLS are stubbornly lingering residues of the past: erosion of the hinterland due to continuing urbanization and the unprofitability of small rural holdings, demographic weakness within the BAC itself due to the high proportion of Spanish speakers and hispanicized Basques, and the lack of a well-known, productive and widespread literacy tradition. In view of the above circumstances (and the psychological counterparts which they engender) realistic Basque RLS-efforts would be forced to accept the long-term inevitability of bilingualism, even if there were no central state requirements in that connection. Given these circumstances, it is clear that there is still an ever-present danger of 'Irelandization' in the long run, because of the lack of secure home, family and neighborhood foundations for converting the vast variety of RLS-efforts that are underway into a safe intergenerational transmission process.

There can be no doubt, however, that short-run time has been gained, whether one compares youngsters with their parents or older youngsters with younger ones. Among those who are 15–17 years old 36% claim to be able to write Basque, whereas only 23% of those 25–29 years old can make this claim. Some 17% of the younger group reports using Basque with their priest whereas only 9% of the older group does so.[18] Relative to their parents, 14- to 18-year-olds are strikingly ahead in claiming to know some Basque (50% vs 13%). In comparison with the inhabitants of the other Autonomous Communities in Spain (Catalonia, Galicia, Valencian, etc.) young Basques (12- to 18-year-olds) are among the most favorable toward the use of their regional language and in identifying with their region. In these two respects they have caught up with and even outdistanced the Catalans, although the latter are still far ahead with respect to actually speaking their own language. A supradialectal standard has gained increased acceptance and the corpus of the language has been dramatically expanded. Most dramatic of all is the explosion in urban and governmental use, thin facades, it is true, over the underlying Spanish, but a growing 'sign of the times'. All in all, progress has been made, a new generation will certainly have been deeply influenced, and the true dimensions of the continuing struggle are now better recognized than before. With proper priorities ( more directly focusing on fostering and propagating stage 6) the future of Basque can be much, much safer than the recent past has been.

Things do not appear to be nearly so rosy for Frisian, but even here they are not entirely bleak. There is much passive goodwill for Frisian, even among those who do not understand it, and even much understanding of Frisian merely due to its similarity to Dutch. The basic problem seems to be in activating this goodwill, along both personal and societal lines. Unfortunately, there are few if any pervasive Frisianizing factors that can be counted upon to really make a difference.

The goodwill that often makes it easier than it used to be to speak Frisian in public, even to interlocutors who respond in Dutch, remains largely unharnessed (or even unharnessable) in terms that are productive of intergenerational transmissibility of Frisian as a mother tongue. The language policies pertaining to education and to administration, the two major areas of language policy struggle thus far, remain legalistically encumbered, contested and essentially unimplemented insofar as their broader possibilities are concerned. There are, of course, still some fanatical '*Djip Friezen*' (= deep Frisians; the designation is a play on words to evoke an association with the expression 'deep freeze") who still dream of a totally Frisian Friesland, both linguistically and demographically, but even they are totally uncoordinated and generally ineffectual. Not that there is a let-up of activity. The dispute about the official use of Frisian placenames continues to be very intense. Pro-Frisian 'demonstration societies' and even a secret society have claimed considerable media attention, as has the formation of the first anti-Frisian society. The resulting uproar seems to have awakened the activists. The first all-Frisian childcare play-group has come into being in Ljouwert. Thus, the struggle is far from over. Indeed, it may go on forever, ineffective though it may generally be insofar as intergenerational transmissibility of Frisian as a mother tongue is concerned.

Those who have grown up Frisian-speaking during the most recent years now encounter an environment that is much more Dutchified, in almost all formal and informal domains, than was the case a generation ago. Modern society, being inherently more volatile than the traditional life that it has constantly eroded, requires a constant stream of innovations in order to make an impression or to be impressed. The Basque scene is so crammed full of such constant innovations that it is hard to tell 'exactly what is really working', since there are so many efforts going on simultaneously. The Frisian scene is rather lethargic in comparison, and it is hard for RLSers there to finally strike out on a course of action since they have such a penchant for prolonged discussion and profound disagreement. Even more unfortunate is the fact that proposed policies directly involving the family are often considered to be too private or personal and, therefore, 'off limits' for RLS policy purposes. A certain disinclination toward policies interpretable as infringing on the family's privacy is a trait that Frisians share with other Netherlanders (although why it is that some things are so interpreted while others — e.g. legal wills, personal prayers and family-selected kindergartens are not — is not at all clear. Such disinclinations stand in the way of thinking language policies through to the inevitable role of the family, home, neighborhood and local community in repairing the damage that has been done to Frisian. There is no way in which education, public administration or even the much touted media can substitute or compensate for the basic family-proximate processes of transmission. Hopefully this realization will take hold before it is too late for stage 6 to be reclaimed and before there will be no alternative but to return to stage 7 as the last arena of natural Frisian for an aging segment of the population. As hard as it may be to build stage 6, and, particularly under modern circumstances it is admittedly very difficult — although not impossible — it is even harder to reach that stage once the retreat to stage 7 has become generalized.[19-21]

## Notes

1.  Navarre, although historically Basque and with a not inconsiderable Basque-speaking population (53,000 as of the early 1980s, equivalent to about 11% of the total population, was granted its own Statute of Autonomy. This 'dismemberment' of the Basque Country (a more inclusive and traditional designation than that of the Basque Autonomous Community) is still vehemently opposed by many Basque nationalists, including, but not limited to, several Basque terrorist groups. Other autonomous regions established at roughly the same time are the Catalan Autonomous Community, Valencia (also dismembered from the CAC) Navarre and Galicia. The situation from the 'Spanish patriotic catechism' is reported in Azevedo (1984).

2.  The figures reported here are from an unpublished 1986 study by Martinez de Luna. Note that 39% of 15- to 17-year-olds and 30% of 25- to 29-year-olds believe that the BAC 'should be Basque-speaking'.

3.  The first cited usage of the term 'normalization' is that of R.L. Ninyoles in his *Idioma y poder social*. Madrid: Tecnos, 1972). The term has remained little used outside of its original Iberian setting. Also see Cobarrubias and Lasa (1987) for a brief discussion of this term and some insight into its different implications *vis-á-vis* the Autonomous Catalan Community and the Autonomous Basque Community. It is in the former case only that 'normalization' primarily implies a return to a former, more normal (= functionally all-embracing and, therefore, essentially monolingual) functionality. See Chapter 10 for further discussion of this concept in connection with Catalan RSL-efforts.

4.  My major sources in this section have been Cobarrubias and Lasa (1987), Secretariat of Language Policy (1986a), Siguan (1988) and notes gathered during my own field-work, primarily in and around San Sebastian during the summers of 1985 and 1986, in Madrid as well during the latter period, and during brief but very intensive visits to Bilbao in mid-1989 and early 1990. Mike Zalbide (San Sebastian/Victoria-Gasteiz) and Nick Gardner (Victoria-Gasteiz) commented extensively on a first draft of my comments and I have relied on their comments quite heavily in order to help me avoid the usual biased characterizations (or caricatures) as to the purported 'primitiveness' or 'backwardness' of Basque culture and society which can still be found in Iberian discussions of the Basque scene.

5.  The Frisian scholarly and social traditions do not include within the designation 'Frisian' either 'City Frisian' or several even smaller and even more discrepant Frisian dialects. We will also adhere to the Frisian tradition in connection with these matters, since to do otherwise would be to impose outside criteria on the definition of what the Frisian speech community is or should be. More generally,

neither linguistic distance nor intercommunicability are as relevant to RLS-efforts as the inside ('emic') view of what constitutes the 'natural [or feasible] language boundaries' to be defended.

6. Frisian is the major indigenous minority language of The Netherlands. Even more severe problems are faced by the country's immigrant minority languages. In the latter connection note the extensive bibliography in Guus Extra and Ton Vallen (1985).

7. My basic sources for this introductory discussion of the Frisian language situation are Boelens (1987), Gorter (1987a and b), Khleif (1982), van der Plank (1987), Smith (1987) and personal fieldwork notes gathered in mid-1982, in early 1983 and in mid-1989.

8. My observations on stages 8 and 7 in the Basque country are primarily based on extensive discussions with Basque educators, scholars and professionals, on the one hand, and with ordinary citizens, on the other hand, during visits to the BAC. The corpus planning efforts referred to are primarily those of UZEI, a private firm set up in 1977, that has by now published dozens of technical nomenclatures. Although these are often criticized as having been constructed in an overly hasty manner, with too little attention to the consultation, try-out, evaluation and revision stages of lexical elaboration, it is quite obvious that a huge amount of work has been accomplished by this firm and that no other (governmentally more responsible) group has accomplished anything comparable during the same brief period.

9. My comments are based on personal observations and interviews and discussions in 1982, 1983 and 1989, as well as on very welcome personal memoranda prepared for my use by Durk Gorter and Koen Zondag. Khleif (1982) has also been most helpful. Gorter has kindly commented extensively on an earlier draft of this chapter and I am well aware of my indebtedness to him throughout the Frisian sections of this chapter.

10. The comments and findings of Anon. (1988b) Azurmendi (1986), Larrañaga (unpublished ms., 1986) and Martinez de Luna (unpublished, 1986) have been particularly helpful to me in the preparation of my remarks re stage 6 in the BAC.

11. In connection with the above discussion of stage 6 in Friesland I have depended on the writings of Khleif (1982), van der Plank (1987), Zondag (1987) and, particularly, a memorandum prepared for my personal use by Zondag.

12. My major sources of information concerning stage 5 in Friesland are Khleif (1982) and special memoranda prepared for my use by Durk Gorter and Koen Zondag. With respect to the BAC, I have relied upon Anon. (1988b), Azurmendi (1986), Cobarrubias and Lasa (1987) and Secretariat for Language Policy (1986c).

13. The Basquization of teachers, the EGA Examinations, the growth of *ikastolas*, and type B and type D schools are well discussed in Anon. (1988b), Artola and Berasategi (1986), Martinez de Luna (unpublished, 1986), Churruca (1986), Cobarrubias and Lasa (1987), Department of Education, Universities and Research (1986, 1987).

14. The complexities of the Frisian school scene are instructively clarified in the writings of Boelens (1987), de Jong (1982), Gorter (1982), Meestringa (1987) and Zondag (ms. and 1982).

15. Basque or Frisian at work are treated in Boelens (1987), Census of 1986 and a memorandum prepared for my use by Azurmendi. Generally speaking, there is a great paucity of exhaustive and systematic attention to stage 3. Accordingly, I have relied on my own field notes in both settings very extensively.

16. The mass media, print and non-print, and the functioning of Basque or Frisian administrative units are treated in memoranda for my use by Boelens, de Vries,

Gorter and Zondag. Useful publications in this connection are those by Boelens (1987), Gorter (1982 and 1988), Khleif (1982), Meestringa (1987), van der Plank (1987) and Anon (1988b), Azurmendi (1986), Cobarrubias and Lasa (1987), Gardner (ms) and Secretariat of Language Policy (1986a and c).

17. My discussion in this section depends substantially on my own fieldwork, in both the Basque Autonomous Community and in Friesland, on several recent occasions. The only additional sources utilized beyond those previously mentioned is Secretariat of Language Policy (1986b).

18. One of the major predictors of Basque use and of pro-Basque attitudes are Catholic (and even 'Very Catholic") involvements and practices. Other powerful predictors are affiliation with nationalist and left-wing parties, and female gender. Cumulative multiple prediction is urgently needed to determine just how much of the variance in Basque use, is accounted for by each of these and other relevant respondent characteristics taken one at a time, as well as how much they account for when taken all together.

19. Beyond those references already cited, I have found the following items to be useful and provocative in fostering my familiarity with the BAC and its RLS-efforts: Anon. (1988b), Anon. (1989), Clark (1980), Etxebarría (unpublished 1988), EIFE-2 (1989), Gardner (1986, 1988, 1989), Labayen (1965), Lasa (1968), Zalbide (personal communication).

20. Beyond those references already cited, I have found the following items to be helpful and stimulating in fostering my familiarity with RLS-efforts in Friesland: Gorter (unpublished 1988), Gorter et al. (1984), Keppley Mahmood (1989), Ytsma (1986), Zondag (undated) and Zondag (personal communication).

21. None of those whom I have cited or whose help I have acknowledged throughout this chapter are in any way responsible for (or, necessarily, even in agreement with) the interpretations and conclusions that I have arrived at on the basis of their invaluable assistance. This chapter was completed during the first quarter of 1990.

# References

## (a) References pertaining to Basque

ANON. 1988a The determination of the Basques. *Contact* 5, 2, 1–2.

— 1988b, *Cooperation Between the Public Institutions and the Popular Organizations in the Normalisation of the Language.* Donostia: Euskarazko Kulturaran Batzarrea.

— 1989, There are one hundred and twenty choirs in the Basque Country. *Euskal Etxeak* No. 6–7, 13.

ARTOLA, Ihñaki and BERASATEGI, Jose Mari 1986, *Basquising School Atmosphere.* Vitoria-Gasteiz: Department of Education, Universities and Research, Gobierno Vasco. Mimeo.

AZVEDO, Milton 1984, The reestablishment of Catalan as a language of culture. *Hispanic Linguistics* 1, 305–30.

AZURMENDI AYERBE, María-José 1986, La juventud de euskadi en relación con el Euskara. In Elso JAVIER *et al. Juventud Vasca 1986.* Vitoria-Gasteiz: Gobierno Vasco.

CENSUS OF 1986: Preliminary results. Vitoria-Gasteiz: Goberno Vasco. Mimeo.

CHURRUCA, Juan 1986, *Seis Años de Autonomía en Educación*. Vitoria-Gasteiz: Department of Education, Universities and Research, Gobierno Vasco.

CLARK, Robert P. 1980, Euskadi: Basque nationalism in Spain since the Civil War. In Charles R. FOSTER (ed.) *Nations Without a State: Ethnic Minorities in Western Europe*. New York: Praeger, 76–100.

COBARRUBIAS, Juan and LASA, Carmen Garmendia 1987, Language policy and language planning efforts in Spain. In Lorne LAFORGE, (ed.) *Proceedings of the International Colloquium on Language Planning*. Quebec City: Laval University Press, 132–92.

DEPARTMENT OF EDUCATION, UNIVERSITIES AND RESEARCH 1986, *Literacy Training and Basquisation of the Teaching Staff*. Vitoria-Gasteiz: Basque Government.

— 1987, *EGA Certificate of Proficiency*. Vitoria-Gasteiz: Basque Government.

EIFE-2 1989, *Influence of Factors on the Learning of Basque*. Gastiez: Central Publications Service of the Basque Government.

ETXEBARRÍA, Maitena 1988, La modernización de la lengua vasca en la administración. Mimeo.

EXTRA, Guus and VALLEN, Tom (eds) 1985 *Ethnic Minorities and Dutch as a Second Language*. Dordrecht: Foris.

GARDNER, Nick 1986, Basque in public administration. Vitoria-Gasteiz: Department of Education, Universities and Research, Gobierno Vasco. Mimeo.

— 1988, What sort of public service Basque language examinations are feasible? Vitoria-Gasteiz: Department of Education, Universities and Research, Gobierno Vasco. Mimeo.

— 1989, Language planning in the Autonomous Community of the Basque Country, 1975–1989. Vitoria-Gasteiz: Department of Education, Universities and Research, Gobierno Vasco.

LABAYEN, Antonio María 1965, Creación de la academia de Lengua y Declamación Euskara. Appendix 2 in his Teatro Euskaro. San Sebastian-Donostia: Auñamendi, 139–51.

LARAÑAGA, Iñaki 1986, La situación del euskara en el ámbito familiar: investigaciones relizadas y en proyecto en relación con la transmisión familiar del euskara: San Sebastian, Siadeco. Mimeo.

LASA, Fr. José Ignacio 1968, Iturriaga, adelantado de las artes pedagógicas sobre el vascuence. In his *Sobre la Enseñanza Primaria en el País Vasco*. San Sebastian-Donostia: aunamendi, 147–60.

MARKHAM, James M. 1980, Basque ikastolas: saving a heritage. *New York Times*, January 6, p. 21 (Education).

ROS, Maria, CANO, J. and HUKI, Carmen 1988, Language and intergroup perception in Spain. In William B. GUDYKUNST (ed.) *Language and Ethnic Identity*. Clevedon: Multilingual Matters, 87–103.

SECRETARIAT OF LINGUISTIC POLICY 1986a, *Secretariat of Linguistic Policy*. Vitoria-Gasteiz: Basque Government.

— 1986b, *The Advisory Board on the Basque Language*. Vitoria-Gasteiz: Basque Government.

— 1986c, *Basic Law of the Standardization of the Use of Basque*. Vitoria-Gasteiz: Basque Government.

SIGUAN, Miguel 1988, Bilingual education in Spain. In Christina Bratt PAULSTON (ed.) *International Handbook on Bilingualism and Bilingual Education*. New York: Greenwood, 449–73.

*(b) References pertaining to Frisian*

Boelens, K. 1987, *The Frisian Language* (revised, by D. Gorter and K. Zondag). Leeuwarden/Ljouwert: Provincial Government of Friesland.

De Jong, Sikko 1982, Objectives of the bilingual schools in Friesland: Correspondence and deviation between theory and practice. In K. Zondag (ed.) *Bilingual Education in Friesland*. Frjentsjer/Franeker: T. Wever, 1–35.

Gorter, Durk 1982, Education in Frisian and public opinion. In K. Zondag (ed.) *Bilingual Education in Friesland*. Frjentsjer/Franeker: T. Wever, 96–126.

— 1987a, Aspects of language choice in the Frisian-Dutch bilingual context: neutrality and asymmetry. In Gearóid Mac Eoin, Anders Ahlquist and Donncha O'Haudha (eds) *Third International Conference on Minority Languages (General Papers)*. Clevedon: Multilingual Matters, 121–32.

— 1987b, Surveys of the Frisian language situation: some considerations of research methods on language maintenance and language shift. *International Journal of the Sociology of Language* 68, 41–56.

— 1988, The case of Frisian in the Netherlands. Mimeo.

Gorter, Durk, *et al.* 1984 *Taal yn Fryslân*. Ljouwert: Fryske Akademy.

— 1988, *Language in Friesland*. Ljouwert: Fryske Akademy.

Keppley Mahmood, Cynthia 1989, *Frisian and Free*. Prospect Heights: Waveland.

Khleif, Bud B. 1982, Ethnicity and language with reference to the Frisian case; Issues of schooling, work and identity. In K. Zondag (ed.) *Bilingual Education in Friesland*. Frjentsjer/Franeker: T. Wever, 1975–204.

Meestringa, Theun 1987, English as a foreign language in Frisian bilingual primary schools. *International Journal of the Sociology of Language* 64, 59–70.

Smith, Jim 1987, Review of 'Taal yn Fryslân' (1984). *International Journal for the Sociology of Language* 64, 121–4.

Van Der Plank, P. H. 1987, Frisian language use and ethnic identity. *International Journal of the Sociology of Language* 64, 9–20.

Zondag, Koen 1982, Background to the educational system of the Netherlands and Friesland. In his (ed.) *Bilingual Education in Friesland*. Frjentsjer/Franeker: T. Wever, 1–35.

— 1987, This morning the church presents a comedy. *International Journal of the Sociology of Language*. 64, 71–80.

— Undated. Early biliteracy in a monoculture.

# 7 Four American Examples: Navajo, Spanish and Yiddish (Secular and Ultra-Orthodox)

The United States is not just a country like all other countries, it is an entire world. Huge, rich, highly urbanized, ethno-religiously diverse and relatively recently populated, language shift has become part of its still-forming national ethos. Although initially settled by anglophone 'Pilgrim Fathers' who left the religiously tolerant Netherlands and voyaged to the New World precisely because their children were losing English and becoming linguistically Dutchified, the maintenance of other languages was never consensually declared to be a part of the 'American Dream' and, instead, the displacement of other mother tongues by English became a popular expectation and, more than that, even a verity, particularly since the early days of this century. A brief reversal of this trend during the 'ethnic revival' of the mid-60s to the mid-70s has contributed to the recent insecurity and the self-centeredness of the anglo and anglified middle class, characteristics which have expressed themselves via conservative politics more generally and via such scapegoating as efforts on behalf of English Only ('English Official') amendments[1,2] to state and federal constitutions.

Nevertheless, although language shift has come to be one of the most widely shared and widely expected 'American experiences', on the one hand, language maintenance and RLS-efforts have been a constant feature of two centuries of 'sidestream' American life, on the other hand. The full and stirring story of these manifold language maintenance (LM) and RLS-efforts has been documented by several sociolinguists[3] and this chapter will merely attempt to briefly review the current situations in this connection with respect to three ethnolinguistic groups (one of them considered in terms of its two major sociolinguistic sub-groupings) out of the scores that constitute the total LM/RLS reality in the United States: namely, the situations of one indigenous language (Navajo), one colonial language that has recently been augmented by large-scale immigration (Spanish) and one immigrant language (Yiddish). The basic similarity of the story that we have to tell about such initially very different cases (different in size, in historical depth within the USA, in social structure, in interaction with and dependence upon the 'mainstream', and in degree of concentration) is indicative of the powerful and basically similar societal influences associated with and dominated by the anglo mainstream, similarities which overcome all of the above differences and which point almost all minority ethnolinguistic development in the same direction. Their implications for minorities elsewhere, whether indigenous or immigrant, should be evident.

## The Current State of Navajo

The Navajos are over 200,000 in number and more than half of them are concentrated in Arizona alone. Almost all of the others are in New Mexico, with more minor numbers being in Utah and Colorado. These four states are contiguous, meeting at right angles with each other ('Four Corners'), and the Navajo Reservation itself is either within or borders upon them all. Although specific treaties presumably regulate the relations between the United States and the Navajo Nation, the Navajos are far from being a free and independent people as the existence of such treaties seemingly implies. Both much of American law in general and of Bureau of Indian Affairs regulations in particular, apply to the Navajos (i.e. have been imposed upon them) and have consequences for their self-government, their economic development and well-being and their relations with their Amerindian and anglo neighbors. They have been forced to engage in livestock reduction (1930s), relocation (50s and 60s) and propelled into hostilities and arbitration with neighboring tribes (40s and to this very day), all of these processes contributing, on the one hand, to a loss of Navajoness and, on the other hand, to the growth of the 'Xmen-via-Yish' phenomenon.

While the Navajos clearly constitute the largest intact Amerindian ethnocultural entity in the USA today, and although they are primarily concentrated in a relatively inaccessible and inhospitable reservation, it is, nevertheless, already the case that roughly half of their number are no longer Navajo-speaking, particularly those who have relocated in Navajo Reservation towns or off the Reservation entirely, as well as those who have more recently returned to the Reservation (often with non-Navajo spouses and minimally Navajo-enculturated children), after extended periods of off-Reservation work, education and personal contacts. Life on the Reservation provides all the rewards of living among one's own and participating in one's own ethnocultural traditions. On the other hand, it is a relatively hard life and one which is supported largely by sheep-raising and by government-financed work (or 'make-work') of various kinds (including work at government-financed Navajo Community Schools, see below).

Both unemployment and underemployment are high (indeed, among the very highest in the USA) and in the midst of seemingly affluent America the

Reservation strikes all those who are familiar with 'the outside' as a Third-World-like pocket of poverty. Jobs requiring English offer only some economic relief (and even less psychic gratification), but these inexorably lead away from contact with and involvement in an Xmen-via-Xish life-style, whether traditional or modified. The new, constantly growing, Xmen-via-Yish life-style may be generally regretted by adults but is even more generally viewed as inevitable and even promising by the youngsters who constitute the bulk of the Navajo population (average age about 18). The reservation area is huge (25,000 square miles, or roughly the size of West Virginia) and rich in largely unexploited mineral resources. These resources are, at present, largely owned or controlled by outside economic interests and there seems to be little prospect for correcting this state of affairs, although Navajo-instigated lawsuits have long been underway in attempts to do just that.

Since the arrival of the Whitemen, the persistence of Navajo has primarily depended (and successfully so) on its seemingly unbridgeable cultural, physical and economic distance from anglo-society. In recent years, however, this separation has lessened dramatically, what with improvements and expansions of the mass-communication media and of all of the major arteries of vehicular traffic. As a result, most Navajos are now bilingual. In 1976, English competence was rated as 'high' among 42% of those who still spoke primarily Navajo and, in addition, another 23% already spoke English primarily, with 10% of that number being English monolinguals.[4] Although Navajos are still among the more maintenance-effective minority mother tongue groups in the USA today, their growing anglification began to set in a generation ago. Of the parents of current school-aged children (4–17 years old), 11.5% use more English than Navajo (or even only English) in their daily lives. Among the school-aged children themselves this is true of 34%. Indeed, among those children both of whose parents are English-dominant bilinguals, 84% primarily speak English; and even among parents both of whom are primarily or only Navajo speakers, 17% of their children are primarily English speakers (a percentage which rises precipitously if only one parent, particularly the mother, is primarily English-speaking). Obviously, the Navajos are finding it increasingly difficult to compartmentalize English effectively into only certain functions and, unless this situation is reversed, further attrition of their traditional language is a foregone conclusion. On the other hand, a growing number of tribal leaders have come to be concerned, albeit still only informally, with fostering, protecting and restoring both Navajo language use and the observance of the authentic traditions with which that use has so long been associated. Thus, while there is now no tribal organization concerned explicitly with the current state or the future of Navajo (the now defunct Bilingual Education Unit in the tribe's Division of Education having formerly served this function), the slow shift to English is now noticeable even in Reservation-interior communities. It is even more noticeable, of course, in more urbanized Reservation areas. In the latter, however, there are also some few signs of active RLS sentiments and efforts, so that the overall picture is both more negative and more diversified or differentiated than it long used to be. Both maintenance and RLS-efforts are underway that help maintain substantial indigenous regulation and direction of Navajo culture change. Unfortunately, however, generations of passive dependence on such quickly disappearing factors as isolation or distance from anglo influences as the prime protectors of the Navajo way of life has left its definite mark, although it is badly in need of replacement. It remains to be seen whether such replacement will be anything other than too little and too late.

## The Current State of Spanish (Focusing on Puerto Ricans in New York)

Spanish is obviously the major non-English mother tongue in the USA today, although due to the sizeable number of its illegally immigrated speakers there is no certainty as to the exact number of its speakers or mother tongue claimants. Estimates as to speakers vary widely (between 15 million and 25 million, the mean between these two extremes, 20 million, probably being a safe compromise figure for the late 1980s) and the continuation and magnitude of the largely illegal immigration, an obvious imponderable, may well be the major determinant of the long-term maintenance of Spanish in the continental USA. However, even at its maximum, Spanish mother tongue accounts for less than 10% of the total population of the country (the proportion attained by German prior to World War I) and Spanish speakers themselves are by no means a demographically or culturally unified 'block'. Indeed, the extent to which their diversity and dispersion should be focused upon, rather than the mainstream tendency to lump them together as 'Hispanics', is another imponderable of major importance in any forecast of the future.

The label 'Hispanics' is a misnomer if it is taken to imply a single, unified ethnocultural entity. It is only in the USA, and only in relatively recent years at that, that the Mexican-Americans ('Chicanos'), Puerto Ricans ('Boricuas'), Cubans and other Caribbeans, and Central and South Americans, the four major segments of the total 'Hispanic' contingent, have interacted appreciably and begun to realize and accept the common fate, common perceptions on the part of outsiders, common cultural features and, in some parts of the country, residential propinquity and social class disadvantages, that primarily bind them together. Although they have increasingly begun to prefer the designation 'Latinos', particularly in the more communally mixed Northeastern and North Central regions of the USA, the differences between them are still extensive. The Mexican-Americans, by now primarily urbanized and primarily characterized as of recent immigration, still have a sizeable rural population in the American Southwest as well as a small upper class, both of which date back to Spanish colonial days. The Puerto Ricans are primarily concentrated in the urban megalopolis that stretches from Boston through New York and Philadelphia to Washington and generally manifest all of the manifold cultural dislocations of poverty and (im)migration (often of several '[im]migration, return and re-[im]migration' cycles). The Cubans are concentrated in southern Florida and boast a sizeable and very enterprising 'white' middle class (buttressed by wealthy Latin Americans arriving from other countries of origin). Their economic ascendency has aroused the envy and opposition of their anglo counterparts (although the more recent 'Mariel boatlift Cubans' are primarily rural, poor and more obviously 'non-white'). Thus, while most Hispanics are blamed for being poor, uneducated, dislocated and dependent on public assistance, others are blamed for being wealthy, highly competitive and successfully enterprising.

The other Caribbean and Central or South American derived Hispanics basically present a profile similar to Puerto Ricans, with the added disadvantages of the scars of recent, war-related, personal tragedies in their erstwhile homelands. Except for the Cubans, many Hispanics also frequently suffer from widespread mainstream bias against 'people of color' (this is so even though not all of them, by any means, are visibly identifiable. Most lighter skinned Hispanics of mixed ancestry are still commonly not regarded as 'white' by non-Hispanic Whites, although they are fully accepted by 'white Hispanics' on the basis of shared ethnicity; see Denton and Massey, 1989). Finally, possibly except for the majority of Cubans, most of them suffer from political impotence, due partly to their illegal status, partly to their internal fractionization and partly to their lack of orientation *vis-à-vis* American political reality. This latter weakness may yet be reversed somewhat during the coming years, as the unifying label ('Hispanics' or 'Latinos'), on the one hand, and an American-born leadership group, on the other hand, both come to the fore.

The Spanish language maintenance and RLS situations are probably as complex as the ethnocultural sketch provided above, and, if anything, even more handicapped by a lack of adequate and recent data.[5] The best available information indicates that the total number of Spanish mother tongue claimants is in the neighborhood of 12 to 13 million, of whom slightly more than half are American-born.[6] These, like the total Hispanic population of the country, are overwhelmingly concentrated in California, Texas, Florida, New Mexico, Arizona and New York, with just over half of the total being in the first two states alone. The language maintenance potential of this high degree of concentration is further reinforced by the fact that some 88% of the parents of school-aged Hispanic children are active speakers of Spanish. On the negative side of the ledger, however, is the fact that over 30% of these children are already English monolinguals, this percentage rising to 55% where both parents are native-born and primarily English-speaking, and to 80% where the mother is native-born and monolingually English-speaking. Except where one parent is still a Spanish monolingual (regardless of place of birth), the vast majority of Hispanic children of school age are primarily English speakers, even though, as can be deduced from the information provided above, nearly 70% of them still speak Spanish on occasions.

The occasional use of Spanish is itself currently structured in a fashion which is more indicative of language shift than of language maintenance. The younger generations more frequently speak Spanish to those who are older than they are (their parents, grandparents and other members of these two older generations) than they do to those who are of their own or of a younger generation.[7] This pattern has been documented for Texas, California and New York, as has the growing tendency among adults and children alike to mix the two languages, particularly when speaking Spanish amongst themselves, and to do so by means of entire English phrases, on the one hand, and by English phrasal calques (i.e. entire phrases translated word for word from English) within their Spanish, on the other hand.[8] Putting all of these pieces of the puzzle together, imperfectly though they may fit, and adding to them other signs of galloping social change among Hispanics on the USA mainland (e.g. their increasing Protestantization, co-option into anti-bilingual education efforts and co-option into the pro-'English Official' movement), leaves one with the definite impression of a major language shift tidal wave underway under the surface, masked as yet by the large number of monolingually Spanish recent arrivals. Although Spanish on the USA mainland is certainly not faced by any danger of total attrition, huge portions of it are faced by serious weakening and by an unfortunately implied relationship with such negative factors as illegal status, foreign nativity, unwillingness to Americanize and poverty. Accordingly, language maintenance and RLS-efforts have recently come to be of interest even in connection with this giant of the non-English language scene in the USA. As Table 7.1 reveals, without further immigration, both the total number of Hispanics and the proportion of Spanish-only or Spanish-dominant Hispanics will shrink dramatically during the next century.

## The Current State of Yiddish, Secular and Ultra-Orthodox

On the whole, the situation of Yiddish is much weaker than that of either of the two languages discussed above. It generally lacks both the mainstream

TABLE 7.1   *Estimated numbers of Hispanics and English-Spanish bilinguals in the USA, into the last quarter of the twenty-first century, without further Hispanic migration (and without substantial RLS-efforts)*

| Year | Estimated population | Percent aged 40+ | Percent English bilingual |
|------|------|------|------|
| 2001 | 12.24 | 45.3 | 54.3 |
| 2006 | 11.93 | 48.5 | 56.3 |
| 2011 | 11.64 | 54.4 | 58.2 |
| 2016 | 11.22 | 59.2 | 60.1 |
| 2021 | 10.47 | 63.1 | 62.5 |
| 2026 | 9.91 | 69.4 | 64.2 |
| 2031 | 9.11 | 73.2 | 66.0 |
| 2036 | 8.36 | 77.5 | 67.6 |
| 2041 | 7.57 | 80.1 | 69.4 |
| 2046 | 6.46 | 80.9 | 71.8 |
| 2051 | 5.76 | 83.4 | 73.7 |
| 2056 | 5.04 | 85.5 | 75.6 |
| 2061 | 4.31 | 87.0 | 76.9 |
| 2066 | 3.61 | 87.8 | 79.3 |
| 2071 | 2.61 | 87.9 | 82.5 |
| 2076 | 2.18 | 88.0 | 84.9 |

*Source*: Veltman, 1990

separation of interior-Reservation Navajo, on the one hand, and the numbers (and, most particularly, the self-replenishing [im]migrational potential) of Spanish, on the other hand. Although its position is generally similar to that of various other pre-World War I immigrant languages in the USA today (particularly to those that have experienced no significant immigrational reinforcement since then and are not expecting any such reinforcement in the foreseeable future either, e.g. Dutch, Norwegian, Swedish, Danish), both external and internal characteristics of the Jewish community combine to make the overall situation of Yiddish incomparably more precarious. The Nazi-inspired and primarily Nazi-conducted Holocaust annihilated six million European Jews during World War II, some five million of whom constituted the heartland of this language's authentic Eastern European ethnocultural base. Since then, massive upward social mobility in the USA (and the cultural and linguistic Americanization that both contributed to and resulted therefrom) and a similar mobility plus half a century of governmental ethno-religious repression in the USSR (from roughly the mid-1930s to the very late 80s) and, finally, the triumphantly Hebrew-focused emphases in Israel, all combined to tear away additional millions of speakers from this language. As a result of all of the foregoing genocidal cataclysms and cultural dislocations, the total number of Yiddish mother tongue claimants worldwide has shrunk from over 10 million before World War II to somewhat over three million today. Of this latter number, nearly half are in the USA and, accordingly, the future of Yiddish in the USA (where it has consistently been one of the top six non-English languages during the entire twentieth century) will go a long way toward determining the future of this language throughout the entire world.[9]

The Yiddish mother tongue population in the USA — some million and a quarter all in all — is not only overwhelmingly urbanized (and, therefore, overly exposed to the language and culture of mainstream American life), but it is also overwhelmingly concentrated in the Greater New York City Metropolitan Area and in the Greater Los Angeles Metropolitan Area — two of the major social change capitals of the USA. Whatever potential assets may derive from the concentration factor *per se* are further vitiated, however, by several concurrent marked weaknesses of Yiddish from the language maintenance point of view. Among foreign-born Yiddish mother tongue claimants in the USA today, nearly two thirds are already English monolinguals (although many still understand the language) and English is even the language primarily used by over 90% of those who arrived in the USA as recently as during the 1960s. Among native-born Yiddish mother tongue claimants roughly 80% are English monolinguals and nearly 97% are primarily English speakers. Even among the remaining small number of school-aged children who are still of Yiddish mother tongue today (perhaps some 125,000 all in all) only 50% come from homes where the language is still actively spoken. Among American-born children who do come from such homes, nearly 60% are English monolinguals. The total number of active Yiddish speakers in the USA today (including those who are primarily speakers of English but whose Yiddish is still occasionally implemented and adequate for, at the very least, ordinary conversational purposes) is probably no more than 300,000 with school-aged children accounting for roughly 10% of this number.[10] Clearly, the attrition of Yiddish in the USA is far advanced and only drastic and carefully selected steps have any chance of stemming continued attrition in the future.

Another significant factor that must be appreciated in connection with the apparent disarray within the Yiddish mother tongue sector of American Jewry is the extreme nature of the secular vs. ultra-Orthodox distinction within the ranks of its major users and advocates. The secularists (most commonly referred to as 'Yiddishists' but also known as 'Yiddish secular nationalists' in some accounts) arose in late nineteenth- and early twentieth-century Eastern Europe, in the context of other minority nationalist movements within the Czarist and Austro-

Hungarian Empires. They define their Jewishness not in the traditional ethno-religious terms based upon biblical, talmudic and post-talmudic rabbinic sources and authorities, but in modern ethno-national terms based upon language, litera-ture and such modern institutions as schools, theaters and the periodical press, and such modern authorities as the writers, teachers and scholars contributing to the foregoing. Yiddishist secularism in Eastern Europe also frequently had cul-tural autonomist or Zionist goals and a laborite orientation that fractionated over the entire left-wing spectrum from democratic socialism through communism to anarchism. Although productively active in its pro-Yiddish efforts in the USA prior to World War II, secular Yiddishism has weakened drastically since the Holocaust, neither having the Eastern European heartland of Yiddish to draw upon for the replenishment of rapidly anglifying American Jewry nor being able to maintain cultural boundaries between itself and English-speaking Jews (or even non-Jews) who also defined themselves primarily in modern, secular cul-tural terms. Nevertheless, weakened though the secularists are today, they still remain a notable and conscious force on behalf of Yiddish in American Jewish life.[11]

Far less consciously Yiddish-oriented, but far more successful at the inter-generational transmission of the language in daily life, are the ultra-Orthodox, particularly the Hasidic ultra-Orthodox,[12] whose major numbers in the USA trace back to the post World War II decade. Here, Yiddish is not a verity unto itself, as it is in the secular circles sketched above, but the language is adamantly maintained as part of the scrupulously traditional home and community life-style which is the hallmark of ultra-Orthodox life. Jewish vs. non-Jewish and ultra-Orthodox vs. non-ultra-Orthodox boundaries are minutely defined and pre-served, and Yiddish functions significantly in both of these connections as 'quasi sanctified', even though relatively little attention is devoted to it directly.[13]

Although quite different in their demographic compositions, both of the above-mentioned sub-groups are now quite atypical, linguistically as well as in terms of their Jewish priorities and emphases, in American Jewish life. Between the roughly 50,000 relatively aged but conscientiously active secularists, on the one hand (many of whom have become increasingly positive toward religious traditionalism during recent years), and the roughly 150,000 ultra-Orthodox, on the other hand (many of whom have become quite adept at utilizing the most modern 'secular' methods of fostering their communal goals), there stretches the bulk of American Jewry, still well over five million in all, with probably no more than 100,000 Yiddish speakers of near-native competence among them. Although approximately a million and a quarter of the foregoing had Yiddish as their childhood mother tongue, and although many of those can still understand the Yiddish punchline to a joke and may sprinkle their informal English (particularly when speaking to one another) with Yiddish loans and even with established Yiddish-derived phraseological calques,[14] active use or facility in the language has long since been lost by most of them and, in the lion's share of cases, may never have existed to begin with (given that the definition of 'mother tongue' utilized by the United States Census pertains to the language of the household during one's infancy rather than to one's own first language). The roughly 300,000 speakers of Yiddish in the USA today are not a negligible number, but of this number fully 50% are aged 65 and over while only some 20% are aged 20 and under. Of these almost all are active members of ultra-Orthodox communities. The virtually overwhelming language shift process *vis-à-vis* Yiddish in America since the beginning of this century is doubtlessly one of the most rapid and far-going in the annals of major immigrant languages throughout all of American history. RLS-efforts are obviously urgently needed, and very carefully focused efforts at that, if Yiddish is to be more than a passive vestige of the past, on the one hand, or an active indicator of one branch of extreme orthodoxy, on the other.

## 'Current State' Summary

The nature of the respective threats facing Navajo, Spanish and Yiddish are in some ways quite different. Navajo is faced by the threat of growing economic, demographic and cultural encroachment of the outside anglo world, and not only into its territory but even into its most intimate cultural processes. Spanish is faced by the threat of increasing curtailment of immigration and a growing demographic diffusion and socioeconomic mobility, such that the language will leave behind its current centers of preponderant and traditional concentration for relocation in a large variety of less Hispanic urban centers throughout America. Yiddish is threatened by the inability of Yiddish secularist modernity to maintain itself *vis-à-vis* the competing modernities (Jewish and non-Jewish) via English and, therefore, by the further peripheralization of Yiddish into the status of an ultra-Orthodox marker alone in the future, regardless of how multifaceted and central its past may have been. The phenomenon of Xmen-via-Yish (in this chapter, the reader will need to exercise care not to confuse 'Yish' with 'Yiddish') already represents the overwhelming mainstream in the American Jewish case. It constitutes a rapidly growing precedent in the Spanish case and a worrisome new one in the Navajo case. In each instance, the precedents result from the difficulties faced by all American minorities (and by American immigrant minorities in particular) to substantially regulate or moderate the ethnolinguistic influences stemming from the Anglo-American culture that surrounds them and to which they not only *have* but also commonly *seek* easy access. RLS-efforts, therefore, face the difficult balancing act of re-establishing and

maintaining ethnolinguistic boundaries, at least in part of the total life-space of
the minorities involved, while not closing off access to those general American
opportunities and experiences that are desired. It is a dilemma not unknown by
minorities in other parts of the modern world, a world in which the notion of
maintaining ethnolinguistic boundaries is suspect of 'ghettoization', even though
this is self-imposed and even though no such suspicion accompanies majority
efforts along the same lines.

*Stage 8: Reassembling the languages and/or acquiring them on an individual basis during adulthood*

None of the languages we are discussing are 'so far gone' as to need to be
reassembled as linguistic systems before further RLS-efforts can be undertaken.
Exemplary or adequate dictionaries, formal grammars and textbooks at all levels
of advancement and sophistication exist for each of them,[15] although most
American Jews are by now so estranged from Yiddish that they may not be
aware of the fact that this is so (and has long been so) in connection with this
language as well. Indeed, so vestigial is Yiddish in most American Jewish social
networks, that the uninformed grandchildren of former Yiddish speakers, judg-
ing by the Yiddish deficiencies that they note in their own circles, have reported
it to be no more than a reduced 'pidgin', totally incapable of handling the complexity and the sophistication of modern life. Others, who may interact occasionally with fluent native speakers of Yiddish, tend to view the Yiddish that
they hear from them as 'unnatural', 'scholastic' or even 'funny' or 'ludicrous'.
Thus, rather than those who no longer speak the language considering themselves *deficient*, it is the laggard speakers and the language itself that are widely
judged to be deficient instead. Often, it is this very image of being in linguistic
disarray (an image that sometimes even extends into the circles of those who are
still fluently speaking the language itself), rather than any more objective disarray, that Yiddish RLS-efforts need to overcome. In this context it should come
as no surprise that the bulk of those learning Yiddish today do so in adulthood
and, except in ultra-Orthodox circles, as a matter of individual 'interest' rather
than communally integrated experience.

*Stage 7: The maintenance of a vibrant and natural adult Xish-speaking society*

Most Hispanic adults are still fluent speakers of Spanish, just as most
Navajo adults are still fluent speakers of Navajo and as ultra-Orthodox Jewish
adults are still fluent speakers of Yiddish. In all three cases, most adults commonly speak their ethnic mother tongues to each other, even though most of them are
bilingual and could well speak English to each other about most aspects of their
daily lives. Adult community life is still primarily non-English in connection
with interactions with neighbors, most neighborhood shopping, participation in

local community-sponsored activities and associations with recreational, charitable, mutual assistance and popular cultural agendas. Navajo religious ceremonials are far less invariably in Navajo, clearly so if the decrease in long (five- or nine-day) 'sings' and the increased membership in the pan-Indian (and, therefore, necessarily non-Navajo) Native American Church and other Christian churches are considered. Hispanic worship in Spanish is also less widely available than might be expected, both because of the still relatively meager supply of Spanish-speaking priests[16] and because of the steadily growing proportion of youngsters in many parishes whose Spanish is already rather marginal. Ultra-Orthodox Jewish services are completely in traditional Hebrew/Aramaic, but rabbinic sermons, male talmudic study and argumentation, female review of the weekly Torah lection and pulpit announcements are invariably conducted in Yiddish. Generally speaking, the most crucial RLS-efforts needed on behalf of Navajo, Spanish and ultra-Orthodox Yiddish are not at the stage 7 level, precisely because so many Xmen are still Xish speakers in all three instances. Also, the link between the generations is most often still intact so that not only do stage 7 activities reach a goodly proportion of young people as well, but the links between the adult community and the intergenerational family (stage 6) are many and functional. However, the situation for Yiddish in secularist circles is almost completely non-functional precisely in the latter connection.

For non-ultra-Orthodox adult American Jews who are still fluent Yiddish speakers there is, theoretically, still a vibrant and natural (i.e. socially integrated) Yiddish-speaking life, particularly in New York. The Yiddish secularist scene there is obviously much weaker than it was twenty (or even ten) years ago but it still sponsors a fair number of periodical publications and offers lectures, song concerts, theater performances, literary readings and special commemorative events on frequent occasions. Unfortunately, few if any younger individuals, or non-Yiddish speakers of whatever age, ever attend or are even aware of these ongoing activities. Those who are attitudinally positive toward Yiddish, and their number is much larger than the number of speakers (as was also the case in connection with Irish, Basque and Frisian), are much more likely to attend English translations of originally Yiddish theatrical or song material, or to read English translations of Yiddish novels, short stories and poetry,[17] than to savour the originals or to prepare themselves to ever be able to do so. It sometimes seems that as more and more American Jews become aware of the riches of secular Yiddish culture via the plentifully available English translations, so plentiful, indeed, that the bulk of the most outstanding works in this language may soon be available in that fashion (and, to a lesser degree, also in French, Spanish and Modern Hebrew), the fewer will be the secularists who will be able either to enjoy these works in the original or to make additional contributions of their own to these various areas of secular Yiddish cultural creativity.

Rather than evincing any ability to attract to its ranks the vast majority of Jewish adults for whom Yiddish *per se* is already a closed book, it now seems doubtful that aging secularist Yiddish society (average age now in the high 70s) can maintain its own much diminished ranks, even in the Greater New York Metropolitan Area, through to the end of this century. In order to be able to do so, it would have to find a stage 6 connection with the young, a connection which (as we will soon see) is still almost entirely lacking. Even the vast amount of Yiddish-in-translation is not exploited in ways that might tend to foster the secularist stage 7 itself (e.g. bilingual editions of literary texts, theatrical performances and literary texts in 'simple Yiddish', etc.). Actually, one might conclude that the bulk of such translations serve to further validate the claim of 'Xmen-via-Yish', a claim which is self-defeating insofar as secularist Yiddish RLS is concerned.

*Stage 6: Creating the intergenerationally continuous Xish-speaking community via providing and stressing the link to family life, residential concentration and neighborhood institutions*

In the four minority language communities in the USA that we are examining most speakers of Xish are also speakers of Yish (English), and even in the one instance in which this is not yet clearly and obviously the case, Navajo, the presence within the family of even one English-dominant bilingual parent results in a huge proportion of children speaking either English only or English usually. Obviously, the link to the younger generation is under stress and requires special attention even in those cases (Navajo, Spanish and ultra-Orthodox Yiddish) where stage 7 is generally still in reasonably good shape. How is this special attention exemplified? At various interior settlements in the Navajo territory, Rock Point among them (from which most of our concrete Reservation-interior examples will be drawn), children still spend a substantial amount of their out-of-school time engaged in a parentally supervised or parentally proximate environment, whether at work (assisting the family in chores or in economically pertinent activity) or in crafts, dances and other traditional skills and pursuits, some of which actually went through an appreciable revival in the 60s and 70s, although it should also be said that much of that interest has subsided since then. Even the school domain is one that involves appreciable adult involvement, particularly in the tribally managed 'contract schools' (as distinct from the more usual Bureau of Indian Affairs schools, on the one hand, or the Public School District schools, on the other hand). The 'contract schools' not only employ more Navajo teachers, for their much more extensive Navajo curricula, but they also employ many community adults as custodians, cooks, cafeteria workers, teachers' aids and specialists in Navajo extra-curricular activities. The result of this planned involvement of adults in what might ordinarily be considered a 'youth preserve', and of planned youth involvement in what had come to be considered 'adult activities' had, as not entirely unanticipated side-effects, a salubrious effect on strengthening the role of Navajo in family and in youth activities more generally in the Reservation-interior communities. A generation ago, a further result of these efforts was to both enable and require young Navajo lawyers and other specialists hired by the tribal councils (to protect and litigate on behalf of additional Navajo mineral and land rights) to attend tribal council meetings and to increasingly provide their spoken reports and professional advice in Navajo, rather than doing so exclusively in English, thereby stressing that the competence to do so in Navajo is part of an educated young person's responsibility rather than, as was previously generally assumed, being in conflict with that responsibility.[18]

However, more than a quarter of all Navajos (and over a third of the young folks among them) now live in Navajo towns (or even in off-Reservation anglo towns) and the above-sketched 'classic picture' is distinctly over and done with there and weakening almost everywhere else. The omnipresent 'religious prac-tices' (like all non-Western cultures, Navajo does not really recognize any aspect of individual or communal behavior that is not religiously imbued), whether indigenous or Christian, are, as already mentioned, decreasingly in Navajo, but so are almost all social and recreational activities more generally, with the exception of Navajo song and dance *per se*. All in all, English is growing and Navajo is shrinking in almost all home-family-community areas, but substantial-ly less so in the Reservation-interior settlements than elsewhere.

Ultra-Orthodox Yiddish society, although almost entirely urban, is very similar to Reservation-interior Navajo society in all of the above respects, even though knowledge and out of home-and-neighborhood use of English may be even more widespread among adults here than among their Navajo counterparts. However, Yiddish is stressed at home, in the neighborhood, and as the vernacular (as distinct from their textual language) at school and at play. All adult newcomers to the community who opt to accept its ways and beliefs, are expected to become fluent in Yiddish, be they Israeli or even Sefardi,[19] in order to interact normally with all lay and clerical members of the community. In recent years, there have been an increasing number of children's story-books and textbooks in Yiddish as well as children's games and song-tapes in Yiddish. Again, children are normatively present at a great variety of adult (and adult-supervised) activities — these are invariably conducted in Yiddish, whether these be rabbinic sermons, talmudic study sessions or the meetings of women's charitable societies — both because the very high birth rate constantly outdistances the community's childcare facilities, as well as because informal learning by example is held in high repute. Essentially, it is the voluntary boundedness of the total ultra-Orthodox community, implementing cultural

boundaries *vis-à-vis* non-Orthodox Jews as well as *vis-à-vis* non-Jews, that
basically guarantees the strong intergenerational links that characterize it. The
ultra-Orthodox live together, travel to work together via their own buses (men in
the front seats, praying and studying), work together, pray together during work
hours, study together for hours each day before or after prayers, vacation
together in their own resorts and, in all ways possible, minimize their cultural
dependence on 'outsiders'. All adults are bilingual, acquiring English in school
and, particularly, in commercial or in 'outreach' contacts with English-speaking,
non-observant Jews. However, English has no more than this lingua franca
function in most ultra-Orthodox (particularly in Hasidic) circles. It is the
language of the 'outside' and few if any 'inside' functions are allocated to it. In
accord with this approach, the community's young are also fully Yiddish-
speaking, there being little alternative to that vernacular within the normal
rounds of adolescent or young adult community membership.

In the Reservation-interior Navajo and ultra-Orthodox communities the link
with the younger generation is at the level of normal, everyday life. Although it
is not entirely the case that no special attention whatsoever is given to 'youth
programs', it is, nevertheless, the case that most efforts that involve the young,
whether they be traditional or consciously planned, are largely in Xish (i.e. in
the ethnic mother tongue) in the normal course of events.

Among Puerto Ricans in New York the normal intergenerational link is
reinforced by a larger number of consciously planned and purposively organized
activities that simultaneously aim at keeping children 'out of trouble' and in a
Spanish-speaking environment consisting of adults who know them and whom
they know. Such efforts are all the more important because Puerto Ricans in
New York (in many ways the most disadvantaged Spanish-speaking group and
the one on which we will generally focus) do not typically control or sponsor
schools of their own that could serve as their own institutionalized links to their
young ones. Furthermore, there is also a lack of adequate community control
over local religious institutions, particularly so in the Catholic case (which is
also the dominant case). All in all, therefore, there is substantial reliance on
Spanish language-related influences, from informal institutions, on the one hand,
such as the local *bodega* (a neighborhood store, to which children are sent several times a day for minor purchases, that combines features of a grocery store,
pharmacy and folksy community center, but, unfortunately, one which is now
being crowded out by supermarkets and by Korean or other Asian-owned competitors) and, on the other hand, on hometown associations, folk-dance troupes,
*beisbol* or *futbol* (Latin American soccer) clubs, national celebrations (not only
those of Puerto Rican origin but those of the entire variety of Latino origins now
frequently united by intermarriage and simple neighborhood proximity), holiday
celebrations (e.g. *el dia de los reyes* (January 6, celebrated by every conceivable

community organization, the biggest such celebration being organized by El Museo del Barrio, complete with a camel-led parade in which thousands of children participate), fundraisers (via dances, picnics, excursions), *batutera* clubs (baton-twirling for girls), social clubs, fashion shows, and a fairly endless round of 'showers', weddings, baptisms and birthday parties.

The number and variety of the above Hispanic activities testifies to a still vibrant, ethnic community life and to a life-style in which adult-sponsored activities for children (or for adults and children together) can still often make up for the slowly increasing lack of Spanish at home and in the immediate family. It is not unusual for children from the primarily English-speaking Hispanic homes to still learn to understand and to speak Spanish via years of participation in the above-mentioned activities and institutions. However, as the formerly compact Hispanic neighborhoods begin to thin out, due to both the in-migration of more recent (and non-Hispanic) arrivals in those same neighborhoods and the slow, but nevertheless noteworthy, out-migration of Hispanics to a variety of new and better (safer, better housing or occupationally more advantageous) neighborhoods, many of the above activities too are beginning to thin out, reach somewhat fewer youngsters, lose their effectiveness as language learning vehicles and require more and more adult effort to keep them going across generational (and, particularly, across immigrant generational) lines. If and when newer Hispanic immigrants cease flocking to New York the continued efficacy of these methods would become questionable — just as the formerly omnipresent *bodega* itself has now become a 'threatened institution' — within less than a score of years.[20]

In secularist Yiddish-speaking circles the linkages with young people that were so plentiful in earlier years, particularly prior to the closing of mass immigration from Eastern Europe in the early 1920s but also continuing on, to some extent, to World War II, have virtually disappeared. The lack of geographic concentration, itself a consequence of social mobility and anglification, makes it virtually impossible for even the small number of remaining young secularist Yiddish speakers to meet and interact with any frequency, either with their elders or with one another. Efforts to re-establish a geographic concentration for the few (no more than a hundred in all) young, secular Yiddish speakers now launching their own families, are met with incredulity and impatience, probably because they are understood neither functionally nor theoretically/philosophically. It is fair to say that there is virtually no societally structured intergenerational ethnolinguistic continuity among Yiddish secularists in New York today (and even less outside of New York) and such meager continuity as does still obtain exists on an atypical and individual family basis alone.

The rich and widespread attitudinal positiveness toward Yiddish and the intellectual admiration for the Yiddish secularist world that gave modern Jewry and even the world at large so much (literature, songs, social movements) do not and cannot, by themselves, lead to language learning, language use, language fluency or language transmission to another generation. There are thousands of young people who have 'nothing but admiration' for Yiddish, but 'nothing but admiration' is not enough to lead them to a more active and societally organized stance vis-à-vis the language. 'Nothing but admiration' leads to circles of admirers (part-time/sometime students, fans, audiences at events largely in translation). 'Nothing but admiration' is not enough. From the point of view of RLS it is really nothing at all.[21] If Yiddish secularism is to be anything more than an individually idiosyncratic and societally peripheral phenomenon before the end of this century, an innovative and unprecedented concentration on stage 6 probably provides its last chance for survival outside of the annals of history. Without at least a few successes at this stage, its stage 7 glories too will turn into exercises in translation for Xmen-via-Yish.

*Stage 5: Literacy via community schools that do not aim at meeting the compulsory education requirements*

For a variety of reasons, none of the groups that we are discussing invests much activity or effort in stage 5 type schools. The acquisition of literacy is still a relatively recent aspiration for Navajos (and for Navajo). Traditionally, only selected elders were literate in Navajo and such literacy focused on various sanctified and curative rituals and traditions that were (and, very commonly, still are) considered to be extremely powerful lore and, therefore, necessarily of restricted circulation. With the establishment of a government-financed but Tribal Council-controlled ('contract') school in Rock Point (we will consider this type of school under stage 4a, below) the notion of Navajo literacy was considerably expanded, but this expansion existed only in a few Reservation-interior localities and has, therefore, reached only a small part of the younger generation, many of whom have little need for Navajo literacy even after graduation from the 'contract' school. The use of Navajo literacy for adult communication between Navajo settlements is meager indeed. As a result, the only stage 5 type schools in the Navajo territory are those maintained by various Christian denominations in connection with teaching Navajo translations of various Christian texts. These efforts too are rare and, at any rate, are hardly of the kind that will give Navajo literacy either much functional or much prestige value, leading as they must to untranslated (English) Christian texts.

Navajo needs its own societal institutions for fostering the broader and more conscious unity and community that literacy, literacy institutions and widely read Navajo texts can help cultivate. This is particularly true as the number of type 4a schools (see below) ceases to grow due to the lack of either inside or outside funding. Type 5 schools are not only more affordable, but they can more easily work at adult literacy in addition than can schools that serve in lieu of compulsory education. Type 5 schools can more easily become active forces on behalf of fostering a supra-local 'community of interest' at the adult level, with RLS as an avowed (rather than as a disguised or muted) aspect of such unity. The contrived routines that parents of pupils in type 4a schools went (and currently go) through in order to get the pupils to exercise their Navajo literacy (at a time when the parents themselves have no such literacy at their own command) — such as asking their youngsters to make reminder-notes concerning things the parents should remember, or concerning shopping needs — would become unnecessary, and would be replaced by societally more meaningful and appropriate literacy if such literacy were intergenerationally shared via type 5 schooling for parents (or for parents and children alike).[22]

The ultra-Orthodox Yiddish-speaking world prizes literacy very highly, but this relates almost completely to Hebrew literacy (for which type 4a schools are carefully maintained). A modicum of formal and even more informal Yiddish-literacy exposure is provided for girls (usually on a family or neighborhood basis), but, by and large, both boys and girls are expected to transfer their school-based Hebrew-reading and writing skills to Yiddish without much formal attention being devoted to this process (due to the common alphabet and roughly similar orthographic conventions utilized by both languages). Although Yiddish literacy is not particularly prized or highlighted, the fact that the language has become an ultra-Orthodox marker, and the existence of a small but significant body of ultra-Orthodox Yiddish literature (periodicals, story-books, holiday readings, pamphlets reporting recent talks by leading rabbis and such staples, some of them over a century old, as accounts of the lives of famous rabbis, popular histories and moralistic readings, translations of the prayer-book and of the Old Testament), gives Yiddish literacy a recognized if limited ethnocultural role alongside of the more prestigious and sanctified role of Hebrew literacy. As a result, there is probably nearly universal adult literacy in Yiddish among the ultra-Orthodox, even though there are few neighborhood schools especially for this purpose (and these few are for girls alone) and little directed attention is devoted to such literacy even in type 4a schools. This is not to be taken as a sign that stage 5 is generally unimportant but, rather, that within ultra-Orthodox circles its goals, as far as children are concerned, are accomplished by other appropriate cultural means, particularly by the large, intensive and constantly growing number of type 4a schools.

On the other hand, separate male and female adult groups for study and for fellowship are plentifully available in ultra-Orthodox neighborhoods, and adult literacy in Yiddish (both reading and writing), were it to be added to their programs, would be particularly useful for the growing contingents of recent Jewish 'converts' to ultra-Orthodoxy (known as *baley-tshuve*, literally 'returnees'). The lack of Yiddish literacy among the latter — and their weaknesses even with respect to Yiddish oralcy — threatens to expose ultra-Orthodoxy to more English and to more immediate models of Xmen-via-Yish than ultra-Orthodoxy has ever heretofore encountered within its own ranks.[23]

Among American Hispanics the attainment of functionally minimal Spanish reading literacy is quite widespread, and only a few years of school attendance in Spanish (in a pre-immigrational setting) or even in English (in the continental USA) are needed for such rudimentary proficiency to obtain. The near-perfect grapho-phonemic nature of Spanish spelling and the rough similarity between Spanish and English orthographic conventions seem to be sufficient for this purpose, although an everyday life-style among lower- and working-class Hispanics that requires hardly any literacy at all results in a command of literacy in general and of Spanish literacy in particular that is halting and insecure. Unfortunately, there are pitifully few stage 5 type schools for Spanish literacy in Greater New York City (or in the USA as a whole, for that matter) — whether for adults or for youngsters — and many of those few that do exist are maintained as a result of continental Spanish or other non-local support.

Nevertheless, relative to other minority groups in the USA, there is still a large (and often scrappy) Spanish periodical press, although English publications for Hispanics are growing rapidly in number, circulation, influence and appeal to the young. The absence of a strong role for Spanish literacy or of community-controlled schools to foster such literacy, whether among children or adults, obviously weakens Spanish maintenance efforts in New York (and elsewhere in the USA as well) because it demotes a world language with a truly outstanding literary heritage to the role of an uneducated patois, a role which also weakens the political potential of Hispanics and the attractiveness of the language for the American-born generations whose members are necessarily exposed to and influenced by the advantages of literacy in English.[24] Just as the building and preserving of Spanish-speaking neighborhoods is a necessary arena for RLS-efforts among Hispanics, so type 5 schools and centers (being natural outgrowths of neighborhood efforts) are crucial literacy-engendering agencies that would plug Hispanics back into their own reading and writing traditions, at least at a belle-lettristic level, and impart thereby a new dignity to their own language, as well as a new link-medium from one urban center to another. Type 5 efforts for the improvement of adult and child literacy are particularly important for Spanish in New York (and probably elsewhere in the USA as well), given that Spanish medium type 4a schools are still substantially beyond the reach of most Hispanics. For its own good *vis-à-vis* English and *vis-à-vis* the level of unity that only literacy can sustain, Spanish needs to cultivate its own literacy garden.

Yiddish secularist literacy is almost universal and derives, on the one hand, from the major focus on modern Yiddish literature within the ranks of the secularists, and, on the other hand, from the older generation's childhood attendance at type 5 or 4a Orthodox schools in Eastern Europe or in the USA (and their subsequent transfer to Yiddish of the Hebrew literacy that was acquired in those schools) and the younger generation's former attendance at (now largely defunct) Yiddish secular supplementary schools in the USA, precisely of the type 5 variety, which stressed Yiddish literacy even more than oralcy. The latter schools formerly existed in all larger urban areas in the USA and probably numbered close to 200 in all at their peak (prior to World War II). Today, they have practically ceased to exist, numbering perhaps some two dozen in all, and those few that still function meet for so few hours per week (usually Sunday mornings) that stable Yiddish literacy is no longer a manageable goal for their students, particularly given the fact that these students no longer speak Yiddish to their parents or grandparents or even hear it spoken at home. Many synagogue-affiliated afternoon and Sunday schools — by no means within the secularist fold — have also taken to offering Yiddish for a few hours per week, and many more are entirely willing to do so if only proper texts and teachers were available for this purpose; but here again, it is mostly 'Yiddish appreciation' rather than Yiddish oralcy or literacy that is, or would be, aimed at. Nevertheless, Yiddish literacy continues to play a major role in secularist circles, providing an international (even if small) audience for the best journals and books and, even more importantly, providing the sense of worldwide perspectives and of a far-flung community of interest and orientation. Clearly, the retention of stage 5 is shaky in current secular Yiddishist circles, primarily because so few adults or youngsters are attracted to the schools maintained for this purpose and because of the ineffectiveness of such minimalist schools as still do exist when neither oralcy nor community are available as either prerequisites or co-requisites of literacy. This is but another example of how the attainment of prior stages is often necessary if subsequent ones are to be either possible or effective means of RLS.[25]

In summary, before crossing the 'continental divide' to functions that require greater dependence upon and interaction with the non-Xish world, it should be clear that ultra-Orthodox Yiddish occupies one extreme of the maintenance continuum and secularist Yiddish the opposite extreme, with Navajo and Spanish being intermediate between the two but still closer to the retentivist pole than to its opposite. The absolutely fundamental role of control of an intergenerational residential environment (stage 6) is well illustrated by all four cases, a control that immigrant groups in general find difficult to achieve and that even indigenous groups cannot long maintain under modern interactive circumstances unless they are able and willing to detach from maximal participation in and self-modeling upon the surrounding mainstream secular world. Even the attainment of community literacy, so necessary for wider concurrent unity (contact with other Xish speakers elsewhere) and for the widespread attainment of optimal historical continuity, is of secondary importance relative to the attainment and maintenance of intergenerational home-family-neighborhood-community processes. Indeed, only with the attainment of intergenerational transmissibility of the language does self-contained and self-regulated literacy become not only a theoretical plus but a functional possibility as well.

Secular Yiddishism in America today has not retained this fundamental stage and without it, its 'higher' literary and cultural sophistication adds nothing to its intergenerational transmissibility. Navajo and ultra-Orthodox Yiddish have a secure grip on stage 6 and, therefore, their lack of notable activity on the 'higher' fronts (including stage 5) does them no serious intergenerational harm. Spanish, in between these two extremes, unfortunately still shows little awareness of its true dependence on neighborhood solidarity. That is where the real (even if quiet) struggle for Spanish maintenance is being fought and and it is there that it will be either won or lost by the turn of the century, most probably even with ongoing immigration and certainly without it. The subsequent battle for control of the larger contextual worlds, their media and their institutions, is still far off in the future for Spanish. *That* battle may never be fought at all — and certainly it will have no chance whatsoever of influencing RLS — if stages 6 and 5 are not won to begin with.

*Stage 4a: Schools that are under Xish control and that can be attended 'in lieu of compulsory education'*

In the early to mid-70s a small number of schools that were being operated for Navajo pupils by the Federal government's Bureau of Indian Affairs were turned over to local tribal councils to be operated under contract with the Bureau. The funding for these schools was still almost entirely Federal (even if it was not always entirely BIA funding), but the responsibility for curriculum, staffing and operations was transferred to the local Navajo authorities. These 'contract schools', although relatively few in number, soon became centers of pedagogic, curricular and extra-curricular innovation and their greater stress on Navajo as a co-medium of instruction was part and parcel of their historically unique role. They generally taught all ethnically encumbered subjects in Navajo, but also often taught other subjects in this medium as well, whenever suitably trained indigenous staff and specially prepared curricular materials were available to enable them to do so (Holm and Holm, 1990).[26]

These schools produced the first-ever generation of Navajo-literate youngsters and helped revive many of the half-forgotten songs, dances, crafts and traditions that had been ignored (or prohibited) by BIA schools and public schools serving Navajo pupils. The 'contract schools' became veritable community centers. They represented the return of education to community control and, in addition, they provided major sources of employment and major avenues of supervision of the growing generation. Last but not least, some of the schools also taught English more successfully and became national models of effective locally controlled bilingual/bicultural education. Their only weak spot was their utter dependence on governmental funding and more recently, since severe cutbacks in such funding became government policy, these schools too have become weaker in most respects. While their future may or may not be entirely at risk (only some 10% of all Navajo children now attend such schools, roughly two-thirds of all Navajo children attending public schools, and about one quarter attending type 4b Bureau of Indian Affairs schools), it is now doubtful whether their impact can once again be as strong and as stimulating, even in their own rural communities, as was formerly the case. Obviously, this is a type 4a school which is not entirely the master of its own fate, in the model of true type 4a schools elsewhere. Its dependence on others may lead to its downfall, unless Navajo funding can be found for it, when and if other local resources come sufficiently under tribal control. The real control, rather than merely the BIA sub-contracted operation, of Navajo type 4a schools must become an important goal for Navajos, building such control upon prior, solid stage 6 foundations.

Ultra-Orthodox youngsters invariably study in type 4a schools that are organized, maintained and conducted by their own parents and community leaders. There are approximately 120 such Yiddish medium day schools (known as *yeshi'ves*) today, elementary and secondary, almost all of them in the Greater New York Metropolitan Area. Boys and girls almost always study in separate schools and their respective curricula differ appreciably after the first few years of instruction. The Judaic curriculum of the boys is increasingly focused on the study of Hebrew/Aramaic Talmud,[27] while that of the girls ultimately stresses home and family life. In either case, the medium of instruction is primarily Yiddish for the Judaic courses to which as many as five or six hours a day may be devoted during six days of the week (i.e. on every day but the Saturday sabbath). English is taught (usually as a second language) and used as the language of instruction for two or three hours per day, in accord with the requirements of the State Education Department of New York. The traditional curricular pattern calls for the Judaic courses to be taught in the morning and the English (i.e. secular) courses to be taught in the afternoon. The level of English proficiency that is aimed at is no more than that which may be required in offices and businesses serving the general public. Post-secondary general education is not encouraged but intellectually outstanding boys are encouraged to continue in post-secondary Judaic (usually: rabbinic) studies, and many males actually continue to devote some time to such studies on a daily basis throughout their lives.

By dint of long exposure to Yiddish as the medium of Judaic study (it is rarely taught as a language in its own right) the few pupils who do not come from Yiddish-speaking homes (Sefardic children or English-speaking children of parents who have just recently adopted the ultra-Orthodox way of life) acquire facility in the language (particularly for the purposes of ultra-Orthodox Judaic studies). Although purists will undoubtedly claim that ultra-Orthodox Yiddish lacks the grammatical refinement and the lexical breadth of secularist Yiddish, ultra-Orthodox usage is obviously fluent and fully appropriate to the life-style and interests of its speech community and the *yeshi'ves* have obviously been instrumental in strengthening the language, particularly among males and by cementing its sanctity-by-association with hallowed textual studies.

Neither Spanish nor secularist Yiddish have any approximation to either the Navajo contract schools or to the ultra-Orthodox *yeshi'ves*. For secularist Yiddish, the two attempts to found type 4a all-day schools in New York in recent years both failed, the last such attempt (under the auspices of the major Yiddish secularist organization, the Workmen's Circle) being abandoned even before the school itself could begin functioning. For Spanish, the closest approximations to type 4a Spanish medium all-day schools under Hispanic community control are the very few Catholic parochial schools in which a modicum of attention is given to teaching in Spanish and to Hispanic studies more generally. These are very few in number relative to the huge child population involved and may actually be educationally inferior to, less effective in any RLS sense than, and even outnumbered by the private English medium ethnic schools conducted by Cuban-Americans in the Greater Miami area. In the latter schools Spanish is the language of all interpersonal interaction (between staff, parents and students) and it is taught as a subject, but it is not a medium of instruction in any course outside of the Spanish course *per se*.[28] All in all, type 4a schools are still a minor force on the Spanish RLS front, whether in New York City or in the USA as a whole. This is obviously an important but neglected front, not only in Greater New York City but throughout the USA. Unfortunately, Hispanics are still unaccustomed to the idea of founding and maintaining their own schools, whether of type 5 or of type 4a. Instead, they are accustomed to being schooled by others in type 4b schools in which the RLS situation is understandably poor or worse than poor.

*Type 4b schools: Schools for Xish pupils but under Yish control*

As has been mentioned previously, there are also type 4b schools for Navajo pupils. Those operated by the BIA as well as some of those conducted by local school districts (some of which are entirely off Reservation and some

of which serve districts that are partially on and partially off the Reservation)
are under no particular obligation to offer instruction in Navajo and many do
not do so. At best, they offer transitional 'Title VII' bilingual education,
engaged in frankly as a means of transferring Navajo children to English-only
instruction 'as quickly and as painlessly as possible'. The process *is* quick, of
course, so much so that even it becomes 'unnecessary' after the early
elementary grades, and it bypasses Navajo literacy entirely, but it is hardly
painless insofar as RLS goals are concerned. Furthermore, it usually yields
poor results in English as well, low grades in general and, finally, results in
complete withdrawal from school at the earliest opportunity. Who could ask
for anything less? Type 4b schooling for Navajo youngsters has been
disappointing for many decades (and, not infrequently, even punitive too). It
has absolutely no value, to put it mildly, as far as RLS is concerned.
Nevertheless, it is the modal educational pattern for Navajo children today and
for the foreseeable future. The damage done by type 4b schools is substantial
even if such schools initially offer bilingual education in the earliest grades,
before transitioning Navajo pupils entirely to English-only instruction. The
attitude of the staff is condescending or hostile and Navajo culture is ignored,
at best, and belittled, ridiculed or trivialized, at worst.

The damage done by type 4b schools in the Navajo case is largely duplicat-
ed and sometimes even surpassed in the Hispanic case via the relatively massive
'Title VII' bilingual education efforts currently still underway for Hispanic children, under public education auspices. The orientation is typically and begrudg-
ingly transitional, as required by the Federal and several of the state funding
laws that support these efforts, and the transition to English-only instruction is
made as early as possible, usually by or in the third grade. The result is that not
only is nothing positive accomplished for the children's Spanish but their
English too is only moderately benefited. Even so, only some 20% of all
Hispanic children considered to be LEP (Limited English Proficient) receive
bilingual education. Their academic achievement therefore remains low in all
areas and their drop-out rate is very high, regardless of whether or not bilingual
education has been received. In recent years several scholars have argued that
type 4b schools cannot even achieve their avowed English missions without
greatly expanding the Spanish literacy portion of their programs, both in terms
of hours per week and in terms of total number of years of Spanish instruction.[29]
Those few type 4b schools that have followed professional advice in this connection (e.g. the Oyster Bay School in Washington, D.C., the Potter Thomas
School in Philadelphia, the 'Two Way' bilingual programs in P.S. 84, Manhattan,
in Port Washington, New York and in the Coral Way Elementary School in Dade
County, Florida), have all attained excellent academic results, both in English
and in Spanish and for anglo and Hispanic students alike.

A mere handful of public schools in the Greater New York City Area and elsewhere in New York State, and just a few handfuls throughout the USA as a whole, have been able to break out of the compensatory-transitional mold of type 4b education for Hispanics. Those that have, as we have just seen, have usually instituted patterns of instruction that retain Spanish as a co-medium throughout their programs, on the one hand, and have involved Hispanic and non-Hispanic children in simultaneous bilingual education, on the other hand, thereby converting it into an enrichment program rather than retaining the grudging, minimalistic, transitional, compensatory characteristics for economically, culturally and racially disadvantaged minorities that type 4b schooling is almost everywhere else. Unfortunately, these few model public bilingual education programs are much too few in number to be of any significance relative to the overall language maintenance or RLS situations of Puerto Rican and other Hispanic pupils in New York City or elsewhere. Indeed, they are perfect examples of what could be done, but is very rarely done, when minorities are almost completely dependent on 'others' for the education of the younger generations. The lesson such schools teach RLS advocates is that they cannot depend on type 4b schools to achieve RLS goals. If type 4a schools are out of the question (due to lack of means and personnel) then type 5 schools (i.e. community schools not in lieu of compulsory education) must be organized by whatever means and with the best personnel available.

*Stages 3, 2 and 1: Work sphere, mass media, higher education and government*

The demographic concentration of Navajo and ultra-Orthodox Yiddish speakers leads to the use of these languages in the intra-Xmen worksphere (stage 3a, so to speak), as it also frequently does for Spanish. This state of affairs applies to neighborhood businesses controlled by Xmen and, more infrequently, also to those controlled by Ymen interested in competitively maintaining and increasing their Xish clienteles. Obviously, this is an important but limited economic base for the languages involved, but anyone who is eager to move beyond this base, into the Yish economic world, is hard put to do so in Xish. Among Navajos in particular, Xish is of little if any value for getting a job beyond the lowest levels of intra-Xish interaction; and even these jobs rarely *require* Navajo, since so many (particularly younger) Navajos are also English-speaking. Among Spanish and Yiddish speakers there *are* a few examples of large Xish enterprises serving the general public, particularly among Cuban-Americans and ultra-Orthodox Jews. In these enterprises intra-Xmen communication continues in Xish while the public is served in Yish. These enterprises typically hire Xish-speaking employees (almost all of whom also speak English) and they are often purposely drawn from the extended family and neighbors of the owners so that there is not only an ethnic bond between the employees but a family-neighborhood bond as well. As such, they are, once again, extensions of the most crucial stage of all: stage 6. Nevertheless, after all is said and done, there are proportionally few employment opportunities of this kind for as large and as economically depressed a group as Hispanics, and even the ultra-Orthodox world may not be able to secure economic mobility on this family-linked basis if and when such mobility becomes a serious rival (which it is not as yet) to community continuity and boundary maintenance. In the latter case, provisions will need to be made for voluntary Xish study groups, lunch table groups, prayer groups and other Xish interest groups (in a more modern context: bowling, hobby, vacation, savings, etc.) in order to provide Xish speaking/writing opportunities in a Yish setting.

A modicum of local governmental services (those of the police, firefighters, postal employees, hospital staff, social workers and other government counselors and trainers) are presented in all of the languages that we are considering in this chapter, but this is normally done on an 'if available' basis and depends on Yish budgetary circumstances and goodwill. Indeed, several states, some 20 in all (and their number is slowly but constantly growing), explicitly reject any *obligation* to offer services in languages other than English, and pressure is mounting to adopt a Federal constitutional amendment to remove any such obligation at the Federal level as well (both of these developments being the outgrowths of 'Official English' agitation on the part of the US English movement).[30] Nevertheless, even where the obligation to do so does not exist in law, various critical governmental services in Spanish (and to a much lesser degree in Navajo and Yiddish) may well continue, based on notions of professional responsibility to serve immigrants, the poor, the sick, the old, etc. in the language in which those unfortunates are most fluent. This is hardly a reliable stance, nor is it one that contributes to RLS because it is based on (and fosters) a dependent, rather than a positive, image of Xish.

Table 7.2 indicates the situation *vis-à-vis* the mass media in the three languages we have been considering in this chapter. Navajo and Spanish are clearly focused on the spoken word, while Yiddish is focused on the written word. This is a reflection of the greater literacy tradition among secular as well as ultra-Orthodox Yiddish speakers in general, as well as a reflection on the ultra-Orthodox objection to radio and television (particularly the latter) because these foreign-controlled media can and do bring into their homes oral and visual messages that are offensive to ultra-Orthodox cultural values. With rare exceptions, the Navajo and Yiddish media are largely dependent on amateur and amateurish local talent, often characterized by meager professionalism and also with meager audiences, budgets and time-slots available to them. Their RLS contribution is minimal, both because they cannot really compete with the quality and diversity

TABLE 7.2   *Mass media in Navajo, Yiddish and Spanish, 1982–83*

|  | Periodic publications | | | Radio programs[a] | | TV programs[a] | |
|---|---|---|---|---|---|---|---|
|  | n | Mean frequency | Mean circulation | n | Mean frequency | n | Mean frequency |
| Navajo[b] | 2 | ? | ? | 24 | ? | ? | ? |
| Yiddish | 36 | m | 10,350 | 16 | <1 hr/wk | 1 | <1 hr/wk |
| Spanish | 174 | w | 32,500 | 845 | 2 hr/wk | 154 | 2 hr/wk |

*Source*: Fishman *et al.*, 1985

[a] 'Programs' = 'program-stations', i.e., any station that broadcasts several different programs in the *same* language is counted only once, but any station that broadcasts programs in *x* languages is counted *x* times. Some of the same stations that broadcast in Spanish also broadcast in Yiddish.

[b] Holm (Memorandum, 1989) reports only a Rock Point newspaper in Navajo, a new 50,000 watt Tribal radio station devoting some program time to Navajo, a low-powered school TV station (also at Rock Point) devoting some time to Navajo programs, as well as some Navajo broadcasting on both radio and TV in a few non-Navajo towns located near the Reservation.

*Note*: m = monthly, w = weekly

of English media and also because of their general lack of a culturally appropriate RLS youth orientation.

Relative to the Navajo and Yiddish mass media the Spanish media constitute a much larger universe and benefit, therefore, from the availability of some nationally syndicated programs (and, near the Mexican border, also from international programming). Nevertheless, it too is of dubious RLS value. The press, particularly the more profitable daily press, is often not Hispanic-owned (and, therefore, possibly less interested in language and culture maintenance than it might otherwise be) and its language is often highly deficient. Indeed, the newly developing English language press for Hispanics often reveals more RLS concern than does its Spanish counterpart. The non-print media are largely devoted to vocal and orchestral music and, even when the spoken word is emphasized, rarely present models worth emulating. All in all, there is no evidence that the Hispanic mass media have had any noteworthy language maintenance or RLS aspirations and even less evidence that they have had any consequences at all along such lines.[31]

At the higher educational level (stage 1) there is almost nothing of any RLS significance to report. For Navajo there is only one tertiary level institution, the still struggling Navajo Community College in Tsaile, Arizona. It offers a small number of courses, conferences, symposia and meetings on Navajo concerns, most of these being conducted in Navajo, by Navajos and for Navajos, but it has relatively few students, a very limited array of courses (not all of them yielding college credit) and increasingly uncertain prospects as Federal funding for higher education is cut back. It has obviously not reached the level of effectiveness that some had initially expected.

Although Yiddish is taught as a foreign language in some 50–60 American colleges and universities, there are no more than a handful where more than an elementary course is available. The YIVO Institute for Jewish Research (once named the Yiddish Scientific Institute but renamed in the 60s in order to 'reach a wider audience') and Columbia University jointly offer an intensive summer program in Yiddish, with courses at various levels. Columbia University alone offered a graduate major in Yiddish (in the Linguistics Department; the discontinuation of this department now makes the continuation of the full Yiddish program more dubious), in addition to undergraduate courses at various levels. The YIVO also offers a number of graduate courses in Eastern European and American Jewish history, sociology and folklore, among them frequent courses in Yiddish literature.

Very few of the foregoing courses are offered in Yiddish and the nationwide total number of all students involved in these courses, whatever their medium of instruction, can hardly be more than a thousand per year. Few students attending these courses achieve fluency in the language, although the level of knowledge attained 'about Yiddish', and the degree of 'Yiddish appreciation' that is developed in particular, resulting from such courses are often noteworthy. The students and faculty involved in these efforts are primarily from the secular or religiously uncommitted sectors and the concurrent and subsequent demographic dispersion of these individuals makes it difficult for their courses to have either RLS goals or consequences of any societal significance whatsoever. Similarly, although the National Yiddish Book Exchange (Amherst, Mass.; see note 17) makes out-of-print Yiddish books available to these students at a mere fraction (25%) of their regular price, the resulting acquisition of small libraries may foster individual literacy but does nothing to foster societal RLS.

Spanish too enjoys hardly any RLS prospects at the college level. There are two colleges that offer Spanish medium course work, one a public junior college (Eugenio Maria de Hostos, a unit within the City University of New York system) and the other a private four-year college (Boricua). Neither of them plays a significant intellectual or societal role in Hispanic community life in New York City and they are both almost literally unheard of elsewhere. There is also a modicum of Spanish medium higher education in Texas and in California, none

of it really under Hispanic community control; and, of course, Spanish is taught
and offered as both a graduate and an undergraduate major in hundreds of institutions of higher education throughout the USA. Although many Hispanic students attend these courses and constitute the bulk of the country's Spanish
majors (and also the bulk of current as well as prospective teachers of Spanish
at American secondary and tertiary institutions), this entire realm is not linked to
Hispanic community life and generally is not designed to (and does not) produce
individuals who are committed to or involved in either language maintenance or
RLS. For the country's Hispanic youth, only a minor proportion of which attend
tertiary academic institutions, the Spanish that they encounter in these institutions may be a refresher course, an 'easy A' or an easy occupational alternative,
but is not a step toward Spanish in their own personal family lives nor toward
Hispanic community RLS responsibility. For these academic programs to
become such, they would need to cultivate greater community links as well as
community-oriented RLS obligations. In the absence of such links and obligations, higher education for Hispanics accomplishes, at best, only the occupational mobility which finally allows some (not many) Hispanics to catch up
economically with the white mainstream (Stolzenberg, 1990). In most cases this
is not only not an RLS contribution but a process that has anti-RLS consequences of major significance.

## Summary

In this chapter we have reviewed three of the more encouraging minority
language situations in the USA, situations that clearly discredit, at least in part,
the widespread assumption that there is no long-range hope for non-English languages in the United States. The distinctly discouraging situation of Yiddish secularism is very similar to that of many other immigrant languages in the USA
that have not enjoyed any major immigrational replenishment since World War
I. The RLS situation of secular Yiddish is even more precarious than the others,
however, because it has no 'homeland' across the oceans where the language is
still safe and sound, regardless of what happens in the future to its speakers in
the USA. The substantial strength of ultra-Orthodox Yiddish is also no consolation to secular Yiddishists because these two sectors are virtually completely
separated from each other, each representing a completely unacceptable life-
style to the other.

Of the 'encouraging three' (insofar as RLS prospects are concerned),
Spanish is so massive that its constantly ongoing attrition *vis-à-vis* the second
and subsequent generations, particularly among urban dwellers, proceeds with

little intercommunal attention and even less intra-communal awareness. Nevertheless, even though monolingual Spanish speakers continue to arrive in appreciable numbers and even though these newcomers serve as a language learning resource for some youngsters who have not acquired Spanish at home, both the number and the proportion of Hispanic Xmen-via-Yish is growing very rapidly and will soon become a challenge and a threat to the generally unconscious but widespread notion of Xmen-via-Xish. Overall, there has been a significant narrowing of the differences between Hispanics and the American mainstream during the past quarter century and most social processes are working toward the incorporation of more and more Hispanics into American life on terms comparable to those of the European ethnics (notwithstanding the worsening economic circumstances of Puerto Ricans). Both circumstances offer a poor prognosis for RLS success. Indeed, the emergence of what may become an intergenerational Puerto Rican underclass is an ominous development with negative ramifications extending far beyond RLS itself. A prolonged economic downturn in the USA, together with the inevitably vastly intensified efforts to stop illegal immigration, could intensify and bring to the fore the language shift that has already occurred and is occurring daily. RLS efforts at stages 6, 5 and 4a are seriously deficient and would be more effective ultimately if they could be more widely discussed, appreciated, planned and initiated *now*.

The same is true with respect to the slower but nevertheless ongoing attrition of Navajo and ultra-Orthodox Yiddish. The governmental largesse of the 60s and early 70s that made some off-Reservation Navajos return and readopt Navajo customs and practices has slowed to a trickle. Unless major lawsuits that seek to reclaim Navajo control of major natural resources are favorably and quickly settled (and there does not seem much prospect at all for either) the immigration of the young to off-Reservation or Navajo town residence, work, education and the founding of families will intensify and the inroads of anglo-conducted and controlled education, mass media, youth culture and employment potential will burgeon on the Reservation as well. Intensified community planning for language maintenance and RLS at stages 6, 5 and 4a should begin now rather than when language shift accelerates further and when the early benefits of advanced planning must necessarily be sharply reduced.

Ultra-Orthodox (particularly Hasidic) Yiddish is probably best able of all of the languages we have reviewed in this chapter to substantially maintain its own cultural boundaries into the twenty-first century. Stage 6 boundary maintenance *vis-à-vis* the Jewish and non-Jewish modern worlds is a hallowed tradition and a conscious and rewarded obligation. Yiddish is not a sanctified component of this hallowed tradition but it is a recognized part of the way of life through which the tradition is implemented and experienced. The only major problems that could arise for it are in connection with the major efforts from *within* to attract and influence non-Yiddish speaking 'returnees', on the one hand, and major influences stemming both *from within and from without* to diversify occupationally and scatter residentially, on the other hand. The ultra-Orthodox tradition has never espoused or encouraged either of these latter efforts and processes before. However, should these become much intensified in ultra-Orthodox circles both of them would probably encourage greater intragroup use of English for quite different reasons. The cultivation of 'returnees' might legitimize the first major breach of the boundaries and, indeed, those ultra-Orthodox groups that are already most involved in 'outreach' efforts have already significantly increased their use of English and, correspondingly, decreased their use of Yiddish. There is little evidence that ultra-Orthodoxy is overly concerned with the language shift consequences of this development. As the only intergenerationally successful non-English mother tongue group living entirely in an urban context, the ultra-Orthodox deserve the careful attention of RLS-interested specialists, regardless of how their ongoing encounter with modernity turns out.

The needs of Navajo are greatest for control of stages 5 and 4a, both in interior and in non-interior locales; of Spanish for control of stages 6 and 5; of Jewish ultra-Orthodoxy for expansion of stage 5 (for teaching Yiddish to 'returnees', in the context of teaching the ultra-Orthodox life-style) and stage 3 (for regulating social mobility via the Yish sector without thereby leaving Yiddish behind); and of Yiddish secularism for control of stage 6, without which it will soon be no more than a memory that is generally accessible only via translation. Our stage model not only differentiates these groups appropriately but provides a rational agenda for their differential RLS-efforts.

The similarity of the Yiddish secularist plight to that of other American immigrant groups that primarily arrived prior to World War I (all of whom have gone through nearly three-quarters of a century of insufficient immigrational replenishment to make up for their language shift losses), dramatically highlights the question of why interior-Navajo, Spanish speakers and ultra-Orthodox Yiddish speakers are in such relatively better (albeit far from untroubled) circumstances. The numerical massiveness of Spanish speakers tends to be misleading, since it is not the millions of Hispanic newcomers and their children who have experienced any particular success *vis-à-vis* intergenerational mother tongue transmission. They are too recent, at any rate, for the three-generational rule of thumb to come into play, and too dislocated by urban blight and mainstream dependency to be 'good bets' for becoming RLS exemplars when their third generations begin to give way to the fourth, roughly early in the twenty-first century. The backbone of intergenerational mother tongue transmission within the Hispanic fold are those hundreds of thousands of quiet Chicanos in New Mexico, Arizona and Texas who still have a rural and small town counterpart and hinterland to their gradual and relatively undislocated urbanization. The latter too have RLS problems to cope with, but both their problems and their assets are more similar to those of the substantially self-regulatory Navajos of the interior, on the one hand, and the ultra-Orthodox Yiddish speakers, on the other hand. They still have some demographic and cultural space of their own. They too are Americanizing, but they are not so caught up in the race for modernization, nor are they so plugged into the mainstream media, youth culture and value system that their own internal cultural voices can no longer be heard. It is all a matter of degree, but it makes all the difference in the world.

In the American mainstream sociopolitical climate, focused as it is on individual liberties and insensitive as it is to the needs for cultural (i.e. group) protection, voluntary semi-detachment from the mainstream is the price that many of the Navajos, ultra-Orthodox Yiddish speakers and Southwestern Spanish language islands may need to pay for their relative self-regulatory capacity *vis-à-vis* their own ethnocultural and ethnolinguistic practices. The mainstream American stance toward those practices is not essentially different from (indeed, it is merely a variant of) the Western democratic ethic in its disregard for and disinclination toward cultural boundaries that are not politically protected, and even then the inevitability of cultural leveling is taken for granted while the 'politicization of culture' by minorities is decried as a disturbance of the mainstream-dominated quest for undisturbed advantage and civility. The four American cases that we have examined here indicate that even within such an inhospitable climate for RLS — a climate that plagues all of the cases reviewed in this volume — there are local cultural 'arrangements' that, if *consciously* attended to, can foster substantially self-regulatory solutions to the problems and opportunities of RLS and sociocultural life more generally. Boundary maintenance *vis-à-vis* friendly neighbors is difficult, much more so than such maintenance under more adverse circumstances, but it is possible (without closing off desired interactions with the mainstream) and it is imperative if intergenerational mother tongue transmission is to be attained and maintained in the modern world.[32, 33]

## Notes

1. The 'ethnic revival' of the mid-60s to the mid-70s was not a substantive 'revolution', as is sometimes mistakenly intimated, but it was also not a complete failure, not even on the elusive language and ethnicity front, on which it has left behind some long-term subjective identificational gains. For a detailed discussion of the minority language maintenance impact of the 'ethnic revival' see my final chapter ('Epilogue: The rise and fall of the ethnic revival') in Fishman, 1985a.
2. The best overall treatment of the 'English Official/English Only' efforts is Marshall (1986) which should be read in conjunction with Churchill (1986) for additional perspective. A few other worthwhile sources (among many) are Fishman (1988), Macias (1986, 1989), Woolard (1990), Zentella (1988c) and *EPIC Events*, the

newsletter of the English Plus Information Clearinghouse (established under the joint auspices of the National Forum and the Joint National Committee for Languages, 227 Massachusetts Ave., N.E., Suite 120, Washington D. C. 20002). The position of 'US English' (the nationwide organization on behalf of 'English Official') was tellingly presented in its now defunct newsletter *Up-date: US English* and in a selection of pro-English Official papers in Adams and Brink, eds (1990) and in Imhoff (1990). Adams and Brink also provide a good sampling of Federal and state bills that have been introduced on behalf of 'English Official', as well as a sampling of anti-'English Official' points of view.

3. The fullest presentations of minority language maintenance efforts in the United States are Fishman *et al.* (1966), selected chapters in Ferguson and Heath (1981), Veltman (1983) and Fishman *et al.* (1985). Older but still very valuable works are Kloss, 1940–1942 and 1963, as well as his more recent 1977 and 1985.

4. The estimates that I cite of Navajo and/or English use among Navajos are from Veltman (1983) and from the Federal government's 1975 *Survey of Income and Education* (the latter's estimates re Navajo apply only to New Mexico and Arizona). Anglification has probably increased during the intervening years since these studies appeared. For general information about Navajos and other Amerindian peoples see Cornell (1988). For the making and breaking of United States treaties with the Navajos see Brugge (1971), Correll (1979) and Marshall (1981).

5. My Spanish maintenance and shift figures are derived from Waggoner (1981), Veltman (1983), Lopez (1982a, 1982b), Portes and Truelove (1987), Fishman (1987a) and Swicegood *et al.* (1988). For more general information re Hispanics in the USA consult Bean and Tienda (1987) (and the plentiful bibliography cited there) as well as the flow of US Bureau of the Census reports on housing, health, employment, income and education of Hispanics in general and of the major sub-categories under this general designation.

6. Puerto Ricans are counted as 'native-born' in US Census statistics, in view of Puerto Rico's status as a 'free, associated' Commonwealth. Statistics on Mainland-born vs. Island-born language maintenance among Mainland-resident Puerto Ricans are not currently available. If such figures were available they might provide information on Puerto Ricans that was more comparable to that on native-born vs. foreign-born Mexican-Americans and Cuban-Americans.

7. Generational data with respect to Hispanic language maintenance in the USA is available in Fishman *et al.* (1966), Skrabanek (1970), Hudson and Bills (1982), Lopez (1982a and 1982b), and Veltman (1983). English interference in Spanish on the US mainland is copiously documented in Attinasi *et al.* (1982), Elías-Olivares (1976), Lavandera (1981), Milán (1976), Otheguy *et al.* (1989), Peñalosa (1980), Poplack (1979, 1981), Pousada and Poplack (1979), Silva-Corvalán (1989), Solé (1977), Valdés (1980) and Zentella (1978, 1981 and 1985).

8. On code-mixing and calquing, see particularly García *et al.* (1985a) and Otheguy (1982, 1983 and (*et al.*) 1989).

9. The best estimates of worldwide and country-by-country pre-war and post-war Yiddish mother tongue claiming are those provided in Fishman and Fishman (1978) and Fishman (1985b).

10. My figures for Yiddish-speaking in the USA are cited and extrapolated from Veltman, 1983. Preschool-aged Yiddish-speaking children may well be far more numerous than indicated here due to the high and continually rising birthrate in Hasidic circles which are generally only indifferently reached by the USA and other censuses (Oxford, 1981, 1982).

11.  On Yiddish secularism see Goldsmith (1976). For further contextualization of the development of conscious and Jewishly creative secularism within the broader field of Jewish modernization see Goodman (1967, 1972, and 1976), Lehrer (1966), Fishman (1954, 1986), Simon (1954, 1970) and Golumb (1962, 1968).

12.  'Ultra-Orthodox' is itself a relative term, used here to denote more punctilious, extensive and exclusive observance of rituals and customs than that current among 'mainstream', 'modern' or 'centrist' Orthodox, rather than a designation of a totally fixed set of timeless beliefs and observances. The two major subdivisions of the ultra-Orthodox are the Hasidim (also spelled khasidim or khasidem) and the Misna'gdim (Israeli pronunciation: Mitnagdi'm), with the former characterized by emphases on mysticism, zeal, joy and allegiance to particular rabbis regarded as having special powers of intercession with God, and the latter characterized by a stress on exacting observance and in-depth study of traditional sources, rather than on emotion and motivation. The overlap of beliefs and observances between the two camps is very considerable. For a recent introduction to the world of the Hasidim see Rabinowicz, 1988.

13.  Although historical sources reveal a number of ultra-Orthodox calls to the defense of Yiddish (see Weinreich, 1980: 283–4; Fishman, 1987b: 78–80) such conscious calls are, nevertheless, few and far between given the ultra-Orthodox focus on the traditionally sanctified and rabbinically elaborated commandments. For the most recent ultra-Orthodox call to advocate, defend and use Yiddish as the vernacular of everyday life, see the entire issue of *B'darkey hatoyre* (1985/1986, No. 4) devoted to this matter, as well as my analysis of this issue in *Afn shvel* (1987, No. 266, pp. 3–6). For recent ultra-Orthodox doubts about the need to retain Yiddish in their type 4a schools see the exchange of rabbinic views and parental opinions in the *Jewish Observer* May 1988, June 1988 and March 1989, specifically Fryshman (1988 and 1989) and Bender (1988). My analysis of this protracted discussion can be found in Fishman (1989). For the quasi-sanctified nature of Yiddish in a significant sector of the ultra-Orthodox community see Glinert and Shilhav (in press).

14.  For extensive (even though non-scholarly) examples and discussions of the influence of Yiddish on American English slang and humor, business usage, entertainment media usage, advertising, etc., see Rosten (1968, 1982 and 1989). Rosten also provides a few references to the scholarly literature on this topic. For a more reflective and analytic labor of love along these lines, see Samuel (1971). For the contrasted topic of how Jewish cultural specificity (including the influences of Yiddish and Hebrew) has resulted in a 'Jewish English' see Gold (1981).

15.  There is obviously no need to document the existence of an ample and varied set of dictionaries and grammars for Spanish (even including New World Spanish in general and United States Mainland Spanish, and various regional varieties thereof, more particularly). The major Navajo effort along these lines is Young and Morgan (1987). For examples of recent Yiddish dictionaries and grammars see U. Weinreich (1968), Birnbaum (1979), Mark *et al.* (1961–1980) and Mark (1978), Schaechter (1986a, 1986b) and Katz (1988). For a brief review of major Yiddish dictionaries during the past four centuries see Fishman (in press [1991]). Work on Yiddish linguistics more generally is fully inventoried in Bratkowsky (1988). See Fishman (1990) for a selection of papers on Yiddish sociolinguistic topics and Peltz (1987) for an example of ongoing fieldwork of this kind within the American Yiddish context.

16.  Hispanic Pentecostals in New York, as well as elsewhere in the USA, are currently more likely to be exposed to and engaged in Spanish-speaking services and church

activities and events, due to their more intimate, grass-roots functioning, than are Hispanic Catholics who most often attend larger churches which also serve a variety of other ethnolinguistic groups and which, therefore, more often utilize English as a lingua franca of the church. However, the growing Protestantization of USA Hispanics may lead them inexorably into English language religious units of the American mainstream.

17. For two recent collections of Yiddish verse in English translation see Harshav and Harshav (1988) and Howe, Wisse and Shmeruk (1987). There are several excellent collections of translated short stories, essays, novellas, journalism and other prose genres, a fine example of which is Leftwich (1987 [1969]). Yiddish secularism has also given birth to the National Yiddish Book Exchange (Amherst, Mass.), a nationwide retrieval effort which gathers up and resells to individual collectors and to college and university libraries and departments the millions of abandoned Yiddish books whose immigrant owners have died or are of advanced age and whose children have no use for them. This may be designated as an 'Xmen for Xish via Yish' effort that has charitable and archival value rather than RLS value.

18. The Native American Scholarship Fund was established in 1986 to help finance the tertiary level training of Amerindians who will commit themselves to specialize in mathematics, engineering, hard sciences, business, computer science and school teaching/administration for the purposes of meeting tribal Amerindian needs. This is still a very small and weak organization, however, as evidenced by the modesty of its 1988 goal of raising enough money to sponsor a total of ten scholarships.

19. Sefardim are Jews who trace their origins back to the Iberian peninsula. After their expulsion in 1492 they resettled, in major numbers, in North Africa, the Balkans and The Netherlands. Sefardim possessed — and to a minor extent still utilize to this very day — their own Jewish vernacular, usually referred to as Judesmo or Ladino but known by other names as well. As a result of their distinctive history, Sefardim acquired no Yiddish, except in those few resettlement areas (e.g. in the 'Old Settlement' in pre-World War I Ottoman-controlled Palestine) where they lived alongside Yiddish-speaking Jews (the latter being known as Ashkenazim, i.e. derived from Central [and subsequently Eastern] Europe).

20. The cited examples of the still frequent links that Spanish has with the neighborhood and extended family life of all generations, including children, adolescents and young adults, are derived from a memorandum prepared for me by Ana Celia Zentella. Additional information along these lines can be gleaned from Attinasi et al. (1982).

21. The need to re-establish stage 6 as the overriding need in connection with attaining and safeguarding Yiddish in secularist circles is spelled out in my article in *Afn shvel*, 1988, No. 270, pp. 4-8. This approach has received neither support nor recognition from other secularist intellectuals. The only currently ongoing organized youth activity in connection with Yiddish secularism is that of 'Yugntruf: Youth for Yiddish', an organization of college and post-college young folks which publishes an annual journal (*Yugntruf*), nominally conducts a once a week nursery-kindergarten (*Pripetshik*; also see note 25, below), convenes an annual conference and camping week and cooperates with various adult organizations on a variety of joint programs and publication efforts. Most recently, a volume of Yiddish short stories, poems and essays has been published, most of which were written by Yugntruf members. The prevalence of higher stage activities in the absence of (and at the expense of) more fundamental home-and-neighborhood solidification is quite striking in the work of Yugntruf. The few remaining Yiddish secularist youngsters, for

most of whom Yiddish is a hobby or cause rather than an aspect of daily home and neighborhood life, are essentially copying all of the weaknesses of their elders who are involved in the world of Yiddish secularism. In the ultra-Orthodox ranks youth activities take the form of school and club charity work, study contests and trips to sites of Orthodox interest which, while they do not focus on Yiddish, are invariably conducted in Yiddish and constitute a direct outgrowth of family and neighborhood priorities.

22. The problems, prospects and processes of achieving and maintaining literacy in Navajo have been instructively discussed in the work of Spolsky (1975) and in Spolsky and Wayne Holm (1971). My comments on adult and adolescent literacy at Rock Point are based upon correspondence with Wayne Holm and personal field-work observations. For missionary-sponsored literacy efforts in Navajo see Wallis (1968). The Rock Point contract school's operations and achievements are fully described in Rosier and Holm (1980) and in Holm and Holm (1990). The larger Navajo self-governing process is documented in Iverson (1981), Pollock (1984) and Wilkins (1987). It is this process that gives the Tribal Council ultimate authority over the contract schools.

23. Although the ultra-Orthodox invariably achieve literacy in Yiddish (and females may even obtain some instruction in how to conduct correspondence with family and friends in Yiddish) the above-mentioned article in *B'darkey hatoyre* (see note 13) rarely mentions Yiddish literacy (never mentioning Yiddish writing at all) and hews close to the traditional line of literacy in Hebrew and oralcy in Yiddish, particularly for males. Yiddish is not primarily presented as a language of value in and of itself, but as the language implementing daily ultra-Orthodox life, maintaining the boundaries of the ultra-Orthodox community and a means of avoiding the language (and, therefore, the ways and the company) of the gentiles. As such its literacy functions are generally restricted to reading approved ultra-Orthodox periodicals, moralistic chapbooks, biographies of rabbis and historical accounts.

24. For an insightful discussion of the Hispanic press, in Spanish and in English, in the USA, see García *et al.* (1985b) and Gertner *et al.* (1985). It is interesting to note a greater occurrence of Spanish language advocacy in the Hispanic press in English than in the Hispanic press in Spanish. The former is more ideologically conscious regarding Hispanic activism more generally, whereas the latter is more traditionally involved in daily Hispanic life (and in language use), largely without ideological consciousness. The major burden of RLS is to combine the positive aspects of these two positions, utilizing the assets of each for a more powerful and purposive outcome.

25. For references to the history and development of secular Yiddishist supplementary schools in the USA see Fishman (1965: 21–7) and the bibliographic references cited there. More extensive discussions may be found in Kazhdan (1947, 1956) and Gutman (1972). Particular mention should be made of the single secular Yiddish nursery-kindergarten (*Pripetshik* [= hearth]) that is in existence today. It has under 30 enrollees and meets only on Sunday mornings.

26. Special curricular materials have been needed even for such seemingly universal subject areas as arithmetic, geography and algebra because Navajo culture and grammar tend to render these subjects more difficult than they would be for English speakers. In this connection see Pinxten (1987).

27. The Talmud (completed between 400 and 500 CE) is the classic collection of initially orally transmitted Jewish law and tradition. Its Hebrew and Aramaic (Judeo-

Aramaic) texts and their interpretations by subsequent generations of rabbinic scholars are the main subjects of traditional Jewish study to this very day. They also constitute the basis for ongoing rabbinic re-interpretation of these ancient laws and
traditions in order to render them applicable to modern circumstances. For centuries
the Talmud has been studied, argued and discussed in the vernacular of the students
and, accordingly, its association with Yiddish is strong among Ashkenazim in general and among the ultra-Orthodox in particular. To this very day many students of
Talmud coming from non-Yiddish-speaking homes acquire a mastery of Yiddish by
dint of long years of exposure to teachers and fellow students engaged in Talmud
study via Yiddish.

28. The private Cuban-sponsored schools in and around Miami have been provocatively
written up in García and Otheguy (1987). These schools generally carry on the
names and traditions of their progenitor institutions that functioned for the equivalent clienteles in pre-Castro Cuba.

29. The extent to which bilingual education remains unavailable in the USA even for
students (primarily Hispanic students) of limited English proficiency is reviewed by
Oxford *et al.* (1981), Waggoner (1984) and Crawford (1989). The curricular/peda-
gogical inadequacies of type 4b bilingual education even for those who have access
to it are constructively criticized by Ruíz (1988). For the benefits of more prolonged
and intensive instruction in the minority languages utilized in type 4b schooling see
Cummins (1979, 1980a, 1980b, 1980c and 1984). The superiority of type 4a education, both in connection with academic attainment more generally and in connection
with mother tongue mastery and RLS specifically is clearly documented by Byram
(1986).

30. As of this date (mid-1990) a dozen and a half states have adopted 'English Official'
legislation, a handful have defeated it (two adopting 'English Plus' legislation), and
several proposed constitutional amendments pertaining to it at the Federal level have
not yet been reported out of appropriate Congressional committees for general legislative discussion. Increased Federal attention in this connection and court cases
testing the constitutionality of such legislation may be expected in the near future,
one recent ruling having invalidated Arizona's English Official legislation as being
contrary to the freedom of speech provisions of the USA Constitution. Generally, it
has proven to be very difficult to discredit the popular association of proposed
'English Official' legislation with patriotism, fiscal prudence and acculturative propriety.

31. See the above-mentioned studies of Gertner *et al.* (1985) and García *et al.* (1985b)
pertaining to the Spanish press in New York, Miami and Los Angeles.

32. Further references, not cited above, that have also proved useful in the preparation
of this chapter are: (a) In connection with Navajo/Navajos: Thompson (1975), White
(1983), Adair *et al.* (1988), Tolan (1989); (b) In connection with Spanish/Hispanics:
Peng *et al.* (1982), Jorge and Moncarg (1987), Gann and Duignan (1987), Broznan
(1988), García *et al.* (1988), US Bureau of the Census (1988), Zentella (1988b),
Denton and Massey (1989), Griego (1990); In connection with Yiddish/Jews:
Landale and Guest (1990).

33. I am greatly indebted to Wayne Holm, Ana Celia Zentella, Ofelia García and David
E. Fishman for their assistance and criticisms with respect to the first drafts of the
Navajo, Hispanic and Yiddish sections of this chapter. Although this chapter could
not have been written without their help, they are, of course, not responsible for any
errors of fact or interpretation that may remain.

REVERSING LANGUAGE SHIFT

# References

ADAIR, John, DEUSCHLE, Kurt W. and BARNETT, Clifford R. 1988, *The People's Health; Anthropology and Medicine in a Navajo Community*. Albuquerque: University of New Mexico Press.

ADAMS, Karen and BRINK, Daniel 1990, *Perspectives on Official English*. Berlin: Mouton.

ATTINASI, John *et al.* 1982 [second printing: 1988], *Intergenerational Perspectives on Bilingualism: From Community to Classroom*. New York: Center for Puerto Rican Studies, CUNY.

BEAN, Frank D. and TIENDA, Marta 1987, *The Hispanic Population of the United States*. New York: Russell Sage.

BENDER, Yaakov 1988, Mamme loshon is precious, but is it talking to us? *Jewish Observer* June, 31–6.

BIRNBAUM, Solomon A. 1979, *Yiddish: A Survey and a Grammar*. Toronto: University of Toronto Press.

BROZNAN, Nadine 1988, Study Tracks Hispanic Community. *New York Times* December 18, 74.

BRATKOWSKY, Joan G. 1988, *Yiddish Linguistics: A Multilingual Bibliography*. New York: Garland.

BRUGGE, David M. 1971, *The Story of the Navajo Treaties*. Window Rock: Research Section, Navajo Parks and Recreation Department, Navajo Tribe.

BYRAM, Michael S. 1986, *Minority Education and Ethnic Survival; Case Study of a German School in Denmark*. Clevedon: Multilingual Matters.

CHURCHILL, Stacey 1986, *The Education of Linguistic and Cultural Minorities in the OECD Countries*. Clevedon: Multilingual Matters.

CORNELL, Stephen 1988, *The Return of the Native; American Indian Political Resistance*. New York: Oxford University Press.

CORRELL, J. Lee 1979, *Through White Men's Eyes: A Chronological Record of the Navajo People from Earliest Times to the Treaty of June 1, 1868*. Window Rock: Navajo Heritage Center.

CRAWFORD, James 1989, *Bilingual Education: History, Politics, Theory and Practice*. Trenton: Crane.

CUMMINS, J. 1979, *Linguistic Interdependence and the Educational Development of Bilingual Children*. Los Angeles: National Dissemination and Assessment Center.

— 1980a, *Construct of Language Proficiency in Bilingual Education*. Washington: Georgetown University Press.

— 1980b, The entry and exit fallacy in bilingual education. *NABE Journal* 4 (3), 25–39.

— 1980c, The cross-lingual dimension of language proficiency: implications for bilingual education and the optimal age issue. *TESOL Quarterly* 14 (2), 97–111.

— 1984, Wanted: a theoretical framework for relating language proficiency to academic achievement among bilingual students. In Charles RIVERS (ed.) *Language Proficiency and Academic Achievement*. Clevedon: Multilingual Matters, 20–7.

DENTON, Nancey A. and MASSEY, Douglass S. 1989, Racial identity among Caribbean Hispanics. *American Sociological Review* 54, 790–808.

ELÍAS-OLIVARES, Lucía 1976, Ways of Speaking in a Chicano Speech Community: A Sociolinguistic Approach. Ph.D. Dissertation, University of Texas: Austin.

FERGUSON, Charles A. and HEATH, Shirley Brice (eds) 1981, *Language in the USA*. Cambridge: Cambridge University Press.

FISHMAN, Joshua A. (= Fishman, Shikl) 1954, Sekulere yidishkeyt. *Yidisher kemfer* 35 (no. 1054), 35–40.
— 1965, *Yiddish in America*. [*International Journal of American Linguistics* 31, no. 2.] Also published as a monograph: The Hague: Mouton.
— 1985a, Epilogue: the rise and fall of the ethnic revival. In his (*et al.*) *The Rise and Fall of the Ethnic Revival*. Berlin: Mouton, 489–526.
— 1985b, The lively life of a 'dead' language (or 'everyone knows that Yiddish died long ago'). In Nessa WOLFSON and Joan MANES (eds) *Language of Inequality*. Berlin: Mouton, 207–22.
— 1986, Der tsushtayer fun veltlekhkeyt tsum yidishn lebn. *Tsukunft* 92 (no. 11–12), 201–28.
— 1987a, What is happening to Spanish on the US Mainland? *Ethnic Affairs*, 1, 12–23.
— 1987b, A naye farteydikung fun yidish in di khareydishe krayzn. *Afn shvel* 266, 3–6.
— 1988, 'English only': its ghosts, myths and dangers. *International Journal of the Sociology of Language* 74, 125–40.
— 1989, Yidish bay di khareydem: frishe koykhes un naye tsores. *Afn shvel* 276, 1–5.
— (ed.) 1990, *Yiddish: Turning to Life: Sociolinguistic Studies and Interpretations*. Amsterdam: John Benjamins.
— (in press), Yiddish dictionaries. *Worterbicher/Dictionaries/Dictionnaires*. Berlin: Walter de Gruyter.
FISHMAN, Joshua A. *et al.* 1966, *Language Loyalty in the United States*. The Hague: Mouton.
— 1985, *Rise and Fall of the Ethnic Revival*. Berlin: Mouton de Gruyter.
FISHMAN, Joshua A. and FISHMAN, David E. 1978, Yiddish in Israel; A case study of efforts to revise a monocentric language policy. In J. A. FISHMAN (ed.) *Advances in the Study of Societal Multilingualism*. The Hague: Mouton, 185–262.
FRYSHMAN, Bernard 1988, A little mamme loshn about Yiddish. *Jewish Observer* May, 23–5.
— 1989, Mamme loshon: the third side of the coin (letters from parents plus final remarks by Fryshman and Bender). *Jewish Observer* March, 29–42.
GANN, L. H. and DUIGNAN, P. J. 1987, *The Hispanics in the United States: A History*. Boulder: Westview.
GARCÍA, Ofelia *et al.* 1985a, Written Spanish in the United States; an analysis of the Spanish of the ethnic press. *International Journal of the Sociology of Language* 56, 85–98.
— 1985b, The hispanic press in the United States: content and prospects. In J. A. FISHMAN *et al. The Rise and Fall of the Ethnic Revival*. Berlin: Mouton, 343–62.
GARCÍA, Ofelia and OTHEGUY, Ricardo 1987, The bilingual education of Cuban-American children in Dade County's ethnic schools. *Language and Education* 1, 83–95.
GARCÍA, Ofelia *et al.* 1988, Spanish language use and attitudes; a study of two New York City communities. *Language in Society* 17, 475–511.
GERTNER, Michael *et al.* 1985, Language and ethnicity in the periodical publications of four American ethnic groups. In J. A. FISHMAN *et al. The Rise and Fall of the Ethnic Revival*. Berlin: Mouton, 305–41.
GLINERT, Lewis and SHILHAV, Yosseph (in press), Holy land, holy language; language and territory in an ultraorthodox Jewish ideology. *Language in Society*.
GOLD, David L. 1981, The speech and writing of Jews. In Charles A. FERGUSON and Shirley Brice HEATH (eds) *Language in the USA*. Cambridge: Cambridge University Press, 273–92.

GOLDSMITH, Emanuel 1976, *Architects of Yiddishism*. Rutherford: Fairleigh Dickenson University Press. [Re-issued, 1987, as *Modern Yiddish Culture*. New York: Shapolsky.]

GOLUMB, Avrom 1962, *Integrale yidishkeyt: teoriye un praktik*. Mexico City: Author.

— 1968, *Tsvishn tsvey tkufes*. Tel Aviv: Perets.

GOODMAN, Saul (= Gutman, Shoyel) 1967, *Traditsiye un banayung*. New York: Matones.

— 1972, *Der derekh fun sholem aleykhem institut*. New York: Sholem Aleichem Folk Institute.

— 1976, *The Faith of Secular Jews*. New York: Ktav.

GRIEGO, Ricardo J. 1990, The role of the university in maintaining New Mexico's enchantment. Mimeo: University of New Mexico, Albuquerque.

HARSHAV, Benjamin and HARSHAV, Barbara (eds) 1988, *American Yiddish Poetry: A Bilingual Anthology*. Berkeley: University of California Press.

HOLM, Agness and HOLM, Wayne 1990, Rock Point, a Navajo way to go to school; a valediction. *The Annals of the American Academy of Political and Social Science* 508, 170–84.

HOWE, Irving, WISSE, Ruth and SHMERUK, Khone (eds) 1987, *Penguin Book of Modern Yiddish Verse*. New York: Viking Penguin.

HUDSON, Alan and BILLS, Garland 1982, Intergenerational language shift in an Albuquerque barrio. In Jon AMASTAE and Lucia ELIAS-OLIVARES (eds) *Spanish in the United States*. Cambridge: Cambridge University Press, 135–53.

IMHOFF, Gary (ed.) 1990, *Learning in Two Languages*. New Brunswick: Transaction Publishers.

IVERSON, Peter 1981, *The Navajo Nation*. Westport: Greenwood.

JORGE, A. and MONCARG, R. 1987, The Golden Cage; Cubans in Miami. *International Migration Review* 25, 267–82.

KATZ, Dovid 1988, *Grammar of the Yiddish Language*. London: Duckworth.

KAZHDAN, Kh. Sh. 1947, *Di geshikhte fun yidishn shulvezn in umophengikn poyln*. Mexico City: Kultur un hilf.

— 1956, *Fun kheyder un 'shkoles' biz tsisho; dos ruslendishe yidntum in gerangl far shul, shprakh, kultur*. Mexico City: Mendelson Fund.

KLOSS, Heinz 1940–1942, *Volksgruppenrecht in den Vereinigten Staaten von Amerika*. Essen: Essener Verlagsanstalt. 2 vols.

— 1963, *Das Nationalitätenrecht der Vereinigten Staaten von Amerika*. Vienna: Bräumuler.

— 1977, *The American Bilingual Tradition*. Rowley: Newbury.

— 1985, *Deutsch als Muttersprache in den Vereinigten Staaten*. Stuttgart: Steiner.

LANDALE, Nancey S. and GUEST, Avery M. 1990, Generation, ethnicity and occupational opportunity in late 19th century America. *American Sociological Review* 55, 280–96.

LAVANDERA, Beatriz R. 1981, *Lo quebramos, but only in performance*. In Richard P. DURAN (ed.) *Latino Language and Communication Behavior*. Norwood: Ablex, 49–68.

LEFTWICH, Joseph (ed.) and trans. 1987 [1969], *Great Yiddish Writers of the Twentieth Century*. Northvale: Aronson.

LEHRER, Leybush (= Lerer, Leybush) 1966, *In gayst fun traditsiye*. Tel Aviv: Perets.

LOPEZ, David E. 1982a, *Language Maintenance and Shift in the United States Today: The Basic Patterns and Their Social Implications*. Los Alamitos: National Center for Bilingual Research.

— 1982b, *The Maintenance of Spanish Over Three Generations in the United States*. Los Alamitos: National Center for Bilingual Research.

MACÍAS, Renaldo 1986, The English language ideology in the United States. *Social Education* 42, 97–100.

— (ed.) 1989, *Are English Language Amendments in the National Interest?* Claremont: Tomas Rivera Center.

MARK, Yudl 1978, *Gramatik fun der yidisher klal-shprakh*. New York: Kultur-kongres.

— *et al.* 1961–1980, *Der groyser yidisher verterbukh*. New York [vol. 1 and vol. 2] and New York–Jerusalem [vol. 3 and vol. 4]: Komitet.

MARSHALL, Rudolph S. 1981, The Human Capital Loss to the Navajo Tribe Due to Nonfulfillment of the June 1, 1868 Treaty Between the Navajo Tribe and the United States of America. Ph. D. Dissertation, Stanford University.

MARSHALL, David 1986, Language rights and the English language amendment. *International Journal of the Sociology of Language* 60, 7–76. (Also see remarks concerning this paper by 20 commentators from throughout the world, on the pages immediately following.)

MILÁN, William 1976, *New York City Spanish: Myths, Structure and Status*. New York: Institute for Urban and Minority Education (Report Series No. 1).

OTHEGUY, Ricardo 1982, Una visión comunicativa del calco lingüístico como factor explicativo de la influencia del inglés sobre el español de los Estados Unidos. Mimeo: City University of New York.

— 1983, Linguistic calquing as an innovation in the message, not a mixture of systems. Mimeo: City University of New York.

— *et al.* 1989, Transferring, switching and modeling in West New York Spanish: an intergenerational study. *International Journal of the Sociology of Language* 79, 41–52.

OXFORD, Rebecca *et al.* 1981, Projections of non-English language background and limited English proficient persons in the United States to the year 2000; educational planning in the demographic context. *NABE Journal* 5, 1–29.

OXFORD, Rebecca 1982, Letter and tables re Yiddish LEP and NELB estimates from 1976 to 2000, providing further details pertaining to Oxford *et al.* 1981.

PELTZ, Rakhmiel 1987, Who's speaking Yiddish in South Philadelphia today? Jewish language in urban America. *International Journal of the Sociology of Language* 67, 145–66.

PEÑALOSA, Francisco 1980, *Chicano Sociolinguistics: A Brief Introduction*. Rowley: Newbury House.

PENG, Samuel S. *et al.* 1982, Estimation of the number of children with limited English proficiency: a review of analytic procedures. *NABE Journal* 7, 37–52.

PINXTEN, Rik 1987, *Towards a Navajo Indian Geometry*. Ghent: Boeken Reeks.

POLLOCK, Floyd A. 1984, *A Navajo Confrontation and Crisis*. Tsaile: Navajo Community College Press.

POPLACK, Shana 1979, Sometimes I'll start a sentence in English y termino en español; towards a typology of code-switching. *Working Papers*, No. 4. New York: Centro de Estudios Puertorriquenos.

— 1981, Syntactic structure and social function of code-switching In Richard P. DURAN (ed.) *Latino Language and Communicative Behavior*. Norwood: Ablex, 169–84.

PORTES, Alejandro and TRUELOVE, Cynthia 1987, Making sense of diversity; recent research on hispanic minorities in the United States. *American Review of Sociology* 13, 359–85.

POUSADA, Alicia and POPLACK, Shana 1979, No case for convergence; The Puerto Rican
   Spanish verb system in a language contact situation. *Working Papers*, No. 5. New
   York: Centro de Estudios Puertorriquenos.
RABINOWICZ, Harry M. 1988, *Hasidism: The Movement and Its Masters*. Northvale:
   Aronson.
ROSIER, Paul and HOLM, Wayne 1980, *The Rock Point Experience: A Longitudinal Study
   of a Navajo School Program*. Washington: Center for Applied Linguistics.
ROSTEN, Leo C. 1968, *The Joys of Yiddish*. New York: McGraw-Hill.
—  1982, *Hooray for Yiddish!* New York: Simon and Schuster.
—  1989, *The Joys of Yinglish*. New York: McGraw-Hill.
RUÍZ, Richard. 1988, Bilingualism and bilingual education in the United States. In
   Christina Bratt PAULSTON (ed.) *International Handbook of Bilingualism and
   Bilingual Education*. New York: Greenwood, 539–60.
SAMUEL, Maurice 1971, *In Praise of Yiddish*. Chicago: Regnery.
SCHAECHTER, Mordkhe (= Shekhter, Mordkhe) 1986a, *Laytish mame-loshn*. New York:
   Yidish-lige.
—  1986b, *Yiddish II*. Philadelphia: ISHI.
SILVA-CORVALÁN, Carmen 1989, Past and present perspective on language change in U.S.
   Spanish. *International Journal of the Sociology of Language* 79, 53–66.
SIMON, Solomon (= Saymen, Shloyme) 1954, *Tokh-yidishkeyt*. Buenos Aires: Yidbukh.
—  1970, *Emune fun a dor*. New York: Matones.
SKRABENEK, R. L. 1970, Language maintenance among Mexican-Americans.
   *International Journal of Comparative Sociology* 11, 272–82.
SNIPP, C. Matthew 1989, *American Indians: The First of This Land*. New York: Russell
   Sage.
SOLÉ, Yolanda R. 1977, Continuidad/descontinuidad en el español tejano. *The Bilingual
   Review/Revista Bilingue* 4, 189–99.
SPOLSKY, Bernard 1975, Prospects for the survival of the Navajo language. In Dale
   KINKAD et al. (eds.) *Linguistics and Anthropology; In Honor of C. F. Voegelin*.
   Lisse: de Ridder, 596–606.
SPOLSKY, Bernard and HOLM, Wayne 1971, Literacy in the vernacular; The Case of
   Navajo. In Ralph W. EWTON, Jr and Jacob ORNSTEIN (eds) *Studies in Language and
   Linguistics, 1972–73*. El Paso: University of Texas at El Paso, 239–51.
STOLZENBERG, Ross M. 1990, Ethnicity, geography and occupations of U.S. Hispanic
   men. *American Sociological Review* 55, 143–54.
SWICEGOOD, Gray et al. 1988, Language usage and fertility in the Mexican-origin popu-
   lation of the United States. *Demography* 25, 17–33.
THOMPSON, Hildegard 1975, *The Navajos' Long Walk for Education; A History of Navajo
   Education*. Tsaile Lake: Navajo Community College Press.
TOLAN, Sandy 1989, Showdown at Window Rock. *New York Times Magazine* November,
   26–31, 36–40, 74–6.
UNITED STATES BUREAU of the CENSUS 1988, *The Hispanic Population in the United
   States, March 1988. (Advance Report)*. Washington: United States Government
   Printing Office.
VALDÉS, Guadalupe 1980, Code-switching as deliberate verbal strategy: a micro-
   analysis of direct and indirect requests among bilingual Chicano speakers. In
   Richard P. DURAN (ed.) *Latino Language and Communicative Behavior*. Norwood:
   Ablex, 95–108.
VELTMAN, Calvin 1983, *Language Shift in the United States*. Berlin: Mouton.

—  1990, The status of the Spanish language in the United States at the beginning of the 21st century. *International Migration Review* 24, 124–48.

WAGGONER, Dorothy 1981, Educational attainment of language minorities in the United States. *NABE Journal* 6, 1–18.

—  1984, The need for bilingual education: estimates from the 1980 census. *NABE Journal* 8, 1–14.

WALLIS, Ethel E. 1968, *God Speaks Navajo*. New York: Harper and Row.

WEINREICH, Max 1980, *History of the Yiddish Language*. Chicago: University of Chicago Press. (Translation by Shlomo Noble and Joshua A. Fishman of the first two volumes of the four volume Yiddish original [1973].)

WEINREICH, Uriel 1968, *College Yiddish*. New York: YIVO. (Reprinted repeatedly, revised and also translated into Hebrew.)

WHITE, Richard 1983, *The Roots of Dependency*. Lincoln: University of Nebraska Press.

WILKINS, David E. 1987, *Dine Bibeehazaanii: A Handbook of Navajo Government*. Tsaile: Navajo Community College Press.

WOOLARD, Kathryn 1990, Voting rights, liberal voters and the Official English movement; an analysis of campaign rhetoric in San Francisco's Proposition 'O'. In Karen ADAMS and Daniel BRINK (eds) *Perspectives on Official English*. Berlin: Mouton.

YOUNG, Robert W. and MORGAN, William Sr 1987 [1980], *The Navajo Language: A Grammar and Colloquial Dictionary*. (Revised edn.) Albuquerque: University of New Mexico Press.

ZENTELLA, Ana Celia 1978, Code-switching and interactions among Puerto Rucan children. *Working Papers in Sociolinguistics* No. 50. Austin: Southwest Educational Development Laboratory.

—  1981, 'Ta bien; you could answer me in cualquier idioma. In Richard P. DURAN (ed.) *Latino Language and Communicative Behavior*. Norwood: Ablex, 109–32.

—  1985, The fate of Spanish in the United States: The Puerto Rican Experience. In Nessa WOLFSON and Joan MANES (eds) *Language of Inequality*. Berlin: Mouton, 42–59.

—  1988a, Memorandum.

—  1988b, The language situation of Puerto Ricans. In Sandra Lee MCKAY and Sau-ling Cynthia WONG (eds) *Language Diversity: Problem or Resource?* Cambridge: Newbury, 140–65.

—  1988c, Language politics in the USA: The English-only movement. In Betty CRAIGE (ed.) *Literature, Language and Politics*. Athens: University of Georgia Press, 39–53.

# 8   Maori: The Native Language of New Zealand

## Background

The Maoris are the indigenous people of New Zealand (in the Maori language itself, the name of the country is Aotearoa, or 'Land of the Long White Cloud'). Up until recently, the downward trends for the Maori language and culture were so unrelieved and precipitous that their very existence to the end of the twentieth century was questioned by Maoris and pakehas (i.e. European-derived New Zealanders) alike. Accordingly, the recent small and partial successes that Maori has experienced are not only noteworthy but also striking and even have about them a quasi-miraculous mystique.

There has long been a small number of conscientious advocates of the Maori language, and even the Maori tradition itself showed an awareness of the importance of the language for the continuity of the Maori cultural heritage (note such proverbs as 'Without Maori there is no Maoriness' and 'Language is the very life force of Maoriness'), but the odds to be overcome in fostering Maori language and culture under modern circumstances seemed to be truly insuperable. The combined social, cultural, economic, physical (medical) and demographic onslaught of conquest, culture contact, modernization, urbanization and discrimination on the initially rural, pre-modern and pre-industrial Maoris was not only dislocative but dislocative with a genocidal vengeance. Indeed, from 1857 to 1896 the total number of Maoris (defined as persons of half or more Maori ancestry) decreased from roughly 56,000 to roughly 42,000 (a decrease of 25% in only 40 years), a reflection of the Western-derived diseases and multiple problems and disadvantages which depleted the Maoris both psychologically and corporeally. Even by 1921 their numbers, though increasing, had barely returned to the level of 1857, three-quarters of a century before. Since then, however, there has been a remarkable demographic recovery, testimony to the dietary, birthrate and longevity benefits that are among the usual, worldwide fruits of the first century of modernization, once its initial debits are overcome. Today, the Maoris constitute over 10% of the more than three million total population of New Zealand (and estimates going as high as 400,000 are also on record), thus representing a considerable presence, both in absolute and in relative terms.

However, the physical resurgence, dramatic though it has been, has by no means been accompanied by a parallel social, cultural or ethnolinguistic resurgence. Quite the contrary: until very recently it seemed to be the case that the more Maori living and health standards improved, the more their traditions and their language languished. Those who spoke Maori either natively or fluently became an increasingly smaller proportion of all Maoris (perhaps no more than some 50,000 (maximally 70,000) today), while those who even still understood it (but could not employ it overtly) were no more than 100,000 and both of these sub-populations, particularly the population of fluent native speakers, were overwhelmingly beyond 40 years of age (indeed, even beyond 50 years of age) and, therefore, well beyond child-bearing age as well. Even today, when some new and important improvements have occurred in RLS-efforts on behalf of Maori, it is still true that 'there are more fluent speakers passing away each day than there are speakers of comparable ability coming up to take their place'.[1] Not only were next to none of the Maori children growing up in the cities of New Zealand being raised as native speakers of Maori, but even the steadily decreasing rural minority among Maoris was also overwhelmingly raising its little ones as English speakers. Indeed, Maori speaking *communities* had almost disappeared from the scene and those youngsters who were learning Maori as a second language had practically no natural sociocultural milieux in which to utilize it or from which to derive ordinary communicative support for it.

## The Aftermath of Demographic Resurgence

The physical resurgence of the Maoris not only provided an opportunity for organized cultural re-examination among Maoris themselves, but it also made it inevitable that the New Zealand anglo mainstream would also engage in some re-examination of its policies and attitudes toward the Maori people, Maori culture and Maori language. Much of this re-examination produced mere tokenism, particularly in the earlier years. Thus, the Maori Social and Economic Advancement Act of 1945 established a body of Maori Tribal Executives, one of whose functions was 'To preserve, revive and maintain the teaching of Maori arts, crafts, language, genealogy and history in order to perpetuate Maori culture. [12 (a) (v)]', without providing any means whatsoever whereby these particular functions might be carried out, in contrast to the Act's very explicit procedures for 'preventing and abating [Maori] nuisances' and the 'regulation and licensing of [Maori] billiard rooms'. The latter provisions reveal the degree and prevalence of Maori personal and sociocultural dislocation and the extent to which these were becoming worrisome for the mainstream's peace and comfort. More recently, however, both the levels of Maori ethnocultural consciousness and culture planning, as well as the levels of pakeha awareness of the cultural desiderata for Maori well-being and for a trouble-free relationship between pakeha and Maori societies, have improved considerably and with promising (although still indeterminate) results. Taken together, although not often acting in concert, these two different streams of consciousness, that of the mainstream and that of the Maoris themselves, have produced some tangible RLS results. Clearly, one development without the other would have been far less fruitful than was the case when the two were in tandem with each other.

By the 1960s, and in accord with the usual dynamics of the rise of non-mainstream proto-elites, there had appeared a young, well educated and verbally accomplished Maori intelligentsia of a pro-'Xmen with Xish' orientation. Whereas their predecessors, a generation or two earlier, had stressed a program of action characterized by the slogan 'Seek the knowledge of the pakeha!', the intelligentsia of the 60s had already attained that knowledge and those few who had not transethnified in the process were fully and painfully aware of the continuation of Maori disadvantage and of mainstream discrimination nonetheless. The much-heralded, Western-sponsored millennium had not arrived, neither for them personally nor for Maoris collectively, and, instead, the originally genuine co-occurrence of race, ethnicity and language had fallen apart to such a degree that anomie was rampant and that most younger Maoris did not know enough Maori even to be able to bury their dead with dignity. Chagrin and disappointment, both with the Maori condition and with the mainstream that promised much vaguely but that delivered little (whether of material or psychological value) concretely, was heightened by the new contrastive awareness that these exceptional Maori young people had arrived at by virtue of armed forces service abroad and civilian manpower mobilization during World War II.

Growing interaction with the increasing number of Polynesians settling in New Zealand and bringing to that country a much higher level of language maintenance in languages closely related to Maori, and general exposure (via visitors, travel and the media) to the ethnic revival then impacting the entire Western world, may also have helped, but it was due primarily to internal developments and processes that there came to be a new and stronger Maori impatience with the tokenism that was forthcoming from pakeha authorities via such steps as the proclamation of a once a year 'Maori Language Week', the official adoption of native Maori pronunciations for Maori place names, and the traditional entitlement of Maori MPs to occasionally use their language (without translation into English!) when addressing Parliament. Something more was needed and needed urgently if the Maori language and culture were to survive at all, most particularly if they were to attain the modernization and revitalization that both of them required.[2]


## Legal maneuvers

One of the most telling straws in the wind that a new type of modern Maori leader was appearing on the scene was the fact that public and widely publicized appeals to the government began to be made in connection with issues previously only discussed within the small circle of pro-RLSers *per se*. An early example of the above was the petition to Parliament circulated in the late 60s and early 70s by the Nga Tama Toa (= 'Warrior Sons', even though this organization also included many female members as well), a radical, activist youth movement, demanding a greater role for the Maori language in government, in the media and in the various other public institutions of the country. A surprising 30,000 signatures were gathered and delivered to Parliament, testimony to the fact that the small band of activists could elicit the support of a large group — and, potentially, of a huge group — of followers, something that could not be ignored by New Zealand authorities who had long been convinced that tokenism alone would satisfy the cultural goals of most Maoris.

Nevertheless, the only immediate reaction to the petition was a largely decorative 1974 amendment to the Maori Affairs Act which 'officially' recognized Maori as 'the ancestral language of ... the population ... of Maori descent' and which enabled the Minister of Maori Affairs 'from time to time to take such steps as he deems appropriate for the encouragement of the learning and use of the Maori language (in its recognized dialects and variants), both within and without the Department'. It required another five years before it became crystal clear, via Supreme Court and Court of Appeal rulings, that this 'recognition' had absolutely no practical meaning whatsoever, indeed, that it was meaningless as far as the courts were concerned since it was simply a statement of fact and neither *required* nor *implemented* any governmental expansion of the use of Maori, either with Maoris or by Maoris. For those who had placed great hopes on the legislative route to strengthening the position of Maori this was a severe disappointment indeed. For many it clearly implied that other types of remedial action were urgently needed, but there were also those who advocated further legalistic steps of a more sweeping and fundamental sort.

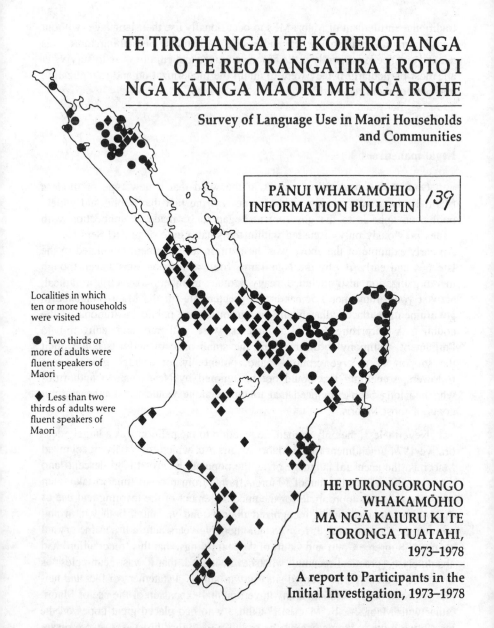

# TE TIROHANGA I TE KŌREROTANGA O TE REO RANGATIRA I ROTO I NGĀ KĀINGA MĀORI ME NGĀ ROHE

Survey of Language Use in Maori Households and Communities

PĀNUI WHAKAMŌHIO INFORMATION BULLETIN 139

Localities in which ten or more households were visited

● Two thirds or more of adults were fluent speakers of Maori

◆ Less than two thirds of adults were fluent speakers of Maori

HE PŪRONGORONGO WHAKAMŌHIO MĀ NGĀ KAIURU KI TE TORONGA TUATAHI, 1973–1978

A report to Participants in the Initial Investigation, 1973–1978

FIGURE 8.1 *Cover page of a 'Report to Participants in the Survey of Language Use in Maori Households and Communities', 1973–1978* (*Source*: Wellington, Maori Unit, New Zealand Council for Educational Research, 1988).

## The Waitangi Tribunal

In 1840 a Treaty of Waitangi had been signed between the British Crown and 45 Maori chiefs, whereby the former committed itself to protect the *taonga*, i.e. all those things of material and spiritual value to the Maori, in return for the latter's fealty to the Crown. Because of insistent claims by the new Maori leadership of the post-World War II era that the Crown had not kept to all points of its commitment, many of which pertained to Maori land and fishing rights, the entire legal status of the Treaty was reviewed in 1975 and the resulting Treaty of Waitangi Act was subsequently revised again in 1986, largely as a result of recommendations made that very year by the Waitangi Tribunal that had been established in order to review Maori unhappiness in connection with a variety of Treaty matters. The Tribunal also made several recommendations that dealt explicitly and urgently with the Maori language, all of them derived from its fundamental agreement with various Maori submissions that their language too was a *taonga* and, accordingly, had been guaranteed protection by the Crown, a guarantee not adhered to in the nearly century and a half that had passed since the original 1840 Treaty. The Tribunal urged the government of New Zealand to undertake various steps that would require Maori in education, the courts, the media, and the public service and, in addition, that a governmental Maori Language Commission be established that would foster the language, 'watch over its progress and set standards for its use' (presumably via its annual *Report* to the New Zealand House of Representatives). Subsequent to the above, in 1987, an act was adopted declaring Maori to be an official language of New Zealand and purporting to implement most of the recommendations of the Tribunal.

Clearly, much further legal maneuvering will be required before it becomes apparent what all of these seemingly momentous decisions will amount to in the everyday life of the language. Thus far, the implementation of the Tribunal's recommendations and of the Maori Language Act is not nearly as momentous as the recommendations and the Act themselves. Maori has certainly taken on some of the trappings of a national language (e.g. using Maori too, i.e. in addition to English, on the letterheads and advertisements of governmental agencies, delivering a few words of ceremonial welcome or of preface in Maori, on the part of many governmental dignitaries and various governmental departments, and encouraging agency personnel to learn Maori in additional departments outside of the Department of Education [which had done so earlier]), but all of these attempts to associate Maori with the symbols of New Zealand nationhood fall far, far short of what is really required in practical terms if the language is to survive as a vernacular, let alone if it is to survive in communities and in a social life of its own rather than being a ceremonial appendage to White society, culture and institutions. These attempts do not translate themselves into a self-motivated and insightful program of concrete and urgent RLS actions and, as we have noted earlier, Maori is hardly in a position to wait patiently for endless further foot-dragging to end, as courts are asked to rule over the myriad matters that should, could or must derive from earlier legal and statutory actions. Reversing language shift depends on the proper actions at the proper time and in the optimal sequence and, therefore, it is to a review of recent actions (rather than Acts) pertaining to Maori that we now turn. Just as the earlier obituaries pertaining to Maori were premature, so the recent trumpetings that it has now risen 'from its death-bed, revived and revitalized as a living language' may well also be somewhat premature, to say the least.[3]

### Stage 6: Family, neighborhood, community

The Maori language, qua linguistic system and qua language-in-culture system, does not need to be painstakingly reassembled out of the fading memories of isolated 'old timers' but substantial language teaching efforts to individual adults are, as we will soon see, underway and urgently required (stage 8). Many of the grandparents who now constitute the major corps of active and fluent Maori speakers are themselves still integrated into real, ongoing, intergenerational communities, that is, they are socially and culturally active folks rather than largely separated off into hospitals or old-age homes. In these communities the grandparents engage in richly traditional Maori language-related daily rounds of life and ritual occasions (stage 7), although these are often and inevitably more intergrandparent oriented than intergenerationally oriented (because of the vast and dislocative sociocultural change that has impacted the past three generations of Maoris). Nevertheless, even though these grandparents, like all grandparents everywhere, are 'getting along in years', they can still be activized as a force for RLS, a force for re-establishing intergenerational language links, the very same links that most of them let fall in the past when they ceased speaking 'Maori only' with their own children. The latter is said not to blame them for their past lapses, given that the housing policy of the Department of Maori Affairs was one of scattering the Maoris (who were massively relocating in urban areas) throughout a large number of different pakeha-dominated neighborhoods, rather than concentrating them in neighborhoods primarily of their own, thereby breaking the authority and the life-pattern that the older generation was accustomed to. However, the same Department of Maori Affairs that acted so counter-productively *vis-á-vis* Maori sociocultural continuity on the urban resettlement front (much like the culturally counter-productive actions of the American 'Bureau of Indian Affairs') fostered two efforts in the late 1970s and early 1980s that had (and still have) great potential for going beyond stages 8 and 7 in the direction of re-establishing the basic family-neighborhood-community nexus of all languages that are in good sociocultural health.

The *aatarangi* movement, which got underway in 1979–80, attempted (and continues to do so today) to promote adult learning and relearning of Maori via a community-based program. Basically, it teaches those who are already Maori speakers (primarily grandparents) to become language teachers and, thereupon, either to teach others to become teachers or teach others to become speakers. The *aatarangi* teachers are unpaid volunteers and they are often referred to as 'barefoot teachers', thus capturing some of the motivational fervor that this term (and also the term 'barefoot doctors') had, and in part still has, in its original mainland Chinese context.[4] Their work involves relatively brief but intensive training in the different situations in which Maori is traditionally used, ranging from informal conversation at home and when chatting with friends and neighbors, to the more formal and poetic language of important gatherings of the traditional tribes. After a few days of teaching by example, by exhortation and *in situ*, the teachers then move on to a different cluster of relatives and friends and the erstwhile students then each become teachers in their own right. More recently the *aatarangi* movement has also interacted and fused with a related one, the Family Development Program (*Tu Tangata Whanau*). The urban neighborhood centers established by the latter program use the *marae* or traditional extended family concept as their basis of operation and orientation in re-establishing Maori cultural norms of hospitality, caring, spirituality and sharing, behavioral norms for which the spoken Maori language is considered essential.

Finally, it should be added that at about the same time that the *aatarangi* movement began, Maori Language Boards were set up around the country to stimulate language efforts in the traditional Maori tribal districts that still remain in several rural areas. All in all, therefore, several efforts have been underway to activate grandparents to teach and parents to learn and transmit, so that the previous cultural self-denegration of Maoris would cease and so that their language would have basic and appropriate everyday sociocultural functions to implement.[5] However, except during distinctly atypical (and usually passing) periods of ideological fervor, there is only 'so much' language learning that adults are likely to engage in, and given that most Maoris are already speaking one language (English) quite effectively for all major life-purposes, it is not to be expected that many of them will voluntarily undertake the further dislocation of their lives which transferring to another language entails, even when that other language is ethnohistorically 'their own', unless other, reinforcing incentives are available. Lacking a neighborhood (intra-Maori) economic base of any importance, a major additional incentive, obviously, is that which derives from the younger generations and the emotional, cognitive, behavioral (and verbal) gratifications that they dispense to the older ones.

A very natural, and vastly popular, outgrowth of the *whanau* program have been the *kohanga reos* (= language nests), which, since 1982, have begun to fulfill in urban life many of the educative functions of the increasingly vanishing rural *marae*. Many of the same grandparents who are active in the *kohanga reo* would, in former years, have been involved in analogous language-in-culture socialization of the very young in pre-urban Maori settings. At the primarily urban *kohanga reos*, Maori-speaking grandparents (and any parents or other adults, varying in age from 16 to 96, who care to offer their services and who can do so in fluent Maori, all of whom are referred to as *Kaiawhi* ['embracers']) typically provide 4–8 hours of daily childcare (the interschool range varying from two to as many as 10 hours per day) to pre-schoolers, most of whom have absolutely no speaking knowledge (and very little if any comprehension either) of Maori. What is additionally significant is that this care is not only provided entirely in Maori but that it is provided at a time in children's language socialization when English-speaking society and culture have not yet strongly impacted their lives. However, what is really involved is not only child language-in-culture socialization but community building and good childcare as well. Not only are elders recognized as rich resources of language-in-culture knowledge (thereby adding to their self-esteem as well as to their societal usefulness), not only is an adult–child ratio maintained which is often better (when all the volunteer teachers show up to render their volunteer service) than that required by New Zealand childcare regulations, not only is the problem of language maintenance attacked at its core (i.e. at the intergenerational transmission nexus), but the Maoris themselves have accepted the responsibility of transmitting the language, rather than waiting for the government to do 'something' on its behalf, and have hit upon a way of doing so that is linked to a distinct vision of being 'Maori-via-Maori', namely the *whanau* (family) and *iwi* (tribal) affiliation,[6] and were recognized and complimented precisely for doing so by the Waitangi Tribunal itself.

Having acknowledged the powerful potential of the *kohanga reos*, particularly for a language that was almost literally without child-speakers, and noting their rapid growth, from four in 1982 to roughly 520 in 1988 with a total enrollment of some 8,000 children, we must also be careful not to exaggerate their current effectiveness or their carry-over into the future. Not all of them, by any means, are pedagogically effective, nor is their nearly total reliance on an untrained, volunteer staff a completely unmixed blessing, neither in the educative connection nor even in connection with childcare *per se*. While a large proportion of Maori pre-schoolers now attend these centers, there are probably even more who still do not do so. Finally, the growing dependence of these centers on funding by the Department of Maori Affairs[7] may ultimately turn out to be a fatal flaw, not only because government priorities are subject to change, particularly as overall budget crises grow more severe, but because this dependence undercuts local and national Maori responsibility for their own ethnolinguistic fate.

In addition, as linguists are not slow to point out, the grass-roots nature of the staffing, the day-to-day management and the program-definition of the rural *kohanga reos* sometimes leads to the preservation or even intensification of the rural dialectal diversity of Maori. This tends to counteract the emergence of a national standard Maori (needed for later Maori literacy) and even competes with the emergence of a more inclusive, unified, supra-local Maori self-concept and identity such as that which the primarily urban and dialectally heterogeneous *kohanga reos* do tend to foster. Most serious of all, however, is the lack of explicit feedback from the *kohanga reos* to the homes, families and neighborhoods from which the children are derived. The *kohanga reos* are not used to help render Maori-speaking the children's overwhelmingly English-speaking parents and older siblings, parents and siblings who are often Maori-positive in a passive way (sufficiently so to send their youngest family members to the *kohanga reos*), but who have not yet, by and large, become even minimally Maori-speaking themselves.

Such parental involvement and 'relinguification' could be made a prerequisite for *kohanga reo* participation, an RLS goal that must be attained if the Maori language socialization of the young is to have a secure post-childcare base in everyday life. Without such a home, family and neighborhood niche the former dislocation of stage 6 is not yet really rectified or repaired, particularly so since subsequent RLS stages, as we will note below, are also still rather shaky and cannot, therefore, be expected to help maintain the Maori proficiency that some of the *kohanga reo* 'graduates' have acquired.

*Stage 5: Voluntary literacy-imparting schools*

No such institutions as those that we have envisaged for stage 5 have been created for Maori. This may, in large part, be a result of the meager literacy tradition for Maori as a whole. However, the lack of such agencies completely under Maori community control and outside of substantial mainstream regulation makes the acquisition of Maori literacy totally dependent on stages that require substantial mainstream approval and/or support. This, in turn, tends to weaken the ideologizing, energizing and unifying role that literacy could play in the formation of stronger intercommunal ties and in the development of a distinctly Maori modernity. It would seem to be a natural goal for the *kohanga reos* to set for themselves, both for post-daycare children and, particularly, for the adults that these children are related to. Like the goal of relinguifying the Maori home, the goal of rendering 'Maori-literate' the Maori adult is a logical outreach function that the combined *aatarangi* and *whanau* movements also need to acknowledge and activate. This extension of their current efforts would be part and parcel of the 'internal struggle' to create a new Maori-via-Maori reality; and no 'external struggle' can be successful until the internal one is completed, and self-sufficiently so. Unfortunately, the somewhat atavistic *aatarangi* emphasis on oral Maori alone tends to overlook the almost universalistic level of adult Maori literacy that missionaries brought to the Maoris by the 1850s (within a decade of the signing of the Treaty of Waitangi). Even as late as the first decades of this century it was not unusual for traditional Maori families to teach their children to read Maori at home, before the young ones began going to (English) school. This literacy tradition has been forgotten and now needs to be revived and extended to adults, either via new institutions created for this very purpose or via child-centered institutions that can be extended into the evening hours in order to help both old and young to return to Maori literacy, and to return Maori literacy to the individual and to the societal life of the Maori people.

*Stage 4: Type 4a schools that teach in Maori and type 4b schools that teach (a little) Maori*

If the very future of the *kohanga reos* is in doubt without the support of the Ministry of Maori Affairs, in doubt because the Maoris are so generally unable and even more generally unaccustomed to financing their own basic RLS institutions (with the possible exceptions of the *marae, marae* gatherings, and certain radio efforts, all of which have benefited from substantial Maori funding, in addition to whatever public funding they may also have acquired), then it should come as no surprise that there are only a handful of type 4a schools, schools essentially conducted under Maori community auspices and in which Maori children can fulfill at least the elementary-level compulsory education requirements. The need for precisely such schools is now obvious, since *kohanga reo* 'graduates' who go on to bilingual education public schools of the more commonly available 4b type (offering 4–5 hours a week of Maori instruction) lose their Maori fluency within a matter of months of beginning to do so. This sad state of affairs led 400 *kohanga reo* teachers, meeting in November 1987, to call for 'a Maori education authority independent of the Education Department', i.e. in effect, calling essentially for Maori schools (initially, elementary schools) under Maori control but paid for by the government. This meeting was soon (1988) followed by the Matawaia Declaration which focused on the administration of Maori education and called for an independent Maori Education Authority in order to 'establish Maori control and autonomy of education from pre-school to Adult education' (R. Benton, personal memorandum). One year later, this Declaration had still not met with a positive or clear governmental response and remained very much on the Maori RLS agenda.

The few schools of the 4a type that have been established to date have come about due to the pressure of parents whose children have just completed (or are just about to complete) their local *kohanga reo*. This pressure is exerted upon a local school principal (preferably a cooperative one), upon a not unwilling local elementary school committee, and upon a District Senior Inspector, to set aside some space (to begin with: one room) in the local elementary school, to appoint a certified teacher who happens to be able to teach in Maori (almost no in-service certification programs and no pre-service programs at all for such teachers currently being available), together with a fluently Maori-speaking teacher's aide, so that their children can be or continue to be taught primarily in Maori. The parents' hope is to add class after class, as new contingents arrive year after year from nearby *kohanga reos*, until a completely or substantially Maori school will coexist with the regular English-language-of-instruction elementary school under the same roof.[8] The genesis, growth and continuation of such all-Maori schools[9] depends on such a complex and rare combination of pakeha good will, cooperation and financing that the initiation of many more schools of this type does not seem particularly likely unless the Waitangi Tribunal's stipulation that 'instruction in Maori should be available as a right to the children of parents who seek it' is explicitly implemented at a statutory level.

Meanwhile, the reports from the current small number of type 4a schools (they are usually referred to as 'immersion' or as 'Maori-oriented' in the New Zealand literature) are encouraging indeed, for they stress not only a direct focus on Maori as the medium of instruction but an indirect focus on Maori as the language of school life as well, through the creation of physical and social 'Maori space'[10]: Maori decorations, Maori cultural styles of pupil–teacher and pupil–pupil interaction, Maori cultural styles of welcoming guests (including non-Maori-speaking guests for whom Maori ceremonial welcoming remarks are translated, just as their non-Maori replies are then translated into Maori, regardless of whether or not these replies — normally in English — have been understood). Thus, it is clear, both linguistically and extra-linguistically, that these schools are under Maori community control.

What is not clear is whether there will be many more such schools than the pitifully small handful that now exist, since those that now exist are entirely supported by and dependent upon public tax funds. It is true that the Waitangi Tribunal recommendations foresaw such schools to the extent that Maori parents desired them; nevertheless, the Tribunal's recommendations are merely that (recommendations without the force of law), and as long as Maori parents themselves are neither Maori-speaking nor RLS-conscious (a stage 6 task!) there is no certainty that they will prefer type 4a schools to the type 4b schools that are much more plentifully available and much less Maori-focused. At the moment (late 1989) the pressure for a Maori Education Authority and for 'giving Maori a greater place in formal education' is increasing but the ultimate success of this pressure is still in doubt.

Perhaps the most encouraging stage 4a development, particularly in the light of the above-mentioned governmental footdragging, is the recent emergence (toward the very end of the 80s) of five *kura kaupapa Maori* ('Maori agenda schools') intended almost exclusively for the 'graduates' of the *kohanga reos*. These are '*ikastola*-like' one- or two-teacher schools that are primarily parent-supported (although in some cases some public funding is also 'unofficially' leaked to them). Clearly these are community products and community building-blocks as well. Since the 150th anniversary of the signing of the Treaty of Waitangi will be celebrated in 1990, it is hoped by RLS leaders that the occasion will be utilized to announce major changes in connection with publicly supporting such schools as will as in connection with approving and supporting a Maori Education Authority more generally. In both connections, apparently, there are still public authorities who need to be convinced that a primarily Maori medium education for Maori children (i.e, for those children whose parents opt for such education for them) would be 'truly educational' rather than 'mentally crippling'. Obviously, RLS advocates and the pakeha establishment still have very different views of the value of Maori (Benton, personal memorandum).

Even type 4b schools, with their few hours of Maori language instruction (and, therefore, also referred to, quite confusingly, as 'bilingual schools') are a vast improvement over the New Zealand schools of former years, public schools as well as church schools, that not only typically taught no Maori at all but that punished ('strapped') Maori children for speaking Maori to each other on the school grounds, much as Chicano children were once punished for speaking Spanish in Texas and in other parts of the American Southwest. From Sir George Grey's Education Ordinance of 1847 (pertaining to the financing of Church of England, Catholic and Wesleyan (Methodist) mission schools), through Sir Apirana Ngata's dictum of the 1930s (to the effect that 'English first, English second, English third and English last' constituted the very best education for Maori children), through to the Play Centre movement of the 1970s (admonishing Maori parents not to speak Maori to their children if they really had their children's best interests at heart), a rather recurring pakeha view, even if unstated in official policy, has been to educate Maori children without any Maori at all whenever possible.

Little by little, however, a minimalistic and tokenistic elective study of Maori has nevertheless crept into the schools, first at the secondary level (where it would have the least chance of being mastered) and then at the elementary level, and is now quite widely available at both of these levels today, but also widely ineffective concerning language fluency, let alone RLS. Such efforts are classical examples of 'too little and too late' and although they are said to have 'symbolic value' it is hard to be sure just what they are symbols of, since they may actually be turning more Maori students off than on. Like any other subject that is made widely available in New Zealand's schools, Maori as a second or foreign language does not lack for teachers, textbooks, curricula or students (including non-Maori students). What it does lack is real life, real results, real societal impact when measured from the point of view of the urgent RLS needs of a severely weakened language and culture.

All in all, therefore, there is little reason to be satisfied with the RLS role of education in the Maori case at this time. Type 4a schools are few in number and hardly any certified teachers are being prepared for such schools. Type 4b schools are more plentiful but totally ineffectual at best and harmful to RLS at worst. They lack coordinated programs and, minimalistic as they are, even they are totally optional as far as any governmental commitment to Maori is concerned. Given this state of affairs, it would seem even more urgent that the *kohanga reo* schools adopt literacy functions as well, wherever possible, both for children and for adults, otherwise the Maori speakers of the future will not only be fewer in number than those of the past, but they will have to cope with the growing burden of contrastive illiteracy as well. The pseudo-problems and pseudo-solutions that constantly preoccupy the New Zealand educational authorities (e.g. purported decentralization to mask the increasing centralization of budgetary decisions, on the one hand, and the awarding of laughably [actually 'cryably'] small extra allowances for type 4b programs) amount to little more than temporizing until a bad RLS situation becomes even worse. The most general governmental bias views Maori only in minimalistic oral or touristic perspective, a perspective that is patronizing and impoverishing as far as RLS goals are concerned.

### Stages 3, 2 and 1: Pie in the sky?

The remaining three stages along our comparative reversing sociolinguistic dislocation scale can be handled briefly, because they generally constitute no more than gleams in the eyes of a few stubborn idealists rather than any substantial reality or genuine RLS opportunity. The lower work sphere (stage 3) either insofar as it pertains to Maoris serving pakehas or pakehas serving Maoris (the intra-Maori work sphere belongs, in our scheme, to stage 6) is still entirely in English. Neither the Maori Trust Boards, Land Incorporations or Foundations, although they constitute Maoridom's wealthiest enterprises, and even though most of their shareholders are derived from the grandparents' generation and are, therefore, typically, Maori-speaking themselves, have attempted to establish Maori-speaking employment opportunities for the Maori masses.

Except for a very few general newspapers that deign to publish Maori notices and messages on a few days out of the week, there is no Maori periodic press. There is a Maori medium high school and a Maori medium junior college, the latter still curricularly quite truncated. Radio is doing somewhat more in Maori, particularly the still weak and intermittent local and private radio efforts which have gained quite a following. The national networks, on the other hand, give no more than 15 (!) minutes per day of news in Maori, and Maori on television was still quite unheard of until 1980.[11] In that year, a one-minute Maori comment in observance of Maori Language Week elicited so many racist reactions and negative comments that nothing of consequence has been attempted in Maori on television thereafter, and even the brief news report in Maori has been shifted to an inconvenient viewing time, thereby losing most of its audience. Nevertheless, the number and the insistence of the requests on behalf of radio and television in Maori (some of them being legal briefs related to Waitangi Treaty interpretations) are both increasing and some greater symbolic recognition of Maori may soon be forthcoming as a result.

However, the pakeha establishment can afford to play games with issues such as these. At the same time that the Maori Language Commission (established 'to foster the Maori language', in accord with one of the Waitangi Tribunal's more nebulous recommendations) and various Maori activists are advocating 'demographically proportionate' government services and mass media in Maori, there is actually some sentiment in government circles for the 'devolution' of the Department of Maori Affairs, one of the oldest governmental departments in all New Zealand, and for turning over its funds and responsibilities to the largely defunct and disorganized Maori tribes. This is patently a thinly disguised attempt to cripple Maori RLS, rather than to help it.

All in all, the resistance to Maori goals at these upper levels is quite unreconstructed, leading some Maori spokesmen to focus on them all the more. While such reactions are quite understandable, the pursuit of these stages at this time may represent little more than the pursuit of a will-o'-the-wisp, i.e. a pursuit that is 'of no consequence to language survival and growth if the fundamental process of [intergenerational] transmission is cut off'.[12] The 'fundamental process' is exactly where an intelligent concentration of scarce resources belongs, if only because Maori TV, should it ever come into being on a 'demographically proportionate' basis, would hardly be able to compete successfully (as an RLS thrust) with the mammoth English programming with which it would obviously be compared. Some encouraging progress has recently been made via the *kohanga reo* and *kura kaupapa* Maori schools, which provide the major opportunities for developing home-family-neighborhood RLS-efforts capable of further judicious grass-roots expansion into stages 5 and 6.

Maori is still dying year by year and effective first aid and major surgery are needed urgently, rather than stressing such elective non-essentials as token mass media programs, the token use of Maori in government offices, signs and letterheads, wildly luxuriant corpus planning for 'Maori in the modern sector', literary prizes for writers, and Maori-speaking telephone operators and clerks at government agencies. All of the above-mentioned are merely symbolic flourishes, given the lack of substance with respect to the societal co-management which they imply, or even any substantially self-regulatory intergenerational Maori home-family-neighborhood life on which such efforts must be firmly based if they are to contribute to RLS *per se* (rather than merely to jobs for a few dozen disaffected intellectuals). What would be fine goals once stages 6 to 4 are fully nailed down would merely be hollow victories, masked defeats and hopeless distractions otherwise. Even were they to be granted (who knows, another Waitangi Tribunal might make more explicit recommendations with respect to them), they would not stop the arterial bleeding of Maori any more than they have of Irish or even of Basque.[13]

# Concluding Comments

Stock comparisons of the current position of Maori with the late nineteenth, early twentieth century — 'revival' of Hebrew — a pie in the sky comparison that appeals to all threatened languages — are quite fallacious, particularly when that revival (or revernacularization, as it is now more correctly termed) is still generally so poorly understood in terms of its own basic sociological dynamics (see Chapter 10, below). That revival was not accomplished by waiting patiently for children who finished Hebrew medium elementary schools to get married and have Hebrew mother tongue children of their own. The revival was based upon prior adult ideological commitment to spoken Hebrew and it was finally accomplished by creating Hebrew-as-a-second-language settlements (= homes, families, neighborhoods) without even waiting for elementary schools to be organized. To wait for the graduates of the *kohanga reos* and of the Maori immersion schools to get married and have Maori mother tongue children of their own would be to assume that one could afford to wait for another generation, while the majority of Maori children continued to attend contraindicated schools, remain Maori illiterates and completely dependent on Yish society in myriad ways, and to assume that this would not be a wait during which there would most probably be more attrition than continuity even in the ranks of the *kohanga reo* 'graduates' themselves, given that most of them would have no type 4a elementary schools to go on to. Rather than wait for such an 'iffy' intergenerational connection a generation hence, rather than struggle inconsequentially for Maori on government letterheads and in 10% of children's television ('proportional representation'!), it would be far better to focus meager resources parsimoniously on stage 6 and then to aim squarely at stages 5 and 4a in terms of major new worlds to conquer.

The Maori case is obviously complicated by the small number of remaining fluent speakers (fewer by far than of the other individual cases presented in this volume), by the dispersion of these remaining fluent speakers, their relatively meager resources, their advanced age and the general atmosphere of antipathy and racism that they so often encounter in the mainstream. These are heavy burdens indeed, and it is no wonder, therefore, that a 'now or never' climate apparently pervades so much of the thinking and efforts of RLS activists. What is more, the Waitangi Treaty claims upon New Zealand tend to orient these activists primarily toward what the government can do for the Maori language and culture as well as toward steps yielding maximally visible 'pay offs'. As a result, there is a corresponding paucity of self-reliance and of sequentially planned goals. At a time when the initial *whanau/kohanga reo/kura kaupapa* Maori successes should be built upon and extended into full-fledged, self-regulated and young-adult focused stage 6, 5 and 4a operations, scarce funds and limited strengths are frequently funneled into symbolic 'atmosphere effects' such as mass media presence and intertranslatability with English in the popular econotechnical realm. The danger for Maori is that these latter goals may well be accomplished and yet the intergenerational mother tongue transmission of the language may not be materially advanced thereby. The biological clock is ticking for Maori. Who can serve as models of native-like Maori language-in-culture, of authenticity oriented Maori Xmen-via-Xish life, suitably modernized of course, when the grandparents are all gone? Will this clock be heard, or will the noise of an artificial life-support system (consisting of media, hype and kindergartens plus a few schools operating in a vacuum) succeed in drowning out the ticking?[14, 15]

## Notes

1. The demographic and linguistic statistics pertaining to Maoris and Maori are cited from N. Benton (1987), R. Benton (1984, and letter of March 28, 1988), T. S. Karetu (mimeo. undated, c. 1987) and Reedy (1982). Further statistical details are provided by a host of excellent studies conducted and 'published' (frequently in xeroxed form) by the New Zealand Council for Educational Research, which has had a Maori Unit since 1972. The final quotation is from T.S. Karetu's undated mimeographed 'Translation into English of the Maori Language Commission's Submission to New Zealand's Commission on Social Policy', the original title of which was 'Ko te Whakapakehatanga o te tapaetanga i te reo Maori'. Karetu is the current Commissioner of Maori Language, heading the Maori Language Commission

established in 1987 in response to the recommendations of the Waitangi Tribunal (see below). Similar pessimistic sentiments are revealed, here and there, in R. Benton (1984) and Reedy (1982).

2.  Further information concerning the precursors of the Maori revival efforts of the late 70s and early 80s is available in R. Benton (1984), Reedy (1982) and Spolsky (1989). R. Benton (1981) is an incomparable source in this connection and provides an exhaustive and immensely useful bibliography as well.

3.  Concerning the so-called 'official' status of Maori and various degrees of unhappiness with that formulation see most of the above-mentioned references but also David (1986) and Karetu interview, June 29, 1988. Clearly, many stage 2 and even stage 1 recommendations have been made when stages 6, 5 and 4 are still in question. The closing triumphal quotation is from Spolsky (1989). Further details on the Waitangi Tribunal are given in Benton (1987a).

4.  The *aatarangi* 'teaching method' is a local Maori adaptation, advanced by a well known Maori writer and broadcaster, Katarina Matairi, of the 'Silent Way' methodolgy of Caleb Gattengo. For an extensive discussion and evaluation of this methodology in its original form see Earl W. Stevick's *Teaching Languages: A Way and Ways*. (Rowley, MA: Newbury House, 1980). For a personal perspective on a week-long Maori immersion 'experience' for adults, see Nicholson (1990).

5.  The *aatarangi* and *whanau* movements are further discussed in most of the previously cited sources. Both of these movements also receive support from the Maori Trustees and the Maori Education Foundation. For a discussion of the 'invention' of Maori traditions, much like the European, American and Afro-Asian precedents along these lines, both by cultural activists as well as by anthropologists, see Hanson (1989).

6.  Some local observers have the mistaken impression that the *kohanga reos* were inspired by the successful Canadian model of 'immersion' bilingual education. There seems to be neither empirical nor theoretical support for this assumption. Canadian 'immersion' efforts involved middle-class anglo parents who volunteered to have their children's elementary education conducted entirely via French medium instruction, with only a single session per day being devoted to the study of English *after the third grade*. The *kohanga reos* were not initially for middle-class Maoris, they are not for elementary but for pre-school education and *childcare*, and they teach not another tongue, one unrelated to the Maori tradition, but the parents' ethnic heritage language. The inspiration for the *kohanga reo* movement is quite indigenous, both in its goals and in its methods. The Irish *naionrai* and the Basque *ikastolas* are parallels but they were even more unknown among Maori elders who 'invented' the first *kohanga reos* than were the Canadian immersion schools of the time. An initial influential promoter of the *kohanga reo* movement was John Rangihau, a consultant to the Department of Maori Affairs, who had previously asked the Department to support the first type 4b bilingual school (in Ruatoki) as its expression of personal thanks to him for his many years of service to the Department, and who subsequently contributed greatly to the mushrooming of *kohanga reos* throughout New Zealand. The name '*kohanga reo*' has been attributed to Sir James Henare and Mrs Tilly Reedy.

7.  In 1989 the Department of Maori Affairs budgeted the equivalent of roughly 12 million dollars (US) for its total support to some 520 *kohanga reos*, or roughly $23,000 per *kohanga reo* per year. This amounted to 4% of the Department's total budget for that year. The total annual budget of New Zealand's Department of Education was roughly 1.5 billion dollars (US) in that year. Planning, administration and control of

each *kohanga reo* is the responsibility of the local parents. They set budgets, which include payments to the two supervising *kaiawhi* (typically, the only paid staff members), fees to be levied, the *koha* (gifts-in-kind) of parents unable to make financial commitments, and seek other sources of financial support and voluntary staffing help. The *kaiawhi* are selected by them and are often members of their own residential communities.

8.  The separate functioning of two schools under one roof is also a well known budgetary solution to the educational needs of small language and religious groups in The Netherlands, particularly in Friesland, where religious and non-religious government-sponsored schools often share the same building.

9.  One secondary school and one embryonic tertiary school of this 'all-Maori' type also have come into being. It is noteworthy, in this connection, that New Zealand's primary education law does not require any set number of hours per year of instruction via English, or even the teaching of English *per se* (it does require 'oral and written language' including (since 1975) 'elements of the Maori language'), in order that schools meet the requirements of government certification for attendance in lieu of compulsory education. If this requirement is not altered, it would statutorily simplify the establishment of all-Maori type 4a elementary schools. The teaching of English is mandatory for secondary schools, but, otherwise, the use of English as the medium of instruction is not required. For the first reasonably accessible documentation of the *kura kaupapa* Maori schools see Rata, 1989.

10. 'Maori space' is Spolsky's designation for the well known sociolinguistic principle of language maintenance via domain and situational language compartmentalization. Spolsky (1989) utilizes the spelling *kohunga* (rather than *kohanga*) *reo*, but seems to be the only one to do so.

11. For an informative discussion of the greater benefits of local (community-based) Maori radio programs relative to national network Maori radio programs, see Waikerepuruo, 1988.

12. Of all the sources I have cited, Reedy (1982) appears to be most dubious that mass media programs in Maori and other stage 3, 2, and 1 solutions will really solve the basic problems of Maori. This quotation is from his 1982 essay, written when he was Assistant Secretary of the Department of Maori Affairs. Reedy is now Secretary of that Department. I have not found this view repeated among more recent and equally qualified observers (although some have communicated with me privately along these lines) and must conclude, therefore, that there is a serious problem of setting priorities among pro-Maori RLS activists today, a problem that becomes increasingly severe as the *kohanga reos* become increasingly routinized and viewed as primarily offering inexpensive childcare and as stages 3, 2, and 1 remain intractably beyond the reach of those most focused on RLS while receiving the lion's share of their attention and effort. For an effective pro-Maori TV statement see Benton (1985b).

13. Some tokenism on these fronts may be expected, given New Zealand's legal precedents of Commissions, Tribunals and legal avenues of redress of Waitangi Treaty obligations. While not all such Maori efforts at obtaining redress will necessarily fail, the implementation of any successful petitions to redress grievances is infinitely more dubious, when and if any such petitions are granted.

14. Further sources, not explicitly cited in this chapter but useful in its preparation, are R. Benton (1984, 1987b), Department of Education (1983), and Hirsch (1987).

15. I am greatly indebted to Richard Benton for his unstinting assistance to me in the preparation of this chapter. Timoti S. Karetu's and Rangi Nicholson's cooperation is

also gratefully acknowledged. Except for a few bibliographic entries which were added somewhat later, this chapter was completed in the final months of 1989.

## References

BENTON, Nena B. Eslao 1987, The Kahawai and the Shark; Perceptions of School Experience and Other Influences on the Maintenance and Use of the Maori Language. Mimeo.

BENTON, Richard A. 1981, *The Flight of the Amokura; Oceanic Languages and Formal Education in the South Pacific*. Wellington: New Zealand Council for Educational Research.

— 1983–84, Smoothing the pillow of a dying language; official policy toward the Maori language in New Zealand since World War II. *Philippine Journal of Linguistics*. 14–15, 24–39. Published simultaneously in Andrew GONZALEZ (ed.) 1984, *Panagini: Essays in Honor of Bonifacio P. Sibayan on his Sixty-Seventh Birthday*. Manila: Linguistic Society of the Philippines, 24–39.

— 1984, *Te rito o te korari; Maori Language and New Zealand's National Identity*. Wellington: Maori Unit, New Zealand Council for Educational Research.

— 1985a, Maori, English and Maori English. In John B. PRIDE, (ed.) *Cross-Cultural Encounters: Communication and Mis-Communication*. Melbourne: River Seine, 110–20.

— 1985b, The role of television in the survival of the Maori language. *Te Wahanga Maori Occasional Papers*, No. 18, 12 pp.

— 1987a, If It's Worth Doing, Is It Worth Doing Badly? Policy and Practice in Maori Education. Mimeo.

— 1987b, Schools as agents for language revival in Ireland and New Zealand. In Bernard SPOLSKY (ed.) *Language and Education in Multilingual Settings*. Clevedon: MUltilingual Matters, 53–76.

— 1988, The Matawaia Declaration: some educational and administrative implications. *Te Wahanga Maori Working Paper*, No. 9, 26 pp.

DAVID, Robie 1986, Maoris campaign for status language. *Language Monthly*, 36, September, 27.

DEPARTMENT OF EDUCATION [NEW ZEALAND] 1983, Education and Cultural and Linguistic Pluralism: New Zealand. Paris Center for Educational Research and Innovation, Organization for Economic Co-operation and Development. Mimeo.

HANSON, Allan 1989, The making of the Maori: culture invention and its logic. *American Anthropologist* 91, 890–902.

HIRSCH, Walter (ed.) 1987, *Living Languages; Bilingualism and Community Languages in New Zealand*. Auckland: Heinemann.

KARETU, Timoti S. Undated (1988?), Translation into English of the Maori Language Commission's Submission to New Zealand's Commission on Social Policy. [Original title: *Ko te Whakapakehatanga o te tapaetanga i te reo Maori*]. Mimeo.

NICHOLSON, Rangi 1990, Maori language total immersion courses for adults in Aotearoa/New Zealand: a personal perspective. In Jon REYHNER (ed.) *Effective Language Education Practices and Native Language Survival; Proceedings of the Ninth Annual International Native American Language Issues Institute*. Choctaw: NALII, 107–20.

RATA, Elizabeth 1989, Kura kaupapa Maori. *PPTA Journal* 3, 30–2.

REEDY, Tamati Muturangi 1982, Fostering the Growth of Indigenous Languages. Mimeo.

SPOLSKY, Bernard 1989, Maori, bilingual education and language revitalization. *Journal of Multilingual and Multicultural Development* 10, 89–106. (This paper was kindly made available to me by the author when it was still in rough draft form)

WAIKEREPURO, Huirangi 1988, 'Te tino rangatiratanga o o ratou whenua': The choice between network and regional radio for Maoridom. (Evidence in opposition to an application by the Broadcasting Corporation for warrants for a Maori radio network.) Mimeo.

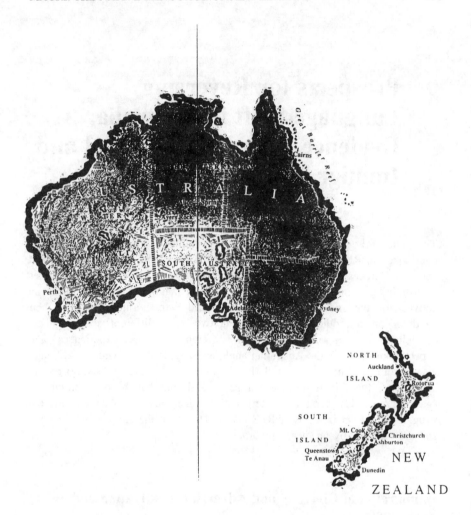

# 9 Prospects for Reversing Language Shift in Australia: Evidence from its Aboriginal and Immigrant Languages

The amazingly variegated country and continent of Australia is often overlooked in RLS discussions but, actually, some of the most interesting and contrasted processes and policies are to be encountered there. The Aborigines ('Austraindians' might be the American term for that continent's pre-European natives), on the one hand, and the post-World War II immigrants and their children, on the other hand, represent two very different sociolinguistic constellations and, also, two very different sets of experiences and expectations *vis-á-vis* the Australian anglo and anglified mainstream. Although the 'bottom line' may be a similarly disappointing (or even shocking) one in both cases, there is nevertheless a great deal that has been accomplished against great odds, certainly in terms of idealism and ennoblement through struggle, if not yet in terms of RLS *per se*. However, the story is not over yet and the future is by no means preordained.

## Immigrational Diversity and Adversity: Cultivation and Resistance

Since the end of World War II, 'White' (i.e. non-Aboriginal) Australia has undergone a massive immigrational transfusion and transformation. A society that had preferred to remain under-populated during the pre-war years, rather than risk the cultural diversity that would be introduced by Orientals, other Asians (e.g. from India or Indonesia), 'Kanaka' (Pacific Islanders) and even by non-anglo Europeans, decided that its political and economic future had much more to lose than to gain from such exclusiveness. Although Europeans remained the immigrants of choice, various West Asian, South Asian, East Asian, South East Asian and Pacific Island immigrants were also admitted.

Some two million non-angloceltic newcomers arrived in a country of roughly seven to eight million inhabitants all in all, and, at least initially, were received with relatively little racism and were acknowledged to be upright, family and mobility oriented citizens and worthy contributors to Australia's commercial and economic development.

With the coming to power of the Labour Party in 1972 (at a time that coincided with the 'ethnic revival', i.e. with an upsurge of self-conscious identity explorations among minority ethnics in Australia and, toward the tail-end of that process, in much of the Western world more generally), new immigrants found a particularly receptive environment also on the cultural front, with a degree of governmental assistance and acceptance that might well have been unprecedented in English mother tongue countries anywhere previously, including Australia itself. Although the 'peak of positiveness' attained in the early 80s has now been passed and voices of opposition and criticism are heard more often, the fact still remains that one out of every 12 Australians now speaks a language other than English at home (CLOTEs is the acronym by which the 'Community Languages Other Than English' are sometimes referred to, the more widespread designation simply being 'community language') and the amounts and kinds of support and recognition that these immigration-based languages receive is still noteworthy, even if their futures are far from assured.

## The Aboriginal Scene: Plus ça Change ...?

The Aboriginal scene has also undergone considerable change since the end of World War II and its re-evaluation in historical perspective has become more common, particularly given that 1988 represented the 200th anniversary of British settlement in Australia. Almost all are agreed that the first 125–150 years of this period constitute a shameful (and, in many cases, even a genocidally catastrophic) story of the destruction of traditional Aboriginal peoples via the expropriation of their traditional lands, the despoiling of their sacred sites, and their inhuman treatment in various ways, not stopping short of mass expulsions, forced re-settlement in inhospitable regions, mass poisonings, shootings and the separation of families (particularly the forced — and often Church-sponsored — separation of children from their parents).

The results were an initially huge increase in Aboriginal mortality (due to both maltreatment by Europeans and contagion from European diseases against which Aborigines had, as yet, developed no resistance) resulting in the total population dropping from more than a quarter million to roughly 80,000 in little over a century and a half. Although a demographic recovery has subsequently occurred, Aboriginal life is still marked by some of the highest rates of alcoholism, illness, discriminatory arrest and detention, unemployment, suicide and other indices of personal and social dislocation to be found anywhere in the world. For those who imagine that nothing could be worse than North and South American policies *vis á vis* the Amerindians it should be pointed out (without in any way seeking to apologize for those policies) that hundreds of treaties were signed (and broken) with Amerindians by the various American authorities, whereas Australia's Aborigines were long not really considered to be humans at all and, therefore, little in the way of treaties or negotiations of any kind were undertaken with them to begin with, and what little there was, whether oral or written, was subsequently simply ignored. They were merely 'expendable objects' and particularly so for the cattlemen, sheep raisers and mineral (or other natural resources) investors.

A change for the better was heralded in a 1967 referendum which gave the Federal ('Commonwealth') government authority in Aboriginal affairs, which, in turn, enabled a more enlightened approach to get underway when the Labour Party came to power (1972). State and Federal governments instituted provisions for recognizing and returning Aboriginal lands, for protecting Aboriginal sacred sites and for permitting Aborigines a measure of self-regulation with respect to their settlements, the education of their children and the use of their languages in the public media in their vicinity. Many of these promises have been subsequently abandoned or seriously compromised and others have led to little more than endless delays, legal wranglings, successive investigatory commissions, public recriminations (some of which have attained international notoriety, whether for their pro- or anti-Aboriginal positions), revived and vociferous racism and bitter political infighting.

The interested reader will find no difficulty in locating the extensive literatures dealing with all of these matters: the original horrors, the new promises, the continuing disappointments and the endless struggles (most recently, particularly in connection with the Aboriginal Land Rights issue).[1] Even as late as 1989, Survival International USA delivered thousands of signatures collected in 36 states and in 21 countries to the Australian embassy in Washington, supporting Aboriginal demands for land rights legislation. In the previous year, a Royal Commission on [Aboriginal] Deaths in [Police] Custody was established, with provision for Aboriginal input into its final report (due in 1990). We can only refer to all of these matters in passing — although the issues involved, particularly the issue of returning traditional lands, are basic ones for the very survival of Aboriginal languages and cultures — but we must remember to keep them in mind as we turn our focused attention to the RLS-efforts that accompany them.

*Stage 8: Reassembling the language*

None of the European or other immigrant languages are at an advanced state of disrepair and, even were that to be the case in connection with the oldest and smallest among them, the necessary 'repairs' would probably be undertaken elsewhere, in their respective home countries, rather than in Australia. In connection with the continent's Aboriginal languages, however, there are hundreds of languages and dialects (yes, hundreds) that require such repair and Australia proper is obviously the main location in which such repairs are and must be undertaken.

The exact number of Aboriginal languages and dialects that were spoken when Europeans first came to Australia is difficult to ascertain. The recently published *Language Atlas: Pacific*[2] lists over 700 languages and dialects but other specialists (e.g. Black, 1983) usually refer to a lower figure, namely, 'nearly 270 distinct languages'. If the former estimate is accepted it becomes clear that 80% of this number are either already extinct or have so few remaining speakers (less than 100) that their early demise is virtually a foregone conclusion. If the latter estimate is preferred, the results are nearly the same. Only some 50 languages remain that are relatively widely spoken (and often written) and of these only 18 have at least 500 speakers and, taken together, account for 25,000 of the approximately 30,000 remaining speakers of Aboriginal languages in Australia today.[3] Pessimistic observers conclude that only some two or three of these will retain any substantial vitality into the twenty-first century. Clearly, modern Australia has been a veritable graveyard of indigenous languages and the study of dying languages as well as the reassembly of dead and momentarily expiring ones has become a major linguistic occupation and preoccupation. Although such efforts add considerably to scholarly (and, ultimately, to the intelligent layman's) appreciation of human diversity, ingenuity and, in more recent days (since 'last living speakers' have also begun to be more intensively studied) cultural dedication as well, they provide scant comfort for the Aboriginal RLS advocate. Unfortunately, this is all the comfort that there can be in many cases.

*Stage 7: The elderly among themselves: learning, relearning and use without intergenerational family or integrated community functions*

At this stage several of the older immigration-based languages (and some of the newer ones too, where the most rapid sociocultural change has occurred) enter our story. Particularly in small immigrant communities in the more rural hinterlands, outside of the major urban areas, but in some of the old ethnic neighborhoods of the latter as well, it is not an uncommon occurrence for 'oldtimers' to get together with each other and to use the 'old language' when they do. There are innumerable small gatherings full of good fellowship and quiet camaraderie, programs of considerable cultural (literary, musical, educational)

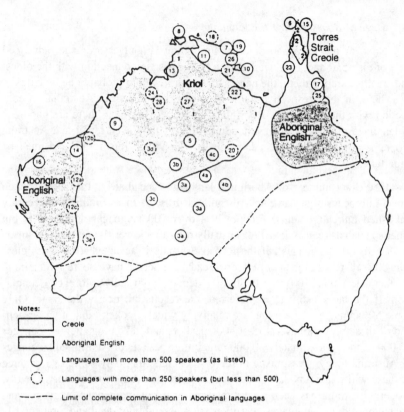

Notes:

◻   Creole

◻   Aboriginal English

◯   Languages with more than 500 speakers (as listed)

◌   Languages with more than 250 speakers (but less than 500)

- - - - -   Limit of complete communication in Aboriginal languages

N.B.: The numbers of speakers of each language are approximations listed for guidance only.

| Language | Speakers | Language | Speakers |
|---|---|---|---|
| 1. Kriol | 15 000 | 12. Western Desert, western | 900 total |
| 2. Torres Strait creole | 15 000 | a. Manyjilyjarra | 500 |
| 3. Western Desert, eastern | 3 000 total | b. Yulharidja | 200 |
| a. Pitjantjatjara | 1 000 | c. Martu Wangka | 200 |
| b. Pintupi and Luritja | 800 | 13. Murrinh-Patha | 800 |
| c. Kgaanyatjarra | 700 | 14. Nyangumarta | 700-800 |
| d. Gugadja | 300 | 15. Miriam | 700? |
| e. Wangkatja | 200-300 | 16. Yindjibarndi | 600 |
| 4. Aranda dialects: | 3 000 total | 17. Guugu Yimidhirr | 600 |
| a. Western Aranda | 1 000 | 18. Burarra | 400-600 |
| b. Eastern Aranda | 1 000 | 19. Dhangu dialects: | |
| c. Anmatjirra | 800 | a. Gaalpu | 200 |
| 5. Warlpiri | 2 800 | b. Wangurri | 150 |
| 6. Kala Lagaw Ya | 2 800 | 20. Alyawarra | 400-500 |
| 7. Dhuwal-Dhuwala dialects | 1 600-1 700 | 21. Nunggubuyu | 300-400 |
| | total | 22. Garawa | 300-400 |
| a. Gupapyungu | 450 | 23. Wik-Munkan | 300 |
| b. Gumarj | 250 500 | 24. Kitya | 300 |
| c. Djambarrpuyngu | 250-450 | 25. Kuku-Yalanji | 300 |
| 8. Tiwi | 1 400 | 26. Ritharngu | 300 |
| 9. Walmajarri | 1 300 | 27. Gurindji | 250 |
| 10. Anindilyakwa | 1 000 | 28. Djaru | 250 |
| 11. Gunwinggu | 900 | **Source:** Australian Institute of Aboriginal Studies | |

FIGURE 9.1 *Prominent Australian Aboriginal Languages (Source:* Senate Standing Committee on Education and the Arts, 1984)

sophistication, at which not a single person of childbearing age or younger is or can be present. At this stage ethnic languages continue to be spoken with complete proficiency, even if code-switching to English is often quite common, but the intergenerational heirs of these languages are 'conspicuous by their scarcity'. Because of the relative recency of massive post-World War II immigration to Australia this scenario is not yet common among Italian, German, Croatian, Greek, Macedonian, Chinese, Vietnamese, Russian, Hebrew or other languages of recent arrivals (but note that there are now no direct linguistic heirs of the earlier waves of German, Italian or Chinese speakers). Various recent language policies of Australian authorities and institutions have also tended to slow down some of the processes whereby this stage assumes 'typical' proportions. Nevertheless, unless subsequent stages soon become more successful than they have been thus far, this is the stage that will become clearly predominant during the 90s. Once this stage becomes predominant, a virtual sociocultural revolution in the lives of young people is required before it can again be superseded on an intergenerational and community-wide basis.

It is among Aborigines, particularly among those who are speakers of languages other than the top 18, that we not only most often find this stage but that we find it in its most painfully enfeebled manifestations. Thus, a brochure inviting Gooris (more usually 'Kooris', an increasingly popular indigenous self-designation applying to and uniting all Aborigines and favored by some as a collective term to replace Aborigine/Aboriginal) to participate in a series of six weekly seminars about Bundjalung,[4] a language of Southeast Australia that is now down to its last few dozen speakers, promises that the seminars will enable them to 'learn more about a language that existed in these areas, learn the sounds of Bundjalung, and … use … Bundjalung words and phrases in … everyday (English) conversation'. This, indeed, is a type of Reversing Language Shift, but it is RLS of the last possible and most urgent kind. The fact that it can no longer lead to proficiency (not to mention intergenerational proficiency, which now seems to be an unobtainable goal for Bundjalung and scores of other Aboriginal languages) makes it no less important and, possibly, no less contributory to identity and self-concept.

Another Aboriginal venture at this stage has to do with the collective preparation and subsequent enjoyment of 'alphabet books' in a few language communities. These books (booklets would be the more appropriate characterization) contain one English letter (upper and lower case) on each page, as well as an English word beginning with that letter, the indigenous equivalent of that word, and a folksy illustrated story or explanation related to the indigenous word. Local linguists and teachers have taken to preparing such alphabet books in ways that maximize local participation in the selection of the words whose indigenous equivalents are felt to be of greatest use or interest, and in the joint authorship of the accompanying stories. Wherever possible, local artists are approached to illustrate the booklets, and the entire interactive process is tape-recorded so as to preserve other indigenous words and phrases that often are utilized in the discussions that surround and constitute the total enterprise. These booklets are then allowed to circulate among the participants (and particularly among the oldest members of their communities) in try-out versions and are then revised before finally being published by school or other local developmental authorities.

Although indigenous people often feel that these little alphabet books help them 'repossess their history', these publications have sometimes also become very popular among tourists and other non-Aborigines in the local areas who have bought many copies of them at airports and other local shops. Minor though these books may be in terms of more functionally ambitious RLS proper, they have been experienced as local triumphs in symbolic and interpersonal respects pertaining to the indigenous identities involved. Indeed, it is for this reason that these efforts are discussed for the first time here, rather than in stage 8, above, or in stages 6 or 4a, below. Adults who fully realize the extent of the Xish language attrition and culture change that is going on round about them are the prime movers, and possibly the prime benefactors, in connection with these 'little alphabet books'. They see them as symbolic of a former, all-encompassing way of life, a pattern which youngsters can no longer reassemble in their mind's eye, and which would vanish without a trace were it not for the booklets produced in order to impart a whiff of their authentic flavor.[5] Under the new National Language Policy (see below), the National Aboriginal Language Program now provides some support for such and similar initiatives, a welcome but basically ineffectual RLS departure from the uncaring policies of the recent past.

A basic problem for the intergenerational transmission of immigrant languages in Australia (some would say: 'the basic problem') is the fact that they do not have their own relatively inviolate space, their own concentrated communities in which their own language-and-culture can dominate or at least where like-minded RLS-minded families can easily reinforce one another by dint of daily interaction and implementation of similar norms and values. Such relatively self-contained communities (in rural areas) and neighborhoods (in urban areas) are not uncommon during the early first generation years and the oldest children in immigrant families frequently grew up in such settings. However, differential social mobility leads to residential mobility as well and the primary settlements are slowly eroded as the most successful immigrants leave them behind for more comfortable, more attractive and more prestigious quarters.

Secondary settlement areas are, almost without exception, urban or suburban (contributing to the early demise or enfeeblement of rural ethnic communities), of low population density and ethnically mixed or 'non-ethnic' in composition. Language maintenance becomes dependent not on natural, daily neighborhood interaction but on relatively infrequent institutional and extra-neighborhood 'visits' to co-ethnic stores, schools, clubs, churches, family and friends (some of whom have remained in the 'old neighborhoods' and are, therefore, inevitably tainted by the stigma of 'not having made it'), visits that are too scattered to provide a critical mass *vis-á-vis* either natural language use or cultural implementation for a new generation that never experienced the full-blown 'real thing'. Younger children of immigrants are largely socialized in such contexts and second generation ethnics tend to raise their own families in these contexts, again almost without exception.

These secondary settlement areas themselves are not sufficiently self-regulatory *vis-á-vis* ethnolinguistic socialization and *vis-á-vis* the implementation of daily Xish language-in-culture to foster the reliable intergenerational transmission of immigrant languages in open and mobility-affording host contexts. The 'visits to ethnic addresses and points of interest' are clearly insufficient to substitute for what is lacking in daily life. Such visits can contribute to identifying with the symbols of ethnic culture but they are not sufficient for maintaining a full and evolving ethnolinguistic repertoire, let alone the substantially self-regulatory ethnolinguistic social boundaries on which ethnolinguistic intergenerational continuity ultimately depends. As Xishness withdraws into a more selective corner of the total life space it gets along with only snatches of Xish (linguistically), 'Xish appreciation' at best, just as it is increasingly based on memories of, stories about, and judicious ('inoffensive') selections from Xish culture. The path to functioning as Xmen-via-Yish is paved with good intentions and is well underway in most post-World War II immigrant-derived communities in Australia today. The lack (indeed, the increasing lack) of intergenerational linkages and Xish community-wide functions for the immigrant languages is becoming increasingly evident, to outside scholars and policy makers and to inside Xmen alike.[6]

*Stage 6: Family-neighborhood-community based language maintenance in which the link to the younger generation is established and retained*

That which the immigrant languages have generally been unable to do, particularly in the larger urban centers of southeastern Australia (Melbourne and Sydney) in which most of them are so overwhelmingly concentrated, has, to a very modest degree, been accomplished by a very few Aboriginal languages in the remoter areas of central, western and northwestern Australia. Actually, there is a two-part tale to be told in this connection, one chapter of which exemplifies the negative consequences of a type of intergenerational concentration in which ethnocultural self-regulation is either minimal or out of the question entirely, and the other chapter of which exemplifies intergenerational concentration precisely for the purpose of attaining greater ethnocultural self-regulation. The first chapter, another sad chapter in the long Aboriginal tale of suffering under white rule, deals with the forced removal (under the Protection Acts) of most Aborigines in the northern and central regions of the country into 'settlements', 'missions' or 'reserves'. The Acts, ostensibly passed in order to protect Aborigines from being gunned down on their own lands, in fact gave the local authorities the right to legally force Aborigines off their land and then transfer or assign these lands to White individuals or companies.

Both by design and by ignorance, ethnoculturally diverse (and, therefore, also linguistically diverse) and, often, traditionally antagonistic Aboriginal populations were resettled together, under the administration of white managers, on impoverished soil and in climatically severe locations considered to be of no conceivable agricultural, pastoral or mineral value to Whites. Here, the very hopelessness of their situation resulted both in Aboriginal sociocultural dislocation and anomie (since it was impossible to observe traditional site-related ceremonies and practices there) and in rampant Aboriginal personal dislocation (alcoholism, violence, widespread illness and malnutrition, increased infant mortality, shortened life-spans, etc.). Many Aborigines still live under such wretched conditions today, even though their legal circumstances have changed with the granting of citizenship and political rights in the 60s, because of a combination of inertia, discrimination and lack of the necessary skills that would make it possible for them to compete successfully for the rewards available to other minorities within mainstrean society. Under these horrendous circumstances RLS is impossible, even though intergenerational communities exist. Negative self-concepts and negative views toward Aboriginal cultures abound, concepts that foster further language shift and ludicrous identification with the oppressor, rather than with one's own heritage.

Beginning in the 60s, roughly at the same time as the first beginnings of the 'ethnic revival' in much of the rest of the world (but, probably, in no way directly linked to that still insufficiently understood more general phenomenon), there began a self-directed movement to leave the above-mentioned disruptive settings and to resettle in 'outstations' where Aborigines could more completely regulate their own lives by concentrating primarily on otherwise unpopulated or 'undesirable' traditional lands. Most of these first 'outstations' — receiving no governmental support or assistance and being actively discouraged or opposed by white authorities — failed and were subsequently abandoned. However, after a decade of continued efforts along these lines, and, finally, with encouragement from newly supportive governmental spokesmen and programs, an increasing number of outstations began to stabilize in the 70s. By now, there are nearly 600 such settlements (not all of them being permanently occupied at any particular time due to the seasonal movements in which some groups traditionally or innovatively participate), the total universe of such settlements being very varied in many demographic, material and cultural respects.

These communities, most of them very small in terms of the number of residents living in them, now accommodate approximately 10,000 inhabitants all in all, or only between 3% and 4% of the entire Aboriginal population, most of whom live in country towns and urban centers, either unable or unwilling to move to outstations. Life in the outstations is far from easy, but it is a life in accord with one or another Aboriginal culture and, therefore, a life that is also played out in the appropriate vernacular and liturgical languages pertaining to these cultures. More and more of these outstations are also beginning to provide supportive contexts for Aboriginal customs, Aboriginal music (traditional and new), and Aboriginal foods and for such innovations as Aboriginal literacy and, more generally, for the self-regulated adoption and adaptation of modern artifacts and knowledge, on the one hand, and their combination with Aboriginal counterparts, on the other hand. A common slogan in such settlements (and one that we will encounter again in our discussion of schooling, below) is 'both ways' or 'two ways', implying that *it is not a total isolation from the modern world that is desired at all, but, rather, an ability to retain that which is selected from the tradition alongside that which is adopted from the outside*, and to do both the one and the other under community control of the decision-making, implementation and evaluation processes.

Neither the current importance nor the future stability of the outstations should be exaggerated. Most Aboriginal cultures and languages cannot possibly benefit from them because of the physical remoteness and limited economic prospects of these settlements. Nevertheless, they provide interesting and important examples of how RLS depends on 'first things first' and how stage 6 becomes the launching pad for further crucial stages, the relationship between the outstations and the Aboriginal land rights efforts being a particularly intimate and symbiotic one.[7]

Immigrant languages in Australia have yet to consciously develop and maintain intergenerationally intact communities that are similarly self-regulating in cultural respects and, therefore, that have similar RLS potential. Their conceptual, residential and occupational over-identification with and involvement in mainstream modernity submerges them entirely in processes that they can neither control nor mitigate. All of their language maintenance efforts, discussed below, are, therefore, built on shifting sands and are unlikely to result in intergenerational mother tongue transmission beyond the second generation, language shift often taking place within the very first (the immigrant) generation itself.

> *Stage 5: Literacy via agencies or institutions that are entirely under Xish control and that do NOT need to meet or satisfy Yish standards re compulsory education*

Immigrant languages in Australia are served by impressively large numbers of community-supported ethnic group schools. These schools meet during after-school hours or on weekends, primarily in quarters of their own (although sometimes quarters are rented from public schools, libraries or other public agencies) and do not intend to meet compulsory education requirements (although Australian public school authorities can grant 'academic credits', upon examination, in connection with many of the languages that students acquire in these schools). The two parenthetical phrases inserted above imply that immigrant ethnic group schools are not totally outside of the public reward (and control) system in Australia, but they are still primarily self-contained and, as such, deserve to be considered here.

There are various estimates of the number of schools and pupils that are involved in stage 5 efforts pertaining to immigrant languages in Australia. A 1985 government report estimated that in 1983 there were over 65,000 students attending 1,200 ethnic schools (primarily in the states of Victoria, in which Melbourne is located, and New South Wales, in which Sydney is located) and studying 51 different languages. In addition, there were more than twice as many more studying in 'insertion classes' run by ethnic community organizations, for at least one hour once a week, but held in public schools during regular school hours. The language maintenance emphases of these schools, their co-emphases on the transmission of traditional and authentic cultural values and behaviors which foster language learning, and the extreme variety of languages that the totality of these schools encompass were also governmentally recognized as making noteworthy contributions to the non-English language resources that are considered to be of value to Australia (based on the fact that an estimated 65% of the students attending these schools speak at home the language that they are studying in their ethnic school) and, therefore, as meriting a measure of financial support from both the Commonwealth and the State governments.

Greater collaboration between the ethnic community supplementary schools and the public schools is envisaged in South Australia in accord with the recent Kisoylous Report (and similar moves are underway in Victoria), in which sharing of teachers, exchange of credits and other such measures are envisaged. The sophistication and the sympathetic stance revealed by these recent governmental views and arrangements is further attested to by the recognition that such support and collaboration could entail an inevitable degree of loss of autonomy for the schools (the government wanting to set some standards re adequacy of facilities, curricular soundness and teacher certification in the schools receiving its support) and that any 'other measures which may further weaken this autonomy should be treated with some caution'.[8]

While it is difficult to estimate either the degree of language mastery actually attained in these schools or the amount of government support that they receive, let alone the language maintenance consequences of such support, it is quite clear that these schools are being encouraged, on the one hand, and increasingly influenced, on the other hand. The funding of curriculum and educational materials centers for these schools, the institution of teaching credentials and the organization of seminars for teachers already credentialed, and the recognition (via certification) of students from these schools who have reached a sufficient level of achievement, these are all encouraging signs of appreciation which maintenance and RLS activists would be happy to attain in all other modern, Westernized countries throughout the world. On the other hand, it is worrisome that there is no sign at all that the efforts of these schools, whether with or without governmental help, have generally had any demonstrably positive consequences insofar as RLS is concerned, particularly given the ongoing residential mobility and 'thinning out' of Australia's urban second generation population which makes attendance at these schools an increasingly 'time consuming' pursuit. The more recent budgetary squeeze in Australian education, particularly in education that is not directly oriented toward increased production and technological capacity, has also added a strong element of doubt as to how much longer governmental co-funding of ethnic group schools will continue. In addition, the increasing governmental stress on the major diplomatic and commercial languages of the Pacific rim (Japanese, Mandarin, Korean, Indonesian) also tends to downplay (and to eat up funds that might otherwise be available for) instruction of most ethnic community languages.

The additional fact that these schools almost completely overlook the maintenance and cultivation of literacy among their graduates (and in their parental support-constituencies as well) is yet another reason to doubt whether they ultimately can make a reliable contribution to RLS. Without any corresponding and vibrant adult literacy with which to link up, second or third generation childhood literacy in an immigrant language tends to be little more than a fleeting rite of initiation, a *rite de passage* that marks a stage which is left behind almost as soon as it is reached.[9]

In the Aboriginal sector, community-operated literacy imparting institutions, whether for children or for adults, are still few and far between and particularly so under auspices that have nothing to do with meeting the educational requirements that have been governmentally instituted. Examples of such programs on a small scale are the one-week and two-week adult courses in Alyawarre (400–500 speakers), Warumungu (? speakers), Warlmanpa (? speakers) and Warlpiri (2,800 speakers) conducted in and around Tennant Creek, Northern Territory, by the Barkly Region Aboriginal Language Center. There are also a few tertiary level institutions located in areas near Aboriginal concentrations (e.g. the Institute for Aboriginal Development in Alice Springs, N.T.) that offer vernacular literacy courses at a non-degree adult education level, often, but not always, as preliminary to their more focused efforts to foster English reading and writing. In addition, there are also missionary groups that offer vernacular literacy courses to adult Aborigines (and to younger Aborigines as well) in conjunction with their more basic Christianizing and Bible study emphases. All in all, however, the disparity between Australian governmental assistance to ethnic community stage 5 schools for immigrants and their children and its thinly disguised lack of interest in the establishment of networks of such schools for Aborigines is quite marked, notwithstanding the support for a few Aboriginal community schools under the program providing grants for ethnic community schools more generally. The first constituency is being helped to pass into an 'Xmen-via-Yish' (English) stage by means of generously subsidized cooption into the Yish system; the other, by a surfeit of what is, at best, a variant of benign neglect.

*Stage 4a: Xish-sponsored and conducted schools that are attended in lieu of meeting compulsory education requirements*

There seems to be no complete census of the all-day schools teaching ethnic 'community languages' and sponsored primarily by the various immigrant-based ethnic groups in Australia. I would estimate that there are no more than 50 such schools, all in all, and probably fewer than that, all but a few handfuls of them being at the elementary school level, with approximately 10,000 students. The lion's share of these schools are under religious auspicies, Hebrew (and, much more rarely, Yiddish too) being taught in the Jewish ones, Greek in most of the Orthodox ones and Italian, German, Polish, Spanish, Portuguese, Vietnamese and perhaps a very few other languages too in the multi-ethnic Catholic ones. All of these schools receive direct and indirect governmental funds which cover a very sizeable proportion of their costs, the remaining costs being covered by tuition fees and community fund-raising efforts. The amount of time devoted to ethnic community language acquisition and, subsequently, to ethnic community language use in the study of other ethnic subjects varies tremendously, from no more than a few hours per week (and as an elective subject to boot) and only in certain years of study, to approximately half of the entire school day in all years of instruction. The results also vary greatly, from little more than passive language appreciation all the way through to fluent speech and creative writing.

In the infrequent cases where these schools still correspond to stable population concentrations in primary settlement ethnic neighborhoods, they, their teachers and their lay school boards undoubtedly make a contribution to intergenerational language maintenance, at least into the adolescent years, when out-of-community influences and opportunities begin to become predominant among pupils. Social mobility and its resulting residential dislocations become the ultimate arbiters of whether the ethnic day-school education provided with so much voluntary dedication and ethnic community effort has any intergenerational impact on the RLS front, or whether it remains little more than a residual memory as far as everyday language use is concerned. The latter outcome already appears to be far more typical than the former one and may be expected to become increasingly so.

In the Aboriginal ranks such schools (usually referred to as 'independent schools') are both few in number and small in size — no more than nine or ten in all, as of early 1989, the exact number being somewhat difficult to pin down due to the fact that there are a few schools of an interstitial type that reveal both type 4a and type 4b characteristics. These are government-funded but under Aboriginal curricular, personnel and administrative control (like the Navajo 'contract schools') and are all situated in areas in which a good bit of Aboriginal self-regulation in many other respects is also common. Most of the type 4a schools initially came into being thanks to the support received from church and other charitable funds. Several, located in very remote areas, were established by Aborigines contrary to the explicit advice and warnings of the State educational authorities, who were convinced that 'there is no practical possibility of the children in homeland centres receiving a complete school program [particularly insofar as English and mathematics are concerned] at a level comparable to that in [the government's] central schools'.[10] The criterion for this judgment was doubtlessly the future success of Aboriginal students in communicating with white Australians and 'getting ahead' in social contexts dominated by them. But this could no longer be an appropriate criterion of a desirable school program for parents who opted to live in settings where their own culture, rather than that of white Australia alone, would be a major component of everyday life. It should also be noted that not all independent Aboriginal schools are in 'outstations' — indeed, several of them are in towns and urban areas (e.g. in Townsville, Perth, Alice Springs, etc.) but that it was there that the notion of autonomous Aboriginal life-style and educational process first took hold.

One of the very first independent Aboriginal schools was the one established in Strelley, Western Australia, in 1976. It soon developed several campuses in neighboring communities, all of them administered entirely by local Aboriginal school boards. These schools were noteworthy for their emphases on the traditional Aboriginal religious lore and laws of the region that they served, thus providing the ultimate justification for stressing vernacular languages as well. Interestingly and appropriately enough, the school programs were preceded by extensive *adult vernacular literacy programs* (one in Nyangumarta [roughly 800 speakers] and the other in Manjiljarra [roughly 500 speakers]). In this fashion, *children were later socialized into the educated use of languages that their elders could already read and write*, literacy thereupon uniting the generations rather than separating them. English too is taught, of course, but as a foreign language.

Of the handful of other independent and vernacular-stressing schools (and, it should be noted, not all independent Aboriginal schools are vernacular-stressing, if for no other reason than the fact that most Aborigines no longer control a vernacular that they can stress and, therefore, other guiding educational rationales must be operative among a segment of Aborigines seeking greater independence from white society), the best known by far is the Yipirinya (= 'caterpillar', a reality in local fauna and a character in local Aboriginal lore) School in Alice Springs (south-central Northern Territory). Its fame is partly based on its long struggle (1979–1984) for governmental recognition (and, therefore, financial assistance) since the Northern Territory educational authorities seemed to be set on making an example of it (due to its Aboriginal curricular content, shortened in-school-day as a result of frequent school-sponsored visits to the 'bush', and preference for and reliance upon uncertified Aboriginal — and, often, on elderly Aboriginal — teachers). After five years of inadequate funding (supplied by church and charitable organizations, both from Australia and abroad), terribly inadequate quarters, and inadequate ability to attain its own programmatic goals, the school was not only 'registered' by the authorities (after a Supreme Court decision in its favor), but vindicated by 'higher authorities'. The House of Representatives' Select Committee on Aboriginal Education (1985) came to the conclusion, partly on the basis of the notoriety attained by the Yipirinya School's struggle, that 'the existence of alternatives in Aboriginal education … constitutes a strength in the community. Also, as expressions of Aboriginal self-determination and … community control, Aboriginal independent schools should be encouraged' and 'recurrent funding … should be made available' to them so that they could operate without undue hardships. This, at long last, represented the extension to Aboriginese of the facilitative approach to independent education that had long been available to Australia's immigrant ethnic groups.

The Yipirinya School was initially set up by parents living in the Aboriginal peripheral camps outside of Alice Springs because the local public schools consistently alienated their children both from education and from Aboriginal life. The Yipirinya School, run by an all-Aboriginal school council which makes all curricular, policy and administrative decisions and is the official 'principal' of the school, aims at combining both Aboriginal culture and 'whitefella skills'.[11] The school is still a relatively tiny one (roughly 60 students in its primary division and 25 in its post-primary division, the latter not yet having been 'registered' by the Northern Territory Education Department) but, nevertheless, it is necessary for it to trichotomize its vernacular efforts, Mparntwe Arrente (approximately 1,000 speakers), Western Arrente (approximately 1,000 speakers) and Luritja (approximately 800 speakers together with a variety also known as Pintupi) all being utilized with different student groups drawn from nine different Aboriginal camps in and around Alice Springs.

As in the Navajo and Maori schools that we have discussed in Chapters 7 and 8, the Yipirinya School makes substantial use of older members of the local Aboriginal cultures in connection with its traditional studies, both on and off campus (e.g. in weekly expeditions into the 'bush' where familiarization with Aboriginal lore and its relationship to local flora and fauna is acquired in a more natural setting directly related to the very tales, songs, dances and religious practices being taught). On the other hand, non-Aboriginal teachers are employed by the School Council to teach English and other non-Aboriginal subject matter, thereby further emphasizing the distinction between what is 'own' and what is 'foreign'. A new intergroup consensus as to the overall success of the school is evidenced by the fact that it has recently begun to plan additional new buildings (above and beyond those recently completed), these plans being pursued with funds from the Commonwealth educational authorities. Thus, against great odds, the long and painful struggle for another (the ninth) independent Aboriginal school, a school that is able to pick and choose its own way in the difficult quest for 'two ways' education for Aboriginal children, seems to be drawing to a successful — even if only locally significant — conclusion. Above all, finally, Yipirinya is an example of how RLS requires that language and culture be pursued together, holistically and intergenerationally, with enough, unembarrassed, voluntary self-separation from the mainstream so that distinctiveness can be attained, maintained and selectively modified and combined with the culture of the surrounding 'big brother'. In 1988, when the Yipirinya School moved from its inadequate, initial 'mobile home' structure into a larger, governmentally funded new site in Alice Springs, this was taken (and rightfully so) as a positive indication of a new stage in the recognition of its hard-won autonomy.

Some of the other independent schools have succeeded against even greater cultural odds than those faced by the Yipirinya School. At the Kulkarriya Community School children have been guided back to Walmajarri-at-school, after they and their older siblings (and, indeed, most adults under 30 years of age) had already shifted to Kriol and to English. This was done as a result of parental/grandparental insistence and careful supervision of their new community school. Local observers now expect these children to begin utilizing Walmajarri in their out-of-school and community interactions in the near future. If the language can then be societally nurtured until these youngsters have children of their own, preferably via intensifying stage 6 and 5 efforts for young and middle-aged adults too, thereby recreating a community that functions increasingly via the language, then a revival of Walmajarri can be said to have occurred.

### Stage 4b: Xish programs in Yish schools

The more dubious effectiveness of pursuing the RLS goal of fostering Xmen-via-Xish by being an invited guest in institutions obviously controlled by Yish authorities is evident in Australia in conjunction with both immigrant and Aboriginal languages. In the immigrant fold this approach is exemplified by the roughly 56,000 children attending 'insertion classes' which are sponsored in whole or in part by ethnic schools or organizations — although paid for by public education funds — and held *during regular school hours in the very quarters of the full-time public schools*. As in the case of the ethnic schools *per se* (see stage 5, above) a large variety of immigrant languages are instructed in this fashion (although, generally, during fewer hours per week) and a large number of part-time teachers are involved (and require State certificates in order to be retained for this purpose). However, the relative insignificance of this effort for RLS purposes is revealed by the fact that only 22% of all students in insertion classes are studying a language which is also spoken in their homes.

There are, of course, some positive outcomes of these efforts as well as of the even more mainstream-embedded efforts to introduce more and more community languages into the standard foreign language offerings of the public schools (elementary and secondary) themselves.[12] Among such positive outcomes are certainly (a) the 33% increase during recent years (1976–1986) in the number of candidates opting to be examined in foreign languages upon high school graduation (the absolute numbers rising from 20,000 to 30,000 during this period, and increasing again in 1987, despite overall declines in school enrollments and in foreign language enrollments) and (b) a similar increase in the number of tertiary level students preparing to become language teachers in general and 'ethnic community language' teachers in particular, and, therefore, a notable increase and a growing diversification in the language offerings of the tertiary institutions themselves.[13]

When all is said and done, however, these outcomes may help broaden and deepen Australian education and may even contribute somewhat to strengthening Australia's trade and political contacts with much of the rest of the world (both of these outcomes being rewarded and fostered from a variety of in-school and post-school sources of recognition and reinforcement), but their contribution to RLS is more likely to be extremely negligible, particularly so in light of the basic weaknesses in stage 6 (see above). Languages which have no assured environments and functions of their own can still be learned, but they are by and large ever so much more quickly lost, with the entire acquisition and loss experience being shrugged off as a frivolity of childhood and adolescence. RLS cannot be built out of such intergenerationally disconnected stuff, although such efforts contribute to 'interest in the language' and, thereby, may buy some time (at the most, until the native-speaking grandparents are gone; at the least, far less time than that) during which more substantive attempts can be launched.

*Stage 3: The Xish work spheres (serving Xmen and/or Ymen)*

There is very little to report in connection with RLS efforts in Australia at the stage 3 level. Even when the immigrant-derived population is occupationally clustered, such clustering is not of an intergenerational nature due to the social and demographic mobility of the second generations. As a result, the work sphere is not an organized RLS facilitator, not even when Xmen work together with each other nor even when other Xmen are their major employers or customers. Indeed, all of the usual immigrant stereotypes and negative associations *vis-á-vis* their own languages as disadvantages are encountered at work among both first and second generation immigrants, even though there are still many workplaces in which older immigrant workers continue informally to use their own languages among themselves. Significantly enough, such negative views are encountered, both overtly and covertly, even in such government-sponsored or co-sponsored enterprises on behalf of fostering 'multiculturism' as the ethnic schools (whether full-time or part-time), insertion classes and radio/television programming (see stage 2, below). Even in these contexts it is common to hear English spoken between those very individuals whose job responsibilities are, temporarily, those of ethnic mother tongue custodianship. Almost all of these folks, and particularly the second generation contingents among them, reveal that their work is 'just a job' and that they see no future in their language, neither individually nor socioculturally.

The situation is somewhat different among a substantial proportion of young Aborigines only in the 'outstations'. As might be expected, these are virtually always encountered speaking their own languages 'at work', particularly since the Western distinctions between 'home' and 'work' are not really applicable in such settings. Interestingly enough, the Aborigines living in these outstations have also been judged (by a white researcher commissioned by the Ministry of Aboriginal Affairs) to constitute 'the most economically independent [Aborigines] in the Northern Territory'.[14] Work and economic factors more generally are aspects of culture. RLS obtains when language and culture (including language and work) are intergenerationally integrated. When such integration between language and culture is not possible in the work sphere, all is not lost. But it becomes even more crucial to achieve that integration in the more foundational and self-regulated domains of the total interaction between language and culture.

*Stage 2: Local mass media and governmental services*

As will be evident from our previous chapters, local mass media and governmental services can make positive contributions to RLS only to the extent that they are directly related to and connected to fundamental family-neighborhood-community functioning. They may well extend the vocabulary and help foster the 'modernity' images of the languages associated with them, thereby improving the attitudes toward these languages among their speakers. But the impact of this attitudinal improvement is soon lost insofar as RLS is concerned, unless that impact is explicitly and quickly fed back to the establishment, functioning and protection of the families, neighborhoods and communities in which these languages can be intergenerationally transmitted as mother tongues. Such 'feedback' contributions of the mass media and governmental services must be specifically planned and kept in mind. This is not merely because threatened languages cannot easily wait for generations until indirect effects may possibly build up sufficient 'atmosphere effect' to influence intergenerational mother tongue transmission. The need for positive feedback to stage 6 is also crucial because, if left to their own devices, local mass media and governmental services easily become negative RLS factors, because even when conducted partially in Xish they tend to tie their clienteles into larger, Yish-centered listening and viewing patterns too, indeed, into larger frames of reference than Xish or Xmen-via-Xish *per se*.

The Australian Department of Immigration and Ethnic Affairs estimated that there were about 100 immigrant-based ethnic newspapers in Australia in 1984, modally weeklies, with a combined readership (including both subscribers and pass-along readers) of approximately half a million. Even now, however, when the period of mass immigration is still relatively recent history, these periodical publications typically have a rather meager second generation readership (even when they introduce special youth sections in English or undertake to publish in both Xish and English in each of their sections). Apparently, second generation literacy in Xish is too weak and its commitments to Xish (or even to Xishness) too peripheral to require an Xish press, in whatever language, for their satisfaction. Accordingly, as is also the case in the USA, most Xish periodicals never make the transitions either to bilingual or to all-English formats. Such transitions assume an Xmen-via-Yish market and there is either no such market out there or it doesn't require a press of its own for its functioning. In either case, lacking the more fundamental supports at earlier stages, there is very little that the immigrant press is able to do that is immediately translatable into RLS payoff.[15]

Hardly any periodical press seems to exist in Aboriginal languages too (and there are also only a very few publishers who specialize in simple books and brochures in such languages), probably because of the continuing rarity of adult and adolescent literacy in these languages. During the coming decade or two, this may change at several of the larger Aboriginal settlements, some of which already publish weekly, monthly or irregular news-sheets (e.g. the Amjinginyi newsletter of the Barkly Region Aboriginal Languages Center), provided that the youngsters educated at the independent schools remain concentrated in their home communities, rather than spreading out and settling elsewhere in numbers too small and too diffused to contribute to effective family, neighborhood and community building.

The absence of any substantial second generation interest in the immigrant-based foreign language press is generally paralleled by a lack of interest on the part of that same generation in foreign language radio, on the one hand, and the much more substantial second generation interest in foreign language television and films, on the other hand. Of course, the level of interest in the latter may benefit considerably from the English subtitles with which they are both commonly accompanied. All in all, a great deal of attention and a sizeable amount of funding is currently being lavished on non-print media utilizing immigrant-based languages with very meager (if any) evidence of positive RLS consequences being derived therefrom. The positive social climate and public acceptability of ethnic community languages to which television and radio contribute is 'something', of course, but that 'something' is, in itself, not effective RLS, precisely because it is not intergenerationally linked from the point of view of mother tongue transmission.

In 1984, 40 radio stations throughout Australia broadcast in immigrant-based community languages for a total of nearly 600 hours per week (or an average of 15 hours per week per station). Four of these stations, in Adelaide, Brisbane, Melbourne and Sydney respectively, were full-time ethnic radio stations. To take the last-mentioned as an example, Radio 2EA broadcast in 53 'community languages of Australia' in 1985 (see Table 9.1), the more prominent of which (Greek, Italian, Arabic, Turkish and 'Yugoslav' — Serbian, Croatian, Slovenian and/or Macedonian) had daily or twice-daily broadcasts. These broadcasts and their counterparts elsewhere attracted a Commonwealth Government subsidy of $650,000, not counting the subsidies paid to stations to train the personnel involved in producing the programs and in presenting them. Nevertheless, it should be observed (as, indeed, it was observed by the media

TABLE 9.1 *The non-English radio channel in Sydney, Newcastle and Wollongong (1985) broadcasts in 53 community languages every week* (*Source:* Radio 2EA brochure)

| Time | Monday | Tuesday | Wednesday | Thursday | Friday | Saturday | Sunday |
|---|---|---|---|---|---|---|---|
| 06:00 | Greek | Greek | Greek | Greek | Greek | Greek | Greek |
| 06:45 | Arabic | Arabic | Arabic | Arabic | Arabic | Arabic | Arabic |
| 07:30 | Croatian | Macedonian | Croatian | Serbian | Macedonian | Croatian | Slovenian |
| 08:15 | Italian | Italian | Italian | Italian | Italian | Italian | Italian |
| 09:00 | Assyrian | Polish | Polish | Armenian | Turkish | Hungarian | Dutch |
| 10:00 | German | Maltese | German | Portuguese | German | Lithuanian | Jewish[b] |
| 11:00 | Dutch | Ukrainian | Russian | Hungarian | Urdu | German | Ukrainian |
| 11:30 | Dutch | Ukrainian | Russian | Hungarian | Hindustani | German | Ukrainian |
| 12:00 | Spanish | Maltese | Spanish | Maltese | Spanish | Maltese | Maltese |
| 13:00 | Norwegian | Music | Aborigian | Laotian | Khmer | Spanish | German |
| 13:30 | Bengali | 'Insight' | Aboriginal | Laotian | Music | Spanish | German |
| 14:00 | Tamil/Gujarati[c] | French | Vietnamese | Spanish | Jewish[b] | Music | Polish |
| 14:30 | Sinhalese/Punjabi[c] | French | Vietnamese | Spanish | Jewish[b] | Music | Polish |
| 15:00 | Arabic | Mandarin | Cantonese | Arabic | Russian | Russian | Arabic |
| 16:00 | Vietnamese | Korean | Swedish | Dutch | Tongan | Latvian | French |
| 16:30 | Vietnamese | Korean | Danish | Dutch | Fijian | Latvian | French |
| 17:00 | Turkish | Turkish | Turkish | Turkish | Turkish | Turkish | Turkish |
| 17:45 | Italian | Italian | Italian | Italian | Italian | Italian | Italian |
| 18:30 | Greek | Greek | Greek | Greek | Greek | Greek | Greek |
| 19:15 | Cantonese | Armenian | Jewish[b] | Mandarin | Assyrian | Romanian | Hindustani |
| 20:15 | Portuguese | Byelorusian | German | Slovak | Pilipino | Finnish | Czech |
| 21:15 | Hungarian | Spanish | Spanish | Ukrainin | Vietnamese | Estonian | Spanish |
| 22:15 | Serbian | Slovenian | Macedonian | Croatian | Serbian | Macedonian | Croatian |
| 23:00 | Celtic[a] | Serbian | Latvian | French | Arabic | German | Special |

[a] 1st Monday in Month: Gaelic-Scottish
2nd Monday in Month: Welsh
3rd Monday in Month: Gaelic-Irish

[b] Presented in Hebrew, Yiddish and English
[c] Alternate Weeks

authorities themselves) that most of the programs were focused on entertainment (rather than on information) and that they were most successful in reaching the poorly educated with little knowledge of English (and, therefore, least successful in reaching a second generation listenership).

The situation with respect to immigrant language television and films is somewhat similar to what we have presented above for radio. Such broadcasts are much more recent in origin but they have already been expanded from Sydney and Melbourne to Canberra, all State capitals and several other cities (see Table 9.2). In 1985–86, 29 languages were involved for an average of five and a quarter hours per day, constituting half of the total broadcast hours on the channel set aside for this purpose (Channel 0/28). These programs are considered to have informational and intercultural functions as well, due to their built-in community service announcement (three minutes out of every hour) and subtitles. It has become clear that these telecasts and films have a wide English-speaking following as well (particularly for their classic foreign films and for their in-depth news coverage); what is totally unclear (or even distinctly dubious) is whether they have any genuine RLS value. To have such, they would need to be much more conscientiously focused on home, family, child and youth material which could be copied and distributed for VCR cassette use in homes, community centers and schools. The social psychological impact of the mass media, strong though it may be either momentarily or cumulatively, is, in itself, not a safe bet for RLS. Families simply do not pass on threatened languages to their children because of a few hours per week of mass media programming, nor do children become mother tongue speakers of Xish on that basis.

Broadcasting in Aboriginal languages, so important because of the relative lack of literacy even in the most retentive Aboriginal communities, took a major leap ahead in 1980 — notwithstanding the small and scattered audiences involved — when an Aboriginal group in Alice Springs formed CAAMA (Central Australian Aboriginal Media Association). The Association now has a $100,000 budget provided by the Commonwealth Government (very little really and constantly at risk of being discontinued) and broadcasts for part of its 16-hour radio day in English and part (more than half) in Pitjantjatjara, Warlpiri and Arandic (Arrente). There are also a few other radio stations broadcasting regularly in Aboriginal languages, all of them very short of funds for this purpose although some of them have produced very worthwhile (indeed, even prizewining) programs.

There are also, at present, only roughly a dozen stations in all of Australia that even present programs for Aboriginal listeners in English. Audio-tapes of *Aboriginal News*, the newsletter of the Queensland Department of Employment, Education and Training, are produced in various Aboriginal languages by the

TABLE 9.2 *English and non-English language television in Australia, 1985–86*

| Language | Number of hours | % of total program time |
|---|---|---|
| Arabic | 77.02 | 2.42 |
| Armenian | 4.30 | 0.13 |
| Bahsa Indonesian | 13.73 | 0.43 |
| Bulgarian | 12.23 | 0.38 |
| Chinese languages[a] | 82.76 | 2.60 |
| Czech | 83.74 | 2.63 |
| Danish | 35.09 | 1.10 |
| Dutch | 37.74 | 1.18 |
| English[a] | 1313.76 | 41.24 |
| Farsi | 0.85 | 0.03 |
| Finnish | 15.00 | 0.47 |
| Flemish | 3.60 | 0.11 |
| French | 154.92 | 4.86 |
| Gaelic | 1.05 | 0.03 |
| Georgian | 1.28 | 0.04 |
| German | 158.48 | 4.98 |
| Greek | 225.83 | 7.09 |
| Hebrew | 12.35 | 0.39 |
| Hungarian | 33.07 | 1.04 |
| Icelandic | 3.12 | 0.10 |
| Indian languages[a] | 26.49 | 0.83 |
| Italian | 297.65 | 9.34 |
| Japanese | 59.36 | 1.86 |
| Maltese | 7.27 | 0.23 |
| Marathi | 1.92 | 0.06 |
| More than one language | 2.26 | 0.07 |
| No dialogue | 31.06 | 0.98 |
| Norwegian | 12.01 | 0.38 |
| Pidgin English | 3.78 | 0.12 |
| Polish | 86.49 | 2.72 |
| Portuguese | 19.83 | 0.62 |
| Russian | 24.09 | 0.76 |
| Spanish | 117.11 | 3.68 |
| Swedish | 30.60 | 0.96 |
| Tagalog | 1.48 | 0.05 |
| Thai | 4.04 | 0.13 |
| Turkish | 30.66 | 0.96 |

TABLE 9.2 *Continued*

| Language | Number of hours | % of total program time |
|---|---|---|
| Ukrainian | 4.59 | 0.14 |
| Welsh | 1.27 | 0.04 |
| Yiddish | 1.48 | 0.05 |
| Yugoslav languages[a] | 151.90 | 4.77 |
| | 3185.26 | 100.00 |

[a]Breakdown as follows:

| | | |
|---|---|---|
| *Chinese languages* | | |
| Cantonese | 34.29 | 1.08 |
| Mandarin | 48.47 | 1.52 |
| *English* | | |
| English | 620.64 | 19.48 |
| English (SBS TV Productions) | 693.12 | 21.76 |
| *Indian languages* | | |
| Bengali | 9.82 | 0.31 |
| Hindi | 16.67 | 0.52 |
| *Yugoslav languages* | | |
| Croatian | 6.79 | 0.21 |
| Macedonian | 13.26 | 0.42 |
| Serbian | 40.21 | 1.26 |
| Serbo-Croatian | 66.46 | 2.09 |
| Slovenian | 25.18 | 0.79 |

(*Source:* Lo Bianco, 1987)

Townsville Aboriginal and Islander Media Association in order to get around the problem of Aboriginal illiteracy. All in all, however, the Aboriginal market is too small, and too scattered, for many successful media programs in Aboriginal languages and it would require heavy governmental subsidization for this number to grow significantly in the future. Once again, the contrast between policy with respect to the immigrant-based languages and policy with respect to the Aboriginal languages is a painful one indeed.

In 1987 CAAMA's television offshoot, IMPARJA (from the Arrente word for 'track' or 'footprint'), was founded and began broadcasting in Aboriginal languages for three-quarters of an hour/week [!], that being all of the time that could be spared due to competitive financial pressures. Somewhat prematurely, a local Aboriginal RLS activist has concluded that 'now [that] we have our own TV and video we can put our own things on ... We can fight fire with fire'. Unfortunately, that is neither a wise policy (presenting 'Dallas' dubbed in Warlpiri is a total waste of time and money) nor a feasible one in practical terms. Unless carefully watched and counterbalanced, the overall growth in English media availability in the remoter areas (due to the rapid growth of satellite-directed broadcasting and rebroadcasting) and the further acceptance of English as an Aboriginal language merely because it is the only feasible Aboriginal lingua franca, is likely to be many, many times greater than the growth of its Aboriginal counterparts. Playing with fire is a dangerous thing to do for those who have very little that they can fall back upon should they get burned. The Aborigines' languages do need modern print and non-print media in their struggles for RLS, but these must be non-competitive with the English media and, instead, must concentrate on fostering the type of Aboriginal life and reinforcing those sociocultural contexts which Aborigines can control and on which RLS depends.[16] Encouraging efforts along these very lines are now underway at taping centers of CAAMA and IMPARJA and at the Video Center of the Barkly Region Aboriginal Languages Center (Northern Territory).

*Stage 1: Higher education, regional or central governmental activity, national media and higher/specialized work sphere*

It is evident from our examination of the prior stages that there is very little of RLS significance to report at this most advanced stage, the stage that is most fully controlled by and for the Yish establishment (unless explicit provisions exist for local cultural autonomy). There are, of course, several ethnic studies/ ethnic languages programs and research centers (and even a few Aboriginal studies/languages programs and research centers) at various major and minor Australian universities, some of which (e.g. Batchelor, Northern Territory) are explicitly teaching about RLS and its needs, processes and priorities. There is also a degree of top-flight media involvement in the large investment that has been made in community language broadcasting and in the more meager support that has been allotted to Aboriginal language broadcasting. More noticeable and more noteworthy than any of the foregoing is the effort to engage in language policy planning at the Commonwealth level and in several of the individual states. Many ethnics and some Aborigines have even been invited to participate in more than a token sense in this planning. Very few Yish establishments throughout the world have done either the one or the other and Australia deserves recognition in both connections,[17] as well as in connection with appropriating or allocating over 90 million dollars for the period 1987–1991 for the purposes of implementing the National Language Policy finally adopted in 1987.

However, when all is said and done, the RLS outlook in Australia is far bleaker than the sheer amount of RLS activity currently ongoing might seem to imply. Aboriginal languages are dying at the rate of one or more a year and language shift continues unabated in the immigrant-based 'community languages' fold. This is a tremendous attrition for a country that recognizes, as few others do, its own dire need for languages other than English and that has shown as much admiration, recognition and support as Australia has for the languages still spoken within its borders. Unfortunately, as we have noted so many times before, good intentions are not enough and the steps taken or about to be taken are either largely unrelated, non-productive or even counter-productive as far as intergenerational RLS-payoff is concerned.

Something (although not much) can still be saved, but it will probably be up to the language communities themselves, more than up to the Government, to point to the required family-home-neighborhood-community foundations of such possible salvation. When the right way is finally recognized, the Aboriginal willingness to withdraw to 'outstations' will be understood in all of its metaphorical power. Self-help and self-regulation in everyday intergenerational mother tongue transmission contexts, safeguarded by boundary setting and boundary preservation, are the *sine qua non* of RLS. Money and planning along such lines by national authorities are unlikely, given the ethos of shared participationism that dominates both democratic and authoritarian regimes today. Small-scale self-regulation and self-help at the local level is the inevitable only way out for the saving remnant that really takes RLS seriously. For the others, 'language appreciation' and Xmen-via-Yish may be the rewards and the consolations of widest currency.[18]

Australian policies and processes constitute a positive but ineffective approach to RLS on behalf of recent immigrant languages and a negative but potentially effective approach to RLS on behalf of Aboriginal languages. Because of its relative proximity to and ultimate commercial connectedness with South and Southeast Asia Australia may well be the first anglo-establishment country to break out of the prison of English monolingualism. However, few of its immigrant language communities and none of its Aboriginal language communities will benefit directly from this self-liberation. Indeed, over the long run (during the next fifty years or so), a few Aboriginal languages associated with 'outstations' and genuine community schools may be far more successful on the RLS scene than any of the recently proliferated immigrant languages currently marked by social mobility and urban demographic dispersion, on the one hand, and by a luxuriant growth of language courses, radio programs and television broadcasts, on the other hand. This will come about because a very few, fortunate (i.e. governmentally benignly neglected) Aboriginal languages are genuinely linked to the intergenerational mother tongue transmission process rooted as it is in home-family-neighborhood and community, whereas no such linkage generally exists in connection with the highly publicized efforts on behalf of immigrant languages. Ultimately, therefore, and with the exception of a few obvious South and Southeast Asian languages plus a few major European tongues that are really needed for Australia's own commercial advancement, Australia will yet be the graveyard of dozens upon dozens of its immigrant languages, through the self-destruction of their community bases, even as it is already the graveyard of an even larger number of its decimated Aboriginal languages.

Efforts that are not sequentially planned from an informed RLS perspective rarely result in RLS, regardless of how colorful and expensive they may be, just as any organized sociopolitical actions that vastly outgrow their demographic foundations must come a cropper. Without the possibility of a solution based upon the territorial principle, such as that which assists various Aboriginal cultures and outstations in their struggles for survival, and without the spirit of *primum mobile* which also applies to Aborigines and to a few isolated immigrant settlements alone, most immigrant speech communities must fall back on their own internal family and community dynamics to generate RLS and even to prime the less-than-RLS efforts of governmental agencies. These speech communities are currently far from being aware of how distant they really are from assuring intergenerational mother tongue transmission of those very languages whose superficial institutional flourishes the government is currently supporting for an increasingly aging first generation.[19]

## Notes

1.  A good starting place for sampling both Aboriginal and Anglo-Australian perspectives during the past century and a half is a volume by Mattingley and Hampton (1988). The issues of *Survival International, Cultural Survival Quarterly* and *pogrom: Zeitschrift der Gesellschaft für bedröhte Völker* are excellent sources of current information (see, e.g., Altman and Dillon, 1986; Duelke, 1984; and Ludwig, 1985). A recent excellent addition to the periodical literature in this area is *Land Rights News* (P.O. Box 3321, Alice Springs, NT 5750, Australia), which is published for the Northern Territory Land Councils but provides a review of news and opinions pertaining to Aborigines and their concerns as well as their accomplishments throughout the country. Thus, its September 1988 issue (Vol. 2, No. 10) includes reports on: the outspoken racism of spokesmen of the Returned Service League, urgent questions raised by the Royal Commission into Aboriginal Deaths in Custody (108 Aboriginal deaths while in custody since 1980), a report by the chairperson of the UN's Working Group on Indigenous Populations urging greater Aboriginal self-management and self-determination in Australia, the protest by Aboriginal spokesmen against the International Labor Organization's minimalist position with respect to the rights of indigenous populations, an extensive listing of tertiary education

offerings and opportunities for Aborigines, an update on the bilingual/bicultural Yipirinya School (to be discussed below), and dozens of brief articles about various ongoing efforts to provide (and to deny) land rights in various parts of Australia.

2.  Stephen Wurm's and Shiro Hattori's (1981) *Language Atlas: Pacific* contains four separate maps covering the various parts of Australia, dividing it into Southeastern, Eastern, Northern and Western regions. This atlas gives estimated numbers of speakers as well as bibliographic references in each case and is an invaluable tool for all those interested in the number, diversity and spatial distribution of the Aboriginal languages.

3.  We will follow Black's (1983) lead by not including creole languages in our discussion of Aboriginal languages. The two major creoles (Kriol and Torres Strait Creole, both of them English-related), each with some 15,000 speakers (including second language speakers), are of considerable importance in their respective areas and represent cases of language genesis and of newly established language-and-ethnicity linkages which should not be lost sight of in considering the manifold cultural dislocations that initially lead to language shift and language death. Creoles are a reminder that authenticity 'comes to be' rather than springs full-formed from the head of Jove. Nevertheless, RLS adherents are attached to their preferred and already legitimated authenticity and are not consoled by the possibility of future authenticities to come. Creole partisans, of course, frequently engage in RLS-efforts of their own, when threatened by contextually more powerful language and culture constellations.

4.  Wurm and Hattori refer to this language as Banjalang (with six dialects) and estimate that it may have had 30 speakers in the late 1970s and early 1980s. Eve Fesl (Director, Aboriginal Languages Center, Monash University), formerly an instructor at the Seminar, estimates 30 speakers today, although she points out that there might be a somewhat larger number if it were possible to count those who hide their language skills in order to avoid the hardships (both for themselves and for their children) visited on former generations of speakers of Aboriginal languages or in order to keep the language from changing as a result of its use by inexperienced 'semi-speakers' (personal communication). The invitation to the series referred to mentions that 'through our language program we hope to reaffirm our cultural relationships. ... We hope to compile the history and stories that were part of our daily lives and traditions. People with language knowledge are invited to share it with us.' The availability and spread of an indigenous aggregative term for all Aborigines (Gooris/Kooris) is suggestive of a growing intergroup identity among them, over and above former and current ethnolinguistic demarcations. The term Goori/Kuri itself stems from the Southeastern coastal area, some 300 miles north of Sydney. Wurm and Hattori list '7?' speakers for Kuri and '9??' for the Yuin-Kuric grouping (10 dialects, all but three of which are extinct).

5.  I am indebted to Tamsin Donaldson, Australian Institute of Aboriginal Studies, for my information about the 'little alphabet books' in general and specifically for details of their construction in several different Aboriginal language settings. Donaldson's paper 'From speaking Ngiyaampaa to speaking English' (1985) is an excellent account of the rapidity of shift in many Aboriginal settings and is a great help in appreciating the special attitude-building role of the 'little alphabet books' at a time when English is already the common vehicle of communication among all but the oldest members of a particular group.

6.  For the scholarly documentation of the above processes, see: Clyne, 1982, 1985, and 1988; McAllister, 1986; and Pauwels, 1988 (the latter being an excellent collection of recent papers on 'the future of ethnic languages in Australia'). While the number

of claimants of community languages other than English is still rising for languages most of whose speakers are either recent arrivals or whose immigration is still ongoing (e.g., Arabic, Spanish, Vietnamese, Chinese, etc.), intergenerational maintenance is usually very poor beyond the second generation and is even often poor beyond the first, if not within the first generation itself.

7.  The material variety of the outstations is nicely described and summarized in 'Desert Homeland Centres — Their Physical Development', Department of Aboriginal Affairs Occasional Reports, 1977 (August), No. 4. I am not entirely sure of how widespread the designation 'Homeland' has become but it seems to me to have a distinctly more positive designation than 'outstation'. *Land Rights News* is a good source of information about publication houses (such as Magabala Books) and a variety of musical groups that have come into being to serve the outstations in general and RLS-efforts in particular. Most of my information on the 'outstations' is derived from material placed at my disposition by Eve Fesl.

8.  The governmental report referred to here is that of the Senate Standing Committee on Education and the Arts, 1984. Another very useful source for this discussion (but even more so, in connection with our discussion of radio and television, stage 2) is that of Foster and Stockley (1984). I am grateful to Joseph Lo Bianco, Michael Clyne, and Manfred Klarberg for providing me with various published and unpublished governmental, organizational and private reports pertaining to ethnic community schools and other related immigrant-RLS issues in Australia.

9.  The attainment of adult literacy in community languages is the goal of the government-sponsored, multi-ethnic Victorian School of Languages, which teaches 30 languages in over a dozen centers in the metropolitan Melbourne and Geelong (Victoria's second largest city) areas. This school is not under ethnic auspices (although some of its branches are mono-ethnic and are even conducted on mono-ethnic institutional premises), however, and, although its students attend of their own volition, it feeds back relatively little to the strengthening of community ethno-linguistic stability because most of its students are pursuing very focused, instrumental language goals. Many of its students are of high school age or older and utilize its courses in order to qualify for high school certification in the community language which they initially acquired in childhood but subsequently largely ceased to speak. Also not included in our discussion are the many non-ethnic proprietary schools now teaching Japanese in order to meet the needs of Australia's rapidly expanding commercial ties with Japan. I am indebted to Annette Schmidt (Australian Institute for Aboriginal Studies, Canberra) for providing me with much valuable information regarding the adult literacy efforts (and other adult education efforts) in various Aboriginal languages.

10. This quotation is from the 'Report of the House of Representatives Select Committee on Aboriginal Education 1985', p. 116. The bulk of my information on Aboriginal type 4a schools is derived from Eve Fesl's dissertation (1989), *Land Rights News*, 1988, 2, no. 10 ('Yipirinya: Making two-way education a reality'), Lo Bianco 1987, Senate Standing Committee on Education and the Arts report *A National Language Policy* (1984), von Tesmar (1988) and very informative and lengthy correspondence with Annette Schmidt, Stephen Harris (Batchelor College, Batchelor, Northern Territory) and Eirlys Richards (Summer Institute of Linguistics, Berrimah, Northern Territory).

11. The contrastive juxtaposition and combination of own *culture* vs. foreign (Western) *skills* constantly reoccurs in late European (i.e. in Eastern and Southern European) and in Afro-Asian nationalisms, the former being viewed as humanistically and

philosophically superior and nourishing to the soul, while the latter are 'merely' technically advanced but philosophically empty. The complementary nature of these two, own ethnocultural lore and traditions, on the other, and foreign technical 'know-how', on the one hand, implies that there need be no deep-seated ideological conflict between the two and, therefore, that they can be combined under proper indigenous auspices and supervision. Like the ethnonationalisms that came before it, Aboriginal self-determination is not a wholesale rejection of the modern western world, but rather, a defense of thought-and-value systems of their own and a willingness to strengthen that defense by the utilization of modern means, as necessary. For further elaboration of the symbiotic nature of modernizing ethnonationalisms, see my *Language and Nationalism* (1972; republished in its entirety in my *Language and Ethnicity*, 1989).

12. The variety of immigrant languages offered in the foreign language programs of the public schools and the proportion of students studying such languages is probably greater in Australia (particularly in the southeastern states of Victoria, New South Wales and South Australia in which most immigrants have settled) than anywhere else in the Western world. In the state of South Australia, e.g., just to cite evidence outside of the major ethnic enclaves of Melbourne (Victoria) and Sydney (New South Wales), nearly 20% of the elementary school students and 40% of the secondary school students were studying languages, the major enrollments being in German and French but with Italian, Indonesian, Greek, Mandarin and Japanese also being well represented and a considerable contingent being found for Serbocroatian as well. It should also be pointed out that a number of Aboriginal languages are offered in public primary schools in most of the larger Aboriginal settlements in South Australia, enrollment being particularly high (over 600) for Pitjantjatjara (1,200–1,300 speakers in South Australia and Northern Territory).

13. My familiarity with respect to stage 4b developments within the immigrant languages fold derives from my personal fieldwork during a prolonged visit to Australia in 1985 and from extensive discussions and correspondence with Joseph Lo Bianco and Manfred Klarberg. Klarberg's article (1987) on 1976–1986 trends with respect to the High School Certificate examinations in the foreign language field should be of considerable interest to language education authorities elsewhere. The more meager type 4b efforts in conjunction with Aboriginal languages are reviewed in the Senate Standing Committee on Education and the Arts' 1984 report which enumerates 25 'bilingual programs' in government schools for Aborigines. Needless to say, all of the foregoing are of a transitional nature. Lo Bianco's 1987 report also lists a few short-term offerings (fewer than a dozen all in all and of only 1–3 years duration) of Aboriginal languages as 'foreign languages' in public and in Catholic schools. From correspondence with Annette Schmidt I have learned of two type 4b programs involving Aboriginal languages that were recently (1989) discontinued due to the lack of qualified staff and administrative uninterest and/or resistance. I am also very grateful to Dorothy Tunbridge, Adnyamathanha Language and Culture Program, for once more reminding me that type 4b programs that have no real RLS consequences of an overt language use sort may, nevertheless, still have a significant positive impact on reawakening and fostering ethnic identity. Nevertheless, with respect to RLS, such programs ultimately contribute more to Xmen-via-Yish than to Xmen-via-Xish life-patterns.

14. Altman, Jon, *Aboriginal Employment and Education News*, 1988, No. 17, p. 18.

15. The major sources of information concerning the immigrant-based foreign language press in Australia are Gilson and Zubrzycki (1967) and Clyne (1982) and Terezakis

(1982). The Senate Standing Committee on Education and the Arts' 1985 report mentions two forthcoming studies (commissioned by the Department of Immigration and Ethnic Affairs) of the contents of Greek and Arabic newspapers in Sydney and of Turkish and Yugoslav newspapers in Melbourne. Neither of these studies seem to have been released as of early 1989, when the bulk of this chapter was written.

16. Useful information concerning immigrant language and Aboriginal language non-print media is provided in Anon. (1988a, 1988b), Australian Institute of Multicultural Affairs (1982), Clyne (1982), Ethnic Television Review Panel (1980), Jernudd (1969), Language Maintenance Newsletter (School of Australian Linguistics, P.O. Batchelor, N.T. 5791), *Land Rights News*, 1988, 2, No. 10, and The Senate Standing Committee on Education and the Arts (1984). During my 1985 fieldwork visit I also gathered much information from stations/channels and broadcasters in the Melbourne and Sydney areas. Still unreported in any systematic fashion are the more limited RLS-efforts via ethnic theater and ethnic choral groups, both of which function among immigrant groups as well as Aboriginal groups.

17. Several major publications have resulted from these planning efforts, among them Commonwealth Department of Education (1982), Applied Linguistics Association of Australia and Australian Linguistic Society (PLANLangPol Committee) (1983), Senate Standing Committee on Education and the Arts (1984), National Advisory and Coordinating Committee on Multicultural Education (1987) and Lo Bianco (1987). The latter is a report that has potentially major implications for RLS, although, as yet, it addresses this issue indirectly and without the explicit attention that it requires if RLS is to be successfully attained. Language maintenance is on the report's agenda, however: see Table 9.3. The National Language Institute, established in 1989, has a center focusing on 'Language in Society', located at Monash University (Clayton, Victoria). This center could help redirect attention to the fact that RLS is not yet really on the Australian agenda.

18. From the huge literature on Australian Aboriginal and immigrant groups and their languages, I would like to mention just a few, not referred to above, that were of substantial additional help to me in my RLS inquiries in connection with that part of the world. In the immigrant languages sector: Lo Bianco (1989) (also contains information on Aboriginal languages and on sign language [for the deaf] in Victoria) and the successive issues of *Vox* (the journal of the Australian Advisory Council on Languages and Multicultural Education, which began publishing in 1988). In the Aboriginal sector: the successive issues of *Land Rights News* (a publication of the Northern Territory Land Councils, which began publishing in 1987), the successive issues of *Language Maintenance Newsletter* (beginning in 1986), *Aboriginal Australians* (= *Report No. 35* [revised edition, 1988] of the Minority Rights Group, London), Loveday (1982), Prior and Wunungmurra (1987) and Reyburn (1988). Other materials that I found useful or stimulating in the preparation of this chapter, although I have not cited them directly, are Baldauf and Luke (1990), Bavin and Shopen (1988), Collman (1988), Cronin (1988), Foster and Stockey (1988), Johnson (1987), Kalantzis, Cope and Slade (1989), Spurr (1988), and Thieberger (1988).

19. My sincere thanks to Michael Clyne, who enabled me to spend five weeks in Australia in 1985, and to him, Joseph Lo Bianco, Steven Harris, Fred Klarberg and Eve Fesl for their manifold assistance, criticism and encouragement in connection with the preparation of this formulation of the RLS situation in immigrant and Aboriginal Australia. Needless to say, any errors of fact or interpretation are my own.

# References

ALTMAN, Jon and DILLON, Michael 1986 [1985], Aboriginal land rights in Australia. *Cultural Survival Quarterly* 10, 2, 53–4 (adaptation of their article 'Watching brief on Land Rights', *Australian Society*, June 1985).

ANON. 1988a, Maningride media gets a new home. *Land Rights News* 2, No. 10, 2.

— 1988b, FM tests for 'a foot in the door' for TAIM. *Land Rights News* 2, No. 10, 15.

APPLIED LINGUISTICS ASSOCIATION OF AUSTRALIA AND AUSTRALIAN LINGUISTIC SOCIETY (PLANLangPol Committee) 1983, *A National Language Policy for Australia*. Kensington: ALAA/ALS (PC).

AUSTRALIAN INSTITUTE OF MULTICULTURAL AFFAIRS 1982, *Evaluation of Post-Arrival Education Programs and Services*. Melbourne: AIMA.

BALDAUF, Richard Jr and LUKE, Allan (eds) 1990, *Language Planning and Education in Australasia and the South Pacific*. Clevedon: Multilingual Matters.

BAVIN, Edith L. and SHOPEN, Timothy 1988, Walpiri in the 80s: An overview of research into language variation and child language. In B. RIGSBY and S. ROMAINE (eds) *The Language[s?] of Australia*. Sydney: Cambridge University Press.

BLACK, Paul 1983, *Aboriginal Languages of the Northern Territory*. Darwin: School of Australian Linguistics/Darwin Community College.

CLYNE, Michael 1982, *Multilingual Australia: Resources–Needs*. Melbourne: River Seine.

— 1985, Language maintenance and language shift: some data from Australia. In Nessa WOLFSON and Joan MANES (eds) *Language of Inequality*. Berlin: Mouton, 195–206.

— 1988, Community languages in the home: a first progress report. *Vox* 1, 22–7.

COLLMAN, Jeff 1988, *Fringe-Dwellers and Welfare; An Aboriginal Response to Bureaucracy*. St Lucia: University of Queensland Press.

COMMONWEALTH DEPARTMENT OF EDUCATION 1982, *Towards a National Language Policy*. Canberra: Australian Government Publishing Service.

CRONIN, Darryl 1988, Land rights; is that all we really want? *Land Rights News* 2, No. 10, 34–5.

DONALDSON, Tamsin 1985, From speaking Ngiyaampaa to speaking English. *Aboriginal History* 9, 126–47.

DUELKE, Britta 1984, Aborigines in Northern Territory. *pogrom: Zeitschrift für bedröhte Völker* 15, No. 108, 50–5.

ETHNIC TELEVISION REVIEW PANEL 1980, *Programming for the Multicultural/Multilingual Television Service: Objectives and Policies* (Third Report). Canberra: ETRP.

FESL, Eve 1989, Language Policy Formulation and Implementation; An Historical Perspective on Australian Languages. Ph.D. Dissertation, Monash University.

FISHMAN, Joshua A. 1972 [1989], *Language and Nationalism: Two Integrative Essays*. Rowley, MA: Newbury House. Reprinted in its entirety as part of *Language and Ethnicity in Minority Sociolinguistic Perspective*. Clevedon: Multilingual Matters, 97–175 and 269–367.

FOSTER, Lois and STOCKLEY, David 1984, *Multiculturism: The Changing Australian Paradigm*. Clevedon: Multilingual Matters.

— 1988, *Australian Multiculturism: A Documentary History and Critique*. Clevedon: Multilingual Matters.

GILSON, M. and ZUBRZYCKI, J. 1967, *The Foreign Language Press in Australia, 1948–1969*. Canberra: Australian National University.

JERNUDD, Björn H. 1969, Foreign language broadcasting in Victoria. *Babel* 5, No. 2, 24–5.

| POLICY PRINCIPLES | SPECIFIED AS | PROGRAMS RECOMMENDED | ACTION TAKEN |
|---|---|---|---|
| (1) ENGLISH FOR ALL | Adult Literacy | Adult Literacy Action Campaign | Funded as two-year program $1.96m in each of 1987–88 & 1988–89 |
| | English mother tongue & English as second dialect | English Language & Learning Project | Considered but not funded. Costed at $7.5m over 3 years |
| | English as second language | for children   ESL New Arrivals doubling | Additional funding provided   1987–88 $5.7m   1988–89 $13.75m   1989–90 $14.7m |
| | | for adults   Implication of recommendations of Campbell Review of AMEP | Fully funded by DILGEA |
| | | ESL index of needs for Aborigines | Not funded   Costed at $0.1m for 1 year |
| | | ESL teacher education | Not specifically funded but some work may be occurring under ESL Program. Costed at $0.6m over 3 years |
| | | Triennial planning for ESL | Nil cost. No apparent action |
| | | Greater coordination of all Commonwealth programs for adult ESL | Nil cost. No apparent action |
| | | Integration of adult ESL programs at TAFE with those of other adult education providers | Nil cost. No action as yet |
| | English as foreign language | Establishment of independent panel to review accreditation of EFL schools | Being done by DEET without NPL funds |
| (2) SUPPORT FOR ABORIGINAL & TORRES STRAIT ISLANDER LANGUAGES | Language maintenance & learning | National Aboriginal Languages Project | Funded at half level recommended ie $2.5m over 3 years |
| | Language awareness | Inclusion of Aboriginal languages & cultural course in language awareness program for junior secondary school level | Not funded Costed at $0.36m for printing & distribution of existing CDC materials |
| (3) A LANGUAGE OTHER THAN ENGLISH FOR ALL | Language learning • community languages for mother tongue maintenance • community languages as second language • geo-political and economic languages as second language • "enrichment" languages | Australian Second Language Learning Program | Fully funded at $22.5m over 3 years |
| | | Upgrading of Ethnic Schools (to be renamed Part-Time Community Language Schools | Not funded Costed at $1m over 3 years |
| | | Asian Studies Program | Additional program   1987–88 $1.85m   1988–89 $1.95m |
| | Language support | Bicentennial Languages Foundation | Not funded Costed for ABA at $1m |
| | | Language teacher education | Some funding anticipated by States under ASLLP. Explicitly costed at $0.6m over 3 years |

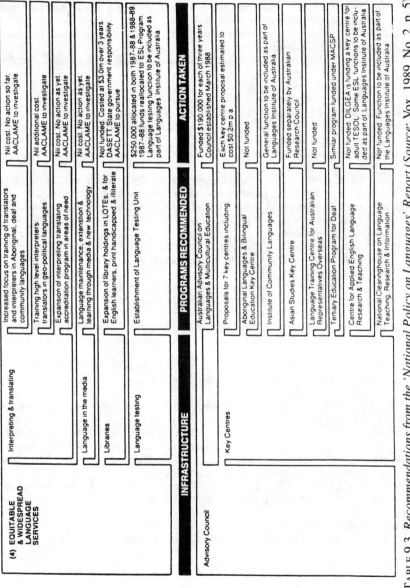

| (4) EQUITABLE & WIDESPREAD LANGUAGE SERVICES | | ACTION TAKEN |
|---|---|---|
| Interpreting & translating | Increased focus on training of translators and interpreters in Aboriginal, deaf and community languages | Nil cost. No action so far. AACLAME to investigate |
| | Training high level interpreters; translators in geo-political languages | Nil additional cost. AACLAME to investigate |
| | Expansion of interpreting translating accreditation program in areas of need | Nil cost. No action as yet. AACLAME to investigate |
| Language in the media | Language maintenance, extension & learning through media & new technology | Nil cost. No action as yet. AACLAME to investigate |
| Libraries | Expansion of library holdings in LOTEs. & for English learners, print handicapped & illiterate | Not funded. Costed at $3.0m over 3 years. DASETT State government responsibility. AACLAME to pursue |
| Language testing | Establishment of Language Testing Unit | $250,000 allocated in both 1987-88 & 1988-89. 1987-88 funds reallocated to ESL Program. Language testing function to be included as part of Languages Institute of Australia |

**INFRASTRUCTURE**

| | PROGRAMS RECOMMENDED | ACTION TAKEN |
|---|---|---|
| Advisory Council | Australian Advisory Council on Languages & Multicultural Education | Funded $190,000 for each of three years Council established March 1988 |
| Key Centres | Proposals for 7 key centres including: | Each key centre proposal estimated to cost $0.2m p a |
| | Aboriginal Languages & Bilingual Education Key Centre | Not funded |
| | Institute of Community Languages | General function to be included as part of Languages Institute of Australia |
| | Asian Studies Key Centre | Funded separately by Australian Research Council |
| | Language Training Centre for Australian Representatives Overseas | Not funded |
| | Tertiary Education Program for Deaf | Similar program funded under MACSP |
| | Centre for Applied English Language Research & Teaching | Not funded DILGEA is funding a key centre for adult TESOL. Some ESL functions to be included as part of Languages Institute of Australia |
| | National Clearinghouse on Language Teaching, Research & Information | Not funded Function to be included as part of the Languages Institute of Australia |

TABLE 9.3 *Recommendations from the 'National Policy on Languages' Report (Source: Vox, 1989, No. 2, p. 5)*

JOHNSON, Steve 1987, The philosophy and politics of Aboriginal language maintenance. *Australian Aboriginal Studies* No. 2, 54–8.

KALANTZIS, Mary, COPE, Bill and SLADE, Diana 1989, *Minority Languages and Dominant Culture*. London: Falmer.

KLARBERG, Fred 1987, The gift of tongues is becoming an appreciating asset. *The Age* June 15, 3.

LO BIANCO, Joseph 1987, *National Policy on Languages*. Canberra: Australian Government Publishing Service.

— 1989, *Victoria: Language Action Plan*. Melbourne: Ministry of Education.

LOVEDAY, P. (ed.) 1982, *Service Delivery to Outstations*. Darwin: Australian National University/North Australia Research Unit.

LUDWIG, Klemens 1985, *Bedröhte Völker: Ein Lexicon natsionaler und religiöser Minderheiten*. Munich: Beck.

MCALLISTER, Ian 1986, Speaking the language; language maintenance and English proficiency among immigrant youth in Australia. *Ethnic and Racial Studies* 9, 24–42.

MATTINGLEY, Christobel and HAMPTON, Kenneth (eds) 1988, *Survival in Our Own Land; Aboriginal Experiences in South Australia Since 1836; Told by Nungas and Others*. Cowandilla: Wakefield.

NATIONAL ADVISORY AND COORDINATING COMMITTEE ON MULTICULTURAL EDUCATION 1987, *Education in and for a Multicultural Society: Issues and Strategies for Policy Making*. Canberra: NACCME.

PAUWELS, Anne (ed.) 1988, The future of ethnic languages in Australia. *International Journal of the Sociology of Language*, No. 72 (entire issue).

PRIOR, John and WUNUNGMURRA, Wali 1987, *Aboriginal Employment in Homelands and Outstations*. Casuarina: Northern Territory Open College/Department of Education.

REYBURN, Bruce 1988, The forgotten struggle of Australia's Aboriginal people. *Cultural Survival Quarterly* 12, No. 3, 7–10.

SENATE STANDING COMMITTEE ON EDUCATION AND THE ARTS 1984, *A National Language Policy*. Canberra: Parliament of the Commonwealth of Australia/Australian Government Publishing Service.

SPURR, Russell 1988, Australia goes Asian. *New York Times Magazine*, December 4, 46–9, 52 and 56.

TEREZAKIS, Maria D. 1982, *The Content of Three Sydney Based Ethnic Newspapers*. Sydney: Macquarie University and Department of Immigration and Ethnic Affairs.

THIEBERGER, Nicholas 1988, *Aboriginal Language Maintenance: Some Issues and Strategies*. La Trobe University, Masters Thesis.

VON TESMAR, Johannes 1988, Die Schule der kleinen Raupen; Die 'Yiprinya School' der Aborigines hat sich durchgesetzt. *pogrom: Zeitschrift für bedröhte Völker* 19, No. 141, 40–1.

WURM, Stephen and HATTORI, Shiro 1981, *Language Atlas: Pacific*. Canberra: Australian Academy of the Humanities, and Tokyo: Japanese Academy.

# 10 Three Success Stories (More or Less): Modern Hebrew, French in Quebec and Catalan in Spain

The nine problematic cases that we have reviewed in previous chapters are by no means all at the same stage of endangerment; indeed, one or two may yet pull out of the endangered category rather completely by the end of the next century (ultra-Orthodox Yiddish and Spanish in particular parts of the USA being the ones that seem most likely to do so, with Navajo, on the one hand, and Basque or Frisian, on the other hand, being rather close behind). Nevertheless, it is fitting to bring our examination of cases to a close by considering three language-and-culture settings which have already done just that: they have traversed the most sensitive and dangerous sections of the difficult path from 'essentially problematic' to 'essentially non-problematic' within the lifetimes of individuals still alive today, sometimes doing so within the course of only one or two generations.

As has been our practice thus far, in our discussion of problematic cases, we will pick our success cases from different parts of the world, one from the Near East (Hebrew), one from the Americas (French in Quebec) and one from Europe (Catalan), although as we will soon see, all three cases have been strongly influenced by European thinking, values, methods and developments. This is an inevitable state of affairs, to the extent that RLS-efforts are often a reflection of late or reactive nationalism and modernization, worldwide processes that are overwhelmingly characterized by dynamics that have their origins and their mainsprings in Europe. Even the return to ultra-Orthodoxy can be partially characterized in this fashion, overtly and consciously rejective of modernization though it be, since it too has learned that the modern world can be held at bay and an essentially authentic minority ethnicity can be maintained with respect to its language-and-culture nexus, only if some of modernity's techniques and methods are selectively and carefully borrowed and even more carefully controlled.

However, similar though these three cases may be in several respects, two errors must be guarded against in discussing their successful RLS-efforts. One is the error of *post hoc ergo propter hoc* reasoning, an error which leads to the mistaken assumption that these three cases could not possibly have failed, i.e. that 'somehow' they 'obviously' had 'success written into their futures' from the very outset because they were never 'really' threatened at all. Were this to be true, there would be nothing to be gained — in so far as building a more generalizable theory and practice of RLS — from examining them. But we must not allow ourselves to be misled by the dubious wisdom of hindsight. Each of these three cases *could* have turned out differently, far less happily, and, indeed, there are still today individuals and organized groups who believe that RLS has not yet fully succeeded in connection with each of them and who worry that the language that is of greatest concern to them is by no means yet 'free' and 'clear'.

Another, equally misleading error, would be to assume that these are the *only* three success cases that *could* have been discussed because there *are* no others. This is patently untrue. The past century is full of success cases, although the roster of failures is not only longer (because RLS is after all difficult to attain and too few have paused to consider, in conceptually integrated terms, what exactly the nature of the difficulty may be or how best to overcome it) but it is also better known (because untrammeled modernization trumpets the failure of RLS, considering such failures to be a vindication of the vulgar myth of modernization as uniformation pure and simple). From the promotion of Guarani to the standardization and defense of Faroese, from the intellectual and elitist revernacularization of Czech to the intellectual modernization and repertoire expansion of Ukrainian, from the unification and dignification of Landsmal to the planned maintenance and cultivation of Sorbian, from the elaboration and functional implementation of Papiamentu to the formation and popular vernacularization of Indonesian, and, more generally, from the rescue of manifold 'doomed' peasant vernaculars to their establishment as languages of literacy and governmental or co-governmental functions, the list is long and distinguished and a testimony to human ingenuity and determination. Successful RLS is part of the pursuit of meaningful identity and the attainment of a cultural future related to one's own cultural past and in accord with one's own definition of what the relationship between the past and the future should be. There is much more successful RLS than smugly provincial modern world knows or cares to know.

The three success cases that will now be presented are presented precisely because there is much to learn from them in connection with RLS-efforts more generally, as well as particularly, encompassing as they do efforts on behalf of a language that was no longer spoken, a language that was still generally spoken but that was no longer literacy, related, and a language generally still widely spoken and read but faced by an opponent contextually very much stronger than it in the world of social mobility, worldwide econotechnical power and modern youth culture.

# Historical Background (Prior to the Beginning of RLS-Efforts)

## The 'miraculous' case of Hebrew

Prior to the beginning of focused efforts on behalf of its vernacularization, toward the very end of the nineteenth century, Hebrew had been successfully passed along generation after generation, for over 2,000 years, as the chief language of formal Jewish prayer, of sacred texts, of rabbinic responsa and of other erudite writing. The degree of facility in *textual* Hebrew acquired by the typical, traditional Jewish male during all of this time varied with *social class* (the Jewish poor — constituting the vast bulk of the population — could not generally afford, or be afforded, the luxury of devoting the endless time to textual study from the age of four or five onward, that such mastery required), *sex* (as a rule, females were either not provided with entré into the textual world of Hebrew at all, or, at most, they were assured only the rudiments of rote prayer-book recitation), and *Orthodoxy* (in those communities, primarily in Western Europe, that experienced early modernization, most educated males typically lost, within the period of a generation or two, their familiarity with, rather than only their devotion to, the vast body of Hebrew-Aramic sacred texts and their accompanying two millennia's worth of worldwide rabbinic commentaries and responsa).

While it is true that the most adept (generally rabbis and other males who had studied through to the level of actual or potential rabbinic ordination) could read and write Hebrew freely within the bounds of traditional subject matter, and that, in the nineteenth century, a few generations of the more modernized among them could use the language in a variety of modern literary genres (secular poetry, essays, journalistic reporting, short stories and novels), it is also true that even they could not and did not converse in that language about the normal rounds and concerns of everyday life. Of course, there were rare occasions when strained conversation utilizing spoken-Hebrew-as-a-lingua-franca did occur, when two Jews met who shared neither a Jewish nor a non-Jewish vernacular (e.g. a Jew from Fez and a Jew from Odessa), but such occasions were both exceedingly rare and exceedingly trying. Indeed, even among the late nineteenth-century modernists and Zionists who agitated on behalf of the spread of modern Hebrew for secular purposes, there were many (including the most illustrious among them, such as Nathan Birnbaum and Theodore Herzl in Western Europe and Moshe-Leyb Lilienblum, Perets Smolenskin and and Akhad Ha-am in Eastern Europe) who did not believe that the vernacularization of Hebrew was readily possible, or who believed that its accomplishment was likely only in the distant future, or who were opposed to it in principle.[1] Within the heartland of unreconstructed Orthodoxy itself, the opposition to vernacularization was well-nigh unanimous into the twentieth century proper, that is, through to the time

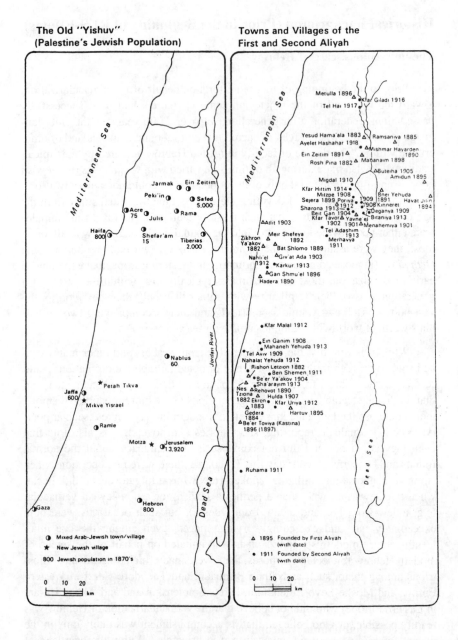

FIGURE 10.1 *Jews in Ottoman Palestine during the pre-Zionist ('Old Yishuv')*
*and the early Zionist periods ('First and Second Aliyahs'), when the functions of*
*Hebrew were changing.* (*Source*: Carta and Aumann, 1983).

that the language had already begun to be revernacularized under modern, Eastern European-derived, secularist auspices among Zionist settlers in Palestine; and, indeed, it is still opposed in some of these circles to this very day.

Thus the RLS problem for Hebrew was one of revernacularizing a language of sanctity and/or literacy. For this largely unprecedented goal to be attained[2] a modern, European-derived and deeply Herderian-influenced language-and-nationality movement had to be formed, one pursuing vital political goals above and beyond language but uncompromisingly opposed to the vibrant Jewish vernaculars then spoken in the diaspora (first and foremost among them Yiddish), as well as to the prestigious world languages familiar to the diaspora Jewish world, a movement which could tear people away from their prior habitual life-patterns and speech-patterns and establish separate settlements in which the old-new language could be consensually vernacularized, not only by those who had no prior vernacular (the very young) but, more essentially, by multilingual adults who had the mettle to persuade themselves and one another to increasingly set their other, very lively vernaculars aside in favor of a still rather stilted Hebrew.

Viewed in this light, what was required, and what was ultimately accomplished, was not some 'miraculous' intervention of the spirit of Jewish election or exceptionality, but, rather, the rare and largely fortuitous co-occurrence of language-and-nationality ideology, disciplined collective will and sufficient societal dislocation from other competing influences to make possible a relatively *rapid and clean break with prior norms of verbal interaction*, both with respect to Hebrew[3] as well as with respect to all other languages in the community's speech repertoire, Jewish and non-Jewish alike. What was ultimately accomplished was not merely the vernacularization of Hebrew but also its re-standardization, its secularization and its association with the entire life-experience of both sexes, rather than only those of males alone. Given the rampant detraditionalization (indeed, anti-clericalism and secular modernization) of the time and of the subsequent half-century, and given the Holocaust that occurred within that period, anything less than *all* of the above startling co-occurrences would have left Hebrew as merely the literacy-bound language of an exotic elite, rather than as the language of a modern and varied nationality and its nation-state.

# French in Quebec and Catalan in the Autonomous Catalan Community

## The spectre that haunts francophone Quebec

French in Quebec and Catalan in the Autonomous Catalan may be seen as characterized by differing degrees of what are fundamentally the same

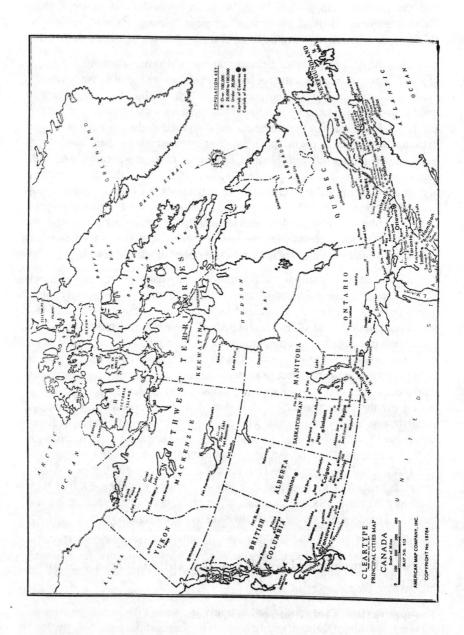

FIGURE 10.2 *Quebec in the Canadian Confederation.*

threatening circumstances: the in-migration of politically more powerfully-connected speakers of languages of broader econotechnical opportunities, on the one hand, and the struggle to engage in RLS-efforts over the opposition of the larger political entity in which they themselves are but a minority. In both instances, the languages in question not only have considerable prestige in their own right and in connection with the highest cultural functions but, at the time that their most recent RLS phase got underway, they had successfully continued to be the spoken, everyday tongues of the bulk of their ethnonational populations. Thus, it was no longer the threat of spoken or even written replacement that threatened them, but, rather, their growing functional displacement in the most statusful pursuits and symbols of government, economy and modern, international mass culture, on the one hand, and the inability to make them co-vernaculars of their respective immigrants, on the other hand.

When Quebec-French RLS-efforts got seriously underway in the late 60s and early 70s, francophones were still over 90% of the total population of the province. Although no disabling legislation had ever been passed against French, nevertheless, only 64% of the francophone labour-force was working at entirely French-speaking jobs. In addition, the more specialized, higher paying, prestigious work sphere was were even more disproportionately in English. To some extent, this was a reflection of the fact that only 7% of francophones had completed university education, whereas over 20% of anglophones in the province had done so. However, even with the same education, anglophones also secured better jobs than francophones did and received better salaries for the same jobs. Indeed, it was totally unimportant for anglophones to learn French at work; it simply didn't result in any wage differential for them. However, a francophone who mastered English and became English-speaking at work immediately earned a sizeable bonus as a result. All in all, the income discrepancy between francophones and anglophones was not only sizeable but it was growing, and francophones were increasingly convinced that unless they could have a government that could tip the scales in their favor economically and culturally, unless they became 'the masters of their own house', they would wind up increasingly disadvantaged socially, economically and culturally in a province in which they were historically and demographically the huge majority.[4] The ultimate francophone language shift horror was not hard to imagine: francophone parents were becoming more concerned about their children's mastery of English than their mastery of French.

How had such a sad state of affairs come into being? An increasing number of French-speaking Quebecers had become convinced, during the 60s, that this was due to conscious exploitation and connivance by American and anglophone-Canadian economic and political leaders, on the one hand, and by the dereliction of their own traditional francophone leaders, on the other hand (both of which were interpreted as long-standing grievances or disadvantages). The Catholic church that had traditionally provided the cultural leadership of Quebec's French-speaking society had emphasized the traditional virtues of family, community and agricultural life, to such an extent that the urban economy was left in anglophone hands, even though the politicians elected to office were themselves primarily francophones. The provincial government of Quebec and the city government of its major metropolis, Montreal, lacked any semblance of a cultural policy and seemed unperturbed at the secondary role of francophones in economic and even in cultural life at either level. The small separatist parties, receiving no more than 6% of the vote in 1966 and perhaps with no more than twice that number of sympathizers, nevertheless found wide and rapidly growing sympathy for their view that the cards were hopelessly stacked against Quebec in an anglo-dominated Canada (and North America) and that francophones were little more than 'the White Niggers of America' (a popular expression which captures all of the nuances of 'internal colonization'), laughed at, looked down upon, exploited and headed for cultural annihilation in their own region.[5] Although there were francophone leaders who cautioned that unbridled nationalism would only exacerbate the economic plight of under-industrialized French Canada and that its cultural authenticity could be safeguarded and fostered without interethnic confrontation and cultural politics,[6] both of the latter developments increasingly came to the fore. At least three factors contributed pervasively and recurringly to the alarm of the Quebecois (Bourhis and Lepicq, 1990): the decline of francophone society in the rest of Canada, making Quebec the last possible major line of defense for French in all of Canada and, indeed, in all of North America, the growing preference for English among non-anglophones immigrants to Quebec (requiring some governmental regulation in the realms of school and work if it was to be reversed, particularly in the light of the falling francophone birthrate in the province) and, finally, the galloping anglophone domination of Quebec's economic activity (fostering a transfer to English, in this domain, among francophones aspiring to social mobility). In each of these connections French increasingly became the symbol and the medium of francophone self-regulatory needs and aspirations, eliciting, in the process, much anglophone opposition, anguish and alarm.

Ever since Federal troops were used to arrest and imprison several hundred independentist 'terrorists' in 1970 (almost all of whom were ultimately released on suspended charges or on lesser charges), and although the vote for separation has never risen above 40% or so, the sentiment for a 'separate (francophone) society' in Quebec, regulating and fostering its own cultural and economic destiny in an openly francophone direction, has continued to attract overwhelming francophone support. One of the major planks in this program is the francization of Quebec's educational, cultural and economic life so as to guarantee that French language and culture will dominate in the province, as befits its historical and its demographic importance there. The model of political independence is latent in the ethnocultural and linguistic solutions that are sought and adopted, not only by the 'Parti quebecois' but by almost all other major parties seeking large and stable constituencies in Quebec. The image of a threat to the dominance of the French language in Quebec, surrounded as it is by a sea of English from within and from without Canada, is the constant spectre that animates these solutions at the grass-roots level and that obtains massive popular support for them.[7] In this context, French, the home, neighborhood and community continuity of which were most probably never really objectively threatened to begin with, has clearly taken center stage, at least emotionally and symbolically, and has become the major rallying call on the Quebec scene, definitely appealing to all those who strive to francicize the most powerful networks and functions of the life of the Province.

### The dilemma that confounds Catalonia: distinguishing between Spanish pressure without and Spanish pressure within

It is frequently forgotten (or entirely unrecognized) that, after the Soviet Union, Spain constitutes the most populous *economically developed multilingual country in the world* and the oldest multilingual state in the world, predating even the Swiss confederation in that respect. Similarly forgotten or overlooked, is the fact that the Catalan contribution to both of these circumstances is and has long been the major one. Catalonia (today's Autonomous Catalan Community) has far outdistanced the Autonomous Basque Community in its RLS-efforts and in the success of its language emphases more generally. Indeed, the absence of any headlines about terrorism and a penchant for quiet, unpublicized but effective efforts, have generally obscured from the world at large the fact that Catalan was once (from the thirteenth to the sixteenth century) the language of a considerable Mediterranean empire and that, outside of Catalonia proper, it is still substantially spoken today (and also co-official) in the Autonomous Valencian Community, in the Balearic Islands, in the French Departement of Pyrenees-Orientales (often referred to as the French Roussillon), and in Andorra (where it is the official language) and in the city of l'Alguer in Sardinia.

RLS-efforts in contemporary Catalonia are substantially motivated by the long and proud historical record of undoubted cultural, political and commercial-industrial accomplishments associated with the Catalan language during prior centuries. Catalan was standardized in grammar and in spelling as far back as the medieval period and its earliest surviving texts, significantly

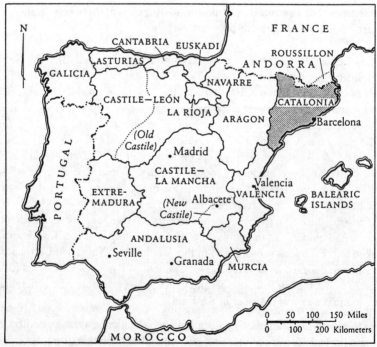

FIGURE 10.3 *The Autonomous Catalan Community and the other Catalan-speaking areas: the Balearic Islands, Roussillon, Andorra and (not shown) the city of Alguer (in Sardinia)* (*Source*: Woolard, 1989).

enough, pertain to non-fictional prose, reflecting the fact that as early as the thirteenth century almost all governmental units had set aside Latin and, instead, utilized Catalan as their language of official record. The first European feudal code in a vernacular, the oldest European maritime code, the first Romance language to be used in science and philosophy, all of these distinctions pertain to Catalan, a language which also enjoyed an uninterrupted record of solid middle- and upper middle-class vernacular use, even during the nineteenth and twentieth centuries, when Spanish (usually referred to as Castilian) finally made serious inroads into all formal domains. In fact, by the twentieth century Catalan has become such an established and beloved symbol of local self-sufficiency (even regional superiority in commerce and industry) and regional resistance to central (Madridian) regulation and obstructionism, that the beleaguered Second Spanish Republic found it advantageous to grant Catalan co-official status (1932), when Catalonia itself was granted a Statute of Autonomy. Little wonder then that Catalonia became a bulwark of the Republic (along with the Basque Country), against the Franco-led rightist insurrection of 1936–1939 which aspired to re-establish a strongly centralized Spanish rule.[8]

Immediately following upon its Civil War victory the Franco-government instituted policies that deprived Catalonia, its culture and its language of any public semblance of their prior independence and recognition. Catalonia's auton-omy was annulled and the region itself was administered from Madrid as four separate provinces. All public use of Catalan was prohibited; Catalan names and toponyms were banned and replaced by Spanish counterparts; Catalan publica-tions, street signs and advertisements or notices were not only discontinued but any disobedience with respect to these prohibitions was punishable (and pun-ished!) by fine, dismissal, arrest and the closing of offending publications, insti-tutions or agencies. The anti-Catalan campaign was so extreme that even ordinary conversational use of the language among ordinary folk could prove to be dangerous, if overheard. The formerly proud language was officially humbled by being declared a 'mere dialect' and those who used it were described in offi-cial propaganda as either 'barking like dogs' or as 'non-Christian'. Only after 20 years of such abuse did the situation begin to ease slowly, as minor, grudging concessions began to be made to the strong popular support and quasi-legal use (particularly in the Church and in the political songs movement known as *Nova Cançó Catalana*) that the language nevertheless enjoyed 'off the record'. Neverthless, there was as much foot-dragging as possible even in this respect and the *implementation* of a 1970 education law which once again permitted the teaching *of* (but still not the teaching *in*) Catalan to children (the teaching of Catalan to adults having already been permitted, in a very few carefully circum-scribed settings, during the 60s) was delayed until 1975, the year in which Franco died.[9]

While the repressive policy of the central authorities had an undeniably negative impact on Catalan use and even on Catalan competence (e.g. an entire generation went through school without any opportunity to acquire or polish Catalan literacy, a limitation that has very recognizable consequences to this very day among most older Catalans), an indirect development of those same years has had even more massive and more devastating consequences for the language. Catalonia had long been one of the most economically advanced areas of Spain and, as a result, its cities (most particularly Barcelona) had long attracted unemployed Spaniards from the rest of the country. These immigrants came in numbers that did not demographically swamp the indigenous (or indigenized) Catalans, and within a generation or more the latest newcomers too were recurringly Catalanized. Indeed, this was part of the uniqueness of Catalonia's relationship with the Castilian 'center'. For generations, the Catalan 'periphery' continued to be economically more advanced than the 'center' and, accordingly, it not only attracted manpower from all over the country (but, particularly, from the impoverished agricultural south of Spain) but it ethnolinguistically transformed those immigrants into its own image. However, the immigration that transpired between 1950 and 1975 was so huge, relative to Catalonia's absorptive capacity, that the rather effortless and rapid ethnolinguistic transformation of its members that had formerly been the rule was no longer possible.[10]

The *economic* consequences of the rapid addition of nearly one and a half million unskilled immigrants to the previous two and a half million 'native Catalans' were not seriously problematic ones for the host population. Indeed, as the newcomers filled the plentiful lower order positions that the booming economy provided, the old-timers quickly moved up into better-paying technical or administrative positions. However, the *cultural and intercultural* consequences became doubly problematic as social class differences compounded the ethnolinguistic differences separating the two populations. Even now, decades after the end of massive immigration (an immigration that would have been even larger had not whole trainloads of newcomers been turned back prior to their arrival) only slightly more than half of the adult population of Catalonia habitually speaks Catalan, a percentage which is halved again in the immigrant 'industrial belt' surrounding Barcelona where Spanish-speaking newcomers and their children, many of the latter born in Catalonia, are overwhelmingly concentrated. Only some 40% pupils attending primary *public* schools in Barcelona are native speakers of Catalan; however, in the *private* schools of the area such speakers are the overwhelming majority. Barcelona proper (as distinct from its 'factory belt') continues to boast one of the highest standards of living in Spain, but those immigrants who are least satisfied economically also have the highest birthrate and are the most likely to cling to Spanish as the medium of their of their everyday life and, therefore, also as the medium of their dissatisfaction with their lot in life.[11]

Catalan RLS-efforts began in earnest with the granting of autonomy by the post-Franco government in 1979. It is three pronged. One of its goals is to attain the symbolic promotion and the functional institutionalization of Catalan in connection with all of the most influential and powerful arenas of modern life. Another of its goals is to overcome the legacy of mother-tongue illiteracy and inferiority that many native, middle-class Catalans have inherited from the Franco years and which even today makes them disinclined to read much in Catalan, to use it with strangers (or even with each other when strangers are present) or with officials. Finally, they aim at activating the passive Catalan that Spanish speakers quickly acquire, due to the basic similarity between the two languages, and at fostering among these speakers a fondness for and an identification with Catalan. In the latter connection, RLS-efforts also seek to counteract any feelings that Spanish speakers may harbor to the effect that Spanish, the nationwide official language ('the language of the Spanish state') and a language which is also specifically protected in that state's very grant of autonomy to Catalonia, is being slighted or subordinated. Of the three success cases that we are considering in this chapter, the revernacularization of Hebrew may have been the most difficult and improbable feat to achieve (considering that it depended on voluntary efforts on a meager demographic base and without any governmental authority at all behind it), but the triple balancing act of Catalan RLS-efforts is, today, as these words are being written, undoubtedly the most difficult one of all.

## The Major RLS-efforts That Were Undertaken on Behalf of Hebrew, French in Quebec and Catalan During the Initial Period of the Gravest Threat to Them

### Hebrew

The initial problem faced by those few that sought to revernacularize Hebrew was a complex one in that daily conversational use of Hebrew could not occur unless traditonal Jewish multilingualism could be overcome, on the one hand, and unless the Hebrew language itself could be modernized and standardized, on the other hand. Eliezer Ben-Yehuda, the widely acclaimed 'father of the revival of Hebrew' probably contributed more to the solution of the latter corpus-planning problem than to the solution of the former, more fundamental status-planning issue. Even in connection with corpus planning, the extent of Ben-Yehuda's effective contributions have probably been greatly exaggerated.

His dictionary came out in alphabetic bits and drabs over a period of decades and was liberally sprinkled with esoteric neologisms that found little favor in the eyes of the actual or prospective community of Hebrew speakers. His Hebrew Language Committee, out of which the illustrious Hebrew Language Academy later developed, was long dormant or inoperative during the very heart of the revernacularization period and, even when active, was excruciatingly slow, pedantic, indecisive and argumentative in its operation. Both his *Complete Dictionary of Ancient and Modern Hebrew* (gathered together from the original newspaper entries in which it had originally appeared over a long period of years and, belatedly, published in book format from 1940 to 1953, such publication coming two full generations after revernacularization had been clearly accomplished) and the Academy were better suited to their roles of *post hoc* symbols of the revernacularization, rather than to functioning as active ingredients, much less causes, of the vernacularization proper, even in the limited corpus-planning area to which they pertain.[12]

If Ben-Yehuda was an ineffective corpus-planner, he was an absolute disaster as a status-planner. A rather eccentric and acerbic character, who rather isolated himself from the new, young, Zionist settlers by living in ultra-religious and linguistically heterogeneous Jerusalem, he was doubly removed from the daily trials and tribulations of modern, secular, Zionist cultural life as it was developing in the new, more homogeneous agricultural settlements in the plains, closer to the Mediterranean coast. His own view of the revernacularization was, understandably, egocentric and revealed no real understanding at all on his part of the social or societal dynamics that were involved and had to be cultivated for revernacularization to occur. He did, however, become the personal symbol of Hebrew as a modern, secular language, a language that defined a modern, secular people.[13]

The teachers and the schools of the new Zionist settlements established during the very first years of this century, twenty-some years after Ben-Yehuda's arrival in Palestine, have also been nominated for the role of prime-movers-and-shakers of the revernacularization of Hebrew. Their ideological commitment, personal example, and pedagogical success (particularly in teaching Hebrew itself as well as all other school subjects via Hebrew, for the first time after two millennia of Hebrew study via other media of instruction) purportedly carried the day, persuading their charges to speak only Hebrew to each other within the four walls of the school and enabling them soon to do so outside of the school itself. Once the pupils carried the language outside of the school, into their after-school life with each other, it was presumably merely a step for them to bring it home and to teach it to their parents. Finally, when these pupils later married one another they then raised the first modern children for whom revernacularized Hebrew was the mother tongue.[14]

Although there is much to be said for the above reconstructed scenario, particularly its focus on stages 6 and 4, it is obviously a gross simplification and idealization of a more complex and a more multi-directional process. If the teachers were really the first to break with the norms which had required Yiddish (or another vernacular) as the language of school instruction, they could hardly be considered free agents in this respect. They were the instructional *and the child-rearing agents* of a very highly ideologized community of pro-Hebrew settlers who generally strongly approved of such action on the part of the teachers and who were actively engaged in Hebrew language learning themselves and, in many cases, even in limited-to-fluent Hebrew language use among themselves. A good proportion of these particular settlers constituted the renowned 'second aliyah', whose members arrived in 1903–1904 and particularly from 1905 to World War I, and who came voluntarily, without being driven out by Czarist pogroms. Many of them had begun speaking Hebrew to each other (usually only occasionally and haltingly, but in some cases with real facility) even while they were still in Russia, prior to their departure for Palestine. They were, of course, very eager to speak Hebrew in Palestine proper and to raise and educate their children in that language, and they made sure to appoint specialists to assist with and to supervise child-rearing in Hebrew from the very earliest days of their children's lives.

Thus, there were clearly many settlers who not only applauded and reinforced the vernacularization undertaken by their children in and out of school, and many families exerted themselves to use Hebrew with their own and with other children much before the latter married and produced children of their own. Finally, subsequent children born to parents whose prior child(ren) had been among the original vernacularizers, almost certainly encountered spoken Hebrew at home, before coming to school and much before the older siblings were of marriageable age. Thus, what was undoubtedly involved was a family–'children's home'–settlement interaction, all going on under rather unified and intense ideological and motivational circumstances, in appreciably self-contained settings that had little interaction with or admiration for their surrounding non-Zionist environments, whether Jewish or gentile, or whether relatively nearby or in far-off Jerusalem.[15] However, if the process of revernacularization within the new settlements of young and committed 'true believers' was a relatively rapid and generally unconflicted one, the process of influencing the rest of Jewish Palestine, particularly the heterogeneous urban centers with their urgent need for an immediately operational and expressive *lingua franca*, with their ideologically different belief systems, some of them (the ultra-Orthodox in particular) strongly opposed to Zionism as well as to the vernacularization of Hebrew, and with their constant influx of refugees coming for asylum rather than Zionist-Hebraist ideological conviction, was a rather long, tedious and often bitter one. However, by the late teens or mid-twenties of this century at the very latest, the revernacularization of Hebrew in the settlements was generally completed (except among the very oldest residents, some of whom never acquired fluency in Hebrew) and the more difficult and far slower task of ver-nacularizing Hebrew among Jewish Palestine's *urban* population began to come to the fore.

## French in Quebec

The (Quebec) Liberal Party that was swept into power in 1960 was the standard-bearer of a 'Quiet Revolution' pursuing modernization, secularization, industrialization and urbanization. These goals aimed at overcoming the eco-nomic backwardness of French Quebec and its entrenched sense of grievance and powerlessness over not being taken seriously or handled fairly by the nine English-speaking provinces of Canada. The 'Quiet Revolution' accomplished much along objective lines, but still left most francophone intellectuals and many ordinary laymen distinctly uneasy and dissatisfied on many fronts. Most of industry and real power in Montreal was still English-controlled. Furthermore, and most crucially insofar as RLS is concerned, the very processes championed by the 'Quiet Revolution' tended to weaken and undermine the dis-tinctive cultural character of French Quebecois life and threatened to make it indistinguishable from the anglophone society which dominated it. Immigrants from Europe and the Third World, sensing the underlying anglophone control of the local opportunity system and its links to the USA (and, therefore, to the lan-guage of the USA), elected English as the language of their own social mobility and of their children's education. De Gaulle's provocative salutation, during his 1967 visit to Montreal world's fair, '*Vive le Quebec libre*', elicited an enthusias-tic response from the crowd that had come to greet him, but it was far from clear what '*libre*' might imply or how to go about achieving that status. The crisis of a hitherto largely rural-based and traditionally religious French culture in con-frontation with a galloping modernization, a process which was not under appre-ciable francophone direction or control, inevitably highlighted language as the flexible, all-encompassing symbol of the combined authenticity, modernization and self-direction that appeared to be necessary for the crisis to be solved.

Although Italian immigrants in Montreal were among the most francized 'new Canadians' in Montreal, they nevertheless overwhelmingly elected English or bilingual (English and French) education for their children. When the trustees of the Saint Leonard School Board tried to reverse this trend by adopting a resolution making French the only language of schooling within its district (1968), a serious riot developed in the streets of Montreal between

Italian Canadians and francophone Montrealers. The bitterness of the latter at being rejected, not only by the anglophones but even by lowly recent arrivals many of whom lived in francophone areas and competed with francophones for employment, was not really assuaged by a 1969 law (Bill 63) which made a few symbolic overtures toward the francophones (e.g. French was declared to be an obligatory second language in non-francophone schools and the soon to be famous or infamous, depending on one's point of view 'Office de la langue francaise' was created to be the watchdog in this connection as well as in connection with the Bill's rather unspecified intentions to 'promote French as a language of work'). More basically, however, Bill 63 disappointed many francophones grievously, as far as their altercation with the 'new Canadians' and their fears for the anglification of francophones were concerned, by establishing freedom of language choice in education.

Francophone efforts to improve their control over their own lives, cultural- ly, politically and economically, began to be more holistic in the 70s. Although the relatively new and independentist 'Parti quebecois' obtained an astounding 24% of the vote in 1970 (a huge turnout for a party constituted only two years earlier), the major event of the year was the kidnapping and murder of Quebec's Labour Minister by a the Front de Libération du Québec, a minuscule group modeled after the urban guerrillas in Latin America and other Third World locales. The (Canadian) Prime Minister's implementation of the War Measures Act in Quebec (with its suspension of civil rights, the 'occupation' of Montreal by the Canadian Army, and the ultimate negotiations for the release of a second governmental kidnap victim in exchange for safe passage to Cuba for the kid- nappers) did more to promote the cause of Quebec independence than anything else that the minority movement on behalf of such independence had accom- plished on its own. Before leaving power, the Liberal-Party-dominated provin- cial government did pass one bill that gratified francophone cultural aspirations. Bill 22 (1974), a replacement for the earlier Bill 63 (1969), made French the official language of Quebec (rather than merely the frequently overlooked co- official language that it had been since long before) and required immigrant chil- dren to prove that they were English-dominant before they could claim the right to English schooling that indigenous anglophone children had always had.[16] With the coming to power of the pro-independence 'Parti quebecois' in 1976, by attracting fully 40% of the votes cast, the stage was set for the next round in the struggle 'to safeguard the French nature of Quebec'.

In retrospect, it seems clear why in a province with a huge francophone majority and where the family-home-community nexus was already safely French, the struggle of that majority on behalf of the community's language and culture would immediately be waged in the political arena pertaining to the work sphere, mass media and governmental operations. The political arena was one that francophones had always controlled numerically anyway, even before their concerns for governmental intervention on behalf of fostering the dominance and direction of their own modernization-and-culture had come to the fore. Intellectuals would argue, and still do,[17] as to whether there was really any productive solution to 'the French problem', i.e. as to whether modernization under any auspices wouldn't inevitably lead to increased interaction with anglo-Canada, with the USA and with the English-language-dominated modern world economy as a whole, a world economy in which no fully distinctive ethnocultures were presumably possible; whether francophone attempts to safeguard their language and culture were not really disguises used by self-seeking intellectuals and an upcoming francophone econotechnical elite in order to stampede the francophone electorate into ever-more extreme nationalist postures aimed at wresting economic control away from a variety of anglo sources of power. Many francophones might even grant some of the above arguments, but they would still generally opt for the promotion of local enterprises controlled by francophones, for the displacement of an anglophone bureaucracy by a francophone one, for greater francophone control over communications and over the mass diffusion of art and culture, and for francophone symbolic domination of all avenues of cultural and economic life in 'their own province'. As that mood became ever more dominant, whether out of resignation *vis-à-vis* the cultural outcomes of the modernization dilemma or out of genuine hope and anticipation for a more francophone reality for themselves and their children, additional steps on behalf of French and in curtailment of English were obviously in the offing as the initial period of greatest danger was left behind and new goals, going beyond mere 'survival in the surrounding ocean of English', were set.

## Catalan

Forty years of repression and degradation by the Franco regime left Autonomous Catalonia with an immediate RLS agenda: the elevation of Catalan and its rightful restoration to all of the most powerful and symbolic functions and processes of modern society. The first and immediate interpretation of RLS was a full-fledged effort to restore Catalan to its old glories as a language of education, of the print and non-print media and of the uppermost reaches of regional government. Book production, which had slowly crept upward during the Franco years (as that regime's originally uncompromising strictures were slowly, very slowly, worn away at the edges), quickly jumped over 300% (from 579 volumes in 1974 to 2,149 in 1981). '[Linguistic] recycling' courses were set up for civil servants, free translations, from Spanish into Catalan, of all public documents were provided, terminologies were prepared in many administrative fields and *recuperacio* (= recovery) of Catalan's earlier 'normal' roles in public domains became the order of the day. Although the *de facto* implementation of Catalan in education proceeded slowly (due to ever so many practical problems pertaining to teachers, texts and curricula) the *de jure* declaration of Catalan as compulsory in primary and secondary education came immediately. Similarly, time on television and radio, space in periodicals (particularly dailies) and presence in cinema films initially increased only slowly, if at all, primarily because most of the major outlets in each of these media were nationwide in scope or in sponsorship. However, progress began to be made in these respects as well, and the founding of all-Catalan or partly-Catalan counterpart outlets slowly took effect and, ultimately, vastly speeded up the entire momentum of RLS.

A 'Charter of the Catalan Language' (also known as the 'Law of Linguistic Normalization') was adopted in 1983 and established parity for Catalan and Spanish in all governmentally encumbered domains, and, in addition, provided specifically for a separate governmental institution dedicated to fostering the use and knowledge of Catalan, the 'Directorate General of Language Policy'. All in all, the first interpretation of 'normalization' required a massive 'operation catch-up' for Catalan insofar as public functions were concerned.[18] This interpretation sought to overcome among native Catalans the deleterious effects of the diglossic pattern that had begun under 'central' (Madridian) economic and cultural pressure well before Franco and that had become even further ingrained during the fascist regime, a pattern that normatively assigned Spanish to literacy, formality and status, and Catalan to little more than domestic and intimate use.

However, even before major decisive victories could be gained in connection with 'normalization of the first kind', a second set of priorities *vis-à-vis* 'normalization' of another kind was not long in coming to the fore. In this connection it came to be recognized that the huge number of Spanish-speaking immigrants could legally exercise their constitutional rights to remain such permanently, utilizing little or no Catalan in their daily lives, thereby, providing Catalan with a constant built-in rival, competitor and threat within the very heart of Catalonia, a threat that exerted a mighty influence on native Catalans themselves and their ability or inclination to pursue 'normalization of the first kind'. The goal of 'normalization of the second kind', therefore, was to encourage Spanish speakers to activate their passive Catalan, so as to speak, read and write it more, primarily by building on their good will toward Catalan and Catalonia as a former opponent of the fascist state and their desire to identify with and feel at home among Catalans. There were now too many of these newcomers, and they were too concentrated residentially and too marked by social class distinctions to be able to count on exogamy or social mobility *per se* as providing foreseeable solutions to their meager use of Catalan. Accordingly, at the same time that 'normalization of the first kind' might persuade Catalans to use more Catalan with one another and with the immigrants and their children, special efforts were instituted to help more of these same immigrants to actively and affectively adopt Catalan as their own language.

In 1982, a 'man in the street' normalization campaign, aimed primarily at reversing Catalan backsliding and immigrant reticence, adopted the slogan '*El catala, cosa de tots*' ('Catalan belongs to everyone'). This sentiment was personified, in poster, newspaper ads and in radio and TV spot commercials, by a winsome ten-year-old cartoon character, 'Norma' (for 'normalization') who, by constant, good natured and even humorous repetition of this slogan, cajoled, motivated and instructed her audience to speak more and better Catalan. The campaign was quite successful, but, as might have been expected, it did not pass without the question being asked 'To whom does Spanish belong [in Catalonia]?' and why couldn't Catalan be fostered, as provided for by the Constitution, as 'Catalonia's *lengua propia*' (own or proper language, the exact meaning being somewhat ambiguous), while at the same time Spanish speakers, also taking advantage of *their* constitutional rights, were served by parallel Spanish language institutions that could be supported via public funds to be specially earmarked for Spanish ethnolinguistic activities of various kinds. Indeed, a 'Manifesto for the Equality of Language Rights', calling for the establishment of permanent and fully official bilingualism in Catalonia, had been signed by 2,300 individuals some two years before (1981). While the chairperson of the Directorate General of Language Policy had quickly declared then that there could be no legitimate charge of discrimination against Spanish when 'all the people of Catalonia unanimously support normalization', great care was obviously exercised in 1983 not to overly intensify the new normalization campaign in order to avoid another massive protest like the one of 1981.[19] However, as it became clear that careful progress was, indeed, being made with both types of normalization, it also became evident to some members of the Directorate General that further careful steps not only had to but could be taken in support of more demanding goals for RLS in Catalonia.

# Relations with the Competitor(s): Diglossia or Displacement?

## Hebrew

In the modern world, all languages have implicit or explicit competitors, whether externally, in the world of international commercial and diplomatic relations, or internally, within their own ethnocultural communities. This is even more true of threatened languages. The very need and drive to engage in RLS-efforts is an indication of worrisome relationships with competitors, particularly and most urgently of the latter (the internal) kind. For Hebrew, there had always been such competitors, even when Jews were still primarily concentrated in ancient Palestine, 'a bridge between continents', part of the fertile crescent, the royal road between Africa and Asia. If this was true even in pre-diaspora Palestine (viz. the foreign influences against which the prophets preached and the Aramaization, Hellenization and Romanization of the court, the nobility and much of the intelligentsia during the Second Commonwealth), it was all the more so in the diaspora, both before and after the destruction of the Second Temple.

Not only has Jewish multilingualism been the rule, rather than the exception, during all of Jewish history, but in this process, a large number of new Jewish vernaculars were created, born out of the superposition of Jewish cultural imperatives and gentile persecution and expulsion upon the co-territorial languages that Jews learned in the various countries of exile in which they found themselves at different periods of their painful, pariah history. While Hebrew (actually Hebrew/Judeo-Aramaic or *leshon ha-kodesh*) was almost always retained for ritual, worship and the study of sacred texts and rabbinic commentaries, Jewish communities in the diaspora commonly utilized a vernacular of their own for internal daily communication and a non-Jewish vernacular for external contacts. Thus, triglossia was the norm for at least many adult males, and women and children approached this norm as closely as their roles, age and personal history permitted. Had modern Zionism been an outgrowth of Jewish traditional life, it might or might not have revernacularized Hebrew, but, even had it done so, it would have almost certainly viewed Hebrew as an intercommunal lingua franca, rather than as the one and only legitimate mother tongue and language of daily life of an independent Jewish Palestine.[20]

However, modern ('political') Zionism was not a direct outgrowth from traditional life, but, rather, on the one hand, sprang from substantially assimilated Western European Jewish exasperation with continued post-emancipation antisemitism, and, on the other hand, from strident Eastern European Jewish secular nationalism, under the strong influence of the other late nationalisms and nation-state aspirations of that part of the world. Like these others, therefore, modern Zionism generally envisaged an internally unified, culturally modernized and homogenized, 'reborn' people, in its old homeland and not only speaking its old language but speaking *only* its old language, insofar as its internal life was concerned. Leading Western Zionists were somewhat slow to adopt this view (even Herzl initially foresaw a Jewish State in which the elite spoke Russian or German and the 'masses', primarily Yiddish), and some Eastern European Zionist groupings also interceded for 'Yiddish too', whether on a temporary or on a more permanent basis, but the monolingual Hebrew bias of most Eastern European Zionists was adamant and only tactically compromising (in line with the adamance of Polish nationalists, Ukrainian nationalists, Lithuanian nationalists, etc., on behalf of their respective national languages). For most, there could be no question but that only Hebrew could rekindle the Jewish 'national soul' and lead it back to the towering moral and cultural grandeur ('albeit in a modern way') of the classical Jewish past. To import an established diaspora Jewish language into Zion struck them as tantamount to 'introducing a pagan idol into the Holy Temple', i.e. polluting and destroying the very promise that a reborn homeland stood for.

Toward the end of the nineteenth century, when the modern Zionist movement began to take shape and to become an active force, the bulk of the Jews whom it sought to enlist on behalf of resettlement in Palestine were from Eastern and East-Central Europe. Their mother tongue was almost invariably Yiddish, then a language of some ten million speakers, and, accordingly, Yiddish was the most usual vernacular that they brought with them to the new settlements and the old and new towns and cities of Palestine. Yiddish too had recently become a vehicle of modern, secular culture, as had Hebrew, and was held in high regard not only by some Eastern European Zionists but by various other contemporary Eastern European Jewish movements, non-Zionist as well as anti-Zionist, religious as well as secular. As a language of everyday life, and even as a language of modern, secular prose, Yiddish could have immediately functioned as the language of Jewish Palestine, many Jews who had come there from North Africa, the Balkans and the Middle East (with other Jewish vernaculars of their own), whether well before, in anticipation of, or immediately after the beginnings of the Zionist movement, having learned it by dint of interaction with the numerically and culturally dominant Eastern Europeans. Indeed, Yiddish was much more fully developed then for all modern purposes than was Hebrew and it could easily have become the language of the Yishuv (the entire Jewish community in Palestine, Zionist and non-Zionist alike) had not steps been taken to suppress it and to besmirch it.

The campaign waged by Hebrasists against Yiddish was bitter and relentless. Yiddish was declared to be loathsome, vulgar, backward and, indeed, a jargon rather than a language at all. Many of these designations had been used before Zionism arrived on the scene, by Eastern and Western European advocates of several distinct carieties of Jewish modernization, but Zionism added to them the epithet of '*galuti*' (diaspora-related, i.e. subservient, weak-kneed, boot-licking) and piled upon the edifice of epithets a storm of physical abuse and hooliganism against the speakers, the organizations, the events and the publications that dared to use Yiddish in public in Palestine. The Zionist objection to Yiddish was, in part, like their objection to Jewish use of any other language for internal purposes in Palestine (indeed, German and French also occasionally suffered from similar outpourings of wrath). Mainstream Zionism could never accept a diglossic arrangement *vis-à-vis* Hebrew, least of all for internal purposes.

However, in many ways the prohibitions against Yiddish were more stringent and the struggle against it more bitter and unrelenting than those that applied to any other language. This was doubtlessly because Yiddish was initially (and even up until World War II) the only other Jewish vernacular that could possibly have been a serious rival to Hebrew, but it was also because virtually all of the revernacularizers of Hebrew spoke Yiddish themselves and, therefore, they had to wrench it out of their own tongues, block it from their own emotions and disconnect it from their own most intimate personal ties.[21] Fifty to sixty years later, another competitor appeared on the scene English, first and foremost as a vital link to Jews in anglophone countries and in the West as a whole. With the near-demise of secular Yiddish (the *coup de grace* was dealt by the Nazi-conducted holocaust rather than by Zionist Hebraism), English, rather than Hebrew, has stepped in to give Jews all over the world — and in Israel too — whatever semblance of a common vernacular they now have. As we will see, below, English does not rival Hebrew as a mother tongue of Jews in Israel, but it does compete with it increasingly in many highly statusful and symbolic functions, and does so, it should be added, at a time when Hebrew itself is no longer surrounded by the soul-stirring passions that protected it during the earliest decades of this century. Thus, Jewish bilingualism remains a widespread fact of daily life, no matter how much the early Zionists railed against it, but the 'companion language' is now a mighty giant on the world scene, rather than a folksy member of the family of Jewish languages.

## French in Quebec

The struggle for Hebrew had to be waged from the speakers' rostrum, in the press, by voluntary associations and by the organized as well as the spontaneous violence of Hebraists and their followers; the Jews in Palestine had no government of their own upon which to fall back in order to champion the language that represented their aspiration for modern, secular statehood, symbolic continuity with the distant past and cross-communal unity. But the French Quebecois, the undoubted majority in the province which they controlled politically, could and did turn to stronger tactics and instruments, namely to their government. The government itself became the chief '*gardien de la langue*'.

As mentioned before, when the 'Parti quebecois' returned to power in 1976 it set out not only to fill the gaps in the Liberal Party's Bill 22 of 1974 but to go considerably further, further perhaps than any language legislation anywhere in the free world. Its Bill 101, more than a year in the planning and discussion stage, became a landmark measure that not only spelled out an all-encompassing language policy but that defined and fostered the relationship between Quebec and the rest of Canada in an adversarial and anti-diglossic direction.

In the Parti's 1977 declaration on language policy (*Livre blanc*), while the Bill was still under debate, it was declared unacceptable to confine the French language 'to a bilingual collective life ... the result of which would be to reduce it to the level of folklore'. Indeed, even familiarity with English as a second language would have to be carefully regulated because 'only when the survival of the French language is assured ... will the English language cease to be the pervasive symbol of perpetual economic and cultural domination' that it still was. Until that far-off date (likened by the opposition to the date of the 'withering away of the state' in communist theory) it was the destiny of the French language to 'accompany, symbolize and support a reconquest by the French-speaking majority in Quebec of that control over the economy which it ought to have. There will no longer be any question of a bilingual Quebec.' It would be the ultimate purpose of Bill 101, the chief architect of that Bill subsequently declared, to help counteract the 'crippling Canadian presence ... that imposes restrictions on Quebec which are as shackles in its attempts to develop its own values and culture'.

The Bill itself was a compendium of measures covering the various domains of modern life. It established a 'Commission de toponymic' to replace English names of towns, rivers and mountains. It required all non-francophone professionals who wished to practice in Quebec to pass French proficiency examinations. It restricted attendance at English-medium schools to those anglophone children at least one of whose parents had attended such schools in Quebec, thereby effectively disqualifying most of the children of 'new Canadians' as well as children of 'old anglo-Canadians' who had come to Quebec from other parts of Canada (until the latter provision was rescinded under pressure in 1983). It required all commercial advertising and public signs to be 'solely in the official language', while permitting the signs of government offices or services to be bilingual, provided the French portion predominated (leading to the elimination from the Montreal telephone book of all English language listings of provincial government services). It required the dubbing or sub-titling in French of all non-French films 'if more than one copy of the film was to be exhibited to the public'. It required that the courts and the legislatures operate entirely in French and all municipalities (even English ones) were required to keep their minutes in French and conduct their official correspondence in French. It declared that only the French version of all Quebec laws was official (a provision later declared to be unconstitutional by the Canadian Supreme Court). But above all, it represented a governmental program for the francization of the workplace.[22]

All businesses had to acquire French names and to use those name alone inside Quebec. Any commercial enterprise with 50 or more employees was required to obtain a francization certificate to prove that it conducted all internal business in French (regardless of whether or not it employed any francophone staff). Regular government inspections were instituted of all businesses with respect to their francization and internal francization committees were required, operating independently of the ownership or management, with whom the government inspectors could meet during their francization inspections. Firms failing, after due warnings, to obtain francization certificates, could be heavily fined and, ultimately, closed. Quotas of francophones were set for every level of administration, up to and including the top administration. The director of the 'Office de la langue francaise', an agency that was given vast new powers and responsibilities in connection with the francization of the workplace, was quite correct in saying that Bill 101 went beyond anything previously undertaken in connection with either corpus planning status planning. Indeed, Bill 101 entered full-force into the new pursuit of 'labor market planning'.

As can be imagined, there was a great deal of anglophone anguish and protest against Bill 101, anguish and protest which have at the time of writing gone on for more than a decade and to little avail. Some of the provisions of Bill 101 have been declared unconstitutional by the Canadian Supreme Court, but fewer have been amended. Quebec governments, whether Liberal or Parti quebecois, have, in effect, taken the position that Canadian courts have no jurisdiction in Quebec because Quebec, though still part of Canada, is both 'a separate society' and a co-founder of Canada, and, therefore, it cannot be overruled by its own creation. Well over 100 major 'head-offices', 15,000 existing positions and 100,000 residents have left the province (including over 12% of the total anglo population of Montreal), but the predominant francophone attitude remains one of *'Ne touchez pas la loi 101'*. Indeed, in subsequent years some of the provisions of the Bill have been tightened up and few indeed have been loosened without Federal intervention, and even that has not usually helped.[23]

Clearly, francophone Quebec (like the early Zionists in Palestine) has rejected a *policy* of widespread bilingualism, let alone of diglossia. It may sound extreme to claim that 'for Quebec, bilingualism is a dangerous menace; only traitors and utopians wish to ignore this', but this claim is supported by pointing to the fate of shrinking francophonie in the rest of Canada, where francophones are (or were) almost always bilingual. To the charge that Quebec is being cruel toward its anglophones and behaving in an unseemly fashion by 'humbling' them (as was claimed by the Commissioner of Official Languages in his 1988 annual report) the answer is given that anglophones in Quebec are still better off

linguistically than are francophones outside of Quebec, that 'the French character of the province is not yet guaranteed' and that 'Francophones need more time
to build a sense of security'. However, the longer the attainment of such security
is delayed, the clearer it becomes that even though the independentists lost the
1980 referendum re negotiating a new 'sovereignty-association' with the rest of
Canada (by a vote of 60% to 40%), Quebec's ethnolinguistic policy often proceeds as if just such an association had actually been approved. As a culturally
sovereign entity, Quebec has neither a need nor a wish for a societal bilingual
accommodation with the fathomless sea of English round about it.[24]

## Catalan

We have seen that in their period of greatest weakness both Hebrew and
French in Quebec functioned in bilingual/diglossic contexts. These contexts
provided safe functions for these languages, functions that sheltered them from
the types of societal competition for which they were not yet sufficiently
accepted. Subsequently, the substantial successes of their RLS-efforts (efforts
that were fully integrated within larger ethnopolitical movements, and
successes that were experienced prior to the attainment of independent
statehood in the case of Hebrew and without any such attainment [thus far] on
the part of Quebec), fundamentally altered the earlier bilingual/diglossic
arrangements and fostered, in their place, the dream and, increasingly, the
reality of a far more internally monolingual society, with their own languages
clearly and quite consensually in the dominant position. There is definite
evidence that Catalan too is being pulled in that same direction, but it is also
evident that in this case it will be 'a long haul' and, ultimately, not as clearly
or as consensually a successful one.

With the granting of autonomy, there was no longer any danger that
Catalan would have to struggle even to maintain its rightful place in intra-
societal communication. Indeed, in 1979 the goal of RLS-efforts became the
attainment of full societal bilingualism in which Catalans could use Catalan
for any and every societal and symbolic function, from the most plebian to the
most elevated. From that initial post-Franco stage, matters have clearly
progressed to a stage that is somewhat 'mixed' at the moment. On the one
hand, there is a definite preference for Catalan in the very highest and most
powerful societal functions and decisions, e.g. in the Generalitat, the
Parliament and the town councils, although the official posture, in accord with
the Constitution, is one of 'official bilingualism'. On the other hand, the
repertoire breadth of most native Catalans is still not what it 'should be', from
the point of view of the Directorate of Language Policy (i.e. their literacy and

formality behavior is still too frequently in Spanish, as is their interaction with non-Catalans), and the active use of conversational Catalan by the bulk of immigrants and their children is far too low. While there has been progress in both of these connections, it has been slow progress at best.

Setting aside the constitutional issue, there are a number of reasons why the struggle against Spanish cannot be conducted more aggressively in Catalonia. Attempts to discredit Spanish among Catalans would have negative repercussions with respect to fostering both the sense of being accepted and a Catalan self-concept among the very considerable Spanish-speaking 'minority' (which, in some demographic and function contexts, actually constitutes a local majority). It is difficult to oppose Spanish, on the one hand, and to appear accepting and attractive to the Spanish-speaking, on the other hand. It is even difficult to foster a Catalan identity among the resident Spanish speakers and, at the same time, to agitate among native Catalans that only someone who uses Catalan in all communications and with everyone is a true and loyal Catalan. Compromises obviously have to be made and the time for maximalist solutions has not (or not yet) arrived.

Catalans who are familiar with the French Quebecois case often point out the Quebecois objections to bilingual education in that context. A well know Catalan language activist has recently featured the Quebecois view that 'Bilingual education can function in an environment where the mother tongue is not threatened. If the mother tongue is in a position of weakness, then bilingual schooling will deliver the final coup de grace.' This is a worrisome realization in a setting where most schools are bilingual and where Catalan immersion schools are still relatively few and far between. Where only slow progress is the best that can be hoped for, particularly in connection with Catalanizing the huge mass of Spanish-speaking immigrants and their children, the ultimate goal of a 'territorial solution' in which Catalonia, like every 'normal nation', will have its own language as the clearly dominant one in its own region and where Spanish will merely be a second language, used for interactions with other regions of Spain, seems far-off indeed. No wonder, then, that there are some who feel disheartened and who, looking excessively at the empty half of the glass, feel that 'the linguistic situation has deteriorated too far for such a goal [the 'normal' goal of the territorial principle, as realized, e.g. in Quebec] to be reached'.[25]

This is probably an overly pessimistic conclusion, particularly since some progress toward Catalanization is being made constantly, both with the immigrant and with the native Catalan population. Perhaps, however, before the ultimate goal can be attained, a new 'reverse diglossia' will have to be at least transitionally attained, with Catalan H and Spanish L.

## The Current Situation: 'Success' and its Residual Problems

### Hebrew

Hebrew has become, in the course of this century, the mother tongue and major spoken language of the vast bulk of the native-born Jewish population of a reborn Jewish state. Its former diglossic relationships with other Jewish vernaculars and with co-territorial non-Jewish vernaculars has been set aside. And yet, some old problems continue, at a much reduced level of intensity, and new ones have appeared on the horizon that need to be watched.

As a haven for persecuted Jews, whether they are committed or alienated, the world over, Israel is constantly experiencing Jewish immigration and, indeed, actively courting such immigration. One result of this immigration, however, is the fact that non-Hebrew-speaking Jews are constantly present in sufficient numbers to require special services and communications in their respective mother tongues, particularly for their adult members, many of whom will never acquire complete proficiency in Hebrew. As long as the 'ingathering of exiles' continues, however, the uniformationist Zionist dream of complete hebraization will remain unattainable and a portion of the country's elite will feel unfulfilled, as a result. The magnitude of this problem is usually understated. The census regularly undercounts the speakers of languages other than Hebrew, and shamelessly does so by as much as 100% in the cases of a large number of diaspora-derived Jewish vernaculars that are 'not supposed to continue to exist' more than two-thirds of a century after the revernacularization of Hebrew occurred. At this point in time, Yiddish is undercounted by as much as 50%, by ignoring the ultra-Orthodox who continue to speak it and whose relations with the secular state are 'strained' (to put it mildly), while Mugrabi/Yahudic (= Judeo-Arabic), Parsic (Judeo-Persian), Judezmo (Judeo-Spanish) and others are ignored completely as separate entities. Although there has been some lip-service about more positive attitudes toward the various Jewish languages and their respective cultural heritages, it is generally limited to a few radio programs and sanctimonious kitsch for residents of old-age homes.[26]

Although the competition from Yiddish has shrunk to clearly insignificant proportions, it has not disappeared entirely and, with the recent demographic explosion of ultra-Orthodoxy in the Jerusalem area, it has, on occasion, again assumed embarrassing dimensions. There is still a major ultra-Orthodox grouping that is completely and intergenerationally Yiddish-speaking and that refuses to recognize the State of Israel in any way and who considers the vernacularization of the Holy Tongue to be sinful. Other, politically more cooperative ultra-Orthodox groupings are also primarily Yiddish-speaking and all ultra-Orthodox groups continue to utilize Yiddish as their major medium of education, particularly for boys. New, essentially Yiddish-speaking, ultra-orthodox neighborhoods have mushroomed in the environs of Jerusalem to cope with the high ultra-Orthodox birthrate. Given the dead-heat between the two major secular political groupings in the country, Likud and Maarach, the small ultra-Orthodox parties are constantly being courted in order to form rather shaky parliamentary majorities with their help. The shakiness of these coalitions makes the support of the small ultra-Orthodox parties even more valuable and enables these small parties to extract major concessions from the major parties that require their support. This surprising state of affairs has recently caused a major Israeli political figure to exclaim in utter horror: 'The future of this country is in the hands of people who speak Yiddish!'[27]

Much more important, however, is the massive use of English, on the one hand, and the massive ignorance of Arabic, on the other hand, among Jews in Israel. Studying English has become a nationwide preoccupation, very much like the preoccupation with learning Hebrew in former generations, and some degree of facility in English is a *sine qua non* for graduation from high school, admission to the university and academic success there, scientific or advanced technological careers, political leadership within Israel itself (it is unthinkable to have a Prime Minister who cannot converse with the President of America or with American Jewish leaders), commercial pursuits with any sort of international connections (either for sales or for purchases), travel abroad, contact with world Jewry and just plain 'being with it', snob appeal and status-signaling among the young and the would-be-young. This is not to say that Hebrew is in any danger whatsoever of being replaced as the mother tongue of almost all native-born Israelis or as the symbol of Jewish independence, but it has suddenly become provincialized and peripheralized in the eyes of many of its speakers, particularly in the eyes of the younger generation and of the intellectuals. It is not so much that English represents a more believable image of modernity than does Hebrew (as English does relative to Arabic among young Israeli Arabs), but that Hebrew is simply no longer 'the heart of the matter' for the younger generation, and the older generation's concern and travail on behalf of Hebrew now seem quaint, if not outright funny, to a good portion of the young who have moved on to more pressing and substantive concerns.[28]

Perhaps it should not surprise us that Hebrew now has little sentiment attached to its use. Indeed, as is the case with English in most English mother tongue countries, Hebrew is now so widely and effortlessly used that it is destined to be little loved, unless, of course, it should somehow become endangered again. When the President of Israel proclaimed the Hebrew year 5750 (equivalent to the last quarter of 1989 and the first three quarters of 1990) as 'the year of the Hebrew language', in honor of the centenary of Ben-Yehuda's founding of the 'Hebrew Language Committee' (later renamed 'The Academy of the Hebrew Language'), the Minister of Education publicly bemoaned the infiltration of 'foreignisms' (actually, almost always Englishisms) into modern Hebrew ('*actuali, banali, combinatsia, dominanti, finansim, moderni, normali, personali, relativi*', etc., etc.), and concluded with the lament 'If only we loved Hebrew as much as Yiddishists love Yiddish or Ladinoists love Ladino'. The Minister of Education grew up in an environment that spoke (and, on occasion, he himself still speaks) both Judezmo and Yahudic. Although he often also calls for preserving the few phonological distinctions between 'Ashkenazi' and 'Sefardi' Hebrew, distinctions that the Minister himself takes pains to maintain via their 'Sefardi' realization only when he is speaking on formal occasions, his own Hebrew 'is full of phonological, grammatical, lexical, semantic, stylistic and paralinguistic Yiddishisms', as is that of most other native speakers of Hebrew today.[29] This may be no more than one sign among dozens of others that Hebrew is totally at home and fully relaxed in the mouths of its current speakers and that it is impossible to achieve in connection with a language that is spoken by one and all the very same standards of purity and affection as those that apply to sacred, written, threatened classical tongues, on the one hand, or threatened vernaculars, on the other.

## French in Quebec

If Hebrew in Israel is now clearly beyond the 'white heat stage' of nationalist fears and aspirations, so far beyond, indeed, that most of the sentimental and ideological attachment to the language has dissipated, the same cannot be said about the state of French in Quebec. Here the argument that the French language and culture will disappear unless the government takes special steps to protect them and to give them advantages over their English counterparts is still frequently heard and widely believed. Bill 101, and the various legal and political maneuvers that it has prompted for over a dozen years after its adoption, provides the best indication of this state of affairs. Indeed, French Quebec adamance in continued support of Bill 101 is sufficiently great to endanger the continuation of the current association of Quebec with Canada and, if further indications are needed of the seriousness with which any threat to French hegemony in Quebec is regarded, this danger to the association with Canada is fully recognized by the pro-French forces without this recognition resulting in any tempering of the views or postures involved on either side. A united Canada may 'muddle through' again, most people believe, but it will not be Quebec that will cave in so as to make that possible.

The British North America Act of 1867, the Constitution of Canada, as it were, could be amended only by an act of the British Parliament, the body which had adopted it in the first place, and since many issues had come up during the ensuing 120 years or more to make amendments to the Constitution desirable, the Canadian Federal government prevailed on Britain (in 1982) to allow it to 'bring the constitution home' and to revise it. Although this 'patriation of the constitution' was accomplished without Quebec's consent or participation, due largely to the exasperation of the Federal Government and the other provinces with Quebec's insistence on doing things its own way and putting its own needs first, it became clear within a few years that unless Quebec's consent was obtained to a new Canadian constitution that it could accept, Quebec would merely continue along the path of considering itself *de facto* independent, even though no *de jure* declaration to that effect was adopted. Federal force could not overcome this problem; indeed, Federal force would merely exacerbate it beyond the bounds of any Federally enforceable solution whatsoever. This realization led to the Lake Meech constitutional accord in 1987.

In return for Quebec's acceptance of the 1982 constitution, a delicate balance was found between French Quebec and the other nine (either predominantly or almost exclusively English) provinces that had a clear majority in the Federal Government. The others recognized Quebec as 'a distinct society' and the Federal Government surrendered some of its powers to the provinces. This accord required the ratification of all ten provincial legislatures within a two-year waiting period, in order to take effect. Although Quebec leaders argued that they could ask for nothing less, if they were to obtain Quebec consent to the accord, and although such consent was finally obtained (notwithstanding the protests of Quebec anglophones, who complained that their rights were being sacrificed) and notwithstanding the even more vociferous complaints of French nationalists (that the very future of the French language itself was being compromised), subsequent Quebec actions definitively limiting the use of English in the province in accord with the spirit of Bill 101 (as detailed by Bill 178 [1988]) have led two other provinces to withhold their approval of the Lake Meech accord and the two-year waiting period is now about to expire.

When the Supreme Court of Canada ruled in 1989 that Quebec could not legally prohibit English commercial signage on the streets of Quebec, the very same Prime Minister of Quebec who had originally campaigned on a promise to abide by the court's decision suddenly opted to disregard it, at least insofar as permitting 'externally visable' English signage was concerned. In supporting its decision, the provincial government cited the Lake Meech accord itself, interpreting it as giving the Province new powers to protect French language and culture via provincial laws favoring the use of French (technically: recognizing the role of the Quebec government in 'preserving and promoting the distinct identity of Quebec'), even if these laws were in conflict with the Canadian Charter of Rights and Freedoms.[30]

Is it really germane to question the sincerity of French-Quebec's trepidations for the future of the French language within its borders, as English advocates always do? Probably not, since a concern remains a concern, whether it is justified or not, and self-interest is no more a francophone habit than an anglophone one. Underlying the francophone insistence on as 'English-free' an environment in Quebec as possible is the conviction that the history of Canada, both prior to and after the British North America Act of 1867, is riddled with innumerable betrayals of the most fundamental promise of all, namely, that made by the Quebec Act of 1771 which guaranteed the protection of French culture in the province. This sense of betrayal, and the constantly self-renewing memory of betrayal, is fed by the awareness that although almost all of the anglophone children in Quebec are currently being provided with public education in English, even though they are a distinct minority there and this education must be subsidized by francophone taxes, only half of the francophone children in the rest of Canada, where they are also a distinct minority, are enabled to attend French schools. From the francophone perspective this is an even more basic denial of rights than is the prohibition against English commercial signs in Quebec. It implies that French in Canada depends entirely on the steadfastness of Quebec, where the French birthrate is slightly lower (12.7/1,000) than it it is in anglo-Canada (14.4/1,000) and where the rate of immigration from abroad is higher while the assimilation of immigrants into French culture is lower. Francophones claim to fear that, if current trends continue, they will become a minority in their own province.

Such fears may demonstrate the supremacy of emotion over reason, particularly when ethnolinguistic issues are on the agenda, as many anglophones claim. Pointing out that the Census of Canada data pertaining to the early 80s indicate that 99.1% of French mother tongue residents of Quebec actually spoke French at home, whereas only 53.1% of English mother tongue residents of Quebec still spoke English at home, 46.6% of them having switched to French at home by the early 80s [as opposed to only 28.7% having done so in 1971], doesn't seem to answer at all to the French fears, suspicions and concerns for the future. Indeed, the latter respond much more spontaneously to efforts to cultivate economic and cultural relations with the rest of the francophone world, on the one hand, and to insistence on unrelenting, politically protected francization as the best guarantee of a durable francization.[31] Thus, though it may very well be that 'the French enjoy making the English suffer' (francophones would add: 'the way the French long suffered under English domination'), this would confirms our initial contention: French in Quebec has not yet arrived at the stage of effort-less and 'taken for granted' existence already reached decades ago by Hebrew in Israel.

## Catalan

If there is some doubt as to the justifiability of the 'sense of endangerment' in connection with French in Quebec, there is no such doubt in connection with Catalan. In fact, the situation is still so 'delicate' there that supporters of RLS need to keep reminding themselves that considerable progress *has* been made, particularly in the past five years, and that there is, indeed, a silver lining to the ethnolinguistic cloud hanging over Catalan. Of course, 'total Catalanization', even along the far from complete lines of 'total hebraization' or 'total franciza-tion', is still an impossible dream, but progress in connection with active Catalan use among Catalans themselves and among Spanish-speaking immigrants and their children is definitely being made. The 1986 census reported that 60% of the population claimed that it 'can speak Catalan' and that among children this proportion rose to 64%, with 55% claiming to do so daily. Even in the Barcelona area, with its high density Spanish-speaking 'industrial belt', the great majority of residents have a 'working knowledge' of Catalan in terms of their work and other minimal daily routines. Given that Catalan speakers continue to predomi-nate as workplace managers, as shop owners and as residents of the best neigh-borhoods, there is obviously a strongly positive economic aura about their language and a strong incentive for others to become more proficient in it, at least as long as the region's economic ascendancy continues. This sentiment is being bolstered by RLS-efforts, via both formal and informal means.

In the educational arena, the number of schools in which Catalan is the main medium of instruction is constantly growing, particularly in the Barcelona industrial belt where over 600 such schools have been established and are achieving encouraging results *vis-à-vis* attaining early bilingual competence. However, problems still abound in this connection, among them the ubiquitous shortage of trained teachers (something we have discovered in so many other RLS-settings the world-over), administrative fragmentation, inability of the out-of-school social environments to reinforce the pupils' school attainments, and, finally, also outcroppings of parental concern (a concern not limited to Spanish-speaking parents) that their children's Spanish not suffer in the process of Catalanization. While there is evidence that this concern is not really justified, it is nevertheless an understandable aspect of the total problem.

Catalanization is also moving ahead at the university level, with two of the three universities within Barcelona proper now offering most of their courses in Catalan and all those outside of Barcelona being almost entirely Catalnized. The university picture is bleakest in connection with textbooks and mimeographed notes, in general, and with science and technology, in particular, although there are, of course, some scientific journals in Catalan as well as an interuniversity effort to prepare Catalan textbooks at least in the introductory liberal arts subjects that nearly all students study. There can be no doubt that, all in all, education is making some contribution to the overall RLS goals.

The mass media are currently still somewhat more problematic, but there too noteworthy progress has been made during the past few years. Barcelona, still a worldwide center of Spanish book publication, now publishes many thousands of Catalan books annually on virtually all topics and in all genres. The daily Barcelona press, on the other hand, as well as the region-wide press circulated throughout Catalonia are both very largely Spanish (commanding over three quarters of the total circulation), although there are two smallish Catalan dailies in Barcelona, as well as weekly supplements or columns in Catalan in the local editions of two of the largest national Spanish dailies. The Catalan press clearly predominates only in connections with distinctly local and regional publications. The government has a program of subsidies for publications in Catalan, but it is clear that the road ahead will be a long and difficult one due to the undiminished power of the national print media.

The radio situation is somewhat better than that of the press, given that there are some 220 radio stations that broadcast mainly or entirely in Catalan. Most of these are local (municipal) stations and, in general, most stations are of the FM variety and are devoted mainly to music. Although the large commercial stations (some 15 in all) are mainly Spanish-using, there is certainly ample Catalan on the radio. The TV situation is not quite as good, but it has lately shown signs of significant improvement, with one (out of three) channels now being Catalan Government-sponsored and completely in Catalan, and with two new such channels, one sponsored by the Catalan Government and the other by the Spanish authorities, scheduled for the near future. Many programs of foreign language provenance (e.g. 'Dallas', 'Sesame Street', 'Batman') are regularly dubbed in Catalan, but this is not yet done for Spanish programs and that, of course, is where the bulk of the competition is located.[32]

Nevertheless, as we have argued throughout this volume, the institutional arenas are not good measures of RLS progress for languages in which the intergenerational transmission system is still in need of the most serious attention. It is in this subtle but crucial area that the picture *vis-à-vis* Catalan is clearly changing for the better, both because Catalan speakers increasingly feel that they have the right to express themselves in Catalan, even in 'mixed company' (particularly since the Spanish speakers present have an increasingly adequate passive and even active control of Catalan), and because Spanish speakers who do not actually indicate a preference for Spanish are correctly assumed to be willing to be communicated with in Catalan. The latter represents a particularly noteworthy change. While both Catalan speakers and Spanish speakers probably still prefer to receive messages in their own native languages, the latter no longer react unfavorably (neither via ridicule nor via reduced solidarity) to non-Catalans who utilize Catalan as a vehicle of communication. Non-native Catalan is, indeed, being heard more and more, by both population sub-groups, and some of those who use it are prestigious and popular figures, including teachers, politicians, radio and television announcers and performers, etc. Slowly but surely, Catalan is ceasing to be merely a cliquish 'ingroup thing' and is competing more effectively as the preferred local language of intergroup communication.

What is recognized as still missing for the largest group of young and young-adult Spanish speakers in and around Barcelona is the opportunity to interact with Catalan speakers in informal, everyday, unthreatening ways. This is hard to arrange, due to the residential segregation that separates the bulk of ordinary Catalan speakers from the bulk of Spanish speakers, both at work and in neighborhood life. A number of interesting and innovative efforts have been launched to help overcome this problem. In Moncada i Reixac, a predominantly Spanish-speaking town of 26,000 in the Barcelona industrial belt, three-day 'immersion colonies' have been organized for four- to seven-year-olds, thanks to Catalan Government funds for this purpose. All of the pre-schoolers in this town are now enrolled in Catalan immersion schools but the 'colonies' enable the children of the town to spend some time with an equal number of Catalan-speaking age-peers from all over Catalonia. A teacher and an assistant are assigned to supervise every five children and the total number of children annually receiving the benefit of this experience is now only about 1,000. Obviously, this program merely represents the experimental beginning of something that must grow a thousand-fold before it can really have societal impact.

Another such pioneering effort is that of the town of l'Hospitalet de Liobregat, a newly mushroomed city in the Barcelona industrial belt which now has some 300,000 (!) predominantly Spanish-speaking inhabitants. A voluntary association of shops has been organized there whose owners and staff have committed themselves to speak Catalan to their customers in order to assist the latter in activating their passive command of the language. All pupils in adult classes in Catalan (more about these, below) receive a list of these shops (all of the shops are also identified by emblems on their doors), so that they can more easily do their shopping and activate their Catalan at the same time. As for special

Catalan conversation groups for Spanish-speaking adults, these have been organized by the provincial government and various local councils. Even here a modicum of ingenuity can be found since the groups are invariably small and led by trained teachers who have specialized in methods of activating a passive knowledge of Catalan.

All of these approaches, and others too, aim at breaking neighborhood habits of intragroup Spanish communication within the industrial zone, thereby greatly shortening the amount of time that is ordinarily needed for the activation of Catalan to take effect, and to make sure that such activation occurs among adults too, rather than only among children. Nevertheless, promising though all of these special efforts are, they are currently merely a drop in the bucket in comparison with what is needed if these goals are to be widely attained in the reasonably near future.[33]

More general 'atmosphere-creating efforts' have also been undertaken in Catalonia. An intensive mass-media campaign aimed at shopkeepers (1986–1987), costing approximately $400,000 in all, encouraged this target group to change their shop signs to Catalan. Some 2,000 signs were changed and sign-painters gave special discounts, in addition to the subsidies, loans and lower interest rates made available by the government for this purpose. Furthermore, restaurants, cafeterias and bars have been assisted to prepare Catalan price lists and menus, an effort that was also backed up by an extensive mass media campaign. Publicity campaigns have also featured Spanish speakers, speaking in broken Catalan, asking their co-workers to help them improve their spoken Catalan. This is a sign that Spanish speakers are no longer afraid, as they were only a few years ago, of being laughed at for speaking Catalan poorly. This too is a sign of progress toward activation. More generally, radio and television interviewers speaking to Spanish speakers have begun to stick adamantly to Catalan, even though their interlocutors still continue in Spanish. This is a widespread signal of a basic intra-Catalan change in the interlocutor-based switching which only a few years ago was considered to be the implicit norm.

On the whole, Catalan RLS activists are far from having arrived at widely implemented solutions to their major problems with Catalans and non-Catalans alike. Even the lower courts and the neighborhood police stations are still not fully Catalanized in practice. Nevertheless, the hardest problems are being tackled and slow progress is being made. Those who believe that the situation is hopeless, that no full normalization of Catalan is possible because Spanish speakers are protected by the Central Government and by the Constitution and have every right to remain Spanish speakers and only Spanish speakers for ever, if they so choose. But Catalan *per se* is no longer diminishing in users or in uses and, indeed, there is good reason to conclude that it is moving ahead on both fronts and in both of the target groups that it must keep in mind. Its ultimate success, if by that we mean the Catalanization of public life in Catalonia, is not a foregone conclusion, but neither was that of Hebrew some 90 years ago nor that of French in Quebec some 30 years ago. Given the continuation and amplification of the intelligent and ample support currently available for RLS-efforts on behalf of Catalan, there is every reason to hope that they will be equally successful by a quarter century from now, as well as considerably less punitive in reaching their goals.

## Conclusions

What can we conclude from these three relatively successful cases? First of all, that success *vis-à-vis* intergenerational mother tongue continuity, is attainable even if, as in the case of Hebrew, no vernacular speech community remains in the language. The vernacularization of Hebrew started at stage 7 and went on to stages 6, 5 (particularly for adults) and 4, in fairly rapid but far from inevitable succession. The schools that vernacularized Hebrew among their pupils *were closely linked to prior homes, families and settlements that fully supported this goal and attempted, less spectacularly perhaps, but no less crucially, to parallel it in a slowly but surely increasing number of pursuits at the adult level.* The higher domains (particularly work sphere outside of the new settlements, mass media and quasi-governmental or symbolic agencies) became vernacularized only substantially later and contributed to the entire process of intergenerational transmission of the new mother tongue only to the extent that this process had safe and sure foundations at stages 6, 5 and 4. Indeed, Ben-Yehuda, whose pre-mature and overly formalized and institutionalized societal efforts tried to turn this progression on its head, by starting at the top and working downwards, was a miserable failure insofar as societally integrative vernacularization and intergenerational mother tongue transmission were concerned.

The French Quebec and Catalan cases crossed over the continental divide more rapidly, as far as focusing on stages 4, 3, 2 and 1 were concerned, because they never lost control of stage 6. Once their ideological clarification had been attained, and given that the French demographic preponderance in Quebec made the anglophone presence non-problematic for stages 6 through 4a, a new breed of francophone leaders in Quebec quickly realized that they could go on the offensive with regard to the francization of stages 3, 2 and 1. However, the close demographic balance in Catalonia made (and still makes) it necessary for RLS leaders there to take a much more long-term view and approach. Nevertheless their aim is fargoing Catalanization, at least in public life and in intergroup communication within Xland, just as it is in Quebec for French and in Israel for Hebrew.

The diglossic emphases that are necessary for self-preservation when RLS-efforts are still concentrated on the weak-side (stages 8 to 5) are counterproductive when circumstances permit these efforts to be concentrated on the strong side. When the worm turns, it can look upward. The Catalan case demonstrates that this can be done far less invidiously than the records of the Hebrew or French Quebec cases reveals. In the end, however, each language remains confronted by a language of wider communication on the world scene, primarily for intergroup communication but, also and inevitably, for certain intragroup processes that are far more than merely metaphorical.

In a sense, the struggle for RLS never ends, particularly at the subjective level, because almost all languages, even those that were never threatened within their own acceptable territorial or functional domains, ultimately encounter contextually stronger competitors. If continental French itself is concerned about fostering the use of French within the borders of France, is there any wonder that francophone Quebec has this concern *vis-à-vis* French in Quebec? It should similarly not surprise us that RLS may be of genuine concern to a whole host of smaller ethnonational languages, not because their very existence is threatened or, more often than not, exposed to patterned avoidance.[34] Accordingly, Hebrew, French in Quebec and Catalan have been only partially successful in their RLS-efforts, buffeted as they are by gigantic languages round about them and annoyed as they may well be by smaller languages within their very midst.

Indeed, the theory and practice of avoiding, counteracting and reversing language shift may well be of interest to all language communities. Such theory and practice constitute aspects of language status planning which have been overlooked for far too long and which have a distinct contribution to make to the larger sociolinguistic enterprise, theoretical and applied, throughout the world.[35, 36]

## Notes

1.  On late nineteenth early twentieth secular hebraist opposition to the revernacularization of Hebrew, primarily based on the assumption that Yiddish would remain the predominant Jewish vernacular, even for lingua franca purposes (as it long was, e.g. at Zionist Congresses, either as such or in a realization facetiously referred to as 'Kongress Deutsch') see Birnbaum (1902, 1905) and, with reference to Ahad Ha-am and Theodore Herzl, see Parfitt (1983).

2.  Even Ben-Yehuda admitted (in the Prolegomenon to his *Complete Dictionary*) that revernacularization was not unprecedented for small communities of fervent believers. This realization strengthened him in his resolve to accomplish this same goal for an entire people.

3.  Prior Hebrew norms also had to be set aside or modified considerably so that the language could be lexically and pragmatically modernized. By the end of the nineteenth century, Hebrew writing was hardly in accord with Biblical norms, although, as a written language, it had changed quite slowly, overall, during the previous 2,500 years. Biblical Hebrew itself also shows much evidence of internal change by the time the final Hebrew-Aramaic books (Daniel, Ezra) were canonized.

4.  Economic and educational statistics for 1970–71 are cited from Arnopolous and Clift (1980) and Vailancourt (1980).

5.  For French-Canadian self-definitions of their situation in an anglo-dominated Canada see Mason Wade (1964 [1946], 1968 [1955]), Vallieres (1971 [1968]), Conseil de la Vie Francaise en Amerique (1967 [1964]) and Porter (1965).

6.  See the writings of Pierre-Elliot Trudeau, later Prime Minister of Canada, for an example of a French Quebec spokesman who opposed French nationalism as a constructive solution to Quebec's problems, and for the advocacy of Federal bilingualism in its place (or see Breton *et al.*, 1964 for a declaration to which Trudeau was a co-signatory).

7.  For introductions (in English) to independentist/separatist reasoning and argumentation, including its heavy stress on language and culture, see Cream and Rioux (1983) and Coleman (1984).

8.  With respect to the earlier centuries of Catalan power and glory, see Azevedo (1984) and Woolard (1989). On the Civil War, see such classic works as Orwell (1952 [1938]), Brenan (1962), Jackson (1965) and Kern (1978). On the francization and hispanization of the topmost elites of nineteenth and twentieth century Catalonia see McDonogh (1980).

9.  For accounts of the persecution of Catalan and Catalonia see Benet (1978), Woolard (1989) and the works on the Civil War cited in note 8, above. The Nova Cançó Catalana movement was, in fact, as much a political as a musical movement. It produced 'folkloristic' singers, most of whom sang songs which they themselves had authored, many of which were either banned or used highly euphemistic expressions ('the mountain's getting old', 'the stake is sure to fall', 'the night will pass away', etc.) in order to avoid being banned.

10. For a discussion of the demographic changes in post-Civil War Catalonia, see Linz (1975). Earlier internal demographic changes, also due to industrialization, are detailed in Vidal-Bendito (1976).

11. For discussions of the interaction between mother tongue and social class, see Badia i Margarit (1969), Shabad and Gunther (1982), Saez (1980), Linz (1975), Turell (1982). On the championing of Spanish and the opposition to Catalanization, see Vallejo *et al.* (1983).

12. For a brief discussion of the various dialectal, historical and stylistic varieties of written Hebrew, across which a compromise, modern written standard was developed, by the latter part of the nineteenth century, see Gold (1989), although he fails to specifically point out the major contribution of the Yiddish/Hebrew writer Mendele to the elaboration and implementation of this compromise. See Glinert (1987) for a discussion of one possible popular written source, among many others not discussed, of modern Hebrew lexical items pertaining to daily life.

13. Ben-Yehuda's own contribution to the revernacularization, see his own writings, 1918a and b, as well as a sympathetic but balanced account of Ben-Yehuda's life and work by Fellman (1973 and 1974).

14. The major protagonist of the 'teachers to pupils in school, to pupils also out of school, to home, to next generation' progression is Nahir (1988), who is largely and essentially followed in this connection by Spolsky (1989). Earlier and more limited presentations of essentially this same point of view are Bar-Adon (1975 and 1977) and, in retrospective reconstruction, focusing on the teachers almost exclusively, Azaryahu (1929) and Arnon (1947).

15. Ben-Yehuda later claimed that he had 'always known' that revernacularization could be accomplished and, indeed, that individuals and small communities *had* accomplished it before him. It is also noteworthy that Hebrew had been used as a market-place *lingua franca* (much like Bazaar Malay) in pre-Ben Yehuda Jerusalem. What is essentially different, then, about the theory here under discussion, is that the new settlements became the linguistic model for the rest of Zionist Palestine, i.e. they defined and led the way toward becoming a Jewish aggregate that viewed itself linguistically and that served as the avant guard of a reconstructed Jewish nation.

16. No attempt will be made here to detail the Canadian-wide federal policies that were formulated at least in great part to assuage or accommodate French Canadian (and specifically, French Quebec) complaints and grievances. Although the federal government proclaimed a policy of multilingualism (1971) that ultimately sought to provide some degree of federal governmental services in French throughout Canada, and particularly in Ottawa, the national capital, French Quebec became progressively less interested in such essentially symbolic gestures and increasingly more concerned with maximizing its own autonomy. For further documentation of the federal and provincial measures and the interaction between them, see Cobarrubias (1985), Bourhis (1984), Coleman (1984), Crean and Rioux (1983) and Federation des Francophones hors Quebec (1978).

17. For arguments against the advisability of the francization of Quebec see Pelletier (1964), Jacobs (1980), Handler (1988) and McKee (1982).

18. Various signs of normalization (defined as maximal functional breadth), as well as various other definitions of this term and of its goals, priorities and assumptions in Catalonia, are to be found in Aracil (1982), Azevedo (1984), Vallverdú (1979a) and Woolard (1986a).

19. For the 1983 'Catalan is for everyone' campaign and the 1981 pro-Spanish protest, as well as the Directorate's reply to it, see Woolard (1986b) and Moll (1982).

20. There is an extensive literature on the birth and development of Jewish vernaculars in Asia, Africa and Europe and their triglossic relationships (functional as well as linguistic) with Hebrew and the major co-territorial non-Jewish vernaculars and written standards. For useful introductions to this topic and to its extensive bibliography see, e.g. the six issues of the now defunct *Jewish Languages Review* (1981–1986), various issues of the *International Journal of the Sociology of Language* [24 (1980), 30 (1981), 37 (1982), 67 (1987)] and Fishman (1985 and 1987a).

21. On the Zionist struggle against Yiddish, see primarily Pilowsi (1985, 1986), Gold (1989), and relevant sections of Fishman and Fishman (1978) and Fishman (1990). None of the foregoing really pays sufficient attention to the terrorism against Yiddish during the 20s and 30s. The full impact of such efforts comes through only in the eye-witness reports of the time, only some of which have been published.

Additional information is constantly surfacing; see, e.g. a very recent note to the editor of the Yiddish (and Bundist) journal *Lebns-fragn* (Tel Aviv, 1989, 38, 448–9), which details the Hebrew University's denial of certificates of immigration to graduates of Yiddish schools in Poland during the 30s, thereby making it impossible for these students to escape from the Holocaust a few years later.

22. The full text of Bill 101 (as well as various analyses and interpretations of that Bill) can be found in Bourhis (1984). Fullerton (1978) contains a briefer but quite adequate summary of the Bill.

23. For examples of the ideological criticism of Bill 101, see Fullerton (1978) and Richler (1983). For evidence that most of the economic and demographic insecurities which motivated the Bill (see, e.g. Laporte, 1974) were already *quite fully reversed before the Bill was enacted*, see La Montagne (1975), demonstrating that just prior to the adoption of the Bill only 0.6% of French Quebecois knew no French and only 2.5% spoke no French at home. Subsequent to the passing of Bill 101 there has been much evidence of the decreasing use of English and the diminishing presence of anglophones in Quebec, the disappearance of former earning differentials between anglophones and francophones in Quebec, increases in French only as the language of home life among francophones, all of these being the continuation of trends that had begun well before Bill 101 was adopted. For details, see McKee (1982).

24. The first quotation is from an article by Marcel Turgeon in *Ici Quebec*, 1977, vol. 1, no. 1. The second quotation is by Michael Roy, the editor of Montreal's *La Presse* and is cited by Wallace (1987b).

25. For discussions of the territorial principle as a desirable goal and the clear rejection of permanent bilingualism as a desirable final state of affairs, see Vallverdú (1979b, 1981), Woolard (1986a, 1986b), Sabater (1980), and Direcció General de Política Lingüística (1983).

26. Israeli censuses commonly report every possible degree of Hebrew present in the population ('Hebrew as only language', 'Hebrew as first language', 'Hebrew as second language', 'Hebrew as third language', etc.). The decline of languages other than Hebrew is frequently studied (see Hofman and Fisherman, 1971, for a more interesting example of such studies). Re conscious undercounts of Jewish languages other than Hebrew see Gold (1989), Isaacs (1989) and Fishman (1989).

27. On the many new, tight-knit, densely populated, Yiddish- speaking ultra-Orhodox neighborhoods in Jerusalem see Shilav and Friedman (1985). On the growth in introductory Yiddish courses in Israeli secular high schools, now encompassing some 3,000 students annually and still expanding, see Dunits (1989). It should also be noted that although Yiddish was initially barred as a subject at the Hebrew University in the 30s, the past quarter century has witnessed the establishment of Yiddish departments or programs there and at almost all of the major Israeli universities. Since its secular revernacularization no longer appears to be possible, its academic study and nostalgic reinterpretation have now become acceptable.

28. Re the growing role of English in Israel see Allony-Fainberg (1977), Cooper and Seckbach (1977), Nadel and Fishman (1977), Ronen, Seckbach and Nadel (1977), Seckbach and Cooper (1977) and Cooper (1985). Re the greater scientific acceptability of English than Arabic for Israeli Arabs (but the equivalence of Hebrew and English in this respect for Israeli Jews), see Cooper, Fishman *et al.* (1977). For Israeli Arabs (and other non-Jewish minorities as well), Hebrew is required from the third grade onward and half of the school day is devoted to 'Jewish subjects' taught in Hebrew. Jewish students, on the other hand, only rarely and reluctantly study

Arabic and even when this is done, it occurs during the final two years of high schools as part of an elective major. As a carry-over from British mandate times, Arabic is co-official in Israel, but, outside of the areas of Arabic territorial concentration, this status pertains only to the courts and to the (unreliable) availability of government forms. About police ignorance of the rights of arrested Arabs to be charged in Arabic, see Fishman and Fisherman (1975). Re the view that Hebrew literature is hopelessly provincial, see Orzion Bartana (*Maariv*, September 1989) to the effect that twentieth century Hebrew literature has become increasingly conceptually impoverished as it has distanced itself from the period of bilingual writing in Hebrew and Yiddish.

29. The lack of apparent affect toward Hebrew among the majority of its current native speakers has been carefully documented by Hofman (1974a, 1974b and 1985). The loss of former Ashkenazi vs. Sefardi markers in the mainstream pronunciation of Israeli Hebrew is reported by Cooper (1985). The current Minister of Education, Yitskhak Navon, is characterized by Gold (1989) as clearly exceptional in his maintaining these differences even on formal occasions.

30. The Lake Meech accord is too recent to have benefited from academic sociolinguistic discussion. For a sample of the recent popular literature on this topic see Anon (1989), Bomboy (1988), Gee (1987), Rose *et al.* (1987) and Wilson-Smith and Rose (1987).

31. Statistics on the intergenerational shrinkage of anglophone Quebec are reported (from the Canadian Census) in De Vries (1986). For the official emphases on francophonie see Bulletin du conseil de la la langue francaise, 1989, 6, no. 1, and for the renewed call to collective responsibility for further francization, see *La francisation en marche*, 1989, 8, no. 1, a publication of the provincial government's Office de la langue francaise.

32. My information on education and the print and non-print media in Catalonia is derived from Direcció General del Patrimonio Escrit (1988/personal communications), Sala (1989), Strubell (1988).

33. My information on innovative regional and local methods for activating the passive familiarity with Catalan of Spanish speakers and their children is derived from Strubell (1984) and Woolard and Galiny (1984 and in press).

34. I have developed this point further in my 'On the peculiar problems of smaller national languages', in Andrew Gonzalez (ed.) 1984, *Panagani: Essays in Honor of Bonifacio P. Sibayan on his Sixty-Seventh Birthday*. Manila: Linguistic Society of the Philippines, 40–5.

35. This entire chapter is based upon innumerable fieldwork visits to Israel and Quebec, and on much correspondence with innumerable specialists there, and upon extensive readings and correspondence on the Catalan case. I have benefited hugely from extensive correspondence, guidance, assistance and criticism from Richard Y. Bourhis (Montreal) and from Miquel Strubell (Barcelona). I have found Woolard's various publications on Catalonia and on Catalan to be a veritable gold mine of information, interpretations and ideas. Needless to say, none of the foregoing are in any way responsible for any errors of fact or interpretation that remain. My greater exposure to Yiddish, English and Spanish (than to Hebrew, French or Catalan), and a general predisposition toward situationally weaker parties may have led to greater attention to anti-RLS views in this chapter than elsewhere in this volume.

36. The huge bibliography on recent sociopolitical studies of French in Quebec and in Canada as a whole is so fully detailed in sources such as Sabourin, Lamarche and

Tarrab (1987) that no partial listing of further worthwhile readings is justified here. The literature on the Hebrew case is only somewhat less voluminous. In addition to the items specifically referred to in this chapter I have also found the following to be useful or stimulating: Spolsky and Cooper (1991), Rabin (1989) and Fisherman (1990). The Catalan literature is the most difficult to locate in libraries outside of Catalonia proper. I would particularly like to mention the following items that have not been cited individually in the body of this chapter: Mey (1989), Johnston (1989), Molla *et al.* (1989).

## Bibliography (of materials cited and recommended)

*Hebrew*

ALLONY-FAINBERG, Yafa 1977, The influence of English on formal terminology in Hebrew. In J. A. FISHMAN *et al.* (eds) *The Spread of English*. Rowley: Newbury House, 223–8.

ANON. (ed.) 1970, *Leket teudot*. Jerusalem: Hebrew Language Academy.

ARNON, Avraham 1947, Shishim shanim bet sefer ivri be-erets yisrael. *Hed ha-khinuch* 21, 9, 8–40.

AZARYAHU (Ozrakovsky), Yosef 1929, Ha-khinuch ha-ivri be-erets yisrael. In David KIMKHI (ed.) *Sefer ha-yovel le-agudat ha-morim (1903–1928)*. Jerusalem: Agudat ha-morim, 57–112.

BACHI, Robert 1956, A statistical analysis of the revival of Hebrew in Israel (and Palestine). *Scripta Hierosolymitana* 3, 179–247.

BAR-ADON, Aaron 1975, *The Rise and Decline of a Dialect*. The Hague: Mouton.

— 1977, On the nativization of modern Hebrew and the role of children in the process. In P. J. HOPPER (ed.) *Studies in Descriptive and Historical Linguistics: Festschrift for Winfred P. Lehman*. Amsterdam: John Benjamins, 481–98.

BEN-YEHUDA, Eliezer 1918a, Tekhiat tsibur ha-ivri be-erets yisrael. In R. SIVAN (ed.) *Ben-yehuda: ktuvim nivkharim*. Jerusalem: Mosad Bialik, 232–8.

— 1918b, Ha-khalom ve-shivro. In R. SIVAN (ed.) *Ben-yehuda: ktuvim nivkharim*. Jerusalem: Mosad Bialik, 55–132.

BIRNBAUM, Nathan 1902, Hebraisch und Judisch. *Ost und West* 2, July. (Translated into English in J. A. FISHMAN 1987, *Ideology, Society and Language: The Odyssey of Nathan Birnbaum*. Ann Arbor: Karoma, 177–82.)

— 1905, Ostjudische Aufgaben. *Bukowinaer Post (Separatdruk)*, July. (Translated into Yiddish in J. A. FISHMAN (in press), A fargesener forkapitl tsu der tshernovitser konferents. *Yivo-bleter*.)

COOPER, Robert L. 1985, Language and social stratification among the Jewish population of Israel. In J. A. FISHMAN (ed.) *Readings in the Sociology of Jewish Languages*. Amsterdam: Brill, 75–81.

COOPER, Robert L. and SECKBACH, Fern 1977, Economic incentives for the learning of a language of wider communication; a case study. In J. A. FISHMAN *et al. The Spread of English*. Rowley, MA: Newbury House, 212–22.

COOPER, Robert L. and FISHMAN, Joshua A. *et al.* 1977, Language, technology and persuasion: three experimental studies. In J. A. FISHMAN *et al.* (eds) *The Spread of English*. Rowley, MA: Newbury House, 197–211.

DUNITS, Mordkhe 1989, Korev 3000 talmidem lernen yidish in dem nayem lernyor in yis-
roel. *Letste nayes*, 3 November.
FELLMAN, Jack 1973, *The Revival of a Classical Tongue*. The Hague: Mouton.
— 1974, The role of Eliezer Ben Yehuda in the revival of the Hebrew language: an
assessment. In J. A. FISHMAN (ed.) *Advances in Language Planning*. The Hague:
Mouton, 427–55.
FISHERMAN, Haya 1990, Attitudes toward foreign words in contemporary Hebrew.
*International Journal of the Sociology of Language* 36, 5–40.
FISHMAN, Joshua A. (ed.) 1980, The sociology of Yiddish. *International Journal of the
Sociology of Language* 24. (Entire issue.)
— (ed.) 1981a, *Never Say Die! A Thousand Years of Yiddish in Jewish Life and Letters*.
The Hague: Mouton.
— (ed.) 1981b, The sociology of Jewish languages. *International Journal of the
Sociology of Language* 30. (Entire issue.)
— (ed.) 1985, *Readings in the Sociology of Jewish Languages*. Leiden: Brill.
— 1987a, Post-exilic Jewish languages and pidgins/creoles: two mutually clarifying
perspectives. *Multilingua* 6, 7–24.
— (ed.) 1987b, Advances in the sociology of Jewish languages. *International Journal
of the Sociology of Jewish Languages* 67. (Entire issue.)
— (Fishman, Shikl) 1989, Yidish bay di khareydim; nayer nakhes un naye tsores. *Afn
shvel* 276, 1–5.
— 1990, *Yiddish: Turning to Life*. Amsterdam: John Benjamins.
FISHMAN, Joshua and FISHMAN, David E. 1978, Yiddish in Israel: A case study of efforts
to revise a monocentric language policy. In J. A. FISHMAN (ed.) *Advances in the
Study of Societal Multilingualism* (pp. 185–262). The Hague: Mouton.
FISHMAN, Joshua A. and FISHERMAN, Haya 1975, The 'official languages' of Israel: their
status in law and police attitudes and knowledge concerning them. In J.-G. SAVARD
and R. VIGNEAULT (eds) *Les etats multilingues: problemes et solutions/Multilingual
Political Systems: Problems and Solutions*. Quebec City: Laval University Press,
497–535.
GLINERT, Lewis 1987, Hebrew-Yiddish diglossia: type and stereotype; implications of the
language of Ganzfried's *Kitzur*. *International Journal of the Sociology of Language*
67, 39–56.
GOLD, David L. 1989, A sketch of the linguistic situation in Israel today. *Language in
Society* 18, 361–88.
HARRIS, Tracy K. (ed.) 1982, The sociology of Judezmo: the language of the Eastern
Sephardim. *International Journal of the Sociology of Language* 37. (Entire issue.)
HOFMAN, John E. 1974a, The prediction of success in language planning: the case of
chemists in Israel. *International Journal of the Sociology of Language* 1, 39–65.
— 1974b, Predicting the use of Hebrew terms among Israeli psychologists.
*International Journal of the Sociology of Language* 3, 53–65.
— 1985, The commitment to modern Hebrew: value or instrument. In J. A. FISHMAN
(ed.) *Readings in the Sociology of Jewish Languages*. Amsterdam: Brill, 51–64.
HOFMAN, John E. and FISHERMAN, Haya 1971, Language shift and maintenance in Israel.
*International Migration Review* 5, 204–26.
ISAACS, Miriam 1988, Yiddish in Orthodox communities of Jerusalem. Paper delivered at
Annual Winter Oxford Yiddish Conference. (Briefly and often inaccurately summa-
rized in *Jerusalem Post*, 1989, 'Living language', June 16, p. 43.
JERUSALEM POST SERVICE 1989, 'Infiltration' of Hebrew is lamented. *The Jewish Week*
(New York), October 27, p. 38.

KORNBERG, Jacques (ed.) 1983, At the crossroads: an introductory essay. In his (ed.) *At the Crossroads: Essays of Ahad Ha-am*. Albany: State University of New York Press, xv–xxvii.

LAPIDE, Pinhas E. 1984, *Hebrew in the Church*. Grand Rapids: Eerdmans.

MAURAIS, Jacque (ed.) 1987, *Politique et aménagement linguistiques*. Paris/Montreal: Conseil de la Langue Française/Le Robert.

NADEL, Elizabeth and FISHMAN, Joshua A. 1977, English in Israel: a sociolinguistic study. In J. A. FISHMAN *et al.* (eds) *The Spread of English*. Rowley, MA: Newbury House, 137–67.

NAHIR, Moshe 1988, Language planning and language acquisition; the 'great leap' in the Hebrew revival. In Christina B. PAULSTON (ed.) *International Handbook of Bilingualism and Bilingual Education*. New York: Greenwood, 275–95.

PARFITT, Tudor 1983, Ahad Ha-am's role in the revival and development of Hebrew. In J. KORNBERG (ed.) *At the Crossroads; Essays on Ahad Ha-am*. Albany: State University of New York Press, 12–27.

PILOWSKI, Arye 1985, Yiddish alongside the revival of Hebrew; public polemics on the status of Yiddish in Eretz Israel, 1907–1929. In J. A. FISHMAN (ed.) *Readings in the Sociology of Jewish Languages*. Leiden: Brill, 104–24.

— 1986, *Yidish tsvishn yo un neyn; yidish un yidish literatur in erets-yisroel, 1907–1948*. Tel Aviv: Veltrat far yidish un yidisher kultur.

RABIN, Chaim 1989, Terminology development in the revival of a language: the case of contemporary Hebrew. In Florian COULMAS (ed.) *Language Adaptation*. Cambridge: Cambridge University Press, 26–38.

RONEN, Meriam, SECKBACH, Fern and COOPER, Robert L. 1977, Foreign loanwords in Hebrew newspapers. In J. A. FISHMAN *et al.* (eds) *The Spread of English*. Rowley, MA: Newbury House, 229–38.

SAULSON, Scott B. 1979, *Institutionalized Language Planning; Documents and Analysis of the Revival of Hebrew*. The Hague: Mouton.

SECKBACH, Fern and COOPER, Robert L. 1977, The maintenance of English in Ramat Eshkol. In J. A. FISHMAN *et al. The Spread of English*. Rowley, MA: Newbury House, 168–78.

SHILAV, Joseph and FRIEDMAN, Menachem 1985, *Growth and Segregation; The Ultra-Orthodox Community of Jerusalem*. Jerusalem: Institute for Jerusalem Studies. (= Study No. 15).

SPOLSKY, Bernard 1989, Language revitalization within a general theory of second language learning. Paper presented at the Fourth International Conference on Minority Languages, Ljouwert/Leeuwarden, June 20–24, 1989.

SPOLSKY, Bernard and COOPER, Robert L. 1991, *The Languages of Jerusalem*. Cambridge: Cambridge University Press.

WEINREICH, Max 1980, *History of the Yiddish Language* (= First two volumes of the four-volume Yiddish original [1973]; translated by Shlomo Noble and Joshua A. Fishman). Chicago: University of Chicago Press.

## French in Quebec

ANON. 1989, The divided nation; Almost two years after its birth, the Meech Lake accord is in danger. *Maclean's* 102, March 20, 18–33.

ARES, Richard 1945, *Notre question nationale*. Montreal: Les Editions de l'Action Nationale.

ARNOPOLOUS, Sheila and CLIFT, Dominique 1980, *The English Fact in Quebec*. Montreal: McGill-Queens University Press.

BEHIELS, Michael D. 1985, *Prelude to Quebec's Quiet Revolution; Liberalism versus New Nationalism, 1945–1960*. Kingston and Montreal: McGill-Queens University Press.

BOMBOY, R. S. 1988, Sovereignty and nationalism in Canada. *Current History* 87, 125 and 136–8.

BOURHIS, Richard Y. (ed.) 1984, *Conflict and Language Planning in Quebec*. Clevedon: Multilingual Matters.

BOURHIS, Richard Y. and LEPICQ, Dominique 1990, Quebec French and language issues in Quebec. In R. POSNER and J. N. GREEN (eds) *Trends in Romance Linguistics and Philology: Bilingualism and Linguistic Conflict in Romance*. Berlin: Mouton.

BRETON, Albert *et al.* 1964, An appeal for realism in politics. *Canadian Forum* 44, no. 520, 29–33. (Pierre-Elliot Trudeau is one of the co-signatories of this statement.)

CHAPUT, Marcel 1961, *Pourquoi je suis separatiste*. Montreal: Editions du Jour.

COBARRUBIAS, Juan (ed.) 1985, *Language Policy in Canada*. Quebec City: International Research Center on Bilingualism.

COLEMAN, William D. 1984, *The Independence Movement in Quebec, 1945–1980*. Toronto: University of Toronto Press.

CONSEIL DE LA VIE FRANCAISE EN AMERIQUE 1967 [French original: 1964], *Nothing More; Nothing Less*. Toronto and Montreal: Holt, Rinehart and Winston.

COOK, Ramsey 1967, *Canada and the French-Canadian Question*. Toronto: Macmillan of Canada.

CREAN, Susan and RIOUX, Marcel 1983, *Two Nations; An Essay on the Culture and Politics of Canada and Quebec in a World of American Pre-Eminence*. Toronto: James Lorimer.

CZARNECKI, Mark 1981, Struggling free from an old yoke. *Maclean's* 94, March 16, 52–3.

D'ANGLEJAN, Alison 1984, Language planning in Quebec: an historical overview and future trends. In Richard Y. BOURHIS (ed.) *Conflict and Language Planning in Quebec*. Clevedon: Multilingual Matters, 29–52.

DAOUST-BLAIS, Denise 1983, Corpus and status language planning in Quebec: a look at linguistic education. In J. COBARRUBIAS and J. A. FISHMAN (eds) *Progress in Language Planning*. Berlin: Mouton, 205–34.

DE VRIES, John 1985, *Towards a Sociology of Languages in Canada*. Quebec City: International Research Center on Bilingualism.

FEDERATION DES FRANCOPHONES HORS QUEBEC 1978 [French original (2 vols) 1977], *The Heirs of Lord Durham; Manifesto of a Vanishing People*. Toronto: Burns and MacEachern.

FULLERTON, Douglas H. 1978, *The Dangerous Delusion; Quebec's Independence Obsession*. Toronto: McClelland and Stewart.

GEE, Marcus 1987, Debates on the morning after. *Maclean's* 100, May 18, 12–13.

HANDLER, Richard 1988, *Nationalism and the Politics of Culture in Quebec*. Madison: University of Wisconsin Press.

JACOBS, Jane 1980, *The Question of Separation; Quebec and the Struggle over Sovereignty*. New York: Random House.

JOHNSON, Daniel 1965, *Egalite ou independance*. Montreal: Les Editions Renaissance.

JUTRAS, Rene 1965, *Quebec libre*. Montreal: Les Editions Actualite.

LACHAPELLE, Réjean 1989, Evolution of language groups and the official languages situation in Canada. Paper presented at the Annual Meeting of the American

Sociological Association (session on 'Relations between English and French in Canada'). San Francisco, August.

LA MONTAGNE, J. 1975, Minority language education in Ontario and Quebec. In R. ARES (ed.) *Les positions — ethniques, linguistique et religieuses — de Canadiens français à la suite du recensement de 1971*. Montreal: Editions Bellarmin.

LAPORTE, Pierre E. 1974, *L'usage des langues dans la vie economique au Quebec*. Quebec: Editeur officielle du Quebec.

— 1984, Status language planning in Quebec: an evaluation. In Richard Y. BOURHIS (ed.) *Conflict and Language Planning in Quebec*. Clevedon: Multilingual Matters, 53–80.

MCKEE, Brian 1982, *A Socio-Demographic Analysis of Language Groups in Quebec*. Ottawa: Department of Sociology and Anthropology, Carlton University.

MALLEA, John R. 1977, *Quebec's Language Policies: Background and Response*. Quebec City: Laval University Press.

MAURAIS, Jacques (ed.) 1987, *Politique et amenagement linguistique*. Quebec City and Paris: Gouvernement du Quebec and Le Robert.

PELLETIER, Gerard 1964, The trouble with Quebec. *Atlantic Monthly* 214, 115–8.

PLASTRE, Guy 1988, Ecologie du bilinguisme en milieu administratif: quelques leçons à tirer de l'expérience canadienne. Paper presented at a conference on language planning, Donostoia (San Sebastian), November 2–4.

PORTER, John 1965, *Vertical Mosaic*. Toronto: University of Toronto Press.

RICHLER, Mordecai 1983, Language problems. *Atlantic Monthly* 251, 10–20.

ROSE, Michael, CLARK, Marc and WALLACE, Bruce 1987, What Bourassa won. *Maclean's* 100, May 11, 11.

SABOURIN, Conrad F., LAMARCHE, Rolande M. and TARRAB, Elca 1987, *La Francité Canadienne, vol. 2: Sociologie et politicologie de la langue*. Montreal: University of Montreal.

SANKOFF, Gillian 1980, *The Social Life of Language*. Philadelphia: University of Pennsylvania Press.

SCHECHTER, Sandra R. 1980, Teaching EFL in a unilingual Quebec. *Canadian Modern Language Review* 36, 201–14.

— in press, L'etat, gardien de la langue: a diachronic view of language policy and planning in Quebec. In Mary E. MCGROARTY and Christian J. FALTIS (eds) *In the Interest of Language: Contexts for Learning and Using Language*. Smith, Denis 1971, *Bleeding Hearts ... Bleeding Country; Canada and the Quebec Crisis*. Edmonton: Hurtig.

SMITH, Denis 1971, *Bleeding Hearts ... Bleeding Country: Canada and the Quebec Crisis*. Edmonton: Hurtig.

VAILLANCOURT, F. 1980, *Differences in Earnings by Language Groups in Quebec, 1970*. Quebec City: International Center for Research on Bilingualism.

VALLEE, Frank G. and DE VRIES, John 1978, Trends in bilingualism in Canada. In J. A. FISHMAN (ed.) *Advances in the Study of Societal Multilingualism*. The Hague: Mouton, 761–92.

VALLIERES, Pierre 1971 [French original: 1968], *White Niggers of America; The Precious Autobiography of a Quebec 'Terrorist'*. New York and London: Monthly Review Press.

— 1972 [French original; 1971], *Choose!* Toronto: New Press.

— 1977, *The Assasination of Pierre Laporte*. Toronto: James Lorimer.

WADE, Mason 1964 [1946], *The French Canadian Outlook; The Unknown North Americans*. Toronto: McClelland and Stewart.

—    1968 [1955], *The French Canadians, 1760-1967 [1945]*. Toronto: Macmillan.
WALLACE, Bruce 1987a, Language on trial. *Maclean's* 100, January 5, 8.
—    1987b, New fury over language. *Maclean's* 100, November 9, 16–17.
WALLER, Harold M. 1988, Linguistic liberty in Canada. *New Leader* 71, No. 13,
     15–17.
WILSON-SMITH, Anthony and ROSE, Michael 1987, Breakthrough. *Maclean's* 100, May
     11, 8–10.


*Catalan*

ARACIL, Lluis V. 1982, Conflicte lingüístic i normalització lingüística a l'Europa nova. In
     his *Papers de Sociolinguistica*. Barcelona: La Magrana, 23–38.
ARGENTE, Joan 1980, Una nació sense estat, un poble sense llengua? *Serra D'Or* 249,
     17.
ARTIGAL, Josep M. 1989, *La immersió a Catalunya*. Vic: Eumo.
AZEVEDO, Milto 1984, The reestablishment of Catalan as a language of culture. *Hispanic
     Linguistics* 1, 305–30.
BADIA I MARGARIT, Antoni 1969, *La Llengua dels Barcelonins; Resultats d'una Enquesta
     sociológico-lingüística*. Barcelona: Edicions 62.
BENET, Josep 1978, *Catalunya sota el Règim Franquista*. Barcelona: Blume.
BRENAN, Gerald 1962, *The Spanish Labyrinth*. Cambridge: Cambridge University
     Press.
CALSAMIGLIA, Helena and TUSON, Amparo 1984, Use of languages and code-switching in
     groups of youths in a *barri* of Barcelona: communicative norms in spontaneous
     speech. *International Journal of the Sociology of Language* 47, 105–21.
DIRECCIÓ GENERAL DEL PATRIMONI ESCRIT I DOCUMENTAL 1988, *The Press in Catalonia
     in the Eighties*. Barcelona: Departament de Cultura de la Generalitat de Catalunya.
DIRECCIÓ GENERAL DE POLÍTICA LINGÜÍSTICA 1983, *Llibre Blanc de la Direcció General
     de Política Lingüística*. Barcelona: Departament de Cultura de la Generalitat de
     Catalunya.
ESTEVA FABREGAT, Claudi 1977, Aculturació lingüística d'immigrats a Barcelona.
     *Treballs de Sociolingüística Catalana* 1, 91–115.
HINA, Horst 1978, *Kastilien und Katalonien in der Kulturdiskussion*. Tubinge: Niemeyer.
JACKSON, Gabriel 1965, *The Second Republic and the Spanish Civil War*. Princeton, NJ:
     Princeton University Press.
JOHNSTON, Hank 1989, Toward an explanation of church opposition to authoritarian
     regimes: religio-oppositional subcultures in Poland and Catalonia. *Journal for the
     Scientific Study of Religion* 28, 493–508.
KERN, Robert W. 1978, *Red Years, Black Years; A Political History of Spanish
     Anarchism, 1911-1937*. Philadelphia: Institute for the Study of Human Interaction.
LINZ, Juan J. 1975, Politics in a multilingual society with a dominant world language: the
     case of Spain. In J.-G. SAVARD and R. VIGNEAULT (eds) *Les etats multilingues: prob-
     lemes et solutions/Multilingual Political Systems: Problems and Solutions*. Quebec
     City: Les presses de l'université Laval, 367–444.
McDONOGH, Gary W. 1980, *Good Families of Barcelona*. Princeton, NJ: Princeton
     University Press.
MEY, Jacob L. 1989, 'Saying it don't make it so'; the *'Una Grande Libre'* of language
     politics. *Multilingua* 8, 333–55.

MOLL, Aina 1982, El difícil i llarg camí de la normalització lingüística. *Avui*, October 21, 1–2.

ORWELL, George 1952 [1938], *Homage to Catalonia*. New York: Harcourt, Brace, Jovanovich.

PAULSTON, Christina B. 1987, Catalan and Occitan: comparative test cases for a theory of language maintenance and shift. *International Journal of the Sociology of Language* 63, 31–62.

PI-SUNYER, Oriol 1980, Dimensions of Catalan nationalism. In Charles R. FOSTER (ed.) *Nations Without a State: Ethnic Minorities in Western Europe*. New York: Praeger, 101–15.

— 1985, Catalan nationalism. In E. A. TIRYAKIAN and R. ROGOWSKI (eds) *New Nationalisms of the Developed West*. Boston: Allen and Unwin, 254–76.

ROS I GARCIA, Maria 1984, Speech attitudes to speakers of language varieties in a bilingual situation. *International Journal of the Sociology of Language* 47, 73–90.

SABATER, Ernest 1980, An approach to the situation of the Catalan language: social and educational use. *International Journal of the Sociology of Language* 47, 29–41.

SAEZ, Armand 1980, Catalunya, gresol o explotadora? Notes sobre immigració i creixement. In J. M. PUIGJANER (ed.) *Immigració i Reconstrucció Nacional a Catalunya*. Barcelona: Blume, 25–42.

SALA, Rafael 1989, Traveling hopefully: Catalan normalization. Paper presented at the Fourth International Conference on Minority Languages. Ljouwert/Leeuwarden (Netherlands), June 20–24.

SHABAD, Goldie and GUNTHER, Richard 1982, Language, nationalism and political conflict in Spain. *Comparative Politics* 14, 443–77.

STRUBELL I TRUETA, Miquel 1984, Language and identity in Catalonia. *International Journal of the Sociology of Language* 47, 91–104.

STRUBELL, Miquel 1988, Primary education in Catalonia. In Alex M. J. RIEMERSMA and Alastair G. S. WALKER (eds) *Report on the EMU Colloquy on 'Lesser Used Languages in Primary Education'*. Ljouwert/Leeuwarden: Fryske Akademy, 15–16.

TURELL, Teresa 1982, El comportament, les actituds i la competencia lingüística dels treballadors dins l'empresa. *Treballs de Sociolinguistica Catalana* 4, 7–31.

VALLEJO, Andrés, LOPEZ, Isaac and MANUECO, Juan Pablo 1983, *La Emigración Castellana*. Madrid: Mostoles Ruodelares.

VALLVERDÚ, Francesc 1979a, *La Normalitzacio lingüística a Catalunya*. Barcelona: Laia.

— 1979b, *Dues Llengües, dues Funcions?* Barcelona: Edicions 62.

— 1981, *El conflicto lingüístico en Catalunya*. Barcelona: Edicions Peninsula.

— 1984, A sociolinguistic history of Catalan. *International Journal of the Sociology of Language* 47, 13–28.

VIDAL-BENDITO, Tomás 1976, *La Despoblación del Campo en Cataluña*. Barcelona: Unbiversidad de Barcelona.

WOOLARD, Kathryn A. 1984, A formal measure of language attitudes in Barcelona: a note from work in progress. *International Journal of the Sociology of Language* 47, 63–71.

— 1985, Language variation and cultural hegemony: toward an integration of sociolinguistics and social theory. *American Ethnologist* 40, 738–48.

— 1986a, The politics of language status planning: 'Normalization' in Catalonia. In Nancy SCHWEDA-NICHOLSON (ed.) *Languages in the International Perspective*. Norwood: Ablex, 91–102.

— 1986b, The 'crisis in the concept of identity' in contemporary Catalonia, 1976–1982. In Gary W. MCDONOGH (ed.) *Conflict in Catalonia: Images of an Urban Society.* Gainsville: University Presses of Florida, 54–71.

— 1989, *Double Talk: Bilingualism and the Politics of Ethnicity in Catalonia.* Stanford: Stanford University Press.

WOOLARD, Kathryn A. and GALINY, Tae-Joong in press, The consequences of political change and language planning for language evaluation in autonomous Catalonia.

# 11 On RLS-Focused Language Planning and on Dialect–Standard Issues and Corpus Planning in Particular

We first briefly introduced the field of 'language planning' in Chapter 4, above. The time has come to look at it again, in order to more fully appreciate its direct relevance to RLS. 'Language planning' is a relatively new area of specialization within the sociology of language. It is concerned with planned behavior toward language or languages, or, more technically put: with the planned allocation of resources to language or languages. Resources are valuable 'commodities', i.e., 'things' or 'efforts' which are sought after but which are not available for the asking, 'things' or 'efforts' such as attention, concern, time, money, manpower, all of which may be disbursed or expended to foster one language rather than another.[1] There are many other kinds of planning besides language planning: e.g. agricultural planning, industrial planning, educational planning, family planning, etc. In some parts of the world there is (and in other parts, there was until very recently) even a type of planning that is referred to as 'culture planning', i.e., planning the types of books that are to be written and published, the types of plays, movies and radio or television programs that are to be produced and presented, etc. Each of these types of planning requires, for its success, societal recognition of the 'authorities' who conduct the planning efforts, or, at the very least, a societal acceptance, however reluctant, of the 'authorities' who implement, evaluate and revise these efforts.

Language planning is a type of planning that is concerned with one or more of the languages utilized within a larger or smaller community. Ethnocultural groups which are in control of their own state apparatuses often delegate language planning to an agency of the central government. Many of these agencies are known as 'academies' (e.g. the French Academy, the Royal Academy of the Spanish Language, the Academy of the Hebrew Language, etc.). However, many well established national languages have no particular governmental agency that is concerned with their societal status or the adequacy of their corpus for the myriad needs of modern technological functioning; English is one such language,

337

and Russian is another. In their cases, and in many others like them, a large number of smaller agencies, whether primarily governmental (as in the USSR), or primarily private or voluntary (as in the USA), attend to some smaller area of language that is of particular concern to them and try to influence usage among their own clienteles.

As the above examples imply, the spirit in which language planning is conducted (the types of rewards or sanctions available to it and the types of organizational forms it assumes) is generally fully in accord with the more widespread 'culture of planning' that characterizes any particular ethnocultural system. Thus, language planning does not have to be totalitarian at all, nor involved in thought control or brainwashing, nor dependent on the police or on censors for its implementation.

Minority groups, including many of those that are particularly in need of and/or engaged in language planning, also frequently support their own language planning academies (e.g. the Frisian Academy, the Committee for Standard Yiddish Spelling, the Hausa Language Board, etc.). However, without a state apparatus of their own, these academies (or language planning agencies) have neither the funds nor the authoritative powers that characterize their counterparts among state-related ethnocultural groups. That is, in the case of most minorities there is necessarily a greater reliance on voluntary support and on voluntary implementation with respect to language planning efforts, rather than on direct or indirect compulsion or the imposition of sanctions from a center of power over people's lives and fortunes.

## Additional Status Planning Efforts Particularly Related to RLS

As was mentioned in an earlier chapter, all RLS-efforts are basically examples of that part of language planning known as 'status planning'. Status planning seeks to allocate societal resources in such ways as to foster the use of a language in more (and in more important) societal functions among larger and larger numbers (and proportions) of individuals. Fostering the home-family-neighborhood-use-function, the school-use function, the work-use function, the media-use function and the governmental-use function, which we have discussed so many times before in connection with various ethnolinguistic groups, are all instances of status planning efforts. Even the corpus planning that RLS requires (e.g. the coining and adoption of new Xish terms required for many if not all of the above functions) ultimately has in mind the facilitation of status planning rather than corpus planning *per se*. We will have more to say about corpus planning later. At this juncture, however, let us turn to a number of status planning issues that cut across all of the above-mentioned functions. Indeed, it is precisely their cross-functional applicability that makes these issues the most appropriate ones to begin with from an RLS point of view.

## Dialect status planning

Many of the languages on behalf of which RLS-efforts are undertaken have, generally, not previously been appreciably utilized in high status functions. Even if such functions have, at times, been discharged in these languages, it remains true that many of their speakers may not have received any of their formal education in schools (nor attended services in churches) in which these languages were the media (or even the co-media) of instruction (or ritualized prayer). Accordingly, most of the constantly shrinking number of mother tongue speakers of threatened languages do very little reading and almost no writing whatsoever in these languages. This functional characterization leaves these languages almost entirely restricted to informal and intimate conversational functions, functions which pertain to life on a small scale. However, this is precisely the functional characterization which corresponds to dialectal (rather than standard) language use. Accordingly, many languages that are in need of and are the recipients of RLS-efforts are designated as 'mere dialects' (with the implication that they are not full-fledged 'languages' at all). This is a demeaning charge, and a potentially damaging one too, particularly since some of the languages in question may actually have no corresponding standard variety and, even if they do have such a variety, it may be one which most speakers do not control, precisely because they have never received either formal education or literacy exposure in these languages.

The above-mentioned lacks, some of them being the lacks of the speakers, others, the lacks of their societies, and still others, the lacks of their languages reflecting their recent and generally current sociocultural functions, are very often associated with attitudinally negative images of Xish among Xmen *per se*, images that must be rectified and overcome if RLS-efforts are to succeed. Dialects often have 'a bad press' among the public at large (even if not among linguists) and their negative social image must be combated, among Xmen and Ymen alike (but particularly among Xmen), as part of the ideological clarification which is a foundational *sine qua non* for all those subsequent RLS functional goals that are more statusful and diverse, above and beyond 'mere oralcy'.

There is a difference, however, as far as RLS is concerned, between a community made up almost exclusively of non-standard 'dialect users' and a community viewed (or self-viewed) as 'using a mere dialect'. The former is often popularly seen as a characterization of the speakers or of their speech communities, while the latter is commonly viewed as a basic characterization of the speech variety being used. Let us examine these two criticisms one at a time, keeping in mind, however, that the former characterization can easily become over-generalized into the latter.

## Using dialect only when a standard is known to exist

Speakers whose Xish repertoire is limited to dialect alone may be embarrassed by that limitation, particularly if they realize that Yish has a standard ('more educated', 'urban', 'cultured') variety and, most particularly, if they know that Xish has such a variety too but they do not know how to use it. Under such circumstances speaking the Xish dialect often comes to be viewed as implying that the community of speakers is lacking in all social graces and societal accomplishments. They and their dialect are believed 'to smell of pigs' and 'to be coarse' (or stupid, gross, ugly, etc., etc.). Such self-views are reflections of the destruction of Xish self-esteem, due to decades of negative comparisons with Yish political power, economic advantage and modern sophistication. It takes time, understanding and careful treatment to overcome such inferiority feelings and the authenticity and beauty of the dialect is one of the major verities that needs to be defined and defended in this process.

It must be pointed out that Ymen too inevitably also speak dialects other than their standard dialect; that they all have had to learn the standard dialect from formal exposure to it in church, in school, in print, in public lectures, etc. Indeed, almost all children everywhere in the world start out as dialect speakers and come to the above formal institutions speaking varieties that are not identical to the variety of those institutions. Mothers and their children, or lovers with one another, or any two people who are fond of each other, speak informally and, therefore, dialectally. Even after the standard is learned there is a definite permanent place in one's verbal repertoire for the dialect, particularly because the standard will primarily have formal and written functions and implications or connotations. It would be ludicrously out-of-place for playmates or others united by an informal, intimate relationship to speak to each other as if they were bishops or prime ministers or even teachers, as if they were 'talking books' rather than two ordinary and very human human beings who have known each other for a long time, been through many intimate moments and endless shared experiences and who must, therefore, show that they are cognizant of their shared past, intimacy, interdependence and affection when they speak to each other. The way in which this is done (and done by Ymen too) is for two such people to speak dialect to one another. Dialect is the language of the ordinary, informal, spontaneous and affectionate heart.

Of course, informality, spontaneity and affect are not appropriate for all human interactions and, therefore, one must generally learn the standard variety too, particularly if one is to engage successfully in formal speech behaviors as well as in reading and writing. But that does not mean that those who command the formal variety 'never come home again'. Of course they come home and when they are 'comfortably at home' (figuratively as well as literally), they relax and may very well speak informally, in the dialect with which they grew up. All dialects reveal *where* one's childhood home is or was, i.e., all dialects are not only informality markers but also regional markers (i.e. they 'give away' where one's first intimate experiences, with parents, friends and relatives, transpired) or social class markers (i.e. their facile use reveals the extent to which one has been uninfluenced by the world of books and formal education more generally). Thus, it is not despite their connotations but because of them that they must be loved and honored, just as one is commanded to love and honor one's mother and one's father. The dialect is part of the foundational, 'small-scale', untutored love and honor, out of which and upon which all future, more encompassing, 'larger-scale' love and honor can develop. Where the foundation is weak or non-existent, nothing solid can be erected subsequently, even though many individuals may also seek to transcend their origins and to go on to a broader sphere of activity (and identity) too.

Such arguments are not merely RLS 'self-confidence strategies'. They are not merely intended to enable dialect speakers to lift their heads *vis-à-vis* Ymen. They are empirical truths as well, and, above all, they provide a foundation for stages 7 and 6, on the one hand, and for the intracultural and intercultural diglossia that RLS must seek to develop among Xmen, most particularly when RLS-efforts are at their earliest, most sensitive stages. Such arguments clearly imply that *dialect may very well not be adequate for everything* that is of individual or societal concern. For certain pursuits the Xish standard may be consensually required and for others, Yish itself may well be needed. The fact that no dialect is 'free standing', nor sufficient unto itself for each and every imaginable societal activity, is implicit in the very concept of 'dialect'. A *'dialect' (or 'sociolect') is always a dialect/sociolect of some more encompassing system of dialects/sociolects*. It is the system *in toto* (a theoretical construct if there ever was one) that is referred to as the 'language'; each of its dialects/sociolects, including the 'dialect of the school', being sociofunctionally and/or geographically restricted. None of them, not even the ones associated with the most formal and distinguished functions (the one usually referred to as 'the standard' or the 'the standard dialect'), can discharge all of the functions that the entire system encompasses and discharges (or seeks to encompass and discharge) through its entire repertoire of varieties.

## If, initially, there is no 'standard dialect'

The realities of modern life are undeniably such that a 'standard dialect' is frequently needed, even if it be merely the 'dialect of the school', so that a speech community or its more accomplished members can utilize Xish in written communications, on more formal spoken-interaction occasions, and in interactions between speakers of dialects that are so divergent from one other as to be mutually incomprehensible and, therefore, requiring a common-ground accessible to both sides. Nevertheless, where no 'standard dialect' has been elaborated or agreed upon in the past, pro-RLSers sometimes resist the creation (or, more usually, the selection) of a standard. The arguments against a standard are usually of three different but related types.

Most common of all is the argument that the standard, whatever dialect may be chosen or elaborated for that honor, will be a stilted and artificial variety for the native speakers of all other varieties and, indeed, even for the native speakers of that very variety *per se* (all of whom speak less bookishly and less 'correctly' than the school-norm specifies). While this observation is doubtless true, it overlooks the fact that the standard variety need not be as obligatory in speech as in writing. Indeed, all dialects should remain valid in speech, particularly in informal and intimate speech within their own traditional speech networks and communities. Orthoepic recriminations really have no place in any secure speech economy. Only a rather limited number of individuals, in any case (even in the case of the most standardized and secure 'international languages') can speak the standard dialect effortlessly and at length, without revealing in one way or another (via a tell-tale phonological, lexical or grammatical slip) 'where they are from', i.e., the regional and/or social class dialect which is their true mother tongue. Accordingly, most native speakers of regional dialects (or of intra-regional social class dialects/ sociolects) will only need to make use of the standard dialect in connection with rare literacy pursuits and in connection with a relatively small number of spoken interactions. If the latter interactions sound artificial and stilted to other-dialect speakers, it is only because they are. Speaking like a book, or like a school-marm, or like a language instructor, or as if one is making a speech from the throne, the pulpit or the speaker's platform, *is*, for most folks, an artificial (or at least a highly unusual) thing to do and normal, everyday speech should not be constrained along such lines in any dialect area. This is not a distinctively RLS problem, but, rather, one which has been faced (and often solved) throughout the world, wherever written and formal standards have come into being.

A similarly widespread dialect–standard issue, i.e., one that is also related, even though not distinctively so, to RLS problems, is the issue of 'unfair advantage'. While it is true that the standard dialect that is officially propagated in school, in formal broadcasting or in other formal speech events, and in most written communication is not really identical with any actually spoken informal dialect, nevertheless, the standard dialect is inevitably closer to one particular dialect or dialect cluster than to others. Accordingly, the speakers whose native, informal varieties are closer to the standard *ab initio*, will have an easier time mastering the standard, both in formal speech and in writing, than will speakers of the other dialects that are more discrepant from the standard. Depending on the degree of divergence of the other dialects from the standard, this may place them and their children at a substantial advantage. It is, of course, wisest (particularly for RLS purposes) not to pick a highly divergent dialect for the role of the standard, but even where the divergences between the standard and the other dialects are not particularly egregious, there is no denying that speakers of standard-proximate dialects will have some advantage over speakers of standard-nonproximate dialects with respect to acquiring the standard.

Without special compensatory efforts, this initial advantage may easily translate itself into a certain number of jobs, scholarships or other tangible benefits. In the long run, only compensatory planning efforts (e.g. in terms of the location of industrial or commercial ventures or of other reward-giving undertakings) can compensate for this linguistic advantage. In the short run, however, the gains realized via increased interregional standard dialect/written communication must also be accompanied by obvious locally focused dialect-related rewards (such as the dialect-using programs provided by Radio na Gaeltachta in Ireland and by radio and television in Italy, Germany, Norway and other countries where dialect differences are quite marked). Thus, whether a standard comes to be viewed as 'worth the price' is ultimately dependent not on corpus planning alone but on diverse aspects of sociocultural and econotechnical planning that are aimed in an interregionally equalizing direction. *Such interregional equalization is not essentially a dialect–standard issue* but one that must be tackled on many other fronts rather than on the dialect–standard front alone, if it is to be effectively attained. If and when it is attained, interdialectal rivalries and inequities will fade, even if they may not entirely disappear.

More obviously and directly related to RLS concerns, given that increased mother tongue transmission is so central to such concerns, is the question of the possibly negative impact of a recently selected and cultivated 'artificial' standard on spoken varieties that are seriously weakened and struggling for their very existence. Under such circumstances, when children come home from school speaking, reading and writing a dialect other than that of their home, neighborhood and community, this may well constitute an additional psychological burden for the already weak and fading intergenerational transmission capacity of local Xish. Parents who get the impression that their local Xish is 'not real Xish' or 'not proper Xish' may choose to give up Xish entirely rather than continue their halting efforts on its behalf.

This problem can be best handled by making sure that RLS-efforts recognize, utilize and dignify the local dialect (certainly in early elementary schooling and even in other formal agencies and functions), alongside or even in preference to the incipient standard. This is exactly what Basque educational authorities have done *vis-à-vis* their major non-standard dialect (which some few adherents regard to be the basis of a separate and rival standard), going so far, indeed, as to publish textbooks for the early elementary years in that variety. Ireland too has adopted a similarly permissive dialectal approach, recognizing thereby both non-native 'revivalist' Irish and the various still spoken Gaeltacht dialects. Pre-World War II Germany also essentially followed such a dialectally permissive approach, as did (and does) Italy, even though their languages are by no means threatened or without long-recognized standard varieties (see Fishman and Salmon, 1972; Zuanelli-Sonino, 1989).

*Teachers must always be situationally acceptive of dialect speech in the elementary classroom*, whether RLS is involved or not, and they must cultivate dialect acceptance among their pupils, regardless of whether one, two or many dialects are present in the classroom. This same kind of tolerance toward spoken dialects must also be cultivated among adults. The standard comes not to displace or replace the dialects, but to complement them in functions which they do not generally discharge and, therefore, in functions that do not compete with their own. Given this type of genuine admiration for and cultivation of dialect speech, RLS-efforts should be able to rally and foster the local supporters of Xish in various localities, leaving the acquisition of the standard variety for later, when local sensitivities are sufficiently satisfied so that repertoire-building can become both feasible and acceptable.[2] RLS must come to realize that most adults who have already completed their schooling may never acquire the 'new' standard, whether written or spoken, and that, whether old or new, most of them may also never need more than a passive command of the standard at any rate.

## If no standard can be agreed upon

Circumstances may arise such that no written standard can be agreed upon, either due to the severity of the interregional rivalries, or due to the very substantial degree of divergence between the various regional varieties, or, as is most common, due to both of the above reasons combined. This must be recognized as a complicating factor, but it is not the end of the world. There are many languages, large and small, that do not boast a single standard. 'Mighty English' is one such language, different regional spoken standards being perfectly acceptable both within and between the British Isles, the United States, Australia and New Zealand, and anglophone Africa, Asia and the Caribbean. This does not prove to be a serious problem for the continued spread of English (and this is so even though differences between the various written varieties are also quite noticeable). The absence of a single standard for Irish is somewhat more problematic. Local indigenous Gaeltacht varieties are widely retained in speech and also, to a lesser extent, in writing, on the one hand, whereas the efforts of Revivalists focus on the standard, on the other hand. Ultra-Orthodox Yiddish written usage is marked by adherence to no particular norm other than the studied avoidance of the somewhat different norms associated with the secular (and once secular-nationalist) YIVO, on the one hand, and Soviet usage, on the other. The various Romansch communities of Switzerland have no single written norm, a condition that also typifies the Ladin and Friulian communities of Northern Italy. In the latter cases, different editions of textbooks are prepared for learners of Xish in different communities, although this is often both an additional cost as well as an irritant *vis-à-vis* Xish, among both Xmen and Ymen. Apparently, in the eyes of many local beholders, 'really respectable' languages just don't operate in this fashion (although some of them really do, English among them, but that seems to be acceptable if at least they are sociopolitically self-regulating and not undergoing language shift).

Admitting that it is far better for RLS-efforts if a single written standard exists (or can be consensually agreed upon by most speakers and users of Xish), because weakened languages are generally not able to afford the multiplicity of standards that marks robust English and a few other major languages the world over (many of which are polycentric), it must also be admitted that it doesn't pay to force a written standard, much less a spoken one, on an adamantly unwilling or seriously ailing speech community. The hostility, opposition, fractionization and patterned evasion that result from unwanted standards exact a price which is far greater, both in morale and in actual language use, than the price exacted by multicentrism without an overarching, unifying standard. On the other hand, the absence of such a standard must not become the excuse for apathy and defeatism *vis-à-vis* RLS-efforts, a stance which is often noted among the Ladins, to their great detriment. Some speech communities are simply not ready for a standard (with its broader language and identity implications), and others may never be ready, and, if that is so, then that is as much a simple fact of life as is ongoing language shift *per se* and RLSers must seek ways and means of working around

it, at the same time that they continue to address a minor portion of their total
efforts to returning, from time to time, to re-examine the objective and subjective need for rectifying this state of affairs. Obviously a standard, particularly a
written one, will be far more necessary if and when stage 4 is reached and surpassed than otherwise and major efforts toward that end might best be placed on
the back-burner until the time for them is really both safe and ripe.


## Finally, Corpus Planning, in Moderation, is Definitely Needed Too

We have already discussed or implied two of the three aspects of the total
'standardization' process: graphization, and normification. In the modern world,
standard dialects are written languages and they have definite written conventions, as far as writing system, orthography and grammatical structure are concerned. One cannot simply write them as one natively speaks them, just as one
cannot spell them as one likes nor invent their letters as one goes along. For all
of these reasons, one has to learn how to write them, even when they are proximate to one's own native dialect, in special institutions that are established for
this purpose. The fact that 'nobody actually speaks that way' is an additional
part of the reason why the standard written dialect has to be learned by dint of
conscious effort and is normally not acquired as effortlessly as is native dialectal
speech itself.

However, another, and final, aspect of standardization remains to be discussed and it too is related to the very fact that the standard variety will be used
in conjunction with topics that are relatively recondite and, therefore, not like
normal conversational topics at all, in terms of their lexical demands. The standard dialect needs to be used in conjunction with topics which usually do not
arise in intimate and informal conversation, e.g. topics pertaining to science and
technology, to large-scale commerce and industry, to legal and medical questions
and complications that so typically and recurringly arise, not to mention the
urban consumer technology that has become part and parcel of everyone's daily
existence, for better or for worse. Most local dialects simply are lexically inadequate for these topics, all of which are substantially removed from rural or small
town experience, on the one hand, or even from the normal daily interaction of
average urban citizens, on the other hand. As the actual or potential language of
middle and even part of higher education, of at least a few somewhat specialized
publications, of legal pronouncements and legal documents, of organizational
and even some governmental deliberations and records, standard Xish will be in
need (or hopes to be in need) of lexical modernization and expansion. This goal

is pursued via special boards or committees (also frequently referred to as 'language academies') that are charged with 'corpus planning'.

Corpus planning is by no means limited entirely and exclusively to lexical elaboration for modernization purposes, but that is its most usual and ultimately its most crucial task, together with the preparation of the nomenclatures, dictionaries or handbooks in which the neologisms created by corpus planners are defined and communicated to their potential users or clienteles. The task of coining new terms for Xish is not an inordinately difficult one, but it *is* substantially more difficult to coin felicitous terms that will be quickly and widely accepted and utilized, in place of the Yish counterpart terms that are usually available first and that often already enjoy wide currency by the time the Xish neologisms finally come into being. Accordingly, 'successful corpus planning' is much harder than mere corpus planning, the latter activity being one in which most mortals dabble from time to time and to no apparent societal effect.

Successful corpus planning is even more crucial in connection with RLS than it is in connection with language planning for unthreatened languages. In the unthreatened case, a corpus planning *faux pas* now and then is bad enough. Neither the users of unthreatened Yish nor its corpus planners need be unduly alarmed about coming up with a 'lulu' now and then (a 'lulu' being a proposed neologism that is so unpopular that it is not only roundly rejected but scornfully laughed out of court). No one concludes from such mishaps that the language is 'on the ropes and sinking quickly'. In the case of threatened Xish, however, ridicule from within and without the speech community is quite another matter. It amounts to a public declaration that the language itself is ridiculous and that its attempts to cope with modernity are obviously destined to fail or, what is worse, to be completely and hopelessly ludicrous, esoteric and 'out of touch'. Accordingly, given the very severe attitudinal and usage penalties to be paid for corpus planning failures in the threatened languages arena, pro-RLSers must engage in such planning with the utmost care, sophistication and sensitivity to speech community preferences and flexibility-related characteristics.

Market research methods are useful tools in order to determine the probable acceptance (and also the probable criticisms) of new coinages before the latter are widely disseminated. The 'model of the good language' itself needs to be fully explored and consensually accepted before corpus planning 'products' are 'launched': Should the standard be patterned after region A or region B or should it be a compromise between the two? Does neologism A evoke any patterned disinclination or opposition and if so, among which sub-group(s) of the population? Indeed, this approach of pilot testing neologisms has been successfully followed in various 'unthreatened' contexts too (e.g. in Sweden), thus effectively breaking with the implicit tradition of so much of corpus planning in bygone days, when it was simply assumed that the language somehow 'belonged to the planners' (were they not the authorities as to what was linguistically good, bad or possible?) and that the speech community would ultimately and necessarily 'fall into line' with whatever it was that the planners suggested.

A favorable climate of opinion is necessary for corpus planning to succeed in a marketing or usage sense, rather than to be merely an intra-linguistic game. The neologisms must be such as to be maximally acceptable to their intended clienteles, or, at least, such as to elicit a minimum of fuss and discord. Generally speaking, corpus planning products are quickly adopted only by a small segment of their intended 'consumers', namely, by 'captive audiences' dependent upon the planners and their associated authorities for their livelihoods or for their ranks and privileges (e.g. armed forces personnel, government officers and their staffs, applicants or prospective applicants for authority- or government-controlled positions, perquisites, permits or licenses). Unfortunately, there are few if any such 'captive audiences' in connection with threatened languages, since threatened languages, almost by self-evident definition, have few authorities who can dispense with or withhold widely meaningful sanctions or rewards. Thus, the use and utility of Xish corpus planning neologisms may be rather restricted at best, realistically speaking, to the inner circle of 'true believers', and it is this inner circle that must remain solidary rather than fractionated or turned off by corpus planning. Xish cannot afford to lose any of those who are most committed to it and must attempt to expand its lexicon (or revise its orthography or engage in any other kind of corpus planning) gingerly and carefully, by means of judicious and relatively risk-free modifications or innovations.[3]

Finally, to tie back to our previous discussion of dialects, it should be remembered that a multiplicity of contending, viable dialects is a problem for RLS-oriented corpus planning and, should such contenders exist, every effort is required to draw upon their respective lexical stocks too, whenever possible, in connection with neologism formation. By doing so the standard may be able to both call upon and attract the loyalists of various dialects and upon their clienteles as well, in the ongoing effort to modernize 'threatened Xish', rather than to allow it to become merely a jumble of antiquated as well as discordant dialects.

## Language Planning that Helps and Language Planning that Hinders

The dialect/standard issue is initially a status-planning issue within Xish rather than between Xish and Yish. It is potentially strengthening for RLS to explain that Xish dialects are not shameful things at all but, rather, totally legitimate expressions of local life in its most intimate, informal and authentic persons, places and topics. It is also potentially helpful to clarify patiently why a particular dialect or compromise between dialects has been (or should be) chosen as the standard dialect (for written and formal spoken communication), because without a consensually recognized and unifying standard, RLS will necessarily be handicapped with regard to its appeal to those whose life-style is modern/urban, a life-style in which written, formal and extra-local communication are all crucial aspects of the total repertoire. In modern times, Xish RLS-efforts themselves will almost certainly be handicapped, rather than either helped or left unaffected, both absolutely and relatively speaking, without a standard. The fact that various 'Big Brothers' can get away without a single, overarching standard is neither here nor there in the pejorative arena in which threatened languages must struggle for their existence.

So far so good. But from here on in language planning can run into trouble and cause trouble for the RLS-effort, both in connection with the actual choice of a standard and the modernization or development of the standard to make it usable in a larger array of modern pursuits. Movements on behalf of weakened and threatened languages are in no position to force the decisions or dictates of a small circle of 'language authorities' upon unwilling, resistant or hostile speakers of various dialects or sociolects, no matter how linguistically sophisticated these authorities might be, particularly if some of the speakers of these other varieties have harbored disappointed aspirations that their own variety would be selected for the standard role. In this connection, much more than linguistic sophistication is called for. Historical perspective is needed to anticipate problems. Political skills are needed to work out compromises and trade-offs between various interested parties, regions and interests. The spirit of compromise, in terms of 'half a pie is better than none', is necessarily part of the very stuff of RLS, particularly at the early stages when it is necessary to pick priorities wisely and to maximize the slender forces and the potential allies that are within reach.

In the spirit of compromise it may be necessary to make special provisions for one or another variety, other than the standard, to share in at least a few of the status functions associated with the standard and to do so for a period of time. The truly operative (rather than the merely pro-forma) selection of a standard is dictated by long-term successful economic and political developments in the course of RLS itself, rather than at the moment when a committee of linguists or other language authorities hands down its decision. This is worth repeating, particularly to linguists: it is status planning, not corpus planning, that is the engine of all language planning success. Accordingly, it behooves one and all to make inclusive or permissive, rather than exclusive (excluding), decisions, particularly initially, both with respect to the selection of a standard dialect and with respect to the corpus planning undertaken on its behalf. If RLS succeeds over the long run, there will be time enough for more focused and potentially excluding decision making, hopefully at a time when Xish is better able to pay the inevitable price that such decision making exacts. A flexible standard (one with a sufficient number of permissible alternatives to satisfy various dialectal preferences, e.g. the acceptability of either British or American pronunciation or spelling of English throughout the English-speaking world) is not only much better than no standard at all; it is also better than a standard that exacts a huge price in terms of compliance and, therefore, in terms of RLS support.

## The Special Case of Corpus Planning under 'Ausbau' Circumstances

Whether in connection with defining a standard or in connection with lexical expansion and modernization, the need for moderation in corpus planning that is sensitive to and in accord with the realities of RLS status planning is particularly great in those cases where Xish is 'genetically' very close to Yish to begin with. Under such circumstances, Xish is frequently viewed (and not only by Ymen) as lacking the basic autonomy of corpus to be considered a 'truly separate' language. This view adds a layer of seeming linguistic dependence to the economic, social, cultural and political dependence that usually exists between Xish and Yish even when the latter is linguistically poles apart from the former. This additional parameter of dependence often presents an additional heavy burden for pro-Xish RLS-efforts.

Of the twelve cases that we have reviewed in earlier chapters of this volume Frisian and Netherlandish are obviously sufficiently close genetically to cause this type of problem to plague the weaker of the two, Frisian. However, during the Franco years, Catalan too was cast in this light (as a 'mere dialect' of Spanish and, therefore, as deserving no particular cultivation or recognition) by the authorities in Madrid; and during the nineteenth century, when Yiddish was still widely spoken by Jews in Germany (or even by Jews in Poland or elsewhere in Eastern Europe where German was once widely known and respected), this was the light in which Yiddish was widely viewed *vis-à-vis* German. In all three instances, corpus planning efforts were instituted on behalf of Xish to combat the negative interpretation of such seemingly excessive phonological, lexical and grammatical similarity to Yish by (a) stressing and (b) increasing the differences between Xish and the stronger rivals. Such efforts are referred to today as being of an *'Ausbau'* nature, or, literally, as 'building away', i.e., consciously making Xish less like Yish than it might otherwise be.[4]

The fact that neither pro-RLS Catalans, Frisians or ultra-Orthodox Yiddish activists currently consider the genetic similarity of their languages to their rivals as being among their chief problems, is a good indication of the substantially perspectival nature of the entire autonomy issue. The deeper genetic similarities between Xish (Xish$_1$, Xish$_2$ and Xish$_3$) and Yish (Yish$_1$, Yish$_2$ and Yish$_3$) remain substantially as they were (for they are largely impervious to *Ausbau* efforts), but the 'level of self-confidence' differences between their communities of speakers has narrowed sufficiently for the genetic differences to be reinterpreted as pluses, because they make it far easier for Xmen-via-Yish (or even Ymen) to learn to understand or even to use Xish than would otherwise be the case. The further fact that Catalan is so much better off from an RLS point of view than Frisian is also a sure sign that language distance *per se* is a very weak determinant of RLS success. Linguistic genetic similarity does not hamper otherwise self-regulatory sociocultural communities. Neither Urdu *vis-à-vis* Hindi, Macedonian *vis-à-vis* Bulgarian or Croatian *vis-à-vis* Serbian are materially inconvenienced by genetic similarity *per se*, and the fact that such similarity does so often materially inconvenience threatened languages is a result of the larger sociocultural, econotechnical and political disadvantages to which they are exposed and the reinterpretation of linguistic facts in the light of the power discrepancies between them and their neighbors.

The above facts and developments may serve as a lesson to Xish linguists not to go overboard in their *Ausbau* efforts. When Xish is still on the weak side of the diglossic functional continuum an overly aggressive stress on removing its similarities *vis-à-vis* Yish may be dislocative, both in informal and in literacy-related functions. Certainly, the relatively small (and decreasing) band of fluent speakers and accomplished writers of Xish should not be made to feel embarrassed because of their use of 'excessive Yisms' in their Xish. Rather, the spirit of dialectal tolerance should be invoked, on the one hand, while those few exemplars who can understandably and expressively utilize 'pure Xish' (i.e. a variety maximally different from Yish) should certainly do so, on the other hand. While RLS is still on the weak side of the diglossic 'continental divide' its objectives should be to increase use, fluency and acceptance of the Xish that is still native-like in nature, rather than to denigrate any of those who could be allies and activists. Above all, *Ausbau* efforts should avoid puristic recommendations that are generally reacted to as being laughable, stilted, 'wooden' or 'odd'. Such recommendations will merely alienate the good will that Xish language specialists could otherwise effectively activate for crucial functional efforts both before and after the 'continental divide' is crossed. It is the crossing of the 'divide' plus the tenor of intergroup relations between Xmen and Ymen, rather than the *Ausbau* efforts themselves, that ultimately determine the success of *Ausbau*.

Perhaps the basic lesson for pro-Xish linguists is that *Ausbau* efforts must foster but not outstrip the language consciousness and the self-regulatory capacities of the bulk of the Xish speech-and-writing community at any particular time. The similarity between Xish and Yish may, at times, have to be shrugged off as no more indicative of a lack of self-regulatory rights and capacities than those that exist between the equally self-regulatory genetically similar 'couples' that we have mentioned above. There are also some advantages to genetic similarity, as we have also seen above. These should be taken advantage of fully, particularly during the early stages of the RLS struggle. Ultimately, the major contributions to *Ausbau* and of *Ausbau* to RLS must come at the later stages of what is, at best, a long and difficult process.

## Conclusions

Language planning efforts of various kinds must be oriented toward being problem solving and must guard against becoming (or even being viewed by Xmen as becoming) problem creating. That is especially true for the various types of corpus planning, including the definition and selection of a standard for Xish and the expansion or modernization of the Xish lexicon in order to render it more intertranslatable with Yish and other languages of international modernity. It is sometimes difficult for the few pro-RLS linguists to think of themselves as problem causing, especially since they are usually aware of the sterling contributions that scores of linguists have made, particularly during the past two centuries, to successful nationalist movements. However, in the last decade of the twentieth century and throughout the twenty-first century the needs and priorities of seriously threatened languages (Xish 'on the weak side') will be quite different from those of successful nationalist movements in earlier times. It is then, when the RLS movement that they are trying to serve is on 'the weak side', after two centuries of modernization have eroded its potential, that sympathetic linguists must particularly learn to differentiate between status planning that helps and that hinders and, most particularly of all, between corpus planning that helps and that hinders.

## Notes

1.  Some of the major recent references to the language planning literature are Joan Rubin *et al.*, 1977; J. Cobarrubias and J. A. Fishman, eds, 1983; L. Laforge, ed., 1987; and Robert L. Cooper, 1990. An ongoing familiarity with the field of language planning and its most recent literature can be attained via perusing the *New*

    *Language Planning Newsletter*, published by the Central Institute of Indian Languages (Mysore, India).

2.  There are many sociolinguistic studies and discussions pertaining to attitudes toward dialectal varieties, those that do have and those that do not (yet) have standard dialect counterparts. The following may be of particular interest in the context of language shift and reversing language shift: W. Braunstein *et al.*, 1979; K. Deprez, 1984; J. Köberl and J. Stükler, 1984; T. Priestly (in press); and Ellen B. Ryan, 1979. Compromise standard dialects, i.e. standards that are not structurally identical to formal speech in any single dialect area, are much more common than usually meets the eye or than tends to be admitted or remembered in subsequent generations. The Pilipino/Filipino and the Yiddish standard are merely two frequently reported upon examples from a much longer list of such compromise standard dialects.

3.  The 'image of the good language' which guides corpus planners, and the judicious market research approach to corpus planning in order to avoid massive rejection of corpus 'products' are discussed in J. A. Fishman, 1983, and K.-H. Dahlstedt, 1976.

4.  The term '*Ausbau* language' is contrasted with its opposite, '*Abstand* language', i.e. 'distance language', a designation for any language that is genetically so dissimilar from another that neither could be taken for dialects of the other, regardless of the power differentials that might exist between their respective speech communities. Accordingly, Basque (*vis-à-vis* Spanish) and Irish, Spanish, Navajo, French in Quebec, Hebrew, Maori and Australian Aboriginal languages (*vis-à-vis* English) are all 'Abstand' languages, with the case of Yiddish and English being somewhat moot since they are both basically Germanic in genetic classification. The terms themselves, '*ausbau*' and '*abstand*', were initially suggested by Heinz Kloss (1967). The measurement and theory of genetic classification are both still inexact and highly conflicted fields of linguistic activity (see Greenberg, 1987) and the popular interpretation of such classification is, of course, even more inexact and subject to cultural and ideological bias. On the other hand, the very looseness of the popular classifications and self-classifications make it possible for successful RLS-efforts to bring about dramatic changes in autonomy judgments, as the Catalan/Spanish and many other cases throughout the world and throughout history amply demonstrate.

# References

BRAUNSTEIN, W., KOBERL, J. and STUCKLER, J. 1979, Vorurteile gegen Dialektsprechern. *Klagenfurter Beitrage zur Sprachwissenschaft* 5, 1–19.

COBARRUBIAS, J. and FISHMAN, J. A. (eds) 1983, *Progress in Language Planning*. Berlin: Mouton.

COOPER, Robert L. 1990, *Language Planning*. Oxford: Oxford University Press.

DAHLSTEDT, K.-H. 1976, Societal ideology and language cultivation: The case of Sweden. *International Journal of the Sociology of Language* 10, 17–50.

DEPREZ, K. 1984, Why do Antwerpians consider Netherlandis language varieties as 'cultured', 'pleasant', 'beautiful', 'rich'? In K. DEPREZ (ed.) *Sociolinguistics in the Low Countries*. Amsterdam: Benjamins, 237–85.

FISHMAN, J. A. 1983, Modeling rationales in corpus planning: modernity and tradition in images of the good corpus. In J. COBARRUBIAS and J. A. FISHMAN (eds) *Progress in Language Planning*. Berlin: Mouton, 107–18.

FISHMAN, Joshua A. and LUEDERS-SALMON, Erica 1972, What has the sociology of language to say to the teacher? On teaching the standard variety to speakers of dialectal varieties. In Courtney CAZDEN *et al.* (eds) *Functions of Language in the Classroom.* New York: Teachers College Press, 67–83. Reprinted in my (1972) *Language in Sociocultural Change.* Stanford: Stanford University Press, 340–55.

GREENBERG, Joseph H. 1987, [Author's precis of his *Language in the Americas*, followed by critical comments by several anthropological linguists and concluding with the author's rebuttal]. *Current Anthropology* 28, 647–67.

KLOSS, Heinz 1967, 'Abstand languages' and 'Ausbau languages'. *Anthropological Linguistics* 9, No. 7, 29–41.

KÖBERL, J. and STÜKLER, J. 1984, Sind Dialektsprecher dummer? *Grazer Linguistische Studien* 21, 131–41.

LAFORGE, L. 1987, *Proceedings of the International Colloquium on Language Planning.* Quebec City: Laval University Press.

PRIESTLY, Tom (in press), 'Our dialect sounds stupid'; The importance of attitudes to so-called sub-standard language codes as a factor in the (non-)retention of Slovene in Carinthia, Austria.

RUBIN, Joan *et al.* 1977, *Language Planning Processes.* Belin: Mouton.

RYAN, Ellen B. 1979, Why do low-prestige language varieties persist? In H. GILES and R. ST CLAIR (eds) *Language and Social Psychology.* Oxford: Blackwell, 145–57.

ZUANELLI-SONINO, Elisabetta (ed.) 1989, Italian Sociolinguistics: Trends and Issues. *International Journal of the Sociology of Language* No. 76 (entire issue).

# 12 The Intergenerational Transmission of 'Additional' Languages for Special Purposes

## Intergenerational Mother Tongue Continuity

In stable, substantially self-regulatory societies, mother tongues reveal intergenerational continuity. Although some degree of language change is constantly ongoing, parents and children can, nevertheless, justifiably be said to speak 'the same language', at least by and large; that is, the mother tongue of the parents is usually and normatively handed on to their children and this is so on a society-wide basis. Indeed, intergenerational ethnocultural continuity so largely subsumes intergenerational mother tongue continuity, that we have come to expect the one when the other obtains and have largely lost the sense of 'the wonder of it all' which is at the base of all scientific inquiry. Once we begin to ask questions about this seemingly 'natural and effortless' process, the many things that could (and sometimes do) go awry begin to become more obvious. Even if we set aside the many still problematic aspects of language acquisition *per se* (after all, as many as 10% of all children acquire speech imperfectly or 'problematically') and focus only on the topic of intergenerational code continuity, many questions come to mind.

Many parents have learned 'additional languages' during or after their own childhood. Why aren't those languages which are acquired as 'additional languages' for generation $G_1$, and which must have been learned because of the rewards or advantages with which they were associated, handed on as mother tongues to the children that constitute generation $G_2$? At any given time, at least half of the post-elementary school non-English mother tongue world seems to be learning English. Why isn't this language (particularly in all those places where it is well learned) then handed on to the next generation as its mother tongue, thereby saving that generation much time, effort and expense, and thereby maximizing for it the benefits to be derived from English, the very benefits (and even additional benefits as well) for which their parents originally exerted themselves to acquire English? Indeed, given all the trials and tribulations of 'small national languages' (Fishman, 1984), it is really quite surprising that most of these languages normally do continue to experience seemingly effortless inter-generational continuity and that they are not voluntarily replaced by those very languages of wider communication that the mother tongue speakers of smaller national languages so regularly master in their ongoing search for both the inter-regional and international advantages that their own mother tongues cannot pro-vide. Why English is *generally not* handed on by English-speaking parents among Netherlanders to their children, and why, therefore, it has to be learned anew by those children after Dutch has already been acquired, while the so much 'less useful' Dutch is handed on by these same parents to their children, is a riddle worth pondering for all those interested in RLS. Why isn't Dutch a threatened language, given that almost all middle-class Netherlanders past ele-mentary school age speak English too and, indeed, do so rather well at that?

## Intergenerational Continuity of Minority Mother Tongues

Some light on the above questions has been shed by research and theoretical formulations pertaining to the intergenerational transmission of minority (or sub-national) languages. In this context, intergenerational mother tongue continuity is very frequently not only endangered but largely or entirely unattained (even in the democratic Netherlands). The basic issue can now be understood as being one of boundary maintenance and control, both *between ethnocultures* as well as between domains *within ethnocultures*. National languages, even small national languages, are substantially protected by political boundaries and by social boundaries and social institutions that are politically protected. These help sepa-rate populations into insiders and outsiders and they define the cultural desiderata — including language — which are required for inside membership. Where minority cultures are sufficiently intact to protect their cultural boundaries (and, of course, interested in doing so), they institute counterpart ethnocultural defens-es for *their* mother tongues. Where such socio-cultural counterparts to political boundaries are in place, even small minorities can attain intergenerational mother tongue continuity (viz. the Old Order Amish and the Hasidic Jews in the USA); lacking them, even large ones cannot do so (viz. the experience of millions of German Americans, Polish Americans, Franco-Americans, Italian Americans, etc. [Fishman *et al.*, 1985]) who have lost their ethnic mother tongues.

Boundaries, political or ethnocultural, imply separation of populations, the control of boundary crossings, the regulation of imports, the definition of desir-able and undesirable cross-boundary relations. Minority ethnocultures, whether indigenous or immigrant, are often prohibited from or incapable of exercising such controls. They are required/compelled to use outside institutions, person-nel, norms and procedures for sensitive functions in connection with familial, religious, educational and economic pursuits. Their internal ethnocultural norms and standards with respect to their reliance upon and their requirement of established indigenous behaviors, observances, institutions and authorities, are weakened and in disarray, often marked more by patterned evasion than by patterned implementation. Democratic governments may not utilize compulsion in attaining these end-results among their minorities, but they accomplish the same, or even greater, destruction of minority boundary maintenance via fostering interactive dependency and relatively open access to educational, economic and political rewards for the most fully transethnified and translinguified individuals of Xish provenance. As a result of such conscious and unconscious 'democratic' Yish policies, ethnocultural minorities not only learn the 'outside' language but displacively use it with one another, on the 'inside', *for advantages which also obtain even within the weakened and transculturating minority community itself.* Such 'inside' use of the 'outside' language is a prime indicator of the erosion of substantially self-regulated ethnocultural boundaries and increasingly robs intergenerational mother tongue continuity of even its most protected and intimate ethno-identificational advantages and functions. Unless RLS-efforts can reverse this situation, it spells the beginning of the end. The outside language not only maintains its unchallenged advantages re 'outside' interactions and rewards, but it attains unrestricted inside advantages as well, thereby rendering the inside language an unnecessary redundancy and tending to vitiate the distinction between inside and outside as a whole (Fishman, 1981).

Note that the crucial problem of intergenerational minority mother tongue continuity is not that of maintaining all ethnocultural boundaries *vis-à-vis* the 'outside'. Almost all Old Order Amish and Hasidic Jews have learned to speak, read and write a regionally unmarked variety of English. Indeed, Old Order Amish schools (being schools of type 4a in our typology) typically devote only *a morning a week* to their sanctified religious 'classical' which they refer to as 'Luther German', and *no instructional time at all* to Pennsylvania German, their everyday vernacular. The crucial problem for intergenerational minority ethnocultural continuity in general, and for mother tongue continuity in particular, is regulating the extent to which outside desiderata can be utilized for inside pursuits. If the outside language is basically used for indigenously monitored interactions with outsiders, then it cannot become the mother tongue of the next generation. In any intact and essentially self-regulating ethnoculture, one's children are, by definition, insiders, not outsiders, and are communicated with and socialized in the language of insiders, the ethnocultural mother tongue. The cultural posture whereby one language is reserved for one set of ethnoculturally approved and essentially self-regulated functions (e.g. outside relations) and another language is reserved for another set of ethnoculturally approved and essentially self-regulated functions (e.g. inside relations) is referred to as diglossia (or as situational diglossia) in the sociolinguistic literature (Fishman, 1980a; Britto, 1986). In its most general terms, diglossia both represents and requires the maintenance of intercultural and intracultural boundaries. Whereas the latter may not be possible without some degree of the former, it is the latter *per se* which is necessary for intergenerational mother tongue continuity.

If we understand that it is the maintenance of stage 6 intracultural boundaries that is the minimally essential requirement for intergenerational minority mother tongue maintenance and transmission, then we can more easily understand why it is that small national languages, on the one hand, and additional languages of wider communication or languages for special purposes, on the other hand, generally achieve such vastly different kinds of intergenerational continuity. Let us first examine an example of the unhampered intergenerational continuity of a small national language.

Like most other small national languages, Dutch (or, more formally correct, Netherlandish) has no problem transmitting itself intergenerationally, even though most adults (and almost all young folks and younger adults, i.e. adults of child-bearing age) have acquired English fluency. Even when 100% of all post-elementary school Netherlanders will know English (a goal which is almost certainly close to having been achieved), each new generation of Dutch offspring will still have to learn the language as an additional language and will do so primarily outside of their own homes. Each new generation of Dutch children will start off as Dutch mother tongue monolinguals and will, therefore, initially only speak Dutch at home, with their parents, siblings, relatives, friends and neighbors. As they subsequently acquire English in school and via mass media exposure (including exposure to the increasingly ubiquitous English-programmed personal computer), the above pattern will generally nevertheless remain unaltered. Even if they may then discuss a very few and substantively restricted topics in English with some of the above-mentioned individuals, such discussions will be few in number, exceptions to the rule, topically circumscribed and defined in terms of metaphorical interaction in a different set of role relationships (e.g. advanced technology 'nuts, pseudo-experts or experts'), rather than in terms of the more basic and intimate home, family, neighborhood or ethnonational community relationships.

## Intergenerational 'Additional Language' Continuity within the Ethnonational Mainstream

The above example enables us to realize why the intergenerational continuity of additional languages is not displacive and, therefore, not problematic in the case of ethnocultures in control of their own polities. Such societies control their own educational and media systems (our stages 4 and 2) and, therefore, can assure that generation after generation of students will be taught the same additional language(s), just as long as it is deemed instrumentally, sentimentally or humanistically advantageous for them to do so. Controlling, as they do, their intercultural boundaries for their own advantage (which, of course, does not mean freezing them), they can discontinue fostering one additional language (e.g. German), or relegate it to briefer study during the later elementary or secondary school years (e.g. French), while introducing another (e.g. English) and giving it earlier as well as more intensive curricular exposure. Furthermore, and much more crucially, controlling as well their intracultural boundaries, they need not be concerned that such more intensive exposure will threaten the national language (and the mother tongue of most students), since Dutch intracultural requirements for participation in Dutch family and neighborhood-community life, Dutch education, Dutch religious life, Dutch economic life, a goodly share of Dutch mass media and all of Dutch governmental services oriented toward the general public will remain unaltered and uncompromised.

No one will ever say to a Dutch youngster whose English is poor 'You are not a good Dutchman; you have neglected an important means of expressing and implementing Dutchness. You can only lead an archaic and provincial Dutch life, and, were you to be taken as a model, Dutch culture itself would be impoverished by the example that you are setting.' Obviously, the now institutionalized intergenerational continuity of 'English as the favorite additional language in the Netherlands', stable though this may be, is not confused with Dutchness, any more than is the stability of the school's (and of society's) stress on other advanced skills. *Vis-à-vis* Dutchness, both English and algebra are viewed as highly desired aspects of a well educated and advantageously educated person. However, English is always an addition to Dutchness and, basically, an outside-oriented addition in terms of its curricular rationale and socio-pedagogic orientation. It is not intended to be, nor will it be, barring the severe dislocation of Dutch ethnocultural self-regulation, an inside language of Dutch society at large.[1] The very means and locus of responsibility for its acquisition and intergenerational transmission is primarily via out-of-home agencies. This should be a consolation for all RLSers who find it impossible to conquer stage 6. There *is* life without stage 6; unfortunately, it is not intergenerational mother tongue/vernacular life.

# Intergenerational Additional Language Continuity of Religious Classicals

In addition to the schools, the entertainment media and the import-export or tourist-oriented facets of the national economy, all of which are important in the spread of English in non-English mother tongue settings, there is yet another major avenue of intergenerational continuity for additional languages. Church Latin, Koranic Arabic, Prayerbook and Old Testament Hebrew, Talmudic Aramaic, Luther Bible German, Old Church Slavonic, Ecclesiastic Greek, Ecclesiastic Armenian and Coptic are just a few Euro-mediterranean examples of religious classicals that have long been maintained on an intergenerational basis. In some cases, these languages are 'target (i.e. textual) languages' to which ample school time is devoted over the course of many years. In other cases, they are 'merely' learned by virtue of repeated use in religious services and in home rituals, with no explicit school time being assigned to them. In some cases, the power of the secular state authority is added to that of religious authority, in order to require and to subsidise school attention to these languages. In other cases, the separation of church and state is clear and sharp, and it is the church itself that must accomplish this intergenerational transmission.

'Church itself', of course, is a simplification of ethnocultural reality, a simplification which the Western European tradition of legal separation between church and state tends to foster. Churches are very commonly (indeed, nearly always) not only ethnoculturally encumbered but, also, ethnoculturally quite specific. Religions are not only part and parcel of ethnocultural life, but indigenous (or indigenized) religions are usually quite specifically legitimized in ethnocultural terms as well. Even the so-called 'universal religions' have developed quite specific ethnocultural variants or 'local coloring', and the overwhelming majority of ethnocultures are still religiously quite homogeneous. Therefore, when we say that a given religious classical language achieves intergenerational continuity due to the 'church itself', we must keep in mind that this means not only due to church attendence *per se* but due to church schools, church youth groups, church influence on home ritual practices, etc. Indeed, the church (the term 'church' being used here as a generic, to signify both the central authority and the local religious unit of whatever religious tradition, whether Christian or not) is a core aspect of the ethnoculture and a reflection of, as well as an instrument of, the ethnoculture's boundary maintenance processes and capacity.

To some extent, religious classicals are similar to the position of English in Holland. No matter how highly regarded, how well taught. how eagerly learned or how well mastered, they remain additional languages for narrow, specific purposes, and they remain such generation after generation, without becoming mother tongues. In other respects, however, religious classicals are similar to ethnocultural mother tongues. They are definitely 'inside'-related and, indeed, they are requirements for ethnocultural membership, until and unless church authorities decide otherwise. Xmen-via-Yish discontinuities are definitely possible within the religious fold. Latin is no longer the common ritual language of the Roman Catholic church; Hebrew has been minimized in Reform Jewish worship; Ecclesiastic Armenian has been de-emphasized in the churches of the Armenian Prelacy in the USA, and Ecclesiastic Greek is no longer the exclusive language of ritual services in the Greek Orthodox Church in the USA. The Missouri Synod Luther Church has been practically de-Germanized during the past 30 years.

Note, however, that except for the Latin example, all of the other examples, above, pertain to religion among immigrant, minority ethnocultural ethno-religious groups whose churches are relatively unprotected by strong boundary maintenance mechanisms *vis-à-vis* their surrounding 'outside' (mainstream) host contexts. As a result, it was the mother tongue of the host contexts that could not be denied, neither in their churches nor in their daily lives. However, where the immigrant-minority situation does not obtain, or where minority–host relations are less incorporative than they are in the USA, that is, where indigenous/indigenized churches serve indigenous/indigenized populations that are fully set off from one another ethnoculturally, then religious classicals regularly remain intergenerationally continuous without either becoming mother tongues or being displaced by them. They do so by punctiliously regulating the differences between ethnocultural behaviors of one kind (e.g. the sermon, announcements, social activities) and ethnocultural behaviors of other kinds (e.g. the holy service and other rituals); i.e. by controlling boundaries within the 'inside'.

## Intergenerational Continuity of Religious Classicals among Minorities

Ethnocultural minorities with religious classicals are engaged in a two-front struggle. Not only must they seek to maintain control of their intragroup boundaries as far as their ethnocultural mother tongues are concerned (e.g. Pennsylvania German, Yiddish, demotic Greek, Palestinian Arabic, etc.), but they must also seek to do the same insofar as their religious classicals are concerned (i.e, Luther Bible German, Classical Hebrew/(Judeo-)Aramaic, Ecclesiastic Greek, Koranic Arabic). Generally the two 'fronts' are closely related to each other and success or failure on the one is related to success or failure on the other. Nevertheless, when differentials develop between the two boundary maintenance 'fronts', it is regularly the religious classical that is maintained longer in its culturally specific functions than is the mother tongue. The religious domain has more authoritative (and, therefore, more resistant) boundaries than does the 'secular' (i.e. less religiously influenced) ethnocultural system with which it is associated. The language use of the former is sanctified, and protected by ritualization, both of which are protectively encapsulating *vis-à-vis* the inroads of everyday secular life. The whole posture of religious classicals is tradition-and-stability ('eternity') oriented rather than progress-and-change oriented. As a result, American Jews (and most diaspora Jews everywhere) are much more protective of Prayerbook/Old Testament Hebrew and Talmudic Aramaic than they are of Yiddish (or Judezmo, Parsic, Yahudic, or other post-exilic Jewish diaspora languages). Similarly, Greek-Americans preserve at least some (and often more than just 'some') Ecclesiastic Greek in their church services, while Arab-Americans and Chinese-Americans continue to prepare their children in Koranic Arabic and Classicized Cantonese or Mandarin hallowed texts, even after they have all become fully English-speaking 'third generation ethnics' (Fishman, 1980b).

Because 'religion' is concerned with eternals rather than with everyday passing events, it is more conservative, less compromising or adapting and more compelling insofar as boundary maintenance is concerned. The home-supported neighborhood-community maintained school and the home-supported neighborhood-community maintained church (both pertaining to stage 5) are the institutions that are relied upon for the intergenerational continuity of these religious classicals for specific purposes, languages that never become and are never intended to become vernaculars or mother tongues. Their relative isolation from the vicissitudes of daily secular life and high-culture power-plays helps protect them when Yish spreads into and overcomes the latter domains. Their relative shelteredness and unimportance *vis-à-vis* 'real power' in the modern world also enables them to retain their relatively uninterrupted institutional effectiveness for the transmission of non-vernacular classical religious tongues.

## Intergenerational Continuity of Heritage Languages as Non-Vernaculars for Specific Purposes among Minorities

Ethnolinguistic minorities that have already undergone the process of language shift, due to insufficient boundary maintenance of the intra- and intercommunal kinds that we have discussed above, nevertheless frequently attempt to assure intergenerational continuity of their erstwhile mother tongues (now often referred to as 'heritage languages' to connote their *past* — rather than their present — currency as languages of everyday life), so that these can be utilized for specific and delimited ethnicity-encumbered 'special events'. Efforts on behalf of heritage languages normally proceed via the establishment of stage 5 or 4a schools to transmit, *de novo* to each successive school-age generation, a language that was formerly acquired at home and then merely reinforced or polished at school for repertoire expansion purposes. Since such home-supported-but-school-based heritage languages correspond neither to an outside nor even to an appreciable inside societal reality, they are generally only meagerly or marginally mastered at best. Nevertheless, parental (and grandparental) devotion may be sufficient to enable teachers to prepare children to perform well (via school-assembly recitations, folksong concerts, dramatic presentations, institutionalized holiday celebrations, etc.) on ethnic festivals and family occasions throughout the calendar cycle.

However, notwithstanding the parental interest and the teacher dedication that generally undergird the schools that continue to teach children heritage languages which even their parents understand poorly if at all, the level of mastery attained by the children soon reaches a plateau during the early elementary school years and then declines during adolescence, as the rewards, experiences and orientations of out-of-home life in Yish, even ethnic group life in Yish, become predominant. Be this as it may, the heritage language (an erstwhile mother tongue) may continue to be taught as an additional language on an inter-generational basis, albeit usually to a shrinking clientele, for very restricted and quite ritualized (even if secular) purposes. Heritage language learning can become a *rite de passage* for the young, but, unlike religious classicals, they have no really safe out-of-school institutional base of their own, given that they are only rarely used at home, in the neighborhood or in church, if at all. The her-itage language school may persist in teaching the language, but, barring a renewed influx of young immigrant speakers of any given heritage language, it will be little more than a relic of bygone days in societal terms because, like var-ious other recondite subjects, it has no real functional validity outside the school that is entrusted with its instruction. Long-term prospects for intergenerational continuity under such circumstances are not good, precisely because of the extreme attrition of heritage languages *vis-à-vis* most aspects of home and neighborhood functioning at the very same time that *respect for the memory of such functioning* in the past is their only claim to church (stage 6) or school (stages 5 or 4a) attention. As that memory fades with time, so, inevitably, does that attention.

## What Features Characterize the Attainment of Intergenerational Continuity of Additional Languages for Special Purposes?

Various languages of wider communication and various religious classicals have achieved long-term intergenerational continuity, both among mainstream and minority populations, and have succeeded in doing so without either aiming at or attaining mother tongue status. In many cases their continuity is even better than that attained by Irish or Frisian, where vernacularization and intergenerational mother tongue status *have* been pursued. The relative success and longevity of intergenerational continuity efforts on behalf of 'additional languages' must lead RLS advocates and activists to ask themselves what can be learned from such efforts and to wonder whether the mother tongue goal is really a necessary or only an expendable feature of their ultimate goal: fostering the prevalence of Xmen-via-Xish.

What features characterize the long-term attainment of intergenerational continuity of additional languages for special purposes? First of all, all of the cases we have mentioned are characterized by a very clear motivational and ideological clarity with respect to functional issues. It is very clear 'what English is for' in the Netherlands, just as it is clear what Ecclesiastic Greek is for in the Greek Orthodox diaspora world. Although these are not static affairs and there is some room for minority opinions (which may ultimately lead to changes in both motives and ideologies), the functional and motivational/ideological clarity that obtains in connection with additional languages is an expression of a communal 'vote of confidence' that these languages are really needed and that considerable resources, material and psychological, can be counted upon in order to support the quest for their intergenerational continuity. We are definitely not dealing with a serious 'Xmen-via-Yish' opposition *vis-à-vis* the functions for which English in the Netherlands and Greek in the Greek Orthodox diaspora are desired.

Such an implicit (and often explicit) 'vote of confidence' would, of course, be highly advantageous for RLS-efforts as well, but, given the fact that such efforts normally get underway after serious erosion of Xish has already occurred and after the 'Xmen-via-Yish' alternative is well established, a 'vote of no-confidence' has already been cast among many whom RLS movements must seek to influence and 'convert'. This, then, is an important distinction. RLS-efforts often deal with much more conflicted ethnocultural issues than does the typical or modal case of the intergenerational acquisition of languages of wider communication and religious classicals.

Secondly, the repertoire range at which the intergenerational continuity of additional languages (ICAL) normally aims is far narrower than the repertoire range at which most RLS-efforts aim. ICAL normally aims at a rather narrow repertoire range, does not attempt any identity transformation and relies on only a very few and quite specific institutions for language acquisition and implementation. ICAL is also unconflicted in these connections and it does not face a bitter, long-standing internal struggle between those who seek broader and those who are satisfied with narrower functions and institutional bases. RLS seeks mother tongue functions and, therefore, identity transformation or intensification. Even when RLS explicitly recognizes the need for an ultimate bilingual 'compromise solution' (such explicit recognition often being absent), it inevitably strains toward increased functions and more varied institutional supports. At the very least, it seeks to occupy the entire internal (intra-Xish) daily-life space, whereas ICAL efforts are more modest, in many ways, seeking to occupy only a corner of family-neighborhood-community or work life. The anomaly is clear: the initially stronger and more consensual effort also pursues more modest and institutionally more sheltered goals while the weaker, more conflicted and more exposed effort often pursues more difficult and all-encompassing goals.

Third, ICAL functions are not only more restricted but they are often also more protected than the functions that RLS advocates pursue. Daily life is amorphous and tends to flow into any and all pursuits. Business and religion have their definite times, role relations and places. They have institutional boundaries (schools, churches, offices) which protect them. These boundaries keep them from intruding and also keep other times, role relations, and places from intruding on them. RLS-efforts are often 'all over the map', which not only dilutes their impact but also makes it harder for them to find a safe niche of their own, where they can breathe free from outside competition and interference. The 'safe zones' of ICAL are not only more easily and fully bounded, but they are the very zones that are crucial for their intergenerational continuity *per se*. RSL-efforts not only often disregard the need for 'safe zones', but show little awareness of the fact that those functions that are of greatest concern to them, the mother tongue functions, are crucially linked to the family-neighborhood-community stage. Accordingly, RLS-efforts often suffer from weak boundary separation *vis-à-vis* external interactions, on the one hand, and *vis-à-vis* internal (intracultural) interactions, on the other hand, and, in addition, undertake few if any efforts that are specifically oriented toward the family-neighborhood-community base on which their intergenerational link so crucially depends.

## Conclusions

The fact that ICAL efforts are more clearly and consensually rationalized and motivated, are more functionally focused and delimited, and are better defended within the very functions crucial for their intergenerational continuity, does not mean that RLS-efforts should adopt ICAL goals. Not at all! But it does mean that RLS-efforts would be well advised to learn a few lessons from the ICAL book. They too require clear and consensual functional and motivational/ideological rationales. They too would benefit, at least initially, before they are dominant movements in their respective areas, from early focus on the few functional arenas that are most easily bounded and safeguarded from Yish incursions and most crucial to the intergenerational transmission of vernaculars as mother tongues. These are difficult goals for RLS movements to accomplish, but they do not become more successful (that is: more frequently intergenerationally continuous) by choosing 'more fashionable' but less germane (and less attainable or transmissible) goals.[2] Mother tongue transmission requires mother tongue use for the purposes of intergenerational intimacy and mutual socialization, functions which many RLS movements regrettably overlook.

## Notes

1.  During the 1982–83 academic year, I was fortunate enough to be a Fellow of the Netherlands Institute for Advanced Study (Wassenaar). Since half of the Fellows were Dutch and half were drawn from various parts of the world, the working language of the Institute was English. As a result, it was usual for Dutch Fellows to converse in English if non-Dutch Fellows were present. However, I often observed and overheard Dutch Fellows discussing their work and their mss (commonly written in English) with each other in English as well. Similar conventions have begun to develop at various other Dutch institutions of advanced research and training, even when non-Dutch nationals are much more rarely involved, probably as a result of exposure to and involvement in the professional literature. Many such institutions, including NIAS, have in-house journals published in English. Nevertheless, the use of English between Dutch scholars remains functionally restricted. This carefully delimited and restricted use of an outsider language among insiders (insiders who quickly return to Dutch when they are not discussing 'business') is indicative of the extent to which the ultimate (even if unseen) 'interlocutor' in such discussions is apparently the outer, international, English-dominated scientific community.
2.  This chapter is an expanded and thoroughly revised version of a paper that initially appeared in Kurt R. Jankowsky, ed., 1985, *Scientific and Humanistic Dimensions of Language*. Amsterdam: John Benjamins, 551–7.

## References

BRITTO, Francis 1986, *Diglossia: A Study of the Theory with Application to Tamil*. Washington, D.C.: Georgetown University Press.

FISHMAN, Joshua A. 1980a, Bilingualism and biculturism as individual and as societal phenomena. *Journal of Multilingual and Multicultural Development* 1, 3–15. Also reprinted in J. A. FISHMAN 1989, *Language and Ethnicity in Minority Sociolinguistic Perspective*. Clevedon: Multilingual Matters, 181–201.

— 1980b, Minority language maintenance and the ethnic mother tongue school. *Modern Language Journal* 64, 167–72.

—    1981, Language maintenance and ethnicity. *Canadian Review of Studies in Nationalism* 8, 229–48. Also reprinted in J. A. FISHMAN 1989, *Language and Ethnicity in Minority Sociolinguistic Perspective.* Clevedon: Multilingual Matters, 202–23.

—    1984, On the peculiar problems of smaller national languages. In Andrew GONZALEZ (ed.) *Panagani; Essays in Honor of Bonifacio Sibayan on his Sixty-seventh Birthday.* Manila: Linguistic Society of the Philippines, 40–5; Simultaneously published in *Philippine Journal of Linguistics*, 1983–84, 40–5. Also reprinted in J. A. FISHMAN, *Language and Ethnicity in Minority Sociolinguistic Perspective.* Clevedon: Multilingual Matters, 368–75.

FISHMAN, Joshua A. *et al.* 1985, *The Rise and Fall of the Ethnic Revival: Sociolinguistic Perspective on Language and Ethnicity.* Berlin: Mouton de Gruyter.

MACNAMARA, John 1974, Successes and Failures in the movement for the restoration of Irish. In Joan RUBIN and Bjorn H. JERNUDD (eds) *Can Language be Planned?* Honolulu: University Press of Hawaii, 65–94.

# 13 Limitations on School Effectiveness in Connection with Mother Tongue Transmission

*$15 MILLION FUND TO ENCOURAGE SHARED VALUES*

A Grant Benefits a Program that has Helped Children of the Poor

The Rockefeller Foundation will spend $15 million in the next five years expanding a program that seeks to better the educational performance of poor children, especially from minorities, by promoting a shared belief in the value of education among teachers, parents and pupils. ...

The [experimental] program requires that the local schools be managed by an 'active partnership' of school staff and student's parents that work to improve student self-confidence and ultimately their performance.

... The program is based on the belief that like all youth, children from poor families must learn proper values and behavior to be psychologically ready for schooling and must want to do well in school.

... Parents have to believe in the school ... and the school staff has to believe in the parents. Working together is a way to break down the distrust and suspicion, to show they all have the children's interest at heart.

(*New York Times*, January 24, 1990, p.B7)

## 'The School Can Do It!'

Most modern RLS movements have quickly and naturally, almost as a matter of course, moved to emphasize schools and schooling as the central thrust and process of the entire RLS endeavor. Perhaps it is time that someone asked the question that few of them actually stopped to ask: 'How much can the school, in and of itself (even the type 4a school, overlooking for the moment that many RLS movements have actually opted for the initially more dubious and problematic type 4b school), reasonably be expected to do for RLS in general, e.g. in connection with fostering the early acquisition and more fluent mastery of Xish, and most particularly, for fostering the cumulative, intergenerational transmissibility of any language which is still all too seldom a mother tongue?' Clearly, without the intergenerational transmissibility that we have stressed throughout our discussion, every new generation must begin again at 'point zero', i.e. monolingual in Yish and in need of a tremendous societal 'catch-up' operation in order to merely wind up where the prior generation had left off, without the benefit of the head start that an incremental increase in mother tongue use so obviously provides for any RLS movement.

The assumption that 'proper schooling' can really help a threatened ethnolinguistic entity to break out of this vicious cycle (the cycle of running harder and harder in order to finally end up, at best, in the same, or nearly in the same, place, generation after generation) is quite widespread, particularly among educators and other language-conscious segments of the lay public, and even among many sociolinguists too, although the latter should really know better. This assumption, that 'the school can do it', is symptomatic of two features of modern RLS movements: (a) it is a declaration of faith (albeit an exaggerated declaration, to be sure) in the view that practical, day-to-day educational steps *can* be taken that will be 'good for RLS', and (b) it is a reflection of the peculiarly modern and even the democratic nature of those very types of social change with which RLS movements are increasingly required to cope.

Given that RLS movements are particularly apt to attract and to activate teachers, teachers being the native, garden-variety form of RLS activist, their faith in schooling as the cure (and often as the sole cure) for 'whatever ails society' is a very understandable professional bias. The faith that teachers have in the school is also an expression of their much sought after positive self-concept, a pursuit that they engage in at the same time that they valiantly try to maintain their own sanity and to fight off 'burn-out' while society heaps more and more fundamentally societal problems and responsibilities on the already over-burdened shoulders of the school. The over-optimism of teachers that schools and schooling *per se* can solve society's problems (equivalent though it be to a conviction on the part of medical practitioners that they can lead society to the fountain of eternal youth) feeds the very societal over-reliance on the school that then leads to teacher 'burn-out'. There is an inherent conflict here which frequently goes unrecognized (even when parents and teachers work in concert, which they do all too rarely — often only in connection with expensive, foundation-funded, experimental programs).

However, the 'school can solve it' approach to social problems is also widespread throughout much of modern (and particularly in modern democratic) society, reaching far beyond the circle of school teachers. Its great appeal derives not only from its simplicity but from the fact that most other social institutions that traditionally contributed in major ways to the enculturation of the young (the family, the church, the youth movement, the armed forces) have suffered serious decreases in power and in influence. These decreases, therefore, leave the school as the only major societal institution that is still able to reach most children for many hours per day over the course of several years (in the West: for some 10–12 years). The view of the school as an 'all-purpose problem solver' is particularly common in modern, pluralistic, democratic societies because such societies lack the compulsory, unifying youth movement and political party which are assigned major responsibilities for the socialization of children and youth in more traditional and authoritarian societies (where solutions to all sorts of major societal problems are also quite elusive). Thus, this new role of the school as 'social influencer of last resort' is really often a role gained by default. Common though this role may be, covering the waterfront from arguably youth-related issues like the AIDS crisis to issues that have no special relationship to youth at all, like this summer's water shortage or counteracting the coming 'greenhouse effect', the ubiquity of the school's involvement does not in any way bolster the effectiveness of the school in connection with actually solving any societal problems whatsoever. Indeed, the school's willy-nilly involvement in societal problem solving may often seriously weaken it in connection with its own academic and orientational responsibilities.

The unsuitability and the inefficiency of tackling societal problems via reliance on the school becomes even clearer when one realizes that the power and role of the school to influence the home-neighborhood-community complex, the complex that is at the very core of RLS as a whole and, in particular, at the heart of the nativization effort (the effort to increasingly reinstate Xish as the characteristic mother tongue or co-mother tongue of Xmen), has itself become weaker and more peripheral in the life of its own proper primary clienteles: pupils and their parents.

## The School and the Task of Fostering Xish as a Mother Tongue

The general considerations reviewed above (that the traditional societal institutions of socialization have become weaker and that, therefore, the school has been assigned new and diverse socialization and social problem solving responsibilities, even though it too has become a weaker influence on the young than heretofore) have nothing uniquely to do with RLS. However, another reason why many look to the school in conjunction with RLS in general and the improvement of Xish mother tongue status in particular is somewhat more unique, even if equally mistaken. This reason posits a model of language which does not essentially differentiate between language and other school subjects (e.g. mathematics, science, geography), all of which usually start at or near 'point zero' generation after generation and are only weakly (if at all) intergenerationally transmitted.

First of all, let us pause to remember that very few students retain into adulthood the facts of geography, science or history, on the one hand, or the modes of reasoning inculcated in algebra or trigonometry, on the other hand, that are conveyed to them in elementary and secondary school. Survey after survey in all Western settings reveals a huge proportions of 'don't know' and totally incorrect responses to questions pertaining to school-based subjects, beginning with the earliest post-school years and snowballing thereafter. Indeed, in connection with algebra the loss-curve is so steep as to lead to the conclusion that teaching algebra to the generality of highschool students, before they have the faintest experience of the societal uses of algebra, is probably a waste of time, at worst, or, at best, an outcropping of discredited 'faculty psychology' and its dubious convictions that 'the mind is a muscle' which grows stronger when exercised by difficult matter (regardless of how alien). The extensive attrition of the bulk of school learning over time is doubtlessly due to the substantial post-school societal reinforcement or reward that is required if post-school retention of most subject matter content is to widely obtain. Thus, the building of societal reward processes must come prior to any growth in post-school retention or utilization of school learning.

The corresponding need for out-of-school (including both pre-school and post-school) reinforcement is doubly or triply great in conjunction with various aspects of language learning and this is so due to the communicational and identificational roles of language. Thus, if the school can pretend to be an independent agency as far as mathematics or geography acquisition and retention are concerned (although, basically, this too is no more than an unfounded pretense), merely because the school is the major agency for implanting such subjects in the minds of the young, no such pretense at all is possible as far as language acquisition and retention are concerned. Without considerable and repeated societal reinforcement schools cannot successfully teach either first or second languages and, furthermore, where such reinforcement is plentifully available, languages are acquired and retained even if they are not taught in school. A major part of the spread of English and other *lingua francas* during the past generation can be directly attributed to such out-of-school societal reinforcements.

The foregoing, while it strongly implies that the school cannot stand alone on the language front, does not mean that the school is totally unimportant in connection with the attainment of many instructional language goals; however, the importance of the school is best designated as 'initiatory' and 'contributory' rather than as substantially 'unique' or 'independent'. Schools are often important in initiating second language acquisition and some very few atypical students attain a modest fluency in that respect, even without direct societal support. Schools often initiate literacy acquisition, with respect to both reading and writing. In addition, schools often initiate repertoire expansion, that is, they introduce students to cultivated speech (often via extensive exposure to cultivated reading and writing), i.e. to non-vernacular varieties (often referred to as H varieties) of the mother tongue that differ from the daily, spoken, informal and 'untutored' varieties.

Finally, schools are often important in connection with enriching their students' attitudinal and overt-implementational commitments to language by providing and stressing the historical, cultural and moral rationales for such commitments. Via lessons and discussions about language and via actively involving students in school-and-society projects on behalf of language, schools are often the first agencies to articulate what many adults strongly believe but which few can articulate well, namely, that for any given ethnohistorical aggregate a given language with which it has been long and intimately associated is more than just an interchangeable 'means of communication', because it also symbolically implements and activates the historically associated culture that it quintessentially expresses. By repeatedly implementing and activating its associated culture and by doing so with positive affect, a language creates a social bond between the community of users of that language and its historically associated culture, symbolism and identity.

However, in all of the above respects in which schooling admittedly plays a significant role in connection with some aspect of language use and behavior toward language, it still requires extensive and recurring pre-school, out-of-school and post-school societal reinforcement, particularly if its initiatory efforts are to become cumulative and intergenerationally transmissible, i.e. if any particular language or variety under consideration is to attain a more widespread mother tongue or co-mother tongue role. The mother tongue role is reserved for those languages that are simultaneously early-childhood-acquired (not necessarily transmitted by the biological mother, but most commonly so) and emotion-intimacy-identity infused and, therefore, societally binding on this basis. Most RLS movements not only pursue this societally binding function, but they seek to do so on a cumulative, intergenerationally self-transmissible basis, thereby obviating the need to re-establish the link between Xish and its related ethnocultural identity anew, generation after generation.

Indeed, it is precisely because of both the communicational and the extra-communicational (affect-identity-societally binding) functions of language that threatened mother tongues and co-mother tongues require even more societal pre-school, out-of-school and after-school linkages and reinforcements if they are to become self-maintaining within the entire Xmen-via-Xish idea and life-style. In the case of threatened languages that are still infrequently realized as mother tongues, pre-school, out-of-school and post-school reinforcements are urgently needed in order to foster the bonds of identity and mutuality with their associated 'culture and society' complexes. Indeed, such bonds are imperative if cumulative intergenerational transmissibility is to be attained *in the mother tongue role*. Needless to say, such bonds *can* be supported and nurtured by the school, but, both quite soon as well as increasingly, such bonds depend on much more than the school itself. They also depend much more basically on out-of-school factors than on in-school factors, that is, out-of-school factors provide the strongest affective and instrumental reinforcements for taking that extra step from functional mastery and language spread to the discharge and transmission of the affect-identity-societal bonding mother tongue role *per se*. After all, children arrive in the school already talking, i.e. at an age when it is too late for the school to influence mother tongue transmission from parents to children. Furthermore, the lapse between the end of schooling and the beginning of a subsequent generation is far too long for the school itself to be able to bridge that hiatus without the assiduous cooperation, intervention and influential follow-up by other-than-school institutions and processes.

## More Basic than the School: The Family-Neighborhood-Community Arena

More fundamental than the school by far, insofar as making an acquired language which was not a mother tongue of generation I into the mother tongue or co-mother tongue of generation II is concerned is the entire family-neighborhood-community arena in which the school plays only a circumscribed role. A language which is not normatively operative throughout this intimate, affect-related and societally binding arena is not subsequently handed on as, or transmuted into, a mother tongue merely by virtue of the school's attention. Regardless of the rewards attained in adolescent and adult life in conjunction with the acquisition and mastery of X (e.g. English as a second language), almost all members of each successive generation will still begin anew in conjunction with it, at or near point zero. This is so unless and until a new generation arises that will introduce it to the subsequent one *much before schooling commences* and break through to its utilization and retention in the affective intimacy of the family-neighborhood-community identity-and-society binding experience. Only such an experience, and not the school, will initiate an intergenerational mother tongue transmission experience. The basic RLS question is exactly how this early, intimately affective, societally binding functional change can come about and how it can become a self-priming process intergenerationally once it does come about. This is a substantially different role and responsibility *vis-à-vis* Xish than the school can really discharge, pro-Xish though it may be.

It is often hard to appreciate the fact that the language or co-language of school, media, work and government does not automatically or necessarily become the mother tongue of the next generation, neither when the original shift from X to Y takes place nor when the RLS shift from Y to X is desired, unless and until a particular language obtains a secure niche in the early pre-school and co-school intimate socialization processes at the family-neighborhood-community level (stage 6 in our earlier discussions). The school cannot be reasonably expected to compensate for the absence, weakness or opposition of the foregoing arena, *not even in connection with such societally more neutral subjects as mathematics and science*, because the school itself is dependent on that very same arena for the effectiveness of its own, more limited, less intimate, less societally binding, less ethnocultural identity forming instruction.

Even the much touted mass media are insufficiently interpersonal, child-oriented, affect-suffused, societally binding to attain cumulative intergenerational mother tongue transmission, particularly so since the proportion of Yish utilized by the media will long (and perhaps always) be greater than the proportion of Xish. Nor can the work sphere or the government function *in loco parentis* insofar as mother tongue attainment or transmission are concerned. The favorable outcomes of the Hebrew, Catalan and Quebec French cases *did not begin with* work, media or government Xization; they began with the acquisition of a firm family-neighborhood-community base or, better yet (in the Catalan and Quebec French cases), with the fact that such a base had never widely been lost from the outset. Even Hebrew, which was intergenerationally transmitted as a language of prayer and of the study of sacred texts for nearly 2,000 years prior to its revernacularization, depended for its transmissibility as a second or third language not on the community-school (stage 5a or 4a) *per se* but on a strong out-of-school societal consensus, the unwavering institutional support of the synagogue and its clerical leadership and on a quasi-compulsory omnipresent voluntary network of post-school adult study centers in which the school's studies were continually reinforced and expanded upon within the male population.

What media, work sphere, and government agencies and institutions can do for science, mathematics and geography (i.e. the ability to sentimentally and instrumentally reinforce the school's efforts so that each of these subjects 'takes hold' in the lives of at least a few individuals, although even then these consequences rarely attain the intergenerational transmissibility which is synonymous with the mother tongue role) they *cannot* do with respect to converting a non-mother tongue into a mother tongue or co-mother tongue. Schools simply come insufficiently early in individual development and are generally also insufficiently undisputed, affect-laden, intimacy- and identity-focused or societally binding for such purposes.

This does not mean, however, that school-media-work sphere-government cannot contribute at all to converting a non-mother tongue into a mother tongue or a co-mother tongue. However, all that the latter 'higher order agencies' can do ('higher order' not by virtue of intrinsic importance for intergenerational transmission but by virtue of their distance from the very crux of such transmission) is to constructively focus societal resources (attention, funds, manpower, intelligence and dedication) on the family-neighborhood-community complex and on the problems and opportunities that it and it alone presents for the attainment of the mother tongue role. In particular, the schools, media, work sphere and government can underscore the fact that successful mother tongue fostering requires fostering the *idea of the language*, the total language and culture complex of Xmen-via-Xish, rather than merely the language alone or first and foremost. And certainly the activization of this complex among the parents of the next generation requires and entails more than the school alone.

## The Increasing Weakness of the Direct Home–School Link

A further vitiating factor which undermines the role of the school in the total RLS enterprise, a factor which simultaneously makes it more difficult for the school to strengthen the family's efforts on behalf of Xish, just as it also makes it more difficult for the family to strengthen the school's efforts on behalf of Xish or any other subject or medium of instruction, is the increasing interposition of the many new child-socialization agencies required by modern, urban life. Indeed, modern, urban life is characterized by the growing peripheralization of the family *vis-à-vis* the total child-socialization process, on the one hand, and by the bureaucratic fragmentation of the agencies that have arisen to complement the family in connection with this process, on the other hand. RLS-efforts in general and mother tongue transmission and stabilization efforts in particular are rendered much more complex and problematic by such modern, urban developments as the shrinking proportion of children being raised in two-parent families and the growing proportion of children being raised in families in which all available adults are working full-time.

Due to the rapid increase in one-parent families, resulting from the rising divorce rate and the growing unmarried parent rate, on the one hand, and the unavailability of either a parent or a parent-surrogate during the child's entire waking day (modern living quarters and geographic mobility both mean that once-ubiquitous grandparents are now simply unaccommodatable or unavailable), children, from the very earliest months on, seldom have anyone at home to care for them, feed them, help them with school work or even *simply to talk to them*. What was still the norm just a generation ago, namely, pre-school and elementary school-aged children growing up in two-parent families in which at least one adult — usually the mother — did not work full-time until the children had at least finished elementary school, has become a distinctly rare and even surprising (if not quaint or archaic) phenomenon in many modern cities the world over. 'Hard data' from the United States Bureau of the Census shows what must be a generally less documented worldwide trend, namely that the parental time even potentially available to children (total time minus time in paid work) fell appreciably between 1960 and 1986.[1] As a result of these profound changes in urban family structure and function, pre-school and school-aged children are increasingly exposed to early socialization experiences (*and that means to early language experiences*) provided by a large and varied number of employees of new neighborhood/community agencies. These new agencies sooner or later come to constitute the lion's share of the neighborhood and the community insofar as modern life is concerned and, therefore, they must also do so insofar as RLS-efforts and, particularly, mother tongue fostering and transmitting efforts are concerned.

During pre-school years, often from the time a child is just a few weeks old, 'child care' is provided by 'child care agencies', for 6, 8 and even 10 hours a day and for 5, 6 and even 7 days per week. Many working parents want some free hours for themselves when they get home from work in the evenings and a free day (or two) for themselves on weekends. As in the kibbutz of old, young children are primarily cared for by child care specialists and are with their parent(s) during only relatively few hours per week. The after-school hours, during the elementary grades (and, at times, even during the secondary grades) are spent in organized play groups, homework assistance groups, hobby or special interest (sports, music/dance, computer) groups, and mealtime (breakfast, lunch and/or dinner) groups. These neighborhood-community agencies are not at all limited in availability to middle-class children, because public funding is increasingly being provided in order that lower-class urban children can also 'benefit' from them. All in all, they constitute a powerful new reality in child socialization and education, a reality which not only changes the entire tenor of school — home relations but one that has dramatic and worrisome implications and consequences for all RLS-efforts, mother tongue fostering efforts first and foremost among them, as well.

As should be readily apparent, the fragmentation of the family's former responsibilities produces a situation which weakens the school as an RLS agency, precisely because many new agencies intervene between it and the family nexus of intergenerational language transmission. The linguistic behaviors, skills and values of the young are now being developed (and, as time goes by, will tend to be developed even more and more) by a whole host of helpers, counsellors and specialists who are not only prior to, outside of and after the school but also outside of the family as well. While it is still too early to say whether language socialization is being hurt or helped, advanced or delayed, by the changes that have occurred and that are accelerating, it is already clear that the new helpers, counsellors and specialists must increasingly be RLS-provided and RLS-coordinated (with each other, with the school and with the family), particularly if urban RLS-efforts are to stay abreast of social change and attempt to regulate or utilize on behalf of RLS in general and on behalf of the strengthening of the Xish mother tongue role in particular the social change that has already occurred and that must inevitably occur in ever-accelerating fashion. Thus, it is not only the school which is becoming ever more questionable as an RLS agency, but its links to the home and, indeed, the very impact of the home itself (unaided) in the mother tongue transmission process is also becoming increasingly 'mediated'. Vastly more RLS attention to neighborhood-community building is needed now and even more will be needed in the post-modern future.

However, as always, the glass is also partially full in connection with the foregoing widespread social changes. The weakening of the socialization and language socialization roles and responsibilities of both the family and the school, as well as the interposition of many new agencies between the two of them, may also benefit RLS and foster the strengthening of the Xish mother tongue role. This would be particularly likely to occur in all those contexts where there are few parents who are fluent Xish speakers or who have strongly positive Xish language attitudes. The manifold new agencies of child (and of child language) socialization are easier to finance, influence, regulate, supervise and reward than are the thousands of discrete family units in any particular locality. Rather than bemoan the peripheralization of the school and of the family, RLS advocates and activists need to find ways and means of establishing, maintaining and improving the various child care, play and socialization agencies that have already mushroomed and that can be expected to continue to do so for the foreseeable future. At any rate, there is no turning the clock back. The utilization of the school for RLS purposes must increasingly become merely only one step in an integrated, stagewise progression of steps, rather than the first, last and most crucial step that it has often been made out to be in the past.

To depend exclusively or even largely on the school is now needlessly to court disaster re mother tongue socialization, as the Irish and the Maori examples discussed above amply reveal. Modern, urban society has recently become even more complex than was formerly the case. To buttress the RLS potential of the school via the post-school instrumental reward system is to overlook the fact that *that* system also needs to find its long and 'iffy' way back to the intergenerational transmission nexus before RLS can be attained. It is now becoming clearer than ever that it is not enough to create Xish-at-work requirements or Xish media. Xish job-holders (or Xish media listeners) must marry their ideological and practical counterparts and raise their children from birth in Xish, in neighborhoods intensively served by the full panoply of Xish neighborhood and child (language) socialization agencies (including Xish-stressing schools). Only after the intergenerational transmission system is in good operational order can the higher order agencies be concentrated upon, and even when that is done these too must be consciously tied back to lower order reality.

## The Increasingly Complicated 'Core Complex', Yet One Still Too Often Overlooked

The attainment of the mother tongue role is not a goal that the school itself can begin to approximate. This was always so and has steadily been becoming even more so of late. The early socialization (and language socialization) years are particularly in need of modern, urban RLS attention. These are years when the traditional, formal school is not yet operative in the lives of children. During these early years parents require birthing instruction, parenting instruction, child care provision and child health provision. RLS-efforts would be wise to invest greatly in operating such agencies and services, i.e. to becoming 'prime providers' in these very areas so that the services of these *modern realizations of neighborhood and community* can be available *in Xish*, at the lowest possible price and to the largest number of recipients. The modern family-neighborhood-community may not be much like the golden, idealized myth of intimacy and authenticity that classical RLS theory has usually imagined and longed for; however, it remains the locus of mother tongue transmission, of ethnocultural bonding, and needs to become the new focus of Xmen-via-Xish efforts in the modern, urban age. The provision *in Xish* of the new family services offered by these new agencies of neighborhood and community will not only update the image of Xish, rendering it relevant to *life as it is*, rather than only to life as it was or as it might be, but they will inevitably update Xish and Xishness themselves.

The *New York Times* recently (May 14, 1989) commented on how American English itself is changing due to the revolution which locates the bulk of early childcare outside of the family. Parents and children now speak about 'quality time', the brief time that parents themselves devote to their children (as contrasted with the much more plentiful 'quantity time' available to the agency-related child care providers), of 'enhancement classes', the pre-gymnastics, pre-dance, pre-swimming, pre-cooking, pre-reading groups for the very young (indeed, for pre-schoolers, some of whom may still be 'pre-walking'), of 'friending out', i.e. of a child's relative success in making friends in the various activity groups in which he or she participates and in each of which a different sub-set of children may be encountered, and of the evils of 'hoovering', eating at an overly rapid rate in the meal-group (i.e. sucking in one's food like a Hoover vacuum cleaner sucks in the dust). The language or co-languages that accompany all of these new activities have all of these new terms and are 'relevant' therefore to the fragmented intimacy and the scheduled affect of modern, urban childhood and of the modern parent — child family-neighborhood-community experience. For all of this the school alone is just not enough; indeed, it is no longer at the heart of the matter, being both too little and too late for mother tongue acquisition and retention. Indeed, the foundation-funded experimental program that we cited at the beginning of this chapter may very well fail, precisely because it is predicated on an outdated and vanishing model of home — school relationships. But where and if that simplistic model is still functional, the experiment's belated recognition that 'schools cannot do it alone' is essentially what should not be lost on school-focused RLS circles. Their job is a much more difficult one than most of them have ever imagined.


## Concluding Sentiments

The over-reliance on the school with respect to the attainment of RLS goals is merely an example of the more widespread tendency to seek out and depend upon one-factor solutions to a very involved, multivariate problem. The 'school alone can do it' view has parallels in the view that 'the media alone can do it' and, on an even more widespread basis, in the view that 'controlling the work sphere (the economy) alone can do it'. In addition to being simplistic, these views also lead RLS-efforts to bank on processes that are distant from the immediate nexus of mother tongue transmission and that feed back to reinforce that nexus only haphazardly and after considerable delay. They may serve to reinforce Xish horizontally, by broadening the scope of its functions, but they do too little to foster it vertically, by contributing to its intergenerational transmissibility. Such broadening efforts enable minority (or minoritized) languages whose intergenerational transmissability is no longer in serious doubt, to move energetically into the higher status spheres of modern life. Their precedents mesmerize RLSers who labor on behalf of intergenerationally weaker, infinitely more threatened language-in-culture constellations. The resulting mismatch of priorities can be not only disappointing (as in the case of Irish) but devastating as well (as in the case of Scottish Gaelic, with only some 80,000 speakers and a well nigh complete reliance on the school and other higher order 'props'). What is sauce for the goose is by no means necessarily sauce for the gander.

But even appropriately focused RLS-efforts on behalf of seriously threatened languages are becoming increasingly difficult to institute and will doubtlessly become even more so. As urban neighborhoods and communities become ever more fragmented and difficult to serve, RLS-efforts will require increasingly more integrative focus and sophistication in order to make a dent in the preponderantly Yish order of things. Probably only very few and very fortunate RLS movements will succeed in 'putting it all together'. Dedication itself will not make the difference. More and more, it will be the shrewd pursuit of appropriate priorities that will differentiate between 'also rans' and those who have a real chance of coming out ahead.

## Notes

1.  Rapalus, Peter 1990 Expert on family economics wonders: are we 'underinvesting' in our children? *Campus Report* (Stanford University). February 7, p. 4.

# 14 Theoretical Recapitulation: What is Reversing Language Shift (RLS) and How Can it Succeed?

It is no exaggeration to say that millions of people throughout the world are consciously engaged in efforts to reverse language shift and that many hundreds of thousands do so as members of movements whose explicit goal is RLS. Yet the efforts of these millions and the goals of these hundreds of thousands have been relatively little mentioned in the social science literature and have remained only infrequently referred to even in the sociolinguistic literature. Part of the reason for this ethically unjustified and intellectually as well as practically disappointing state of affairs, it seems to me, is that both the social sciences as a whole and sociolinguistics in its own right have sliced up their treatments of social movements in general, and reformatory or protest social movements in particular, in such a way that RLS never clearly appears as the distinctive phenomenon that it is.

This is not terribly surprising. The modern, Western social sciences have only very recently come to recognize socially patterned language use and socially manifested behavior toward language as topics to be reckoned with. Sociolinguistics itself, on the other hand, even in its more RLS-sympathetic (although less intensively cultivated) 'macro' or 'sociology of language' pursuits, has not yet arrived at a sufficiently refined taxonomy of language status planning to explicitly provide for the consideration of RLS activity. As a result, very refined terminological and conceptual distinctions are made with respect to the 'minus' side of the ledger (we speak of language attrition–shift–endangerment–loss–death and can itemize many studies of each way-station along this increasingly negative progression), while the 'plus' side remains rather gross and undifferentiated and studies of revival, restoration, revitalization and restabilization remain proportionately few and far between. At the same time, language 'status planning', of which RLS is a sub-category, is overly identified with central governmental efforts, hardly the most likely or the most sympathetic auspices for minority RLS-efforts.

The most general reason for the neglect of RLS is probably the fact that RLS is an activity of minorities, frequently powerless, unpopular with outsiders and querulous amongst themselves; it is an activity that is very often unsuccessful and that strikes many intelligent laymen and otherwise intelligent social scientists as 'unnatural', i.e. as counter to some supposedly 'natural' drift of historical events or the 'obvious' direction of social change. It is hard for self-serving mainstream intellectual spokesmen and institutions to be sympathetic to the lingering, cantankerous, neither fully alive nor fully dead quality of many (perhaps most) efforts on behalf of receding minority languages (and the majority of sidestream scholars too are ultimately dependent on the mainstream for their perspectives, if not for their very livelihoods). Indeed, RLS-efforts are often like the 'gomers' or 'crocks' that constantly reappear in the emergency rooms of major metropolitan hospitals: elderly, complaining individuals who neither die nor get better and for whom nothing effective can seemingly ever be done. Most young doctors, like most majority spokesmen in other fields, learn to 'meet 'em, greet 'em and street 'em', i.e. to make light of the complaints of these embarrassing unfortunates and to turn to other, more tractable cases as expeditiously as possible. 'Crocks' take up scarce resources (staff time, energy, funds, supplies, equipment) and contribute disproportionately to staff burn-out. They are no more than obviously 'suspect' and unpopular reminders of the failure of modern medicine to be able to cope with chronic social and individual health problems, particularly those that are characterized by a goodly overlay of social pathology, on the one hand, and that are seemingly irreversible, on the other. Minority cultures that are struggling for their very lives, for dignity, attention and affirmative action are also inevitably suspect and unpopular. Both RLS-efforts and 'gomers' are unwelcome testimony to shortcomings of the mainstream and to the tremendous will of the neglected and the 'different' to lead their own lives and to find their own satisfactions, regardless of outside pronouncements that nothing can or should be done for them.

## RLS among the 'Social Movements'

RLS-efforts may very well consist of the efforts of individuals, even, on occasion, of the activity of an isolated individual, but they are much more characteristically socially patterned and organized activities of the type that sociologists refer to as 'social movements'. But where, exactly, do RLS-efforts belong in the long array of types of social movements studied by social scientists? RLS movements not only differ in many respects from the 'collective behavior' phenomena (crowds, mobs, panic scenes, riots, etc.) that sociologists and social psychologists of an earlier generation so frequently studied, but they also differ interestingly from the types of bona fide social movements that have elicited more recent sociological attention. Like the latter, RLS-efforts have definite goals, they are enduring and organized, and like some of them too, they are commonly enacted outside of 'normal' institutional channels (e.g. outside of mainstream political parties, voluntary organizations, schools, media, etc.) and, indeed, are often oppositional to such institutions and tend to set up alternative social institutions, organizations and structures of their own.

However, there is often about RLS-efforts a very palpable degree of affect, a sentimental (rather than merely an instrumental) bonding, a stress on real or putative ethno-kinship, an aspiration toward consciousness and identity (re)formation, a heightened degree of altruistic self-sacrifice and a disregard for 'least effort' advantages, to the degree that RLS behavior often impresses outsiders as bordering on the 'irrational' and the 'mystic'. It is perhaps the latter characteristics that have tended to elicit fear, suspicion and rejection in the mainstream and that have led to frequent charges that RLS-efforts are a species of 'collective behavior' after all, rather than manifestations of the 'social movement behaviors' of the comfortably rational and familiarly materialistic mainstream or mainstream-proximate types. These fears and suspicions have raised a series of roadblocks to the appreciation of RLS and other ethnic 'behavior-and-identity' movements during the past century and a half.

## 'Irrational' Ethnocultural Behavior-and-Identity Movements

There is, of course, a long history to the charges of 'irrationality' by those who are in control of secure ethnocultural establishments of their own, against those who are without such control and seeking to attain it. Lord Acton criticized the 'preposterous' ethnocultural claims aroused by Herder and fostered by the French Revolution among the peoples without states, and 'therefore without histories', throughout Europe. Subsequently, many of these claims were sufficiently powerful to be attacked from below (rather than from above as was the case with Lord Acton), by Marx and Engels, in their efforts to foster a new and presumably more rational proletarian identity. Again and again, ethnicity has been delegitimized in the West (by both secular and Church spokesmen) as anti-modern, anti-intellectual, irrational, anti-progressive and anti-civil. Little wonder then that modern social science should also be heir to this tradition,[1] particularly given the fact that so much of modern social science is American and America views itself (and its identity) as universalistically supra-ethnic, rather than as parochially ethnic in the deeply traditional (and self-styled deeply historical) Old World sense.

One of the earliest social science attempts to understand the seemingly non-modern and anti-modern identity re-establishment efforts of small peoples was Ralph Linton's early 40s analysis of 'nativistic movements' among small, over-run, indigenous peoples in the colonial empires established by the modern West. Linton described as 'nativistic' any conscious, organized attempt on the part of a society's members to revive or perpetuate selected aspects of their severely dislocated culture. Although Linton differentiated between 'revivalistic' and 'perpetuative' nativism, as well as between 'magical' and 'rational' efforts on behalf of either, he devoted major attention to the revivalistic–magical quadrant in his four-fold table and considered nativism as a whole to be a reaction to the unbearable oppression, dislocation and domination of Western rule. Implicitly, therefore, there is a non-Western flavor to the entire phenomenon, such that the cultural self-protective efforts of small Western populations at the mercy of non-Westerners would not only be deemed 'perpetuative' and 'rational' but might be said *not* to be nativistic at all, but, rather, protective of Western civilization. Clearly, Linton did not anticipate either 'revivalistic' or 'perpetuative' RLS-efforts within the very West itself (where, indeed, the lion's share of such efforts have occurred) and his conceptualization of cultural behaviors is excessively dichotomous; it is either X or Y, Western or non-Western, whereas most RLS-efforts envisage more complex, more contextual and situational repertoires com-posed of ingredients of Xishness and Yishness.

Anthony Wallace, writing in the mid 50s, a dozen years after Linton, as well as Bernard Barber, writing just a few years before Linton, contributed an interest in 'messianism' to the discussion of nativistic efforts. For Barber, mes-sianism is the mystic solution to a cultural impasse; it is an attempt to find supernaturally derived stability and hope in a culture which is otherwise in real-istic shreds and tatters. For Wallace, messianism, nativism and millennarism are all types of 'revitalization', i.e. movements which emphasize the elimination of alien persons, customs, values and/or artifacts. Thus, both Barber and Wallace focus essentially on irrational and backward-looking solutions, and, as a result, would not have much to say about the bulk of RLS-efforts which are really attempts to arrive *at self-regulated modernization*, i.e. at Xish modernization that is in the spirit of and under the aegis of Xishness as defined by 'Xmen-with-Xish'.

Western social science seems to be primarily telling us that modernization and authenticity preoccupations cannot go together, just as authenticity preoccu-pations and rationality cannot go together. The seeming anomaly of moderniza-tion, rationality, affectivity and authenticity, the cornerstones of RLS, are theoretically unprovided for because such a complex combination strikes mod-ern social science as perversely contradictory, as 'so near and yet so far' from the mainstream ethos. The true complexity of modern minority movements is elusive, doubly so since such movements are contraindicated given the simplistic theories according to which mainstream processes and virtues are considered simultaneously prototypical, normal and inescapable.

In many ways, Russell Thornton's mid-80s retrospective analysis of the Amerindian Ghost Dance movements of 1870 and 1890 hews close to the irrational and backward-looking characterizations encountered in Wallace's discussion of revitalization movements, as one might expect from a consideration of manifestations that predicted demographic/cultural recovery as a by-product of dances that would bring the dead back to life. Nevertheless, Thornton does add one crucial new twist to the discussion thus far: a realization that such movements are at least phenomenologically rational and that they may be sufficiently motivating to be productive 'resource mobilization' as well. However, Thornton's magnanimous admission that the Ghost Dances 'were deliberate responses ... that probably made sense to the Indians involved ... [and] in terms of their culture ... [were] essentially rational acts' is not only a condescending tautology but implies that no such rationality would obtain from the point of view of modern, Western culture.

Setting aside the fact that Thorntone overlooks the frequency with which modern Western populations engage in efforts to protect *their* sanctities (sanctities that are obviously above and beyond the rational), the rationality of goals and the rationality of means must always be analytically separated. RLS is usually a thoroughly modern enterprise in terms of the rationality of its means (thus any implied equation between RLS and ghost dances being totally out of order), while its goals admittedly partake of the rationality of modern religious and ideological verities that a major portion of mankind considers to be worth struggling toward, regardless of price in time, effort and resources. Still provocatively interesting for us today, however, more so than any of Thornton's judgmental comments, are his conclusions that the Amerindian efforts to which he refers were most extensively and rewardingly engaged in by those very cultures that had been most dislocated and that, *in toto*, these efforts were basically attempts to re-establish group boundaries. Neither of these considerations requires notions of 'irrationality' but rather, as Thornton fully realized, are fully consistent with 'resource mobilization' and 'relative deprivation' theories within the social sciences.

A further step along the path of re-rationalizing and demystifying revitalization movements was recently taken by Duane Champagne. He realizes that there are basic similarities between the revitalization movements that occur in structurally less differentiated societies and the reform or guided cultural change movements that occur in structurally more differentiated (= more modern) ones. Both types of efforts utilize the most effective means available to their societies, those of the latter societies being organizationally, institutionally, materially and conceptually more advanced and, therefore, more capable of accepting the inevitability of cultural change and able to influence its outcome via political and economic means. Champagne's analysis should once and for all remove the penumbra of backwardness and irrationality from efforts of the RLS type. Such efforts may fail or prevail, depending on rationally analyzable factors (i.e. they do so on the basis of means and circumstances totally like those that govern the success and failure of the other social movements with which they must compete), differing from their contemporary competitors more with respect to ends than to means. Indeed, given the scarcity of means that most RLS-efforts have at their disposition, a good case can be made that they often *attempt to be more rational* with respect to their deployment than is frequently the case for movements that are socially ascendant.[2] All in all, attempts to convince the modern mind of the rationality of ethnocultural behavior-and-identity reintensification movements have experienced some success during the past half century, but much greater impact in this direction is still necessary before RLS-efforts will be commonly viewed as the natural, thoughtful and constructive undertakings that their participants take them to be.

## RLS, 'Backward Looking' Resistance to Change, and Cultural Conservatism

Another oft-repeated stereotypic charge is that RLS and related re-ethnification or ethnic re-intensification movements are backward looking ('past-oriented'), conservative, change-resistant dinosaurs. Of course, most basic philosophical values tend to have their origins in the past and small cultures that are now in particular danger of erosion naturally recognize a past when that was not (or not as much) the case. RLS-efforts are very sensitive, due to their very goal-consciousness *per se*, to the constant diminution in the numbers or proportions of speakers/users of the language-in-culture on behalf of which they struggle, to the incursions of time, to the fact that things were better 'then' than they are 'now'. But this does not need to make them more 'backward looking' (if by that we mean: seriously pursuing a return to and a preservation of the past) than are most other opponents of present evils, injustices and dislocations. Shall we designate as 'backward looking' all those who remember when urban neighborhoods were much safer, cleaner and far less polluted than they are today, merely because they strive toward a closer approximation to past superior standards in these respects? Many others, besides RLSers, yearn for social and cultural arrangements that will foster stronger family bonds of affection, mutual care and concern, respect, ethical behavior and commitment. It would be nonsense to designate such concerns as necessarily 'backward looking'.

Many others, besides RLSers, realize that local communities must be more fully involved in their schools, health agencies, playgrounds, zoning regulations, and child care services, if they are to overcome the problems and inefficiencies of the growing massification, bureaucratization and deterioration of modern society. One does not need to be a member of either the Old Order Amish or the Institute of Cultural Conservatism to bemoan the general lack of intellectual concern for the moral and spiritual dimensions of modern life and, accordingly, it is unfounded to accuse those RLSers who have any or all of the above concerns of displaying a stultifying opposition to modernity. As some social scientists have already recognized, 'defenders' of the core values of modern democratic systems are apt to perceive and point out real threats to the well-being of that system. Such defense should really be viewed as part of the process of change, part of the direction-finding or direction-setting field of forces that we call change, otherwise the empty cycle of 'change for the sake of change alone' will be upon us.[3] RLSers have sometimes been accused of goal fixation to the point of forgetting why the goal is being pursued to begin with. But certainly this charge also applies to those who are 'modernists in principle' while forgetting the humanistic religious, philosophical and ideological goals that make life human, purposeful and worthwhile.

But in reality, RLSers are not merely defenders of some mystical, mythical and bygone past; they are actually 'change-agents on behalf of persistence'. Very few social scientists indeed have been inclined to conceptualize and analyze the relationship between change and persistence, probably because of our modern fascination with the dynamics of change *per se*. But all change is interspersed with persistence as well, just as all persistence is interspersed with ongoing change. Persistence no more means equilibrium than change means chaos. The forces and processes of change co-exist, *in a single process*, with the forces and processes of persistence and what most social scientists mistakenly call 'change' is really the by-product of the *interaction* of persistence and change. Actually, the power of persistence helps provide the direction and generate the resultant of the total dynamics that are operative at any time and place. Ethnolinguistic persistence involves a basic continuity in the meaning of symbols. For RLSers a given language is the first and foremost of these symbols, as is their interpretation of that language as being truly fundamental to identity and continuity. Although RLS is rendered difficult by the values, movements and processes opposed to it, it is also rendered difficult by its inevitable interweaving with ongoing sociocultural change. Experienced RLSers realize that all cultures are constantly changing and that their goal is merely to influence and direct this change, so that it will not contradict or overpower the core of their cultural system, rather than legislate change out of existence.

Identity persistence and ethnocultural persistence are not synonymous, of course. The former is purely phenomenological and is no basic criterion of RLS, i.e. it can be attained without RLS, while the latter involves a studied persistence of behaviors, i.e. *commitments to implemented interpretations* (of life, of relationships, of history, of symbols). RLS requires societal boundary maintenance, rather than merely being the result of such boundary maintenance. Language is a prime boundary-maker and protector, because it not only implies and reflects core boundaries but because it constantly creates and legitimizes them as well. RLS seeks to avoid the dislocations that inevitably result from the destruction and substitution of core symbols, behaviors, boundaries and values, possible though it may be to come through such destruction and substitution with one's phenomenological social identity intact. It is not change *per se* that is opposed by RLSers but changes in a core behavioral complex in which the language is generatively and regeneratively linked to the protected cultural core.

For the persisters, language is both corpus and message and the authentic message without the authentic corpus is as empty as the authentic corpus without the authentic message. Nevertheless, a corpus can and must generate endless novel messages too, since the novel ones not only enable the authentic ones to achieve their contrastive sanctity but assure that sanctity of a new life, timeliness and vigor as well. As Spicer recognized ever so long ago, 'a people that endures ... embodies the most important kind of social unit which men can create: a living, cumulative interpretation [and here I would add: enactment] of human life ... collective purpose and destiny'. Only by persisting in the midst of change, only by indigenizing change, only by taming and refashioning change (thereby taming and refashioning persistence too) does RLS reflect a creative guarantee as to its living potential, rather than degenerate into some totally lifeless, antiquarian oddity. It is not the return of the past that RLS seeks, but the mining of the past so that the core that animated it can continue to be implemented.[4] For all of its fascination with change, much of the thoughtful West is also 'past appreciative'. For all of their use of the past, most RLS movements and efforts are future-oriented.

We have noted, above, several dimensions along which RLS movements do not neatly fit into the customary sociological classifications of social movements. RLS-efforts cut across the usually recognized demarcations. They are oppositional to the direction of social change and to their own exclusion from the regulation of social change, but they do not reject social change in principle. They recognize the putative kinship bond between their members, a

suprarational hallmark of all ethnicity movements, but they seek rational
resource mobilization and optimal planning toward the accomplishment of
RLS goals. However, there is yet another, non-classificatory and even more
fundamental reason why the bulk of Western social science, with all of its
fascination with and even overt support for social change, has had so little
interest in and sympathy for the type of guided social change (planned social
change) that RLS implies.


## The Oppressiveness of Tradition and the Pursuit of 'Authenticity' as Complete Individual Liberty

Although RLS is a type of sociocultural change, it is simply not the type of
social change that the social science literature has classically and generally
attended to. There is, of course, some recognition of a 'cultural paradigm' in
mainstream social science discussion of social change, a paradigm that views
innovation as an ongoing process that is literally impossible without continuity
of beliefs, values, behaviors and symbol systems. However, social theory knows
much more about fostering change (the 'structural paradigm') and *advancing
individual authenticity via liberation from repressive societal regulation*, than it
knows about voluntarily fostering continuity via anchoring, re-anchoring or re-
interpreting a particular cultural tradition.

Voluntarism is assumed only in the destruction of tradition and never in
its implementation, development, recovery or defense. Indeed, change for
change's sake has come to occupy a somewhat hallowed position in social
theory and has influenced the social sciences as well. John Stuart Mill
(1806–1873), well before the mid-nineteenth century, fully and seemingly
irrevocably equated tradition with unhappiness. Thereafter, the view that
humans can 'be themselves' ('be authentic') *only if they live without any
imposed social structure at all* has occupied a central niche in Western social
thought. Indeed, even before Mill, Edmund Burke (1729–1797) had
proclaimed that repression was a basic fact of social life ('power for some and
obedience for the rest'), and Montesquieu (1689–1755) and Jean Jacques
Rousseau (1712–1776) had anticipated him by declaring that to maximize
one's happiness each individual required freedom to shape a happiness that
would be *completely of his own design*. If the need for 'group liberation' was
acknowledged at all (as it was by Montesquieu, who, nevertheless,
concentrated on sexual, religious and political groups but was typically
oblivious to ethnocultural ones) such liberation was justified on the basis of
the happiness that would be derived from being *freed from ties to groupness*,

i.e. authenticity was viewed as liberation *from* groupness rather than as liberation *of* groupness or *for* groupness.

Only Rousseau vacillated, late in life, recognizing that the emptiness and alienation of the totally free required for their alleviation those very communal bonds that decreased individual freedom. He reconciled the two, individual happiness and communal affiliation, only in utopian terms and recognized, even so, that utopias themselves were, therefore, at odds with the openness and the constant changeability of urban modernity. Among the more or less systematic schools of social thought only the Herderians, the nationalists, the racists and the Marxists defended carefully selected (and very different) affiliative ideals for any length of time after the flawed and failed Spring of '48, and none of these were ever really taken seriously by the mainstream of Western social science. Furthermore, before the recent appearance of the new, post-industrial left, the Marxists themselves were as classically anti-ethnic as were the bourgeois thinkers.[5]

Perhaps of greater import for recent theoretical opposition to planned ethnicity-fostering culture change, such as RLS, is the 'alternative society' or 'commune movement' of the 60s and 70s. It harks back to Montesquieu in its abhorence of mechanistic, dehumanizing, competitive and materialistic societal ties and by emphasizing individualistic and counter-culture, rather than mainstream or traditional cultural definitions of 'success'. The new 'life-style', studiously supra-ethnic in nature, stressed openness, intimacy, flexibility, cooperation and altruistic sacrifice, *Gemeinschaft* features that theoreticians had once ascribed to the ethnically integrated, small community but which the communes derived independently from their anti-establishment vantage point.[6] Their revolt was against mainstream rather than for sidestream 'tradition' and few of their followers recognized that minority groups had been rebels before them, and, at times, more disciplined, organized and effective rebels at that.

Many RLS-efforts actually reveal a close similarity to the anti-establishment and anti-materialistic *Gemeinschaft* strivings of the 'communes', thereby underscoring even more the void that so often (and so needlessly) separates the ethnic dimension and the radical dimensions of modern social criticism. Clearly, however, 'traditionless authenticity' and 're-ethnifying authenticity' are poles apart, regardless of the term 'authenticity' that they share. Their common stress on achieving self-regulatory status is often overlooked, primarily because the former is individualistic and the latter is group-cultural in orientation *vis-à-vis* the attainment of happiness. The perfect combination of both might well be optimal, but requires as much acceptance of the claims of (minority) ethnocultures as of the claims of individuality. Modern Western thought has generally been more willing to suffer the pains of the latter rather than grant the legitimacy of the former.

## Recent Growth in Theory Pertaining to Ethnicity

A final area of attempted rapprochement and accommodation between Western social theory and ethnic re-intensification efforts pertains more directly to an understanding of ethnicity *per se*. The ethnic revival of the mid-60s to the mid-70s roused both bourgeois and leftist thinkers from the stupor that had clouded their thinking about ethnicity for over a century. It came to be belatedly recognized by those who sought to grapple with the far-flung (although not overly deep) ethnic stirrings in most parts of the First and Second Worlds, that many of the myths and biases that had previously colored their views of ethnicity (irrationality, backward-looking focus, conservativism, oppression of individual 'authenticity' culminating in sociocultural/political oppression) were substantially erroneous or unfounded. Ethnicity did not involve attempts to preserve the traits of either static or pre-modern cultures. The transitions between and the combinations of traditional and modern behaviors and sentiments were actually exceedingly varied and constantly ongoing in all populations, including those that were non-state forming. States and non-states differed not only in market articulation and in power but in social organization and in historically deep cultural manifestations. The greater power of the state ('the most successful predatory form of social organization') might force irreversible changes upon non-state societies, but this was not as predictable an outcome toward the end of the twentieth century as it had been in the nineteenth, given the relative increase in non-state resources and in the use of modern methods in all spheres of life (including non-state spheres), while the finite nature of state resources became ever more apparent. Indeed, the influences of non-state entities on their surrounding 'host' states came to be increasingly evident.

Resource mobilization theory (Jenkins, 1983), important though it continued to be for the study of social movements, seemed to provide less new insight into the persistence of indigenous sidestream ('peripheral') ethnicity than had initially been hoped. Sidestream ethnicity resists reduction to the level of grievances (and to manipulable, largely specious grievances at that) and the ethnic revival requires for its explanation additional factors, above and beyond the combination of minority grievances (old or new) and increased minority resources. Declining status inequalities between 'central' and indigenous 'peripheral' populations became quite noticeable—due both to the growing ethnic middle class which, nevertheless, did not forgo its cultural identity as a means of social mobility, and the growing competitiveness of the latter *vis-à- vis* social rewards (including the reward of acknowledged cultural legitimacy). Indeed, the unexpected versatility of re-invigorated ethnic movements clearly highlighted their ability not only to maintain an indigenous leadership but to tap and activate indigenous resources of dedication as well.

The ability of universality and particularism to develop and co-exist simultaneously within the very same populations was a rude awakening for both Marxist and non-Marxist theorists who had assumed that industrialization, urbanization, modernization and the spread of education would inevitably reduce ethnic consciousness and lead to the demise of narrower loyalties in favor of broader ones. This prediction was not confirmed, narrower and broader loyalties being far more syncretistic than theory-conscious intellectuals had imagined, and the post-industrial Left was forced to identify with rather than continue to reject the cultural self-regulatory aspirations of ethnic minorities in the West itself. Bourgeois thinkers too went through much soul-searching and reformulation in the light of the evident significance of ethnicity within mainstream academia itself. Ethnicity efforts came to be viewed as reformist of mainstream insensitivity, much like pro-environmental, anti-sexist and anti-bigness or anti-industrial-growth efforts. However, even this is not the entire story, since ethnicity efforts *are* sometimes allied with conservative political, religious and moral reform efforts as well. Ultimately, however, although much has changed in mainstream thought concerning ethnicity since Lord Acton, most recent developments in ethnicity theory still treat ethnicity as *reactive to* or as *transformational of* other, more basic material circumstances and aspirations.

This evident disinclination (even after 150 years of painful and reluctant theoretical change) toward accepting ethnicity in its own right, as a permeable, changeable but ultimately also quite robust and recurring identity-values-behavior complex, a complex that situationally influences aspects of mainstream as well as sidestream life, even under the most modern circumstances, remains a blindspot in social theory that only further 'rethinking' can overcome. The ultimate theoretical contribution of RLS research and theory to general social science theory is not only their assistance in developing a sociology of RLS-efforts *per se* but, in addition, their rich potential for providing further empirical and theoretical perspective contributory toward the rethinking of ethnicity as such.[7] Rather than being viewed as threats to the state or as by-products of split labor markets or even of boundary maintenance processes *per se*[8] (none of which, by the way, give signs of disappearing from the horizon in the foreseeable future), ethnicity and ethnicity movements must come to be appreciated more ethnographically and phenomenologically, i.e. more from the point of view of the insider who experiences them rather than from the point of view of the outsider who views them, telescopically or microscopically, from afar without appreciating, therefore, their affective significance. So terrified are most Western thinkers of the charge of 'primordialism' that they refuse to understand the recurring appeal of primordialism to common folk the world over. Like physicians who refuse to appreciate the common man's dread of cancer or AIDS, they therefore, unknowingly but intrapunitively, limit their own ability to understand the condition that they are presumably concerned with.

The ethnic rejection of the notion that mainstream identity represents one's sole and complete identity (and, indeed, the growing search for sidestream roots) implies an acceptance of self and one's origins that is also rich in its potential for better understanding of others, and of inevitable links to others, as well. If the simplistic ethnic myth of fixed, homogeneous and completely bounded cultures must give way to a more realistic sense of the changeability and intersectedness of all cultures, the awareness of this myth, on the one hand, and, on the other hand, the absolute necessity of undertaking attempts to cultivate the threads of intimacy, involvement and historical relevance, so that meaningful, unalienated social existence remains possible, are often better realized by minorities than by the majorities that smugly disregard, abuse or regulate them. The real question for modern life and for RLS is not whether this is a discrete or interacting world, but, rather, given an incredibly complex field of interacting forces, how one (not just minority ethnics but any social movement) can build a home that one can still call one's own and, by cultivating it, find community, comfort, companionship and meaning in a world whose mainstreams are increasingly unable to provide these basic ingredients for their own members. Mainstream social theory generally refuses to recognize the basically normal affiliative expression, heightened by contrastivity and adversity, that RLS and minority ethnicity movements more generally represent, perhaps because the mainstream itself has abnormally lost this voluntary affective identification of one member with another. Renaming its own galloping alienation 'liberty' does not in any way actually foster liberty or reverse alienation.

> *RLS Theory: A perspective for rational effort to build and safeguard Gemeinschaft aspirations so that they will be in touch with but not inundated by the world at large*

The eight-stage analysis of and prescription for RLS that has been presented here is an alternative planning theory in the sense that it attempts to bridge the gap between social science and societal reform (Albrecht and Gill-Chin, 1986). Planning scientists and planning practitioners tend to look down on one another, trading charges of conceptual poverty and lack of realism (and, therefore, lack of validity). Most of the explanatory theories advanced in language planning, for example, do not reveal, and, therefore, cannot provide, insight into the struggle of some societies toward intergenerational linguistic continuity. Appropriate RLS status planning can only occur if the societal link between generations is constantly kept in mind and if every putative RLS-effort is tested by the question 'how will this effort reach into and reinforce the intergenerational link?'— a link that must take place early, affectively and verbally if RLS is to come about. This does not mean that well-grounded RLS theory can provide us with a blueprint for the future. The future cannot be reduced to a series of technical applications of theoretically formulated steps, neither in economic planning, in agricultural planning, in educational planning, in family planning nor in RLS planning. The best that RLS theory can do is to provide greater societal perspective for negotiating the difficult priorities that any RLS-effort inevitably involves. As with all other types of social planning, RLS planning will inevitably be accompanied by unexpected side-effects and even negative consequences. However, there is no alternative modern route to social problem solving than the route via planning. For the advocates of RLS there is, therefore, no dilemma as to whether RLS planning should occur. If there is a dilemma it deals with the *how* of RLS, i.e. with a systematic overall approach that can guide the efforts that must be undertaken.

To begin with, even before concrete efforts are undertaken, RLS involves 'consciousness heightening and reformation'. The importance of ideological clarification and awareness for the process of directed cultural change can easily be exaggerated but it cannot be denied. RLS behaviors cannot challenge conventional institutions and mainstream-derived ideas as to the role of Xish without fully clarifying the ideal of Xmen-with-Xish. It is hard enough to row against the current; it is virtually impossible to do so without knowing where one would like to get to and why. Any organized activity, particularly ethnically related organized activity, immediately raises questions of right and wrong, desirability and undesirability, legitimacy and illegitimacy, possibility and impossibility. RLS advocates must explore these issues as frankly and as openly as their surrounding political culture permits, i.e. not only with each other but with those who are RLS-uninterested and with those who are RLS-opposed as well. It is always easier to communicate only with those who are already converted; however, those who do so inevitably face the danger of ceasing to explain basic premises even to themselves.

The premises that Xmen are not Ymen and that Xish culture (daily and life-cycle traditional observances, distinctive artifacts, beliefs and values, exemplary literature, art, music, dance, etc.) is not Yish culture must not be skipped over, no more than the premises that Xish culture is worth maintaining, that it can do so only if it becomes more self-regulatory, that one of its main props and creations is its own language and that the latter must be fostered in as many domains of individual and social life as are intraculturally acceptable and feasible. Any such exploration will inevitably be difficult and initially 'touchy'. It forces to the confrontational surface hitherto quiescent assumptions of what being a good Xman entails. Unless these assumptions are clarified and consensualized, at or soon after the outset, all RLS-efforts coming thereafter will be conflicted and contested from within. The goal of fostering commitment to and implementation of a society of authentic 'Xmen-with-Xish' is a difficult one to attain, all the more so if language shift is already far along and the phenomenon of Xmen-via-Yish has already spread, taken root and proved itself to be rewarding. The hoped-for benefits of RLS must be clearly spelled out and its implied, suspected or alleged debits must be openly faced. People cannot be tricked into supporting RLS. They must be convinced to accept a definition of their 'best interest' and 'most positive future' that depends upon and derives from RLS and from the rewards and self-regulatory capacity of the Xmen-with-Xish stance. The first ones to do so will obviously be pioneers and must be particularly ready to work hard in order to attain very sparse results. All this becomes possible only when the RLS enterprise can count on the participation of maximally dedicated and ideologically oriented individuals. The crucial

---

### STAGES OF REVERSING LANGUAGE SHIFT:
### SEVERITY OF INTERGENERATIONAL DISLOCATION
(read from the bottom up)

1. Education, work sphere, mass media and governmental operations at higher and nationwide levels
2. Local/regional mass media and governmental services.
3. The local/regional (i.e. non-neighborhood) work sphere, both among Xmen and among Ymen.
4b. Public schools for Xish children, offering some instruction via Xish, but substantially under Yish curricular and staffing control.
4a. Schools in lieu of compulsory education and substantially under Xish curricular and staffing control.

II. *RLS to transcend diglossia, subsequent to its attainment*

5. Schools for literacy acquisition, for the old and for the young, and not in lieu of compulsory education.
6. The intergenerational and demographically concentrated home-family-neighborhood: the basis of mother tongue transmission.
7. Cultural interaction in Xish primarily involving the community-based older generation.
8. Reconstructing Xish and adult acquisition of XSL.

I. *RLS to attain diglossia (assuming prior ideological clarification)*

---

FIGURE 14.1 *Toward a theory of reversing language shift*

importance of self-aware ideological communities for the process of cultural change is well documented[9] ("solidarity' seems to be the currently fashionable blanket term or codeword for this state of affairs, but it seems to me to be much preferable that its referent be spelled out in terms of social domains and directed efforts, than that yet another codeword be bandied about), even though it is quite clear, and will become even clearer in what we still have to say, below, that consciousness and ideology are not enough. They are merely the first of many concerns, all of which, taken together, constitute a theory and a model of the intergenerational transmission of language, culture, society and identity.

*Stages 8 to 5: RLS on the 'weak side': in pursuit of diglossia*

A theory of RLS must make provision for pre-existing differences in Xish sociolinguistic disarray, so that when *Zeitgeist* and material opportunities for renewed RLS present themselves, the resulting upsurge in effort can take off from different points, appropriate to the situation at hand. In that spirit, and in the spirit of knowing 'what comes next', the notion of a graded series of RLS priorities is offered here as a heuristic theoretical stance, rather than as a fully proven verity. Real life is always full of more complexities and irregularities than theory can provide for. As a result, there may be less implicationality or reproduceability in real life than the theory implies.[10] Nevertheless, the notion of graded priorities in RLS-efforts, even if it is less than perfectly validated, has two virtues: (a) the virtue of more parsimoniously and forcefully directing attention to the crucial issues of self-reliance and of 'first things first', and (b) the virtue of constantly directing attention to the absolutely crucial question of the link to intergenerational continuity. The first virtue is a significant one, because RLS, like all minority-based efforts, is more likely than not to be characterized by a serious shortage of resources. Accordingly, it is important to focus the meager resources that *are* available in as judicious and self-reliant a way as possible. The second virtue constitutes a reminder that RLS must not be carried away by the most fashionable technologies or the most glamorous institutions that are so very much 'in the public eye'. When all is said and done, any and all seriously intended RLS-efforts must still stand the acid test of fostering demonstrable transmissibility across the intergenerational link. It is the achievement of that transmissability, rather than the modernity and glamour of the means employed, that characterizes a good investment of RLS time and effort. Of the eight post-ideological steps that I have in mind, four are particularly urgent and germane to RLS-efforts at their earliest and weakest stages, when political conflict and power goals cannot be afforded, allies are few and far between, and self-help is, therefore, the only dependable approach in pursuit of basic sociolinguistic stability in the midst of pervasive language shift.

*Stage 8*, the reassembly of the Xish language model *per se*, is an obviously rock-bottom stage at which RLS can begin, once adequate ideological clarification has been attained. This stage applies not only for total language communities, as Australian Aboriginal examples indicate, but also for particularly dislocated local variants of languages that are possibly still in good repair elsewhere, although they are often locally inaccessible; indeed, wherever fluent native speakers are no longer available and where even second language speakers command dubious fluency and correctness, a prior stage of re-establishing community norms of Xish grammar, phonology, intonation and prosody, ideomaticity and semantic typologies is highly desirable. This may call for the importation of outside specialists and teaching–learning materials that can provide models of the variety or varieties of Xish that are to be 'oralized' and/or 'litericized'. The alternative is to indigenize a historically inauthentic, non-native local variety of Xish. This is no sin, of course, and has occurred in many places (e.g. among revivalist Irish speakers, as well as among some Amerindian and Aboriginal language advocates), but it obviously exposes an ethnolinguistic authenticity movement, such as RLS, to the particularly difficult-to-rebut or embarrassing charge of inauthenticity. Although such charges are ultimately answerable (precisely because mainstream authenticity also has about it a goodly proportion of conscious and unconscious innovation), it is probably better if one can avoid this issue to begin with and, thereby, to be free to turn RLS attention to code implementation rather than to remain preoccupied with issues of code definition and specification.

The role of linguists is most obvious at this stage, although not of linguists alone. Linguists are notoriously poor at motivating and organizing the societal devotion that is required if stage 8 is to be transcended and if RLS is to become a social movement rather than merely a monograph or a textbook.

*Stage 7* is a remarkably gratifying one, on the one hand, and a remarkably misleading one, on the other hand, insofar as the true state of RLS affairs is concerned. The fact that there is a large, still active, elderly population ('elderly' being defined as 'past child-bearing age') that organizes and partakes of endless Xish public events, rituals, ceremonies, concerts, lectures, courses, contests, readings, songfests, theatrical presentations, radio and television programs and publications is, of course, a tremendous societal achievement and a great joy to those individuals who are personally involved in and enriched by these activities. However, from the point of view of RLS, all of these activities are merely rallies of the 'last Mohicans'. They serve to enthuse the already enthusiastic, to convince the already convinced. At best, they may be said to keep motivation high among the already committed and, in that way, to keep open the possibility that other means of RLS, via efforts that are linked to and involve the younger generations, may still be devised, adopted, implemented and emphasized.

It is hard for a thousand 'old-timers' who attend an absolutely first rate 'pageant for Xish' to believe that on the morning after Xish is still no better off than it was on the night before. However, that is really the case, quite regardless of how many 'young guests' were also present on any one such particular occasion or another, because 'special events' of this kind are just that; as such they are simply not linked into the ongoing, normal, daily family socialization pattern. Their audiences disperse and there is no necessary carry-over from the ideological and esthetic highs that these events often attain, to the concrete rounds of daily life and, most particularly, to the child socialization nexus on which RLS ultimately really depends. This is not to say that stage 7 is ultimately useless; it is merely to say that it is ultimately useless if it too, like stage 8, cannot be transcended. Stage 7 efforts may even occasionally receive Yish governmental support (as in the case of the Heritage Language programs in Canada), but this is a sure sign of their recognized and appreciated tokenism ("folkloric potential') as far as further possible and necessary efforts are concerned if RLS is really to be intergenerationally activated and restabilized.

*Stage 6*, consisting of home-family-neighborhood-community reinforcement (and of organized RLS activity squarely aimed at each of the foregoing), constitutes the heart of the entire intergenerational transmission pursuit and the *sine qua non* of the initial stages thereof. It may be merely metaphorically enlightening to believe, as Kenneth Burke claimed, that 'men build their cultures by huddling together, nervously loquacious, at the edge of an abyss', but it is inescapably true that the bulk of language socialization, identity socialization and commitment socialization generally takes place 'huddled together', through intergenerationally proximate, face-to-face interaction and generally takes place relatively early in life at that. Spicer, one of the few social scientists to have invested a professional lifetime in the study of 'persistent (though stateless) peoples', put it this way in his final summary: '... [T]he persistence of configurations of identity symbols depends on the kind of communication possible in local community organizations, uniting household groups. It is in the milieu of the effective local community ... that the basis for choosing to identify with an enduring people becomes established'.[11]

Unfortunately, knowing that RLS must always feed into and connect up with the interaction of children and their parents or other affectionate socializers in natural, daily home-family-neighborhood-community life if intergenerational transmissibility is to be attained, is no guarantee at all that such linkages can be brought about. In modern, democratic contexts it is not at all easy to plan or engineer RLS-efforts that focus directly on home-family-neighborhood-community building. Although many Jewish settlements and kibbutzim in Ottoman Palestine became bastions of Hebrew language revernacularization, they functioned in this fashion at the tremendous price of tearing themselves away both from the Jewish life round about them in Palestine as well as from the Jewish life, primarily Yiddish-speaking Eastern European, from which most of the revivers of spoken Hebrew and their followers had come. That they could make a virtue out of this double alienation is merely a testimony to the self-sufficient life-style that they were able to establish and the robustness of the sociocultural boundaries that they long maintained between themselves and other Jews (whom they obviously viewed as 'Xmen-via-Yish'). Even so, many of the Hebrew-revernacularizing townlets and kibbutzim failed, as have almost all of the experimental communities established too expressly for language maintenance or RLS purposes.

We will examine some of the difficulties and solutions that pertain to this stage below, after we have reviewed all of the stages. At this point, it must suffice to say that *if this stage is not satisfied, all else can amount to little more than biding time*, at best generation by generation, without a natural, self-priming social mechanism having been engendered thereby. For a language that has shrunk to 10% of its former 'realm', remaining at 10% may seem like an accomplishment of sorts, but it is also a confirmation to 90% of the population that the ideal of 'Xmen-via-Yish' is really the more viable alternative. That is why simply maintaining the stage 7 *status-quo-ante* is an undesirable long-term 'solution' for endangered languages. Attaining stage 6 is a necessary, even if not a sufficient, desideratum of RLS. Unlike other stages, when stage 6 is transcended it is not merely 'left behind'; quite the contrary: all subsequent stages must be diligently tied back to and connected with stage 6 if they too are to contribute to the living reality of RLS rather than merely to its propagandistic hoopla, one-upmanship or hype. It is here that the revolutionary link-up between Xish and 'childhood through youth' is accomplished and retained (Levitt and Rubenstein, 1972).

*Stage 5* entails formal linguistic socialization. Although such socialization does not need to be restricted to literacy and literacy alone, that indeed is by far the lion's share of what this stage entails in modern settings. Whether restricted to literacy or not, this stage adds additional varieties to the learner's repertoire, above and beyond those that can be acquired in the largely oral and familiar interaction within most family, neighborhood and community intergenerational situations. The availability of more formal varieties (and, in modern life, reading/writing essentially involves more formal varieties than does most of speech) gives Xish a range which enables it to be more comfortable *vis-à-vis* the predictably greater ranges that are normally available in Yish and Zish, due to the intergroup, governmental and econotechical functions of the latter. Xish religious, legal and oral traditions can all be tapped for the elaboration of such more formal varieties and the attainment of literacy in one or another of these varieties contributes to the attainment and solidification of wider intracommunal bonds and the cultivation of additional support opportunities for RLS. Clearly, stage 5 entails a kind of schooling, one that may initially be open and attractive to adults as well as to children. However, it does not involve schooling in lieu of compulsory Yish regulated/administered education, and, as a result, can avoid many of the expenses and most of the Yish control-and-approval requirements that such education generally entails.

Stages 8 to 5 constitute the 'program minimum' of RLS. These stages do not involve major costs and they do not crucially depend on Yish cooperation. They are generally of the 'do it yourself' variety and, as such, can be approximated in almost all types of political and economic climates. They are particularly appropriate for numerically and politically weak language-in-culture settings and are not restricted in applicability to permissive democratic settings, although the latter are always more facilitative insofar as overt organizational efforts are concerned. RLS concentration on these four initial steps, particularly *on any subgrouping of them that also includes stage 6*, generally presumes a stable bilingual model of Xish society in which Y/X diglossia is attained and maintained by surrendering to Yish all effective control over the more modern and interactive media and pursuits.

Such diglossia is not a rare or impossible goal, nor is it a goal which inevitably consigns its adherents or practitioners to poverty, backwardness, non-participationism or isolation from the mainstream. Compulsory and higher education, economic opportunity and governmental service may still be entirely open to those who espouse and maintain the lower level Xmen-via-Xish position, but, except for presumably minor and voluntary Yish accommodations via translation, usually in connection with absolutely crucial public welfare services and whatever media and political visibility Xish can obtain by means of the numbers and funds at its own disposal, the bulk of such opportunities will clearly be available to them only in Yish. That being the case, the future of Xish rests squarely on the relative impermeability of the intergroup boundaries and on the non-negotiability of the 'Xmen-via-Xish' position at stages 6 and 5.

This being the case, a case which is often described and experienced, justly or unjustly, as 'second class citizenship', it is clear why RLS movements often seek to push on beyond these stages into the upper reaches of sociosymbolic life. However, it should be clear that just as not to do so constitutes an unjustified foreclosing of RLS opportunity and sociolinguistic potential, so the premature crossing over of RLS-efforts into the arena of the second four stages runs the risk of burdens and challenges that may be excessive, non-productive and even dangerous for the entire RLS enterprise. The choice between these two types of risk is a fateful one, indeed.

*Stages 4 to 1: RLS on the strong side, or transcending diglossia in search of increased power-sharing*

It is upon crossing the 'continental divide', from the pursuit of diglossia to the pursuit of more than just that, that legal provisions for Xish increasingly begin to have to be made. To make them earlier would be an instance of *legis sine moribus vanae*. Not to make them at this stage would soon be tantamount to political foolishness. Education in lieu of compulsory schooling involves an intrusion of the state into the life of the home, family, neighborhood and community. Most democratic states provide for the possibility of substantially curtailing or substantively modifying (or pro-RLS orienting) this intrusion by means of private, parochial or proprietary schools. Such schools must still follow the minimal essentials of the approved general curriculum, employ state certified teachers in conjunction with teaching those minimal essentials and maintain facilities and schedules that meet state specifications pertaining to fire, safety, health and attendance standards. Otherwise, however, they are free to lengthen the school day and the school year to facilitate the addition of courses and experiences that are particularly desirable to them. The maintenance of such relatively independent schools (type 4a schools in our complete typology) obviously entails major costs for RLS advocates and their supporters. These costs can sometimes be avoided if Xish-speaking parents and actually or potentially Xish-speaking children are sufficiently concentrated and if the Yish authorities are sufficiently cooperatively inclined to justify and to permit special RLS public school programs (type 4b) for minority language children. Generally, such programs are reluctantly and unreliably offered, are really compensatory in nature and orientation and inferior in educational quality. They do not foster either the image or the reality of Xish cultural self-regulation and this has an inescapably negative impact on the self-esteem of Xish pupils, parents and other adults alike. They are particularly unsuitable to the attainment of the goals of weak and inexperienced RLS movements, and the more centralized the Yish educational establishment is, the more unsatisfactory such schools are if the local attainment of RLS success *per se* is utilized as the criterion of 'success'.

Even where schools of the 4b type do not suffer from outright or hidden sabotage by the governmental authorities on whose personnel, funds and approval they depend, they present the danger of leading away from the Xish community of orientation and can yield positive results only if sufficiently surrounded by and embedded within an RLS-oriented family-neighborhood-community field of forces. Several localized examples of RLS-oriented type 4b schools exist to indicate that this goal is not impossible of attainment, but, on the whole, this attainment is rare and often depends on the prior or concurrent establishment in nearby areas of cultural autonomy arrangements

that transcend schooling *per se*. In essence, they represent the conversion of
compensatory 4b programs into self-regulatory 4a programs via the attainment
of a political accommodation at a governmental level higher than the local
school authority. In the absence of such higher and transcendent
considerations, which obviously aim at dovetailing schooling with stage 6
institutions and processes, there is absolutely no reason to assume that
schooling (even type 4a schooling) is either a guarantee of or even a prop for
successful RLS. RLS movements must guard against allowing the academic
affiliations and professional biases of friendly academicians (which tend to
make them view education as the universal panacea for any and all problems)
to lead these movements prematurely to assume that Xish schooling is 'the
basic solution' to RLS problems. The Irish experience alone should disabuse
us of that fallacy.

Unreconstructed schools of type 4b, even more so than schools of type 4a,
are a bridge between the immediate and the larger, less Xish, less controllable
environment. Only the demographically and economically strong can cross this
bridge with relative safety by providing the societal support that schools themselves need in order to successfully extend RLS-efforts outward into the larger
Xish community. No such extension can succeed before the basic family-neighborhood-community support of Xish is in place and putting and keeping it in
place is becoming more and more problematic even for mainstream schools. We
will return to this point below.

*Stage 3* pertains to the non-neighborhood worksphere in general, i.e., with
the more influential work sphere which cannot be contained within Xish neigh-
borhood/community limits. This is a tremendously influential setting for RLS-
efforts and, indeed, one which pervades and colors all of social life, particularly
in modern, secular contexts. With its necessary implications for social status and
mobility the work sphere has become the most fully rationalized and cross-
nationally, cross-ethnically, and cross-linguistically connected domain of modern functioning. As such, it is a particularly difficult area for RLS to penetrate,
influence and control. The growing predominance of multinational firms and the
frequent rotation of their office incumbents, plus the fact that services or products are provided to an ethnolinguistically very heterogeneous clientele and that
there is a constant growth and change of technology, products and services,
these are all features that prove to be linguistically and socioculturally problematic for all but the largest 'establishment languages'. The insuperable roadblocks
which they frequently represent insofar as RLS is concerned must be realistically viewed in that perspective, although opportunities for RLS will also obtain,
depending on the overall degree of modernization and development that the
Xish and Yish economies have attained.[12]

However, even when aspects of everyday or even higher- work sphere operations *can* be altered to accommodate local RLS pressures, the link between the work sphere (higher or lower) and intergenerational language transmission is far from direct or obvious. Individual or group economic circumstances certainly influence such RLS concerns as the rate of selection of own-group and own-language marriage partners, the rate of childbearing, the neighborhood of residence, the preferred language of family life, of child-socialization and of the medium of instruction selected for one's children. These are all 'lower order' (i.e., more fundamental) concerns than the work sphere itself and must also be tackled directly, as indicated earlier, rather than only indirectly via RLS efforts pertaining to the work sphere *per se*. Thus, while it is true that the work sphere must be 'captured', particularly for those seeking a maximum of cultural autonomy (rather than a diglossic H/L arrangement), it is also true that it is quite difficult to do so and that in doing so the forging of direct links to stage 6 must be constantly kept in mind. The formation of 'contract groups' that work together in Xish (in the lower work sphere) and of service centers or counters operating in Xish, or of Xish 'cells', 'branches', 'floors' or 'networks' in larger firms, these are all possible tactics for introducing and maintaining Xish at work, but it is the indirectness of any positive link between work and stage 6 that must constantly be kept in mind and innovatively tackled and directed in a pro-RLS fashion.

*Stage 2* is concerned with lower governmental services, i.e. those that have direct, daily contact with the citizenry, including the local mass media. As with the work sphere, these must be viewed as more than merely factors in the 'creation of a climate' for RLS (many language movements pay far too much attention to such symbolic, 'atmospheric' goals) and even as more than the creation of contexts for Xish use. The services and media entailed at this stage reach into the very neighborhoods and, indeed, into the very homes that constitute the nuclei of RLS and of Xish life itself. The importance of Xishizing these services and influences is beyond question, *but only to the extent that their links to stage 6 are focused upon.* Without such links the Xishization of these services and influences constitute no more than a holding pattern; they buy time but they do not become self-priming RLS devices, particularly since there will always be more Yish than Xish services and media units. The location and staffing of these services and the content and orientation of their programs cannot themselves function as intergenerational transmission linkages. Such linkages must be there to begin with, maintained by far more direct family, neighborhood and community-building processes, before governmental services and lower mass media can make transmissible contributions to RLS, to identity formation, to community organization and to socialization of the young.

404                                                                    REVERSING LANGUAGE SHIFT

It is doubtless harder to build Xish neighborhoods and to assist Xish-speaking families than to broadcast for x minutes per day in Xish on radio or television. The former, however, are immediate building-blocks of intergenerational transmission whereas the latter are obviously not, unless very skillfully aimed, revised, fine-tuned, and evaluated specifically *vis-à-vis* criteria of intergenerational mother tongue transmission. We must not turn our backs on the media in the RLS struggle, but they are far from being cure-alls or even vitamins. Yish media can weaken stage 6 more than Xish media can strengthen it. This is a dilemma that must be faced by fostering stage 6 *per se*, more directly, rather than by fostering RLS indirectly via the media.

Finally, *stage 1* may be reached, the stage at which Xish cultural autonomy is recognized and implemented, even in the upper reaches of education, work, media and government operations, and particularly within the region (or regions) of Xish concentration. It is at this stage that the pressures for taking the step from autonomy to independence become greatest, and when philosophies of the 'naturalnesss of Xish monolingualism in all domains of life' come to be advanced (and not only at the individual and societal levels but even at the neurological level as well: see, e.g., Laponce, 1984/1987). Once again, it must be clear that it is not some very general, unfocused, amorphous 'atmosphere effect' or process of osmosis that is of primary RLS concern in this connection, but, rather, precisely what it is that stage 1 can do for stage 6 that really counts. The communications, rewards and opportunity structures emanating from 'on high' influence family, neighborhood and community processes via a very long, involved and impersonal chain of indirect influences and, therefore, their contributions to RLS are, ultimately, equally indirect and uncertain. While stage 1 can make a definite contribution to RLS, this contribution must be successfully translated into intergenerationally transmissible stage 6 processes and interactions before it will have more than bureaucracy-building and elite-building effects. Stages 3 to 1 are not only difficult for Xish to penetrate (due to their Yish locus of control and their Yish-dominated, even if heterogeneous, clienteles), but they all link back to mother tongue acquisition only in a roundabout fashion and with considerable time-lapse, if at all. They may help shape adult identity and language use, much more so than they help implant basic identity and mother tongue use in the young. Were this not so, much of the indigenous non-English mother tongue world, so dependent on English-speaking jobs, English-speaking media and English-speaking governmental functioning, would be of English mother tongue and of Anglo-American ethnicity by now, whereas this is obviously not the case in any part of that world, even when intergenerationally interacting with and dependent upon the English behemoth.

FIGURE 14.2 *Graded Intergenerational Dislocation Stages (GIDS) in thirteen monitored RLS settings.*

Abbreviations: AA = Australian Aborigines (selected cases), AIR = Australian Immigrant (post WW2), B = Basque, C = Catalan, FQ = Francophone Quebec, F = Frisian, H = Hebrew, I = Irish, M = Maori, NR = Navajo (selected reservation community 1), S = Spanish: New York City Puerto Ricans, YO = Yiddish Ultra-Orthodox (NYC), YS = Yiddish Secular (NYC); IC = Ideological clarification; Numbers = GIDS stages (X = stage[s] currently receiving most attention in RLS-efforts); Ts = Total dislocation score.

| # | AA | AIR | B | C | FQ | F | H | I | M | NR | S | YO | YS | # |
|---|----|-----|---|---|----|---|---|---|---|----|---|----|----|---|
| 1 | | | X | X | X | X | | | | | | | | 1 |
| 2 | | X | X | X | | X | X | | | | | | | 2 |
| 3 | | | X | X | | | | | | | | X | | 3 |
| 4b | | | | | | X | | | X | | X | | | 4b |
| 4a | X | X | X | | | | | X | X | | X | | | 4a |
| 5 | | | | | | | | | X | | | | X | 5 |
| 6* | +− | − | − | + | + | − | + | − | | +− | +− | + | − | 6* |
| 7 | X | X | | | | X | | X | X | X | X | | X | 7 |
| 8 | X | | X | | | | | X | X | | | | X | 8 |
| IC* | +− | + | + | + | + | + | +− | +− | +− | +− | +− | +− | +− | IC* |
| Ts** | 19 | 13 | 18 | 6 | 1 | 13 | 1 | 21 | 24 | 11 | 11 | 7 | 20 | Ts** |
| | AA | AIR | B | C | FQ | F | H | I | M | NR | S | YO | YS | |

\* Average Ts for − or +− at stage 6: 15.75; at IC: 14.13
   Average Ts for +        at stage 6: 3.75; at IC: 10.20

\*\* Languages ranked by the *sum* of their GIDS scores (Ts):

| | + on 6 | | + on IC |
|---|---|---|---|
| 1 = FQ, H | X | X | X |
| 6 = C | X | | X |
| 7 = YO (NYC) | X | | |
| 10 = S (NYCPR) | | | |
| 11 = NR | | | |
| 13 = AIR, F | | X | X |
| 18 = B | | | X |
| 19 = AA | | | |
| 20 = YS (NYC) | | | |
| 21 = I | | | |
| 24 = M | | | |

## Problems of Focusing on 'Lower Order' Neighborhood and Community Organization

Figure 14.2 reaffirms the crucial nature of stage 6 in differentiating between the more and the less successful cases that we have discussed in this volume, and also reveals the even more crucial importance of stage 6 than ideological clarification *per se*. Of course, our stagewise discussion, above, clearly implies that there are weaknesses to RLS-efforts 'on the strong side', just as there are undeniable strengths to RLS-efforts 'on the weak side'. Clearly, the 'strong side', with its stress on the institutions of modernity and on the structures of cultural autonomy (control of education, the work sphere, media, governmental services) is more than most RLS movements can realistically aspire to in the foreseeable future. Equally clear is the fact that even when such props for RLS *are* attained, *they must still be translated into the lower order processes of stage 6* if a self-priming intergenerational transmissibility system is be constituted and set into motion. The 'strong side' itself is not such a system, although it may adequately trickle down to that system once that system is in operation. Thus, the key to RLS is stage 6 and it is to some of the problems of stage 6-building that we now turn.

Stage 6 may be viewed as an arena for 'collective action' and, therefore, as politically encumbered and, in accord with the theory of such action, as subdivisible into interest articulation, organization, mobilization and opportunity utilization. Adopting the 'collective action' approach to stage 6 would help alert us to the fact that beliefs, resources and actions do not always come together in unproblematic ways. Particularly when they are at their early stages, RLS-efforts find it difficult to convince others that sociocultural change is needed and that established power and interests can be influenced and modified by minorities with clearly focused views and a stagewise program of goals and priorities. Another early difficulty is the over-reliance on voluntary and part-time leadership and on part-time/leisure-time activists. One route that has been much used to temper such over-reliance is the involvement of individuals whose normal work responsibilities include participation in or attention to social action, e.g., teachers, professors, social workers, lawyers, etc. However, these too can rarely offer full-time commitment and are usually establishment-regulated and establishment-dependent in many ways. Moreover, much of the literature on collective action and social action is too general in its orientation to be of direct relevance to RLS-efforts or to early RLS-efforts in particular. In the latter connection, the accumulated body of theory and data pertaining to organizational functioning, to neighborhood organization and to interest-group processes may be more helpful.

Those who believe that all significant political action occurs at the national level need to be disabused of that perspective, particularly at early stages of RLS activity. Many of the most salient and explosive domestic political issues are fully recognizable as struggles between local residents and the local 'outcroppings' of nationwide authorities or of non-local interests more generally. Furthermore, the question of how powerless persons can gain power in local affairs is of the greatest importance to a real understanding of democratic politics. The fundamental task of the RLS neighborhood organizer is to find RLS incentives that will induce self-interested local residents to support and become active on behalf of an RLS nursery, RLS day-care center, RLS housing cluster, RLS cooperative market, RLS employment center, RLS recreational center, RLS homework/tutoring group, RLS work transportation service, legal aid service, credit union, etc. Incentives are crucial in understanding the difficulties which RLS spokesmen and ideologists face in their efforts to attract and organize larger groups of Xmen on behalf of RLS. The success of interest-group organizations, and that is what RLS-efforts are, depends on much more than ideological appeals, and all such appeals must be heavily intermingled with concrete inducements or services such as the foregoing (Horwitt, 1989).

As modern *Gesellschaft* forces continue to expand, the incentives of RLS-sponsored neighborhood care, companionship and assistance in managing one's work, health and family problems become ever more meaningful, particularly in poorer neighborhoods. An RLS stress on human relationships in modern life, on local accountability, on neighborhood collective responsibility for all who live there, on self-help activities focused upon priority concerns of the local residents, becomes ever more meaningful as both parents are in increasingly the workforce, as public education deteriorates and as individual family means cannot provide for the old, the sick, the newborn, nor a place to play or study for the young. Voluntary organizations serving such needs are not merely wishy-washy expressions of piety and good intentions but vital experimenters and innovators on the way to social and cultural reform. They help people to find identity and purpose, self-realization and fulfillment, the very things that RLS must stand for both ideologically and practically. Particularly in the current climate of conservative politics and budget cutting, more people-oriented help and self-help becomes both a particularly important and a particularly effective context for introducing and fostering RLS.

RLS neighborhood building efforts must obviously relate local spiritual beliefs, family values, informal neighboring and self-help notions to Xish and to the ideal of Xmen-via-Xish. In response to Durkheim's well-known dictum that 'it is impossible to artificially resuscitate a particularistic spirit which no longer has any function', RLS must stress the functionality of Xish in terms of locally and non-bureaucratically satisfying the deeply cherished values and needs of all ordinary, rank-and-file Xmen. But, obviously, neighborhoodism has a strong political component and potential, and the energy and effectiveness of the networks generated by RLS neighborhoodism will be tied to the fact that they satisfy needs, make demands, have goals and address concrete purposes. RLS neighborhoods must be battling neighborhoods, struggling for social, cultural, economic, political and personal dignity. Action needs an image of community that local residents can identify with and that fosters commitment as a type of functional equivalence to kinship among non-kin. As distinct from its role among ideologists and linguists, Xish cannot be pursued in and of itself, for its own sake, among ordinary folk. It must be part of the warp and woof of social life and make a meaningful difference in the neighborhood *Gemeinschaft*-life and in the *Gemeinschaft*-strivings of ordinary people.

All social movements try, in their own ways, to fulfill needs and strivings. RLS-efforts must be able to do so even better than others, because kinlike affect and mutual support are part of the basic promise of the ethnicity message and of the authenticity message and, therefore, are not only suitable but necessary parts of the distinctiveness of RLS-efforts. Neighborhoods built on such distinctiveness and affect can go on to build Xish schools (at stages 5, 4a and even neighborhood-controlled public schools of type 4b), Xish worksites and move toward other selected goals 'on the strong side' too.[13]

Sometimes the above advice, and the entire approach on which it is based, strikes RLS activists as contra-intuitive and as self-limiting. It is obviously harder to build Xish families, neighborhoods and communities than to establish Xish schools, publications or non-print media. However, the former immediately provides a base for intergenerational continuity and a point of departure for stages that can come after it and can be supported by it, whereas the latter do not because they are too restricted in time and place and have no daily, intimate, socialization foundation underlying them. At best, they can contribute to the 'spirit' necessary for such a foundation to be laid, but they do not lay it themselves. Thus, the approach being advanced here does not counsel ignoring the higher order domains, but, rather, counsels the necessity of a prior, firmly established child-socialization base to which they can contribute and from which they themselves, in turn, can derive the political support which they require, given that they will always be outweighed by their Yish counterparts. Thus, it is by no means a return to simple village life that stage 6 envisages but, rather, an attempt to find or fashion the pattern of urban reality that is most constructive *vis-à-vis* the complex dislocative challenges facing RLS today.

# Difficulties of Focusing on RLS via 'Lower Order' Family Processes

The affective and affiliative emphases that derive from the kinship-ethnicity dimension of RLS-efforts not only directly imply the home, neighborhood and community, as the fundamental link to the intergenerational transmission of Xish, but they also and equally directly imply the family, as the very building block of such transmission. It is in the family that social support and transactions with the community have traditionally been initiated and nurtured; it is also in the family that social commitments have traditionally been nurtured. Above all, it is in the family that a peculiar bond with language and language activities (conversation, games, stories, songs, proverbs and felicitous expressions, verbalized emotion, verbal ritual and verbal play) is fostered, shared and fashioned into personal and social identity. Unfortunately, the 'traditional' family has become harder and harder to find and to maintain. It has been eroded by the very same universalizing macro-forces that erode small languages and caring neighborhoods.

Good RLS neighborhood organization, therefore, must include programs designed to provide social support for older adolescents, for young couples and for families (particularly young families) through the provision of RLS-oriented social workers and counsellors, the organization of parent groups for a variety of purposes but for RLS-parenting as well, the organization of drop-in centers for assistance with any and all family problems, but for assistance with RLS as well. Such initially 'formal support systems' should aim at generating informal or internal support systems within the families and neighborhoods they serve so that the latter will have less and less need for the formal supports. RLS family support efforts cannot be oblivious to the fact that all competent parenting (not to mention RLS-oriented parenting) must be grounded in the norms, values and behaviors of a particular culture. Nowadays, parents must often be taught not only enjoyable parenting but also to recognize, implement and enjoy their own culture and this inevitably becomes part of the task of RLS.

Of course, all of the above assumes that it is possible to break out of the impersonality and uniformity of *Gesellschaft* and to ameliorate the loss of *Gemeinschaft* without thereby creating more bureaucratic problems than one solves. RLS-inspired neighborhood and family services must constantly be founded on consultation and cooperation, on self-liquidation of formal structures as genuine self-participation increases, and, above all, on the realization that it is unrealistic to expect reversals within a few years of the myriad neighborhood and family problems that have evolved over the past century or more. Naturally, all planning entails some unexpected negative side-effects as well. Nevertheless, these can be minimized if RLS-efforts are conducted in an experimental, consultative, self-correcting and self-liquidating fashion.

The Yish mainstream itself has failed at correcting the very neighborhood and family problems that RLS must face if it is to succeed. Certainly RLS should distance itself from the Orwellian vision of a war-ravaged world in which the functions of the family have been taken over by stultifying and impersonal child-rearing institutions. Quite the contrary! RLS should be at the forefront of returning communities, neighborhoods and families to the values, norms and behaviors that have preferential and historical validity for them. Many of the problems of Yish society itself are due to the very fact that most larger societal systems will not work without important input from the family. Although it is far from clear that RLS-efforts will be more successful than others that have attempted to influence family patterns, its inevitably smaller scale and its greater focus on the young, the old, the sick, the poor and the neglected are its greatest safeguards and its basic strengths. The small successes that it can attain (small in the light of the enormity of the problems that it must tackle) will be beacons of promise for others who are willing to be involved in an ennobling struggle even though it is a struggle that they may not fully win.[14]

The basic dilemma of RLS-efforts everywhere is that their success requires overcoming the very problems of modern life that the strongest societies and cultures have not been able to overcome. The basic strength of RLS-efforts is that they can afford to take a less ponderous, more grass-roots approach to these problems and, thereby, seek to come to the attention of and become more identified with those whose lives they aim to influence.

## The School: The Bridge between 'The Weak Side' and 'The Strong Side' Approaches to RLS

For maximal RLS success some type of school must be an integral part of the family-neighborhood axis of child socialization and identity-commitment formation. Schools cannot succeed, whether their goal be RLS or merely history or mathematics instruction, if the relationship between teachers, parents and students is distant and if these parties are estranged from each other, from the curriculum and from self and community actualizing experience. 'Schools are the children of the community', it has been wisely said, but this adage is little more than novel verbiage, 'educationese', because the state of affairs that it describes has become an impossible dream, purely 'pie in the sky' as far as most education is concerned. On the one hand, mainstream parents and communities have little to say about what goes on in the school that their children attend. On the other hand, mainstream schools themselves do not seem to comprehend the extent to which the schools had been challenged, every bit as much as has the family, as the major force in providing children with the skills, attitudes and behaviors upon which decency and success in modern life increasingly depend.

Precisely because such a high proportion of families are either of the 'single parent' variety or of the 'both parents working' variety (only some 7% of American families currently consist of two parents, *one of whom stays at home at least during the years in which the children are attending elementary school*), student participation in neighborhood and community activities has become much more crucial for later success than ever before. Childcare/playgroup arrangements that involve contact with adult specialists in tutoring, computers, dance, drama, writing, library research, athletics, scouting and after-school jobs contribute to an amazing widening of perspective and learning experiences, as well as to a diversification of interests and interactive competence, that have great significance not only for academic success but for success in the larger society thereafter.

The above out-of-school agencies and activities have substantially usurped the traditional role of the family as the major partner of the school, and, in addition, they are all neighborhood/community-related arenas of crucial language use, language views and language competencies. The stage 5 school can attempt to be the institutional resource that corresponds to Xish in this connection. So can type 4a schools to some extent, although they probably require an auxiliary agency, such as the stage 5 school, in order to divide up the day and the onerous responsibilities of constantly relating Xish to childlife, to local needs and resources, to changing demands of the work sphere, to the entertainment sphere and to the burgeoning knowledge sphere. The RLS-school must no longer be concerned only with ethnically encumbered attitudes, knowledge, skills and beliefs, but with relating Xish to the rapidly changing world in which languages must constantly scramble in order to find a place for themelves, most particularly so if diglossic arrangements with that world-at-large are ideologically unacceptable or simply tactically impossible.[15]

## Additional Concerns and Perspectives

The foregoing remarks are not intended to make it seem that RLS is impossible or doomed to failure. They are intended to make it clear why it is so hard to succeed at it. Successful RLS implies remaking social reality and that is very hard for minorities to do. The social meaning of being a minority is that one is forced to spend almost all of one's cultural resources on damage control, that is, on merely staying alive within a cultural reality that is not of one's own making and not even under one's own substantial ability to influence. If we add to these widely generalizable difficulties (a) those of also engaging in and achieving acceptance of a modicum of corpus planning, at least in order to stay abreast of 'popular modernity', (b) those of traditional second languages which cannot count on the usual home and neighborhood process for their intergenerational transmissibility, (c) those of purported national and official languages which cannot come close to fully controlling the 'high side' even within their own territorial borders, also (d) the particular problems of 'expected short-gevity' that beset urban, immigrant minorities, then one may well conclude that the task is not only a formidable one but a hopeless one as well. However, such a pessimistic conclusion is belied by the success cases we have glanced at, Hebrew in Ottoman and Pre-Mandate Palestine, Catalan in Spain, French in Quebec and in the dozens of others that have been reported upon elsewhere (see, e.g. Ellis and mac a'Ghobhainn, 1971). *None of these successes was pre-ordained or occurred without struggle and reverses* and all of them qualified as 'successes', whether or not their leaders admitted it to the rank-and-file, well before cultural autonomy was attained. In addition to the eminently hopeful status of Navajo, ultra-Orthodox Yiddish and even Spanish in various corners of the USA, Basque seems not only salvageable but even improving and that of Irish-as-a-second-language has stabilized. The latter accomplishment is something which appeared quite impossible only some two generations ago and remains widely unrecognized even today because it leaves 'the language' at a lower level of utilization than was generally aimed at.

Rebuilding society or guiding the meandering currents of social change is very hard, even for those who are in control. The eight-stage model, with its stress on the foundational nature (not the exclusive importance) of stage 6, must not be 'fluffed off' by the conundrum that 'all stages are more fully interdependent than the model maintains'. Such a view provides no insight into the direction and the timing of intergenerational mother tongue transmission and how it differs from influence processes more generally. Such a view disregards the very limited successes of countless RLS-efforts (Frisian, Irish, Maori and American/Australian immigrational languages being foremost among them) that have been overly influenced by its blandishments. Such an analysis provides no guide to action because it has no approach as to priorities and no evaluative perspective as to the differences between long-range and short-range 'success'. Such a comment merely promotes busywork in all directions, thereby foreclosing all prospects of success in connection with solving what is a most difficult problem at any rate. It is similarly not advisable to point to the myriad 'additional factors' that can be appended to or derived from the eight-stage RLS model. Untold learning, interactional, communicational, attitudinal and other psychosocial, intercultural and interlinguistic dimensions can be proliferated *ad infinitum*. But to do so is to ultimately obfuscate the intergenerational transmission issue rather than to clarify it, by endlessly delaying the realization that RLS-efforts must attempt to do a few crucial things well and early, rather than be delayed until academics can shed light on all possible interpersonal, intergroup and inter-linguistic issues related to it.

## Concluding Sentiments

There is often a regrettable and probably inescapable gap between the experiences and concerns of ordinary men and women, focused as they commonly are on the concrete processes and requirements of daily life, and the reflections of scientists and other intellectuals, focused on confirmable evidence, parsimonious generalizations and integrative theories. This difference in perspective, however, should not make it impossible for those interested in the latter to realize that all their higher order constructs must still be validated against the processes and requirements that preoccupy the former. All theories of RLS must clearly suggest how they can be translated into the actual flow of intergenerational transmissibility that is effected via the daily lives of ordinary people and the traditions and values of ongoing cultures.

The weakest can never successfully compete with the strongest *vis-à-vis* the control of universities, the mass media, good jobs and the impersonal and unrelenting governmental prerogatives related to mass modernization and post-modernization. Initially, those who are weak can only compete for control over their own intimacy and then strive to go on from there, from the firm foundation of their own 'little culture' to the possibly greater regulation of selected corners of their own modernity. They must begin their RLS-efforts close to the direct intergenerational mother tongue transmission nexus and move on, slowly and gingerly, from there, doing so only as those processes that stand further from that nexus can be both regulated and focused more fully on that link itself.

The recent unisex revolution in the Western world is a good example of the soundness of this approach. New out-of-home roles and opportunities for women are becoming institutionalized, far above and beyond the lagging requirements of the law, because this revolution was initiated and transmitted via home-family-neighborhood-community role changes in the daily life-experiences and interactions between ordinary men and women. Without this plebian beginning and the success which that beginning attained in its own ranks and at its own level, any new laws that would have been adopted would merely have been 'on the books' (as are many language laws today), as further examples of the tokenism and the pious fraud that frequently stand in the way of any more genuine amelioration of the condition of the downtrodden. However, the centrality of the family and of the small-scale processes which constitute and build informal, face-to-face intimacy and affection (Donahue, in press; Poster, 1978) insofar as the intergenerational transmission of mother tongue and cultural identity are concerned, does not imply that these institutions and processes *per se* and alone are sufficient for the ultimate success of such revolutions. It has been the burden of our argument throughout this volume that they are indispensably necessary but not sufficient for the success of RLS, and that they should be aimed at directly and early, not only before other stages in the struggle are focused upon but in order that these other staged can be successfully grounded once they are focused upon.

The impending demise of ethnolinguistic minorities has been prematurely predicted, with or without crocodile tears, over and over again during the past two centuries (Fishman, 1983/1985). Such predictions are no more than thinly disguised 'death wishes' that urge threatened cultures to hurry up and die today (or to submit quietly to euthanasia) rather than tomorrow. Equally harmful to the hidden RLS capacities of many threatened languages, however, are the premature 'societal control wishes' of many RLS advocates that aim immediately at the top of the mountain without realizing that the base must first be traversed.

Many aspects of RLS still remain relatively unexamined, even in as lengthy a treatment as the present one has been. The psychological dimensions of RLS still require systematic exploration, whether we turn to such matters as 'Xish self-esteem', 'perceived linguistic vitality' or 'tapping Yish guilt' on behalf of Xish RLS purposes. All of these certainly deserve attention, as does the insufficiency of the innocently inchoate dream of 'happy, reciprocal pluralism, period'. On the other hand, an unexaggerated recognition of the economic and political antagonism that may well come to the fore when 'the worm turns' is also overdue. The latter are not uniquely or particularly embarrassments of RLS, since cultural imperialism, erosion and subjugation are every bit as conflict-engendering, if not more so, than RLS. If we have shied away from addressing such issues fully in this volume it is not because they are less worthy but because the sociological dimensions of RLS-efforts *per se* have been particularly ignored in the past.

RLS-efforts go on and on, paying homage to human persistence in building the kind of ethnocultural life that is more consistent with deeply held ethnolinguistic convictions. Indeed, RLS is a peculiarly and admirably human endeavor, after all is said and done, an endeavor to rebuild society in accord with an ideal of cultural democracy, justice and equality, to meet felt responsibilities *vis-à- vis* one's identity, to behaviorally implement the traditions to which one subscribes, to safeguard and activate perceived cultural imperatives and sanctities by handing them on to one's children or, at least, to make supreme efforts on their behalf and to 'go down trying', if necessary. The methods and priorities currently most often utilized in this quest can clearly be improved upon; they can be rendered more rational with respect to priorities, more knowledgeable with respect to precedents the world over, more informed *vis-à-vis* the social science theories and findings that might bear upon them. These are the considerations we have tried to stress in our discussions in this volume. In an increasingly interactive world such as ours, one in which both *glasnost* and the 'spirit of 1992' have become major realities during the very years in which this book was being written, RLS-efforts are likely to have reverberations (both expected and unexpected and both positive and negative) that only a tradition of patient, comparative and theoretically integrated study and practice can hope to cope with. In the certainty that RLS-efforts will continue and will even be augmented in the years ahead, may this book continue to be stimulating and useful, even as it implies the kind of 'better world' that all RLSers hope will come to pass.

## Notes

1.  For some of the earliest but still timely Western objections to the legitimacy claims of minority indigenous ethnic groups see Lord Acton (1862 [1907]) and Engels (1866). For the more general and enduring roadblocks to an appreciation of ethnicity in human behavior, see my '*Language, Ethnicity and Racism*', 1977 (reprinted: 1989).

2.  On the rationality/irrationality and modernity/non-modernity of revitalization efforts, in relation to the current cultural planning of our own day and age, see Barber (1941), Champagne (1983), Kehoe (1989), Linton (1943), Wallace (1956), Thornton (1986) and Traugott (1978).

3.  On the dilemmas of forgotten values and those who pursue them, see Institute of Cultural Conservatism (1987) and Klein (1976).

4.  The major work on cultural persistence is still that of Spicer (1980) and his pupils, e.g., Castile (1981) and Moore (1981). Although pioneering and stimulating to this day, this work requires updating and, above all, a more systematic approach to the theory and practice of cultural persistence. Also note Dolitsky and Kuzina (1986) and Kent (1983).

5.  For useful introductions to eighteenth- and nineteenth-century British and French theories of social change and, therefore, to social theory more generally, see Berman (1970), Janos (1986) and Ryan (1969).

6.  Sperber (1976) and Borowski (1984) provide thoughtful reviews of the communes and other alternative life-styles of the 1960s and 1970s and of the various factors which led to the variance in their success and durability.

7.  Ample evidence of recent Marxist and non-Marxist rethinking of ethnicity can be gleaned from Baumgarten (1982), Fishman (1983/1985), Hall (1983), Hechter and Appelbaum (1982), Lipset (1985), McCarthy and Zahn (1973), Nielsen (1980), Olzak (1983), Ragin (1979) and Wax (1974). A rather full review of the literature and a critique of its minor innovations and major inadequacies can be found in Fishman (op. cit.), Olzak (op. cit.) and Yinger (1985).

8.  See Bonacich *et al.* (1972), De Marchi and Boileau (1982), Juliani (1982), Lieberson (1963), Said (1977), Suhrke and Noble (1973), Wolf (1982) and Yinger (op. cit.) for indications of the ubiquitous, relatively permanent and non-threatening nature of ethnicity in many modern contexts.
9.  The importance of the initial and ongoing clarification of goals and beliefs for effective social action is discussed by Aidala (1984), McPherson (1973), Tilly (1978) and Wuthnow (1976).
10. High implicationality has proven to be attainable only in relatively few social behavioral domains (including a few sociolinguistic areas among them; see Rickford, 1987 and in press). Even there scalability may be more attractive because of its apparent conceptual elegance than because of any enhanced predictive or explanatory validity that it attains or provides.
11. See Burke (1954: 136) and Spicer (1980: 358) for the references cited.
12. Geertz clearly sketches the role of economic factors in fostering more pervasive cultural change (see, e.g., his 1963 volume), but he is particularly stimulating for our own RLS concerns in connection with his stress on gradualism and transitionalism with respect to most traditional/*Gemeinschaft* and modern/*Gesellschaft* characterizations and the large variety of combinations between modernity and tradition even when economic modernization is ongoing. Corners and nooks of work sphere RLS may well present themselves even under conditions of ongoing work sphere modernization under Yish impetus.
13. For examples of research and theory on the ability of minorities to influence and wrest concessions from majorities see Hirsch and Gutierrez (1972) and Moscovici et al. (1985). Collective action and social action are reviewed by Tilly (1978) and Crowell (1968). The huge literature on neighborhood organization can be sampled via works such as Arzac (1982), Bulmer (1986), Hallman (1977), O'Brien (1975) and Scott (1981). Bulmer's book constitutes a review and critique of the fruitful pioneering work done in this area by Philip Abrams. Horwitt (1989) performs the same task re Saul Alinsky, albeit in exceptionally laudatory terms. For compendia of the most recent work on organization theory more generally, see Morgan (1986 and 1989) as well as Massarik (1990).
14. Methods, difficulties and doubts re planned efforts to strengthen modern family dynamics are prevocatively reviewed in Curran (1983), Elliot (1986), Fishman and Rosman (1986), McCubbin (1985), Mindick (1986), Moynihan (1986) and Zigler and Weiss (1985).
15. For a fine discussion of the school's changed relationship to the family and the community see Heath and McLaughlin (1987). Also note Smith and Clement (1981).

# References

ACTON, Lord J. E. E. 1907, Nationality. Reprinted in J. N. FIGGIS and R. V. LAWRENCE (eds) *The History of Freedom and Other Essays [by Lord Acton]*. London: Macmillan, 270–300; originally published in *Home and Foreign Review*, 1862, July.
AIDALA, Angela A. 1984, Worldviews, ideologies and social experimentation: clarification and replication of 'The Consciousness Reformation'. *Journal for the Scientific Study of Religion* 23, 44–59.
ALBRECHT, Johann and GILL-CHIN, Lim 1986, A search of alternative planning theory: Use of critical theory. *Journal of Architectural and Planning Research* 3, 117–31.

ARZAC, Adriana A. 1982, The Development of Community Competence through a Neighborhood Organization. Dr.P.H. Dissertation, University of Texas, Houston, School of Public Health.

BARBER, Bernard 1941, Acculturation and messianic movements. *American Sociological Review* 6, 663–669.

BAUMGARTEN, Murray 1982, *City Scriptures*. Cambridge, MA: Harvard University Press.

BERMAN, M. 1970, *The Politics of Authenticity; Radical Individualism and the Emergence of Modern Society*. New York: Atheneum.

BONACICH, E. *et al.* 1972, A theory of ethnic antagonism: the split labor market. *American Sociological Review* 37, 547–59.

BOROWSKI, Karol 1984, *Attempting an Alternative Society*. Norwood, NJ: Norwood Editions.

BULMER, Martin 1986, *Neighbors; The Work of Philip Abrams*. Cambridge: Cambridge University Press.

BURKE, Kenneth 1954, *Permanence and Change*. Los Altos: Hermes (revised edn).

CASTILE, George P. 1981, Issues in the analysis of enduring cultural systems. In G. P. CASTILE and Gilbert KUSHER (eds) *Persistent Peoples: Cultural Enclaves in Perspective*. Tucson: University of Arizona Press, xv–xxii.

CHAMPAGNE, Duane 1983, Social structure, revitalization movements and state building: social change in four native American societies. *American Sociological Review* 48, 754–63.

CROWELL, George 1968, *Society Against Itself*. Philadelphia: Westminster Press.

CURRAN, D. 1983, *Traits of Healthy Family*. Minneapolis: Winston.

DE MARCHI, Bruna and BOILEAU, Anna Maria (eds) 1982, *Boundaries and Minorities in Western Europe*. Milan: Franco Angeli.

DOLITSKY, A. and KUZINA, L. 1986, Cultural change vs. persistence: A case from Old Believer settlements. *Arctic* 39, 223–31.

DONAHUE, Thomas S. in press, The functionalist perspective of the family in the sociology of language: an axiom.

ELLIOT, Faith R. 1986, *The Family: Change or Continuity*. Houndmills: Macmillan Education.

ELLIS, Peter B. and MAC A'GHOBHAINN, Seumas 1971, *The Problem of Language Revival*. Inverness: Club Leabhar.

ENGELS, F. 1866, What have the working class to do with Poland? *Commonwealth*, March 24, March 31 and May 5.

FISHMAN, Charles H. and ROSMAN, Bernice L. (eds) 1986, *Evolving Models for Family Change*. New York: Guilford.

FISHMAN, Joshua A. 1977, Language, ethnicity and racism. Georgetown Round Table on Languages and Linguistics, 297–309; reprinted in his *Language and Ethnicity in Minority Sociolinguistic Perspective*, 1984. Clevedon: Multilingual Matters, 9–22.

— 1983, Epilogue: the rise and fall of the ethnic revival in the United States. *Journal of Intercultural Studies* 4, No. 3, 5–46; reprinted in his (*et al.*) *Rise and Fall of the Ethnic Revival*, 1985. Berlin: Mouton de Gruyter, 489–525.

GEERTZ, Clifford 1963, *Peddlers and Princes; Social Change and Economic Modernization in Two Indonesian Towns*. Chicago: University of Chicago Press.

HALL, Thomas D. 1983, Peripheries, regions of refuge and non-state societies: Toward a theory of reactive social change. *Social Quarterly* 64, 582–97.

HALLMAN, Howard W. 1977, *The Organization and Operation of Neighborhood Councils; A Practical Guide*. New York: Praeger.

HEATH, Shirley B. and MCLAUGHLIN, Milbrey Wallin 1987, A child resource policy:

Moving beyond dependence on school and family. *Phi Delta Kappan* 68, 576–80.

HECHTER, Michael and APPELBAUM, Malka 1982, A theory of ethnic collective action. *International Migration Review* 16, 412–34.

HIRSCH, Herbert and GUTIERREZ, Armando 1972, *Learning to be Militant; Ethnic Identity and the Development of Political Militance in a Chicano Community.* San Francisco: R & E Research Associates.

HORWITT, Sanford D. 1989, *Let Them Call Me Rebel; Saul Alinsky: His Life and Legacy.* New York: Knopf.

INSTITUTE OF CULTURAL CONSERVATISM 1987, *Cultural Conservatism: Toward a New Agenda.* Lanham: University Press of America.

JANOS, Andrew C. 1986, *Politics and Paradigms: Changing Theories of Change in Social Science.* Stanford, CA: Stanford University Press.

JENKINS, J. Craig 1983, Resource mobilization theory and the study of social movements. *Annual Review of Sociology* 9, 527–53.

JULIANI, R. N. 1982, Ethnicity: myth, social reality and ideology. *Contemporary Sociology* 11, 368–70.

KEHOE, Alice Beck 1989, *Ghost Dance Religion: Ethnohistory and Revitalization.* Fort Worth: Holt, Rinehart & Winston.

KENT, Susan 1983, The differential acceptance of cultural change: An archaeological test-case. *Historical Archaeology* 17, 56–63.

KLEIN, Donald 1976, Dynamics of resistance to change: The defenders. In Warren BENNIS *et al.* (eds) *The Planning of Change.* New York: Holt, Rinehart & Winston (third edn), 117–26.

LAPONCE, Jean A. 1984, *Langue et territoire.* Quebec: International Center for Research on Bilingualism; translated into English (1987) as *Languages and Their Territories.* Toronto: University of Toronto Press.

LEVITT, Morton and RUBENSTEIN, Ben 1972, *Youth and Social Change.* Detroit: Wayne State University Press.

LIEBERSON, Stanley 1963, *Ethnic Patterns in American Cities.* New York: Free Press.

LINTON, Ralph 1943, Nativistic movements. *American Anthropologist* 45, 231–40.

LIPSET, Seymour M. 1985, *Consensus and Conflict: Essays in Political Sociology.* New Brunswick: Transaction Books.

MCCARTHY, J. and ZAHN, M. N. 1973, *The Trend of Social Movements.* Morristown: General Learning.

MCCUBBIN, Hamilton I. *et al.* 1985, Family dynamics: strengthening families through action-research. In Robert N. RAPOPORT (ed.) *Children, Youth and Families: The Action Research Relationship.* Cambridge: Cambridge University Press, 126–65.

MCPHERSON, William (ed.) 1973, *Ideology and Change.* Palo Alto: National Press.

MASSARIK, Fred 1990, *Advances in Organization Development.* Norwood: Ablex.

MINDICK, Burton 1986, *Social Engineering in Family Matters.* New York: Praeger.

MOORE, Janet R. 1981, Persistence with change: A property of sociocultural dynamics. In G. P. CASTILE and Gilbert KUSHER (eds) *Persistent Peoples: Cultural Enclaves in Perspective.* Tucson: University of Arizona Press, 228–42.

MORGAN, Gareth 1986, *Images of Organization.* Newbury Park: Sage.

—1989, *Creative Organization Theory.* Newbury Park: Sage.

MOSCOVICI, Serge *et al.* (eds) 1985, *Perspectives on Minority Influence.* Cambridge: Cambridge University Press.

MOYNIHAN, Daniel P. 1986, *Family and Nation.* New York: Harcourt, Brace, Jovanovich.

NIELSEN, F. 1980, The Flemish movement in Belgium after World War II. *American Sociological Review* 45, 76–94.

O'BRIEN, David J. 1975, *Neighborhood Organization and Interest-Group Processes*. Princeton, NJ: Princeton University Press.

OLZAK, Susan 1983, Contemporary ethnicity mobilization. *Annual Review of Sociology* 9, 355–74.

POSTER, Mark 1978, *The Critical Theory of the Family*. New York: Seabury.

RAGIN, C.C. 1979, Ethnic political mobilization. *American Sociological Review* 44, 619–34.

RAO, M.S. 1981, Changing moral values in the context of social-cultural movements. In Adrian C. Mayer (ed) *Culture and Morality: Essays in Honor of Christopher von Furer-Haimendorf*. Delhi: Oxford University Press, 191–208.

RICKFORD, John R. 1987, The haves and have nots; sociolinguistic surveys and the assessment of speaker competence. *Language in Society* 16, 149–78.

— In press, Implicational scaling and critical age limits in models of linguistic variation, acquisition and change. In Charles A. FERGUSON and Thom HUEBNER (eds) *Second Language Acquisition and Linguistic Theory*. Amsterdam: John Benjamins.

RYAN, Bryce 1969, *Social and Cultural Change*. New York: Ronald.

SAID, A. A. (ed.) 1977, *Ethnicity and United States Foreign Policy*. New York: Praeger.

SCOTT, David 1981, *'Don't Mourn for Me, Organize...' The Social and Political Uses of Voluntary Organization*. Sydney: Allen and Unwin.

SMITH, Elsie and CLEMENT, B. G. 1981, A union of school, community and family. *Urban Education* 16, 247–60.

SPERBER, Mae T. 1976, *Search for Utopia*. Middleboro: Country Press.

SPICER, Edward H. 1980, *The Yaquis: A Cultural History*. Tucson: Arizona University Press.

SUHRKE, R. P. and NOBLE L. G. (eds) 1973, *Ethnic Conflict in International Relations*. New York: Praeger.

THORNTON, Russell 1986, *We Shall Live Again; The 1870 and 1890 Ghost Dance Movements as Demographic Revitalization*. Cambridge: Cambridge University Press.

TILLY, Charles 1978, *From Mobilization to Revolution*. Reading: Addison-Wesley.

TRAUGOTT, Mark 1978, Reconsidering social movements. *Social Problems* 26, 38–49.

WALLACE, Anthony 1956, Revitalization movements. *American Anthropologist* 58, 264–281.

WAX, Murray L. 1974, Cultural pluralism, political power and ethnic studies. In Wilton S. DILLON (ed.) *The Cultural Drama: Modern Identitites and Social Ferment*. Washington, D. C.: Smithsonian Institution, 107–20.

WOLF, Eric R. 1982, *Europe and the People Without History*. Berkeley: University of California Press.

WUTHNOW, Robert. 1976, *The Conscious Reformation*. Berkeley: University of California Press

YINGER, J. Milton 1985, Ethnicity. *Annual Review of Sociology* 11, 151–80.

ZIGLER, Edward and WEISS, Heather 1985, Family support systems: An ecological approach to child development. In Robert N. RAPOPORT (ed.) *Children, Youth and Families: The Action Research Relationship*. Cambridge: Cambridge University Press, 166–205.

# Index

*Note:* Page references in italics indicate tables and figures.